D1068984

# THEODORE ROOSEVELT

# THEODORE ROOSEVELT

## THE ROUGH RIDERS
## AN AUTOBIOGRAPHY

THE LIBRARY OF AMERICA

The paper used in this publication meets the
minimum requirements of the American National Standard for
Information Sciences — Permanence of Paper for Printed
Library Materials, ANSI z39.48 — 1984.

Distributed to the trade
in the United States by Penguin Putnam Inc.
and in Canada by Penguin Books Canada Ltd.

Library of Congress Catalog Number: 2004044195
For cataloging information, see end of Notes.
ISBN 1–931082–65–0

———

First Printing
The Library of America — 153

Manufactured in the United States of America

Louis Auchincloss
IS THE EDITOR OF THIS VOLUME

# Contents

# THE ROUGH RIDERS

From a copyrighted Photograph by Rockwood

Theodore Roosevelt

ON BEHALF OF THE ROUGH RIDERS
I DEDICATE THIS BOOK
TO THE OFFICERS AND MEN OF THE
FIVE REGULAR REGIMENTS
WHICH TOGETHER WITH MINE MADE UP THE
CAVALRY DIVISION AT SANTIAGO

THEODORE ROOSEVELT

EXECUTIVE MANSION
ALBANY, N. Y., MAY 1, 1899

# CONTENTS

# ILLUSTRATIONS

7

Hark! I hear the tramp of thousands,
　　And of armed men the hum;
Lo! a nation's hosts have gathered
　　Round the quick-alarming drum—
　　　　Saying, "Come,
　　　　Freemen, come!
Ere your heritage be wasted," said the quick-alarming drum.

"Let me of my heart take counsel:
　　War is not of Life the sum;
Who shall stay and reap the harvest
　　When the autumn days shall come?"
　　　　But the drum
　　　　Echoed, "Come!
Death shall reap the braver harvest," said the solemn-sounding drum.

"But when won the coming battle,
　　What of profit springs therefrom?
What if conquest, subjugation,
　　Even greater ills become?"
　　　　But the drum
　　　　Answered, "Come!
You must do the sum to prove it," said the Yankee-answering drum.
　　　　　　　　　　　　　—BRET HARTE.

# I

## RAISING THE REGIMENT

Dᴜʀɪɴɢ the year preceding the outbreak of the Spanish
War I was Assistant Secretary of the Navy. While my
party was in opposition, I had preached, with all the fervor
and zeal I possessed, our duty to intervene in Cuba, and
to take this opportunity of driving the Spaniard from the
Western World. Now that my party had come to power, I felt
it incumbent on me, by word and deed, to do all I could to
secure the carrying out of the policy in which I so heartily
believed; and from the beginning I had determined that, if a
war came, somehow or other, I was going to the front.

Meanwhile, there was any amount of work at hand in getting ready the navy, and to this I devoted myself.

Naturally, when one is intensely interested in a certain
cause, the tendency is to associate particularly with those who
take the same view. A large number of my friends felt very
differently from the way I felt, and looked upon the possibility of war with sincere horror. But I found plenty of sympathizers, especially in the navy, the army, and the Senate
Committee on Foreign Affairs. Commodore Dewey, Captain
Evans, Captain Brownson, Captain Davis — with these and the
various other naval officers on duty at Washington I used to
hold long consultations, during which we went over and over,
not only every question of naval administration, but specifically everything necessary to do in order to put the navy in
trim to strike quick and hard if, as we believed would be the
case, we went to war with Spain. Sending an ample quantity
of ammunition to the Asiatic squadron and providing it with
coal; getting the battle-ships and the armored cruisers on the
Atlantic into one squadron, both to train them in manœuv-
ring together, and to have them ready to sail against either the
Cuban or the Spanish coasts; gathering the torpedo-boats into
a flotilla for practice; securing ample target exercise, so conducted as to raise the standard of our marksmanship; gathering in the small ships from European and South American
waters; settling on the number and kind of craft needed as

auxiliary cruisers — every one of these points was threshed over in conversations with officers who were present in Washington, or in correspondence with officers who, like Captain Mahan, were absent.

As for the Senators, of course Senator Lodge and I felt precisely alike; for to fight in such a cause and with such an enemy was merely to carry out the doctrines we had both of us preached for many years. Senator Davis, Senator Proctor, Senator Foraker, Senator Chandler, Senator Morgan, Senator Frye, and a number of others also took just the right ground; and I saw a great deal of them, as well as of many members of the House, particularly those from the West, where the feeling for war was strongest.

Naval officers came and went, and Senators were only in the city while the Senate was in session; but there was one friend who was steadily in Washington. This was an army surgeon, Dr. Leonard Wood. I only met him after I entered the navy department, but we soon found that we had kindred tastes and kindred principles. He had served in General Miles's inconceivably harassing campaigns against the Apaches, where he had displayed such courage that he won that most coveted of distinctions — the Medal of Honor; such extraordinary physical strength and endurance that he grew to be recognized as one of the two or three white men who could stand fatigue and hardship as well as an Apache; and such judgment that toward the close of the campaigns he was given, though a surgeon, the actual command of more than one expedition against the bands of renegade Indians. Like so many of the gallant fighters with whom it was later my good fortune to serve, he combined, in a very high degree, the qualities of entire manliness with entire uprightness and cleanliness of character. It was a pleasure to deal with a man of high ideals, who scorned everything mean and base, and who also possessed those robust and hardy qualities of body and mind, for the lack of which no merely negative virtue can ever atone. He was by nature a soldier of the highest type, and, like most natural soldiers, he was, of course, born with a keen longing for adventure; and, though an excellent doctor, what he really desired was the chance to lead men in some kind of hazard. To every possibility of such

Colonel Leonard Wood.

adventure he paid quick attention. For instance, he had a great desire to get me to go with him on an expedition into the Klondike in mid-winter, at the time when it was thought that a relief party would have to be sent there to help the starving miners.

In the summer he and I took long walks together through the beautiful broken country surrounding Washington. In winter we sometimes varied these walks by kicking a foot-ball in an empty lot, or, on the rare occasions when there was enough snow, by trying a couple of sets of skis or snow-skates, which had been sent me from Canada.

But always on our way out to and back from these walks and sport, there was one topic to which, in our talking, we returned, and that was the possible war with Spain. We both felt very strongly that such a war would be as righteous as it would be advantageous to the honor and the interests of the nation; and after the blowing up of the Maine, we felt that it was inevitable. We then at once began to try to see that we had our share in it. The President and my own chief, Secretary Long, were very firm against my going, but they said that if I was bent upon going they would help me. Wood was the medical adviser of both the President and the Secretary of War, and could count upon their friendship. So we started with the odds in our favor.

At first we had great difficulty in knowing exactly what to try for. We could go on the staff of any one of several Generals, but we much preferred to go in the line. Wood hoped he might get a commission in his native State of Massachusetts; but in Massachusetts, as in every other State, it proved there were ten men who wanted to go to the war for every chance to go. Then we thought we might get positions as field-officers under an old friend of mine, Colonel — now General — Francis V. Greene, of New York, the Colonel of the Seventy-first; but again there were no vacancies.

Our doubts were resolved when Congress authorized the raising of three cavalry regiments from among the wild riders and riflemen of the Rockies and the Great Plains. During Wood's service in the Southwest he had commanded not only regulars and Indian scouts, but also white frontiersmen. In the Northwest I had spent much of my time, for many years, either on my ranch or in long hunting trips, and had lived and worked for months together with the cow-boy and the mountain hunter, faring in every way precisely as they did.

Secretary Alger offered me the command of one of these regiments. If I had taken it, being entirely inexperienced in military work, I should not have known how to get it equipped most rapidly, for I should have spent valuable weeks in learning its needs, with the result that I should have missed the Santiago campaign, and might not even have had the consolation prize of going to Porto Rico. Fortunately, I was wise enough to tell the Secretary that while I believed I could learn to command the regiment in a month, yet that it was just this very month which I could not afford to spare, and that therefore I would be quite content to go as Lieutenant-Colonel, if he would make Wood Colonel.

This was entirely satisfactory to both the President and Secretary, and, accordingly, Wood and I were speedily commissioned as Colonel and Lieutenant-Colonel of the First United States Volunteer Cavalry. This was the official title of the regiment, but for some reason or other the public promptly christened us the "Rough Riders." At first we fought against the use of the term, but to no purpose; and when finally the Generals of Division and Brigade began to write in formal communications about our regiment as the "Rough Riders," we adopted the term ourselves.

The mustering-places for the regiment were appointed in New Mexico, Arizona, Oklahoma, and Indian Territory. The difficulty in organizing was not in selecting, but in rejecting men. Within a day or two after it was announced that we were to raise the regiment, we were literally deluged with applications from every quarter of the Union. Without the slightest trouble, so far as men went, we could have raised a brigade or even a division. The difficulty lay in arming, equipping, mounting, and disciplining the men we selected. Hundreds of regiments were being called into existence by the National Government, and each regiment was sure to have innumerable wants to be satisfied. To a man who knew the ground as Wood did, and who was entirely aware of our national unpreparedness, it was evident that the ordnance and quartermaster's bureaus could not meet, for some time to come,

Regimental Drill of the Rough

Colonel Wood.          Lieutenant Colonel Roosevelt.

Riders at San Antonio, Texas.

one-tenth of the demands that would be made upon them; and it was all-important to get in first with our demands. Thanks to his knowledge of the situation and promptness, we immediately put in our requisitions for the articles indispensable for the equipment of the regiment; and then, by ceaseless worrying of excellent bureaucrats, who had no idea how to do things quickly or how to meet an emergency, we succeeded in getting our rifles, cartridges, revolvers, clothing, shelter-tents, and horse gear just in time to enable us to go on the Santiago expedition. Some of the State troops, who were already organized as National Guards, were, of course, ready, after a fashion, when the war broke out; but no other regiment which had our work to do was able to do it in anything like as quick time, and therefore no other volunteer regiment saw anything like the fighting which we did.

Wood thoroughly realized what the Ordnance Department failed to realize, namely the inestimable advantage of smokeless powder; and, moreover, he was bent upon our having the weapons of the regulars, for this meant that we would be brigaded with them, and it was evident that they would do the bulk of the fighting if the war were short. Accordingly, by acting with the utmost vigor and promptness, he succeeded in getting our regiment armed with the Krag-Jorgensen carbine used by the regular cavalry.

It was impossible to take any of the numerous companies which were proffered to us from the various States. The only organized bodies we were at liberty to accept were those from the four Territories. But owing to the fact that the number of men originally allotted to us, 780, was speedily raised to 1,000, we were given a chance to accept quite a number of eager volunteers who did not come from the Territories, but who possessed precisely the same temper that distinguished our Southwestern recruits, and whose presence materially benefited the regiment.

We drew recruits from Harvard, Yale, Princeton, and many another college; from clubs like the Somerset, of Boston, and Knickerbocker, of New York; and from among the men who belonged neither to club nor to college, but in whose veins the blood stirred with the same impulse which once sent the Vikings over sea. Four of the policemen who had served under me, while I was President of the New York Police Board, insisted on coming — two of them to die, the other two to return unhurt after honorable and dangerous service. It seemed to me that almost every friend I had in every State had some one acquaintance who was bound to go with the Rough Riders, and for whom I had to make a place. Thomas Nelson Page, General Fitzhugh Lee, Congressman Odell of New York, Senator Morgan; for each of these, and for many others, I eventually consented to accept some one or two recruits, of course only after a most rigid examination into their physical capacity, and after they had shown that they knew how to ride and shoot. I may add that in no case was I disappointed in the men thus taken.

Harvard being my own college, I had such a swarm of applications from it that I could not take one in ten. What particularly pleased me, not only in the Harvard but the Yale and Princeton men, and, indeed, in these recruits from the older States generally, was that they did not ask for commissions. With hardly an exception they entered upon their duties as troopers in the spirit which they held to the end, merely endeavoring to show that no work could be too hard, too disagreeable, or too dangerous for them to perform, and neither asking nor receiving any reward in the way of promotion or consideration. The Harvard contingent was practically raised by Guy Murchie, of Maine. He saw all the fighting and did his duty with the utmost gallantry, and then left the service as he had entered it, a trooper, entirely satisfied to have done his duty — and no man did it better. So it was with Dudley Dean, perhaps the best quarterback who ever played on a Harvard Eleven; and so with Bob Wrenn, a quarterback whose feats rivalled those of Dean's, and who, in addition, was the champion tennis player of America, and had, on two different years, saved this championship from going to an Englishman. So it was with Yale men like Waller, the high jumper, and Garrison and Girard; and with Princeton men like Devereux and Channing, the foot-ball players; with Larned, the tennis player; with Craig Wadsworth, the steeple-chase rider; with Joe Stevens, the crack polo player; with Hamilton Fish, the ex-captain of the Columbia crew, and with scores of others whose names are quite as worthy of mention as any of those

I have given. Indeed, they all sought entry into the ranks of
the Rough Riders as eagerly as if it meant something widely
different from hard work, rough fare, and the possibility of
death; and the reason why they turned out to be such good
soldiers lay largely in the fact that they were men who had
thoroughly counted the cost before entering, and who went
into the regiment because they believed that this offered their
best chance for seeing hard and dangerous service. Mason
Mitchell, of New York, who had been a chief of scouts in the
Riel Rebellion, travelled all the way to San Antonio to enlist;
and others came there from distances as great.

Some of them made appeals to me which I could not possibly resist. Woodbury Kane had been a close friend of mine
at Harvard. During the eighteen years that had passed since
my graduation I had seen very little of him, though, being
always interested in sport, I occasionally met him on the hunting field, had seen him on the deck of the Defender when she
vanquished the Valkyrie, and knew the part he had played on
the Navajoe, when, in her most important race, that otherwise
unlucky yacht vanquished her opponent, the Prince of Wales's
Britannia. When the war was on, Kane felt it his duty to fight
for his country. He did not seek any position of distinction.
All he desired was the chance to do whatever work he was put
to do well, and to get to the front; and he enlisted as a trooper.
When I went down to the camp at San Antonio he was on
kitchen duty, and was cooking and washing dishes for one of
the New Mexican troops; and he was doing it so well that I
had no further doubt as to how he would get on.

My friend of many hunts and ranch partner, Robert Munro
Ferguson, of Scotland, who had been on Lord Aberdeen's
staff as a Lieutenant but a year before, likewise could not keep
out of the regiment. He, too, appealed to me in terms which
I could not withstand, and came in like Kane to do his full
duty as a trooper, and like Kane to win his commission by
the way he thus did his duty.

I felt many qualms at first in allowing men of this stamp to
come in, for I could not be certain that they had counted the
cost, and was afraid they would find it very hard to serve —
not for a few days, but for months — in the ranks, while I,
their former intimate associate, was a field-officer; but they

hat they knew their minds, and the events showed
/ did. We enlisted about fifty of them from Virginia,
id, and the Northeastern States, at Washington. Be-
owing them to be sworn in, I gathered them together
.plained that if they went in they must be prepared not
y to fight, but to perform the weary, monotonous labor
..ent to the ordinary routine of a soldier's life; that they
must be ready to face fever exactly as they were to face bullets; that they were to obey unquestioningly, and to do their
duty as readily if called upon to garrison a fort as if sent to
the front. I warned them that work that was merely irksome
and disagreeable must be faced as readily as work that was
dangerous, and that no complaint of any kind must be made;
and I told them that they were entirely at liberty not to go,
but that after they had once signed there could then be no
backing out.

Not a man of them backed out; not one of them failed to
do his whole duty.

These men formed but a small fraction of the whole. They
went down to San Antonio, where the regiment was to gather
and where Wood preceded me, while I spent a week in Washington hurrying up the different bureaus and telegraphing my
various railroad friends, so as to insure our getting the carbines, saddles, and uniforms that we needed from the various
armories and storehouses. Then I went down to San Antonio
myself, where I found the men from New Mexico, Arizona,
and Oklahoma already gathered, while those from Indian Territory came in soon after my arrival.

These were the men who made up the bulk of the regiment,
and gave it its peculiar character. They came from the Four
Territories which yet remained within the boundaries of the
United States; that is, from the lands that have been most recently won over to white civilization, and in which the conditions of life are nearest those that obtained on the frontier
when there still was a frontier. They were a splendid set of
men, these Southwesterners — tall and sinewy, with resolute,
weather-beaten faces, and eyes that looked a man straight in
the face without flinching. They included in their ranks men
of every occupation; but the three types were those of the
cow-boy, the hunter, and the mining prospector — the man

who wandered hither and thither, killing game for a l
and spending his life in the quest for metal wealth.

In all the world there could be no better material for soldi
than that afforded by these grim hunters of the mountains
these wild rough riders of the plains. They were accustomed
to handling wild and savage horses; they were accustomed to
following the chase with the rifle, both for sport and as a
means of livelihood. Varied though their occupations had
been, almost all had, at one time or another, herded cattle
and hunted big game. They were hardened to life in the
open, and to shifting for themselves under adverse circumstances. They were used, for all their lawless freedom, to the
rough discipline of the round-up and the mining company.
Some of them came from the small frontier towns; but most
were from the wilderness, having left their lonely hunters'
cabins and shifting cow-camps to seek new and more stirring
adventures beyond the sea.

They had their natural leaders — the men who had shown
they could master other men, and could more than hold their
own in the eager driving life of the new settlements.

The Captains and Lieutenants were sometimes men who
had campaigned in the regular army against Apache, Ute, and
Cheyenne, and who, on completing their term of service,
had shown their energy by settling in the new communities
and growing up to be men of mark. In other cases they were
sheriffs, marshals, deputy-sheriffs and deputy-marshals — men
who had fought Indians, and still more often had waged relentless war upon the bands of white desperadoes. There was
Bucky O'Neill, of Arizona, Captain of Troop A, the Mayor of
Prescott, a famous sheriff throughout the West for his feats
of victorious warfare against the Apache, no less than against
the white road-agents and man-killers. His father had fought
in Meagher's Brigade in the Civil War; and he was himself a
born soldier, a born leader of men. He was a wild, reckless
fellow, soft spoken, and of dauntless courage and boundless
ambition; he was stanchly loyal to his friends, and cared
for his men in every way. There was Captain Llewellen, of
New Mexico, a good citizen, a political leader, and one of the
most noted peace-officers of the country; he had been shot
four times in pitched fights with red marauders and white

Captain Allyn Capron.

Captain Bucky O'Neill.

outlaws. There was Lieutenant Ballard, who had broken up the Black Jack gang of ill-omened notoriety, and his Captain, Curry, another New Mexican sheriff of fame. The officers from the Indian Territory had almost all served as marshals and deputy-marshals; and in the Indian Territory, service as a deputy-marshal meant capacity to fight stand-up battles with the gangs of outlaws.

Three of our higher officers had been in the regular army. One was Major Alexander Brodie, from Arizona, afterward Lieutenant-Colonel, who had lived for twenty years in the Territory, and had become a thorough Westerner without sinking the West Pointer — a soldier by taste as well as training, whose men worshipped him and would follow him anywhere, as they would Bucky O'Neill or any other of their favorites. Brodie was running a big mining business; but when the Maine was blown up, he abandoned everything and telegraphed right and left to bid his friends get ready for the fight he saw impending.

Then there was Micah Jenkins, the Captain of Troop K, a gentle and courteous South Carolinian, on whom danger acted like wine. In action he was a perfect game-cock, and he won his majority for gallantry in battle.

Finally, there was Allyn Capron, who was, on the whole, the best soldier in the regiment. In fact, I think he was the ideal of what an American regular army officer should be. He was the fifth in descent from father to son who had served in the army of the United States, and in body and mind alike he was fitted to play his part to perfection. Tall and lithe, a remarkable boxer and walker, a first-class rider and shot, with yellow hair and piercing blue eyes, he looked what he was, the archetype of the fighting man. He had under him one of the two companies from the Indian Territory; and he so soon impressed himself upon the wild spirit of his followers, that he got them ahead in discipline faster than any other troop in the regiment, while at the same time taking care of their bodily wants. His ceaseless effort was so to train them, care for them, and inspire them as to bring their fighting efficiency to the highest possible pitch. He required instant obedience, and tolerated not the slightest evasion of duty; but his mastery of his art was so thorough and his performance of his own duty so rigid that he won at once not merely their admiration, but that soldierly affection so readily given by the man in the ranks to the superior who cares for his men and leads them fearlessly in battle.

All — Easterners and Westerners, Northerners and Southerners, officers and men, cow-boys and college graduates, wherever they came from, and whatever their social position — possessed in common the traits of hardihood and a thirst for adventure. They were to a man born adventurers, in the old sense of the word.

The men in the ranks were mostly young; yet some were past their first youth. These had taken part in the killing of the great buffalo herds, and had fought Indians when the tribes were still on the war-path. The younger ones, too, had led rough lives; and the lines in their faces told of many a hardship endured, and many a danger silently faced with grim, unconscious philosophy. Some were originally from the East, and had seen strange adventures in different kinds of life, from sailing round the Horn to mining in Alaska. Others had been born and bred in the West, and had never seen a larger town than Santa Fé or a bigger body of water than the Pecos in flood. Some of them went by their own name; some had changed their names; and yet others possessed but half a name, colored by some adjective, like Cherokee Bill, Happy Jack of Arizona, Smoky Moore, the bronco-buster, so named because cow-boys often call vicious horses "smoky" horses, and Rattlesnake Pete, who had lived among the Moquis and taken part in the snake-dances. Some were professional gamblers, and, on the other hand, no less than four were or had been Baptist or Methodist clergymen — and proved first-class fighters, too, by the way. Some were men whose lives in the past had not been free from the taint of those fierce kinds of crime into which the lawless spirits who dwell on the borderland between civilization and savagery so readily drift. A far larger number had served at different times in those bodies of armed men with which the growing civilization of the border finally puts down its savagery.

There was one characteristic and distinctive contingent which could have appeared only in such a regiment as ours. From the Indian Territory there came a number of Indians —

Cherokees, Chickasaws, Choctaws, and Creeks. Only a few were of pure blood. The others shaded off until they were absolutely indistinguishable from their white comrades; with whom, it may be mentioned, they all lived on terms of complete equality.

Not all of the Indians were from the Indian Territory. One of the gamest fighters and best soldiers in the regiment was Pollock, a full-blooded Pawnee. He had been educated, like most of the other Indians, at one of those admirable Indian schools which have added so much to the total of the small credit account with which the White race balances the very unpleasant debit account of its dealings with the Red. Pollock was a silent, solitary fellow — an excellent pen-man, much given to drawing pictures. When we got down to Santiago he developed into the regimental clerk. I never suspected him of having a sense of humor until one day, at the end of our stay in Cuba, as he was sitting in the Adjutant's tent working over the returns, there turned up a trooper of the First who had been acting as barber. Eying him with immovable face Pollock asked, in a guttural voice, "Do you cut hair?" The man answered "Yes"; and Pollock continued, "Then you'd better cut mine," muttering, in an explanatory soliloquy, "Don't want to wear my hair long like a wild Indian when I'm in civilized warfare."

Another Indian came from Texas. He was a brakeman on the Southern Pacific, and wrote telling me he was an American Indian, and that he wanted to enlist. His name was Colbert, which at once attracted my attention; for I was familiar with the history of the Cherokees and Chickasaws during the eighteenth century, when they lived east of the Mississippi. Early in that century various traders, chiefly Scotchmen, settled among them, and the half-breed descendants of one named Colbert became the most noted chiefs of the Chickasaws. I summoned the applicant before me, and found that he was an excellent man, and, as I had supposed, a descendant of the old Chickasaw chiefs.

He brought into the regiment, by the way, his "partner," a white man. The two had been inseparable companions for some years, and continued so in the regiment. Every man who has lived in the West knows that, vindictive though the hatred between the white man and the Indian is when they stand against one another in what may be called their tribal relations, yet that men of Indian blood, when adopted into white communities, are usually treated precisely like anyone else.

Colbert was not the only Indian whose name I recognized. There was a Cherokee named Adair, who, upon inquiry, I found to be descended from the man who, a century and a half ago, wrote a ponderous folio, to this day of great interest, about the Cherokees, with whom he had spent the best years of his life as a trader and agent.

I don't know that I ever came across a man with a really sweeter nature than another Cherokee named Holderman. He was an excellent soldier, and for a long time acted as cook for the head-quarters mess. He was a half-breed, and came of a soldier stock on both sides and through both races. He explained to me once why he had come to the war; that it was because his people always had fought when there was a war, and he could not feel happy to stay at home when the flag was going into battle.

Two of the young Cherokee recruits came to me with a most kindly letter from one of the ladies who had been teaching in the academy from which they were about to graduate. She and I had known one another in connection with Governmental and philanthropic work on the reservations, and she wrote to commend the two boys to my attention. One was on the Academy foot-ball team and the other in the glee-club. Both were fine young fellows. The foot-ball player now lies buried with the other dead who fell in the fight at San Juan. The singer was brought to death's door by fever, but recovered and came back to his home.

There were other Indians of much wilder type, but their wildness was precisely like that of the cow-boys with whom they were associated. One or two of them needed rough discipline; and they got it, too. Like the rest of the regiment, they were splendid riders. I remember one man, whose character left much to be desired in some respects, but whose horsemanship was unexceptionable. He was mounted on an exceedingly bad bronco, which would bolt out of the ranks at drill. He broke it of this habit by the simple expedient of giving it two tremendous twists, first to one side and then to the other, as it bolted, with the result that, invariably, at the second bound its legs crossed and over it went with a smash, the rider taking the somersault with unmoved equanimity.

The life histories of some of the men who joined our regiment would make many volumes of thrilling adventure.

We drew a great many recruits from Texas; and from nowhere did we get a higher average, for many of them had served in that famous body of frontier fighters, the Texas Rangers. Of course, these rangers needed no teaching. They were already trained to obey and to take responsibility. They were splendid shots, horsemen, and trailers. They were accustomed to living in the open, to enduring great fatigue and hardship, and to encountering all kinds of danger.

Many of the Arizona and New Mexico men had taken part in warfare with the Apaches, those terrible Indians of the waterless Southwestern mountains — the most bloodthirsty and the wildest of all the red men of America, and the most formidable in their own dreadful style of warfare. Of course, a man who had kept his nerve and held his own, year after year, while living where each day and night contained the threat of hidden death from a foe whose goings and comings were unseen, was not apt to lose courage when confronted with any other enemy. An experience in following in the trail of an enemy who might flee at one stretch through fifty miles of death-like desert was a good school out of which to come with profound indifference for the ordinary hardships of campaigning.

As a rule, the men were more apt, however, to have had experience in warring against white desperadoes and law-breakers than against Indians. Some of our best recruits came from Colorado. One, a very large, hawk-eyed man, Benjamin Franklin Daniels, had been Marshal of Dodge City when that pleasing town was probably the toughest abode of civilized man to be found anywhere on the continent. In the course of the exercise of his rather lurid functions as peace-officer he had lost half of one ear — "bitten off," it was explained to me. Naturally, he viewed the dangers of battle with philosophic calm. Such a man was, in reality, a veteran even in his first fight, and was a tower of strength to the recruits in his part of the line. With him there came into the regiment a deputy marshal from

Five Bronco-Busters.

Cripple Creek named Sherman Bell. Bell had a hernia, but he was so excellent a man that we decided to take him. I do not think I ever saw greater resolution than Bell displayed throughout the campaign. In Cuba the great exertions which he was forced to make, again and again opened the hernia, and the surgeons insisted that he must return to the United States; but he simply would not go.

Then there was little McGinty, the bronco-buster from Oklahoma, who never had walked a hundred yards if by any possibility he could ride. When McGinty was reproved for his absolute inability to keep step on the drill-ground, he responded that he was pretty sure he could keep step on horseback. McGinty's short legs caused him much trouble on the marches, but we had no braver or better man in the fights.

One old friend of mine had come from far northern Idaho to join the regiment at San Antonio. He was a hunter, named Fred Herrig, an Alsatian by birth. A dozen years before he and I had hunted mountain sheep and deer when laying in the winter stock of meat for my ranch on the Little Missouri, sometimes in the bright fall weather, sometimes in the Arctic bitterness of the early Northern winter. He was the most loyal and simple-hearted of men, and he had come to join his old "boss" and comrade in the bigger hunting which we were to carry on through the tropic mid-summer.

The temptation is great to go on enumerating man after man who stood pre-eminent, whether as a killer of game, a tamer of horses, or a queller of disorder among his people, or who, mayhap, stood out with a more evil prominence as himself a dangerous man — one given to the taking of life on small provocation, or one who was ready to earn his living outside the law if the occasion demanded it. There was tall Proffit, the sharp-shooter, from North Carolina — sinewy, saturnine, fearless; Smith, the bear-hunter from Wyoming, and McCann, the Arizona book-keeper, who had begun life as a buffalo-hunter. There was Crockett, the Georgian, who had been an Internal Revenue officer, and had waged perilous war on the rifle-bearing "moonshiners." There were Darnell and Wood of New Mexico, who could literally ride any horses alive. There were Goodwin, and Buck Taylor, and Armstrong the ranger, crack shots with rifle or revolver. There was many a skilled packer who had led and guarded his trains of laden mules through the Indian-haunted country surrounding some outpost of civilization. There were men who had won fame as Rocky Mountain stage-drivers, or who had spent endless days in guiding the slow wagon-trains across the grassy plains. There were miners who knew every camp from the Yukon to Leadville, and cow-punchers in whose memories were stored the brands carried by the herds from Chihuahua to Assiniboia. There were men who had roped wild steers in the mesquite brush of the Nueces, and who, year in and year out, had driven the trail herds northward over desolate wastes and across the fords of shrunken rivers to the fattening grounds of the Powder and the Yellowstone. They were hardened to the scorching heat and bitter cold of the dry plains and pine-clad mountains. They were accustomed to sleep in the open, while the picketed horses grazed beside them near some shallow, reedy pool. They had wandered hither and thither across the vast desolation of the wilderness, alone or with comrades. They had cowered in the shelter of cut banks from the icy blast of the norther, and far out on the midsummer prairies they had known the luxury of lying in the shade of the wagon during the noonday rest. They had lived in brush lean-tos for weeks at a time, or with only the wagon-sheet as an occasional house. They had fared hard when exploring the unknown; they had fared well on the round-up; and they had known the plenty of the log ranch-houses, where the tables were spread with smoked venison and calf-ribs and milk and bread, and vegetables from the garden-patch.

Such were the men we had as recruits: soldiers ready made, as far as concerned their capacity as individual fighters. What was necessary was to teach them to act together, and to obey orders. Our special task was to make them ready for action in the shortest possible time. We were bound to see fighting, and therefore to be with the first expedition that left the United States; for we could not tell how long the war would last.

I had been quite prepared for trouble when it came to enforcing discipline, but I was agreeably disappointed. There were plenty of hard characters who might by themselves have given trouble, and with one or two of whom we did have to take rough measures; but the bulk of the men thoroughly

understood that without discipline they would be merely a
valueless mob, and they set themselves hard at work to learn
the new duties. Of course, such a regiment, in spite of, or
indeed I might almost say because of, the characteristics which
made the individual men so exceptionally formidable as soldiers, could very readily have been spoiled. Any weakness in
the commander would have ruined it. On the other hand, to
treat it from the stand-point of the martinet and military
pedant would have been almost equally fatal. From the beginning we started out to secure the essentials of discipline,
while laying just as little stress as possible on the nonessen-
tials. The men were singularly quick to respond to any appeal
to their intelligence and patriotism. The faults they committed were those of ignorance merely. When Holderman, in announcing dinner to the Colonel and the three Majors, genially
remarked, "If you fellars don't come soon, everything 'll get
cold," he had no thought of other than a kindly and respectful regard for their welfare, and was glad to modify his form
of address on being told that it was not what could be described as conventionally military. When one of our sentinels,
who had with much labor learned the manual of arms, saluted
with great pride as I passed, and added, with a friendly nod,
"Good-evening, Colonel," this variation in the accepted formula on such occasion was meant, and was accepted, as mere
friendly interest. In both cases the needed instruction was
given and received in the same kindly spirit.

One of the new Indian Territory recruits, after twenty-four
hours' stay in camp, during which he had held himself distinctly aloof from the general interests, called on the Colonel
in his tent, and remarked, "Well, Colonel, I want to shake
hands and say we're with you. We didn't know how we would
like you fellars at first; but you're all right, and you know your
business, and you mean business, and you can count on us
every time!"

That same night, which was hot, mosquitoes were very annoying; and shortly after midnight both the Colonel and I
came to the doors of our respective tents, which adjoined one
another. The sentinel in front was also fighting mosquitoes.
As we came out we saw him pitch his gun about ten feet off,
and sit down to attack some of the pests that has swarmed up

his trousers' legs. Happening to glance in our direction, he nodded pleasantly and, with unabashed and friendly feeling, remarked, "Ain't they bad?"

It was astonishing how soon the men got over these little peculiarities. They speedily grew to recognize the fact that the observance of certain forms was essential to the maintenance of proper discipline. They became scrupulously careful in touching their hats, and always came to attention when spoken to. They saw that we did not insist upon the observance of these forms to humiliate them; that we were as anxious to learn our own duties as we were to have them learn theirs, and as scrupulous in paying respect to our superiors as we were in exacting the acknowledgment due our rank from those below us; moreover, what was very important, they saw that we were careful to look after their interests in every way, and were doing all that was possible to hurry up the equipment and drill of the regiment, so as to get into the war.

Rigid guard duty was established at once, and everyone was impressed with the necessity for vigilance and watchfulness. The policing of the camp was likewise attended to with the utmost rigor. As always with new troops, they were at first indifferent to the necessity for cleanliness in camp arrangements; but on this point Colonel Wood brooked no laxity, and in a very little while the hygienic conditions of the camp were as good as those of any regular regiment. Meanwhile the men were being drilled, on foot at first, with the utmost assiduity. Every night we had officers' school, the non-commissioned officers of each troop being given similar schooling by the Captain or one of the Lieutenants of the troop; and every day we practised hard, by squad, by troop, by squadron and battalion. The earnestness and intelligence with which the men went to work rendered the task of instruction much less difficult than would be supposed. It soon grew easy to handle the regiment in all the simpler forms of close and open order. When they had grown so that they could be handled with ease in marching, and in the ordinary manœuvres of the drill-ground, we began to train them in open-order work, skirmishing and firing. Here their wood-craft and plainscraft, their knowledge of the rifle, helped us very much. Skirmishing they took to naturally, which was fortunate, as practically all our fighting was done in open order.

Meanwhile we were purchasing horses. Judging from what I saw I do not think that we got heavy enough animals, and of those purchased certainly a half were nearly unbroken. It was no easy matter to handle them on the picket-lines, and to provide for feeding and watering; and the efforts to shoe and ride them were at first productive of much vigorous excitement. Of course, those that were wild from the range had to be thrown and tied down before they could be shod. Half the horses of the regiment bucked, or possessed some other of the amiable weaknesses incident to horse life on the great ranches; but we had abundance of men who were utterly unmoved by any antic a horse might commit. Every animal was speedily mastered, though a large number remained to the end mounts upon which an ordinary rider would have felt very uncomfortable.

My own horses were purchased for me by a Texas friend, John Moore, with whom I had once hunted peccaries on the Nueces. I only paid fifty dollars apiece, and the animals were not showy; but they were tough and hardy, and answered my purpose well.

Mounted drill with such horses and men bade fair to offer opportunities for excitement; yet it usually went off smoothly enough. Before drilling the men on horseback they had all been drilled on foot, and having gone at their work with hearty zest, they knew well the simple movements to form any kind of line or column. Wood was busy from morning till night in hurrying the final details of the equipment, and he turned the drill of the men over to me. To drill perfectly needs long practice, but to drill roughly is a thing very easy to learn indeed. We were not always right about our intervals, our lines were somewhat irregular, and our more difficult movements were executed at times in rather a haphazard way; but the essential commands and the essential movements we learned without any difficulty, and the men performed them with great dash. When we put them on horseback, there was, of course, trouble with the horses; but the horsemanship of the riders was consummate. In fact, the men were immensely interested in making their horses perform each evolution with

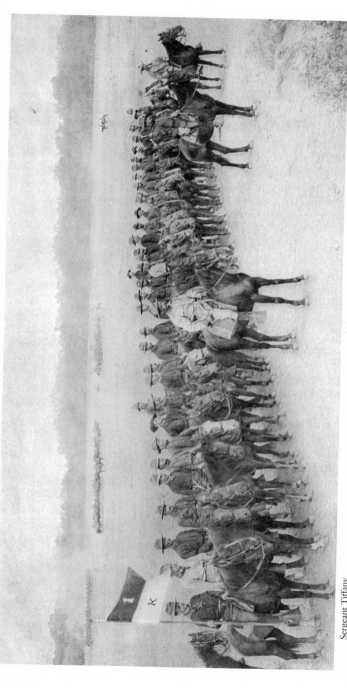

Sergeant Tiffany
with flag.

Lieutenant
Woodbury Kane.

Captain
Jenkins.

Lieutenant
H. K. Devereaux.

Troop K, Rough Riders.

the utmost speed and accuracy, and in forcing each unquiet, vicious brute to get into line and stay in line, whether he would or not. The guidon-bearers held their plunging steeds true to the line, no matter what they tried to do; and each wild rider brought his wild horse into his proper place with a dash and ease which showed the natural cavalryman.

In short, from the very beginning the horseback drills were good fun, and everyone enjoyed them. We marched out through the adjoining country to drill wherever we found open ground, practising all the different column formations as we went. On the open ground we threw out the line to one side or the other, and in one position and the other, sometimes at the trot, sometimes at the gallop. As the men grew accustomed to the simple evolutions, we tried them more and more in skirmish drills, practising them so that they might get accustomed to advance in open order and to skirmish in any country, while the horses were held in the rear.

Our arms were the regular cavalry carbine, the "Krag," a splendid weapon, and the revolver. A few carried their favorite Winchesters, using, of course, the new model, which took the Government cartridge. We felt very strongly that it would be worse than a waste of time to try to train our men to use the sabre — a weapon utterly alien to them; but with the rifle and revolver they were already thoroughly familiar. Many of my cavalry friends in the past had insisted to me that the revolver was a better weapon than the sword — among them Basil Duke, the noted Confederate cavalry leader, and Captain Frank Edwards, whom I had met when elk-hunting on the head-waters of the Yellowstone and the Snake. Personally, I knew too little to decide as to the comparative merits of the two arms; but I did know that it was a great deal better to use the arm with which our men were already proficient. They were therefore armed with what might be called their natural weapon, the revolver.

As it turned out, we were not used mounted at all, so that our preparations on this point came to nothing. In a way, I have always regretted this. We thought we should at least be employed as cavalry in the great campaign against Havana in the fall; and from the beginning I began to train my men in shock tactics for use against hostile cavalry. My belief was that the horse was really the weapon with which to strike the first blow. I felt that if my men could be trained to hit their adversaries with their horses, it was a matter of small amount whether, at the moment when the onset occurred, sabres, lances, or revolvers were used; while in the subsequent mêlée I believed the revolver would outclass cold steel as a weapon. But this is all guesswork, for we never had occasion to try the experiment.

It was astonishing what a difference was made by two or three weeks' training. The mere thorough performance of guard and police duties helped the men very rapidly to become soldiers. The officers studied hard, and both officers and men worked hard in the drill-field. It was, of course, rough and ready drill; but it was very efficient, and it was suited to the men who made up the regiment. Their uniform also suited them. In their slouch hats, blue flannel shirts, brown trousers, leggings and boots, with handkerchiefs knotted loosely around their necks, they looked exactly as a body of cow-boy cavalry should look. The officers speedily grew to realize that they must not be over-familiar with their men, and yet that they must care for them in every way. The men, in return, began to acquire those habits of attention to soldierly detail which mean so much in making a regiment. Above all, every man felt, and had constantly instilled into him, a keen pride of the regiment, and a resolute purpose to do his whole duty uncomplainingly, and, above all, to win glory by the way he handled himself in battle.

*Drawn by Charles Dana Gibson.*

Colonel Theodore Roosevelt.

# II

## TO CUBA

UP TO the last moment we were spending every ounce of energy we had in getting the regiment into shape. Fortunately, there were a good many vacancies among the officers, as the original number of 780 men was increased to 1,000; so that two companies were organized entirely anew. This gave the chance to promote some first-rate men.

One of the most useful members of the regiment was Dr. Robb Church, formerly a Princeton foot-ball player. He was appointed as Assistant Surgeon, but acted throughout almost all the Cuban campaign as the Regimental Surgeon. It was Dr. Church who first gave me an idea of Bucky O'Neill's versatility, for I happened to overhear them discussing Aryan word-roots together, and then sliding off into a review of the novels of Balzac, and a discussion as to how far Balzac could be said to be the founder of the modern realistic school of fiction. Church had led almost as varied a life as Bucky himself, his career including incidents as far apart as exploring and elk-hunting in the Olympic Mountains, cooking in a lumber-camp, and serving as doctor on an emigrant ship.

Woodbury Kane was given a commission, and also Horace Devereux, of Princeton. Kane was older than the other college men who entered in the ranks; and as he had the same good qualities to start with, this resulted in his ultimately becoming perhaps the most useful soldier in the regiment. He escaped wounds and serious sickness, and was able to serve through every day of the regiment's existence.

Two of the men made Second Lieutenants by promotion from the ranks while in San Antonio were John Greenway, a noted Yale foot-ball player and catcher on her base-ball nine, and David Goodrich, for two years captain of the Harvard crew. They were young men, Goodrich having only just graduated; while Greenway, whose father had served with honor in the Confederate Army, had been out of Yale three or four years. They were natural soldiers, and it would be well-nigh impossible to overestimate the amount of good they did the regiment. They were strapping fellows, entirely fearless, modest, and quiet. Their only thought was how to perfect themselves in their own duties, and how to take care of the men under them, so as to bring them to the highest point of soldierly perfection. I grew steadily to rely upon them, as men who could be counted upon with absolute certainty, not only in every emergency, but in all routine work. They were never so tired as not to respond with eagerness to the slightest suggestion of doing something new, whether it was dangerous or merely difficult and laborious. They not merely did their duty, but were always on the watch to find out some new duty which they could construe to be theirs. Whether it was policing camp, or keeping guard, or preventing straggling on the march, or procuring food for the men, or seeing that they took care of themselves in camp, or performing some feat of unusual hazard in the fight — no call was ever made upon them to which they did not respond with eager thankfulness for being given the chance to answer it. Later on I worked them as hard as I knew how, and the regiment will always be their debtor.

Greenway was from Arkansas. We could have filled up the whole regiment many times over from the South Atlantic and Gulf States alone, but were only able to accept a very few applicants. One of them was John McIlhenny, of Louisiana; a planter and manufacturer, a big-game hunter and book-lover, who could have had a commission in the Louisiana troops, but who preferred to go as a trooper in the Rough Riders because he believed we would surely see fighting. He could have commanded any influence, social or political, he wished; but he never asked a favor of any kind. He went into one of the New Mexican troops, and by his high qualities and zealous attention to duty speedily rose to a sergeantcy, and finally won his lieutenancy for gallantry in action.

The tone of the officers' mess was very high. Everyone seemed to realize that he had undertaken most serious work. They all earnestly wished for a chance to distinguish themselves, and fully appreciated that they ran the risk not merely of death, but of what was infinitely worse — namely, failure at the crisis to perform duty well; and they strove earnestly so to train themselves, and the men under them, as to minimize the possibility of such disgrace. Every officer and every man was taught continually to look forward to the day of battle eagerly, but with an entire sense of the drain that would then be made upon his endurance and resolution. They were also taught that, before the battle came, the rigorous performance of the countless irksome duties of the camp and the march was demanded from all alike, and that no excuse would be tolerated for failure to perform duty. Very few of the men had gone into the regiment lightly, and the fact that they did their duty so well may be largely attributed to the seriousness with which these eager, adventurous young fellows approached their work. This seriousness, and a certain simple manliness which accompanied it, had one very pleasant side. During our entire time of service, I never heard in the officers' mess a foul story or a foul word; and though there was occasional hard swearing in moments of emergency, yet even this was the exception.

The regiment attracted adventurous spirits from everywhere. Our chief trumpeter was a native American, our second trumpeter was from the Mediterranean — I think an Italian — who had been a soldier of fortune not only in Egypt, but in the French Army in Southern China. Two excellent men were Osborne, a tall Australian, who had been an officer in the New South Wales Mounted Rifles; and Cook, an Englishman, who had served in South Africa. Both, when the regiment disbanded, were plaintive in expressing their fond regret that it could not be used against the Transvaal Boers!

One of our best soldiers was a man whose real and assumed names I, for obvious reasons, conceal. He usually went by a nickname which I will call Tennessee. He was a tall, gaunt fellow, with a quiet and distinctly sinister eye, who did his duty excellently, especially when a fight was on, and who, being an expert gambler, always contrived to reap a rich harvest after pay-day. When the regiment was mustered out, he asked me to put a brief memorandum of his services on his discharge certificate, which I gladly did. He much appreciated this, and added, in explanation, "You see, Colonel, my real name isn't Smith, it's Yancy. I had to change it, because three or four years ago I had a little trouble with a gentleman, and — er — well, in fact, I had to kill him; and the District Attorney, he had it in for me, and so I just skipped the country; and now, if it ever should be brought up against me, I should like to show your certificate as to my character!" The course of frontier justice sometimes moves in unexpected zigzags; so I did not express the doubt I felt as to whether my certificate that he had been a good soldier would help him much if he was tried for a murder committed three or four years previously.

The men worked hard and faithfully. As a rule, in spite of the number of rough characters among them, they behaved very well. One night a few of them went on a spree, and proceeded "to paint San Antonia red." One was captured by the city authorities, and we had to leave him behind us in jail. The others we dealt with ourselves, in a way that prevented a repetition of the occurrence.

The men speedily gave one another nicknames, largely conferred in a spirit of derision, their basis lying in contrast. A brave but fastidious member of a well-known Eastern club, who was serving in the ranks, was christened "Tough Ike"; and his bunkie, the man who shared his shelter-tent, who was a decidedly rough cow-puncher, gradually acquired the name of "The Dude." One unlucky and simple-minded cow-puncher, who had never been east of the great plains in his life, unwarily boasted that he had an aunt in New York, and ever afterward went by the name of "Metropolitan Bill." A huge red-headed Irishman was named "Sheeny Solomon." A young Jew who developed into one of the best fighters in the regiment accepted, with entire equanimity, the name of "Pork-chop." We had quite a number of professional gamblers, who, I am bound to say, usually made good soldiers. One, who was almost abnormally quiet and gentle, was called "Hell Roarer"; while another, who in point of language and deportment was his exact antithesis, was christened "Prayerful James."

While the officers and men were learning their duties, and learning to know one another, Colonel Wood was straining every nerve to get our equipments — an effort which was complicated by the tendency of the Ordnance Bureau to send whatever we really needed by freight instead of express. Finally, just as the last rifles, revolvers, and saddles came, we were ordered by wire at once to proceed by train to Tampa.

Instantly, all was joyful excitement. We had enjoyed San Antonio, and were glad that our regiment had been organized in the city where the Alamo commemorates the death fight of Crockett, Bowie, and their famous band of frontier heroes. All of us had worked hard, so that we had had no time to be homesick or downcast; but we were glad to leave the hot camp, where every day the strong wind sifted the dust through everything, and to start for the gathering-place of the army which was to invade Cuba. Our horses and men were getting into good shape. We were well enough equipped to warrant our starting on the campaign, and every man was filled with dread of being out of the fighting. We had a pack-train of 150 mules, so we had close on to 1,200 animals to carry.

Of course, our train was split up into sections, seven, all told; Colonel Wood commanding the first three, and I the last four. The journey by rail from San Antonio to Tampa took just four days, and I doubt if anybody who was on the trip will soon forget it. To occupy my few spare moments, I was reading M. Demolins's "Supériorité des Anglo-Saxons." M. Demolins, in giving the reasons why the English-speaking peoples are superior to those of Continental Europe, lays much stress upon the way in which "militarism" deadens the power of individual initiative, the soldier being trained to complete suppression of individual will, while his faculties become atrophied in consequence of his being merely a cog in a vast and perfectly ordered machine. I can assure the excellent French publicist that American "militarism," at least of the volunteer sort, has points of difference from the militarism of Continental Europe. The battalion chief of a newly raised American regiment, when striving to get into a war which the American people have undertaken with buoyant and light-hearted indifference to detail, has positively unlimited opportunity of the display of "individual initiative," and is in no danger whatever either of suffering from unhealthy suppression of personal will, or of finding his faculties of self-help numbed by becoming a cog in a gigantic and smooth-running machine. If such a battalion chief wants to get anything or go anywhere he must do it by exercising every pound of resource, inventiveness, and audacity he possesses. The help, advice, and superintendence he gets from outside will be of the most general, not to say superficial, character. If he is a cavalry officer, he has got to hurry and push the purchase of his horses, plunging into and out of the meshes of red-tape as best he can. He will have to fight for his rifles and his tents and his clothes. He will have to keep his men healthy largely by the light that nature has given him. When he wishes to embark his regiment, he will have to fight for his railway-cars exactly as he fights for his transport when it comes to going across the sea; and on his journey his men will or will not have food, and his horses will or will not have water and hay, and the trains will or will not make connections, in exact correspondence to the energy and success of his own efforts to keep things moving straight.

It was on Sunday, May 29th, that we marched out of our hot, windy, dusty camp to take the cars for Tampa. Colonel Wood went first, with the three sections under his special care. I followed with the other four. The railway had promised us a forty-eight hours' trip, but our experience in loading was enough to show that the promise would not be made good. There were no proper facilities for getting the horses on or off the cars, or for feeding or watering them; and there was endless confusion and delay among the railway officials. I marched my four sections over in the afternoon, the first three having taken the entire day to get off. We occupied the night. As far as the regiment itself was concerned, we worked an excellent system, Wood instructing me exactly how to proceed so as to avoid confusion. Being a veteran campaigner, he had all along insisted that for such work as we had before us we must travel with the minimum possible luggage. The men had merely what they could carry on their own backs, and the officers very little more. My own roll of clothes and bedding could be put on my spare horse. The mule-train was to be used simply for food, forage, and spare ammunition. As it turned out, we were not allowed to take either it or the horses.

It was dusk when I marched my long files of dusty troopers into the station-yard. I then made all dismount, excepting the troop which I first intended to load. This was brought up to the first freight-car. Here every man unsaddled, and left his saddle, bridle, and all that he did not himself need in the car, each individual's property being corded together. A guard was left in the car, and the rest of the men took the naked horses into the pens to be fed and watered. The other troops were loaded in the same way in succession. With each section there were thus a couple of baggage-cars in which the horse-gear, the superfluous baggage, and the travel rations were carried; and I also put aboard, not only at starting, but at every other opportunity, what oats and hay I could get, so as to provide against accidents for the horses. By the time the baggage-cars were loaded the horses of the first section had eaten and drunk their fill, and we loaded them on cattle-cars. The officers of each troop saw to the loading, taking a dozen picked men to help them; for some of the wild creatures, half broken and fresh from the ranges, were with difficulty driven up the chutes. Meanwhile I superintended not merely my own men, but the railroad men; and when the delays of the latter, and their inability to understand what was necessary, grew past bearing, I took charge of the trains myself, so as to insure the horse-cars of each section being coupled with the baggage-cars of that section.

We worked until long past midnight before we got the horses and baggage aboard, and then found that for some reason the passenger-cars were delayed and would not be out for some hours. In the confusion and darkness men of the different troops had become scattered, and some had drifted off to the vile drinking-booths around the stock-yards; so I sent details to search the latter, while the trumpeters blew the assembly until the First Sergeants could account for all the men. Then the troops were arranged in order, and the men of each lay down where they were, by the tracks and in the brush, to sleep until morning.

At dawn the passenger-trains arrived. The senior Captain of each section saw to it that his own horses, troopers, and baggage were together; and one by one they started off, I taking the last in person. Captain Capron had at the very beginning shown himself to be simply invaluable, from his extraordinary energy, executive capacity, and mastery over men; and I kept his section next mine, so that we generally came together at the different yards.

The next four days were very hot and very dusty. I tried to arrange so the sections would be far enough apart to allow each ample time to unload, feed, water, and load the horses at any stopping-place before the next section could arrive. There was enough delay and failure to make connections on the part of the railroad people to keep me entirely busy, not to speak of seeing at the stopping-places that the inexperienced officers got enough hay for their horses, and that the water given to them was both ample in quantity and drinkable. It happened that we usually made our longest stops at night, and this meant that we were up all night long.

Two or three times a day I got the men buckets of hot coffee, and when we made a long enough stop they were allowed liberty under the supervision of the non-commissioned officers. Some of them abused the privilege, and started to get drunk. These were promptly handled with the necessary severity, in the interest of the others; for it was only by putting an immediate check to every form of lawlessness or disobedience among the few men who were inclined to be bad that we were enabled to give full liberty to those who would not abuse it.

Everywhere the people came out to greet us and cheer us. They brought us flowers; they brought us watermelons and other fruits, and sometimes jugs and pails of milk — all of which we greatly appreciated. We were travelling through a region where practically all the older men had served in the Confederate Army, and where the younger men had all their lives long drunk in the endless tales told by their elders, at home, and at the cross-roads taverns, and in the court-house squares, about the cavalry of Forrest and Morgan and the infantry of Jackson and Hood. The blood of the old men stirred to the distant breath of battle; the blood of the young men leaped hot with eager desire to accompany us. The older women, who remembered the dreadful misery of war — the misery that presses its iron weight most heavily on the wives and the little ones — looked sadly at us; but the young girls drove down in bevies, arrayed in their finery, to wave flags in farewell to the troopers and to beg cartridges and buttons as mementos. Everywhere we saw the Stars and Stripes, and everywhere we were told, half-laughing, by grizzled ex-Confederates that they had never dreamed in the by-gone days of bitterness to greet the old flag as they now were greeting it, and to send their sons, as now they were sending them, to fight and die under it.

It was four days later that we disembarked, in a perfect welter of confusion. Tampa lay in the pine-covered sand-flats at the end of a one-track railroad, and everything connected with both military and railroad matters was in an almost inextricable tangle. There was no one to meet us or to tell us where we were to camp, and no one to issue us food for the first twenty-four hours; while the railroad people unloaded us wherever they pleased, or rather wherever the jam of all kinds of trains rendered it possible. We had to buy the men food out of our own pockets, and to seize wagons in order to get our spare baggage taken to the camping ground which we at last found had been allotted to us.

Once on the ground, we speedily got order out of confusion. Under Wood's eye the tents were put up in long streets, the picket-line of each troop stretching down its side of each street. The officers' quarters were at the upper ends of the streets, the company kitchens and sinks at the opposite ends. The camp was strictly policed, and drill promptly begun. For thirty-six hours we let the horses rest, drilling on foot, and then began the mounted drill again. The regiments with which we were afterward to serve were camped near us, and the sandy streets of the little town were thronged with soldiers, almost all of them regulars; for there were but one or two volunteer organizations besides ourselves. The regulars wore the canonical dark blue of Uncle Sam. Our own men were clad in dusty brown blouses, trousers and leggings being of the same hue, while the broad-brimmed soft hat was of dark gray; and very workmanlike they looked as, in column of fours, each troop trotted down its company street to form by squadron or battalion, the troopers sitting steadily in the saddles as they made their half-trained horses conform to the movement of the guidons.

Over in Tampa town the huge winter hotel was gay with general-officers and their staffs, with women in pretty dresses, with newspaper correspondents by the score, with military *attachés* of foreign powers, and with onlookers of all sorts; but we spent very little time there.

We worked with the utmost industry, special attention being given by each troop-commander to skirmish-drill in the woods. Once or twice we had mounted drill of the regiment as a whole. The military *attachés* came out to look on — English, German, Russian, French, and Japanese. With the Englishman, Captain Arthur Lee, a capital fellow, we soon struck up an especially close friendship; and we saw much of him throughout the campaign. So we did of several of the newspaper correspondents — Richard Harding Davis, John Fox, Jr., Caspar Whitney, and Frederic Remington. On Sunday Chaplain Brown, of Arizona, held service, as he did almost every Sunday during the campaign.

There were but four or five days at Tampa, however. We were notified that the expedition would start for destination unknown at once, and that we were to go with it; but that our horses were to be left behind, and only eight troops of seventy men each taken. Our sorrow at leaving the horses was entirely outweighed by our joy at going; but it was very hard indeed to select the four troops that were to stay, and the men who had to be left behind from each of the troops that went. Colonel Wood took Major Brodie and myself to command the two squadrons, being allowed only two squadron commanders. The men who were left behind felt the most bitter heartburn. To the great bulk of them I think it will be a life-long sorrow. I saw more than one, both among the officers and privates, burst into tears when he found he could not go. No outsider can appreciate the bitterness of the disappointment. Of course, really, those that stayed were entitled to precisely as much honor as those that went. Each man was doing his duty, and much the hardest and most disagreeable duty was to stay. Credit should go with the performance of duty, and not with what is very often the accident of glory. All this and much more we explained, but our explanations could not alter the fact that some had to be chosen and some had to be left. One of the Captains chosen was Captain Maximilian Luna, who commanded Troop F, from New Mexico. The Captain's people had been on the banks of the Rio Grande before my forefathers came to the mouth of the Hudson or Wood's landed at Plymouth; and he made the plea that it was his right to go as a representative of his race, for he was the

Chaplain Brown Preaching to the Regiment.

only man of pure Spanish blood who bore a commission in the army, and he demanded the privilege of proving that his people were precisely as loyal Americans as any others. I was glad when it was decided to take him.

It was the evening of June 7th when we suddenly received orders that the expedition was to start from Port Tampa, nine miles distant by rail, at daybreak the following morning; and that if we were not aboard our transport by that time we could not go. We had no intention of getting left, and prepared at once for the scramble which was evidently about to take place. As the number and capacity of the transports were known, or ought to have been known, and as the number and size of the regiments to go were also known, the task of allotting each regiment or fraction of a regiment to its proper transport, and arranging that the regiments and the transports should meet in due order on the dock, ought not to have been difficult. However, no arrangements were made in advance; and we were allowed to shove and hustle for ourselves as best we could, on much the same principles that had governed our preparations hitherto.

We were ordered to be at a certain track with all our baggage at midnight, there to take a train for Port Tampa. At the appointed time we turned up, but the train did not. The men slept heavily, while Wood and I and various other officers wandered about in search of information which no one could give. We now and then came across a Brigadier-General, or even a Major-General; but nobody knew anything. Some regiments got aboard the trains and some did not, but as none of the trains started this made little difference. At three o'clock we received orders to march over to an entirely different track, and away we went. No train appeared on this track either; but at six o'clock some coal-cars came by, and these we seized. By various arguments we persuaded the engineer in charge of the train to back us down the nine miles to Port Tampa, where we arrived covered with coal-dust, but with all our belongings.

The railway tracks ran out on the quay, and the transports, which had been anchored in midstream, were gradually being brought up alongside the quay and loaded. The trains were unloading wherever they happened to be, no attention

Troop H, shortly after Arrival at Tampa.

whatever being paid to the possible position of the transport on which the soldiers were to go. Colonel Wood and I jumped off and started on a hunt, which soon convinced us that we had our work cut out if we were to get a transport at all. From the highest General down, nobody could tell us where to go to find out what transport we were to have. At last we were informed that we were to hunt up the depot quartermaster, Colonel Humphrey. We found his office, where his assistant informed us that he didn't know where the Colonel was, but believed him to be asleep upon one of the transports. This seemed odd at such a time; but so many of the methods in vogue were odd, that we were quite prepared to accept it as a fact. However, it proved not to be such; but for an hour Colonel Humphrey might just as well have been asleep, as nobody knew where he was and nobody could find him, and the quay was crammed with some ten thousand men, most of whom were working at cross purposes.

At last, however, after over an hour's industrious and rapid search through this swarming ant-heap of humanity, Wood and I, who had separated, found Colonel Humphrey at nearly the same time and were alloted a transport — the Yucatan. She was out in midstream, so Wood seized a stray launch and boarded her. At the same time I happened to find out that she had previously been allotted to two other regiments — the Second Regular Infantry and the Seventy-first New York Volunteers, which latter regiment alone contained more men than could be put aboard her. Accordingly, I ran at full speed to our train; and leaving a strong guard with the baggage, I double-quicked the rest of the regiment up to the boat, just in time to board her as she came into the quay, and then to hold her against the Second Regulars and the Seventy-first, who had arrived a little too late, being a shade less ready than we were in the matter of individual initiative. There was a good deal of expostulation, but we had possession; and as the ship could not contain half of the men who had been told to go aboard her, the Seventy-first went away, as did all but four companies of the Second. These latter we took aboard. Meanwhile a General had caused our train to be unloaded at the end of the quay farthest from where the ship was; and the hungry, tired men spent most of the day in

Scene on the Dock at Port Tampa on the Day of Sailing
of the Transports.

the labor of bringing down their baggage and the food and ammunition.

The officers' horses were on another boat, my own being accompanied by my colored body-servant, Marshall, the most faithful and loyal of men, himself an old soldier of the Ninth Cavalry. Marshall had been in Indian campaigns, and he christened my larger horse "Rain-in-the-Face," while the other, a pony, went by the name of "Texas."

By the time that night fell, and our transport pulled off and anchored in midstream, we felt we had spent thirty-six tolerably active hours. The transport was overloaded, the men being packed like sardines, not only below but upon the decks; so that at night it was only possible to walk about by continually stepping over the bodies of the sleepers. The travel rations which had been issued to the men for the voyage were not sufficient, because the meat was very bad indeed; and when a ration consists of only four or five items, which taken together just meet the requirements of a strong and healthy man, the loss of one item is a serious thing. If we had been given canned corn-beef we would have been all right, but instead of this the soldiers were issued horrible stuff called "canned fresh beef." There was no salt in it. At the best it was stringy and tasteless; at the worst it was nauseating. Not one-fourth of it was ever eaten at all, even when the men became very hungry. There were no facilities for the men to cook anything. There was no ice for them; the water was not good; and they had no fresh meat or fresh vegetables.

However, all these things seemed of small importance compared with the fact that we were really embarked, and were with the first expedition to leave our shores. But by next morning came the news that the order to sail had been countermanded, and that we were to stay where we were for the time being. What this meant none of us could understand. It turned out later to be due to the blunder of a naval officer who mistook some of our vessels for Spaniards, and by his report caused consternation in Washington, until by vigorous scouting on the part of our other ships the illusion was dispelled.

Meanwhile the troop-ships, packed tight with their living freight, sweltered in the burning heat of Tampa Harbor. There was nothing whatever for the men to do, space being too cramped for amusement or for more drill than was implied in the manual of arms. In this we drilled them assiduously, and we also continued to hold school for both the officers and the non-commissioned officers. Each troop commander was regarded as responsible for his own non-commissioned officers, and Wood or myself simply dropped in to superintend, just as we did with the manual at arms. In the officers' school Captain Capron was the special instructor, and a most admirable one he was.

The heat, the steaming discomfort, and the confinement, together with the forced inaction, were very irksome; but everyone made the best of it, and there was little or no grumbling even among the men. All, from the highest to the lowest, were bent upon perfecting themselves according to their slender opportunities. Every book of tactics in the regiment was in use from morning until night, and the officers and non-commissioned officers were always studying the problems presented at the schools. About the only amusement was bathing over the side, in which we indulged both in the morning and evening. Many of the men from the Far West had never seen the ocean. One of them who knew how to swim was much interested in finding that the ocean water was not drinkable. Another, who had never in his life before seen any water more extensive that the headstream of the Rio Grande, met with an accident later in the voyage; that is, his hat blew away while we were in mid-ocean, and I heard him explaining the accident to a friend in the following words: "Oh-o-h, Jim! Ma hat blew into the creek!" So we lay for nearly a week, the vessels swinging around on their anchor chains, while the hot water of the bay flowed to and fro around them and the sun burned overhead.

At last, on the evening of June 13th, we received the welcome order to start. Ship after ship weighed anchor and went slowly ahead under half-steam for the distant mouth of the harbor, the bands playing, the flags flying, the rigging black with the clustered soldiers, cheering and shouting to those left behind on the quay and to their fellows on the other ships. The channel was very tortuous; and we anchored before we had gone far down it, after coming within an ace of a bad collision with another transport. The next morning we were all again under way, and in the afternoon the great fleet steamed southeast until Tampa Light sank in the distance.

For the next six days we sailed steadily southward and eastward through the wonderful sapphire seas of the West Indies. The thirty odd transports moved in long parallel lines, while ahead and behind and on their flanks the gray hulls of the war-ships surged through the blue water. We had every variety of craft to guard us, from the mighty battle-ship and swift cruiser to the converted yachts and the frail, venomous-looking torpedo-boats. The war-ships watched with ceaseless vigilance by day and night. When a sail of any kind appeared, instantly one of our guardians steamed toward it. Ordinarily, the torpedo-boats were towed. Once a strange ship steamed up too close, and instantly the nearest torpedo-boat was slipped like a greyhound from the leash, and sped across the water toward it; but the stranger proved harmless, and the swift, delicate, death-fraught craft returned again.

It was very pleasant, sailing southward through the tropic seas toward the unknown. We knew not whither we were bound, nor what we were to do; but we believed that the nearing future held for us many chances of death and hardship, of honor and renown. If we failed, we would share the fate of all who fail; but we were sure that we would win, that we should score the first great triumph in a mighty world-movement. At night we looked at the new stars, and hailed the Southern Cross when at last we raised it above the horizon. In the daytime we drilled, and in the evening we held officers' school; but there was much time when we had little to do, save to scan the wonderful blue sea and watch the flying-fish. Toward evening, when the officers clustered together on the forward bridge, the band of the Second Infantry played tune after tune, until on our quarter the glorious sun sank in the red west, and, one by one, the lights blazed out on troop-ship and war-ship for miles ahead and astern, as they steamed onward through the brilliant tropic night.

The men on the ship were young and strong, eager to face what lay hidden before them, eager for adventure where risk was the price of gain. Sometimes they talked of what they might do in the future, and wondered whether we were to

Transport No. 8 — Yucatan, with Rough Riders on Board,
off for Cuba.

attack Santiago or Porto Rico. At other times, as they lounged in groups, they told stories of their past — stories of the mining camps and the cattle ranges, of hunting bear and deer, of war-trails against the Indians, of lawless deeds of violence and the lawful violence by which they were avenged, of brawls in saloons, of shrewd deals in cattle and sheep, of successful quest for the precious metals; stories of brutal wrong and brutal appetite, melancholy love-tales, and memories of nameless heroes — masters of men and tamers of horses.

The officers, too, had many strange experiences to relate; none, not even Llewellen or O'Neill, had been through what was better worth telling, or could tell it better, than Capron. He had spent years among the Apaches, the wildest and fiercest of tribes, and again and again had owed his life to his own cool judgment and extraordinary personal prowess. He knew the sign language, familiar to all the Indians of the mountains and the plains; and it was curious to find that the signs for different animals, for water, for sleep and death, which he knew from holding intercourse with the tribes of the Southeast, were exactly like those which I had picked up on my occasional hunting or trading trips among the Sioux and Mandans of the North. He was a great rifle shot and wolf hunter, and had many tales to tell of the deeds of gallant hounds and the feats of famous horses. He had handled his Indian scouts and dealt with the "bronco" Indians, the renegades from the tribes, in circumstances of extreme peril; for he had seen the sullen, moody Apaches when they suddenly went crazy with wolfish blood-lust, and in their madness wished to kill whomever was nearest. He knew, so far as white man could know, their ways of thought, and how to humor and divert them when on the brink of some dangerous outbreak. Capron's training and temper fitted him to do great work in war; and he looked forward with eager confidence to what the future held, for he was sure that for him it held either triumph or death. Death was the prize he drew.

Most of the men had simple souls. They could relate facts, but they said very little about what they dimly felt. Bucky O'Neill, however, the iron-nerved, iron-willed fighter from Arizona, the Sheriff whose name was a by-word of terror to

General View of the Landing at Daiquiri — Transports in the Offing.

every wrong-doer, white or red, the gambler who with unmoved face would stake and lose every dollar he had in the
world — he, alone among his comrades, was a visionary, an
articulate emotionalist. He was very quiet about it, never talking unless he was sure of his listener; but at night, when we
leaned on the railing to look at the Southern Cross, he was
less apt to tell tales of his hard and stormy past than he was to
speak of the mysteries which lie behind courage, and fear, and
love, behind animal hatred, and animal lust for the pleasures
that have tangible shape. He had keenly enjoyed life, and he
could breast its turbulent torrent as few men could; he was a
practical man, who knew how to wrest personal success from
adverse forces, among money-makers, politicians, and desperadoes alike; yet, down at bottom, what seemed to interest
him most was the philosophy of life itself, of our understanding of it, and of the limitations set to that understanding. But
he was as far as possible from being a mere dreamer of dreams.
A stanchly loyal and generous friend, he was also exceedingly
ambitious on his own account. If, by risking his life, no matter
how great the risk, he could gain high military distinction, he
was bent on gaining it. He had taken so many chances when
death lay on the hazard, that he felt the odds were now against
him; but, said he, "Who would not risk his life for a star?"
Had he lived, and had the war lasted, he would surely have
won the eagle, if not the star.

We had a good deal of trouble with the transports, chiefly
because they were not under the control of the navy. One
of them was towing a schooner, and another a scow; both, of
course, kept lagging behind. Finally, when we had gone nearly
the length of Cuba, the transport with the schooner sagged
very far behind, and then our wretched transport was directed
by General Shafter to fall out of line and keep her company.
Of course, we executed the order, greatly to the wrath of Captain Clover, who, in the gunboat Bancroft, had charge of the
rear of the column — for we could be of no earthly use to
the other transport, and by our presence simply added just
so much to Captain Clover's anxiety, as he had two transports
to protect instead of one. Next morning the rest of the convoy
were out of sight, but we reached them just as they finally
turned.

Another View of the Landing at Daiquiri.

Until this we had steamed with the trade-wind blowing steadily in our faces; but once we were well to eastward of Cuba, we ran southwest with the wind behind on our quarter, and we all knew that our destination was Santiago. On the morning of the 20th we were close to the Cuban coast. High mountains rose almost from the water's edge, looking huge and barren across the sea. We sped onward past Guantanamo Bay, where we saw the little picket-ships of the fleet; and in the afternoon we sighted Santiago Harbor, with the great war-ships standing off and on in front of it, gray and sullen in their war-paint.

All next day we rolled and wallowed in the seaway, waiting until a decision was reached as to where we should land. On the morning of June 22d the welcome order for landing came.

We did the landing as we had done everything else — that is, in a scramble, each commander shifting for himself. The port at which we landed was called Daiquiri, a squalid little village where there had been a railway and iron-works. There were no facilities for landing, and the fleet did not have a quarter the number of boats it should have had for the purpose. All we could do was to stand in with the transports as close as possible, and then row ashore in our own few boats and the boats of the war-ships. Luck favored our regiment. My former naval aide, while I was Assistant Secretary of the Navy, Lieutenant Sharp, was in command of the Vixen, a converted yacht; and everything being managed on the go-as-you-please principle, he steamed by us and offered to help put us ashore. Of course, we jumped at the chance. Wood and I boarded the Vixen, and there we got Lieutenant Sharp's black Cuban pilot, who told us he could take our transport right in to within a few hundred yards of the land. Accordingly, we put him aboard; and in he brought her, gaining at least a mile and a half by the manœuvre. The other transports followed; but we had our berth, and were all right.

There was plenty of excitement to the landing. In the first place, the smaller war-vessels shelled Daiquiri, so as to dislodge any Spaniards who might be lurking in the neighborhood, and also shelled other places along the coast, to keep the enemy puzzled as to our intentions. Then the surf was high, and the landing difficult; so that the task of getting the men, the ammunition, and provisions ashore was not easy. Each man carried three days' field rations and a hundred rounds of ammunition. Our regiment had accumulated two rapid-fire Colt automatic guns, the gift of Stevens, Kane, Tiffany, and one or two others of the New York men, and also a dynamite gun, under the immediate charge of Sergeant Borrowe. To get these, and especially the last, ashore, involved no little work and hazard. Meanwhile, from another transport, our horses were being landed, together with the mules, by the simple process of throwing them overboard and letting them swim ashore, if they could. Both of Wood's got safely through. One of mine was drowned. The other, little Texas, got ashore all right. While I was superintending the landing at the ruined dock, with Bucky O'Neill, a boatful of colored infantry soldiers capsized, and two of the men went to the bottom; Bucky O'Neill plunging in, in full uniform, to save them, but in vain.

However, by the late afternoon we had all our men, with what ammunition and provisions they could themselves carry, landed, and were ready for anything that might turn up.

# III

## GENERAL YOUNG'S FIGHT
## AT LAS GUASIMAS

JUST BEFORE leaving Tampa we had been brigaded with the First (white) and Tenth (colored) Regular Cavalry under Brigadier-General S. B. M. Young. We were the Second Brigade, the First Brigade consisting of the Third and Sixth (white), and the Ninth (colored) Regular Cavalry under Brigadier-General Sumner. The two brigades of the cavalry division were under Major-General Joseph Wheeler, the gallant old Confederate cavalry commander.

General Young was — and is — as fine a type of the American fighting soldier as a man can hope to see. He had been in command, as Colonel, of the Yellowstone National Park, and I had seen a good deal of him in connection therewith, as I was President of the Boone and Crockett Club, an organization devoted to hunting big game, to its preservation, and to forest preservation. During the preceding winter, while he was in Washington, he had lunched with me at the Metropolitan Club, Wood being one of the other guests. Of course, we talked of the war, which all of us present believed to be impending, and Wood and I told him we were going to make every effort to get in, somehow; and he answered that we must be sure to get into his brigade, if he had one, and he would guarantee to show us fighting. None of us forgot the conversation. As soon as our regiment was raised General Young applied for it to be put in his brigade. We were put in; and he made his word good; for he fought and won the first fight on Cuban soil.

Yet, even though under him, we should not have been in this fight at all if we had not taken advantage of the chance to disembark among the first troops, and if it had not been for Wood's energy in pushing our regiment to the front.

On landing we spent some active hours in marching our men a quarter of a mile or so inland, as boat-load by boat-load they disembarked. Meanwhile one of the men, Knoblauch, a New Yorker, who was a great athlete and a champion swimmer, by diving in the surf off the dock, recovered most of the rifles which had been lost when the boat-load of colored cavalry capsized. The country would have offered very great difficulties to an attacking force had there been resistance. It was little but a mass of rugged and precipitous hills, covered for the most part by dense jungle. Five hundred resolute men could have prevented the disembarkation at very little cost to themselves. There had been about that number of Spaniards at Daiquiri that morning, but they had fled even before the ships began shelling. In their place we found hundreds of Cuban insurgents, a crew of as utter tatterdemalions as human eyes ever looked on, armed with every kind of rifle in all stages of dilapidation. It was evident, at a glance, that they would be no use in serious fighting, but it was hoped that they might be of service in scouting. From a variety of causes, however, they turned out to be nearly useless, even for this purpose, so far as the Santiago campaign was concerned.

We were camped on a dusty, brush-covered flat, with jungle on one side, and on the other a shallow, fetid pool fringed with palm-trees. Huge land-crabs scuttled noisily through the underbrush, exciting much interest among the men. Camping was a simple matter, as each man carried all he had, and the officers had nothing. I took a light mackintosh and a toothbrush. Fortunately, that night it did not rain; and from the palm-leaves we built shelters from the sun.

General Lawton, a tall, fine-looking man, had taken the advance. A thorough soldier, he at once established outposts and pushed reconnoitring parties ahead on the trails. He had as little baggage as the rest of us. Our own Brigade-Commander, General Young, had exactly the same impedimenta that I had, namely, a mackintosh and a tooth-brush.

Next morning we were hard at work trying to get the stuff unloaded from the ship, and succeeded in getting most of it ashore, but were utterly unable to get transportation for anything but a very small quantity. The great shortcoming throughout the campaign was the utterly inadequate transportation. If we had been allowed to take our mule-train, we could have kept the whole cavalry division supplied.

In the afternoon word came to us to march. General Wheeler, a regular game-cock, was as anxious as Lawton to

Rough Riders' Camp at Daiquiri.

get first blood, and he was bent upon putting the cavalry division to the front as quickly as possible. Lawton's advance-guard was in touch with the Spaniards, and there had been a skirmish between the latter and some Cubans, who were repulsed. General Wheeler made a reconnoissance in person, found out where the enemy was, and directed General Young to take our brigade and move forward so as to strike him next morning. He had the power to do this, as when General Shafter was afloat he had command ashore.

I had succeeded in finding Texas, my surviving horse, much the worse for his fortnight on the transport and his experience in getting off, but still able to carry me.

It was mid-afternoon and the tropic sun was beating fiercely down when Colonel Wood started our regiment — the First and Tenth Cavalry and some of the infantry regiments having already marched. Colonel Wood himself rode in advance, while I led my squadron, and Major Brodie followed with his. It was a hard march, the hilly jungle trail being so narrow that often we had to go in single file. We marched fast, for Wood was bound to get us ahead of the other regiments, so as to be sure of our place in the body that struck the enemy next morning. If it had not been for his energy in pushing forward, we should certainly have missed the fight. As it was, we did not halt until we were at the extreme front.

The men were not in very good shape for marching, and moreover they were really horsemen, the majority being cowboys who had never done much walking. The heat was intense and their burdens very heavy. Yet there was very little straggling. Whenever we halted they instantly took off their packs and threw themselves on their backs. Then at the word to start they would spring into place again. The captains and lieutenants tramped along, encouraging the men by example and word. A good part of the time I was by Captain Llewellen, and was greatly pleased to see the way in which he kept his men up to their work. He never pitied or coddled his troopers, but he always looked after them. He helped them whenever he could, and took rather more than his full share of hardship and danger, so that his men naturally followed him with entire devotion. Jack Greenway was under him as lieutenant, and to him the entire march was nothing but an enjoyable outing, the chance of fight on the morrow simply adding the needed spice of excitement.

It was long after nightfall when we tramped through the darkness into the squalid coast hamlet of Siboney. As usual when we made a night camp, we simply drew the men up in column of troops, and then let each man lie down where he was. Black thunder-clouds were gathering. Before they broke the fires were made and the men cooked their coffee and pork, some frying the hard-tack with the pork. The officers, of course, fared just as the men did. Hardly had we finished eating when the rain came, a regular tropic downpour. We sat about, sheltering ourselves as best we could, for the hour or two it lasted; then the fires were relighted and we closed around them, the men taking off their wet things to dry them, so far as possible, by the blaze.

Wood had gone off to see General Young, as General Wheeler had instructed General Young to hit the Spaniards, who were about four miles away, as soon after daybreak as possible. Meanwhile I strolled over to Captain Capron's troop. He and I, with his two lieutenants, Day and Thomas, stood around the fire, together with two or three non-commissioned officers and privates; among the latter were Sergeant Hamilton Fish and Trooper Elliot Cowdin, both of New York. Cowdin, together with two other troopers, Harry Thorpe and Munro Ferguson, had been on my Oyster Bay Polo Team some years before. Hamilton Fish had already shown himself one of the best non-commissioned officers we had. A huge fellow, of enormous strength and endurance and dauntless courage, he took naturally to a soldier's life. He never complained and never shirked any duty of any kind, while his power over his men was great. So good a sergeant had he made that Captain Capron, keen to get the best men under him, took him when he left Tampa — for Fish's troop remained behind. As we stood around the flickering blaze that night I caught myself admiring the splendid bodily vigor of Capron and Fish — the captain and the sergeant. Their frames seemed of steel, to withstand all fatigue; they were flushed with health; in their eyes shone high resolve and fiery desire. Two finer types of the fighting man, two better representatives of the American soldier, there were not in the whole army. Capron was going over his plans for the fight when we should meet the Spaniards on the morrow, Fish occasionally asking a question. They were both filled with eager longing to show their mettle, and both were rightly confident that if they lived they would win honorable renown and would rise high in their chosen profession. Within twelve hours they both were dead.

I had lain down when toward midnight Wood returned. He had gone over the whole plan with General Young. We were to start by sunrise toward Santiago, General Young taking four troops of the Tenth and four troops of the First up the road which led through the valley; while Colonel Wood was to lead our eight troops along a hill-trail to the left, which joined the valley road about four miles on, at a point where the road went over a spur of the mountain chain and from thence went down hill toward Santiago. The Spaniards had their lines at the junction of the road and the trail.

Before describing our part in the fight, it is necessary to say a word about General Young's share, for, of course, the whole fight was under his direction, and the fight on the right wing under his immediate supervision. General Young had obtained from General Castillo, the commander of the Cuban forces, a full description of the country in front. General Castillo promised Young the aid of eight hundred Cubans, if he made a reconnoissance in force to find out exactly what the Spanish strength was. This promised Cuban aid did not, however, materialize, the Cubans, who had been beaten back by the Spaniards the day before, not appearing on the firing-line until the fight was over.

General Young had in his immediate command a squadron of the First Regular Cavalry, two hundred and forty-four strong, under the command of Major Bell, and a squadron of the Tenth Regular Cavalry, two hundred and twenty strong, under the command of Major Norvell. He also had two Hotchkiss mountain guns, under Captain Watson of the Tenth. He started at a quarter before six in the morning, accompanied by Captain A. L. Mills, as aide. It was at half-past seven that Captain Mills, with a patrol of two men in advance, discovered the Spaniards as they lay across where the two roads came together, some of them in pits, others simply lying

in the heavy jungle, while on their extreme right they occupied a big ranch. Where General Young struck them they held
a high ridge a little to the left of his front, this ridge being separated by a deep ravine from the hill-trail still farther to the
left, down which the Rough Riders were advancing. That is,
their forces occupied a range of high hills in the form of an
obtuse angle, the salient being toward the space between the
American forces, while there were advance parties along both
roads. There were stone breastworks flanked by block-houses
on that part of the ridge where the two trails came together.
The place was called Las Guasimas, from trees of that name
in the neighborhood.

General Young, who was riding a mule, carefully examined
the Spanish position in person. He ordered the canteens of
the troops to be filled, placed the Hotchkiss battery in concealment about nine hundred yards from the Spanish lines,
and then deployed the white regulars, with the colored regulars in support, having sent a Cuban guide to try to find
Colonel Wood and warn him. He did not attack immediately,
because he knew that Colonel Wood, having a more difficult
route, would require a longer time to reach the position.
During the delay General Wheeler arrived; he had been up
since long before dawn, to see that everything went well.
Young informed him of the dispositions and plan of attack
he made. General Wheeler approved of them, and with excellent judgment left General Young a free hand to fight his
battle.

So, about eight o'clock Young began the fight with his
Hotchkiss guns, he himself being up on the firing-line. No
sooner had the Hotchkiss one-pounders opened than the
Spaniards opened fire in return, most of the time firing by volleys executed in perfect time, almost as on parade. They had
a couple of light guns, which our people thought were quick
firers. The denseness of the jungle and the fact that they used
absolutely smokeless powder, made it exceedingly difficult to
place exactly where they were, and almost immediately Young,
who always liked to get as close as possible to his enemy,
began to push his troops forward. They were deployed on
both sides of the road in such thick jungle that it was only here
and there that they could possibly see ahead, and some con-

fusion, of course, ensued, the support gradually getting mixed with the advance. Captain Beck took A Troop of the Tenth in on the left, next Captain Galbraith's troop of the First; two other troops of the Tenth were on the extreme right. Through the jungle ran wire fences here and there, and as the troops got to the ridge they encountered precipitous heights. They were led most gallantly, as American regular officers always lead their men; and the men followed their leaders with the splendid courage always shown by the American regular soldier. There was not a single straggler among them, and in not one instance was an attempt made by any trooper to fall out in order to assist the wounded or carry back the dead, while so cool were they and so perfect their fire discipline, that in the entire engagement the expenditure of ammunition was not over ten rounds per man. Major Bell, who commanded the squadron, had his leg broken by a shot as he was leading his men. Captain Wainwright succeeded to the command of the squadron. Captain Knox was shot in the abdomen. He continued for some time giving orders to his troops, and refused to allow a man in the firing-line to assist him to the rear. His First Lieutenant, Byram, was himself shot, but continued to lead his men until the wound and the heat overcame him and he fell in a faint. The advance was pushed forward under General Young's eye with the utmost energy, until the enemy's voices could be heard in the entrenchments. The Spaniards kept up a very heavy firing, but the regulars would not be denied, and as they climbed the ridges the Spaniards broke and fled.

Meanwhile, at six o'clock, the Rough Riders began their advance. We first had to climb a very steep hill. Many of the men, foot-sore and weary from their march of the preceding day, found the pace up this hill too hard, and either dropped their bundles or fell out of line, with the result that we went into action with less than five hundred men — as, in addition to the stragglers, a detachment had been left to guard the baggage on shore. At the time I was rather inclined to grumble to myself about Wood setting so fast a pace, but when the fight began I realized that it had been absolutely necessary, as otherwise we should have arrived late and the regulars would have had very hard work indeed.

Tiffany, by great exertions, had corralled a couple of mules and was using them to transport the Colt automatic guns in the rear of the regiment. The dynamite gun was not with us, as mules for it could not be obtained in time.

Captain Capron's troop was in the lead, it being chosen for the most responsible and dangerous position because of Capron's capacity. Four men, headed by Sergeant Hamilton Fish, went first; a support of twenty men followed some distance behind; and then came Capron and the rest of his troop, followed by Wood, with whom General Young had sent Lieutenants Smedburg and Rivers as aides. I rode close behind, at the head of the other three troops of my squadron, and then came Brodie at the head of his squadron. The trail was so narrow that for the most part the men marched in single file, and it was bordered by dense, tangled jungle, through which a man could with difficulty force his way; so that to put out flankers was impossible, for they could not possibly have kept up with the march of the column. Every man had his canteen full. There was a Cuban guide at the head of the column, but he ran away as soon as the fighting began. There were also with us, at the head of the column, two men who did not run away, who, though non-combatants — newspaper correspondents — showed as much gallantry as any soldier in the field. They were Edward Marshall and Richard Harding Davis.

After reaching the top of the hill the walk was very pleasant. Now and then we came to glades or rounded hill-shoulders, whence we could look off for some distance. The tropical forest was very beautiful, and it was a delight to see the strange trees, the splendid royal palms and a tree which looked like a flat-topped acacia, and which was covered with a mass of brilliant scarlet flowers. We heard many bird-notes, too, the cooing of doves and the call of a great brush cuckoo. Afterward we found that the Spanish guerillas imitated these bird-calls, but the sounds we heard that morning, as we advanced through the tropic forest, were from birds, not guerillas, until we came right up to the Spanish lines. It was very beautiful and very peaceful, and it seemed more as if we were off on some hunting excursion than as if we were about to go into a sharp and bloody little fight.

Of course, we accommodated our movements to those of the men in front. After marching for somewhat over an hour, we suddenly came to a halt, and immediately afterward Colonel Wood sent word down the line that the advance guard had come upon a Spanish outpost. Then the order was passed to fill the magazines, which was done.

The men were totally unconcerned, and I do not think they realized that any fighting was at hand; at any rate, I could hear the group nearest me discussing in low murmurs, not the Spaniards, but the conduct of a certain cow-puncher in quitting work on a ranch and starting a saloon in some New Mexican town. In another minute, however, Wood sent me orders to deploy three troops to the right of the trail, and to advance when we became engaged; while, at the same time, the other troops, under Major Brodie, were deployed to the left of the trail where the ground was more open than elsewhere — one troop being held in reserve in the centre, besides the reserves on each wing. Later all the reserves were put into the firing-line.

To the right the jungle was quite thick, and we had barely begun to deploy when a crash in front announced that the fight was on. It was evidently very hot, and L Troop had its hands full; so I hurried my men up abreast of them. So thick was the jungle that it was very difficult to keep together, especially when there was no time for delay, and while I got up Llewellen's troops and Kane's platoon of K Troop, the rest of K Troop under Captain Jenkins which, with Bucky O'Neill's troop, made up the right wing, were behind, and it was some time before they got into the fight at all.

Meanwhile I had gone forward with Llewellen, Greenway, Kane and their troopers until we came out on a kind of shoulder, jutting over a ravine, which separated us from a great ridge on our right. It was on this ridge that the Spaniards had some of their intrenchments, and it was just beyond this ridge that the Valley Road led, up which the regulars were at that very time pushing their attack; but, of course, at the moment we knew nothing of this. The effect of the smokeless powder was remarkable. The air seemed full of the rustling sound of the Mauser bullets, for the Spaniards knew the trails by which we were advancing, and opened heavily on our position.

Opening at Side of Road through which Left Flank of Rough Riders Deployed.

Moreover, as we advanced we were, of course, exposed, and they could see us and fire. But they themselves were entirely invisible. The jungle covered everything, and not the faintest trace of smoke was to be seen in any direction to indicate from whence the bullets came. It was some time before the men fired; Llewellen, Kane, and I anxiously studying the ground to see where our opponents were, and utterly unable to find out.

We could hear the faint reports of the Hotchkiss guns and the reply of two Spanish guns, and the Mauser bullets were singing through the trees over our heads, making a noise like the humming of telephone wires; but exactly where they came from we could not tell. The Spaniards were firing high and for the most part by volleys, and their shooting was not very good, which perhaps was not to be wondered at, as they were a long way off. Gradually, however, they began to get the range and occasionally one of our men would crumple up. In no case did the man make any outcry when hit, seeming to take it as a matter of course; at the outside, making only such a remark as, "Well, I got it that time." With hardly an exception, there was no sign of flinching. I say with hardly an exception, for though I personally did not see an instance, and though all the men at the front behaved excellently, yet there were a very few men who lagged behind and drifted back to the trail over which we had come. The character of the fight put a premium upon such conduct, and afforded a very severe test for raw troops; because the jungle was so dense that as we advanced in open order, every man was, from time to time, left almost alone and away from the eyes of his officers. There was unlimited opportunity for dropping out without attracting notice, while it was peculiarly hard to be exposed to the fire of an unseen foe, and to see men dropping under it, and yet to be, for some time, unable to return it, and also to be entirely ignorant of what was going on in any other part of the field.

It was Richard Harding Davis who gave us our first opportunity to shoot back with effect. He was behaving precisely like my officers, being on the extreme front of the line, and taking every opportunity to study with his glasses the ground where we thought the Spaniards were. I had tried some volley firing at points where I rather doubtfully believed the Spaniards to be, but had stopped firing and was myself studying the jungle-covered mountain ahead with my glasses, when Davis suddenly said: "There they are, Colonel; look over there; I can see their hats near that glade," pointing across the valley to our right. In a minute I, too, made out the hats, and then pointed them out to three or four of our best shots, giving them my estimate of the range. For a minute or two no result followed, and I kept raising the range, at the same time getting more men on the firing-line. Then, evidently, the shots told, for the Spaniards suddenly sprang out of the cover through which we had seen their hats, and ran to another spot; and we could now make out a large number of them.

I accordingly got all of my men up in line and began quick firing. In a very few minutes our bullets began to do damage, for the Spaniards retreated to the left into the jungle, and we lost sight of them. At the same moment a big body of men who, it afterward turned out, were Spaniards, came in sight along the glade, following the retreat of those whom we had just driven from the trenches. We supposed that there was a large force of Cubans with General Young, not being aware that these Cubans had failed to make their appearance, and as it was impossible to tell the Cubans from the Spaniards, and as we could not decide whether these were Cubans following the Spaniards we had put to flight, or merely another troop of Spaniards retreating after the first (which was really the case) we dared not fire, and in a minute they had passed the glade and were out of sight.

At every halt we took advantage of the cover, sinking down behind any mound, brush, or tree-trunk in the neighborhood. The trees, of course, furnished no protection from the Mauser bullets. Once I was standing behind a large palm with my head out to one side, very fortunately; for a bullet passed through the palm, filling my left eye and ear with the dust and splinters.

No man was allowed to drop out to help the wounded. It was hard to leave them there in the jungle, where they might not be found again until the vultures and the land-crabs came, but war is a grim game and there was no choice. One of the men shot was Harry Heffner of G Troop, who was mortally wounded through the hips. He fell without uttering a sound, and two of his companions dragged him behind a tree. Here he propped himself up and asked to be given his canteen and his rifle, which I handed to him. He then again began shooting, and continued loading and firing until the line moved forward and we left him alone, dying in the gloomy shade. When we found him again, after the fight, he was dead.

At one time, as I was out of touch with that part of my wing commanded by Jenkins and O'Neill, I sent Greenway, with Sergeant Russell, a New Yorker, and trooper Rowland, a New Mexican cow-puncher, down in the valley to find out where they were. To do this the three had to expose themselves to a very severe fire, but they were not men to whom this mattered. Russell was killed; the other two returned and reported to me the position of Jenkins and O'Neill. They then resumed their places on the firing-line. After awhile I noticed blood coming out of Rowland's side and discovered that he had been shot, although he did not seem to be taking any notice of it. He said the wound was only slight, but as I saw he had broken a rib, I told him to go to the rear to the hospital. After some grumbling he went, but fifteen minutes later he was back on the firing-line again and said he could not find the hospital — which I doubted. However, I then let him stay until the end of the fight.

After we had driven the Spaniards off from their position to our right, the firing seemed to die away so far as we were concerned, for the bullets no longer struck around us in such a storm as before, though along the rest of the line the battle was as brisk as ever. Soon we saw troops appearing across the ravine, not very far from where we had seen the Spaniards whom we had thought might be Cubans. Again we dared not fire, and carefully studied the new-comers with our glasses; and this time we were right, for we recognized our own cavalry-men. We were by no means sure that they recognized us, however, and were anxious that they should, but it was very difficult to find a clear spot in the jungle from which to signal; so Sergeant Lee of Troop K climbed a tree and from its summit waved the troop guidon. They waved their guidon back, and as our right wing was now in touch with the regulars, I left Jenkins and O'Neill to keep the connection, and led Llewellen's troop back to the path to join the rest of the regiment, which was evidently still in the thick of the fight. I was still very much in the dark as to where the main body of the Spanish forces were, or exactly what lines the battle was following, and was very uncertain what I ought to do; but I knew it could not be wrong to go forward, and I thought I would find Wood and then see what he wished me to do. I was in a mood to cordially welcome guidance, for it was most bewildering to fight an enemy whom one so rarely saw.

I had not seen Wood since the beginning of the skirmish, when he hurried forward. When the firing opened some of the men began to curse. "Don't swear — shoot!" growled Wood, as he strode along the path leading his horse, and everyone laughed and became cool again. The Spanish outposts were very near our advance guard, and some minutes of the hottest kind of firing followed before they were driven back and slipped off through the jungle to their main lines in the rear.

Here, at the very outset of our active service, we suffered the loss of two as gallant men as ever wore uniform. Sergeant Hamilton Fish at the extreme front, while holding the point up to its work and firing back where the Spanish advance guards lay, was shot and instantly killed; three of the men with him were likewise hit. Captain Capron, leading the advance guard in person, and displaying equal courage and coolness in the way that he handled them, was also struck, and died a few minutes afterward. The command of the troop then devolved upon the First Lieutenant, young Thomas. Like Capron, Thomas was the fifth in line from father to son who had served in the American army, though in his case it was in the volunteer and not the regular service; the four preceding generations had furnished soldiers respectively to the Revolutionary War, the War of 1812, the Mexican War, and the Civil War. In a few minutes Thomas was shot through the leg, and the command devolved upon the Second Lieutenant, Day (a nephew of "Albemarle" Cushing, he who sunk the great Confederate ram). Day, who proved himself to be one of our most efficient officers, continued to handle the

Brigadier-General S. B. M. Young.

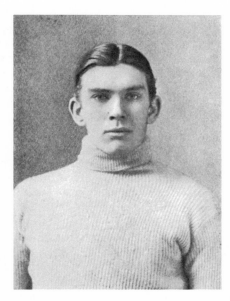

Hamilton Fish, Jr., First Sergeant, Troop L,
Killed in battle at Las Guasimas.

men to the best possible advantage, and brought them steadily forward. L Troop was from the Indian Territory. The whites, Indians, and half-breeds in it, all fought with equal courage. Captain McClintock was hurried forward to its relief with his Troop B of Arizona men. In a few minutes he was shot through the leg and his place was taken by his First Lieutenant, Wilcox, who handled his men in the same soldierly manner that Day did.

Among the men who showed marked courage and coolness was the tall color-sergeant, Wright; the colors were shot through three times.

When I had led G Troop back to the trail I ran ahead of them, passing the dead and wounded men of L Troop, passing young Fish as he lay with glazed eyes under the rank tropic growth to one side of the trail. When I came to the front I found the men spread out in a very thin skirmish line, advancing through comparatively open ground, each man taking advantage of what cover he could, while Wood strolled about leading his horse, Brodie being close at hand. How Wood escaped being hit, I do not see, and still less how his horse escaped. I had left mine at the beginning of the action, and was only regretting that I had not left my sword with it, as it kept getting between my legs when I was tearing my way through the jungle. I never wore it again in action. Lieutenant Rivers was with Wood, also leading his horse. Smedburg had been sent off on the by no means pleasant task of establishing communications with Young.

Very soon after I reached the front, Brodie was hit, the bullet shattering one arm and whirling him around as he stood. He had kept on the extreme front all through, his presence and example keeping his men entirely steady, and he at first refused to go to the rear; but the wound was very painful, and he became so faint that he had to be sent. Thereupon, Wood directed me to take charge of the left wing in Brodie's place, and to bring it forward; so over I went.

I now had under me Captains Luna, Muller, and Houston, and I began to take them forward, well spread out, through the high grass of a rather open forest. I noticed Goodrich, of Houston's troop, tramping along behind his men, absorbed

Major Brodie,
Wounded in the Guasimas Fight.

in making them keep at good intervals from one another and fire slowly with careful aim. As I came close up to the edge of the troop, he caught a glimpse of me, mistook me for one of his own skirmishers who was crowding in too closely, and called out, "Keep your interval, sir; keep your interval, and go forward."

A perfect hail of bullets was sweeping over us as we advanced. Once I got a glimpse of some Spaniards, apparently retreating, far in the front, and to our right, and we fired a couple of rounds after them. Then I became convinced, after much anxious study, that we were being fired at from some large red-tiled buildings, part of a ranch on our front. Smokeless powder, and the thick cover in our front, continued to puzzle us, and I more than once consulted anxiously the officers as to the exact whereabouts of our opponents. I took a rifle from a wounded man and began to try shots with it myself. It was very hot and the men were getting exhausted, though at this particular time we were not suffering heavily from bullets, the Spanish fire going high. As we advanced, the cover became a little thicker and I lost touch of the main body under Wood; so I halted and we fired industriously at the ranch buildings ahead of us, some five hundred yards off. Then we heard cheering on the right, and I supposed that this meant a charge on the part of Wood's men, so I sprang up and ordered the men to rush the buildings ahead of us. They came forward with a will. There was a moment's heavy firing from the Spaniards, which all went over our heads, and then it ceased entirely. When we arrived at the buildings, panting and out of breath, they contained nothing but heaps of empty cartridge-shells and two dead Spaniards, shot through the head.

The country all around us was thickly forested, so that it was very difficult to see any distance in any direction. The firing had now died out, but I was still entirely uncertain as to exactly what had happened. I did not know whether the enemy had been driven back or whether it was merely a lull in the fight, and we might be attacked again; nor did I know what had happened in any other part of the line, while as I occupied the extreme left, I was not sure whether or not my flank was in danger. At this moment one of our men who had dropped out, arrived with the information (fortunately false) that Wood was dead. Of course, this meant that the command devolved upon me, and I hastily set about taking charge of the regiment. I had been particularly struck by the coolness and courage shown by Sergeants Dame and McIlhenny, and sent them out with small pickets to keep watch in front and to the left of the left wing. I sent other men to fill the canteens with water, and threw the rest out in a long line in a disused sunken road, which gave them cover, putting two or three wounded men, who had hitherto kept up with the fighting-line, and a dozen men who were suffering from heat exhaustion — for the fighting and running under that blazing sun through the thick dry jungle was heart-breaking — into the ranch buildings. Then I started over toward the main body, but to my delight encountered Wood himself, who told me the fight was over and the Spaniards had retreated. He also informed me that other troops were just coming up. The first to appear was a squadron of the Ninth Cavalry, under Major Dimick, which had hurried up to get into the fight, and was greatly disappointed to find it over. They took post in front of our lines, so that our tired men were able to get a rest, Captain McBlain, of the Ninth, good-naturedly giving us some points as to the best way to station our outposts. Then General Chaffee, rather glum at not having been in the fight himself, rode up at the head of some of his infantry, and I marched my squadron back to where the rest of the regiment was going into camp, just where the two trails came together, and beyond — that is, on the Santiago side of — the original Spanish lines.

The Rough Riders had lost eight men killed and thirty-four wounded, aside from two or three who were merely scratched and whose wounds were not reported. The First Cavalry, white, lost seven men killed and eight wounded; the Tenth Cavalry, colored, one man killed and ten wounded; so, out of 964 men engaged on our side, 16 were killed and 52 wounded. The Spaniards were under General Rubin, with, as second in command, Colonel Alcarez. They had two guns, and eleven companies of about a hundred men each: three belonging to the Porto Rico regiment, three to the San Fernandino, two to the Talavero, two being so-called mobilized companies from the mineral districts, and one a company of engineers; over twelve hundred men in all, together with two guns.*

General Rubin reported that he had repulsed the American attack, and Lieutenant Tejeiro states in his book that General Rubin forced the Americans to retreat, and enumerates the attacking force as consisting of three regular regiments of infantry, the Second Massachusetts and the Seventy-first New York (not one of which fired a gun or were anywhere near the battle), in addition to the sixteen dismounted troops of cavalry. In other words, as the five infantry regiments each included twelve companies, he makes the attacking force consist of just five times the actual amount. As for the "repulse," our line never went back ten yards in any place, and the advance was practically steady; while an hour and a half after the fight began we were in complete possession of the entire Spanish position, and their troops were fleeing in masses down the road, our men being too exhausted to follow them.

General Rubin also reports that he lost but seven men killed. This is certainly incorrect, for Captain O'Neill and I went over the ground very carefully and counted eleven dead Spaniards, all of whom were actually buried by our burying squads. There were probably two or three men whom we missed, but I think that our official reports are incorrect in stating that forty-two dead Spaniards were found; this being based upon reports in which I think some of the Spanish dead were counted two or three times. Indeed, I should doubt whether their loss was as heavy as ours, for they were under cover, while we advanced, often in the open, and their main lines fled long before we could get to close quarters. It was a

*See Lieutenant Müller y Tejeiro, "Combates y Capitulación de Santiago de Cuba," page 136. The Lieutenant speaks as if only one échelon, of seven companies and two guns, was engaged on the 24th. The official report says distinctly, "General Rubin's column," which consisted of the companies detailed above. By turning to page 146, where Lieutenant Tejeiro enumerates the strength of the various companies, it will be seen that they averaged over 110 men apiece; this probably does not include officers, and is probably an under-statement anyhow. On page 261 he makes the Spanish loss at Las Guasimas, which he calls Sevilla, 9 killed and 27 wounded. Very possibly he includes only the Spanish regulars; two of the Spaniards we slew, over on the left, were in brown, instead of the light blue of the regulars, and were doubtless guerillas.

very difficult country, and a force of good soldiers resolutely handled could have held the pass with ease against two or three times their number. As it was, with a force half of regulars and half of volunteers, we drove out a superior number of Spanish regular troops, strongly posted, without suffering a very heavy loss. Although the Spanish fire was very heavy, it does not seem to me it was very well directed; and though they fired with great spirit while we merely stood at a distance and fired at them, they did not show much resolution, and when we advanced, always went back long before there was any chance of our coming into contact with them. Our men behaved very well indeed — white regulars, colored regulars, and Rough Riders alike. The newspaper press failed to do full justice to the white regulars, in my opinion, from the simple reason that everybody knew that they would fight, whereas there had been a good deal of question as to how the Rough Riders, who were volunteer troops, and the Tenth Cavalry, who were colored, would behave; so there was a tendency to exalt our deeds at the expense of those of the First Regulars, whose courage and good conduct were taken for granted. It was a trying fight beyond what the losses show, for it is hard upon raw soldiers to be pitted against an unseen foe, and to advance steadily when their comrades are falling around them, and when they can only occasionally see a chance to retaliate. Wood's experience in fighting Apaches stood him in good stead. An entirely raw man at the head of the regiment, conducting, as Wood was, what was practically an independent fight, would have been in a very trying position. The fight cleared the way toward Santiago, and we experienced no further resistance.

That afternoon we made camp and dined, subsisting chiefly on a load of beans which we found on one of the Spanish mules which had been shot. We also looked after the wounded. Dr. Church had himself gone out to the firing-line during the fight, and carried to the rear some of the worst wounded on his back or in his arms. Those who could walk had walked in to where the little field-hospital of the regiment was established on the trail. We found all our dead and all the badly wounded. Around one of the latter the big, hideous land-crabs had gathered in a grewsome ring, waiting for life to be extinct.

One of our own men and most of the Spanish dead had been found by the vultures before we got to them; and their bodies were mangled, the eyes and wounds being torn.

The Rough Rider who had been thus treated was in Bucky O'Neill's troop; and as we looked at the body, O'Neill turned to me and asked, "Colonel, isn't it Whitman who says of the vultures that 'they pluck the eyes of princes and tear the flesh of kings'?" I answered that I could not place the quotation. Just a week afterward we were shielding his own body from the birds of prey.

One of the men who fired first, and who displayed conspicuous gallantry was a Cherokee half-breed, who was hit seven times, and of course had to go back to the States. Before he rejoined us at Montauk Point he had gone through a little private war of his own; for on his return he found that a cowboy had gone off with his sweetheart, and in the fight that ensued he shot his rival. Another man of L Troop who also showed marked gallantry was Elliot Cowdin. The men of the plains and mountains were trained by life-long habit to look on life and death with iron philosophy. As I passed by a couple of tall, lank, Oklahoma cow-punchers, I heard one say, "Well, some of the boys got it in the neck!" to which the other answered with the grim plains proverb of the South: "Many a good horse dies."

Thomas Isbell, a half-breed Cherokee in the squad under Hamilton Fish, was among the first to shoot and be shot at. He was wounded no less than seven times. The first wound was received by him two minutes after he had fired his first shot, the bullet going through his neck. The second hit him in the left thumb. The third struck near his right hip, passing entirely through the body. The fourth bullet (which was apparently from a Remington and not from a Mauser) went into his neck and lodged against the bone, being afterward cut out. The fifth bullet again hit his left hand. The sixth scraped his head and the seventh his neck. He did not receive all of the wounds at the same time, over half an hour elapsing between the first and the last. Up to receiving the last wound he had declined to leave the firing-line, but by that time he had lost so much blood that he had to be sent to the rear. The man's wiry toughness was as notable as his courage.

Camp of the Rough Riders after the Guasimas Fight.

Helping a Wounded Rough Rider to the Rear
after the Guasimas Fight.

We improvised litters, and carried the more sorely wounded back to Siboney that afternoon and the next morning; the others walked. One of the men who had been most severely wounded was Edward Marshall, the correspondent, and he showed as much heroism as any soldier in the whole army. He was shot through the spine, a terrible and very painful wound, which we supposed meant that he would surely die; but he made no complaint of any kind, and while he retained consciousness persisted in dictating the story of the fight. A very touching incident happened in the improvised open-air hospital after the fight, where the wounded were lying. They did not groan, and made no complaint, trying to help one another. One of them suddenly began to hum, "My Country 'tis of Thee," and one by one the others joined in the chorus, which swelled out through the tropic woods, where the victors lay in camp beside their dead. I did not see any sign among the fighting men, whether wounded or unwounded, of the very complicated emotions assigned to their kind by some of the realistic modern novelists who have written about battles. At the front everyone behaved quite simply and took things as they came, in a matter-of-course way; but there was doubtless, as is always the case, a good deal of panic and confusion in the rear where the wounded, the stragglers, a few of the packers, and two or three newspaper correspondents were, and in consequence the first reports sent back to the coast were of a most alarming character, describing, with minute inaccuracy, how we had run into an ambush, etc. The packers with the mules which carried the rapid-fire guns were among those who ran, and they let the mules go in the jungle; in consequence the guns were never even brought to the firing-line, and only Fred Herrig's skill as a trailer enabled us to recover them. By patient work he followed up the mules' tracks in the forest until he found the animals.

Among the wounded who walked to the temporary hospital at Siboney was the trooper, Rowland, of whom I spoke before. There the doctors examined him, and decreed that his wound was so serious that he must go back to the States. This was enough for Rowland, who waited until nightfall and then escaped, slipping out of the window and making his way back to camp with his rifle and pack, though his wound must have made all movement very painful to him. After this, we felt that he was entitled to stay, and he never left us for a day, distinguishing himself again in the fight at San Juan.

Next morning we buried seven dead Rough Riders in a grave on the summit of the trail, Chaplain Brown reading the solemn burial service of the Episcopalians, while the men stood around with bared heads and joined in singing, "Rock of Ages." Vast numbers of vultures were wheeling round and round in great circles through the blue sky overhead. There could be no more honorable burial than that of these men in a common grave — Indian and cow-boy, miner, packer, and college athlete — the man of unknown ancestry from the lonely Western plains, and the man who carried on his watch the crests of the Stuyvesants and the Fishes, one in the way they had met death, just as during life they had been one in their daring and their loyalty.

On the afternoon of the 25th we moved on a couple of miles, and camped in a marshy open spot close to a beautiful stream. Here we lay for several days. Captain Lee, the British attaché, spent some time with us; we had begun to regard him as almost a member of the regiment. Count von Götzen, the German attaché, another good fellow, also visited us. General Young was struck down with the fever, and Wood took charge of the brigade. This left me in command of the regiment, of which I was very glad, for such experience as we had had is a quick teacher. By this time the men and I knew one another, and I felt able to make them do themselves justice in march or battle. They understood that I paid no heed to where they came from; no heed to their creed, politics, or social standing; that I would care for them to the utmost of my power, but that I demanded the highest performance of duty; while in return I had seen them tested, and knew I could depend absolutely on their courage, hardihood, obedience, and individual initiative.

There was nothing like enough transportation with the army, whether in the way of wagons or mule-trains; exactly as there had been no sufficient number of landing-boats with the transports. The officers' baggage had come up, but none of us had much, and the shelter-tents proved only a partial protection against the terrific downpours of rain. These occurred

The Spot where Seven Rough Riders were Buried
after the First Day's Fight at Las Guasimas.

almost every afternoon, and turned the camp into a tarn, and the trails into torrents and quagmires. We were not given quite the proper amount of food, and what we did get, like most of the clothing issued us, was fitter for the Klondyke than for Cuba. We got enough salt port and hardtack for the men, but not the full ration of coffee and sugar, and nothing else. I organized a couple of expeditions back to the sea-coast, taking the strongest and best walkers and also some of the officers' horses and a stray mule or two, and brought back beans and canned tomatoes. These I got partly by great exertions on my part, and partly by the aid of Colonel Weston of the Commissary Department, a particularly energetic man whose services were of great value. A silly regulation forbade my purchasing canned vegetables, etc., except for the officers; and I had no little difficulty in getting round this regulation, and purchasing (with my own money, of course) what I needed for the men.

One of the men I took with me on one of these trips was Sherman Bell, the former Deputy Marshal of Cripple Creek, and Wells-Fargo Express rider. In coming home with his load, through a blinding storm, he slipped and opened the old rupture. The agony was very great and one of his comrades took his load. He himself, sometimes walking, and sometimes crawling, got back to camp, where Dr. Church fixed him up with a spike bandage, but informed him that he would have to be sent back to the States when an ambulance came along. The ambulance did not come until the next day, which was the day before we marched to San Juan. It arrived after nightfall, and as soon as Bell heard it coming, he crawled out of the hospital tent into the jungle, where he lay all night; and the ambulance went off without him. The men shielded him just as school-boys would shield a companion, carrying his gun, belt, and bedding; while Bell kept out of sight until the column started, and then staggered along behind it. I found him the morning of the San Juan fight. He told me that he wanted to die fighting, if die he must, and I hadn't the heart to send him back. He did splendid service that day, and afterward in the trenches, and though the rupture opened twice again, and on each occasion he was within a hair's breadth of death, he escaped, and came back with us to the United States.

The army was camped along the valley, ahead of and behind us, our outposts being established on either side. From the generals to the privates all were eager to march against Santiago. At daybreak, when the tall palms began to show dimly through the rising mist, the scream of the cavalry trumpets tore the tropic dawn; and in the evening, as the bands of regiment after regiment played the "Star-Spangled Banner," all, officers and men alike, stood with heads uncovered, wherever they were, until the last strains of the anthem died away in the hot sunset air.

# IV

## THE CAVALRY AT SANTIAGO

ON JUNE 30TH we received orders to hold ourselves in readiness to march against Santiago, and all the men were greatly overjoyed, for the inaction was trying. The one narrow road, a mere muddy track along which the army was encamped, was choked with the marching columns. As always happened when we had to change camp, everything that the men could not carry, including, of course, the officers' baggage, was left behind.

About noon the Rough Riders struck camp and drew up in column beside the road in the rear of the First Cavalry. Then we sat down and waited for hours before the order came to march, while regiment after regiment passed by, varied by bands of tatterdemalion Cuban insurgents, and by mule-trains with ammunition. Every man carried three days' provisions. We had succeeded in borrowing mules sufficient to carry along the dynamite gun and the automatic Colts.

At last, toward mid-afternoon, the First and Tenth Cavalry, ahead of us, marched, and we followed. The First was under the command of Lieutenant-Colonel Veile, the Tenth under Lieutenant-Colonel Baldwin. Every few minutes there would be a stoppage in front, and at the halt I would make the men sit or lie down beside the track, loosening their packs. The heat was intense as we passed through the still, close jungle, which formed a wall on either hand. Occasionally we came to gaps or open spaces, where some regiment was camped, and now and then one of these regiments, which apparently had been left out of its proper place, would file into the road, breaking up our line of march. As a result, we finally found ourselves following merely the tail of the regiment ahead of us, an infantry regiment being thrust into the interval. Once or twice we had to wade streams. Darkness came on, but we still continued to march. It was about eight o'clock when we turned to the left and climbed El Poso hill, on whose summit there was a ruined ranch and sugar factory, now, of course, deserted. Here I found General Wood, who was arranging for the camping of the brigade. Our own arrangements for the night were simple. I extended each troop across the road into the jungle, and then the men threw down their belongings where they stood and slept on their arms. Fortunately, there was no rain. Wood and I curled up under our rain-coats on the saddle-blankets, while his two aides, Captain A. L. Mills and Lieutenant W. E. Shipp, slept near us. We were up before dawn and getting breakfast. Mills and Shipp had nothing to eat, and they breakfasted with Wood and myself, as we had been able to get some handfuls of beans, and some coffee and sugar, as well as the ordinary bacon and hardtack.

We did not talk much, for though we were in ignorance as to precisely what the day would bring forth, we knew that we should see fighting. We had slept soundly enough, although, of course, both Wood and I during the night had made a round of the sentries, he of the brigade, and I of the regiment; and I suppose that, excepting among hardened veterans, there is always a certain feeling of uneasy excitement the night before the battle.

Mills and Shipp were both tall, fine-looking men, of tried courage, and thoroughly trained in every detail of their profession; I remember being struck by the quiet, soldierly way they were going about their work early that morning. Before noon one was killed and the other dangerously wounded.

General Wheeler was sick, but with his usual indomitable pluck and entire indifference to his own personal comfort, he kept to the front. He was unable to retain command of the cavalry division, which accordingly devolved upon General Samuel Sumner, who commanded it until mid-afternoon, when the bulk of the fighting was over. General Sumner's own brigade fell to Colonel Henry Carroll. General Sumner led the advance with the cavalry, and the battle was fought by him and by General Kent, who commanded the infantry division, and whose foremost brigade was led by General Hawkins.

As the sun rose the men fell in, and at the same time a battery of field-guns was brought up on the hill-crest just beyond, between us and toward Santiago. It was a fine sight to see the great horses straining under the lash as they whirled the guns up the hill and into position.

General Sumner, who Commanded the Cavalry Division
During the San Juan Fight.

Our brigade was drawn up on the hither side of a kind of half basin, a big band of Cubans being off to the left. As yet we had received no orders, except that we were told that the main fighting was to be done by Lawton's infantry division, which was to take El Caney, several miles to our right, while we were simply to make a diversion. This diversion was to be made mainly with the artillery, and the battery which had taken position immediately in front of us was to begin when Lawton began.

It was about six o'clock that the first report of the cannon from El Caney came booming to us across the miles of still jungle. It was a very lovely morning, the sky of cloudless blue, while the level, shimmering rays from the just-risen sun brought into fine relief the splendid palms which here and there towered above the lower growth. The lofty and beautiful mountains hemmed in the Santiago plain, making it an amphitheatre for the battle.

Immediately our guns opened, and at the report great clouds of white smoke hung on the ridge crest. For a minute or two there was no response. Wood and I were sitting together, and Wood remarked to me that he wished our brigade could be moved somewhere else, for we were directly in line of any return fire aimed by the Spaniards at the battery. Hardly had he spoken when there was a peculiar whistling, singing sound in the air, and immediately afterward the noise of something exploding over our heads. It was shrapnel from the Spanish batteries. We sprung to our feet and leaped on our horses. Immediately afterward a second shot came which burst directly above us; and then a third. From the second shell one of the shrapnel bullets dropped on my wrist, hardly breaking the skin, but raising a bump about as big as a hickory-nut. The same shell wounded four of my regiment, one of them being Mason Mitchell, and two or three of the regulars were also hit, one losing his leg by a great fragment of shell. Another shell exploded right in the middle of the Cubans, killing and wounding a good many, while the remainder scattered like guinea-hens. Wood's led horse was also shot through the lungs. I at once hustled my regiment over the crest of the hill into the thick underbrush, where I had no little difficulty in getting them together again into column.

Meanwhile the firing continued for fifteen or twenty minutes, until it gradually died away. As the Spaniards used smokeless powder, their artillery had an enormous advantage over ours, and, moreover, we did not have the best type of modern guns, our fire being slow.

As soon as the firing ceased, Wood formed his brigade, with my regiment in front, and gave me orders to follow behind the First Brigade, which was just moving off the ground. In column of fours we marched down the trail toward the ford of the San Juan River. We passed two or three regiments of infantry, and were several times halted before we came to the ford. The First Brigade, which was under Colonel Carroll — Lieutenant-Colonel Hamilton commanding the Ninth Regiment, Major Wessels the Third, and Captain Kerr the Sixth — had already crossed and was marching to the right, parallel to, but a little distance from, the river. The Spaniards in the trenches and block-houses on top of the hills in front were already firing at the brigade in desultory fashion. The extreme advance of the Ninth Cavalry was under Lieutenants McNamee and Hartwick. They were joined by General Hawkins, with his staff, who was looking over the ground and deciding on the route he should take his infantry brigade.

Our orders had been of the vaguest kind, being simply to march to the right and connect with Lawton — with whom, of course, there was no chance of our connecting. No reconnoissance had been made, and the exact position and strength of the Spaniards was not known. A captive balloon was up in the air at this moment, but it was worse than useless. A previous proper reconnoissance and proper look-out from the hills would have given us exact information. As it was, Generals Kent, Sumner, and Hawkins had to be their own reconnoissance, and they fought their troops so well that we won anyhow.

I was now ordered to cross the ford, march half a mile or so to the right, and then halt and await further orders; and I promptly hurried my men across, for the fire was getting hot, and the captive balloon, to the horror of everybody, was coming down to the ford. Of course, it was a special target for the enemy's fire. I got my men across before it reached the

Rough Riders Fording the San Juan River while Moving to the Front.

ford. There it partly collapsed and remained, causing severe loss of life, as it indicated the exact position where the Tenth and the First Cavalry, and the infantry, were crossing.

As I led my column slowly along, under the intense heat, through the high grass of the open jungle, the First Brigade was to our left, and the firing between it and the Spaniards on the hills grew steadily hotter and hotter. After awhile I came to a sunken lane, and as by this time the First Brigade had stopped and was engaged in a stand-up fight, I halted my men and sent back word for orders. As we faced toward the Spanish hills my regiment was on the right with next to it and a little in advance the First Cavalry, and behind them the Tenth. In our front the Ninth held the right, the Sixth the centre, and the Third the left; but in the jungle the lines were already overlapping in places. Kent's infantry were coming up, farther to the left.

Captain Mills was with me. The sunken lane, which had a wire fence on either side, led straight up toward, and between, the two hills in our front, the hill on the left, which contained heavy block-houses, being farther away from us than the hill on our right, which we afterward grew to call Kettle Hill, and which was surmounted merely by some large ranch buildings or haciendas, with sunken brick-lined walls and cellars. I got the men as well-sheltered as I could. Many of them lay close under the bank of the lane, others slipped into the San Juan River and crouched under its hither bank, while the rest lay down behind the patches of bushy jungle in the tall grass. The heat was intense, and many of the men were already showing signs of exhaustion. The sides of the hills in front were bare; but the country up to them was, for the most part, covered with such dense jungle that in charging through it no accuracy of formation could possibly be preserved.

The fight was now on in good earnest, and the Spaniards on the hills were engaged in heavy volley firing. The Mauser bullets drove in sheets through the trees and the tall jungle grass, making a peculiar whirring or rustling sound; some of the bullets seemed to pop in the air, so that we thought they were explosive; and, indeed, many of those which were coated with brass did explode, in the sense that the brass coat was ripped off, making a thin plate of hard metal with a jagged edge, which inflicted a ghastly wound. These bullets were shot from a .45-calibre rifle carrying smokeless powder, which was much used by the guerillas and irregular Spanish troops. The Mauser bullets themselves made a small clean hole, with the result that the wound healed in a most astonishing manner. One or two of our men who were shot in the head had the skull blown open, but elsewhere the wounds from the minute steel-coated bullet, with its very high velocity, were certainly nothing like as serious as those made by the old large-calibre, low-power rifle. If a man was shot through the heart, spine, or brain he was, of course, killed instantly; but very few of the wounded died — even under the appalling conditions which prevailed, owing to the lack of attendance and supplies in the field-hospitals with the army.

While we were lying in reserve we were suffering nearly as much as afterward when we charged. I think that the bulk of the Spanish fire was practically unaimed, or at least not aimed at any particular man, and only occasionally at a particular body of men; but they swept the whole field of battle up to the edge of the river, and man after man in our ranks fell dead or wounded, although I had the troopers scattered out far apart, taking advantage of every scrap of cover.

Devereux was dangerously shot while he lay with his men on the edge of the river. A young West Point cadet, Ernest Haskell, who had taken his holiday with us as an acting second lieutenant, was shot through the stomach. He had shown great coolness and gallantry, which he displayed to an even more marked degree after being wounded, shaking my hand and saying, "All right, Colonel, I'm going to get well. Don't bother about me, and don't let any man come away with me." When I shook hands with him, I thought he would surely die; yet he recovered.

The most serious loss that I and the regiment could have suffered befell just before we charged. Bucky O'Neill was strolling up and down in front of his men, smoking his cigarette, for he was inveterately addicted to the habit. He had a theory that an officer ought never to take cover — a theory which was, of course, wrong, though in a volunteer organization the officers should certainly expose themselves very fully, simply for the effect on the men; our regimental toast on the transport running, "The officers; may the war last until each is killed, wounded, or promoted." As O'Neill moved to and fro, his men begged him to lie down, and one of the sergeants said, "Captain, a bullet is sure to hit you." O'Neill took his cigarette out of his mouth, and blowing out a cloud of smoke laughed and said, "Sergeant, the Spanish bullet isn't made that will kill me." A little later he discussed for a moment with one of the regular officers the direction from which the Spanish fire was coming. As he turned on his heel a bullet struck him in the mouth and came out at the back of his head; so that even before he fell his wild and gallant soul had gone out into the darkness.

My orderly was a brave young Harvard boy, Sanders, from the quaint old Massachusetts town of Salem. The work of an orderly on foot, under the blazing sun, through the hot and matted jungle, was very severe, and finally the heat overcame him. He dropped; nor did he ever recover fully, and later he died from fever. In his place I summoned a trooper whose name I did not know. Shortly afterward, while sitting beside the bank, I directed him to go back and ask whatever general he came across if I could not advance, as my men were being much cut up. He stood up to salute and then pitched forward across my knees, a bullet having gone through his throat, cutting the carotid.

When O'Neill was shot, his troop, who were devoted to him, were for the moment at a loss whom to follow. One of their number, Henry Bardshar, a huge Arizona miner, immediately attached himself to me as my orderly, and from that moment he was closer to me, not only in the fight, but throughout the rest of the campaign, than any other man, not even excepting the color-sergeant, Wright.

Captain Mills was with me; gallant Shipp had already been killed. Mills was an invaluable aide, absolutely cool, absolutely unmoved or flurried in any way.

I sent messenger after messenger to try to find General Sumner or General Wood and get permission to advance, and was just about making up my mind that in the absence of orders I had better "march toward the guns," when Lieutenant-Colonel Dorst came riding up through the storm of bullets with the welcome command "to move forward and support the regulars in the assault on the hills in front." General Sumner had obtained authority to advance from Lieutenant Miley, who was representing General Shafter at the front, and was in the thick of the fire. The General at once ordered the first brigade to advance on the hills, and the second to support it. He himself was riding his horse along the lines, superintending the fight. Later I overheard a couple of my men talking together about him. What they said illustrates the value of a display of courage among the officers in hardening their soldiers; for their theme was how, as they were lying down under a fire which they could not return, and were in consequence feeling rather nervous, General Sumner suddenly appeared on horseback, sauntering by quite unmoved; and, said one of the men, "That made us feel all right. If the General could stand it, we could."

The instant I received the order I sprang on my horse and then my "crowded hour" began. The guerillas had been shooting at us from the edges of the jungle and from their perches in the leafy trees, and as they used smokeless powder, it was almost impossible to see them, though a few of my men had from time to time responded. We had also suffered from the hill on our right front, which was held chiefly by guerillas, although there were also some Spanish regulars with them, for we found their dead. I formed my men in column of troops, each troop extended in open skirmishing order, the right resting on the wire fences which bordered the sunken lane. Captain Jenkins led the first squadron, his eyes literally dancing with joyous excitement.

I started in the rear of the regiment, the position in which the colonel should theoretically stay. Captain Mills and Captain McCormick were both with me as aides; but I speedily had to send them off on special duty in getting the different bodies of men forward. I had intended to go into action on foot as at Las Guasimas, but the heat was so oppressive that I found I should be quite unable to run up and down the line and superintend matters unless I was mounted; and, moreover, when on horseback, I could see the men better and they could see me better.

A curious incident happened as I was getting the men started forward. Always when men have been lying down under cover for some time, and are required to advance, there is a little hesitation, each looking to see whether the others are going forward. As I rode down the line, calling to the troopers to go forward, and rasping brief directions to the captains and lieutenants, I came upon a man lying behind a little bush, and I ordered him to jump up. I do not think he understood that we were making a forward move, and he looked up at me for a moment with hesitation, and I again bade him rise, jeering him and saying: "Are you afraid to stand up when I am on horseback?" As I spoke, he suddenly fell forward on his face, a bullet having struck him and gone through him lengthwise. I suppose the bullet had been aimed at me; at any rate, I, who was on horseback in the open, was unhurt, and the man lying flat on the ground in the cover beside me was killed. There were several pairs of brothers with us; of the two Nortons one was killed; of the two McCurdys one was wounded.

I soon found that I could get that line, behind which I personally was, faster forward than the one immediately in front of it, with the result that the two rearmost lines of the regiment began to crowd together; so I rode through them both, the better to move on the one in front. This happened with every line in succession, until I found myself at the head of the regiment.

Both lieutenants of B Troop from Arizona had been exerting themselves greatly, and both were overcome by the heat; but Sergeants Campbell and Davidson took it forward in splendid shape. Some of the men from this troop and from the other Arizona troop (Bucky O'Neill's) joined me as a kind of fighting tail.

The Ninth Regiment was immediately in front of me, and the First on my left, and these went up Kettle Hill with my regiment. The Third, Sixth, and Tenth went partly up Kettle Hill (following the Rough Riders and the Ninth and First), and partly between that and the block-house hill, which the infantry were assailing. General Sumner in person gave the Tenth the order to charge the hills; and it went forward at a rapid gait. The three regiments went forward more or less intermingled, advancing steadily and keeping up a heavy fire. Up Kettle Hill Sergeant George Berry, of the Tenth, bore not only his own regimental colors but those of the Third, the

Little Texas — Colonel Roosevelt's War Horse.

color-sergeant of the Third having been shot down; he kept
shouting, "Dress on the colors, boys, dress on the colors!" as
he followed Captain Ayres, who was running in advance of
his men, shouting and waving his hat. The Tenth Cavalry lost
a greater proportion of its officers than any other regiment in
the battle — eleven out of twenty-two.

By the time I had come to the head of the regiment we
ran into the left wing of the Ninth Regulars, and some of the
First Regulars, who were lying down; that is, the troopers
were lying down, while the officers were walking to and fro.
The officers of the white and colored regiments alike took the
greatest pride in seeing that the men more than did their duty;
and the mortality among them was great.

I spoke to the captain in command of the rear platoons,
saying that I had been ordered to support the regulars in the
attack upon the hills, and that in my judgment we could not
take these hills by firing at them, and that we must rush them.
He answered that his orders were to keep his men lying where
they were, and that he could not charge without orders. I
asked where the Colonel was, and as he was not in sight, said,
"Then I am the ranking officer here and I give the order to
charge" — for I did not want to keep the men longer in the
open suffering under a fire which they could not effectively
return. Naturally the Captain hesitated to obey this order
when no word had been received from his own Colonel. So I
said, "Then let my men through, sir," and rode on through
the lines, followed by the grinning Rough Riders, whose attention had been completely taken off the Spanish bullets,
partly by my dialogue with the regulars, and partly by the
language I had been using to themselves as I got the lines forward, for I had been joking with some and swearing at others,
as the exigencies of the case seemed to demand. When we
started to go through, however, it proved too much for the
regulars, and they jumped up and came along, their officers
and troops mingling with mine, all being delighted at the
chance. When I got to where the head of the left wing of
the Ninth was lying, through the courtesy of Lieutenant
Hartwick, two of whose colored troopers threw down the
fence, I was enabled to get back into the lane, at the same time
waving my hat, and giving the order to charge the hill on our

right front. Out of my sight, over on the right, Captains McBlain and Taylor, of the Ninth, made up their minds independently to charge at just about this time; and at almost the same moment Colonels Carroll and Hamilton, who were off, I believe, to my left, where we could see neither them nor their men, gave the order to advance. But of all this I knew nothing at the time. The whole line, tired of waiting, and eager to close with the enemy, was straining to go forward; and it seems that different parts slipped the leash at almost the same moment. The First Cavalry came up the hill just behind, and partly mixed with my regiment and the Ninth. As already said, portions of the Third, Sixth, and Tenth followed, while the rest of the members of these three regiments kept more in touch with the infantry on our left.

By this time we were all in the spirit of the thing and greatly excited by the charge, the men cheering and running forward between shots, while the delighted faces of the foremost officers, like Captain C. J. Stevens, of the Ninth, as they ran at the head of their troops, will always stay in my mind. As soon as I was in the line I galloped forward a few yards until I saw that the men were well started, and then galloped back to help Goodrich, who was in command of his troop, get his men across the road so as to attack the hill from that side. Captain Mills had already thrown three of the other troops of the regiment across this road for the same purpose. Wheeling around, I then again galloped toward the hill, passing the shouting, cheering, firing men, and went up the lane, splashing through a small stream; when I got abreast of the ranch buildings on the top of Kettle Hill, I turned and went up the slope. Being on horseback I was, of course, able to get ahead of the men on foot, excepting my orderly, Henry Bardshar, who had run ahead very fast in order to get better shots at the Spaniards, who were now running out of the ranch buildings. Sergeant Campbell and a number of the Arizona men, and Dudley Dean, among others, were very close behind. Stevens, with his platoon of the Ninth, was abreast of us; so were McNamee and Hartwick. Some forty yards from the top I ran into a wire fence and jumped off Little Texas, turning him loose. He had been scraped by a couple of bullets, one of which nicked my elbow, and I never expected to see him again. As I ran up to the hill, Bardshar stopped to shoot, and two Spaniards fell as he emptied his magazine. These were the only Spaniards I actually saw fall to aimed shots by any one of my men, with the exception of two guerillas in trees.

Almost immediately afterward the hill was covered by the troops, both Rough Riders and the colored troopers of the Ninth, and some men of the First. There was the usual confusion, and afterward there was much discussion as to exactly who had been on the hill first. The first guidons planted there were those of the three New Mexican troops, G, E, and F, of my regiment, under their Captains, Llewellen, Luna, and Muller, but on the extreme right of the hill, at the opposite end from where we struck it, Captains Taylor and McBlain and their men of the Ninth were first up. Each of the five captains was firm in the belief that his troop was first up. As for the individual men, each of whom honestly thought he was first on the summit, their name was legion. One Spaniard was captured in the buildings, another was shot as he tried to hide himself, and a few others were killed as they ran.

Among the many deeds of conspicuous gallantry here performed, two, both to the credit of the First Cavalry, may be mentioned as examples of the others, not as exceptions. Sergeant Charles Karsten, while close beside Captain Tutherly, the squadron commander, was hit by a shrapnel bullet. He continued on the line, firing until his arm grew numb; and he then refused to go to the rear, and devoted himself to taking care of the wounded, utterly unmoved by the heavy fire. Trooper Hugo Brittain, when wounded, brought the regimental standard forward, waving it to and fro, to cheer the men.

No sooner were we on the crest than the Spaniards from the line of hills in our front, where they were strongly intrenched, opened a very heavy fire upon us with their rifles. They also opened upon us with one or two pieces of artillery, using time fuses which burned very accurately, the shells exploding right over our heads.

On the top of the hill was a huge iron kettle, or something of the kind, probably used for sugar refining. Several of our men took shelter behind this. We had a splendid view of the charge on the San Juan block-house to our left, where the

Charge of the Rough Riders at San Juan Hill.

infantry of Kent, led by Hawkins, were climbing the hill. Obviously the proper thing to do was to help them, and I got the men together and started them volley-firing against the Spaniards in the San Juan block-house and in the trenches around it. We could only see their heads; of course this was all we ever could see when we were firing at them in their trenches. Stevens was directing not only his own colored troopers, but a number of Rough Riders; for in a mêlée good soldiers are always prompt to recognize a good officer, and are eager to follow him.

We kept up a brisk fire for some five or ten minutes; meanwhile we were much cut up ourselves. Gallant Colonel Hamilton, than whom there was never a braver man, was killed, and equally gallant Colonel Carroll wounded. When near the summit Captain Mills had been shot through the head, the bullet destroying the sight of one eye permanently and of the other temporarily. He would not go back or let any man assist him, sitting down where he was and waiting until one of the men brought him word that the hill was stormed. Colonel Veile planted the standard of the First Cavalry on the hill, and General Sumner rode up. He was fighting his division in great form, and was always himself in the thick of the fire. As the men were much excited by the firing, they seemed to pay very little heed to their own losses.

Suddenly, above the cracking of the carbines, rose a peculiar drumming sound, and some of the men cried, "The Spanish machine-guns!" Listening, I made out that it came from the flat ground to the left, and jumped to my feet, smiting my hand on my thigh, and shouting aloud with exultation, "It's the Gatlings, men, our Gatlings!" Lieutenant Parker was bringing his four Gatlings into action, and shoving them nearer and nearer the front. Now and then the drumming ceased for a moment; then it would resound again, always closer to San Juan hill, which Parker, like ourselves, was hammering to assist the infantry attack. Our men cheered lustily. We saw much of Parker after that, and there was never a more welcome sound than his Gatlings as they opened. It was the only sound which I ever heard my men cheer in battle.

The infantry got nearer and nearer the crest of the hill. At last we could see the Spaniards running from the rifle-pits as the Americans came on in their final rush. Then I stopped my men for fear they should injure their comrades, and called to them to charge the next line of trenches, on the hills in our front, from which we had been undergoing a good deal of punishment. Thinking that the men would all come, I jumped over the wire fence in front of us and started at the double; but, as a matter of fact, the troopers were so excited, what with shooting and being shot, and shouting and cheering, that they did not hear, or did not heed me; and after running about a hundred yards I found I had only five men along with me. Bullets were ripping the grass all around us, and one of the men, Clay Green, was mortally wounded; another, Winslow Clark, a Harvard man, was shot first in the leg and then through the body. He made not the slightest murmur, only asking me to put his water canteen where he could get at it, which I did; he ultimately recovered. There was no use going on with the remaining three men, and I bade them stay where they were while I went back and brought up the rest of the brigade. This was a decidedly cool request, for there was really no possible point in letting them stay there while I went back; but at the moment it seemed perfectly natural to me, and apparently so to them, for they cheerfully nodded, and sat down in the grass, firing back at the line of trenches from which the Spaniards were shooting at them. Meanwhile, I ran back, jumped over the wire fence, and went over the crest of the hill, filled with anger against the troopers, and especially those of my own regiment, for not having accompanied me. They, of course, were quite innocent of wrong-doing; and even while I taunted them bitterly for not having followed me, it was all I could do not to smile at the look of injury and surprise that came over their faces, while they cried out, "We didn't hear you, we didn't see you go, Colonel; lead on now, we'll sure follow you." I wanted the other regiments to come too, so I ran down to where General Sumner was and asked him if I might make the charge; and he told me to go and that he would see that the men followed. By this time everybody had his attention attracted, and when I leaped over the fence again, with Major Jenkins beside me, the men of the various regiments which were already on the hill came with a rush, and we started across the wide valley which lay between us and the Spanish intrenchments. Captain Dimmick, now in command of the Ninth, was bringing it forward; Captain McBlain had a number of Rough Riders mixed in with his troop, and led them all together; Captain Taylor had been severely wounded. The long-legged men like Greenway, Goodrich, sharp-shooter Proffit, and others, outstripped the rest of us, as we had a considerable distance to go. Long before we got near them the Spaniards ran, save a few here and there, who either surrendered or were shot down. When we reached the trenches we found them filled with dead bodies in the light blue and white uniform of the Spanish regular army. There were very few wounded. Most of the fallen had little holes in their heads from which their brains were oozing; for they were covered from the neck down by the trenches.

It was at this place that Major Wessels, of the Third Cavalry, was shot in the back of the head. It was a severe wound, but after having it bound up he again came to the front in command of his regiment. Among the men who were foremost was Lieutenant Milton F. Davis, of the First Cavalry. He had been joined by three men of the Seventy-first New York, who ran up, and, saluting, said, "Lieutenant, we want to go with you, our officers won't lead us." One of the brave fellows was soon afterward shot in the face. Lieutenant Davis's first sergeant, Clarence Gould, killed a Spanish soldier with his revolver, just as the Spaniard was aiming at one of my Rough Riders. At about the same time I also shot one. I was with Henry Bardshar, running up at the double, and two Spaniards leaped from the trenches and fired at us, not ten yards away. As they turned to run I closed in and fired twice, missing the first and killing the second. My revolver was from the sunken battle-ship Maine, and had been given me by my brother-in-law, Captain W. S. Cowles, of the Navy. At the time I did not know of Gould's exploit, and supposed my feat to be unique; and although Gould had killed his Spaniard in the trenches, not very far from me, I never learned of it until weeks after. It is astonishing what a limited area of vision and experience one has in the hurly-burly of a battle.

There was very great confusion at this time, the different regiments being completely intermingled — white regulars, colored regulars, and Rough Riders. General Sumner had kept a considerable force in reserve on Kettle Hill, under Major Jackson, of the Third Cavalry. We were still under a heavy fire and I got together a mixed lot of men and pushed on from the trenches and ranch-houses which we had just taken, driving the Spaniards through a line of palm-trees, and over the crest of a chain of hills. When we reached these crests we found ourselves overlooking Santiago. Some of the men, including Jenkins, Greenway, and Goodrich, pushed on almost by themselves far ahead. Lieutenant Hugh Berkely, of the First, with a sergeant and two troopers, reached the extreme front. He was, at the time, ahead of everyone; the sergeant was killed and one trooper wounded; but the lieutenant and the remaining trooper stuck to their post for the rest of the afternoon until our line was gradually extended to include them.

While I was re-forming the troops on the chain of hills, one of General Sumner's aides, Captain Robert Howze — as dashing and gallant an officer as there was in the whole gallant cavalry division, by the way — came up with orders to me to halt where I was, not advancing farther, but to hold the hill at all hazards. Howze had his horse, and I had some difficulty in making him take proper shelter; he stayed with us for quite a time, unable to make up his mind to leave the extreme front, and meanwhile jumping at the chance to render any service, of risk or otherwise, which the moment developed.

I now had under me all the fragments of the six cavalry regiments which were at the extreme front, being the highest officer left there, and I was in immediate command of them for the remainder of the afternoon and that night. The Ninth was over to the right, and the Thirteenth Infantry afterward came up beside it. The rest of Kent's infantry was to our left. Of the Tenth, Lieutenants Anderson, Muller, and Fleming reported to me; Anderson was slightly wounded, but he paid no heed to this. All three, like every other officer, had troopers of various regiments under them; such mixing was inevitable in making repeated charges through thick jungle; it was essentially a troop commanders', indeed, almost a squad leaders', fight. The Spaniards who had been holding the trenches and the line of hills, had fallen back upon their supports and we were under a very heavy fire both from rifles and great guns.

At the point where we were, the grass-covered hill-crest was gently rounded, giving poor cover, and I made my men lie down on the hither slope.

On the extreme left Captain Beck, of the Tenth, with his own troop, and small bodies of the men of other regiments, was exercising a practically independent command, driving back the Spaniards whenever they showed any symptoms of advancing. He had received his orders to hold the line at all hazards from Lieutenant Andrews, one of General Sumner's aides, just as I had received mine from Captain Howze. Finally, he was relieved by some infantry, and then rejoined the rest of the Tenth, which was engaged heavily until dark, Major Wint being among the severely wounded. Lieutenant W. N. Smith was killed. Captain Bigelow had been wounded three times.

Our artillery made one or two efforts to come into action on the firing-line of the infantry, but the black powder rendered each attempt fruitless. The Spanish guns used smokeless powder, so that it was difficult to place them. In this respect they were on a par with their own infantry and with our regular infantry and dismounted cavalry; but our only two volunteer infantry regiments, the Second Massachusetts and the Seventy-first New York, and our artillery, all had black powder. This rendered the two volunteer regiments, which were armed with the antiquated Springfield, almost useless in the battle, and did practically the same thing for the artillery wherever it was formed within rifle range. When one of the guns was discharged a thick cloud of smoke shot out and hung over the place, making an ideal target, and in a half minute every Spanish gun and rifle within range was directed at the particular spot thus indicated; the consequence was that after a more or less lengthy stand the gun was silenced or driven off. We got no appreciable help from our guns on July 1st. Our men were quick to realize the defects of our artillery, but they were entirely philosophic about it, not showing the least concern at its failure. On the contrary, whenever they heard our artillery open they would grin as they looked at one another and remark, "There go the guns again; wonder how soon they'll be shut up," and shut up they were sure to be. The light battery of Hotchkiss one-pounders, under Lieutenant

View from San Juan Hill of the First Hill and Block-house Captured on the First of July.

J. B. Hughes, of the Tenth Cavalry, was handled with conspicuous gallantry.

On the hill-slope immediately around me I had a mixed
force composed of members of most of the cavalry regiments,
and a few infantrymen. There were about fifty of my Rough
Riders with Lieutenants Goodrich and Carr. Among the rest
were perhaps a score of colored infantrymen, but, as it happened, at this particular point without any of their officers. No
troops could have behaved better than the colored soldiers had
behaved so far; but they are, of course, peculiarly dependent
upon their white officers. Occasionally they produce non-
commissioned officers who can take the initiative and accept
responsibility precisely like the best class of whites; but this
cannot be expected normally, nor is it fair to expect it. With
the colored troops there should always be some of their own
officers; whereas, with the white regulars, as with my own
Rough Riders, experience showed that the non-commissioned
officers could usually carry on the fight by themselves if they
were once started, no matter whether their officers were killed
or not.

At this particular time it was trying for the men, as they
were lying flat on their faces, very rarely responding to the bullets, shells, and shrapnel which swept over the hill-top, and
which occasionally killed or wounded one of their number.
Major Albert G. Forse, of the First Cavalry, a noted Indian
fighter, was killed about this time. One of my best men,
Sergeant Greenly, of Arizona, who was lying beside me, suddenly said, "Beg pardon, Colonel; but I've been hit in the leg."
I asked, "Badly?" He said, "Yes, Colonel; quite badly." After
one of his comrades had helped him fix up his leg with a first-
aid-to-the-injured bandage, he limped off to the rear.

None of the white regulars or Rough Riders showed the
slightest sign of weakening; but under the strain the colored
infantrymen (who had none of their officers) began to get a
little uneasy and to drift to the rear, either helping wounded
men, or saying that they wished to find their own regiments.
This I could not allow, as it was depleting my line, so I jumped
up, and walking a few yards to the rear, drew my revolver,
halted the retreating soldiers, and called out to them that I
appreciated the gallantry with which they had fought and

would be sorry to hurt them, but that I should shoot the first man who, on any pretence whatever, went to the rear. My own men had all sat up and were watching my movements with the utmost interest; so was Captain Howze. I ended my statement to the colored soldiers by saying: "Now, I shall be very sorry to hurt you, and you don't know whether or not I will keep my word, but my men can tell you that I always do;" whereupon my cow-punchers, hunters, and miners solemnly nodded their heads and commented in chorus, exactly as if in a comic opera, "He always does; he always does!"

This was the end of the trouble, for the "smoked Yankees" — as the Spaniards called the colored soldiers — flashed their white teeth at one another, as they broke into broad grins, and I had no more trouble with them, they seeming to accept me as one of their own officers. The colored cavalrymen had already so accepted me; in return, the Rough Riders, although for the most part Southwesterners, who have a strong color prejudice, grew to accept them with hearty good-will as comrades, and were entirely willing, in their own phrase, "to drink out of the same canteen." Where all the regular officers did so well, it is hard to draw any distinction; but in the cavalry division a peculiar meed of praise should be given to the officers of the Ninth and Tenth for their work, and under their leadership the colored troops did as well as any soldiers could possibly do.

In the course of the afternoon the Spaniards in our front made the only offensive movement which I saw them make during the entire campaign; for what were ordinarily called "attacks" upon our lines consisted merely of heavy firing from their trenches and from their skirmishers. In this case they did actually begin to make a forward movement, their cavalry coming up as well as the marines and reserve infantry,* while their skirmishers, who were always bold, redoubled their activity. It could not be called a charge, and not only was it not pushed home, but it was stopped almost as soon as it began, our men immediately running forward to the crest of the hill with shouts of delight at seeing their enemies at last come into

*Lieutenant Tejeiro, p. 154, speaks of this attempt to retake San Juan and its failure.

Lieutenant J. McIlhenny,
Promoted for Gallantry.

Lieut. Horace K. Devereux,
Wounded at San Juan Hill.

Lieutenant S. Coleman,
Promoted for Gallantry.

Lieutenant W. E. Dame,
Promoted for Gallantry.

the open. A few seconds' firing stopped their advance and drove them into the cover of the trenches.

They kept up a very heavy fire for some time longer, and our men again lay down, only replying occasionally. Suddenly we heard on our right the peculiar drumming sound which had been so welcome in the morning, when the infantry were assailing the San Juan block-house. The Gatlings were up again! I started over to inquire, and found that Lieutenant Parker, not content with using his guns in support of the attacking forces, had thrust them forward to the extreme front of the fighting line, where he was handling them with great effect. From this time on, throughout the fighting, Parker's Gatlings were on the right of my regiment, and his men and mine fraternized in every way. He kept his pieces at the extreme front, using them on every occasion until the last Spanish shot was fired. Indeed, the dash and efficiency with which the Gatlings were handled by Parker was one of the most striking features of the campaign; he showed that a first-rate officer could use machine-guns, on wheels, in battle and skirmish, in attacking and defending trenches, alongside of the best troops, and to their great advantage.

As night came on, the firing gradually died away. Before this happened, however, Captains Morton and Boughton, of the Third Cavalry, came over to tell me that a rumor had reached them to the effect that there had been some talk of retiring and that they wished to protest in the strongest manner. I had been watching them both, as they handled their troops with the cool confidence of the veteran regular officer, and had been congratulating myself that they were off toward the right flank, for as long as they were there, I knew I was perfectly safe in that direction. I had heard no rumor about retiring, and I cordially agreed with them that it would be far worse than a blunder to abandon our position.

To attack the Spaniards by rushing across open ground, or through wire entanglements and low, almost impassable jungle, without the help of artillery, and to force unbroken infantry, fighting behind earthworks and armed with the best repeating weapons, supported by cannon, was one thing; to repel such an attack ourselves, or to fight our foes on anything like even terms in the open, was quite another thing. No possible number of Spaniards coming at us from in front could have driven us from our position, and there was not a man on the crest who did not eagerly and devoutly hope that our opponents would make the attempt, for it would surely have been followed, not merely by a repulse, but by our immediately taking the city. There was not an officer or a man on the firing-line, so far as I saw them, who did not feel this way.

As night fell, some of my men went back to the buildings in our rear and foraged through them, for we had now been fourteen hours charging and fighting without food. They came across what was evidently the Spanish officers' mess, where their dinner was still cooking, and they brought it to the front in high glee. It was evident that the Spanish officers were living well, however the Spanish rank and file were faring. There were three big iron pots, one filled with beef-stew, one with boiled rice, and one with boiled peas; there was a big demijohn of rum (all along the trenches which the Spaniards held were empty wine and liquor bottles); there were a number of loaves of rice-bread; and there were even some small cans of preserves and a few salt fish. Of course, among so many men, the food, which was equally divided, did not give very much to each, but it freshened us all.

Soon after dark, General Wheeler, who in the afternoon had resumed command of the cavalry division, came to the front. A very few words with General Wheeler reassured us about retiring. He had been through too much heavy fighting in the Civil War to regard the present fight as very serious, and he told us not to be under any apprehension, for he had sent word that there was no need whatever of retiring, and was sure we would stay where we were until the chance came to advance. He was second in command; and to him more than to any other one man was due the prompt abandonment of the proposal to fall back — a proposal which, if adopted, would have meant shame and disaster.

Shortly afterward General Wheeler sent us orders to intrench. The men of the different regiments were now getting in place again and sifting themselves out. All of our troops who had been kept at Kettle Hill came forward and rejoined us after nightfall. During the afternoon Greenway, apparently not having enough to do in the fighting, had taken advantage of a lull to explore the buildings himself, and had found a number of Spanish intrenching tools, picks, and shovels, and these we used in digging trenches along our line. The men were very tired indeed, but they went cheerfully to work, all the officers doing their part.

Crockett, the ex-Revenue officer from Georgia, was a slight man, not physically very strong. He came to me and told me he didn't think he would be much use in digging, but that he had found a lot of Spanish coffee and would spend his time making coffee for the men, if I approved. I did approve very heartily, and Crockett officiated as cook for the next three or four hours until the trench was dug, his coffee being much appreciated by all of us.

So many acts of gallantry were performed during the day that it is quite impossible to notice them all, and it seems unjust to single out any; yet I shall mention a few, which it must always be remembered are to stand, not as exceptions, but as instances of what very many men did. It happened that I saw these myself. There were innumerable others, which either were not seen at all, or were seen only by officers who happened not to mention them; and, of course, I know chiefly those that happened in my own regiment.

Captain Llewellen was a large, heavy man, who had a grown-up son in the ranks. On the march he had frequently carried the load of some man who weakened, and he was not feeling well on the morning of the fight. Nevertheless, he kept at the head of this troop all day. In the charging and rushing, he not only became very much exhausted, but finally fell, wrenching himself terribly, and though he remained with us all night, he was so sick by morning that we had to take him behind the hill into an improvised hospital. Lieutenant Day, after handling his troop with equal gallantry and efficiency, was shot, on the summit of Kettle Hill. He was hit in the arm and was forced to go to the rear, but he would not return to the States, and rejoined us at the front long before his wound was healed. Lieutenant Leahy was also wounded, not far from him. Thirteen of the men were wounded and yet kept on fighting until the end of the day, and in some cases never went to the rear at all, even to have their wounds dressed. They were Corporals Waller and Fortescue and Trooper McKinley of

Troop E; Corporal Roades of Troop D; Troopers Albertson, Winter, McGregor, and Ray Clark of Troop F; Troopers Bugbee, Jackson, and Waller of Troop A; Trumpeter McDonald of Troop L; Sergeant Hughes of Troop B; and Trooper Gievers of Troop G. One of the Wallers was a cow-puncher from New Mexico, the other the champion Yale high-jumper. The first was shot through the left arm so as to paralyze the fingers, but he continued in battle, pointing his rifle over the wounded arm as though it had been a rest. The other Waller, and Bugbee, were hit in the head, the bullets merely inflicting scalp wounds. Neither of them paid any heed to the wounds except that after nightfall each had his head done up in a bandage. Fortescue I was at times using as an extra orderly. I noticed he limped, but supposed that his foot was skinned. It proved, however, that he had been struck in the foot, though not very seriously, by a bullet, and I never knew what was the matter until the next day I saw him making wry faces as he drew off his bloody boot, which was stuck fast to the foot. Trooper Rowland again distinguished himself by his fearlessness.

For gallantry on the field of action Sergeants Dame, Ferguson, Tiffany, Greenwald, and, later on, McIlhenny, were promoted to second lieutenancies, as Sergeant Hayes had already been. Lieutenant Carr, who commanded his troop, and behaved with great gallantry throughout the day, was shot and severely wounded at nightfall. He was the son of a Confederate officer; his was the fifth generation which, from father to son, had fought in every war of the United States. Among the men whom I noticed as leading in the charges and always being nearest the enemy, were the Pawnee, Pollock, Simpson of Texas, and Dudley Dean. Jenkins was made major, Woodbury Kane, Day, and Frantz captains, and Greenway and Goodrich first lieutenants, for gallantry in action, and for the efficiency with which the first had handled his squadron, and the other five their troops — for each of them, owing to some accident to his superior, found himself in command of his troop.

Dr. Church had worked quite as hard as any man at the front in caring for the wounded; as had Chaplain Brown. Lieutenant Keyes, who acted as adjutant, did so well that he

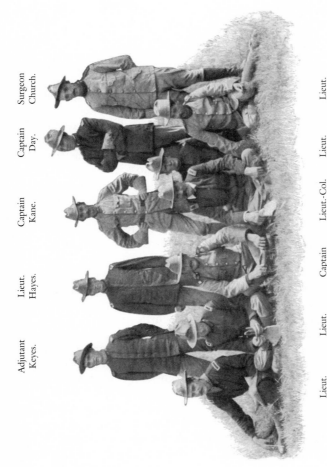

Adjutant Keyes.   Lieut. Hayes.   Captain Kane.   Captain Day.   Surgeon Church.

Lieut. Ferguson.   Lieut. Goodrich.   Captain Frantz.   Lieut.-Col. Brodie.   Lieut. Greenway.   Lieut. Greenwald.

Men Recommended for Promotion for Gallantry in Action.

was given the position permanently. Lieutenant Coleman similarly won the position of quartermaster.

We finished digging the trench soon after midnight, and then the worn-out men laid down in rows on their rifles and dropped heavily to sleep. About one in ten of them had blankets taken from the Spaniards. Henry Bardshar, my orderly, had procured one for me. He, Goodrich, and I slept together. If the men without blankets had not been so tired that they fell asleep anyhow, they would have been very cold, for, of course, we were all drenched with sweat, and above the waist had on nothing but our flannel shirts, while the night was cool, with a heavy dew. Before anyone had time to wake from the cold, however, we were all awakened by the Spaniards, whose skirmishers suddenly opened fire on us. Of course, we could not tell whether or not this was the forerunner of a heavy attack, for our Cossack posts were responding briskly. It was about three o'clock in the morning, at which time men's courage is said to be at the lowest ebb; but the cavalry division was certainly free from any weakness in that direction. At the alarm everybody jumped to his feet and the stiff, shivering, haggard men, their eyes only half-opened, all clutched their rifles and ran forward to the trench on the crest of the hill.

The sputtering shots died away and we went to sleep again. But in another hour dawn broke and the Spaniards opened fire in good earnest. There was a little tree only a few feet away, under which I made my head-quarters, and while I was lying there, with Goodrich and Keyes, a shrapnel burst among us, not hurting us in the least, but with the sweep of its bullets killing or wounding five men in our rear, one of whom was a singularly gallant young Harvard fellow, Stanley Hollister. An equally gallant young fellow from Yale, Theodore Miller, had already been mortally wounded. Hollister also died.

The Second Brigade lost more heavily than the First; but neither its brigade commander nor any of its regimental commanders were touched, while the commander of the First Brigade and two of its three regimental commanders had been killed or wounded.

In this fight our regiment had numbered 490 men, as, in addition to the killed and wounded of the first fight, some had

Captain Woodbury Kane,

Promoted for Gallantry in the Fight of July 1st.

William Pollock,

Pawnee Indian.

EAST AND WEST.

had to go to the hospital for sickness and some had been left behind with the baggage, or were detailed on other duty. Eighty-nine were killed and wounded: the heaviest loss suffered by any regiment in the cavalry division. The Spaniards made a stiff fight, standing firm until we charged home. They fought much more stubbornly than at Las Guasimas. We ought to have expected this, for they have always done well in holding intrenchments. On this day they showed themselves to be brave foes, worthy of honor for their gallantry.

In the attack on the San Juan hills our forces numbered about 6,600.* There were about 4,500 Spaniards against us.†

*According to the official reports, 5,104 officers and men of Kent's infantry, and 2,649 of the cavalry had been landed. My regiment is put down as 542 strong, instead of the real figure, 490, the difference being due to men who were in hospital and on guard at the seashore, etc. In other words, the total represents the total landed; the details, etc., are included. General Wheeler, in his report of July 7th, puts these details as about fifteen per cent. of the whole of the force which was on the transports; about eighty-five per cent. got forward and was in the fight.

†The total Spanish force in Santiago under General Linares was 6,000: 4,000 regulars, 1,000 volunteers, and 1,000 marines and sailors from the ships. (Diary of the British Consul, Frederick W. Ramsden, entry of July 1st.) Four thousand more troops entered next day. Of the 6,000 troops, 600 or thereabouts were at El Caney, and 900 in the forts at the mouth of the harbor. Lieutenant Tejeiro states that there were 520 men at El Caney, 970 in the forts at the mouth of the harbor, and 3,000 in the lines, not counting the cavalry and civil guard which were in reserve. He certainly very much understates the Spanish force; thus he nowhere accounts for the engineers mentioned on p. 135; and his figures would make the total number of Spanish artillerymen but 32. He excludes the cavalry, the civil guard, and the marines which had been stationed at the Plaza del Toros; yet he later mentions that these marines were brought up, and their commander, Bustamente, severely wounded; he states that the cavalry advanced to cover the retreat of the infantry, and I myself saw the cavalry come forward, for the most part dismounted, when the Spaniards attempted a forward movement late in the afternoon, and we shot many of their horses; while later I saw and conversed with officers and men of the civil guard who had been wounded at the same time — this in connection with returning them their wives and children, after the latter had fled from the city. Although the engineers are excluded, Lieutenant Tejeiro mentions that their colonel, as well as the colonel of the artillery, was wounded. Four thousand five hundred is surely an understatement of the forces which resisted the attack of the forces under Wheeler. Lieutenant Tejeiro is very careless in his figures. Thus in one place he states that the position of San Juan was held by two companies comprising 250 soldiers. Later he says it was held by three companies, whose strength he puts at

Our total loss in killed and wounded was 1,071. Of the cavalry division there were, all told, some 2,300 officers and men, of whom 375 were killed and wounded. In the division over a fourth of the officers were killed or wounded, their loss being

---

300 — thus making them average 100 instead of 125 men apiece. He then mentions another echelon of two companies, so situated as to cross their fire with the others. Doubtless the block-house and trenches at Fort San Juan proper were only held by three or four hundred men; they were taken by the Sixth and Sixteenth Infantry under Hawkins's immediate command; and they formed but one point in the line of hills, trenches, ranch-houses, and block-houses which the Spaniards held, and from which we drove them. When the city capitulated later, over 8,000 unwounded troops and over 16,000 rifles and carbines were surrendered; by that time the marines and sailors had of course gone, and the volunteers had disbanded.

In all these figures I have taken merely the statements from the Spanish side. I am inclined to think the actual numbers were much greater than those here given. Lieutenant Wiley, in his book In Cuba with Shafter, which is prac-tically an official statement, states that nearly 11,000 Spanish troops were sur-rendered; and this is the number given by the Spaniards themselves in the remarkable letter the captured soldiers addressed to General Shafter, which Wiley quotes in full. Lieutenant Tejeiro, in his chap. xiv., explains that the volunteers had disbanded before the end came, and the marines and sailors had of course gone, while nearly a thousand men had been killed or captured or had died of wounds and disease, so that there must have been at least 14,000 all told. Subtracting the reinforcements who arrived on the 2d, this would mean about 10,000 Spaniards present on the 1st; in which case Kent and Wheeler were opposed by at least equal numbers.

In dealing with the Spanish losses, Lieutenant Tejeiro contradicts himself. He puts their total loss on this day at 593, including 94 killed, 121 missing, and 2 prisoners — 217 in all. Yet he states that of the 520 men at Caney but 80 got back, the remaining 440 being killed, captured, or missing. When we captured the city we found in the hospitals over 2,000 seriously wounded and sick Spaniards; on making inquiries, I found that over a third were wounded. From these facts I feel that it is safe to put down the total Span-ish loss in battle as at least 1,200, of whom over a thousand were killed and wounded.

Lieutenant Tejeiro, while rightly claiming credit for the courage shown by the Spaniards, also praises the courage and resolution of the Americans, saying that they fought, "con un arrojo y una decision verdaderamente admirables." He dwells repeatedly upon the determination with which our troops kept charging though themselves unprotected by cover. As for the Spanish troops, all who fought them that day will most freely admit the courage they showed. At El Caney, where they were nearly hemmed in, they made a most desper-ate defence; at San Juan the way to retreat was open, and so, though they were seven times as numerous, they fought with less desperation, but still very gallantly.

relatively half as great again as that of the enlisted men —
which was as it should be.

I think we suffered more heavily than the Spaniards did in
killed and wounded (though we also captured some scores
of prisoners). It would have been very extraordinary if the
reverse was the case, for we did the charging; and to carry
earthworks on foot with dismounted cavalry, when these earthworks are held by unbroken infantry armed with the best
modern rifles, is a serious task.

# V

## IN THE TRENCHES

WHEN the shrapnel burst among us on the hill-side we made up our minds that we had better settle down to solid siege work. All of the men who were not in the trenches I took off to the right, back of the Gatling guns, where there was a valley, and dispersed them by troops in sheltered parts. It took us an hour or two's experimenting to find out exactly what spots were free from danger, because some of the Spanish sharp-shooters were in trees in our front, where we could not possibly place them from the trenches; and these were able to reach little hollows and depressions where the men were entirely safe from the Spanish artillery and from their trench-fire. Moreover, in one hollow, which we thought safe, the Spaniards succeeded in dropping a shell, a fragment of which went through the head of one of my men, who, astonishing to say, lived, although unconscious, for two hours afterward. Finally, I got all eight troops settled, and the men promptly proceeded to make themselves as much at home as possible. For the next twenty-four hours, however, the amount of comfort was small, as in the way of protection and covering we only had what blankets, rain-coats, and hammocks we took from the dead Spaniards. Ammunition, which was, of course, the most vital need, was brought up in abundance; but very little food reached us. That afternoon we had just enough to allow each man for his supper two hardtacks, and one hardtack extra for every four men.

During the first night we had dug trenches sufficient in length and depth to shelter our men and insure safety against attack, but we had not put in any traverses or approaches, nor had we arranged the trenches at all points in the best places for offensive work; for we were working at night on ground which we had but partially explored. Later on an engineer officer stated that he did not think our work had been scientific; and I assured him that I did not doubt that he was right,

for I had never before seen a trench, excepting those we captured from the Spaniards, or heard of a traverse, save as I
vaguely remembered reading about them in books. For such
work as we were engaged in, however, the problem of in-
trenchment was comparatively simple, and the work we did
proved entirely adequate. No man in my regiment was ever
hit in the trenches or going in or out of them.

But on the first day there was plenty of excitement connected with relieving the firing line. Under the intense heat,
crowded down in cramped attitudes in the rank, newly dug,
poisonous soil of the trenches, the men needed to be relieved
every six hours or so. Accordingly, in the late morning, and
again in the afternoon, I arranged for their release. On each
occasion I waited until there was a lull in the firing and then
started a sudden rush by the relieving party, who tumbled
into the trenches every which way. The movement resulted on
each occasion in a terrific outburst of fire from the Spanish
lines, which proved quite harmless; and as it gradually died
away the men who had been relieved got out as best they
could. Fortunately, by the next day I was able to abandon this
primitive, though thrilling and wholly novel, military method
of relief.

When the hardtack came up that afternoon I felt much sympathy for the hungry unfortunates in the trenches and hated
to condemn them to six hours more without food; but I did
not know how to get food into them. Little McGinty, the
bronco buster, volunteered to make the attempt, and I gave
him permission. He simply took a case of hardtack in his arms
and darted toward the trenches. The distance was but short,
and though there was an outburst of fire, he was actually
missed. One bullet, however, passed through the case of hardtack just before he disappeared with it into the trench. A
trooper named Shanafelt repeated the feat, later, with a pail of
coffee. Another trooper, George King, spent a leisure hour in
the rear making soup out of some rice and other stuff he found
in a Spanish house; he brought some of it to General Wood,
Jack Greenway, and myself, and nothing could have tasted
more delicious.

At this time our army in the trenches numbered about

Rough Riders in the Trenches.

11,000 men; and the Spaniards in Santiago about 9,000,* their reinforcements having just arrived. Nobody on the firing line, whatever was the case in the rear, felt the slightest uneasiness as to the Spaniards being able to break out; but there were plenty who doubted the advisability of trying to rush the heavy earthworks and wire defences in our front.

All day long the firing continued — musketry and cannon. Our artillery gave up the attempt to fight on the firing line, and was withdrawn well to the rear out of range of the Spanish rifles; so far as we could see, it accomplished very little. The dynamite gun was brought up to the right of the regimental line. It was more effective than the regular artillery because it was fired with smokeless powder, and as it was used like a mortar from behind the hill, it did not betray its presence, and those firing it suffered no loss. Every few shots it got out of order, and the Rough Rider machinists and those furnished by Lieutenant Parker — whom we by this time began to consider as an exceedingly valuable member of our own regiment — would spend an hour or two in setting it right. Sergeant Borrowe had charge of it and handled it well. With him was Sergeant Guitilias, a gallant old fellow, a veteran of the Civil War, whose duties were properly those of standard-bearer, he having charge of the yellow cavalry standard of the regiment; but in the Cuban campaign he was given the more active work of helping run the dynamite gun. The shots from the dynamite gun made a terrific explosion, but they did not seem to go accurately. Once one of them struck a Spanish trench and wrecked part of it. On another occasion one struck a big building, from which there promptly swarmed both Spanish cavalry and infantry, on whom the Colt automatic guns played with good effect, during the minute that elapsed before they could get other cover.

These Colt automatic guns were not, on the whole, very successful. The gun detail was under the charge of Sergeant

---

*This is probably an understatement. Lieutenant Müller, in chap. xxxviii. of his book, says that there were "eight or nine thousand;" this is exclusive of the men from the fleet, and apparently also of many of the volunteers (see chap. xiv.), all of whom were present on July 2d. I am inclined to think that on the evening of that day there were more Spanish troops inside Santiago than there were American troops outside.

(afterward Lieutenant) Tiffany, assisted by some of our best men, like Stephens, Crowninshield, Bradley, Smith, and Herrig. The guns were mounted on tripods. They were too heavy for men to carry any distance and we could not always get mules. They would have been more effective if mounted on wheels, as the Gatlings were. Moreover, they proved more delicate than the Gatlings, and very readily got out of order. A further and serious disadvantage was that they did not use the Krag ammunition, as the Gatlings did, but the Mauser ammunition. The Spanish cartridges which we captured came in quite handily for this reason. Parker took the same fatherly interest in these two Colts that he did in the dynamite gun, and finally I put all three and their men under his immediate care, so that he had a battery of seven guns.

In fact, I think Parker deserved rather more credit than any other one man in the entire campaign. I do not allude especially to his courage and energy, great though they were, for there were hundreds of his fellow-officers of the cavalry and infantry who possessed as much of the former quality, and scores who possessed as much of the latter; but he had the rare good judgment and foresight to see the possibilities of the machine-guns, and, thanks to the aid of General Shafter, he was able to organize his battery. He then, by his own exertions, got it to the front and proved that it could do invaluable work on the field of battle, as much in attack as in defence. Parker's Gatlings were our inseparable companions throughout the siege. After our trenches were put in final shape, he took off the wheels of a couple and placed them with our own two Colts in the trenches. His gunners slept beside the Rough Riders in the bomb-proofs, and the men shared with one another when either side got a supply of beans or of coffee and sugar; for Parker was as wide-awake and energetic in getting food for his men as we prided ourselves upon being in getting food for ours. Besides, he got oil, and let our men have plenty for their rifles. At no hour of the day or night was Parker anywhere but where we wished him to be in the event of an attack. If I was ordered to send a troop of Rough Riders to guard some road or some break in the lines, we usually got Parker to send a Gatling along, and whether the change was made by day or by night, the Gatling went, over any ground and in any weather. He never exposed the Gatlings needlessly or unless there was some object to be gained, but if serious fighting broke out, he always took a hand. Sometimes this fighting would be the result of an effort on our part to quell the fire from the Spanish trenches; sometimes the Spaniards took the initiative; but at whatever hour of the twenty-four serious fighting began, the drumming of the Gatlings was soon heard through the cracking of our own carbines.

I have spoken thus of Parker's Gatling detachment. How can I speak highly enough of the regular cavalry with whom it was our good fortune to serve? I do not believe that in any army of the world could be found a more gallant and soldierly body of fighters than the officers and men of the First, Third, Sixth, Ninth, and Tenth United States Cavalry, beside whom we marched to blood-bought victory under the tropic skies of Santiago. The American regular sets the standard of excellence. When we wish to give the utmost possible praise to a volunteer organization, we say that it is as good as the regulars. I was exceedingly proud of the fact that the regulars treated my regiment as on a complete equality with themselves, and were as ready to see it in a post of danger and responsibility as to see any of their own battalions. Lieutenant Colonel Dorst, a man from whom praise meant a good deal, christened us "the Eleventh United States Horse," and we endeavored, I think I may say successfully, to show that we deserved the title by our conduct, not only in fighting and in marching, but in guarding the trenches and in policing camp. In less than sixty days the regiment had been raised, organized, armed, equipped, drilled, mounted, dismounted, kept for a fortnight on transports, and put through two victorious aggressive fights in very difficult country, the loss in killed and wounded amounting to a quarter of those engaged. This is a record which it is not easy to match in the history of volunteer organizations. The loss was but small compared to that which befell hundreds of regiments in some of the great battles of the later years of the Civil War; but it may be doubted whether there was any regiment which made such a record during the first months of any of our wars.

After the battle of San Juan my men had really become veterans; they and I understood each other perfectly, and trusted

Colonel Roosevelt and Rough Riders at the Point where they Charged Over the Hill at San Juan.

each other implicitly; they knew I would share every hardship and danger with them, would do everything in my power to see that they were fed, and so far as might be, sheltered and spared; and in return I knew that they would endure every kind of hardship and fatigue without a murmur and face every danger with entire fearlessness. I felt utter confidence in them, and would have been more than willing to put them to any task which any crack regiment of the world, at home or abroad, could perform. They were natural fighters, men of great intelligence, great courage, great hardihood, and physical prowess; and I could draw on these qualities and upon their spirit of ready, soldierly obedience to make up for any deficiencies in the technique of the trade which they had temporarily adopted. It must be remembered that they were already good individual fighters, skilled in the use of the horse and the rifle, so that there was no need of putting them through the kind of training in which the ordinary raw recruit must spend his first year or two.

On July 2d, as the day wore on, the fight, though raging fitfully at intervals, gradually died away. The Spanish guerillas were causing us much trouble. They showed great courage, exactly as did their soldiers who were defending the trenches. In fact, the Spaniards throughout showed precisely the qualities they did early in the century, when, as every student will remember, their fleets were a helpless prey to the English warships, and their armies utterly unable to stand in the open against those of Napoleon's marshals, while on the other hand their guerillas performed marvellous feats, and their defence of intrenchments and walled towns, as at Saragossa and Gerona, were the wonder of the civilized world.

In our front their sharp-shooters crept up before dawn and either lay in the thick jungle or climbed into some tree with dense foliage. In these places it proved almost impossible to place them, as they kept cover very carefully, and their smokeless powder betrayed not the slightest sign of their whereabouts. They caused us a great deal of annoyance and some little loss, and though our own sharp-shooters were continually taking shots at the places where they supposed them to be, and though occasionally we would play a Gatling or a Colt all through the top of a suspicious tree, I but twice saw

Spaniards brought down out of their perches from in front of our lines — on each occasion the fall of the Spaniard being hailed with loud cheers by our men.

These sharp-shooters in our front did perfectly legitimate work, and were entitled to all credit for their courage and skill. It was different with the guerillas in our rear. Quite a number of these had been posted in trees at the time of the San Juan fight. They were using, not Mausers, but Remingtons, which shot smokeless powder and a brass-coated bullet. It was one of these bullets which had hit Winslow Clark by my side on Kettle Hill; and though for long-range fighting the Remingtons were, of course, nothing like as good as the Mausers, they were equally serviceable for short-range bush work, as they used smokeless powder. When our troops advanced and the Spaniards in the trenches and in reserve behind the hill fled, the guerillas in the trees had no time to get away and in consequence were left in the rear of our lines. As we found out from the prisoners we took, the Spanish officers had been careful to instil into the minds of their soldiers the belief that the Americans never granted quarter, and I suppose it was in consequence of this that the guerillas did not surrender; for we found that the Spaniards were anxious enough to surrender as soon as they became convinced that we would treat them mercifully. At any rate, these guerillas kept up in their trees and showed not only courage but wanton cruelty and barbarity. At times they fired upon armed men in bodies, but they much preferred for their victims the unarmed attendants, the doctors, the chaplains, the hospital stewards. They fired at the men who were bearing off the wounded in litters; they fired at the doctors who came to the front, and at the chaplains who started to hold burial service; the conspicuous Red Cross brassard worn by all of these non-combatants, instead of serving as a protection, seemed to make them the special objects of the guerilla fire. So annoying did they become that I sent out that afternoon and next morning a detail of picked sharp-shooters to hunt them out, choosing, of course, first-class woodsmen and mountain men who were also good shots. My sharp-shooters felt very vindictively toward these guerillas and showed them no quarter. They started systematically to hunt them, and showed themselves much superior at the guerillas' own game, killing eleven, while not one of my men was scratched. Two of the men who did conspicuously good service in this work were Troopers Goodwin and Proffit, both of Arizona, but one by birth a Californian and the other a North Carolinian. Goodwin was a natural shot, not only with the rifle and revolver, but with the sling. Proffit might have stood as a type of the mountaineers described by John Fox and Miss Murfree. He was a tall, sinewy, handsome man of remarkable strength, an excellent shot and a thoroughly good soldier. His father had been a Confederate officer, rising from the ranks, and if the war had lasted long enough the son would have risen in the same manner. As it was, I should have been glad to have given him a commission, exactly as I should have been glad to have given a number of others in the regiment commissions, if I had only had them. Proffit was a saturnine, reserved man, who afterward fell very sick with the fever, and who, as a reward for his soldierly good conduct, was often granted unusual privileges; but he took the fever and the privileges with the same iron indifference, never grumbling, and never expressing satisfaction.

The sharp-shooters returned by nightfall. Soon afterward I established my pickets and outposts well to the front in the jungle, so as to prevent all possibility of surprise. After dark, fires suddenly shot up on the mountain passes far to our right. They all rose together and we could make nothing of them. After a good deal of consultation, we decided they must be some signals to the Spaniards in Santiago, from the troops marching to reinforce them from without — for we were ignorant that the reinforcements had already reached the city, the Cubans being quite unable to prevent the Spanish regulars from marching wherever they wished. While we were thus pondering over the watch-fires and attributing them to Spanish machinations of some sort, it appears that the Spaniards, equally puzzled, were setting them down as an attempt at communication between the insurgents and our army. Both sides were accordingly on the alert, and the Spaniards must have strengthened their outlying parties in the jungle ahead of us, for they suddenly attacked one of our pickets, wounding Crockett seriously. He was brought in by the other troopers. Evidently the Spanish lines felt a little nervous, for this sputter of shooting was immediately followed by a tremendous fire of great guns and rifles from their trenches and batteries. Our men in the trenches responded heavily, and word was sent back, not only to me, but to the commanders in the rear of the regiments along our line, that the Spaniards were attacking. It was imperative to see what was really going on, so I ran up to the trenches and looked out. At night it was far easier to place the Spanish lines than by day, because the flame-spurts shone in the darkness. I could soon tell that there were bodies of Spanish pickets or skirmishers in the jungle-covered valley, between their lines and ours, but that the bulk of the fire came from their trenches and showed not the slightest symptom of advancing; moreover, as is generally the case at night, the fire was almost all high, passing well overhead, with an occasional bullet near by.

I came to the conclusion that there was no use in our firing back under such circumstances; and I could tell that the same conclusion had been reached by Captain Ayres of the Tenth Cavalry on the right of my line, for even above the cracking of the carbines rose the Captain's voice as with varied and picturesque language he bade his black troopers cease firing. The Captain was as absolutely fearless as a man can be. He had command of his regimental trenches that night, and, having run up at the first alarm, had speedily satisfied himself that no particular purpose was served by blazing away in the dark, when the enormous majority of the Spaniards were simply shooting at random from their own trenches, and, if they ever had thought of advancing, had certainly given up the idea. His troopers were devoted to him, would follow him anywhere, and would do anything he said; but when men get firing at night it is rather difficult to stop them, especially when the fire of the enemy in front continues unabated. When he first reached the trenches it was impossible to say whether or not there was an actual night attack impending, and he had been instructing his men, as I instructed mine, to fire low, cutting the grass in front. As soon as he became convinced that there was no night attack, he ran up and down the line adjuring and commanding the troopers to cease shooting, with words and phrases which were doubtless not wholly unlike those which the Old Guard really did use at Waterloo. As I ran down my own line, I could see him coming up his, and he saved me all trouble in stopping the fire at the right, where the lines met, for my men there all dropped everything to listen to him and cheer and laugh. Soon we got the troopers in hand, and made them cease firing; then, after awhile, the Spanish fire died down. At the time we spoke of this as a night attack by the Spaniards, but it really was not an attack at all. Ever after my men had a great regard for Ayres, and would have followed him anywhere. I shall never forget the way in which he scolded his huge, devoted black troopers, generally ending with "I'm ashamed of you, ashamed of you! I wouldn't have believed it! Firing; when I told you to stop! I'm ashamed of you!"

That night we spent in perfecting the trenches and arranging entrances to them, doing about as much work as we had the preceding night. Greenway and Goodrich, from their energy, eagerness to do every duty, and great physical strength, were peculiarly useful in this work; as, indeed, they were in all work. They had been up practically the entire preceding night, but they were too good men for me to spare them, nor did they wish to be spared; and I kept them up all this night too. Goodrich had also been on guard as officer of the day the night we were at El Poso, so that it turned out that he spent nearly four days and three nights with practically hardly any sleep at all.

Next morning, at daybreak, the firing began again. This day, the 3d, we suffered nothing, save having one man wounded by a sharp-shooter, and, thanks to the approaches to the trenches, we were able to relieve the guards without any difficulty. The Spanish sharp-shooters in the trees and jungle nearby, however, annoyed us very much, and I made preparations to fix them next day. With this end in view I chose out some twenty first-class men, in many instances the same that I had sent after the guerillas, and arranged that each should take his canteen and a little food. They were to slip into the jungle between us and the Spanish lines before dawn next morning, and there to spend the day, getting as close to the Spanish lines as possible, moving about with great stealth, and picking off any hostile sharp-shooter, as well as any soldier who exposed himself in the trenches. I had plenty of men who possessed a training in wood-craft that fitted them for this work; and as soon as the rumor got abroad what I was planning, volunteers thronged to me. Daniels and Love were two of the men always to the front in any enterprise of this nature; so were Wadsworth, the two Bulls, Fortescue, and Cowdin. But I could not begin to name all the troopers who so eagerly craved the chance to win honor out of hazard and danger.

Among them was good, solemn Fred Herrig, the Alsatian. I knew Fred's patience and skill as a hunter from the trips we had taken together after deer and mountain sheep through the Bad Lands of the Little Missouri. He still spoke English with what might be called Alsatian variations — he always spoke of the gun detail as the "góndêtle," with the accent on the first syllable — and he expressed a wish to be allowed "a holiday from the gondetle to go after dem gorrillas." I told him he could have the holiday, but to his great disappointment the truce came first, and then Fred asked that, inasmuch as the "gorrillas" were now forbidden game, he might be allowed to go after guinea hens instead.

Even after the truce, however, some of my sharp-shooters had occupation, for two guerillas in our rear took occasional shots at the men who were bathing in a pond, until one of our men spied them, when they were both speedily brought down. One of my riflemen who did best at this kind of work, by the way, got into trouble because of it. He was much inflated by my commendation of him, and when he went back to his troop he declined to obey the first Sergeant's orders on the ground that he was "the Colonel's sharp-shooter." The Lieutenant in command, being somewhat puzzled, brought him to me, and I had to explain that if the offence, disobedience of orders in face of the enemy, was repeated he might incur the death penalty; whereat he looked very crestfallen. That afternoon he got permission, like Fred Herrig, to go after guinea-hens, which were found wild in some numbers round about; and he sent me the only one he got as a peace offering. The few guinea-hens thus procured were all used for the sick.

Dr. Church had established a little field hospital under the shoulder of the hill in our rear. He was himself very sick and had almost nothing in the way of medicine or supplies or apparatus of any kind, but the condition of the wounded in the big field hospitals in the rear was so horrible, from the lack of attendants as well as of medicines, that we kept all the men we possibly could at the front. Some of them had now begun to come down with fever. They were all very patient, but it was pitiful to see the sick and wounded soldiers lying on their blankets, if they had any, and if not then simply in the mud, with nothing to eat but hardtack and pork, which of course they could not touch when their fever got high, and with no chance to get more than the rudest attention. Among the very sick here was gallant Captain Llewellen. I feared he was going to die. We finally had to send him to one of the big hospitals in the rear. Doctors Brewer and Fuller of the Tenth had been unwearying in attending to the wounded, including many of those of my regiment.

At twelve o'clock we were notified to stop firing and a flag of truce was sent in to demand the surrender of the city. The negotiations gave us a breathing spell.

That afternoon I arranged to get our baggage up, sending back strong details of men to carry up their own goods, and, as usual, impressing into the service a kind of improvised pack-train consisting of the officers' horses, of two or three captured Spanish cavalry horses, two or three mules which had been shot and abandoned and which our men had taken and cured, and two or three Cuban ponies. Hitherto we had simply been sleeping by the trenches or immediately in their rear, with nothing in the way of shelter and only one blanket to every three or four men. Fortunately there had been little rain. We now got up the shelter tents of the men and some flies for the hospital and for the officers; and my personal baggage appeared. I celebrated its advent by a thorough wash and shave.

Later, I twice snatched a few hours to go to the rear and visit such of my men as I could find in the hospitals. Their patience was extraordinary. Kenneth Robinson, a gallant young trooper, though himself severely (I supposed at the time mortally) wounded, was noteworthy for the way in which he tended those among the wounded who were even more helpless, and the cheery courage with which he kept up their spirits. Gievers, who was shot through the hips, rejoined us at the front in a fortnight. Captain Day was hardly longer away. Jack Hammer, who, with poor Race Smith, a gallant Texas lad who

View of San Juan Hill and Block-house, showing the Camp of the United States Forces.

was mortally hurt beside me on the summit of the hill, had been on kitchen detail, was wounded and sent to the rear; he was ordered to go to the United States, but he heard that we were to assault Santiago, so he struggled out to rejoin us, and thereafter stayed at the front. Cosby, badly wounded, made his way down to the sea-coast in three days, unassisted.

With all volunteer troops, and I am inclined to think with regulars, too, in time of trial, the best work can be got out of the men only if the officers endure the same hardships and face the same risks. In my regiment, as in the whole cavalry division, the proportion of loss in killed and wounded was considerably greater among the officers than among the troopers, and this was exactly as it should be. Moreover, when we got down to hard pan, we all, officers and men, fared exactly alike as regards both shelter and food. This prevented any grumbling. When the troopers saw that the officers had nothing but hardtack, there was not a man in the regiment who would not have been ashamed to grumble at faring no worse, and when all alike slept out in the open, in the rear of the trenches, and when the men always saw the field officers up at night, during the digging of the trenches, and going the rounds of the outposts, they would not tolerate, in any of their number, either complaint or shirking work. When things got easier I put up my tent and lived a little apart, for it is a mistake for an officer ever to grow too familiar with his men, no matter how good they are; and it is of course the greatest possible mistake to seek popularity either by showing weakness or by mollycoddling the men. They will never respect a commander who does not enforce discipline, who does not know his duty, and who is not willing both himself to encounter and to make them encounter every species of danger and hardship when necessary. The soldiers who do not feel this way are not worthy of the name and should be handled with iron severity until they become fighting men and not shams. In return the officer should carefully look after his men, should see that they are well fed and well sheltered, and that, no matter how much they may grumble, they keep the camp thoroughly policed.

After the cessation of the three day's fighting we began to get our rations regularly and had plenty of hardtack and salt pork, and usually about half the ordinary amount of sugar and coffee. It was not a very good ration for the tropics, however, and was of very little use indeed to the sick and half sick. On two or three occasions during the siege I got my improvised pack-train together and either took or sent it down to the sea-coast for beans, canned tomatoes, and the like. We got these either from the transports which were still landing stores on the beach or from the Red Cross. If I did not go myself I sent some man who had shown that he was a driving, energetic, tactful fellow, who would somehow get what we wanted. Chaplain Brown developed great capacity in this line, and so did one of the troopers named Knoblauch, he who had dived after the rifles that had sunk off the pier at Daiquiri. The supplies of food we got in this way had a very beneficial effect, not only upon the men's health, but upon their spirits. To the Red Cross and similar charitable organizations we owe a great deal. We also owed much to Colonel Weston of the Commissary Department, who always helped us and never let himself be hindered by red tape; thus he always let me violate the absurd regulation which forbade me, even in war time, to purchase food for my men from the stores, although letting me purchase for the officers. I, of course, paid no heed to the regulation when by violating it I could get beans, canned tomatoes, or tobacco. Sometimes I used my own money, sometimes what was given me by Woody Kane, or what was sent me by my brother-in-law, Douglas Robinson, or by the other Red Cross people in New York. My regiment did not fare very well; but I think it fared better than any other. Of course no one would have minded in the least such hardships as we endured had there been any need of enduring them; but there was none. System and sufficiency of transportation were all that were needed.

On one occasion a foreign military attaché visited my headquarters together with a foreign correspondent who had been through the Turco-Greek war. They were both most friendly critics, and as they knew I was aware of this, the correspondent finally ventured the remark, that he thought our soldiers fought even better than the Turks, but that on the whole our system of military administration seemed rather worse than that of the Greeks. As a nation we had prided ourselves on our business ability and adroitness in the arts of peace, while outsiders, at any rate, did not credit us with any especial war-like prowess; and it was curious that when war came we should have broken down precisely on the business and ad-ministrative side, while the fighting edge of the troops cer-tainly left little to be desired.

I was very much touched by the devotion my men showed to me. After they had once become convinced that I would share their hardships, they made it a point that I should not suffer any hardships at all; and I really had an extremely easy time. Whether I had any food or not myself made no differ-ence, as there were sure to be certain troopers, and, indeed, certain troop messes, on the lookout for me. If they had any beans they would send me over a cupful, or I would suddenly receive a present of doughnuts from some ex-roundup cook who had succeeded in obtaining a little flour and sugar, and if a man shot a guinea-hen it was all I could do to make him keep half of it for himself. Wright, the color sergeant, and Henry Bardshar, my orderly, always pitched and struck my tent and built me a bunk of bamboo poles, whenever we changed camp. So I personally endured very little discomfort; for, of course, no one minded the two or three days preced-ing or following each fight, when we all had to get along as best we could. Indeed, as long as we were under fire or in the immediate presence of the enemy, and I had plenty to do, there was nothing of which I could legitimately complain; and what I really did regard as hardships, my men did not object to — for later on, when we had some leisure, I would have given much for complete solitude and some good books.

Whether there was a truce, or whether, as sometimes hap-pened, we were notified that there was no truce but merely a further cessation of hostilities by tacit agreement, or whether the fight was on, we kept equally vigilant watch, especially at night. In the trenches every fourth man kept awake, the others sleeping beside or behind him on their rifles; and the Cossack posts and pickets were pushed out in advance beyond the edge of the jungle. At least once a night at some irregular hour I tried to visit every part of our line, especially if it was dark and rainy, although sometimes, when the lines were in charge of some officer like Wilcox or Kane, Greenway or Goodrich, I became lazy, took off my boots, and slept all night through.

Sometimes at night I went not only along the lines of our own brigade, but of the brigades adjoining. It was a matter of pride, not only with me, but with all our men, that the lines occupied by the Rough Riders should be at least as vigilantly guarded as the lines of any regular regiment.

Sometimes at night, when I met other officers inspecting their lines, we would sit and talk over matters, and wonder what shape the outcome of the siege would take. We knew we would capture Santiago, but exactly how we would do it we could not tell. The failure to establish any depot for provisions on the fighting-line, where there was hardly ever more than twenty-four hours' food ahead, made the risk very serious. If a hurricane had struck the transports, scattering them to the four winds, or if three days of heavy rain had completely broken up our communication, as they assuredly would have done, we would have been at starvation point on the front; and while, of course, we would have lived through it somehow and would have taken the city, it would only have been after very disagreeable experiences. As soon as I was able I accumulated for my own regiment about forty-eight hours' hardtack and salt pork, which I kept so far as possible intact to provide against any emergency.

If the city could be taken without direct assault on the intrenchments and wire entanglements, we earnestly hoped it would be, for such an assault meant, as we knew by past experience, the loss of a quarter of the attacking regiments (and we were bound that the Rough Riders should be one of these attacking regiments, if the attack had to be made). There was, of course, nobody who would not rather have assaulted than have run the risk of failure; but we hoped the city would fall without need arising for us to suffer the great loss of life which a further assault would have entailed.

Naturally, the colonels and captains had nothing to say in the peace negotiations which dragged along for the week following the sending in the flag of truce. Each day we expected either to see the city surrender, or to be told to begin fighting again, and toward the end it grew so irksome that we would have welcomed even an assault in preference to further inaction. I used to discuss matters with the officers of my own regiment now and then, and with a few of the officers of the

neighboring regiments with whom I had struck up a friendship — Parker, Stevens, Beck, Ayres, Morton, and Boughton.
I also saw a good deal of the excellent officers on the staffs
of Generals Wheeler and Sumner, especially Colonel Dorst,
Colonel Garlington, Captain Howze, Captain Steele, Lieutenant Andrews, and Captain Astor Chanler, who, like
myself, was a volunteer. Chanler was an old friend and a
fellow big-game hunter, who had done some good exploring
work in Africa. I always wished I could have had him in my
regiment. As for Dorst, he was peculiarly fitted to command
a regiment. Although Howze and Andrews were not in my
brigade, I saw a great deal of them, especially of Howze, who
would have made a nearly ideal regimental commander. They
were both natural cavalry-men and of most enterprising na-
tures, ever desirous of pushing to the front and of taking the
boldest course. The view Howze always took of every emergency (a view which found prompt expression in his actions
when the opportunity offered) made me feel like an elderly
conservative.

The week of non-fighting was not all a period of truce; part
of the time was passed under a kind of nondescript arrangement, when we were told not to attack ourselves, but to be
ready at any moment to repulse an attack and to make preparations for meeting it. During these times I busied myself
in putting our trenches into first-rate shape and in building
bomb-proofs and traverses. One night I got a detail of sixty
men from the First, Ninth, and Tenth, whose officers always
helped us in every way, and with these, and with sixty of my
own men, I dug a long, zigzag trench in advance of the salient
of my line out to a knoll well in front, from which we could
command the Spanish trenches and block-houses immediately
ahead of us. On this knoll we made a kind of bastion consisting of a deep, semi-circular trench with sand-bags arranged
along the edge so as to constitute a wall with loop-holes. Of
course, when I came to dig this trench, I kept both Greenway
and Goodrich supervising the work all night, and equally of
course I got Parker and Stevens to help me. By employing as
many men as we did we were able to get the work so far advanced as to provide against interruption before the moon
rose, which was almost midnight. Our pickets were thrown

Gen. Wheeler.    Col. Roosevelt.

Gen. Wood.

A Consultation at General Wheeler's Head-quarters.

far out in the jungle, to keep back the Spanish pickets and prevent any interference with the diggers. The men seemed to think the work rather good fun than otherwise, the possibility of a brush with the Spaniards lending a zest that prevented its growing monotonous.

Parker had taken two of his Gatlings, removed the wheels, and mounted them in the trenches; also mounting the two automatic Colts where he deemed they could do best service. With the completion of the trenches, bomb-proofs, and traverses, and the mounting of these guns, the fortifications of the hill assumed quite a respectable character, and the Gatling men christened it Fort Roosevelt, by which name it afterward went.*

During the truce various military attachés and foreign officers came out to visit us. Two or three of the newspaper men, including Richard Harding Davis, Caspar Whitney, and John Fox, had already been out to see us, and had been in the trenches during the firing. Among the others were Captains Lee and Paget of the British army and navy, fine fellows, who really seemed to take as much pride in the feats of our men as if we had been bound together by the ties of a common nationality instead of the ties of race and speech kinship. Another English visitor was Sir Bryan Leighton, a thrice-welcome guest, for he most thoughtfully brought to me half a dozen little jars of devilled ham and potted fruit, which enabled me to summon various officers down to my tent and hold a feast. Count von Götzen, and a Norwegian attaché, Gedde, very good fellows both, were also out. One day we were visited by a travelling Russian, Prince X., a large, blond man, smooth and impenetrable. I introduced him to one of the regular army officers, a capital fighter and excellent fellow, who, however, viewed foreign international politics from a strictly trans-Mississippi stand-point. He hailed the Russian with frank kindness and took him off to show him around the trenches, chatting volubly, and calling him "Prince," much as Kentuckians call one another "Colonel." As I returned I heard him remarking: "You see, Prince, the great result of this war is that it has united the two branches of the Anglo-Saxon

*See Parker's "With the Gatlings at Santiago."

Bomb-proofs Behind the Main Trenches Before Santiago.

(The position taken by the Rough Riders in their second charge on July 1st.)

people; and now that they are together they can whip the world, Prince! they can whip the world!" — being evidently filled with the pleasing belief that the Russian would cordially sympathize with this view.

The foreign attachés did not always get on well with our generals. The two English representatives never had any trouble, were heartily admired by everybody, and, indeed, were generally treated as if they were of our own number; and seemingly so regarded themselves. But this was not always true of the representatives from Continental Europe. One of the latter — a very good fellow, by the way — had not altogether approved of the way he was treated, and the climax came when he said good-by to the General who had special charge of him. The General in question was not accustomed to nice ethnic distinctions, and grouped all of the representatives from Continental Europe under the comprehensive title of "Dutchmen." When the attaché in question came to say farewell, the General responded with a bluff heartiness, in which perhaps the note of sincerity was more conspicuous than that of entire good breeding: "Well, good-by; sorry you're going; which are you anyhow — the German or the Russian?"

Shortly after midday on the 10th fighting began again, but it soon became evident that the Spaniards did not have much heart in it. The American field artillery was now under the command of General Randolph, and he fought it effectively. A mortar battery had also been established, though with an utterly inadequate supply of ammunition, and this rendered some service. Almost the only Rough Riders who had a chance to do much firing were the men with the Colt automatic guns, and the twenty picked sharp-shooters, who were placed in the newly dug little fort out at the extreme front. Parker had a splendid time with the Gatlings and the Colts. With these machine guns he completely silenced the battery in front of us. This battery had caused us a good deal of trouble at first, as we could not place it. It was immediately in front of the hospital, from which many Red Cross flags were flying, one of them floating just above this battery, from where we looked at it. In consequence, for some time, we did not know it was a hostile battery at all, as, like all the other Spanish batteries, it was using smokeless powder. It was only by the aid of powerful glasses that we finally discovered its real nature. The Gatlings and Colts then actually put it out of action, silencing the big guns and the two field-pieces. Furthermore, the machine guns and our sharp-shooters together did good work in supplementing the effects of the dynamite gun; for when a shell from the latter struck near a Spanish trench, or a building in which there were Spanish troops, the shock was seemingly so great that the Spaniards almost always showed themselves, and gave our men a chance to do some execution.

As the evening of the 10th came on, the men began to make their coffee in sheltered places. By this time they knew how to take care of themselves so well that not a man was touched by the Spaniards during the second bombardment. While I was lying with the officers just outside one of the bomb-proofs I saw a New Mexican trooper named Morrison making his coffee under the protection of a traverse high up on the hill. Morrison was originally a Baptist preacher who had joined the regiment purely from a sense of duty, leaving his wife and children, and had shown himself to be an excellent soldier. He had evidently exactly calculated the danger zone, and found that by getting close to the traverse he could sit up erect and make ready his supper without being cramped. I watched him solemnly pounding the coffee with the butt end of his revolver, and then boiling the water and frying his bacon, just as if he had been in the lee of the roundup wagon somewhere out on the plains.

By noon of next day, the 11th, my regiment with one of the Gatlings was shifted over to the right to guard the Caney road. We did no fighting in our new position, for the last straggling shot had been fired by the time we got there. That evening there came up the worst storm we had had, and by midnight my tent blew over. I had for the first time in a fortnight undressed myself completely, and I felt fully punished for my love of luxury when I jumped out into the driving downpour of tropic rain, and groped blindly in the darkness for my clothes as they lay in the liquid mud. It was Kane's night on guard, and I knew the wretched Woody would be out along the line and taking care of the pickets, no matter what the storm might be; and so I basely made my way to the kitchen

Sergeant Guitilias, a Veteran
of the Civil War.

The Standard-bearer of the
Rough Riders, and attached
to the dynamite-gun.

Trooper Morrison, formerly
a Baptist Minister.

tent, where good Holderman, the Cherokee, wrapped me in dry blankets, and put me to sleep on a table which he had just procured from an abandoned Spanish house.

On the 17th the city formally surrendered and our regiment, like the rest of the army, was drawn up on the trenches. When the American flag was hoisted the trumpets blared and the men cheered, and we knew that the fighting part of our work was over.

Shortly after we took our new position the First Illinois Volunteers came up on our right. The next day, as a result of the storm and of further rain, the rivers were up and the roads quagmires, so that hardly any food reached the front. My regiment was all right, as we had provided for just such an emergency; but the Illinois new-comers had of course not done so, and they were literally without anything to eat. They were fine fellows and we could not see them suffer. I furnished them some beans and coffee for the elder officers and two or three cases of hardtack for the men, and then mounted my horse and rode down to head-quarters, half fording, half swimming the streams; and late in the evening I succeeded in getting half a mule-train of provisions for them.

On the morning of the 3d the Spaniards had sent out of Santiago many thousands of women, children, and other non-combatants, most of them belonging to the poorer classes, but among them not a few of the best families. These wretched creatures took very little with them. They came through our lines and for the most part went to El Caney in our rear, where we had to feed them and protect them from the Cubans. As we had barely enough food for our own men the rations of the refugees were scanty indeed and their sufferings great. Long before the surrender they had begun to come to our lines to ask for provisions, and my men gave them a good deal out of their own scanty stores, until I had positively to forbid it and to insist that the refugees should go to head-quarters; as, however hard and merciless it seemed, I was in duty bound to keep my own regiment at the highest pitch of fighting efficiency.

As soon as the surrender was assured the refugees came streaming back in an endless squalid procession down the Caney road to Santiago. My troopers, for all their roughness and their ferocity in fight, were rather tender-hearted than otherwise, and they helped the poor creatures, especially the women and children, in every way, giving them food and even carrying the children and the burdens borne by the women. I saw one man, Happy Jack, spend the entire day in walking to and fro for about a quarter of a mile on both sides of our lines along the road, carrying the bundles for a series of poor old women, or else carrying young children. Finally the doctor warned us that we must not touch the bundles of the refugees for fear of infection, as disease had broken out and was rife among them. Accordingly I had to put a stop to these acts of kindness on the part of my men; against which action Happy Jack respectfully but strongly protested upon the unexpected ground that "The Almighty would never let a man catch a disease while he was doing a good action." I did not venture to take so advanced a theological stand.

# VI

## THE RETURN HOME

Two or three days after the surrender the cavalry division was marched back to the foothills west of El Caney, and there went into camp, together with the artillery. It was a most beautiful spot beside a stream of clear water, but it was not healthy. In fact no ground in the neighborhood was healthy. For the tropics the climate was not bad, and I have no question but that a man who was able to take good care of himself could live there all the year round with comparative impunity; but the case was entirely different with an army which was obliged to suffer great exposure, and to live under conditions which almost insured being attacked by the severe malarial fever of the country. My own men were already suffering badly from fever, and they got worse rather than better in the new camp. The same was true of the other regiments in the cavalry division. A curious feature was that the colored troops seemed to suffer as heavily as the white. From week to week there were slight relative changes, but on the average all the six cavalry regiments, the Rough Riders, the white regulars, and the colored regulars seemed to suffer about alike, and we were all very much weakened; about as much as the regular infantry, although naturally not as much as the volunteer infantry.

Yet even under such circumstances adventurous spirits managed to make their way out to us. In the fortnight following the last bombardment of the city I enlisted no less than nine such recruits, six being from Harvard, Yale, or Princeton; and Bull, the former Harvard oar, who had been back to the States crippled after the first fight, actually got back to us as a stowaway on one of the transports, bound to share the luck of the regiment, even if it meant yellow fever.

There were but twelve ambulances with the army, and these were quite inadequate for their work; but the conditions in the large field hospitals were so bad, that as long as possible we kept all of our sick men in the regimental hospital at the front. Dr. Church did splendid work, although he himself was suffering much more than half the time from fever. Several of the men from the ranks did equally well, especially a young doctor from New York, Harry Thorpe, who had enlisted as a trooper, but who was now made acting assistant-surgeon. It was with the greatest difficulty that Church and Thorpe were able to get proper medicine for the sick, and it was almost the last day of our stay before we were able to get cots for them. Up to that time they lay on the ground. No food was issued suitable for them, or for the half-sick men who were not on the doctor's list; the two classes by this time included the bulk of the command. Occasionally we got hold of a wagon or of some Cuban carts, and at other times I used my improvised pack-train (the animals of which, however, were continually being taken away from us by our superiors) and went or sent back to the sea-coast at Siboney or into Santiago itself to get rice, flour, cornmeal, oatmeal, condensed milk, potatoes, and canned vegetables. The rice I bought in Santiago; the best of the other stuff I got from the Red Cross through Mr. George Kennan and Miss Clara Barton and Dr. Lesser; but some of it I got from our own transports. Colonel Weston, the Commissary-General, as always, rendered us every service in his power. This additional and varied food was of the utmost service, not merely to the sick but in preventing the well from becoming sick. Throughout the campaign the Division Inspector-General, Lieutenant-Colonel Garlington, and Lieutenants West and Dickman, the acting division quartermaster and commissary, had done everything in their power to keep us supplied with food; but where there were so few mules and wagons even such able and zealous officers could not do the impossible.

We had the camp policed thoroughly, and I made the men build little bunks of poles to sleep on. By July 23d, when we had been ashore a month, we were able to get fresh meat, and from that time on we fared well; but the men were already sickening. The chief trouble was the malarial fever, which was recurrent. For a few days the man would be very sick indeed; then he would partially recover, and be able to go back to work; but after a little time he would be again struck down. Every officer other than myself except one was down with sickness at one time or another. Even Greenway and Goodrich succumbed to the fever and were knocked out for a few days. Very few of the men indeed retained their strength and energy, and though the percentage actually on the sick list never got over twenty, there were less than fifty per cent. who were fit for any kind of work. All the clothes were in rags; even the officers had neither socks nor underwear. The lithe college athletes had lost their spring; the tall, gaunt hunters and cow-punchers lounged listlessly in their dog-tents, which were steaming morasses during the torrential rains, and then ovens when the sun blazed down; but there were no complaints.

Through some blunder our march from the intrenchments to the camp on the foothills, after the surrender, was made during the heat of the day; and though it was only some five miles or thereabouts, very nearly half the men of the cavalry division dropped out. Captain Llewellen had come back, and led his troop on the march. He carried a pick and shovel for one of his sick men, and after we reached camp walked back with a mule to get another trooper who had fallen out from heat exhaustion. The result was that the captain himself went down and became exceedingly sick. We at last succeeded in sending him to the States. I never thought he would live, but he did, and when I met him again at Montauk Point he had practically entirely recovered. My orderly, Henry Bardshar, was struck down, and though he ultimately recovered, he was a mere skeleton, having lost over eighty pounds.

Yellow fever also broke out in the rear, chiefly among the Cubans. It never became epidemic, but it caused a perfect panic among some of our own doctors, and especially in the minds of one or two generals and of the home authorities. We found that whenever we sent a man to the rear he was decreed to have yellow fever, whereas, if we kept him at the front, it always turned out that he had malarial fever, and after a few days he was back at work again. I doubt if there were ever more than a dozen genuine cases of yellow fever in the whole cavalry division; but the authorities at Washington, misled by the reports they received from one or two of their military and medical advisers at the front, became panic-struck, and under the influence of their fears hesitated to bring the army home, lest it might import yellow fever into the United States. Their panic was absolutely groundless, as shown by the fact that when brought home not a single case of yellow fever developed upon American soil. Our real foe was not the yellow fever at all, but malarial fever, which was not infectious, but which was certain, if the troops were left throughout the summer in Cuba, to destroy them, either killing them outright, or weakening them so that they would have fallen victims to any disease that attacked them.

However, for a time our prospects were gloomy, as the Washington authorities seemed determined that we should stay in Cuba. They unfortunately knew nothing of the country nor of the circumstances of the army, and the plans that were from time to time formulated in the Department (and even by an occasional general or surgeon at the front) for the management of the army would have been comic if they had not possessed such tragic possibilities. Thus, at one period it was proposed that we should shift camp every two or three days. Now, our transportation, as I have pointed out before, was utterly inadequate. In theory, under the regulations of the War Department, each regiment should have had at least twenty-five wagons. As a matter of fact our regiment often had none, sometimes one, rarely two, and never three; yet it was better off than any other in the cavalry division. In consequence it was impossible to carry much of anything save what the men had on their backs, and half of the men were too weak to walk three miles with their packs. Whenever we shifted camp the exertion among the half-sick caused our sick-roll to double next morning, and it took at least three days, even when the shift was for but a short distance, before we were able to bring up the officers' luggage, the hospital spare food, the ammunition, etc. Meanwhile the officers slept wherever they could, and those men who had not been able to carry their own bedding, slept as the officers did. In the weak condition of the men the labor of pitching camp was severe and told heavily upon them. In short, the scheme of continually shifting camp was impossible of fulfilment. It would merely have resulted in the early destruction of the army.

Again, it was proposed that we should go up the mountains and make our camps there. The palm and the bamboo grew to the summits of the mountains, and the soil along their sides was deep and soft, while the rains were very heavy, much more so than immediately on the coast — every mile or two inland bringing with it a great increase in the rainfall. We could, with much difficulty, have got our regiments up the mountains, but not half the men could have got up with their belongings; and once there it would have been an impossibility to feed them. It was all that could be done, with the limited number of wagons and mule-trains on hand, to feed the men in the existing camps, for the travel and the rain gradually rendered each road in succession wholly impassable. To have gone up the mountains would have meant early starvation.

The third plan of the Department was even more objectionable than either of the others. There was, some twenty-five miles in the interior, what was called a high interior plateau, and at one period we were informed that we were to be marched thither. As a matter of fact, this so-called high plateau was the sugar-cane country, where, during the summer, the rainfall was prodigious. It was a rich, deep soil, covered with a rank tropic growth, the guinea-grass being higher than the head of a man on horseback. It was a perfect hotbed of malaria, and there was no dry ground whatever in which to camp. To have sent the troops there would have been simple butchery.

Under these circumstances the alternative to leaving the country altogether was to stay where we were, with the hope that half the men would live through to the cool season. We did everything possible to keep up the spirits of the men, but it was exceedingly difficult because there was nothing for them to do. They were weak and languid, and in the wet heat they had lost energy, so that it was not possible for them to indulge in sports or pastimes. There were exceptions; but the average man who went off to shoot guinea-hens or tried some vigorous game always felt much the worse for his exertions. Once or twice I took some of my comrades with me, and climbed up one or another of the surrounding mountains, but the result generally was that half of the party were down with some kind of sickness next day. It was impossible to take heavy exercise in the heat of the day; the evening usually saw a rain-storm which made the country a quagmire; and in the early morning the drenching dew and wet, slimy soil made walking but little pleasure. Chaplain Brown held service every Sunday under a low tree outside my tent; and we always had a congregation of a few score troopers, lying or sitting round, their strong hard faces turned toward the preacher. I let a few of the men visit Santiago, but the long walk in and out was very tiring, and, moreover, wise restrictions had been put as to either officers or men coming in.

In any event there was very little to do in the quaint, dirty old Spanish city, though it was interesting to go in once or twice, and wander through the narrow streets with their curious little shops and low houses of stained stucco, with elaborately wrought iron trellises to the windows, and curiously carved balconies; or to sit in the central plaza where the cathedral was, and the clubs, and the Café Venus, and the low, bare, rambling building which was called the Governor's Palace. In this palace Wood had now been established as military governor, and Luna, and two or three of my other officers from the Mexican border, who knew Spanish, were sent in to do duty under him. A great many of my men knew Spanish, and some of the New Mexicans were of Spanish origin, although they behaved precisely like the other members of the regiment.

We should probably have spent the summer in our sick camps, losing half the men and hopelessly shattering the health of the remainder, if General Shafter had not summoned a council of officers, hoping by united action of a more or less public character to wake up the Washington authorities to the actual condition of things. As all the Spanish forces in the province of Santiago had surrendered, and as so-called immune regiments were coming to garrison the conquered territory, there was literally not one thing of any kind whatsoever for the army to do, and no purpose to serve by keeping it at Santiago. We did not suppose that peace was at hand, being ignorant of the negotiations. We were anxious to take part in the Porto Rico campaign, and would have been more than willing to suffer any amount of sickness, if by so doing we could get into action. But if we were not to take part in the Porto Rico campaign, then we knew it was absolutely indispensable to get our commands north immediately, if they were to be in trim for the great campaign against Havana, which would surely be the main event of the winter if peace were not declared in advance.

Our army included the great majority of the regulars, and was, therefore, the flower of the American force. It was on every account imperative to keep it in good trim; and to keep it in Santiago meant its entirely purposeless destruction. As soon as the surrender was an accomplished fact, the taking away of the army to the north should have begun.

Every officer, from the highest to the lowest, especially among the regulars, realized all of this, and about the last day of July, General Shafter called a conference, in the palace, of all the division and brigade commanders. By this time, owing to Wood's having been made Governor-General, I was in command of my brigade, so I went to the conference too, riding in with Generals Sumner and Wheeler, who were the other representatives of the cavalry division. Besides the line officers all the chief medical officers were present at the conference. The telegrams from the Secretary stating the position of himself and the Surgeon-General were read, and then almost every line and medical officer present expressed his views in turn. They were almost all regulars and had been brought up to life-long habits of obedience without protest. They were ready to obey still, but they felt, quite rightly, that it was their duty to protest rather than to see the flower of the United States forces destroyed as the culminating act of a campaign in which the blunders that had been committed had been retrieved only by the valor and splendid soldierly qualities of the officers and enlisted men of the infantry and dismounted cavalry. There was not a dissenting voice; for there could not be. There was but one side to the question. To talk of continually shifting camp or of moving up the mountains or of moving into the interior was idle, for not one of the plans could be carried out with our utterly insufficient transportation, and at that season and in that climate they would merely have resulted in aggravating the sickliness of the soldiers. It was deemed best to make some record of our opinion, in the shape of a letter or report, which would show that to keep the army in Santiago meant its absolute and objectless ruin, and that it should at once be recalled. At first there was naturally some hesitation on the part of the regular officers to take the initiative, for their entire future career might be sacrificed. So I wrote a letter to General Shafter, reading over the rough draft to the various Generals and adopting their corrections. Before I had finished making these corrections it was determined that we should send a circular letter on behalf of all of us to General Shafter, and when I returned from presenting him mine, I found this circular letter already prepared and we all of us signed it. Both letters were made public. The result was immediate. Within three days the army was ordered to be ready to sail for home.

As soon as it was known that we were to sail for home the spirits of the men changed for the better. In my regiment the officers began to plan methods of drilling the men on horseback, so as to fit them for use against the Spanish cavalry, if we should go against Havana in December. We had, all of us, eyed the captured Spanish cavalry with particular interest. The men were small, and the horses, though well trained and well built, were diminutive ponies, very much smaller than cow ponies. We were certain that if we ever got a chance to try shock tactics against them they would go down like nine-pins, provided only that our men could be trained to charge in any kind of line, and we made up our minds to devote our time to this. Dismounted work with the rifle we already felt thoroughly competent to perform.

My time was still much occupied with looking after the health of my brigade, but the fact that we were going home, where I knew that their health would improve, lightened my mind, and I was able thoroughly to enjoy the beauty of the country, and even of the storms, which hitherto I had regarded purely as enemies.

The surroundings of the city of Santiago are very grand. The circling mountains rise sheer and high. The plains are threaded by rapid winding brooks and are dotted here and there with quaint villages, curiously picturesque from their combining traces of an outworn old-world civilization with new and raw barbarism. The tall, graceful, feathery bamboos rise by the water's edge, and elsewhere, even on the mountain-crests, where the soil is wet and rank enough; and the splendid royal palms and cocoanut palms tower high above the matted green jungle.

Generally the thunder-storms came in the afternoon, but once I saw one at sunrise, driving down the high mountain valleys toward us. It was a very beautiful and almost terrible sight; for the sun rose behind the storm, and shone through the gusty rifts, lighting the mountain-crests here and there, while the plain below lay shrouded in the lingering night. The angry, level rays edged the dark clouds with crimson, and turned the downpour into sheets of golden rain; in the valleys the glimmering mists were tinted every wild hue; and the remotest heavens were lit with flaming glory.

One day General Lawton, General Wood and I, with Ferguson and poor Tiffany, went down the bay to visit Morro Castle. The shores were beautiful, especially where there were groves of palms and of the scarlet-flower tree, and the castle itself, on a jutting headland, overlooking the sea and guarding the deep, narrow entrance to the bay, showed just what it was, the splendid relic of a vanished power and a vanished age. We wandered all through it, among the castellated battlements, and in the dungeons, where we found hideous rusty implements of torture; and looked at the guns, some modern and some very old. It had been little hurt by the bombardment of the ships. Afterward I had a swim, not trusting much to the shark stories. We passed by the sunken hulks of the Merrimac and the Reina Mercedes, lying just outside the main channel. Our own people had tried to sink the first and the Spaniards had tried to sink the second, so as to block the entrance. Neither attempt was successful.

On August 6th we were ordered to embark, and next morning we sailed on the transport Miami. General Wheeler was with us and a squadron of the Third Cavalry under Major Jackson. The General put the policing and management of the ship into my hands, and I had great aid from Captain McCormick, who had been acting with me as adjutant-general of the brigade. I had profited by my experience coming down, and as Dr. Church knew his work well, although he was very sick, we kept the ship in such good sanitary condition, that we were one of the very few organizations allowed to land at Montauk immediately upon our arrival.

Soon after leaving port the captain of the ship notified me that his stokers and engineers were insubordinate and drunken, due, he thought, to liquor which my men had given them. I at once started a search of the ship, explaining to the men that they could not keep the liquor; that if they surrendered whatever they had to me I should return it to them when we went ashore; and that meanwhile I would allow the sick to drink when they really needed it; but that if they did not give the liquor to me of their own accord I would throw it overboard. About seventy flasks and bottles were handed to me, and I found and threw overboard about twenty. This at once put a stop to all drunkenness. The stokers and engineers were sullen and half mutinous, so I sent a detail of my men down to watch them and see that they did their work under the orders of the chief engineer; and we reduced them to obedience in short order. I could easily have drawn from the regiment sufficient skilled men to fill every position in the entire ship's crew, from captain to stoker.

We were very much crowded on board the ship, but rather better off than on the Yucatan, so far as the men were concerned, which was the important point. All the officers except General Wheeler slept in a kind of improvised shed, not unlike a chicken coop with bunks, on the aftermost part of the upper deck. The water was bad — some of it very bad. There was no ice. The canned beef proved practically uneatable, as we knew would be the case. There were not enough vegetables. We did not have enough disinfectants, and there was no provision whatever for a hospital or for isolating the sick; we simply put them on one portion of one deck. If, as so many of the high authorities had insisted, there had really been a yellow-fever epidemic, and if it had broken out on shipboard, the condition would have been frightful; but there was no yellow-fever epidemic. Three of our men had been kept behind as suspects, all three suffering simply from malarial fever. One of them, Lutz, a particularly good soldier, died; another, who was simply a malingerer and had nothing the matter with him whatever, of course recovered; the third was Tiffany who, I believe, would have lived had we been allowed to take him with us, but who was sent home later and died soon after landing.

I was very anxious to keep the men amused, and as the quarters were so crowded that it was out of the question for them to have any physical exercise, I did not interfere with their playing games of chance so long as no disorder followed. On shore this was not allowed; but in the particular emergency which we were meeting, the loss of a month's salary was as nothing compared to keeping the men thoroughly interested and diverted.

By care and diligence we succeeded in preventing any serious sickness. One man died, however. He had been suffering from dysentery ever since we landed, owing purely to his own fault, for on the very first night ashore he obtained a lot of fiery liquor from some of the Cubans, got very drunk, and had to march next day through the hot sun before he was entirely sober. He never recovered, and was useless from that time on. On board ship he died, and we gave him sea burial. Wrapped in a hammock, he was placed opposite a port, and the American flag thrown over him. The engine was stilled, and the great ship rocked on the waves unshaken by the screw, while the war-worn troopers clustered around with bare heads, to listen to Chaplain Brown read the funeral service, and to the band of the Third Cavalry as it played the funeral dirge. Then the port was knocked free, the flag withdrawn, and the shotted hammock plunged heavily over the side, rushing down through the dark water to lie, till the Judgment Day, in the ooze that holds the timbers of so many gallant ships, and the bones of so many fearless adventurers.

We were favored by good weather during our nine days' voyage, and much of the time when there was little to do we simply sat together and talked, each man contributing from the fund of his own experiences. Voyages around Cape Horn, yacht races for the America's cup, experiences on foot-ball teams which are famous in the annals of college sport; more serious feats of desperate prowess in Indian fighting and in breaking up gangs of white outlaws; adventures in hunting big game, in breaking wild horses, in tending great herds of cattle, and in wandering winter and summer among the mountains and across the lonely plains — the men who told the tales could draw upon countless memories such as these of the things they had done and the things they had seen others do. Sometimes General Wheeler joined us and told us about the great war, compared with which ours was such a small war — far-reaching in their importance though its effects were destined to be. When we had become convinced that we would escape an epidemic of sickness the homeward voyage became very pleasant.

On the eve of leaving Santiago I had received from Mr. Laffan of the *Sun*, a cable with the single word "Peace," and we speculated much on this, as the clumsy transport steamed slowly northward across the trade wind and then into the Gulf Stream. At last we sighted the low, sandy bluffs of the Long Island coast, and late on the afternoon of the 14th we steamed through the still waters of the Sound and cast anchor off Montauk. A gun-boat of the Mosquito fleet came out to greet us and to inform us that peace negotiations had begun.

Next morning we were marched on shore. Many of the men were very sick indeed. Of the three or four who had been closest to me among the enlisted men, Color-Sergeant Wright was the only one in good health. Henry Bardshar was a wreck, literally at death's door. I was myself in first-class health, all the better for having lost twenty pounds. Faithful Marshall, my colored body-servant, was so sick as to be nearly helpless.

Bob Wrenn nearly died. He had joined us very late and we could not get him a Krag carbine; so I had given him my Winchester, which carried the government cartridge; and when he was mustered out he carried it home in triumph, to the envy of his fellows, who themselves had to surrender their beloved rifles.

For the first few days there was great confusion and some want even after we got to Montauk. The men in hospitals suffered from lack of almost everything, even cots. But after these few days we were very well cared for and had abundance of all we needed, except that on several occasions there was a shortage of food for the horses, which I should have regarded as even more serious than a shortage for the men, had it not been that we were about to be disbanded. The men lived high, with milk, eggs, oranges, and any amount of tobacco, the lack of which during portions of the Cuban campaign had been felt as seriously as any lack of food. One of the distressing features of the malarial fever which had been ravaging the troops was that it was recurrent and persistent. Some of my men died after reaching home, and many were very sick. We owed much

The Rough Riders at Camp Wikoff.

to the kindness not only of the New York hospitals and the Red Cross and kindred societies, but of individuals, notably Mr. Bayard Cutting and Mrs. Armitage, who took many of our men to their beautiful Long Island homes.

On the whole, however, the month we spent at Montauk before we disbanded was very pleasant. It was good to meet the rest of the regiment. They all felt dreadfully at not having been in Cuba. It was a sore trial to men who had given up much to go to the war, and who rebelled at nothing in the way of hardship or suffering, but who did bitterly feel the fact that their sacrifices seemed to have been useless. Of course those who stayed had done their duty precisely as did those who went, for the question of glory was not to be considered in comparison to the faithful performance of whatever was ordered; and no distinction of any kind was allowed in the regiment between those whose good fortune it had been to go and those whose harder fate it had been to remain. Nevertheless the latter could not be entirely comforted.

The regiment had three mascots; the two most characteristic — a young mountain lion brought by the Arizona troops, and a war eagle brought by the New Mexicans — we had been forced to leave behind in Tampa. The third, a rather disreputable but exceedingly knowing little dog named Cuba, had accompanied us through all the vicissitudes of the campaign. The mountain lion, Josephine, possessed an infernal temper; whereas both Cuba and the eagle, which have been named in my honor, were extremely good-humored. Josephine was kept tied up. She sometimes escaped. One cool night in early September she wandered off and, entering the tent of a Third Cavalry man, got into bed with him; whereupon he fled into the darkness with yells, much more unnerved than he would have been by the arrival of any number of Spaniards. The eagle was let loose and not only walked at will up and down the company streets, but also at times flew wherever he wished. He was a young bird, having been taken out of his nest when a fledgling. Josephine hated him and was always trying to make a meal of him, especially when we endeavored to take their photographs together. The eagle, though good-natured, was an entirely competent individual and ready at any moment to beat Josephine off. Cuba was also oppressed at times by Josephine, and was of course no match for her, but was frequently able to overawe by simple decision of character.

In addition to the animal mascots, we had two or three small boys who had also been adopted by the regiment. One, from Tennessee, was named Dabney Royster. When we embarked at Tampa he smuggled himself on board the transport with a 22-calibre rifle and three boxes of cartridges, and wept bitterly when sent ashore. The squadron which remained behind adopted him, got him a little Rough Rider's uniform, and made him practically one of the regiment.

The men who had remained at Tampa, like ourselves, had suffered much from fever, and the horses were in bad shape. So many of the men were sick that none of the regiments began to drill for some time after reaching Montauk. There was a great deal of paper-work to be done; but as I still had charge of the brigade only a little of it fell on my shoulders. Of this I was sincerely glad, for I knew as little of the paper-work as my men had originally known of drill. We had all of us learned how to fight and march; but the exact limits of our rights and duties in other respects were not very clearly defined in our minds; and as for myself, as I had not had the time to learn exactly what they were, I had assumed a large authority in giving rewards and punishments. In particular I had looked on court-martials much as Peter Bell looked on primroses — they were court-martials and nothing more, whether resting on the authority of a lieutenant-colonel or of a major-general. The mustering-out officer, a thorough soldier, found to his horror that I had used the widest discretion both in imposing heavy sentences which I had no power to impose on men who shirked their duties, and, where men atoned for misconduct by marked gallantry, in blandly remitting sentences approved by my chief of division. However, I had done substantial, even though somewhat rude and irregular, justice — and no harm could result, as we were just about to be mustered out.

My chief duties were to see that the camps of the three regiments were thoroughly policed and kept in first-class sanitary condition. This took up some time, of course, and there were other matters in connection with the mustering out which had to be attended to; but I could always get two or three hours a day free from work. Then I would summon a number of the officers, Kane, Greenway, Goodrich, Church, Ferguson, McIlhenny, Frantz, Ballard and others, and we would gallop down to the beach and bathe in the surf, or else go for long rides over the beautiful rolling plains, thickly studded with pools which were white with water-lilies. Sometimes I went off alone with my orderly, young Gordon Johnston, one of the best men in the regiment; he was a nephew of the Governor of Alabama, and when at Princeton had played on the eleven. We had plenty of horses, and these rides were most enjoyable. Galloping over the open, rolling country, through the cool fall evenings, made us feel as if we were out on the great Western plains and might at any moment start deer from the brush, or see antelope stand and gaze, far away, or rouse a band of mighty elk and hear their horns clatter as they fled.

An old friend, Baron von Sternberg, of the German Embassy, spent a week in camp with me. He had served, when only seventeen, in the Franco-Prussian War as a hussar, and was a noted sharp-shooter — being "the little baron" who is the hero of Archibald Forbes's true story of "The Pig-dog." He and I had for years talked over the possibilities of just such a regiment as the one I was commanding, and he was greatly interested in it. Indeed I had vainly sought permission from the German ambassador to take him with the regiment to Santiago.

One Sunday before the regiment disbanded I supplemented Chaplain Brown's address to the men by a short sermon of a rather hortatory character. I told them how proud I was of them, but warned them not to think that they could now go back and rest on their laurels, bidding them remember that though for ten days or so the world would be willing to treat them as heroes, yet after that time they would find they had to get down to hard work just like everyone else, unless they were willing to be regarded as worthless do-nothings. They took the sermon in good part, and I hope that some of them profited by it. At any rate, they repaid me by a very much more tangible expression of affection. One afternoon, to my genuine surprise, I was asked out of my tent by Lieutenant-

Colonel Brodie (the gallant old boy had rejoined us), and found the whole regiment formed in hollow square, with the officers and color-sergeant in the middle. When I went in, one of the troopers came forward and on behalf of the regiment presented me with Remington's fine bronze, "The Bronco-buster." There could have been no more appropriate gift from such a regiment, and I was not only pleased with it, but very deeply touched with the feeling which made them join in giving it. Afterward they all filed past and I shook the hands of each to say good-by.

Most of them looked upon the bronze with the critical eyes of professionals. I doubt if there was any regiment in the world which contained so large a number of men able to ride the wildest and most dangerous horses. One day while at Montauk Point some of the troopers of the Third Cavalry were getting ready for mounted drill when one of their horses escaped, having thrown his rider. This attracted the attention of some of our men and they strolled around to see the trooper remount. He was instantly thrown again, the horse, a huge, vicious sorrel, being one of the worst buckers I ever saw; and none of his comrades were willing to ride the animal. Our men, of course, jeered and mocked at them, and in response were dared to ride the horse themselves. The challenge was instantly accepted, the only question being as to which of a dozen noted bronco-busters who were in the ranks should undertake the task. They finally settled on a man named Darnell. It was agreed that the experiment should take place next day when the horse would be fresh, and accordingly next day the majority of both regiments turned out on a big open flat in front of my tent — brigade head-quarters. The result was that, after as fine a bit of rough riding as one would care to see, in which one scarcely knew whether most to wonder at the extraordinary viciousness and agile strength of the horse or at the horsemanship and courage of the rider, Darnell came off victorious, his seat never having been shaken. After this almost every day we had exhibitions of bronco-busting, in which all the crack riders of the regiment vied with one another, riding not only all of our own bad horses but any horse which was deemed bad in any of the other regiments.

Sergeant Darnell Rides the
Third Cavalry Bucker.

McGinty on a Bronco.

Darnell, McGinty, Wood, Smoky Moore, and a score of others took part in these exhibitions, which included not merely feats in mastering vicious horses, but also feats of broken horses which the riders had trained to lie down at command, and upon which they could mount while at full speed.

Toward the end of the time we also had mounted drill on two or three occasions; and when the President visited the camp we turned out mounted to receive him as did the rest of the cavalry. The last night before we were mustered out was spent in noisy, but entirely harmless hilarity, which I ignored. Every form of celebration took place in the ranks. A former Populist candidate for Attorney-General in Colorado delivered a fervent oration in favor of free silver; a number of the college boys sang; but most of the men gave vent to their feelings by improvised dances. In these the Indians took the lead, pure bloods and half-breeds alike, the cowboys and miners cheerfully joining in and forming part of the howling, grunting rings, that went bounding around the great fires they had kindled.

Next morning Sergeant Wright took down the colors, and Sergeant Guitilias the standard, for the last time; the horses, the rifles, and the rest of the regimental property had been turned in; officers and men shook hands and said good-by to one another, and then they scattered to their homes in the North and the South, the few going back to the great cities of the East, the many turning again toward the plains, the mountains, and the deserts of the West and the strange Southwest. This was on September 15th, the day which marked the close of the four months' life of a regiment of as gallant fighters as ever wore the United States uniform.

The regiment was a wholly exceptional volunteer organization, and its career cannot be taken as in any way a justification for the belief that the average volunteer regiment approaches the average regular regiment in point of efficiency until it has had many months of active service. In the first place, though the regular regiments may differ markedly among themselves, yet the range of variation among them is nothing like so wide as that among volunteer regiments,

Color-Sergeant A. P. Wright.

where at first there is no common standard at all; the very best being, perhaps, up to the level of the regulars (as has recently been shown at Manila), while the very worst are no better than mobs, and the great bulk come in between.* The average regular regiment is superior to the average volunteer regiment in the physique of the enlisted men, who have been very carefully selected, who have been trained to life in the open, and who know how to cook and take care of themselves generally.

Now, in all these respects, and in others like them, the Rough Riders were the equals of the regulars. They were hardy, self-reliant, accustomed to shift for themselves in the open under very adverse circumstances. The two all-important qualifications for a cavalryman are riding and shooting — the modern cavalryman being so often used dismounted, as an infantryman. The average recruit requires a couple of years before he becomes proficient in horsemanship and marksmanship; but my men were already good shots and first-class riders when they came into the regiment. The difference as regards officers and non-commissioned officers, between regulars and volunteers, is usually very great; but in my regiment (keeping in view the material we had to handle), it was easy to develop non-commissioned officers out of men who had been round-up foremen, ranch foremen, mining bosses, and the like. These men were intelligent and resolute; they knew they had a great deal to learn, and they set to work to learn it; while they were already accustomed to managing considerable interests, to obeying orders, and to taking care of others as well as themselves.

As for the officers, the great point in our favor was the anxiety they showed to learn from those among their number who, like Capron, had already served in the regular army; and the fact that we had chosen a regular army man as Colonel. If a volunteer organization consists of good material, and is eager to learn, it can readily do so if it has one or two first-class regular officers to teach it. Moreover, most of our captains and lieutenants were men who had seen much of wild

*For sound common-sense about the volunteers see Parker's excellent little book, "The Gatlings at Santiago."

life, who were accustomed to handling and commanding other men, and who had usually already been under fire as sheriffs, marshals, and the like. As for the second in command, myself, I had served three years as captain in the National Guard; I had been deputy sheriff in the cow country, where the position was not a sinecure; I was accustomed to big game hunting and to work on a cow ranch, so that I was thoroughly familiar with the use both of horse and rifle, and knew how to handle cowboys, hunters, and miners; finally, I had studied much in the literature of war, and especially the literature of the great modern wars, like our own Civil War, the Franco-German War, the Turco-Russian War; and I was especially familiar with the deeds, the successes and failures alike, of the frontier horse riflemen who had fought at King's Mountain and the Thames, and on the Mexican border. Finally, and most important of all, officers and men alike were eager for fighting, and resolute to do well and behave properly, to encounter hardship and privation, and the irksome monotony of camp routine, without grumbling or complaining; they had counted the cost before they went in, and were delighted to pay the penalties inevitably attendant upon the career of a fighting regiment; and from the moment when the regiment began to gather, the higher officers kept instilling into those under them the spirit of eagerness for action and of stern determination to grasp at death rather than forfeit honor.

The self-reliant spirit of the men was well shown after they left the regiment. Of course, there were a few weaklings among them; and there were others, entirely brave and normally self-sufficient, who, from wounds or fevers, were so reduced that they had to apply for aid — or at least, who deserved aid, even though they often could only be persuaded with the greatest difficulty to accept it. The widows and orphans had to be taken care of. There were a few light-hearted individuals, who were entirely ready to fight in time of war, but in time of peace felt that somebody ought to take care of them; and there were others who, never having seen any aggregation of buildings larger than an ordinary cow-town, fell a victim to the fascinations of New York. But, as a whole, they scattered out to their homes on the disbandment of the regiment; gaunter than when they had enlisted, sometimes weakened by fever or wounds, but just as full as ever of sullen, sturdy capacity for self-help; scorning to ask for aid, save what was entirely legitimate in the way of one comrade giving help to another. A number of the examining surgeons, at the muster-out, spoke to me with admiration of the contrast offered by our regiment to so many others, in the fact that our men always belittled their own bodily injuries and sufferings; so that whereas the surgeons ordinarily had to be on the look-out lest a man who was not really disabled should claim to be so, in our case they had to adopt exactly the opposite attitude and guard the future interests of the men, by insisting upon putting upon their certificates of discharge whatever disease they had contracted or wound they had received in line of duty. Major J. H. Calef, who had more than any other one man to do with seeing to the proper discharge papers of our men, and who took a most generous interest in them, wrote me as follows: "I also wish to bring to your notice the fortitude displayed by the men of your regiment, who have come before me to be mustered out of service, in making their personal declarations as to their physical conditions. Men who bore on their faces and in their forms the traces of long days of illness, indicating wrecked constitutions, declared that nothing was the matter with them, at the same time disclaiming any intention of applying for a pension. It was exceptionally heroic."

When we were mustered out, many of the men had lost their jobs, and were too weak to go to work at once, while there were helpless dependents of the dead to care for. Certain of my friends, August Belmont, Stanley and Richard Mortimer, Major Austin Wadsworth — himself fresh from the Manila campaign — Belmont Tiffany, and others, gave me sums of money to be used for helping these men. In some instances, by the exercise of a good deal of tact and by treating the gift as a memorial of poor young Lieutenant Tiffany, we got the men to accept something; and, of course, there were a number who, quite rightly, made no difficulty about accepting. But most of the men would accept no help whatever. In the first chapter, I spoke of a lady, a teacher in an academy in the

Colonel Roosevelt's Farewell to the Rough Riders.

Indian Territory, three or four of whose pupils had come into my regiment, and who had sent with them a letter of introduction to me. When the regiment disbanded, I wrote to her to ask if she could not use a little money among the Rough Riders, white, Indian, and half-breed, that she might personally know. I did not hear from her for some time, and then she wrote as follows:

"MUSCOGEE, IND. TER.,
"December 19, 1898.

"MY DEAR COLONEL ROOSEVELT: I did not at once reply to your letter of September 23d, because I waited for a time to see if there should be need among any of our Rough Riders, of the money you so kindly offered. Some of the boys are poor, and in one or two cases they seemed to me really needy, but they all said no. More than once I saw the tears come to their eyes, at thought of your care for them, as I told them of your letter. Did you hear any echoes of our Indian war-whoops over your election? They were pretty loud. I was particularly exultant, because my father was a New Yorker and I was educated in New York, even if I was born here. So far as I can learn, the boys are taking up the dropped threads of their lives, as though they had never been away. Our two Rough Riders students, Meagher and Gilmore, are doing well in their college work.

"I am sorry to tell you of the death of one of your most devoted troopers, Bert Holderman, who was here serving on the Grand Jury. He was stricken with meningitis in the jury-room, and died after three days of delirium. His father, who was twice wounded, four times taken prisoner, and fought in thirty-two battles of the civil war, now old and feeble, survives him, and it was indeed pathetic to see his grief. Bert's mother, who is a Cherokee, was raised in my grandfather's family. The words of commendation which you wrote upon Bert's discharge are the greatest comfort to his friends. They wanted you to know of his death, because he loved you so.

"I am planning to entertain all the Rough Riders in this vicinity some evening during my holiday vacation. I mean to have no other guests, but only give them an opportunity for reminiscences. I regret that Bert's death makes one less. I had hoped to have them sooner, but our struggling young college salaries are necessarily small and duties arduous. I make a home for my widowed mother and an adopted Indian daughter, who is in school; and as I do the cooking for a family of five, I have found it impossible to do many things I would like to.

"Pardon me for burdening you with these details, but I suppose I am like your boys, who say, 'The Colonel was always as ready to listen to a private as to a major-general.'

"Wishing you and yours the very best gifts the season can bring, I am,

"Very truly yours,
"ALICE M. ROBERTSON."

Is it any wonder that I loved my regiment?

# APPENDIX A

## *MUSTER-OUT ROLL*

[Owing to the circumstances of the regiment's service, the paper-work was very difficult to perform. This muster-out roll is very defective in certain points, notably in the enumeration of the wounded who had been able to return to duty. Some of the dead are also undoubtedly passed over. Thus I have put in Race Smith, Sanders, and Tiffany as dead, correcting the rolls; but there are doubtless a number of similar corrections which should be made but have not been, as the regiment is now scattered far and wide. I have also corrected the record for the wounded men in one or two places where I happen to remember it; but there are a number of the wounded, especially the slightly wounded, who are not down at all.]

### FIELD, STAFF, AND BAND.

Theodore Roosevelt . . . . . Colonel . . . . . . . . . . . New York, N.Y.

Alexander O. Brodie . . . . . Lieut. Colonel . . . . . . . Prescott, Ariz.

Henry B. Hersey . . . . . . . Major . . . . . . . . . . . . Santa Fé, N.M.

George M. Dunn . . . . . . . Major . . . . . . . . . . . . Denver, Col.

Micah J. Jenkins . . . . . . . Major . . . . . . . . . . . . Youngs Is., S.C.

Henry A. Brown . . . . . . . Chaplain . . . . . . . . . . Prescott, Ariz.

Maxwell Keyes . . . . . . . . 1st Lt. & Adjt. . . . . . . . San Antonio, Tex.

Sherrard Coleman . . . . . . 1st Lt. & Q. M. . . . . . . Santa Fé, N.M.

Ernest Secker . . . . . . . . . Sergt. Major . . . . . . . . Los Angeles, Cal.

Matthew Douthett . . . . . . Q. M. Sergeant . . . . . . Denver, Col.

Clay Platt. . . . . . . . . . . . . Cf. Trumpeter . . . . . . . San Antonio, Tex.

Joseph F. Kansky . . . . . . . Sad. Sergeant . . . . . . . Tacoma, Wash.

Leonard Wood. . . . . . . . . Colonel . . . . . . . . . . . Cape Cod, Mass.
> Promoted, July 9, 1898, to Brig.-Gen. of U.S. Vols.

Thomas W. Hall. . . . . . . . 1st Lieut. & Adjt.
> Tendered his resignation as 1st Lieut. and Adjt., which took effect Aug. 1, 1898, in compliance with S. O. No. 175, O. G. O., dated July 29, 1898.

Jacob Schwaizer . . . . . . . . 1st Lt. & Q. M. . . . . . . El Reno, O.T.
> Resigned his commission as 1st Lieut., Aug. 4, 1898. Resignation took effect Sept. 7, 1898.

Joseph A. Carr . . . . . . . . . Sergt. Major . . . . . . . . Washington, D.C.
> Discharged at San Antonio, Texas, by way of favor to enable him to accept a commission as 1st Lieut. in the Regiment, May 19, 1898.

Christian Madsen . . . . . . . R. Q. M. Sergt. . . . . . . El Reno, O.T.
> Discharged on Surgeon's certificate of disability at Camp Wikoff, L. I., Aug. 26, 1898.

Alfred E. Lewis . . . . . . . . R. Q. M. Sergt.
> Deserted from Camp at San Antonio, Tex., on or about May 5, 1898.

Ernest Haskell . . . . . . . . . Cadet . . . . . . . . . . . . . West Point.
> Acted with regiment as second lieutenant. Dangerously wounded by Mauser bullet, July 1st.

### THE HOSPITAL CORPS.

Henry La Motte . . . . . . . . Major . . . . . . . . . . Williamsburg, Mass.
James A. Massie . . . . . . . . 1st Lieutenant . . . . Santa Fé, N.M.
*James R. Church . . . . . . 1st Lieutenant . . . . Washington, D.C.
James B. Brady . . . . . . . . . Steward . . . . . . . . . Santa Fé, N.M.
Herbert J. Rankin . . . . . . . Steward . . . . . . . . . Las Vegas, N.M.
Charles A. Wilson . . . . . . Steward . . . . . . . . . Colorado Springs, Col.
John R. Rawdin . . . . . . . . Private.

*Acted as Regimental Surgeon during most of the campaign.

## TROOP A.

### CAPTAIN FRANK FRANTZ.

Frank Frantz . . . . . . . . . . Captain . . . . . . . . . . . . Prescott, Ariz.
John C. Greenway . . . . . . 1st Lieutenant . . . . . . . Hot Springs, Ark.
Joshua D. Carter . . . . . . . 2d Lieutenant . . . . . . . Prescott, Ariz.
William W. Greenwood . . 1st Sergeant . . . . . . . . Prescott, Ariz.
> Shot in left foot and leg in battle, July 1, 1898. Engaged in battles of Las Guasimas, June 24th; San Juan, July 1st.

James T. Greenley . . . . . . Sergeant . . . . . . . . . . . Prescott, Ariz.
> Wounded in leg, July 1, 1898. Engaged in battles of Las Guasimas, June 24th; San Juan, July 1st; and siege of Santiago following.

King C. Henley . . . . . . . . Q. M. Sergeant . . . . . . Winslow, Ariz.
Henry W. Nash . . . . . . . . Sergeant . . . . . . . . . . . Young, Ariz.
Samuel H. Rhodes . . . . . . Sergeant . . . . . . . . . . . Tonto Basin, Ariz.
Robert Brown . . . . . . . . . Sergeant . . . . . . . . . . . Prescott, Ariz.
Charles E. McGarr . . . . . . Sergeant . . . . . . . . . . . Prescott, Ariz.
Carl Holtzschue . . . . . . . . Sergeant . . . . . . . . . . . Prescott, Ariz.
George L. Bugbee . . . . . . Corporal . . . . . . . . . . . Lordsburg, N.M.
Harry G. White . . . . . . . . Corporal . . . . . . . . . . . Richenbar, Ariz.
> Absent from July 2, 1898, in Governor's Island, N.Y., Hospital, on account of wound in leg, received on July 2, 1898. Engaged in battles of Las Guasimas, June 24, 1898; San Juan, July 1, 1898.

Cade C. Jackson . . . . . . . . Corporal . . . . . . . . . . . Flagstaff, Ariz.
Harry B. Fox . . . . . . . . . . Corporal . . . . . . . . . . . Jerome, Ariz.

William Cranfurd . . . . . . . Corporal . . . . . . . . . . San Antonio, Tex.
George A. McCarter . . . . . Corporal . . . . . . . . . . Safford, Ariz.
Rufus H. Marine . . . . . . . Corporal . . . . . . . . . . Flagstaff, Ariz.
John D. Honeyman . . . . . Corporal . . . . . . . . . . San Antonio, Tex.
Emilio Cassi . . . . . . . . . . . Trumpeter . . . . . . . . . Jerome, Ariz.
    Wounded in hand on July 2, 1898.
Frank Harner . . . . . . . . . . Trumpeter . . . . . . . . . Preston, Ariz.
Thomas Hamilton . . . . . . Blacksmith . . . . . . . . . Jerome, Ariz.
Wallace B. Willard . . . . . . Farrier . . . . . . . . . . . . . Cottonwood, Ariz.
Forest Whitney . . . . . . . . Saddler . . . . . . . . . . . . Richenbar, Ariz.
John H. Waller . . . . . . . . Wagoner . . . . . . . . . . . Prescott, Ariz.
    Wounded in left arm in battle of July 1, 1898. Engaged in Las Guasimas, June 24, 1898; San Juan, July 1, 1898; and siege of Santiago following.

## TROOPERS.

Adams, Ralph R., Yonkers, N.Y.
Allen, George L., Prescott, Ariz.
Azbill, John, St. John's, Ariz.
Azbill, William, St. John's, Ariz.
Arnold, Henry N., New York City
Barnard, John C., New York City
Bartoo, Nelson E., Winslow, Ariz.
Belknap, Prescott H. Boston, Brookline, Mass.
Brauer, Lee W., Richmond, Va.
Bugbee, Fred. W., Lordsburg, N.M.
    Wounded in head in battle of San Juan, July 1, 1898. Slight. Mauser rifle.
Bull, Charles C., San Francisco, Cal.
Bulzing, William, Santa Fé, N.M.
Burke, Edward F., Orange, N.J.
Bardshar, Henry P., Prescott, Ariz.
Church, Leroy B., Ithaca, Mich.
Curtis, Harry A., Boston, Mass.
Freeman, Thomas L., Thurber, Tex.
Griffen, Walter W., Globe, Ariz.
Glover, William H., Liberty, Tex.
Hawes, George P., Jr., Richmond, Va.

Haymon, Edward G. B., Chicago, Ill.
Huffman, Lawrence E., Las Cruces, Mex.
Hoffman, Fred., Pueblo, Col.
Hodgdon, Charles E., Prescott, Ariz.
Hogan, Daniel L., Flagstaff, Ariz.
Howard, John L., St. Louis, Mo.
Hubbell, John D., Boston, Mass.
Jackson, Charles B., Prescott, Ariz.
    Wounded in neck at battle of San Juan, July 1, 1898. Nature of injury slight. Mauser rifle.
Johnson, John W., Kingman, Ariz.
Lefors, Jefferson D., Prescott, Ariz.
Lewis, William F., Congress, Ariz.
Larned, William A., Summit, N.J.
Le Roy, Arthur M., Prescott, Ariz.
May, James A., Safford, Ariz.
McCarty, Frank, Flagstaff, Ariz.
Mills, Charles E., Cedar Rapids, Ia.
Murchie, Guy, Calais, Me.
Osborne, George, Bungendera, N.S.W., Australia
O'Brien, Edward, Jerome, Ariz.
    Wounded in head, by shrapnel, morning of July 2, 1898.

Page, William, Richenbar, Ariz.

Perry, Charles B., Perry's Landing, Tex.
> Shot in head, July 2, 1898. Severe.

Paxton, Frank, Safford, Ariz.

Pearsall, Paul S., New York, N.Y.

Pettit, Louis P., Flagstaff, Ariz.

Philip, Hoffman, Washington, D.C.

Pierce, Harry B., Central City, N.M.

Raudebaugh, James D., Flagstaff, Ariz.

Rapp, Adolph, San Antonio, Tex.

Sells, Henry, Flagstaff, Ariz.

Sellers, Henry J., Williams, Ariz.

Sewall, Henry F., New York, N.Y.

Shaw, James A., Prescott, Ariz.

Shanks, Lee P., Paducah, Ky.

Stark, Wallace J., Safford, Ariz.

Sullivan, Patrick J., Prescott, Ariz.

Thomas, Rufus K., Boston, Mass.

Thomson, Joseph F., Jr., Washington, D.C.

Tuttle, Arthur L., Safford, Ariz.

Van Siclen, Frank, Safford, Ariz.

Wager, Oscar G., Jerome, Ariz.

Wallace, Walter D., Flagstaff, Ariz.

Wallace, William F., Flagstaff, Ariz.
> Wounded in neck in battle of San Juan, July 1, 1898.

Wayland, Thomas J., Williams, Ariz.

Webb, Adelbert B., Safford, Ariz.

Weil, Henry J., Kingman, Ariz.

Wilson, Jerome, Chloride, Ariz.

Wrenn, Robert D., Chicago, Ill.

### DISCHARGED.

Garret, Samuel H. . . . . . . . . . . . . . . . . . . . . . . Prescott, Ariz.
> Honorably discharged the service by order of A. G. O. Special Order No. 14, Aug. 24, 1898.

Greenwald, Sam. . . . . . . . . . . . . . . . . . . . . . Prescott, Ariz.
> Discharged by authority of Secretary of War, at Camp Wikoff, Aug. 31, 1898.

McCormick, Willis . . . . . . . . . . . . . . . . . . . . . Salt Lake City, Utah.
> Honorably discharged the service, Aug. 23, 1898. By order Secretary of War.

### KILLED IN ACTION.

O'Neill, William O . . . . . . . . Captain . . . . . . . . Prescott, Ariz.
> Engaged and killed in battle of San Juan, July 1, 1898, by gunshot wound in the head.

Doherty, George H. . . . . . . . Corporal . . . . . . . Jerome, Ariz.
> Engaged and killed in battle of Las Guasimas, June 24, 1898, by bullet wound in the head.

Boyle, James . . . . . . . . . . . . Private . . . . . . . . . Prescott, Ariz.
> Engaged in and mortally wounded at battle of San Juan, July 1, 1898; shot through neck and body; died July 2, 1898.

Champlin, Fred E. . . . . . . . . Private . . . . . . . . . Flagstaff, Ariz.
> Engaged in battle of Las Guasimas, June 24, 1898, and battle of San Juan, July 1, 1898, where he was mortally wounded. Died, July 2, 1898; shot in leg and foot by shrapnel and arm torn off by shell. Left thigh and hand.

Liggett, Edward . . . . . . . . . . Private . . . . . . . . . . Jerome, Ariz.
  Engaged and killed in battle of Las Guasimas, June 24, 1898; shot through the
    body.
Reynolds, Lewis . . . . . . . . . . Private . . . . . . . . . . Kingman, Ariz.
  Engaged in battle of Las Guasimas, June 24, 1898, and San Juan, July 1, 1898.
    Killed on July 1, 1898; shot through the stomach.

### DIED OF DISEASE.

Hollister, Stanley . . . . . . . . . Private . . . . . . . . . . Santa Barbara, Cal.
  Wounded in left thigh in battle, July 2, 1898; severe. Died of typhoid fever in
    general U.S. Hospital, Fortress Monroe, Va., Aug. 17, 1898.
Wallace, Alexander H. . . . . . . Private . . . . . . . . . . Pasadena, Cal.
  Died of typhoid fever at St. Peter's Hospital, Brooklyn, Aug. 31, 1898.
Walsh, George . . . . . . . . . . . Private . . . . . . . . . . San Francisco, Cal.
  Died at sea, aboard S. S. Miami, Aug. 11, 1898, of chronic dysentery; buried at
    sea, Aug. 12, 1898.

### SUICIDE.

De Vol, Harry P. . . . . . . . . . . . . . . . . . . . . . . . . . San Antonio, Tex.
  While in Guard-House, Camp Wikoff, died of self-inflicted wound in the head.

### DESERTER.

Jackson, John W. . . . . . . . . . Private . . . . . . . . . . Jerome, Ariz.
  Deserted the service at Tampa, Fla., July 7, 1898.

# TROOP B.

## Captain James H. McClintock.

James H. McClintock . . . . . . Captain . . . . . . . . . Phoenix, Ariz.
  Wounded at battle of Las Guasimas, June 24, 1898. Wounded in left ankle.
George B. Wilcox . . . . . . . . . 1st Lieutenant . . . . . Prescott, Ariz.
Thomas H. Rymning . . . . . . 2d Lieutenant . . . . . Tucson, Ariz.
William A. Davidson . . . . . . . 1st Sergeant . . . . . . Phoenix, Ariz.
Stephen A. Pate . . . . . . . . . . Q. M. Sergeant. . . . Tucson, Ariz.
  Wounded in right lung before Santiago de Cuba, July 1, 1898.
Elmer Hawley. . . . . . . . . . . . Sergeant. . . . . . . . Phoenix, Ariz.
John E. Campbell . . . . . . . . . Sergeant. . . . . . . . Phoenix, Ariz.
Charles H. Utling . . . . . . . . . Sergeant. . . . . . . . Phoenix, Ariz.
Edward G. Norton . . . . . . . . Sergeant. . . . . . . . Phoenix, Ariz.
David L. Hughes . . . . . . . . . Sergeant. . . . . . . . Tucson, Ariz.
  Wounded in head, July 1, 1898, at battle before Santiago de Cuba.
Jerry F. Lee. . . . . . . . . . . . . Sergeant. . . . . . . . Globe, Ariz.
  Shot in head before Santiago de Cuba, July 1, 1898.

Eugene W. Waterbury . . . . . . Corporal . . . . . . . . Tucson, Ariz.
Walter T. Gregory. . . . . . . . Corporal . . . . . . . Phoenix, Ariz.
Thomas W. Pemberton, Jr. . . Corporal . . . . . . . Phoenix, Ariz.
George J. McCabe. . . . . . . . Corporal . . . . . . . Bisbee, Ariz.
Calvin McCarthy. . . . . . . . . Corporal . . . . . . . Phoenix, Ariz.
Charles E. Heitman. . . . . . . Corporal . . . . . . . Phoenix, Ariz.
Frank Ward . . . . . . . . . . . . Corporal . . . . . . . Globe, Ariz.
Dudly S. Dean . . . . . . . . . . Corporal . . . . . . . Boston, Mass.
John Foster. . . . . . . . . . . . . Bugler . . . . . . . . . Bisbee, Ariz.
Jesse Walters. . . . . . . . . . . . Bugler . . . . . . . . . Phoenix, Ariz.
Frank W. Harmson . . . . . . . Farrier . . . . . . . . . Tucson, Ariz.
Fred A. Pomeroy . . . . . . . . Blacksmith . . . . . . . Kingman, Ariz.
Joseph E. McGinty . . . . . . . Wagoner . . . . . . . . Tucson, Ariz.
Richard E. Goodwin . . . . . . . Saddler. . . . . . . . . Phoenix, Ariz.

## TROOPERS

Boggs, Looney L., Phoenix, Ariz.
Buckholdt, Chas., Kickapoo
  Springs, Tex.
Beebe, Walter S., Prescott, Ariz.
Brady, Fred L., New York, N.Y.
Butler, James A., Albuquerque,
  N.M.
Barrowe, Beekman K., Tampa, Fla.
Colwell, Grant, Phoenix, Ariz.
Collier, Edward G., Globe, Ariz.
Chester, Will M., Oakwell, Tex.
Christian, Benjamin, Norfolk, Va.
Chamberlin, Lowell A.,
  Washington, D.C.
Day, Robert, Santa Fé, N.M.
Drachman, Sol. B., Tucson, Ariz.
Draper, Durward D., Phoenix,
  Ariz.
Eakin, Alva L., Globe, Ariz.
Eads, Wade Q., San Antonio, Tex.
Fitzgerald, Frank T., Tucson, Ariz.
Goss, Conrad F., Tampa, Fla.
Gurney, Frank W., Tampa, Fla.
Hall, John M., Phoenix, Ariz.
  Wounded in shoulder by shrapnel,
    July 1, 1898, before Santiago de
    Cuba. Piece of shell not removed.

Hammer, John S., San Antonio,
  Tex.
  Slightly wounded by shell, July 1,
    1898, before Santiago de Cuba.
    Wounded in leg.
Hildreth, Fenn S., Tucson, Ariz.
Hartzell, Ira C., Phoenix, Ariz.
Haydon, Roy F., Prescott, Ariz.
Henderson, Sibird, Globe, Ariz.
Hildebrand, Louis T., Prescott,
  Ariz.
Heywood, John P., Tampa, Fla.
James, William T., Jerome, Ariz.
Johnson, Anton E., Prescott, Ariz.
King, Geo. C., Prescott, Ariz.
Keir, Alex. S., Bisbee, Ariz.
Laird, Thomas J., Prescott, Ariz.
Merritt, Fred M., Tucson, Ariz.
Merritt, William W., Red Oak, Ia.
McCann, Walter J., Phoenix, Ariz.
  Iron stanchion fell upon right side
    of head, right arm and shoulder,
    while asleep in quarters on
    transport Yucatan, en route for
    Cuba, June 21, 1898.
Middleton, Clifton C., Globe, Ariz.
Misner, Jackson H., Bisbee, Ariz.

McMillen, Albert C., New York, N.Y.

Norton, Gould G., Tampa, Fla.

Orme, Norman L., Phoenix, Ariz.
Shot in left arm and side, June 24, 1898, at Las Guasimas. G. S. left shoulder.

Owens, William A., Jerome, Ariz.

Proffitt, William B., Prescott, Ariz.

Peck, John C., Santa Fé, N.M.

Pollock, Horatio C., Phoenix, Ariz.

Patterson, Hal. A., Selma, Ala.

Roberts, Frank S., San Antonio, Tex.

Rinehart, Robert, Phoenix, Ariz.

Stanton, Richard H., Phoenix, Ariz.

Saunders, Wellman H., Salem, Mass.

Snodderly, William L., Bisbee, Ariz.

Smith, Race H., San Antonio, Tex.
Shot in stomach, breast, and arms by shrapnel, July 2, 1898, before Santiago.

Schenck, Frank W., Phoenix, Ariz.

Stewart, W. Walton, Selma, Ala.

Toland, Jesse T., Bisbee, Ariz.

Truman, George E., San Antonio, Tex.

Townsend, Albert B., Prescott, Ariz.

Tilkie, Charles M., Chicago, Ill.

Van Treese, Louis H., Tucson, Ariz.

Warford, David E., Globe, Ariz.
Shot in both thighs, July 1, 1898, before Santiago de Cuba.

Webb, William W., Prescott, Ariz.

Wiggins, Thomas W., Bisbee, Ariz.
Shot in right hip at Las Guasimas, June 24, 1898. G. S. left hip.

Whittaker, George C., Silver City, N.M.

Wilkerson, Wallace W., Santa Fé, N.M.

Woodward, Sidney H., Kingman, Ariz.

Young, Thomas H., Phoenix, Ariz.

## DISCHARGED.

Bird, Marshall M. . . . . . . . . . . . . . . . . . . . . . . . California.
Discharged on Surgeon's certificate of disability. Fracture of skull and concussion of brain incurred in line of duty, Aug. 8, 1898.

Cronin, Cornelius P. . . . . . . . . . . . . . . . . . . . . . Yuma, Ariz.
Discharged, June 13, 1898, on Surgeon's certificate.

Crimmins, Martin L. . . . . . . . . . . . . . . . . . . . . . New York, N.Y.
Mustered out to accept commission, July 29, 1898.

Goodrich, David M. . . . . . . . . . . . . . . . . . . . . . . Akron, O.
Discharged, May 19, 1898, to accept commission.

Murphy, James E. . . . . . . . . . . . . . . . . . . . . . . . Delrio, Ariz.
Discharged, Sept. 10th, by order of Secretary of War. Shot in head, July 1, 1898, before Santiago de Cuba.

## DIED.

Hall, Joel R. . . . . . . . . . . . . . . . . . . . . . . . . . . . . Seattle, Wash.

Logue, David . . . . . . . . . . . . . . . . . . . . . . . . . . . Globe, Ariz.
Killed, July 1, 1898, before Santiago de Cuba; buried on field of battle.

Norton, Oliver B. . . . . . . . . . . . . . . . . . . . . . . . .
Killed, July 1, 1898, before Santiago de Cuba; buried on field of battle.

Saunders, W. H............................ Salem, Mass.
    Died of fever at Santiago.
Smith, Race W. ......................... San Antonio, Tex.
    Died of wounds received July 2, 1898.
Swetman, John W......................... Globe, Ariz.
    Killed, July 1, 1898, before Santiago de Cuba; buried on field of battle.
Tomlinson, Leroy E. ....
    Sent to hospital boat, June 19, 1898, en route to Cuba; fever. Certificate of death
    dated June 23, 1898. Body and effects sent ashore, care Capt. Stephens, Signal
    Corps, U.S.A. Typhoid fever contracted in line of duty.

## TROOP C.

### Captain Joseph L. B. Alexander.

Joseph L. B. Alexander . . . Captain . . . . . . . . Phoenix, Ariz.
Robert S. Patterson . . . . . 1st Lieutenant. . . . Safford, Ariz.
Hal Sayre, Jr. . . . . . . . . . . 2d Lieutenant. . . . Denver, Col.
Willis O. Huson. . . . . . . . 1st Sergeant . . . . . Yuma, Ariz.
James H. Maxey. . . . . . . . Q. M. Sergeant . . Yuma, Ariz.
Sam W. Noyes . . . . . . . . . Sergeant. . . . . . . . Tucson, Ariz.
Adam H. Klingham . . . . . Sergeant. . . . . . . . Flagstaff, Ariz.
Sumner H. Gerard . . . . . . Sergeant. . . . . . . . New York, N.Y.
John McAndrew. . . . . . . . Sergeant. . . . . . . . Congress Junction, Ariz.
Eldridge E. Jordan . . . . . . Sergeant. . . . . . . . Phoenix, Ariz.
Wilbur D. French. . . . . . . Corporal . . . . . . . Safford, Ariz.
Hedrick M. Warren . . . . . Corporal . . . . . . . Phoenix, Ariz.
Bruce C. Weathers . . . . . . Corporal . . . . . . . Safford, Ariz.
Frank A. Woodin . . . . . . . Corporal . . . . . . . Phoenix, Ariz.
Charles A. Armstrong. . . . Corporal . . . . . . . San José, Cal.
Elisha E. Garrison . . . . . . Corporal . . . . . . . New York, N.Y.
William T. Atkins . . . . . . . Corporal . . . . . . . Selma, Ala.
Oscar J. Mullen . . . . . . . . Corporal . . . . . . . Tempe, Ariz.
Frank Marti . . . . . . . . . . . Trumpeter . . . . . . Jerome, Ariz.
John A. W. Stelzriede . . . . Trumpeter . . . . . . Tempe, Ariz.
James G. Yost . . . . . . . . . Blacksmith . . . . . . Prescott, Ariz.
Frank Vans Agnew . . . . . . Farrier . . . . . . . . . Kissimee, Fla.
Francis L. Morgan . . . . . . Saddler . . . . . . . . White Hills, Ariz.
Jerome W. Lankford. . . . . Wagoner . . . . . . . White Hills, Ariz.

### TROOPERS

Asay, William, Safford, Ariz.
Anderson, Thomas A., San
    Antonio, Tex.
Barthell, Peter K., Kingman, Ariz.
Bradley, Peter, Jerome, Ariz.
Burks, Robert E., Prescott, Ariz.

Byrns, Orlando C., Prescott, Ariz.

Bowler, George P., New York, N.Y.

Carleton, William C., Tempe, Ariz.

Carlson, Carl, Tempe, Ariz.

Cartledge, Crantz, Tempe, Ariz.

Coleman, Lockhart G., St. Louis, Mo.

Danforth, Clyde L., Flagstaff, Ariz.

Danforth, Wm. H., Flagstaff, Ariz.

Dewees, John L., San Antonio, Tex.

Duncan, Arthur G., New York.

Engel, Edwin P., Phoenix, Ariz.

Force, Peter, Selma, Ala.

Gaughan, James, Phoenix, Ariz.

Gibbins, Floyd J., Prescott, Ariz.

Goodwin, James C., Tempe, Ariz.

Gardiner, John P., Boston, Mass.

Gavin, Anthony, Buffalo, N.Y.

Hanson, Ivan M., Phoenix, Ariz.

Hanson, William, Prescott, Ariz.

Herold, Philip M., Phoenix, Ariz.

Howland, Harry, Flagstaff, Ariz.

Hubbell, William C., Nogales, Ariz.

Hall, Edward C., New Haven, Conn.

Kastens, Harry E., Winslow, Ariz.

Marvin, William E., Yuma, Ariz.

Mason, David P., Brownsville, Tex.

Moffett, Edward B., Yuma, Ariz.

Neville, George A., Yuma, Ariz.

Norton, John W., Lockport, Ill.

O'Leary, Daniel, Tempe, Ariz.

Parker, John W., Safford, Ariz.

Payne, Forest B., Phoenix, Ariz.

Pond, Ashley, Detroit, Mich.

Perry, Arthur R., Phoenix, Ariz.

Ricketts, William L., Phoenix, Ariz.

Roederer, John, Prescott, Ariz.

Rupert, Charles W., Prescott, Ariz.

Reed, George W., Tucson, Ariz.

Sayers, Samuel E., Yuma, Ariz.

Scharf, Charles A., Flagstaff, Ariz.

Sexsmith, William, Yuma, Ariz.

Shackelford, Marcus L., Jerome, Ariz.

Shoemaker, John, Phoenix, Ariz.

Skogsburg, Charles G., Safford, Ariz.

Scull, Guy H., Boston, Mass.

Sloan, Thomas H., Phoenix, Ariz.

Somers, Fred B., Flagstaff, Ariz.

Trowbridge, Lafayette, Prescott, Ariz.

Vines, Jesse G., Phoenix, Ariz.

Vance, William E., Austin, Tex.

Wormell, John A., Phoenix, Ariz.

Younger, Charles, Winslow, Ariz.

Wright, Albert P.. . . . . . . . Color Sergeant* . . . . . . Yuma, Ariz.

### DISCHARGED — *Disability.*

Alamia, John B.. . . . . . . . . Private . . . . . . . . . . . . . Port Isabel, Tex.
  Discharged, account epileptic fits, per order O. A. G. O.

Pearson, Rufus W.. . . . . . . Sergeant. . . . . . . . . . . . Phoenix, Ariz.
  Discharged, Aug. 26, 1898, on certificate of discharge signed by Secretary of War General Alger.

*Color Sergeant of Regiment.

## DISCHARGED BY ORDER.

Grindell, Thomas F. . . . . . . . Sergeant . . . . . . . . . . Tempe, Ariz.
 Discharged by telegraph order A. G. O., Sept. 8, 1898.
Hill, Wesley . . . . . . . . . . . . . Private . . . . . . . . . . . Tempe, Ariz.
 Discharged by telegraph order A. G. O., Sept. 8, 1898.
Scudder, William M. . . . . . . . Private . . . . . . . . . . . Chicago, Ill.
 Discharged per special order 204, par. 52, War Department, A. G. O.,
   Washington, D.C., Aug. 30, 1898.
Wallack, Robt. R. . . . . . . . . . Private . . . . . . . . . . . Washington.
 Discharged, July 19, 1898, per par. 27, S. O. 203, War Department, A. G. O.,
   Washington, D.C., Aug. 29, 1898, being appointed 2d Lieutenant for
   Regular Army.

## TRANSFERRED.

Rowdin, John E. . . . . . . . . . . Private . . . . . . . . . . Phoenix, Ariz.
 Transferred, June 8, 1898, per R. O. No. 6, dated Tampa, Fla., June 8, 1898.

## DIED.

Adsit, Nathaniel B. . . . . . . . . Private . . . . . . . . . . Buffalo, N.Y.
 Died, Aug. 1st, at Buffalo, of typhoid fever.
Clearwater, Frank H. . . . . . . . Private . . . . . . . . . . Brownsville, Tex.
 Died at Corpus Christi, Sept. 2, 1898, of typhoid malaria.
Newnhone, Thomas M. . . . . . Private . . . . . . . . . . Phoenix, Ariz.
 Died at hospital Ford McPherson, of typhoid fever, Aug. 4, 1898.

## TROOP D.

### Captain R. B. Huston.

Robert B. Huston . . . . . . . . . Captain. . . . . . . . . . . Guthrie, O.T.
David M. Goodrich. . . . . . . . 1st Lieutenant . . . . . . Akron, Ohio.
Robert H. M. Ferguson . . . . 2d Lieutenant . . . . . . New York City.
Orlando G. Palmer . . . . . . . . 1st Sergeant. . . . . . . Ponco City, O.T.
Gerald A. Webb . . . . . . . . . Sergeant . . . . . . . . . Guthrie, O.T.
Joseph A. Randolph . . . . . . . Sergeant . . . . . . . . . Waukomis, O.T.
Ira A. Hill. . . . . . . . . . . . . Sergeant . . . . . . . . . Newkirk, O.T.
Charles E. Hunter. . . . . . . . . Sergeant . . . . . . . . . Enid, O.T.
Scott Reay . . . . . . . . . . . . . Sergeant . . . . . . . . . Blackwell, O.T.
Paul W. Hunter . . . . . . . . . Sergeant . . . . . . . . . Chandler, O.T.
Thomas Moran . . . . . . . . . . Sergeant . . . . . . . . . Fort Sill, O.T.
Calvin Hill . . . . . . . . . . . . . Corporal. . . . . . . . . Pawnee, O.T.
George Norris. . . . . . . . . . . Corporal. . . . . . . . . Kingfisher, O.T.
John D. Roades . . . . . . . . . Corporal. . . . . . . . . Hennessey, O.T.
 Wounded in battle of Las Guasimas, June 24, 1898. G. S. leg.

Lyman F. Beard . . . . . . . . Corporal . . . . . . . Shawnee, O.T.
Henry Meagher . . . . . . . . . Corporal . . . . . . . El Reno, O.T.
    Wounded in the battle before Santiago, July 1, 1898. Both shoulders.
Alexander H. Denham . . . . Corporal . . . . . . . Oklahoma City, O.T.
    Wounded in battle of Las Guasimas, June 24, 1898. G. S. left thigh.
Henry K. Love . . . . . . . . . Corporal . . . . . . . Tecumseh, O.T.
Harrison J. Holt . . . . . . . . Corporal . . . . . . . Denver, Col.
William D. Amrine . . . . . . . Saddler . . . . . . . . Newkirk, O.T.
Starr W. Wetmore . . . . . . . Trumpeter . . . . . . Newkirk, O.T.
    Wounded in battle before Santiago, July 1, 1898. Right thigh, severe. Missile or
    weapon, Mauser rifle.
James T. Brown . . . . . . . . Trumpeter . . . . . . Newkirk, O.T.
Lorrin D. Muxlow . . . . . . . Wagoner . . . . . . . Guthrie, O.T.

## TROOPERS.

Baily, William, Norman, O.T.
    Wounded in battle before Santiago, July 2, 1898. Right foot. Missile or weapon, Mauser rifle.
Beal, Fred N., Kingfisher, O.T.
    Wounded in battle of Las Guasimas, June 24, 1898. G. S. leg.
Burgess, George, Shawnee, O.T.
Brandon, Perry H., Lancaster, O.T.
Byrne, Peter F., Guthrie, O.T.
Cease, Forrest L., Guthrie, O.T.
Chase, Leslie C., Kingfisher, O.T.
Cook, Walter M., Enid, O.T.
Crawford, William S., Enid, O.T.
Cross, William E., El Reno, O.T.
Crockett, Warren E., Marietta, Ga.
    Wounded in battle before Santiago, July 2, 1898. Leg. Missile or weapon, Mauser rifle.
Cunningham, Solomon M., San Antonio, Tex.
Carlow, Gerald, Boerne, Tex.
David, Icem J., Enid, O.T.
Emery, Elzie E., Shawnee, O.T.
Faulk, William A., Guthrie, O.T.
Hill, Edwin M., Tecumseh, O.T.

Honeycutt, James V., Shawnee, O.T.
Eppley, Kurtz, Orange, N.J.
Green, Charles H., Albuquerque, N.M.
Hatch, Charles P., Newport, R.I.
Holmes, Thomas M., Newkirk, O.T.
    Wounded in battle before Santiago, July 1, 1898. Left leg, severe. Missile or weapon, Mauser rifle.
Haynes, Jacob M., Newkirk, O.T.
Howard, John S., Boerne, Tex.
Ishler, Shelby F., Enid, O.T.
    Wounded in battle of Las Guasimas, June 24, 1898. G. S. right forearm.
Ivy, Charles B., Waco, Tex.
Johnston, Edward W., Cushing, O.T.
    Wounded in battle before Santiago, July 1, 1898. Right thigh.
Joyce, Walter, Guthrie, O.T.
Knox, William F.
Laird, Emmett, Albuquerque, N.M.
Loughmiller, Edgar F., Oklahoma City, O.T.
Lovelace, Carl, Waco, Tex.
Lush, Henry, El Reno, O.T.

McMillan, Robert L., Shawnee, O.T.
    Wounded in battle before Santiago, July 1, 1898. Left shoulder and arm.

McClure, David V., Oklahoma City, O.T.

McMurtry, George G., Pittsburg, Pa.

Miller, Roscoe B., Guthrie, O.T.

Miller, Volney D., Guthrie, O.T.

Munn, Edward, Elizabeth, N.J.

Newcomb, Marcellus L., Kingfisher, O.T.
    Wounded in battle of Las Guasimas, June 24, 1898. G. S. right knee.

Norris, Warren, Kingfisher, O.T.

Palmer, William F., Shawnee, O.T.

Proctor, Joseph H., Pawnee, O.T.

Pollock, William, Pawnee, O.T.

Russell, Albert P., El Reno, O.T.

Sands, George H., Guthrie, O.T.

Schmutz, John C., Germantown, Ohio.

Scott, Cliff D., Clifton, O.T.

Schupp, Eugene, Santa Fé, N.M.

Shanafelt, Dick, Perry, O.T.

Shipp, Edward M., Kingfisher, O.T.

Stewart, Clare H., Pawnee, O.T.

Stewart, Clyde H., Pawnee, O.T.

Tauer, William L., Ponca City, O.T.

Thomas, Albert M., Guthrie, O.T.

Vanderslice, James E., Enid, O.T.

Van Valen, Alexander L., Poughkeepsie, N.Y.

Wolff, Frederick W., San Antonio, Tex.

Wright, William O., Pawnee, O.T.

Wright, Edward L., Guthrie, O.T.

## DISCHARGED.

Shockey, James M. . . . . . . Corporal . . . . . . . . . . Perry, O.T.
    Discharged, July 1, 1898, by order of Asst. Adjt. Gen'l.

Luther, Arthur A. . . . . . . . Farrier . . . . . . . . . . . . Pawnee, O.T.
    Discharged, July 1, 1898, by order of Asst. Adjt. Gen'l.

Page, John F. . . . . . . . . . . Private . . . . . . . . . . . Alva, O.T.
    Discharged by verbal order of Gen'l Wood, Aug. 6, 1898.

Wells, Joseph O. . . . . . . . Private . . . . . . . . . . . St. Joseph, Mich.
    Discharged by order of Asst. Adjt. Gen'l, Aug. 27, 1898.

Simpson, William S. . . . . . Corporal . . . . . . . . . . Dallas, Tex.
    Discharged by reason of promotion into regular army, as 2d Lieut., Sept. 3, 1898.

## TRANSFERRED.

Schuyler, A. McGinnis . . . 1st Lieutenant . . . . . . . Newkirk, O.T.
    Promoted to Captain and transferred to Troop I 1st U. S. V. C., May 19, 1898.

Schweizer, Jacob . . . . . . . 2d Lieutenant . . . . . . . El Reno, O.T.
    Promoted to 1st Lieut. and assigned to duty as Q. M. 1st U. S. V. C., May 19, 1898.

Carr, Joseph A. . . . . . . . . 1st Lieutenant . . . . . . . Washington, D.C.
    Transferred to Troop K 1st U. S. V. C., Sept. 5, 1898. Wounded in battle before Santiago, July 2, 1898. Left testicle. Missile or weapon, Mauser rifle.

*PRIVATES.*

Douthett, Matthew, Guthrie, O.T.
  Appointed Q. M. Sergeant 1st
    U. S. V. C., and assigned to
    duty, Aug. 31, 1898.

Freeman, Elisha L., Ponca City,
  O.T.
  Transferred to Troop K 1st
    U. S. V. C., May 11, 1898.

Folk, Theodore, Oklahoma City,
  N.M.
  Transferred to Troop K 1st
    U. S. V. C., May 11, 1898.

Hulme, Robert A., El Reno, O.T.
  Transferred to Troop K 1st
    U. S. V. C., May 11, 1898.

Jordan, Andrew M., El Reno,
  O.T.
  Transferred to Troop K 1st
    U. S. V. C., May 11, 1898.

McGinty, William, Stillwater,
  O.T.
  Transferred to Troop K 1st
    U. S. V. C., May 11, 1898.

Mitchell, William H., Guthrie, O.T.
  Transferred to Troop K 1st
    U. S. V. C., May 11, 1898.

Staley, Francis M., Waukomis,
  O.T.
  Transferred to Troop K 1st
    U. S. V. C., May 11, 1898.

Smith, Fred, Guthrie, O.T.
  Transferred to Troop K 1st
    U. S. V. C., May 11, 1898.

Weitzel, John F., Newkirk, O.T.
  Transferred to Troop K 1st
    U. S. V. C., May 11, 1898.

Woodward, John A., El Reno,
  O.T.
  Transferred to Troop K 1st
    U. S. V. C., May 11, 1898.

Wilson, Frank M., Guthrie, O.T.
  Transferred to Troop K 1st
    U. S. V. C., May 11, 1898.

Burke, Edward F., Orange, N.J.
  Transferred to Troop A 1st
    U. S. V. C., July 13, 1898.

*DIED.*

Cashion, Roy V . . . . . . . . . Private . . . . . . . . . . . Hennessey, O.T.
  Killed in battle before Santiago, July 1, 1898. Head.

Miller, Theodore W. . . . . . . Private . . . . . . . . . . . . Akron, Ohio.
  Wounded in battle before Santiago, July 1, 1898. Died from effects of wound,
    July 8, 1898. Penetrating neck; severe — totally paralyzed from head down.

*DESERTED.*

Crosley, Henry S. . . . . . . . . Private . . . . . . . . . . . . Guthrie, O.T.
  Dropped from the rolls as deserted, July 8, 1898.

## TROOP E.

### Captain Frederick Muller.

Frederick Muller. . . . . . . . Captain. . . . . . . . . . . . Sante Fé, N.M.
William E. Griffin . . . . . . . 1st Lieutenant . . . . . . Sante Fé, N.M.
John A. McIlhenny . . . . . . 2d Lieutenant . . . . . . New Orleans, La.
John S. Langston . . . . . . . . 1st Sergeant. . . . . . . . Cerrillos, N.M.
Royal A. Prentice . . . . . . . . Q. M. Sergeant . . . . . . Las Vegas, N.M.

Hugh B. Wright . . . . . . . . Sergeant . . . . . . . . . Las Vegas, N.M.
Albert M. Jones . . . . . . . . Sergeant . . . . . . . . . Sante Fé, N.M.
Timothy Breen . . . . . . . . . Sergeant . . . . . . . . . Sante Fé, N.M.
    Wounded and sent to hospital, July 1, 1898. Arm.

Berry F. Taylor . . . . . . . . . Sergeant . . . . . . . . . Las Vegas, N.M.
Thomas P. Ledgwidge . . . . Sergeant . . . . . . . . . Sante Fé, N.M.
John Mullen . . . . . . . . . . . Sergeant . . . . . . . . . Chicago, Ill.
    Wounded and sent to hospital, July 1, 1898. Side and head; severe.

Harman H. Wynkoop . . . . . Corporal . . . . . . . . . Sante Fé, N.M.
    Wounded in line of duty and sent to hospital, July 2, 1898. Returned to duty,
      Sept. 4, 1898.

James M. Dean . . . . . . . . . Corporal . . . . . . . . . Sante Fé, N.M.
    Wounded in line of duty and sent to hospital, June 24, 1898. Returned to duty,
      Aug. 31, 1898. G. S. left thigh.

Edward C. Waller . . . . . . . Corporal . . . . . . . . . Chicago, Ill.
    Wounded in line of duty, July 2, 1898. Scalp, slight.

G. Roland Fortescue . . . . . . Corporal . . . . . . . . . New York, N.Y.
    Slight bullet wound in foot, July 1, 1898.

Edward Bennett . . . . . . . . Corporal . . . . . . . . . Cripple Creek, Col.
Charles E. Knoblauch . . . . Corporal . . . . . . . . . New York, N.Y.
Richard C. Conner . . . . . . . Corporal . . . . . . . . . Sante Fé, N.M.
Ralph E. McFie . . . . . . . . . Corporal . . . . . . . . . Las Cruces, N.M.
Arthur J. Griffin . . . . . . . . Trumpeter . . . . . . . Sante Fé, N.M.
Edward S. Lewis . . . . . . . . Trumpeter . . . . . . . Las Vegas, N.M.
Robert J. Parrish . . . . . . . . Blacksmith . . . . . . . Clayton, N.M.
Grant Hill . . . . . . . . . . . . Farrier . . . . . . . . . . Sante Fé, N.M.
Joe T. Sandoval . . . . . . . . Saddler . . . . . . . . . . Sante Fé, N.M.
Guilford B. Chapin . . . . . . Wagoner . . . . . . . . . Sante Fé, N.M.

### TROOPERS

Ausburn, Charles G., New Orleans, La.
Almach, Roll, Santa Fé, N.M.
Brennan, John M., Santa Fé, N.M.
Baca, Jose M., Las Vegas, N.M.
Beard, William M., San Antonio, Tex.
Cooper, George B., Tampa, Fla.
Conway, James, San Antonio, Tex.
Dettamore, George W., Clayton, N.M.
    Wounded in line of duty and sent to hospital, July 1, 1898.

Davis, Harry A., Boston, Mass.
Dodge, George H., Denver, Col.
Debli, Joseph, Tampa, Fla.
Donavan, Freeman M., Santa Fé, N.M.
Douglas, James B., New York, N.Y.
Easley, William T., Clayton, N.M.
Edwards, Lawrence W.
Fries, Frank D., Santa Fé, N.M.
Francis, Mack, Maynesville, N.C.
Fettes, George, Antonito, Col.
Gisler, Joseph, Santa Fé, N.M.

Gibbs, James P., Santa Fé, N.M.

Gibbie, William R., Las Vegas, N.M.

Grigsby, Braxton, New York, N.Y.

Grigg, John G., San Antonio, Tex.

Gammel, Roy U., Jersey Co., Ill.

Harding, John D., Socoro, N.M.

Hood, John B., New York, N.Y.

Harkness, Daniel D., Las Vegas, N.M.

Hutchison, William M., Santa Fé, N.M.

Hall, John P., Williamson Co., Tex.
Wounded in line of duty and sent to hospital, July 1, 1898.
Returned to duty, Aug. 31, 1898.

Hogle, William H., Santa Fé, N.M.

Hudson, Arthur J., Santa Fé, N.M.

Hulskotter, John, Santa Fé, N.M.

Hutchason, Joseph M., Jimtown, Tenn.

Howell, William S. E., Cerrillos, N.M.

Hadden, David A., San Antonio, Tex.

Hixon, Thomas L., Las Vegas, N.M.

Heard, Judson, Pecos City, Tex.

Hamlin, Warden W., Chicago, Ill.

Jones, Thomas B., Santa Fé, N.M.

Johnston, Charles E., San Antonio, Tex.

Jacobus, Charles W., Santa Fé, N.M.

Knapp, Edgar A., Elizabeth, N.J.

Kingsley, Charles E., Las Vegas, N.M.

Kissam, William A., New York, N.Y.

Lowe, Frank, Santa Fé, N.M.

Ludy, Dan, Las Vegas, N.M.

Livingston, Thomas C., Hamilton Co., Tex.

Lowitzki, Hyman S., Santa Fé, N.M.

Lewis, James.

Merchant, James E., Cerrillos, N.M.

Moran, William J., Cerrillos, N.M.

McKinnon, Samuel, Madrid, N.M.

McKinley, Charles E., Cerrillos, N.M.
Wounded in line of duty, July 1, 1898. Head.

McKay, Charles F., Santa Fé, N.M.

McCabe, Frederick H., Santa Fé, N.M.

McDowell, John C., Santa Fé, N.M.

Morrison, Amaziah B., Las Vegas, N.M.

Mahan, Lloyd L., Cerrillos, N.M.

Martin, Henry D., Cerrillos, N.M.

Menger, Otto F., Clayton, N.M.
Wounded in line of duty, July 1, 1898. Sent to hospital. Left side.

Mungor, William C., Santa Fé, N.M.

Nettleblade, Adolph F., Cerrillos, N.M.

Roberts, Thomas, Golden, N.M.

Ryan, John E., Santa Fé, N.M.
Wounded, July 1, 1898, in line of duty.

Ramsey, Homer M., Pearsall, Tex.

Seaders, Ben. F., Las Vegas, N.M.

Skinner, Arthur V., Santa Fé, N.M.

Schnepple, William C., Santa Fé, N.M.

Scanlon, Edward, Cerrillos, N.M.

Slevin, Edward, Tampa, Fla.

Taylor, William R., New York, N.Y.

Wagner, William W., Bland, N.M.

Wright, George, Madrid, N.M.

Wynkoop, Charles W., Santa Fé, N.M.

Warren, George W., Santa Fé, N.M.

## DISCHARGED.

Dame, William E.. . . . . . . . . . 1st Sergeant . . . . . . . . Cerrillos, N.M.
  Discharged per O. reg. comds., Aug. 10, 1898.
Wesley, Frederick C.. . . . . . . . Sergeant. . . . . . . . . . Santa Fé, N.M.
  Discharged on account of disability, Aug. 26, 1898. Wounded forearm slight,
    July 1, 2, or 3.

## TRANSFERRED BY VERBAL ORDER REGIMENTAL
### COMMANDER, MAY 12, 1898.

Reber, William R. . . . . . . . . . Sergeant . . . . . . . . . . . . . . . . . . . . . .
Price, Stuart R. . . . . . . . . . . . Corporal . . . . . . . . . . . . . . . . . . . . . .
Bernard, William C.. . . . . . . . Trooper . . . . . . . . . . . . . . . . . . . . . . .
Brown, Hiram T.. . . . . . . . . . Trooper . . . . . . . . . . . . . . . . . . . . . . .
Bump, Arthur L. . . . . . . . . . . Trooper . . . . . . . . . . . . . . . . . . . . . . .
Cloud, William. . . . . . . . . . . Trooper . . . . . . . . . . . . . . . . . . . . . . .
Davis, Henry Clay . . . . . . . . . Trooper . . . . . . . . . . . . . . . . . . . . . . .
Duran, Jose L. . . . . . . . . . . . Trooper . . . . . . . . . . . . . . . . . . . . . . .
Easton, Stephen . . . . . . . . . . Trooper . . . . . . . . . . . . . . . . . . . . . . .
Fennell, William A. . . . . . . . . Trooper . . . . . . . . . . . . . . . . . . . . . . .
Fleming, Clarence A. . . . . . . . Trooper . . . . . . . . . . . . . . . . . . . . . . .
Holden, Prince A. . . . . . . . . . Trooper . . . . . . . . . . . . . . . . . . . . . . .
Land, Oscar N. . . . . . . . . . . . Trooper . . . . . . . . . . . . . . . . . . . . . . .
Martin, John . . . . . . . . . . . . Trooper . . . . . . . . . . . . . . . . . . . . . . .
Roberts, John P. . . . . . . . . . . Trooper . . . . . . . . . . . . . . . . . . . . . . .
Stephens, Orregon . . . . . . . . . Trooper . . . . . . . . . . . . . . . . . . . . . . .
Torbett, John G. . . . . . . . . . . Trooper . . . . . . . . . . . . . . . . . . . . . . .
Williams, Thomas C. . . . . . . . Trooper . . . . . . . . . . . . . . . . . . . . . . .
Zigler, Daniel J.. . . . . . . . . . . Trooper . . . . . . . . . . . . . . . . . . . . . . .

## DIED.

Cochran, Irad, Jr.. . . . . . . . . . Trooper . . . . . . . . . . . . . . . . . . . . . . .
  Died, May 26, 1898, San Antonio, Tex. Spinal meningitis.
Miller, John S.. . . . . . . . . . . . Trooper . . . . . . . . . . . . . . . . . . . . . . .
  Died, July 16, 1898, of yellow fever, at Siboney, Cuba.
Judson, Alfred M. . . . . . . . . . Trooper . . . . . . . . . . . . . . . . . . . . . . .
  Died Aug. 17, 1898, of typhoid fever, at Montauk Point, L.I.
O'Neill, John . . . . . . . . . . . . Trooper . . . . . . . . . . . . . . . . . . . . . . .
  Died, Aug. 3, 1898, of dysentery, at Edgmont Key, Fla.

## KILLED.

Green, Henry C. . . . . . . . . . . Trooper . . . . . . . . . . . . . . . . . . . . . . .
  Killed in action, July 1, 1898, near Santiago de Cuba.
Robinson, John F.. . . . . . . . . . Trooper . . . . . . . . . . . . . . . . . . . . . . .
  Killed in action, July 2, 1898, near Santiago de Cuba.

*ALTERATIONS, September 7, 1898.*

Sherrard, Coleman . . . . . . . . 1st Lieutenant . . . . . Santa Fé, N.M.
John A. McIlhenny. . . . . . . . 2d Lieutenant . . . . . New Orleans, La.

## TROOP F.

### Captain Maximilian Luna.

Maximilian Luna . . . . . . . . . Captain . . . . . . . . . Santa Fé, N.M.
Horace W. Weakley . . . . . . . 1st Lieutenant . . . . . Santa Fé, N.M.
William E. Dame . . . . . . . . . 2d Lieutenant . . . . . Santa Fé, N.M.
  Transferred from Troop E to F.
Horace E. Sherman . . . . . . . 1st Sergeant . . . . . . . Santa Fé, N.M.
Garfield Hughes. . . . . . . . . . Sergeant . . . . . . . . . Santa Fé, N.M.
Thomas D. Fennessy . . . . . . Sergeant . . . . . . . . . Santa Fé, N.M.
William L. Mattocks. . . . . . . Sergeant . . . . . . . . . Santa Fé, N.M.
James Doyle. . . . . . . . . . . . Sergeant . . . . . . . . . Santa Fé, N.M.
George W. Armijo . . . . . . . . Sergeant . . . . . . . . . Santa Fé, N.M.
  Wounded in action, June 24th. G. S. wrist.
Eugene Bohlinger. . . . . . . . . Sergeant . . . . . . . . . Santa Fé, N.M.
Herbert A. King. . . . . . . . . . Sergeant . . . . . . . . . Santa Fé, N.M.
Edward Donnelly. . . . . . . . . Corporal . . . . . . . . . Santa Fé, N.M.
John Cullen . . . . . . . . . . . . Corporal . . . . . . . . . Santa Fé, N.M.
Edward Hale . . . . . . . . . . . Corporal . . . . . . . . . Santa Fé, N.M.
Arthur P. Spenser. . . . . . . . . Corporal . . . . . . . . . Santa Fé, N.M.
John Boehnke . . . . . . . . . . Corporal . . . . . . . . . Santa Fé, N.M.
Albert Powers . . . . . . . . . . Corporal . . . . . . . . . Santa Fé, N.M.
  Wounded in action, July 1, 1898.
Wentworth S. Conduit. . . . . . Corporal . . . . . . . . . Santa Fé, N.M.
Ray V. Clark . . . . . . . . . . . Farrier. . . . . . . . . . . Santa Fé, N.M.
  Contusion scalp, slight. Missile shrapnel. Wounded near Santiago de Cuba,
    July 1, 2, or 3, 1898.
Charles R. Gee. . . . . . . . . . . Farrier. . . . . . . . . . . Santa Fé, N.M.
Jefferson Hill . . . . . . . . . . . Wagoner . . . . . . . . . Santa Fé, N.M.
J. Kirk McKurdy . . . . . . . . . Trumpeter . . . . . . . . San Antonio, Tex.
Arthur L. Perry . . . . . . . . . . Bugler . . . . . . . . . . . Santa Fé, N.M.
  Shoulder. Mauser rifle. Wounded near Santiago de Cuba, July 1, 2, or 3, 1898.

### *PRIVATES.*

Albers, H. L., Santa Fé, N.M.
  Wounded in action, June 24, 1898.
  G. S. right wrist.

Albertson, Ed. J., Santa Fé, N.M.
  Wounded in action, June 24. G. S.
  wrist.

Alexander James, Santa Fé, N.M.

Abbott, Chas. G., Santa Fé, N.M.

Adams, Edgar S., San Antonio, Tex.

Alexander, James F., Santa Fé, N.M.

Black, James S., Santa Fé, N.M.

Bailey, Rob't Z., Santa Fé, N.M.
  Wounded in action, June 24th.
    G. S. both legs.

Boschen, John, San Antonio, Tex.

Bell, Wm. A., Tampa, Fla.

Brennan, Jeremiah, Santa Fé, N.M.

Burris, Walter C., Santa Fé, N.M.

Byrne, John, Muscogee, I.T.
  Transferred from Troop L to F.

Bell, John H., Santa Fé, N.M.

Cochran, William O., Santa Fé, N.M.

Clark, Frank J., San Antonio, Tex.

Colbert, Benjamin H., San Antonio, Tex.

Christian, Edward D., Tampa, Fla.

Clelland, Calvin G., Santa Fé, N.M.

Conley, Edward C., Santa Fé, N.M.

Cochran, Willard M., Santa Fé, N.M.

Cherry, Charles C., Santa Fé, N.M.

Dougherty, Louis, Santa Fé, N.M.

De Bohun, John C., Santa Fé, N.M.

Farley, William, Santa Fé, N.M.

Freeman, Will, Santa Fé, N.M.
  Wounded by fragments of shell in
    wrist, July 1, 1898. Left wrist.

Gibbs, Henry M., Santa Fé, N.M.
  Gunshot wound in foot, July 1, 1898.

Gallagher, Wm. D., Santa Fé, N.M.

Goldberg, Samuel, Santa Fé, N.M.
  Wounded in action, July 1, 1898.
    Hip. Mauser rifle.

Glessner, Otis, Santa Fé, N.M.

Green, John D., Santa Fé, N.M.

Hartle, Albert C., Santa Fé, N.M.
  Gunshot wound in testicles, June
    24, 1898.

Hopping, Charles O., Santa Fé, N.M.

Hammer, George, Santa Fé, N.M.

Kennedy, Stephan A., Santa Fé, N.M.

Leffert, Charles E., Santa Fé, N.M.

Lisk, Guy M., Santa Fé, N.M.

Leach, John M., Santa Fé, N.M.

Le Stourgeon, E. Guy, San Antonio, Tex.

Lavelle, Nolan Z., San Antonio, Tex.

Martin, Thomas, Santa Fé, N.M.

Mills, John B., Santa Fé, N.M.

McGregor, Herbert P., Santa Fé, N.M.
  Wounded in action, July 1, 1898.
    Left shoulder. Mauser rifle.

McCurdy, F. Allen, San Antonio, Tex.

Nickell, William E., Santa Fé, N.M.

Nesbit, Otto W., Santa Fé, N.M.

Newitt, George W., Santa Fé, N.M.

Neal, John M., Santa Fé, N.M.

Parmele, Charles A., Santa Fé, N.M.

Quier, Frank T., Santa Fé, N.M.

Raymond, Milliard L., Santa Fé, N.M.

Reed, Harry B., Santa Fé, N.M.

Reed, Clifford L., Santa Fé, N.M.
  Wounded in action, June 24, 1898.
    In arm.

Renner, Charles L., Santa Fé, N.M.

Reynolds, Edwin L., Santa Fé, N.M.

Russell, Arthur L., Santa Fé, N.M.

Rebentisch, Adolph, San Antonio, Tex.
  Gunshot wound in shoulder,
    June 24, 1898. Left shoulder.

Reyer, Adolph T., Santa Fé, N.M.
Rogers, Albert, Santa Fé, N.M.
Rice, Lee C., Santa Fé, N.M.
Staub, Louis E., Santa Fé, N.M.
Shields, William G., Santa Fé,
   N.M.
Stockbridge, Arthur H., Santa Fé,
   N.M.
Sharland, George H., Santa Fé,
   N.M.
Skipwith, John G., Santa Fé, N.M.
Sinnett, James B., Santa Fé, N.M.
Tangen, Edward, Santa Fé, N.M.
Trump, Norman O., Santa Fé,
   N.M.
Vinnedge, George E., Santa Fé,
   N.M.

Wardwell, Louis C., Santa Fé,
   N.M.
Warren, Paul, Santa Fé, N.M.
Watrous, Charles E., Santa Fé,
   N.M.
Weber, Beauregard, Santa Fé, N.M.
Weller, Samuel M., San Antonio,
   Tex.
Winter, John G., San Antonio, Tex.
   Gunshot wounds in shoulder, arm
   and leg, July 1, 1898.
Winter, Otto R., San Antonio, Tex.
Wertheim, Adolph S., San
   Antonio, Tex.
Walsh, John, Santa Fé, N.M.
Wells, Thomas J., Santa Fé, N.M.
Wilson, Harry W., Tampa, Fla.

### DISCHARGED.

Douglass, James. . . . . . . . . Private . . . . . . . . . . . . Santa Fé, N.M.
   Discharged acct. Surgeon's certificate of disability.

### TRANSFERRED.

Keyes, Maxwell . . . . . . . . . 2d Lieutenant . . . . . . . Santa Fé, N.M.
   Promoted to Adjutant, August 1, 1898

### PRIVATES.

Flynn, Joseph F., Santa Fé, N.M.
   Transferred from Troop F to I,
      May 12, 1898, San Antonio, Tex.
Goodrich, Hedrick Ben, Santa
   Fé, N.M.
   Transferred from Troop F to I,
      May 12, 1898, San Antonio, Tex.
Hickey, Walter, Santa Fé, N.M.
   Transferred from Troop F to I,
      May 12, 1898, San Antonio, Tex.
Hogan, Michael, Santa Fé, N.M.
   Transferred from Troop F to I,
      May 12, 1898, San Antonio, Tex.
King, Harry Bruce, Santa Fé, N.M.
   Transferred from Troop F to I,
      May 12, 1898, San Antonio, Tex.

Kerney, George M., Santa Fé, N.M.
   Transferred from Troop F to I,
      May 12, 1898, San Antonio, Tex.
Larsen, Louis, Santa Fé, N.M.
   Transferred from Troop F to I,
      May 12, 1898, San Antonio, Tex.
McCoy, John, Santa Fé, N.M.
   Transferred from Troop F to I,
      May 12, 1898, San Antonio, Tex.
Nehmer, Charles A., Santa Fé,
   N.M.
   Transferred from Troop F to I,
      May 12, 1898, San Antonio, Tex.
Rogers, Leo G., N.M.
   Transferred from Troop F to I,
      May 12, 1898, San Antonio, Tex.

Rafalowitz, Hyman, Santa Fé, N.M.
Transferred from Troop F to I,
May 12, 1898, San Antonio, Tex.

Spencer, Edwards John, Santa Fé, N.M.
Transferred from Troop F to I,
May 12, 1898, San Antonio, Tex.

Schearnhorst, Jr., Carl J., Santa Fé, N.M.
Transferred from Troop F to I,
May 12, 1898, San Antonio, Tex.

Temple, Frank, Santa Fé, N.M.
Transferred from Troop F to I,
May 12, 1898, San Antonio, Tex.

Bawcom, Joseph L., Santa Fé, N.M.
Transferred from Troop F to I,
May 12, 1898, San Antonio, Tex.

### DIED.

Booth, Frank B . . . . . . . . . . . Private . . . . . . . . . . Madison, Wis.
Wounded in action at Las Guasimas, June 24, 1898; died at Key West, August 30, 1898. G. S. right shoulder.

Erwin, William T. . . . . . . . . . Private . . . . . . . . . . Austin, Tex.
Killed in action, June 24, 1898. Las Guasimas. G. S. head.

Endsley, Guy D. . . . . . . . . . . Private . . . . . . . . . . Somerfield, Pa.
Died in Cuba, July 18, 1898, of fever.

### DESERTED.

Thompson, Charles. . . . . . . . Private . . . . . . . . . . . Mercer Co., W. Va.
Deserted at Tampa, Fla., July 27, 1898.

### DISCHARGED.

McIlhenny, John A.. . . . . . . . Corporal . . . . . . . . San Antonio, Tex.
Discharged to accept commission.

## TROOP G.

### Captain William H. H. Llewellen.

William H. H. Llewellen . . . . Captain . . . . . . . . . Las Cruces, N.M.
John Wesley Green . . . . . . . . 1st Lieutenant . . . . . Gallup, N.M.
David J. Leahy . . . . . . . . . . . 2d Lieutenant . . . . . Raton, N.M.
On sick list from July 1st to Sept. 3d from wound received in San Juan battle.
Columbus H. McCaa . . . . . . 1st Sergeant . . . . . . Gallup, N.M.
Jacob S. Mohler . . . . . . . . . . Q. M. Sergeant. . . . Gallup, N.M.
Raymond Morse . . . . . . . . . . Sergeant. . . . . . . . .
Rolla A. Fullenweider . . . . . . Sergeant. . . . . . . . . Raton, N.M.
Matthew T. McGehee . . . . . . Sergeant. . . . . . . . . Raton, N.M.
James Brown . . . . . . . . . . . . Sergeant. . . . . . . . . Gallup, N.M.
Nicholas A. Vyne . . . . . . . . . Sergeant. . . . . . . . . Emporia, Kan.
Raleigh L. Miller. . . . . . . . . . Sergeant. . . . . . . . . Pueblo, Col.
Henry Kirah . . . . . . . . . . . . . Corporal . . . . . . . . Gallup, N.M.

James D. Ritchie . . . . . . . . . . Corporal . . . . . . . Gallup, N.M.

Luther L. Stewart . . . . . . . . . Corporal . . . . . . . Raton, N.M.
>   Wounded in battle, June 24th. Absent since on account of wound. G. S. left forearm.

John McSparron . . . . . . . . . . Corporal . . . . . . . Gallup, N.M.
>   Wounded, July 1st. Absent since on account of wound. Right thigh, severe. Missile, shrapnel.

Frank Briggs . . . . . . . . . . . . . Corporal . . . . . . . Raton, N.M.

Edward C. Armstrong . . . . . . Corporal . . . . . . . . . Albuquerque, N.M.

William S. Reid . . . . . . . . . . Corporal . . . . . . . Raton, N.M.

Hiram E. Williams . . . . . . . . Corporal . . . . . . . Raton, N.M.

George V. Haefner . . . . . . . . Farrier . . . . . . . . . Gallup, N.M.

Frank A. Hill . . . . . . . . . . . . Saddler . . . . . . . . . Raton, N.M.

Thomas O'Neal . . . . . . . . . . Wagoner . . . . . . . . Springer, N.M.

Willis E. Somers . . . . . . . . . Trumpeter . . . . . . . Raton, N.M.

Edward G. Piper . . . . . . . . . Trumpeter . . . . . . . Silver City, N.M.

Alvin C. Ash . . . . . . . . . . . . Trooper . . . . . . . . Raton, N.M.
>   Absence from command since July 1st to Sept. 7th on account of wound received in battle. Wrist, slight. Missile, shrapnel.

### TROOPERS.

Arnold, Edward B., Prescott, Ariz.

Akin, James E., Dolores, Col.

Anderson, Arthur T., Albuquerque, N.M.

Andrews, William C., Sulphur Springs, Tex.

Beck, Joseph H., San Antonio, Tex.

Bishop, Louis B., San Antonio, Tex.

Brumley, Jr., William H., Dolores, Cal.

Brown, Robert, Gallup, N.M.

Brown, Edwin M., San Antonio, Tex.

Brazelton, William H., St. Louis, Mo.

Beissel, John J., Gallup, N.M.

Camp, Cloid, Raton, N.M.

Camp, Marion, Raton, N.M.

Covenaugh, Thomas F., Raton, N.M.
>   Absent since June 24th on account of wound received in battle.

Cody, William E., St. Louis, Mo.

Chopetal, Frank W., Buffalo, N.Y.

Coyle, Michael H., Raton, N.M.
>   Absent on sick leave since June 24th on account of wound in arm received in battle.

Clark, Winslow, Milton, Mass.
>   Absent on sick leave since July 1st on account of gunshot wound through lung received in battle. Right lung, severe. Missile or weapon, Mauser rifle.

Cotton, Frank W., Jennings, La.

Conover, Alfred J., Chicasee, I.T.

Detwiler, Sherman, Muscatine, Ia.

Dunn, Alfred B., Calvert, Tex.

Edmunds, John H., Alleghany, Pa.

Faupel, Henry F., Martington, Ill.

Fornoff, Frederick, Albuquerque, N.M.

Fitch, Roger S., Buffalo, N.Y.

Gibson, William C., Gallup, N.M.

Gevers, Louis, Austin, Tex.
  Absent from July 1st till Aug. 2d on account of gunshot wound in hips received in battle.
Goodwin, John, Gallup, N.M.
Healey, Frank F., Brooklyn, N.Y.
Henderson, John, Gallup, N.M.
  Absent from July 1st to Sept. 2d on account of wound in arm received in battle. Wrist. Missile or weapon, Mauser rifle.
Henshaw, Laten R., El Paso, Tex.
Johnson, Albert John, Raton, N.M.
Kline, John S., San Marcial, N.M.
Keeley, Bert T., Lamy, N.M.
King, Henry A., Massitee, Mich.
Littleton, Elias M., Springer, N.M.
Lincoln, Malcom D., Lucknow, I.T.
Larson, Anton, Silverton, Col.
Lyle, James C., Georgetown, Col.
Miller, Frank P., Los Angeles, Cal.
Meyers, Fred P., Gallup, N.M.
  Reduced from 1st Sergt. to Trooper on account of absence caused by wound received in battle, July 1, 1898. Head, severe.
Moran, Daniel, Gallup, N.M.
Mann, Eugene M., Omaha, Neb.
McCarthy, George H., Los Angeles, Cal.
McKinney, Frank G., Harrison, Ark.
McKinney, Oliver, Cannon City, Col.
McMullen, Samuel J., St. Louis, Mo.

Noish, John, Raton, N.M.
Phipps, T. W., Bland, N.M.
Petty, Archibald, Gallup, N.M.
Pennington, Elijah, San Antonio, Tex.
Preston, Robert A., Stiles, Tex.
Quigg, George H., Gallup, N.M.
Quinn, Walter D., San Marcial, N.M.
Radcliff, William, Gallup, N.M.
Richards, Richard, Albuquerque, N.M.
Rayburn, Harry C., Camden, Ia.
Reid, Robert W., Raton, N.M.
  Absent on sick leave from June 24th to Sept. 8th on account of wound in side received in battle. G. S. to right hip.
Ragland, Robert C., Guthrie, O.T.
Roland, George, Deming, N.M.
  G. S. right side, June 24, 1898.
Stillson, Earl, Topeka, Kan.
Simmons, Charles M., Raton, N.M.
Slaughter, Benjamin, San Antonio, Tex.
Shannon, Charles W., Raton, N.M.
Thomas, Neal, Aztec, N.M.
Travis, Grant, Aztec, N.M.
Van Horn, Eustace E., Halstead, Kan.
Welch, Toney, Durango, Col.
Whittington, Richard, Gallup, N.M.
Whited, Lyman E., Raton, N.M.
Wood, William D., Bland, N.M.
Wright, Clarence, Springer, N.M.

## DISCHARGED.

Swan, George D. . . . . . . . . . . . . . . . . . . . . . . . . . . . . Gallup, N.M.
  Discharged on account of disability.
Thompson, Frank M. . . . . . . . . . . . . . . . . . . . . . . . Aztec, N.M.
  Discharged on account of disability.

### *DESERTED.*

McCulloch, Samuel T.......................... Springer, N.M.
  Deserted from camp at Tampa, Fla., Aug. 4, 1898.

### *DEATHS.*

Green, J. Knox ............................. Rancho, Tex.
  Died at Montauk Point, N.Y., Camp U.S. Troops, Aug. 15, because of sickness
    which originated in line of duty.

Lutz, Eugene A............................. Raton, N.M.
  Detained in yellow-fever hospital by medical authorities when regiment left
    Cuba. Died in same, Aug. 15, 1898.

### *KILLED IN ACTION.*

Haefner, Henry J............................. Gallup, N.M.
  In battle, June 24, 1898.

Russel, Marcus D............................. Troy, N.Y.
  Killed in action, June 24, 1898.

### *TRANSFERRED.*

Arendt, Henry J. ......... Sergeant........... Gallup, N.M.
  Transferred to Troop I, May 12th.

Corbe, M. C............. Trumpeter ..........
  Transferred to Troop K, May 11.

### TROOPERS.

Bailie, Henry C., Gallup, N.M.
  Transferred from Troop I to Troop
    G, Aug. 31, 1898.

Love, William J., Raton, N.M.
  Transferred to Troop I, May 12th.

Morgan, Schuyler C., Hazard, Ky.
  Transferred to Troop I, May 12th.

Morgan, Ulysses G., Hazard, Ky.
  Transferred to Troop I, May 12th.

Odell, William D., Parkersburg,
    W. Va.
  Transferred to Troop I, May 12th.

Donnelly, Rutherford B. H.,
    Jefferson, O.T.
  Transferred to Troop I, May 12th.

Evans, Evan, Gallup, N.M.
  Transferred to Troop I, May 12th.

Groves, Oscar W., Raton, N.M.
  Transferred to Troop I, May 12th.

Jones, William H., Raton, N.M.
  Transferred to Troop I, May 12th.

Kania, Frank, Jamestown, N.D.
  Transferred to Troop K, May 11th.

Pierce, Ed., Chicago, Ill.
  Transferred to Troop I, May 12th.

Saville, Michael, Chicago, Ill.
  Transferred to Troop I, May 12th.

Sinnett, Lee, Maizeville, W. Va.
  Transferred to Troop I, May 12th.

Tait, John H., Raton, N.M.
  Transferred to Troop I, May 12th.

Peabody, Harry, Raton, N.M.
  Transferred to Troop I, May 12th.

McGowan, Alexander, Gallup,
    N.M.
  Transferred to Troop I, May 12th.

Brown, John, Gallup, N.M.
  Transferred to Troop I, May 12th.

Crockett, Joseph B., Raton, N.M.
  Transferred to Troop I, May 12th.

## TROOP H.

### Captain George Curry.

George Curry . . . . . . . . . . . Captain . . . . . . . . . Tularosa, N.M.
William H. Kelly . . . . . . . . 1st Lieutenant . . . . East Las Vegas, N.M.
Charles L. Ballard . . . . . . . . 2d Lieutenant . . . . Roswell, N.M.
Green A. Settle . . . . . . . . . . 1st Sergeant . . . . . . Jackson Co., Ky.
Nevin P. Gutilius . . . . . . . . Sergeant . . . . . . . . Tularosa, N.M.
William A. Mitchell . . . . . . Sergeant . . . . . . . . El Paso, Tex.
Oscar de Montell . . . . . . . . Sergeant . . . . . . . . Roswell, N.M.
Thomas Darnell . . . . . . . . . Sergeant . . . . . . . . Denver, Col.
Willis J. Physioc . . . . . . . . . Sergeant . . . . . . . . Columbia, S.C.
Michael C. Rose . . . . . . . . . Sergeant . . . . . . . . Silver City, N.M.
Nova A. Johnson . . . . . . . . Sergeant . . . . . . . . Roswell, N.M.
Morton M. Morgan . . . . . . Corporal . . . . . . . . Silver City, N.M.
Arthur E. Williams . . . . . . . Corporal . . . . . . . . Las Cruces, N.M.
Frank Murray . . . . . . . . . . . Corporal . . . . . . . . Roswell, N.M.
Morgan O. B. Lewellyn . . . Corporal . . . . . . . . Las Cruces, N.M.
James C. Hamilton . . . . . . . Corporal . . . . . . . . Roswell, N.M.
George F. Jones . . . . . . . . . Corporal . . . . . . . . El Paso, Tex.
Charles P. Cochran . . . . . . . Corporal . . . . . . . . Eddy, N.M.
John M. Kelly. . . . . . . . . . . Corporal . . . . . . . . El Paso, Tex.
Robert E. Ligon . . . . . . . . . Trumpeter. . . . . . . Beaumont, Tex.
Gaston R. Dehumy. . . . . . . Trumpeter. . . . . . . Sante Fé, N.M.
Uriah Sheard . . . . . . . . . . . Blacksmith . . . . . . El Paso, Tex.
Robert L. Martin . . . . . . . . Farrier. . . . . . . . . . Sante Fé, N.M.
John Shaw . . . . . . . . . . . . . Saddler . . . . . . . . . Scott Co., Iowa.
Taylor B. Lewis . . . . . . . . . Wagoner . . . . . . . . Las Cruces, N.M.

### TROOPERS.

Allison, Jovillo, Bentonville, Ark.
Amonette, Albert B., Roswell, N.M.
Bendy, Cecil C., El Paso, Tex.
Black, Columbus L., Las Cruces, N.M.
Bryan, John B., Las Cruces, N.M.
Bogardus, Frank, Las Cruces, N.M.
Brown, Percy, Spring Hill, Tenn.
Baker, Philip S., Clinton, Ia.
Bullard, John W., Guadaloupe, Tex.
Connell, Thomas J., Bennett, Tex.
Corbett, Thomas F., Roswell, N.M.
Cornish, Thomas J., Freestone, Tex.
Crawford, Clinton K., Cincinnati, O.
Cone, John S., Tularosa, N.M.
Duran, Abel B., Silver City, N.M.
Duran, Jose L., Sante Fé, N.M.
Dorsey, Lewis, Silver City, N.M.
Doty, George B., Santa Fé, N.M.

Dunkle, Frederick W., East Las Vegas, N.M.

Douglas, Arthur L., Eddy, N.M.

Eaton, Frank A., Silver City, N.M.

Fletcher, Augustus C., Silver City, N.M.

Frye, Obey B., Flagstaff, Ariz.

Gasser, Louis, El Paso, Tex.

George, Ira W., Quincy, Ill.

Grisby, James B., Deming, N.M.

Hamilton, James M., Deming, N.M.

Herring, Leary O., Silver City, N.M.

Hunt, Le Roy R., Cincinnati, O.

Houston, Robert C., Hillsboro, N.M.

James, Frank W., Marion Co., Ga.

Johnson, Charles, Lund, Sweden.

Johnson, Harry F., Beaumont, Tex.

Johnson, Lewis L., Beaumont, Tex.

Kehoe, Michael J., Ottawa, Canada.

Kehn, Amandus, Silver City, N.M.

Kinnebrugh, Ollie A., El Paso, Tex.

Kendall, Harry J., Coldsborg, Ky.

Lawson, Frank H., Las Cruces, N.M.

Lewis, Adelbert, Beaver Co., Utah.

Lannon, John, Hillsboro, N.M.

Mooney, Thomas A., Silver City, N.M.

Moneckton, William J., San Antonio, Tex.

McAdams, Joel H., Mt. Pilia, Tenn.

McAdams, Richard P., Mt. Pilia, Tenn.

McCarty, Frederick J., Mentzville, Mo.

Murray, George F., Deming, N.M.

Nobles, William H., Silver City, N.M.

Neff, Nettleton, Cincinnati, O.

Owens, Clay T., El Paso, Tex.

Ott, Charles H., Silver City, N.M.

Pace, John, Bentonville, Ark.

Pipkins, Price.

Powell, Lory H., Roswell, N.M.

Pronger, Norman W., Silver City, N.M.

Pollock, John F., Tularosa, N.M.

Piersol, James M., Osborne, Mo.

Roberson, James R., Belle Co., Tex.

Rutherford, Bruce H., Pana, Ill.

Regan, John J., Beaumont, Tex.

Sharp, Emerson E., Wanamaker, Tenn.

Stewart, Newtown, El Paso, Tex.

Scroggins, Oscar, Logan Co., Ill.

St. Clair, Edward C., New Orleans, La.

Saucier, Harry S., New Orleans, La.

Schutt, Henry, Warren, Pa.

Sawyer, Benjamin, Hillsboro, Ill.

Thompson, Alexander M., Deming, N.M.

Traynor, William S., Wilcox, Ariz.

Thomas, Theodore C., Leavenworth, Kan.

Waggoner, Daniel G., Roswell, N.M.

Waggoner, Curtis C., Roswell, N.M.

Wilson, Charles E., Boulder, Col.

Wilkinson, Samuel I., Cincinnati, O.

Woodson, Pickens E., Honey Grove, Tex.

Wheeler, Frank G., Chautauqua Co., N.Y.

Wickham, Patrick A., Socorro, N.M.

## DISCHARGED.

Rynerson, William L. . . . . . . Sergeant . . . . . . . . . . Las Cruces, N.M.
 Discharged from service of U.S. Army by reason of special order No. 145 Hd.
 Qrs., U.S. Army, Washington, D.C.

## TRANSFERRED.

John B. Wiley . . . . . . . . . . . . Sergeant . . . . . . . . . .
 Transferred to Troop I, May 12, 1898.
Joseph F. Kansky . . . . . . . . . Sergeant . . . . . . . . . .
John V. Morrison . . . . . . . . . Sergeant . . . . . . . . . . Santa Fé, N.M.
 Transferred to Troop I, May 12, 1898.

### PRIVATES.

Lee, Robert E., Donabua, N.M.
 Transferred to Troop I, May 12, 1898.
Bennett, Orton A., Jack Co., Tex.
 Transferred to Troop I, May 12, 1898.
Brito, Jose, El Paso, Tex.
 Transferred to Troop I, May 12, 1898.
Brito, Frank C., El Paso, Tex.
 Transferred to Troop I, May 12, 1898.
Cate, James S., Grape Vine, Tex.
 Transferred to Troop I, May 12, 1898.
Casad, C. Darwin, Las Cruces, N.M.
 Transferred to Troop I, May 12, 1898.
Dolan, Thomas P., Ticonderoga, N.Y.
 Transferred to Troop I, May 12, 1898.
Farrell, Frederick P., El Paso, Tex.
 Transferred to Troop I, May 12, 1898.
Frenger, Muna C., Las Cruces, N.M.
 Transferred to Troop I, May 12, 1898.
Hermeyer, Ernest H., Germany
 Transferred to Troop I, May 12, 1898.
Jopling, Cal., Hamilton Co., Tex.
 Transferred to Troop I, May 12, 1898.

Nehmer, William, Staten, Germany.
 Transferred to Troop I, May 12, 1898.
Roediger, August, Charlotte, N.C.
 Transferred to Troop I, May 12, 1898.
Schafer, George, Pinos Altos, N.M.
 Transferred to Troop I, May 12, 1898.
Storms, Morris J., Roswell, N.M.
 Transferred to Troop I, May 12, 1898.
Sullivan, William J., Manchester, Va.
 Transferred to Troop I, May 12, 1898.
Fritz, William H., Windsor, Conn.
 Transferred to Troop I, May 12, 1898.
Eberman, Henry J., Bremen, Germany.
 Transferred from Troop K to Troop H, May 16, 1898. Re-transferred to K, June 8, 1898. Died.
Bucklin, E. W., Chautauqua Co., N.Y.
 Transferred to Troop L, June 8, 1898.
Wright, Grant, Cold Springs, N.Y.
 Transferred to Troop L, June 8, 1898.

### DIED.

Gosling, Frederick W. . . . . . . . . . . . . . . . . . . . . . Bedfordshire, Eng.
 Died in hospital at Camp Wikoff, N.Y., Aug. 19, 1898.
Casey, Edwin Eugene . . . . . . . . . . . . . . . . . . . . . Las Cruces, N.M.
 Died in hospital at Camp Wikoff, N.Y., Sept. 1, 1898.

Ewell, Edward A. . . . . . . . . . . . . . . . . . . . . . . . Adrian, Ill.
    Deserted, June 28, 1898, at Tampa, Fla.

Miller, Samuel . . . . . . . . . . . . . . . . . . . . . . . . . Roswell, N.M.
    Deserted, June 28, 1898, at Tampa, Fla.

## TROOP I.

### Captain Schuyler A. McGinnis.

Schuyler A. McGinnis . . Captain . . . . . . Newkirk, O.T.
Frederick W. Wintge . . . 1st Lieutenant . . Sante Fé, Mex.
Samuel Grenwald. . . . . . 2d Lieutenant . . Prescott, Ariz.
John B. Wylie . . . . . . . . 1st Sergeant . . . Fort Bayard, N. Mex.
Schuyler C. Morgan. . . . Q. M. Sergeant . Durango, Col.
John V. Morrison . . . . . Sergeant. . . . . . Springerville, Ariz.
William R. Reber. . . . . . Sergeant. . . . . .
Basil M. Ricketts . . . . . . Sergeant. . . . . . Lambs' Club, N.Y.
Percival Gassett . . . . . . . Sergeant. . . . . . Dedham, Mass.
James S. Cate. . . . . . . . . Sergeant. . . . . . Grape Vine, Tex.
William H. Waffensmith . Sergeant. . . . . . Raton, N.M.
August Roediger . . . . . . Corporal . . . . . Charlotte, N.C.
Numa C. Freuger. . . . . . Corporal . . . . . Las Cruces, N. Mex.
William J. Sullivan. . . . . Corporal . . . . . Silver City, N.M.
William J. Nehmer. . . . . Corporal . . . . . Silver City, N.M.
Abraham L. Bainter . . . . Corporal . . . . . Colorado Springs, Col.
Hiram T. Brown . . . . . . Corporal . . . . . Albuquerque, N.M.
Errickson M. Nichols. . . Corporal. . . . . . 52 E. 78th St., New York City
George M. Kerney. . . . . Corporal . . . . . Globe, Ariz.
Robert E. Lea . . . . . . . . Trumpeter . . . . Dona Ana, N.M.
Clarence H. Underwood . Trumpeter . . . . Colorado Springs, Col.
Charles A. Nehmer . . . . Blacksmith . . . . Chicago, Ill.
Hayes Donnelly. . . . . . . Farrier . . . . . . . Jefferson, O.T.
Leo G. Rogers. . . . . . . . Saddler. . . . . . . Bogart, Mo.
Everett E. Holt . . . . . . . Wagoner . . . . . Coffeyville, Kan.

### TROOPERS.

Alexis, George D., New Orleans, La.
Arendt, Henry J., Hoboken, N.J.
Armstrong, Charles M.
Adkins, Joseph R.
Bates, William H.
Barrowe, Hallett A.
Bawcom, Joseph L., Bisbee, Ariz.

Bennett, Horton A., Tularosa, N.M.

Brito, Frank C., Pinos Altos, N.M.

Brito, Jose, Los Angeles, Cal.

Brush, Charles A., Hanford, Cal.

Bassage, Albert C., Corning, N.Y.

Casad, Charles D., Mesilla, N.M.

Cloud, William.

Crockett, Joseph B., Topeka, Kan.

Coe, George M., Albuquerque, N.M.

Clark, Frank M., Hiawatha, Kan.

Davis, Henry C., Santa Fé, N.M.

Dolan, Thomas P., Pinos Altos, N.M.

Denny, Robert W., Raton, Mex.

Duke, Henry K., Lipscomb, Tex.

Evans, Evan, Gallup, N.M.

Fennel, William A., Reunion, Md.

Flynn, Joseph F., Albuquerque, N.M.

Geiger, Percy A., Durango, Col.

Gooch, John R., Sante Fé, N.M.

Groves, Oscar W., Raton, N.M.

Goodrich, Ben Hedric.

Giller, Alfred C. Topeka, Kan.

Hermeyer, Ernest H., Roswell, N.M.

Hickey, Walter, Wishua, N.H.

Hogan, Michael.

Jones, William H., Raton, N.M.

Jopling, Cal, La Luz, N.M.

King, Harry B., Raton, N.M.

Larsen, Louis.

Love, William J., Jersey City, N.J.

McCoy, John, Monrovia, Cal.

McGowan, Alexander, Gallup, N.M.

Martin, John, Decanter, Ill.

Miller, Edwin H., Junction City, Kan.

Miller, David R.

Miller, Jacob H., Needles, Cal.

Morgan, U. S. Grant, Durango, Col.

Morris, Ben F. T., Raton, N.M.

Moore, Roscoe E., Raton, N.M.

North, Franklin H., 2 W. 35th St., New York City

O'Dell, William W., Parkersburg, W. Va.

Peabody, Harry, Raton, N.M.

Pierce, Edward, Chicago, Ill.

Price, Stewart R., Plattsburg, Mo.

Rafalowitz, Hyman, Philadelphia, Pa.

Roberts, John P., Clayton, N.M.

Reisig, Max, Y. M. C. A., St. Louis, Mo.

Raulett, Charles, New Orleans, La.

Reidy, John, Ottawa, Kan.

Shornhorst, Carl J. Jr.

Schafer, George, Pinos Altos, N.M.

Sennett, Lee, Marysville, W. Va.

Storms, Morris J., Centerpoint, Tex.

Spencer, Edward John, Clay County, Tex.

Tait, John H.

Temple, Frank, Lafayette, Ind.

Torbett, John T., Yale, Kan.

Tritz, William H., Windsor, Conn.

Townsend, Charles M., Faribault, Minn.

Twyman, John L., Raton, N.M.

Thompson, George.

Williams, Thomas C.

Wiley, Harry B., Santa Fé, N.M.

Wisenberg, Roy O., Raton, N.M.

Zeigler, Daniel J., Como, Mont.

## DISCHARGED.

arry R. . . . . . . . . . . Private . . . . . . . . . Tampa, Fla.
ged at Tampa, Fla., Aug. 5, 1898, per S. O. 153 A. G. O., dated June 30,
and final statements forwarded to A. G. O., Washington, D.C.,
. 3, 1898.

Howard G. . . . . . . . . Private . . . . . . . .
arge to date from Aug. 23, 1898.

## TRANSFERRED.

d, Alfred O. . . . . . . . . . . 1st Sergeant. . . . . .
Transferred, July 18, 1898, to 2d Army Corps, Camp Alger, per telegraphic instructions A. G. O., Washington, D.C.

Cowdin, Elliot C. . . . . . . . . . . Corporal . . . . . . . .
Transferred to Troop L 1st U.S. Vol. Cav., to date June 7, 1898, per verbal order
Reg. Commander.

Fish, Hamilton Jr. . . . . . . . . . Sergeant . . . . . . . .
Transferred to Troop L 1st U.S. Vol. Cav., June 7, 1898, per verbal order Reg.
Commander. Killed in battle, June 24, 1898.

Wilson, Charles A. . . . . . . . . . Private . . . . . . . . .
Transferred to Hosp. Corps 1st U.S. Vol. Cav., June 7, 1898, verbal order Reg.
Commander.

Greenway, John C. . . . . . . . . . 2d Lieutenant . . . .
Promoted 1st Lieut. Troop A 1st U.S. Vol. Cav.

Bailey, Harry C. . . . . . . . . . . . Private . . . . . . . . .
Transferred back to Troop G, Sept. 1, 1898, per verbal order Reg. Commander.

## DIED.

Tiffany, William . . . . . . . . . . . 2d Lieutenant . . . .
Died Aug. 26, 1898.

## DESERTED.

Saville, Michael . . . . . . . . . . Private . . . . . . . . .
Deserted from Camp Wikoff, L. I., Aug. 20, 1898.

Brown, John . . . . . . . . . . . . . Private . . . . . . . . .
Deserted while en route from Camp Wood, San Antonio, Tex., to camp at
Tampa, Fla., June 3, 1898.

Farrell, Fred. P. . . . . . . . . . . Private . . . . . . . . .
Deserted while en route from Camp Wood, San Antonio, Tex., to camp at
Tampa, Fla., June 3, 1898.

# TROOP K.

## CAPTAIN WOODBURY KANE.

Woodbury Kane . . . . Captain . . . . . . 319 Fifth Ave., New York City.
Joseph A. Carr. . . . . . 1st Lieutenant . . 2127 R. St., Washington, D.C.
Horace K. Devereux . 2d Lieutenant . . Colorado Springs, Col.
Wounded at San Juan, July 1, 1898; forearm and arm; Mauser rifle.

Frederik K. Lie . . . . . . 1st Sergeant. . Orgun P.O., N.M.
Thaddeus Higgins . . . . Sergeant. . . . . 210 W. 104th St., New York
Reginald Ronalds . . . . Sergeant . . . . Knickerbocker Club, N.Y. C
Samuel G. Devore . . . . Sergeant . . . . Wheeling, W. Va.
    Wounded at El Poso, July 1st; left forearm; sharpnel.
Philip K. Sweet . . . . . . Sergeant . . . . 226 W. 121st St., New York City
William J. Breen . . . . . Sergeant . . . . 510 E. 144th St., New York City.
Craig W. Wadsworth. . Sergeant . . . . Geneseo, N.Y.
Henry W. Buel . . . . . . Sergeant . . . . 319 Fifth Ave., New York City.
James B. Tailor . . . . . . Corporal. . . . Ardsley on Hudson, N.Y.
Joseph S. Stevens. . . . . Corporal . . . . Narragansett Ave., Newport, R.I.
Maxwell Norman. . . . . Corporal. . . . Newport, R.I.
Edwin Coakley . . . . . . Corporal. . . . Prescott, Ariz.
George Kerr, Jr. . . . . . Corporal. . . . East Downington, Pa.
Henry S. Van Schaick . Corporal. . . . 100 Broadway, New York City.
Frederick Herrig . . . . . Corporal. . . . Pleasant Valley, Kalispel,
                                   Flat Head Co., Mont.
Oscar Land . . . . . . . . Trumpeter . . 720 S. 8th St., Denver, Col.
George W. Knoblauch . Trumpeter . . 205 W. 57th St., New York City.
Benjamin A. Long . . . . Saddler . . . . . New York City.
    Wounded at El Poso, July 1st; left thigh.
Thomas G. Bradley . . . Farrier . . . . . . Potomac, Montgomery Co., Md.
George T. Crucius . . . . Blacksmith. . . 50 Amanda St., Montgomery, Ala.
Lee Burdwell. . . . . . . Wagoner. . . . Langtry, Tex.

### TROOPERS.

Armstrong, James T.

Adams, John H., Selma, Ala.
    Wounded, July 1st.

Bell, Sherman, Colorado Springs, Col.

Bernard, William C., Las Vegas, N.M.

Batchelder, Wallace N., Chester, Pa.

Bump, Arthur L., New London, O.
    Slightly wounded, July 1st.

Cameron, Charles H., McDonald, Pa.

Campbell, Douglass.

Cash, Walter S., Colorado Springs, Col.
    Wounded, July 1st; arm, slight; Mauser rifle.

Cooke, Henry B.

Carroll, John F., Hillsboro, Tex.

Cartmell, Nathaniel M., Lexington, Va.

Clagett, Jesse C., Moters Station, Frederick Co., Md.

Corbe, Max C., El Paso, Tex.

Coville, Allen M., Topeka, Kan.

Crowninshield, Francis B., Marblehead, Mass.

Channing, Roscoe A., 34 Park Place, New York City.

Daniels, Benjamin F., Colorado Springs, Col.

Davis, John, care W. S. Dickinson, Tarpon Springs, Fla.

Easton, Stephen, Santa Fé, N.M.

Eberman, Edwin.

Emerson, Edwin, *Collier's Weekly*, New York City.

Flemming, Clarence A.

Fetcher, Henry, Green Point, Cumberland Co., Pa.

Folk, Theodore, Oklahoma City, O.T.

Freeman, Elisha L., Burden, Kan.

Holden, Prince A., Grayson Co., Tex.

Hulme, Robert A., El Reno, O.T.

James, William F., San Antonio, Tex.

Jordan, Andrew M., Rossa, Tex.

Kania, Frank, Jamestown, N.D.

Langdon, Jesse D., Fargo, N.D.

Marshall, Creighton, 1807 G St., N. W., Washington, D.C.

Maverick, Lewis, San Antonio, Tex.

McGinty, William, Stillwater, O.T.

McKoy, William J., Oshkosh, Wis.

Mitchell, Mason, Lambs' Club, New York City.
  Wounded at El Poso, July 1st; left arm, slight; shrapnel.

Mitchell, William H., Salem, Mass.

Montgomery, Lawrence N., Hempstead, Tex.

Nicholson, Charles P., 1617 John St., Baltimore, Md.

Norris, Edmund S., Guthrie, O.T.

Poey, Alfred.

Pollak, Albin J.

Quaid, William, Newberg, N.Y.

Robinson, Kenneth D., 55 Liberty St., New York City.
  Wounded on July 1st; right side, severe; Mauser rifle.

Reed, Colton, San Antonio, Tex.

Smith, Frederick, Guthrie, O.T.

Smith, George L., Frankfort, Mich.

Smith, Joseph S., 1322 Brown St., Philadelphia, Pa.

Smith, Clarke T., 2008 Wallace St., Philadelphia, Pa.

Stockton, Richard, 218 W. Jersey St., Elizabeth, N.J.

Stephens, Oregon, Purdy, I.T.

Thorp, Henry, Southampton, L.I.

Test, Clarence L., Austin, Tex.
  Transferred from 3d Penn. Inf. and reported for duty with troop at Montauk Point, Aug. 25th.

Toy, J. Frederick, 602 S. 42d St., Philadelphia, Pa.
  Transferred from 3d Penn. Inf. and reported for duty with troops at Montauk Point, Aug. 25th.

Tudor, William, 37 Brimer St., Boston, Mass.

Venable, Warner M., Stephenville, Tex.

Wiberg, Axel E.

Weitzel, John F., care Windsor Hotel, Newkirk, O.T.

Wilson, Frank M., Guthrie, O.T.

Woodward, John A., Taylor, Tex.

Wright, Grant, Cold Springs, N.Y.

Young, James E., 628 W. 37th St., Los Angeles, Cal.

### DISCHARGED.

Maloon, Winthrop L..... Private.....
  Discharged per S. O. No. 141, A. G. O. Dated June 6th.

McMasters, Frederick D. . Private.....
  Discharged per S. O. No. 178, A. G. O. Dated July 30th, Washington, D.C.

Ferguson, Robert M. .... Sergeant ... 55 Liberty St., New York City.
  Discharged, Aug. 10th, 1898.

Worden, John L. . . . . . . . Private . . . . . 27 W. 43d St., New York City.
Discharged by way of favor per telegraphic order from Assistant Secretary of War. Dated Aug. 15th, Washington, D.C.

Cosby, Arthur F. . . . . . . . Private. . . . .
Discharged per S. O. No. 103, A. G. O., Aug. 17th, Washington, D.C., to enable the soldier to accept a commission. Wounded, July 1st; right hand.

Babcock, Campbell E.. . . . Private. . . . . The Plaza, Chicago, Ill.
Discharged, Sept. 5th, to accept commission.

Lee, Joseph J.. . . . . . . . . . Private. . . . . Knoxville, Md.
Discharged per S. O. No. 205, A. G. O., Washington, D.C., Aug. 31st.

## TRANSFERRED.

Duran, Joseph L. . . . . . . . . Private. . . . . . . . . . . . . Santa Fé, N.M.
Transferred to Troop H, this regiment, July 15th.

Brandon, Perry H. . . . . . . . Private. . . . . . . . . . . . . Douglass, Kan.
Transferred to Troop D, this regiment, July 29th.

David M. Goodrich . . . . . . 1st Lieutenant . . . . . . . . Akron, O.
Transferred from Troop D, this regiment, Aug. 11th. Transferred to Troop D, this regiment, Sept. 5th.

## DIED.

Haywood, Henry. . . Sergeant. . . . Police Department, New York City.
Abdomen; Mauser rifle; killed, July 2d. Wounded, July 1st; died in Division Hospital, Cuba, July 2, 1898, from bullet wound received July 1st.

Ives, Gerard M. . . . . Private. . . . . New York
Died at his home, 338 W. 71st St., New York City (date not known), from typhoid fever.

Tiffany, William. . . . Lieutenant. . New York City.
Died of fever.

## DESERTED.

Staley, Frank . . . . . . Private. . . . .
Deserted from troop at San Antonio, Tex., May 1st.

Curzon . . . . . . . . . . Private. . . . .
Deserted from detachment at Tampa, Fla., June 13th.

## PROMOTED.

Jenkins, Micah J. . . . Major . . . . . Youngs Island, S.C.
Promoted to Major, Aug. 11, 1898.

## TROOP L.

### Captain Richard C. Day.

Richard C. Day. . . . . . . . . Captain . . . . . . . . . . . Vinita, I.T.
Shot through left shoulder on line of duty at San Juan. Left shoulder and arm, severe; Mauser rifle.

John R. Thomas . . . . . . . . 1st Lieutenant. . . . . . . Muscogee, I.T.
G. S. wound in right lower leg at Las Guasimas, June 24th. G. S. right leg.

Frank P. Hayes . . . . . . . . . . 2d Lieutenant . . . . . . . San Antonio, Tex.

Elhanan W. Bucklin . . . . . . 1st Sergeant . . . . . . . . Jamestown, N.Y.

Jerome W. Henderlider. . . . Sergeant. . . . . . . . . . Saranac, Mich.

William M. Simms . . . . . . . Sergeant. . . . . . . . . . Vinita, I.T.
Wounded at San Juan, July 1, 1898, in line of duty. Leg; Mauser rifle.

Joe A. Kline . . . . . . . . . . . . Sergeant. . . . . . . . . . Vinita, I.T.
Wounded at San Juan, July 1st, in line of duty. Leg; Mauser rifle.

William W. Carpenter. . . . . Sergeant. . . . . . . . . . Vinita, I.T.
Wounded at San Juan, July 1st, in line of duty. Left thigh; Mauser rifle.

James McKay . . . . . . . . . . Sergeant. . . . . . . . . . Vinita, I.T.

Dillwyn M. Bell . . . . . . . . Sergeant. . . . . . . . . . Guthrie, O.T.
Hurt in back by fragment of shell at El Paso, July 1st. Contusion back, slight; shrapnel.

James E. McGuire . . . . . . . Sergeant. . . . . . . . . . Chelsea, I.T.

George H. Seaver . . . . . . . . Corporal . . . . . . . . . Muscogee, I.T.
Wounded at El Poso, July 2, 1898, in line of duty. Right foot, slight; Mauser rifle.

John W. Davis . . . . . . . . . . Corporal . . . . . . . . . Vinita, I.T.
Wounded at San Juan, July 1, 1898. Right leg and arm; Mauser rifle.

Samuel G. Davis . . . . . . . . Corporal . . . . . . . . . Sardis, Ark.
Wounded at San Juan, July 1, 1898.

Bud Parnell . . . . . . . . . . . . Corporal . . . . . . . . . Muscogee, I.T.

Joseph J. Roger . . . . . . . . . Corporal . . . . . . . . . Tillou, Ark.
Wounded at San Juan, July 1, 1898. Abdomen and arm; Mauser rifle.

George B. Dunnigan. . . . . . Corporal . . . . . . . . . Vinita, I.T.

Maynard R. Williams . . . . Corporal . . . . . . . . . Fairland, I.T.

Elliot C. Cowdin . . . . . . . . Corporal . . . . . . . . . New York City.

Mike Kinney. . . . . . . . . . . Blacksmith . . . . . . . . Imlay, Mich.

John R. Kean . . . . . . . . . . Farrier . . . . . . . . . . . Maxwell, Ont.
Wounded at Las Guasimas, June 24th. G. S. left shoulder and lungs.

Nicholas H. Cochran . . . . . Wagoner . . . . . . . . . Vinita, I.T.

Guy M. Babcock. . . . . . . . Saddler . . . . . . . . . . . Cherryville, Kan.

Thomas F. Meagher . . . . . . Trumpeter . . . . . . . . Muscogee, I.T.
Wounded at Las Guasimas, June 24th. G. S. left forearm.

Frank R. McDonald . . . . . . Trumpeter . . . . . . . . Oolagah, I.T.
Wounded at San Juan, July 1, 1898. Head; Mauser rifle.

TROOPERS.

Adair, John M., Claremore, I.T.
Benson, Victor H.
Carey, Oren E., Clonau, Ia.
Chilcoot, Frederick, Howels, Neb.
Cook, James, Cherokee City, Ark.
Cruse, James, St. Joe, Ark.
Culver, Ed., Muscogee, I.T.
  Wounded at Las Guasimas,
    June 24th. G. S. breast.
Davis, James C., Waggone, I.T.
Damet, John P., Alexander, S.D.
  Wounded at Las Guasimas,
    June 24th. G. S. left shoulder.
Dennis, David C., Nelson, Mo.
Dobson, William H., Muscogee,
  I.T.
Ennis, Richard L., Cornell, Ill.
Evans, James R., Baldwin, Ark.
Gilmore, Maurice E., Muscogee,
  I.T.
Haley, Robert M., Wagoner, I.T.
Hawkins, Charles D., Vinita, I.T.
Heagert, Rudolph, Vinita, I.T.
Holderman, Bert. T., Artopa, Kan.
Hughes, Frank, Vinita, I.T.
Hughes, William E., Vinita, I.T.
Isbell, Thomas J., Vinita, I.T.
  Wounded at Las Guasimas, June 25th.
    G. S. neck, hip, and thumb.
Jones, Levi, Vinita, I.T.
Johns, William S., Hemasville, Mo.
Kinkade, Elyah S., Muscogee, I.T.
Knox, Robert G., Clinton, La.
Lawrence, Richard, La Porte, Ind.
Lane, Edward K., Chetopa, Kan.
Lane, Sanford J., Saupulpa, I.T.
Lentz, Edward, Bowling Green, O.
Lewis, Frank A., Newark, N.J.
Little, Rollie L., West Fork, Ark.
McDonald, Asa W., Bearing Cross,
  Ark.
McCamish, Andrew L., Bethel,
  Kan.

Miller, John S., Garrison, Neb.
Miller, Boot, Chelsea, I.T.
Moore, John J., Vinita, I.T.
Oskison, Richard L., Vinita, I.T.
  Wounded at San Juan, July 1st. Left
    leg; Mauser rifle.
Owens, Edward L., Vinita, I.T.
Parker, Ora E., Dickins, Ia.
  Wounded near Santiago de Cuba,
    July 1, 2, or 3, 1898. Right thigh,
    severe; shrapnel.
Pulley, William O., Marion, Ill.
Philpot, Leigh T., Bryson, Ky.
Poe, Nathaniel M., Adair, I.T.
  Wounded at Las Guasimas,
    June 24th. G. S. foot.
Price, Benjamin W., Eufaula, I.T.
Rich, Allen K., Fort Gibson, I.T.
Robertson, George W., Muscogee,
  I.T.
Robinson, Frank P., Borbora,
  Kan.
Russell, Daniel, Goodland, I.T.
Scobey, Arthur E., Willis Point,
  Tex.
  Wounded at San Juan Hill, June 1,
    1898. Right hand; Mauser rifle.
Sharp, Walter L., Chicago, Ill.
Skelton, James W., Trinity Mills,
  Tex.
Smith, Bert, Vinita, I.T.
Smith, Sylvester S., Vinita, I.T.
Stefens, Luke B., Rio Vista, I.T.
Stidham, Theodore E., Eufaula,
  I.T.
Swearinger, George, Maysville,
  Mo.
Taylor, Warren P., Hillsboro, Tex.
Thompson, Sylvester V.
  Wounded at San Juan, July 1, 1898.
    Left leg and arm; Mauser rifle.
Wetmore, Robert C., Montclair,
  N.J.

Whitney, Schuyler C., Pryor Creek, I.T. Wounded at Las Guasimas, June 24th. G. S. neck.

Wilkins, George W., Vinita, I.T.
Wilson, James E., Madrid, Mo.
Winn, Arthur N., Muscogee, I.T.

### DISCHARGED.

Hutchinson, Charles A. . . . Private. . . . . . . . . . .
Price, Walter W. . . . . . . . . Private. . . . . . . . . . .
Hayes, Frank P. . . . . . . . . . 1st Sergeant . . . . . . .
Discharged, June 24, 1898, to enable him to accept commission as 2d Lieut. in 1st U.S. Vol. Cav.

### TRANSFERRED.

Robert, William J. . . . . . . . Private. . . . . . . . . . .
Transferred to Troop M, June 7, 1898, by order Col. Wood.
Byrne, John. . . . . . . . . . . Sergeant . . . . . . . . . Vinita, I.T.
Transferred to Troop F, July 10, 1898, by order Col. Wood.

### DIED.

Capron, Allyn K. . . . . . . . . Captain . . . . . . . . . Fort Sill, Okla.
Killed at battle of Las Guasimas, June 24, 1898. G. S. lungs.
Fish, Hamilton . . . . . . . . . Sergeant . . . . . . . . . New York City.
Killed at battle of Las Guasimas, June 24, 1898. G. S. heart.
Dawson, Tilden W. . . . . . . Private. . . . . . . . . . . Vinita, I.T.
Killed at battle of Las Guasimas, June 24, 1898. G. S. head.
Santo, William T. . . . . . . . Private. . . . . . . . . . . Chouteau, I.T.
Killed at battle of San Juan, July 1, 1898. Mauser rifle.
Hendricks, Milo A. . . . . . . Private. . . . . . . . . . . Muscogee, I.T.
Mortally wounded at battle of San Juan, July 1st; died in hospital, July 6, 1898. Mauser rifle.
Enyart, Silas R. . . . . . . . . . Private. . . . . . . . . . . Sapulpa, I.T.
Mortally wounded at San Juan, July 1st; died in hosptial, July 6, 1898.

## TROOP M.

### CAPTAIN ROBERT H. BRUCE.

Robert H. Bruce . . . . . . . . Captain . . . . . . . . . . Mineola, Tex.
Ode C. Nichols . . . . . . . . . 1st Lieutenant . . . . . Durant, I.T.
Albert S. Johnson . . . . . . . 2d Lieutenant . . . . . . Oklahoma City, O.T.
Harry E. Berner. . . . . . . . . 1st Sergeant . . . . . . . Durant, I.T.
Joseph L. Smith. . . . . . . . . Q. M. Sergeant . . . . Caddo, I.T.
William E. Lloyd. . . . . . . . Sergeant . . . . . . . . . Durant, I.T.
Frederick E. Nichols . . . . . Sergeant . . . . . . . . . Purcell, I.T.
Morency A. Hawkins. . . . . Sergeant . . . . . . . . . Tioga, Tex.

| | | |
|---|---|---|
| Wilbert L. Poole | Sergeant | Durant, I.T. |
| Otis B. Weaver | Sergeant | Mt. Vernon, Tex. |
| Henry C. Foley | Sergeant | Muscogee, I.T. |
| Samuel Downing | Corporal | Atoka, I.T. |
| Charles S. Lynch | Corporal | Caddo, I.T. |
| John N. Jackson | Corporal | Caddo, I.T. |
| Frank U. Talman | Corporal | So. McAlester, I.T. |
| Hiram S. Creech | Corporal | Durant, I.T. |
| Charles J. Fandru | Corporal | Caddo, I.T. |
| Theodore E. Schulz | Corporal | Tampa, Fla. |
| William G. Jones | Corporal | Ardmore, I.T. |
| Frank Marion | Trumpeter | Muscogee, I.T. |
| Charles J. Hokey | Trumpeter | Krebs, I.T. |
| John McMullen | Wagoner | Ardmore, I.T. |
| John Hall | Farrier | Durant, I.T. |
| Cragg Parsons | Blacksmith | Ardmore, I.T. |
| Luther M. Kiethly | Saddler | Hartshorn, I.T. |
| Samuel Young | Chief Cook | Caddo, I.T. |

## TROOPERS.

Allaun, Jacob, Sapulpa, I.T.
Byrd, Samuel J. W., Muscogee, I.T.
Boydstun, John F., Caddo, I.T.
Barlow, John W., Caddo, I.T.
Barrington, John P., Ardmore, I.T.
Baird, Thompson M., Thurber, Tex.
Brierty, Thomas, Tampa, Fla.
Butler, Peter L., Kiowa, I.T.
Beal, Andy R., Durant, I.T.
Bruce, Peter R., Wagoner, I.T.
Brown, Leon, Ardmore, I.T.
Barney, Leland, Ardmore, I.T.
Burks, Jesse S., Ardmore, I.T.
Case, George, Durant, I.T.
Calhoun, Wesley, Durant, I.T.
Carter, Arthur E., Ardmore, I.T.
Carden, Horace W., Ardmore, I.T.
Cox, Walter, Durant, I.T.
Cooper, Bud G., Muscogee, I.T.
Dorell, Charles, Vinita, I.T.
Duping, Joseph, Muscogee, I.T.

Flying, Crawford D., Muscogee, I.T.
Fairman, Charles E., Ardmore, I.T.
Griffith, Ezra E., Sapulpa, I.T.
Garland, George W., Ardmore, I.T.
Hall, James T., Wagoner, I.T.
Hawes, Frederick W., Dennison, Tex.
Houchin, Willis C., Durant, I.T.
Hamilton, Troy, Hartshorne, I.T.
Howell, William, Muscogee, I.T.
Harris, Chester, Muscogee, I.T.
Hoffman, George B., Somerville, N.J.
Johnson, Bankston, Caddo, I.T.
Johnson, Charles L., Ardmore, I.T.
Johnson, Gordon, Birmingham, Ala.
Jones, Charles L., McAlester, I.T.
Keithly, Ora E., Hartshorn, I.T.
Kings, John, McAlester, I.T.
Kearns, Edward L., Tampa, Fla.

Mitchell, William, Wagoner, I.T.
Madden, Charles E., Brooken, I.T.
Murphy, William S., Caddo, I.T.
McPherren, Charles E., Caddo, I.T.
Maytubby, Bud, Caddo, I.T.
McDaniel, Thomas E., Muscogee, I.T.
McPherson, Charles E., Caddo, I.T.
Morrell, Robert W., Elizabeth, N.J.
Owens, John M., Oologah, I.T.
Pipkins, Virgil A., Brooken, I.T.
Rouse, John L., Durant, I.T.
Rose, Lewis W., Los Angeles, Cal.
Russell, Walter L., Caddo, I.T.
Rynerson, Benjamin A., Durant, I.T.
Reynolds, Benjamin F., Ardmore, I.T.
Ross, William E., Ardmore, I.T.
Roberts, William J., Vinita, I.T.
Sloane, Samuel P., So. McAlester, I.T.
Sykes, Marion, Muscogee, I.T.
Stewart, Henry J., Caddo, I.T.
Thomas, Jesse C., Caddo, I.T.
Tyler, Edwin, Ardmore, I.T.
Vickers, John W., So. McAlester, I.T.
Williams, Benjamin H., So. McAlester, I.T.
Williams, George W., Ardmore, I.T.
Wolfe, John W., Ardmore, I.T.
Webster, David, Durant, I.T.
Wagner, John D., Caddo, I.T.
Woog, Benjamin B., Washington, D.C.
de Zychlinski, William T., Bismarck, N.D.

### TRANSFERRED.

Lane, Sanford G.. . . . . . . . . . Trooper . . . . . . . . . . Sapulpa, I.T.
 Transferred to Troop L 1st U. S. V. C., June 8, 1898, per verbal order Reg. Com.

### DIED OF DISEASE.

Kyle, Yancy. . . . . . . . . . . . . Trooper . . . . . . . . . . McAlester, I.T.
 Died of typhoid fever at Tampa, July 15, 1898. Final statements rendered and
 settled per Capt. Bruce.

As said above, this is not a complete list of the wounded, or even of the dead, among the troopers. Moreover, a number of officers and men died from fever soon after the regiment was mustered out. Twenty-eight field and line officers landed in Cuba on June 22d; ten of them were killed or wounded during the nine days following. Of the five regiments of regular cavalry in the division, one, the Tenth, lost eleven officers; none of the others lost more than six. The loss of the Rough Riders in enlisted men was heavier than that of any other regiment in the cavalry division. Of the nine infantry regiments in Kent's division, one, the Sixth, lost eleven officers; none of the others as many as we did. None of the nine suffered as heavy a loss in enlisted men, as they were not engaged at Las Guasimas.

No other regiment in the Spanish-American War suffered as heavy a loss as the First United States Volunteer Cavalry.

# APPENDIX B

[BEFORE it was sent, this letter was read to and approved by every officer of the regiment who had served through the Santiago campaign.]

[Copy.]

CAMP WIKOFF, September 10, 1898.

TO THE SECRETARY OF WAR.

SIR: In answer to the circular issued by command of Major-General Shafter under date of September 8, 1898, containing a request for information by the Adjutant-General of September 7th, I have the honor to report as follows:

I am a little in doubt whether the fact that on certain occasions my regiment suffered for food, etc., should be put down to an actual shortage of supplies or to general defects in the system of administration. Thus, when the regiment arrived in Tampa after a four days' journey by cars from its camp at San Antonio, it received no food whatever for twenty-four hours, and as the travel rations had been completely exhausted, food for several of the troops was purchased by their officers, who, of course, have not been reimbursed by the Government. In the same way we were short one or two meals at the time of embarking at Port Tampa on the transport; but this I think was due, not to a failure in the quantity of supplies, but to the lack of system in embarkation.

As with the other regiments, no information was given in advance what transports we should take, or how we should proceed to get aboard, nor did anyone exercise any supervision over the embarkation. Each regimental commander, so far as I know, was left to find out as best he could, after he was down at the dock, what transport had not been taken, and then to get his regiment aboard it, if he was able, before some other regiment got it. Our regiment was told to go to a certain switch, and take a train for Port Tampa at twelve o'clock, midnight. The train never came. After three hours of waiting we were sent to another switch, and finally at six o'clock in the morning got possession of some coal-cars and came down in them. When we reached the quay where the embarkation was proceeding, everything was in utter confusion. The quay was piled with stores and swarming with thousands of men of different regiments, besides onlookers, etc. The commanding General, when we at last found him, told Colonel Wood and myself that he did not know what ship we were to embark on, and that we must find Colonel Humphrey, the Quartermaster-General. Colonel Humphrey was not in his office, and nobody knew where he was. The commanders of the different regiments were busy trying to find him, while their troops waited in the trains, so as to discover the ships to which they were allotted — some of these ships being at the dock and some in mid-stream. After a couple of hours' search, Colonel Wood found Colonel Humphrey and was allotted a ship. Immediately afterward I found that it had already been allotted to two other regiments. It was then coming to the dock. Colonel Wood boarded it in mid-stream to keep possession, while I double-quicked the men down from the cars and got there just ahead of the other two regiments. One of these regiments, I was afterward informed, spent the next thirty-six hours in cars in consequence. We suffered nothing beyond the loss of a couple of meals, which, it seems to me, can hardly be put down to any failure in the quantity of supplies furnished to the troops.

We were two weeks on the troop-ship Yucatan, and as we were given twelve days' travel rations, we of course fell short toward the end of the trip, but eked things out with some of our field rations and troop stuff. The quality of the travel rations given to us was good, except in the important item of meat. The canned roast beef is worse than a failure as part of the rations, for in effect it amounts to reducing the rations by just so much, as a great majority of the men find it uneatable. It was coarse, stringy, tasteless, and very disagreeable in appearance, and so unpalatable that the effort to eat it made some of the men sick. Most of the men preferred to be hungry rather than eat it. If cooked in a stew with plenty of onions and potatoes — *i.e.*, if only one ingredient in a dish with other more savory ingredients — it could be eaten, especially if well salted and peppered; but, as usual (what I regard as a great mistake), no salt was issued with the travel rations, and of course no potatoes and onions. There were no cooking facilities on the transport. When the men obtained any, it was by bribing the cook. Toward the last, when they began to draw on the field rations, they had to eat the bacon raw. On the return trip the same difficulty in rations obtained — *i.e.*, the rations were short because the men could not eat the canned roast beef, and had no salt. We purchased of the ship's supplies some flour and pork and a little rice for the men, so as to relive the shortage as much as possible, and individual sick men were helped from private sources by officers, who themselves ate what they had purchased in Santiago. As nine-tenths of the men were more or less sick, the unattractiveness of the travel rations was doubly unfortunate. It would have been an excellent thing for their health if we could have had onions and potatoes, and means for cooking them. Moreover, the water was very bad, and sometimes a cask was struck that was positively undrinkable. The lack of ice for the weak and sickly men was very much felt. Fortunately there was no epidemic, for there was not a place on the ship where patients could have been isolated.

During the month following the landing of the army in Cuba the food-supplies were generally short in quantity, and in quality were never such as were best suited to men undergoing severe hardships and great exposure in an unhealthy tropical climate. The rations were, I understand, the same as those used in the Klondike. In this connection, I call especial attention to the report of Captain Brown, made by my orders when I was Brigade-Commander, and herewith appended. I also call attention to the report of my own Quartermaster. Usually we received full rations of bacon and hardtack. The hardtack, however, was often mouldy, so that parts of cases, and even whole cases, could not be used. The bacon was usually good. But bacon and hardtack make poor food for men toiling and fighting in trenches under the midsummer sun of the tropics. The ration of coffee was often short, and that of sugar generally so; we rarely got any vegetables. Under these circumstances the men lost strength steadily, and as the fever speedily attacked them, they suffered from being reduced to a bacon and hardtack diet. So much did the shortage of proper food tell upon their health that again and again officers were compelled to draw upon their private purses, or upon the Red Cross Society, to make good the deficiency of the Government supply. Again and again we sent down improvised pack-trains composed of officers' horses, of captured Spanish cavalry ponies, or of mules which had been shot or abandoned but were cured by our men. These expeditions — sometimes under the Chaplain, sometimes under the Quartermaster, sometimes under myself, and occasionally under a trooper — would go to the sea-coast or to the Red Cross head-quarters, or, after the surrender, into the city of Santiago, to get food both for the well and the sick. The Red Cross Society rendered invaluable aid. For example, on one of these expeditions I personally brought up 600 pounds of beans; on another occasion I personally brought up 500 pounds of rice, 800 pounds of cornmeal, 200 pounds of sugar, 100 pounds of tea, 100 pounds of oatmeal, 5 barrels of potatoes, and two of onions, with cases of canned soup and condensed milk for the sick in hospitals. Every scrap of the food thus brought up was eaten with avidity by the soldiers, and put new heart and strength into them. It was only our constant care of the men in this way that enabled us to keep them in any trim at all. As for the sick in the hospital, unless we were able from outside sources to get them such simple delicacies as rice and condensed milk, they usually had the alternative of eating salt pork and hardtack or going without. After each fight we got a good deal of food from the Spanish camps in the way of beans, peas, and rice, together with green coffee, all of which the men used and relished greatly. In some respects the Spanish rations were preferable to ours, notably in the use of rice. After we had been ashore a month the supplies began to come in in abundance, and we then fared very well. Up to that time the men were under-fed, during the very weeks when the heaviest drain was being made upon their vitality, and the deficiency was only partially supplied through the aid of the Red Cross, and out of the officers' pockets and the pockets of various New York friends who sent us money. Before, during, and immediately after the fights of June 24th and July 1st, we were very short of even the bacon and hardtack. About July 14th, when the heavy rains interrupted communication, we were threatened with famine, as we were informed that there was not a day's supply of provisions in advance nearer than the sea-coast; and another twenty-four hours' rain would have resulted in a complete break-down of communications, so that for several days we should have been reduced to a diet of mule-meat and mangos. At this time, in anticipation of such a contingency, by foraging and hoarding we got a little ahead, so that when our supplies were cut down for a day or two we did not suffer much, and were even able to furnish a little aid to the less fortunate First Illinois Regiment, which was camped next to us. Members of the Illinois Regiment were offering our men $1 apiece for hardtacks.

I wish to bear testimony to the energy and capacity of Colonel Weston, the Commissary-General with the expedition. If it had not been for his active aid, we should have fared worse than we did. All that he could do for us, he most cheerfully did.

As regards the clothing, I have to say: As to the first issue, the blue shirts were excellent of their kind, but altogether too hot for Cuba. They are just what I used to wear in Montana. The leggings were good; the shoes were very good; the undershirts not very good, and the drawers bad — being of heavy, thick canton flannel, difficult to wash, and entirely unfit for a tropical climate. The trousers were poor, wearing badly. We did not get any other clothing until we were just about to leave Cuba, by which time most of the men were in tatters; some being actually barefooted, while others were in rags, or dressed partly in clothes captured from the Spaniards, who were much more suitably clothed for the climate and place than we were. The ponchos were poor, being inferior to the Spanish rain-coats which we captured.

As to the medical matters, I invite your attention, not only to the report of Dr. Church accompanying this letter, but to the letters of Captain Llewellen, Captain Day, and Lieutenant McIlhenny. I could readily produce a hundred letters on the lines of the last three. In actual medical supplies, we had plenty of quinine and cathartics. We were apt to be short on other medicines, and we had nothing whatever in the way of proper nourishing food for our sick and wounded men during most of the time, except what we were able to get from the Red Cross or purchase with our own money. We had no hospital tent at all until I was able to get a couple of tarpaulins. During much of the time my own fly was used for the purpose. We had no cots until by individual effort we obtained a few, only three or four days before we left Cuba. During most of the time the sick men lay on the muddy ground in blankets, if they had any; if not, they lay without them until some of the well men cut their own blankets in half. Our regimental surgeon very soon left us, and Dr. Church, who was repeatedly taken down with the fever, was left alone — save as he was helped by men detailed from among the troopers. Both he and the men thus detailed, together with the regular hospital attendants, did work of incalculable service. We had no ambulance with the regiment. On the battlefield our wounded were generally sent to the rear in mule-wagons, or on litters which were improvised. At other times we would hire the little springless Cuban carts. But of course the wounded suffered greatly in such conveyances, and moreover, often we could not get a wheeled vehicle of any kind to transport even the most serious cases. On the day of the big fight, July 1st, as far as we could find out, there were but two ambulances with the army in condition to work — neither of which did we ever see. Later there were, as we were informed, thirteen all told; and occasionally after the surrender, by vigorous representations and requests, we would get one assigned to take some peculiarly bad cases to the hospital. Ordinarily, however, we had to do with one of the makeshifts enumerated above. On several occasions I visited the big hospitals in the rear. Their condition was frightful beyond description from lack of supplies, lack of medicine, lack of doctors, nurses, and attendants, and especially from lack of transportation. The wounded and sick who were sent back suffered so much that, whenever possible, they returned to the front. Finally my brigade commander, General Wood, ordered, with my hearty acquiescence, that only in the direst need should any men be sent to the rear — no matter what our hospital accommodations at the front might be. The men themselves preferred to suffer almost anything lying alone in their little shelter-tents, rather than go back to the hospitals in the rear. I invite attention to the accompanying letter of Captain Llewellen in relation to the dreadful condition of the wounded on some of the transports taking them North.

The greatest trouble we had was with the lack of transportation. Under the order issued by direction of General Miles through the Adjutant-General on or about May 8th, a regiment serving as infantry in the field was entitled to twenty-five wagons. We often had one, often none, sometimes two, and never as many as three. We had a regimental pack-train, but it was left behind at Tampa. During most of the time our means of transportation were chiefly the improvised pack-trains spoken of above; but as the mules got well they were taken away from us, and so were the captured Spanish cavalry horses. Whenever we shifted camp, we had to leave most of our things behind, so that the night before each fight was marked by our sleeping without tentage and with very little food, so far as officers were concerned, as everything had to be sacrificed to getting up what ammunition and medical supplies we had. Colonel Wood seized some mules, and in this manner got up the medical supplies before the fight of June 24th, when for three days the officers had nothing but what they wore. There was a repetition of this, only in worse form, before and after the fight of July 1st. Of course much of this was simply a natural incident of war, but a great deal could readily have been avoided if we had had enough transportation; and I was sorry not to let my men be as comfortable as possible and rest as much as possible just before going into a fight when, as on July 1st and 2d, they might have to be forty-eight hours with the minimum quantity of food and sleep. The fever began to make heavy ravages among our men just before the surrender, and from that time on it became a most serious matter to shift camp, with sick and ailing soldiers, hardly able to walk — not to speak of carrying heavy burdens — when we had no transportation. Not more than half of the men could carry their rolls, and yet these, with the officers' baggage and provisions, the entire hospital and its appurtenances, etc., had to be transported somehow. It was usually about three days after we reached a new camp before the necessaries which had been left behind could be brought up, and during these three days we had to get along as best we could. The entire lack of transportation at first resulted in leaving most of the troop mess-kits on the beach, and we were never able to get them. The men cooked in the few utensils they could themselves carry. This rendered it impossible to boil the drinking water. Closely allied to the lack of transportation was the lack of means to land supplies from the transports.

In my opinion, the deficiency in transportation was the worst evil with which we had to contend, serious though some of the others were. I have never served before, so have no means of comparing this with previous campaigns. I was often told by officers who had seen service against the Indians that, relatively to the size of the army, and the character of the country, we had only a small fraction of the transportation always used in the Indian campaigns. As far as my regiment was concerned, we certainly did not have one-third of the amount absolutely necessary, if it was to be kept in fair condition, and we had to partially make good the deficiency by the most energetic resort to all kinds of makeshifts and expedients.

Yours respectfully,

(Signed)                    THEODORE ROOSEVELT,
*Colonel First United States Cavalry.*

Forwarded through military channels.
(5 enclosures.)

*First Endorsement.*

HEAD-QUARTERS FIFTH ARMY CORPS.

CAMP WIKOFF, September 18, 1898.

Respectfully forwarded to the Adjutant-General of the Army.

(Signed)                    WILLIAM R. SHAFTER,
*Major-General Commanding.*

# APPENDIX C

[The following is the report of the Associated Press correspondent of the "round-robin" incident. It is literally true in every detail. I was present when he was handed both letters; he was present while they were being written.]

SANTIAGO DE CUBA, August 3d (delayed in transmission). — Summoned by Major-General Shafter, a meeting was held here this morning at head-quarters, and in the presence of every commanding and medical officer of the Fifth Army Corps, General Shafter read a cable message from Secretary Alger, ordering him, on the recommendation of Surgeon-General Sternberg, to move the army into the interior, to San Luis, where it is healthier.

As a result of the conference General Shafter will insist upon the immediate withdrawal of the army North.

As an explanation of the situation the following letter from Colonel Theodore Roosevelt, commanding the First Cavalry, to General Shafter, was handed by the latter to the correspondent of The Associated Press for publication:

MAJOR-GENERAL SHAFTER.

SIR: In a meeting of the general and medical officers called by you at the Palace this morning we were all, as you know, unanimous in our views of what should be done with the army. To keep us here, in the opinion of every officer commanding a division or a brigade, will simply involve the destruction of thousands. There is no possible reason for not shipping practically the entire command North at once.

Yellow-fever cases are very few in the cavalry division, where I command one of the two brigades, and not one true case of yellow fever has occurred in this division, except among the men sent to the hospital at Siboney, where they have, I believe, contracted it.

But in this division there have been 1,500 cases of malarial fever. Hardly a man has yet died from it, but the whole command is so weakened and shattered as to be ripe for dying like rotten sheep, when a real yellow-fever epidemic instead of a fake epidemic, like the present one, strikes us, as it is bound to do if we stay here at the height of the sickness season, August and the beginning of September. Quarantine against malarial fever is much like quarantining against the toothache.

All of us are certain that as soon as the authorities at Washington fully appreciate the condition of the army, we shall be sent home. If we are kept here it will in all human possibility mean an appalling disaster, for the surgeons here estimate that over half the army, if kept here during the sickly season, will die.

This is not only terrible from the stand-point of the individual lives lost, but it means ruin from the standpoint of military efficiency of the flower of the American army, for the great bulk of the regulars are here with you. The sick list, large though it is, exceeding four thousand, affords but a faint index of the debilitation of the army. Not twenty per cent. are fit for active work.

Six weeks on the North Maine coast, for instance, or elsewhere where the yellow-fever germ cannot possibly propagate, would make us all as fit as fighting-cocks, as able as we are eager to take a leading part in the great campaign against Havana in the fall, even if we are not allowed to try Porto Rico.

We can be moved North, if moved at once, with absolute safety to the country, although, of course, it would have been infinitely better if we had been moved North or to Porto Rico two weeks ago. If there were any object in keeping us here, we would face yellow fever with as much indifference as we faced bullets. But there is no object.

The four immune regiments ordered here are sufficient to garrison the city and surrounding towns, and there is absolutely nothing for us to do here, and there has not been since the city surrendered. It is impossible to move into the interior. Every shifting of camp doubles the sick-rate in our present weakened condition, and, anyhow, the interior is rather worse than the coast, as I have found by actual reconnoissance. Our present camps are as healthy as any camps at this end of the island can be.

I write only because I cannot see our men, who have fought so bravely and who have endured extreme hardship and danger so uncomplainingly, go to destruction without striving so far as lies in me to avert a doom as fearful as it is unnecessary and undeserved. Yours respectfully,

THEODORE ROOSEVELT,
*Colonel Commanding Second Cavalry Brigade.*

After Colonel Roosevelt had taken the initiative, all the American general officers united in a "round robin" addressed to General Shafter. It reads:

We, the undersigned officers commanding the various brigades, divisions, etc., of the Army of Occupation in Cuba, are of the unanimous opinion that this army should be at once taken out of the island of Cuba and sent to some point on the Northern sea-coast of the United States; that can be done without danger to the people of the United States; that yellow fever in the army at present is not epidemic; that there are only a few sporadic cases; but that the army is disabled by malarial fever to the extent that its efficiency is destroyed, and that it is in a condition to be practically entirely destroyed by an epidemic of yellow fever, which is sure to come in the near future.

We know from the reports of competent officers and from personal observations that the army is unable to move into the interior, and that there are no facilities for such a move if attempted, and that it could not be attempted until too late. Moreover, the best medical authorities of the island say that with our present equipment we could not live in the interior during the rainy season without losses from malarial fever, which is almost as deadly as yellow fever.

This army must be moved at once, or perish. As the army can be safely moved now, the persons responsible for preventing such a move will be responsible for the unnecessary loss of many thousands of lives.

Our opinions are the result of careful personal observation, and they are also based on the unanimous opinion of our medical officers with the army, who understand the situation absolutely.

J. FORD KENT,
*Major-General Volunteers Commanding First Division, Fifth Corps.*
J. C. BATES,
*Major-General Volunteers Commanding Provisional Division.*
ADNA R. CHAFFEE,
*Major-General Commanding Third Brigade, Second Division.*
SAMUEL S. SUMNER,
*Brigadier-General Volunteers Commanding First Brigade, Cavalry.*
WILL LUDLOW,
*Brigadier-General Volunteers Commanding First Brigade, Second Division.*
ADELBERT AMES,
*Brigadier-General Volunteers Commanding Third Brigade, First Division.*
LEONARD WOOD,
*Brigadier-General Volunteers Commanding the City of Santiago.*
THEODORE ROOSEVELT,
*Colonel Commanding Second Cavalry Brigade.*

Major M. W. Wood, the chief Surgeon of the First Division, said: "The army must be moved North," adding, with emphasis, "or it will be unable to move itself."

General Ames has sent the following cable message to Washington:

CHARLES H. ALLEN, *Assistant Secretary of the Navy:*

This army is incapable, because of sickness, of marching anywhere except to the transports. If it is ever to return to the United States it must do so at once.

# APPENDIX D

## CORRECTIONS

It has been suggested to me that when Bucky O'Neill spoke of the vultures tearing our dead, he was thinking of no modern poet, but of the words of the prophet Ezekiel: "Speak unto every feathered fowl . . . ye shall eat the flesh of the mighty and drink the blood of the princes of the earth."

At San Juan the Sixth Cavalry was under Major Lebo, a tried and gallant officer. I learn from a letter of Lieutenant McNamee that it was he, and not Lieutenant Hartwick, by whose orders the troopers of the Ninth cast down the fence to enable me to ride my horse into the lane. But one of the two lieutenants of B troop was overcome by the heat that day; Lieutenant Rynning was with his troop until dark.

One night during the siege, when we were digging trenches, a curious stampede occurred (not in my own regiment) which it may be necessary some time to relate.

Lieutenants W. E. Shipp and W. H. Smith were killed, not far from each other, while gallantly leading their troops on the slope of Kettle Hill. Each left a widow and young children.

Captain (now Colonel) A. L. Mills, the Brigade Adjutant-General, has written me some comments on my account of the fight on July 1st. It was he himself who first brought me word to advance. I then met Colonel Dorst — who bore the same message — as I was getting the regiment forward. Captain Mills was one of the officers I had sent back to get orders that would permit me to advance; he met General Sumner, who gave him the orders, and he then returned to me. In a letter to me Colonel Mills says in part:

> I reached the head of the regiment as you came out of the lane and gave you the orders to enter the action. These were that you were to move, with your right resting along the wire fence of the lane, to the support of the regular cavalry then attacking the hill we were facing. "The red-roofed house yonder is your objective," I said to you. You moved out at once and quickly forged to the front of your regiment. I rode in rear, keeping the soldiers and troops closed and in line as well as the circumstances and conditions permitted. We had covered, I judge, from one-half to two-thirds the distance to Kettle Hill when Lieutenant-Colonel Garlington, from our left flank, called to me that troops were needed in the meadow across the lane. I put one troop

(not three, as stated in your account*) across the lane and went with it. Advancing with the troop, I began immediately to pick up troopers of the Ninth Cavalry who had drifted from their commands, and soon had so many they demanded nearly all my attention. With a line thus made up, the colored troopers on the left and yours on the right, the portion of Kettle Hill on the right of the red-roofed house was first carried. I very shortly thereafter had a strong firing-line established on the crest nearest the enemy, from the corner of the fence around the house to the low ground on the right of the hill, which fired into the strong line of conical straw hats, whose brims showed just above the edge of the Spanish trench directly west of that part of the hill.[†] These hats made a fine target! I had placed a young officer of your regiment in charge of the portion of the line on top of the hill, and was about to go to the left to keep the connection of the brigade — Captain McBlain, Ninth Cavalry, just then came up on the hill from the left and rear — when the shot struck that put me out of the fight.

There were many wholly erroneous accounts of the Guasimas fight published at the time, for the most part written by newspaper-men who were in the rear and utterly ignorant of what really occurred. Most of these accounts possess a value so purely ephemeral as to need no notice. Mr. Stephen Bonsal, however, in his book, "The Fight for Santiago," has cast one of them in a more permanent form; and I shall discuss one or two of his statements.

Mr. Bonsal was not present at the fight, and, indeed, so far as I know, he never at any time was with the cavalry in action. He puts in his book a map of the supposed skirmish ground; but it bears to the actual scene of the fight only the well-known likeness borne by Monmouth to Macedon. There was a brook on the battle-ground, and there is a brook in Mr. Bonsal's map. The real brook, flowing down from the mountains, crossed the valley road and ran down between it and the hill-trail, going nowhere near the latter. The Bonsal brook flows at right angles to the course of the real brook and crosses both trails — that is, it runs up hill. It is difficult to believe that the Bonsal map could have been made by any man who had gone over the hill-trail followed by the Rough Riders and who knew where the fighting had taken place. The position of the Spanish line on the Bonsal map is inverted compared to what it really was.

On page 90 Mr. Bonsal says that in making the "precipitate advance" there was a rivalry between the regulars and Rough Riders, which resulted in each hurrying recklessly forward to strike the Spaniards first. On the contrary the official reports show that General

---

*The other two must have followed on their own initiative.
[†]These were the Spaniards in the trenches we carried when we charged from Kettle Hill, after the infantry had taken the San Juan block-house.

Young's column waited for some time after it got to the Spanish position, so as to allow the Rough Riders (who had the more difficult
trail) to come up. Colonel Wood kept his column walking at a smart
pace, merely so that the regulars might not be left unsupported when
the fight began; and as a matter of fact, it began almost simultane-
ously on both wings.

On page 91 Mr. Bonsal speaks of "The foolhardy formation of a
solid column along a narrow trail, which brought them (the Rough
Riders) . . . within point-blank range of the Spanish rifles and within
the unobstructed sweep of their machine-guns." He also speaks as
if the advance should have been made with the regiment deployed
through the jungle. Of course, the only possible way by which the
Rough Riders could have been brought into action in time to support the regulars was by advancing in column along the trail at a
good smart gait. As soon as our advance-guard came into contact
with the enemy's outpost we deployed. No firing began for at least
five minutes after Captain Capron sent back word that he had come
upon the Spanish outpost. At the particular point where this occurred there was a dip in the road, which probably rendered it, in
Capron's opinion, better to keep part of his men in it. In any event,
Captain Capron, who was a skilful as he was gallant, had ample time
between discovering the Spanish outpost and the outbreak of the
firing to arrange his troop in the formation he deemed best. His
troop was not in solid formation; his men were about ten yards
apart. Of course, to have walked forward deployed through the
jungle, prior to reaching the ground where we were to fight, would
have been a course of procedure so foolish as to warrant the summary court-martial of any man directing it. We could not have made
half a mile an hour in such a formation, and would have been at least
four hours too late for the fighting.

On page 92 Mr. Bonsal says that Captain Capron's troop was ambushed, and that it received the enemy's fire a quarter of an hour
before it was expected. This is simply not so. Before the column
stopped we had passed a dead Cuban, killed in the preceding day's
skirmish, and General Wood had notified me on information he had
received from Capron that we might come into contact with the
Spaniards at any moment, and, as I have already said, Captain
Capron discovered the Spanish outpost, and we halted and partially
deployed the column before the firing began. We were at the time
exactly where we had expected to come across the Spaniards. Mr.
Bonsal, after speaking of L Troop, adds: "The remaining troops of
the regiment had travelled more leisurely, and more than half an hour
elapsed before they came up to Capron's support." As a matter of
fact, all the troops travelled at exactly the same rate of speed, although

there were stragglers from each, and when Capron halted and sent back word that he had come upon the Spanish outpost, the entire regiment closed up, halted, and most of the men sat down. We then, some minutes after the first word had been received, and before any firing had begun, received instructions to deploy. I had my right wing partially deployed before the first shots between the outposts took place. Within less than three minutes I had G Troop, with Llewellen, Greenway, and Leahy, and one platoon of K Troop under Kane, on the firing-line, and it was not until after we reached the firing-line that the heavy volley-firing from the Spaniards began.

On page 94 Mr. Bonsal says: "A vexatious delay occurred before the two independent columns could communicate and advance with concerted action. . . . When the two columns were brought into communication it was immediately decided to make a general attack upon the Spanish position. . . . With this purpose in view, the following disposition of the troops was made before the advance of the brigade all along the line was ordered." There was no communication between the two columns prior to the general attack, nor was any order issued for the advance of the brigade all along the line. The attacks were made wholly independently, and the first communication between the columns was when the right wing of the Rough Riders in the course of their advance by their firing dislodged the Spaniards from the hill across the ravine to the right, and then saw the regulars come up that hill.

Mr. Bonsal's account of what occurred among the regulars parallels his account of what occurred among the Rough Riders. He states that the squadron of the Tenth Cavalry delivered the main attack upon the hill, which was the strongest point of the Spanish position; and he says of the troopers of the Tenth Cavalry that "their better training enabled them to render more valuable service than the other troops engaged." In reality, the Tenth Cavalrymen were deployed in support of the First, though they mingled with them in the assault proper; and so far as there was any difference at all in the amount of work done, it was in favor of the First. The statement that the Tenth Cavalry was better trained than the First, and rendered more valuable service, has not the slightest basis whatsoever of any kind, sort, or description, in fact. The Tenth Cavalry did well what it was required to do; as an organization, in this fight, it was rather less heavily engaged, and suffered less loss, actually and relatively, than either the First Cavalry or the Rough Riders. It took about the same part that was taken by the left wing of the Rough Riders, which wing was similarly rather less heavily engaged than the right and centre of the regiment. Of course, this is a reflection neither on the Tenth Cavalry nor on the left wing of the Rough Riders. Each body simply did what it was ordered to do, and did it well. But to claim that the Tenth Cavalry did better than the First, or bore the most prominent part in the fight, is like making the same claim for the left wing of the Rough Riders. All the troops engaged did well, and all alike are entitled to share in the honor of the day.

Mr. Bonsal out-Spaniards the Spaniards themselves as regards both their numbers and their loss. These points are discussed elsewhere. He develops for the Spanish side, to account for their retreat, a wholly new explanation — viz., that they retreated because they saw reinforcements arriving for the Americans. The Spaniards themselves make no such claim. Lieutenant Tejeiro asserts that they retreated because news had come of a (wholly mythical) American advance on Morro Castle. The Spanish official report simply says that the Americans were repulsed; which is about as accurate a statement as the other two. All three explanations, those by General Rubin, by Lieutenant Tejeiro, and by Mr. Bonsal alike, are precisely on a par with the first Spanish official report of the battle of Manila Bay, in which Admiral Dewey was described as having been repulsed and forced to retire.

There are one or two minor mistakes made by Mr. Bonsal. He states that on the roster of the officers of the Rough Riders there were ten West Pointers. There were three, one of whom resigned. Only two were in the fighting. He also states that after Las Guasimas Brigadier-General Young was made a Major-General and Colonel Wood a Brigadier-General, while the commanding officers of the First and Tenth Cavalry were ignored in this "shower of promotions." In the first place, the commanding officers of the First and Tenth Cavalry were not in the fight — only one squadron of each having been present. In the next place, there was no "shower of promotions" at all. Nobody was promoted except General Young, save to fill the vacancies caused by death or by the promotion of General Young. Wood was not promoted because of this fight. General Young most deservedly was promoted. Soon after the fight he fell sick. The command of the brigade then fell upon Wood, simply because he had higher rank than the other two regimental commanders of the brigade; and I then took command of the regiment exactly as Lieutenant-Colonels Viele and Baldwin had already taken command of the First and Tenth Cavalry when their superior officers were put in charge of brigades. After the San Juan fighting, in which Wood commanded a brigade, he was made a Brigadier-General and I was then promoted to the nominal command of the regiment, which I was already commanding in reality.

Mr. Bonsal's claim of superior efficiency for the colored regular regiments as compared with the white regular regiments does not merit discussion. He asserts that General Wheeler brought on the Guasimas fight in defiance of orders. Lieutenant Miley, in his book, "In Cuba with Shafter," on page 83, shows that General Wheeler made his fight before receiving the order which it is claimed he disobeyed. General Wheeler was in command ashore; he was told to get in touch with the enemy, and, being a man with the "fighting edge," this meant that he was certain to fight. No general who was worth his salt would have failed to fight under such conditions; the only question would be as to how the fight was to be made. War means fighting; and the soldier's cardinal sin is timidity.

General Wheeler remained throughout steadfast against any retreat from before Santiago. But the merit of keeping the army before Santiago, without withdrawal, until the city fell, belongs to the authorities at Washington, who at this all-important stage of the operations showed to marked advantage in overruling the proposals made by the highest generals in the field looking toward partial retreat or toward the abandonment of the effort to take the city.

The following note, written by Sergeant E. G. Norton, of B Troop, refers to the death of his brother, Oliver B. Norton, one of the most gallant and soldierly men in the regiment:

On July 1st I, together with Sergeant Campbell and Troopers Bardshar and Dudley Dean and my brother who was killed and some others, was at the front of the column right behind you. We moved forward, following you as you rode, to where we came upon the troopers of the Ninth Cavalry and a part of the First lying down. I heard the conversation between you and one or two of the officers of the Ninth Cavalry. You ordered a charge, and the regular officers answered that they had no orders to move ahead; whereupon you said: "Then let us through," and marched forward through the lines, our regiment following. The men of the Ninth and First Cavalry then jumped up and came forward with us. Then you waved your hat and gave the command to charge and we went up the hill. On the top of Kettle Hill my brother, Oliver B. Norton, was shot through the head and in the right wrist. It was just as you started to lead the charge on the San Juan hills ahead of us; we saw that the regiment did not know you had gone and were not following, and my brother said, "For God's sake follow the Colonel," and as he rose the bullet went through his head.

In reference to Mr. Bonsal's account of the Guasimas fight, Mr. Richard Harding Davis writes me as follows:

We had already halted several times to give the men a chance to rest, and when we halted for the last time I thought it was for this same purpose, and began taking photographs of the men of L Troop, who were so near that they asked me to be sure and save them a photograph. Wood had twice disappeared down the trail beyond them and returned. As he came back for the second time I remember that you walked up to him (we were all dismounted then), and saluted and said: "Colonel, Doctor La Motte reports that the pace is too fast for the men, and that over fifty have fallen out from exhaustion." Wood replied sharply: "I have no time to bother with sick men now." You replied, more in answer, I suppose, to his tone than to his words: "I merely repeated what the Surgeon reported to me." Wood then turned and said in explanation: "I have no time for them now; I mean that we are in sight of the enemy."

This was the only information we received that the men of L Troop had been ambushed by the Spaniards, and, if they were, they were very calm about it, and I certainly was taking photographs of them at the time, and the rest of the regiment, instead of being half a hour's march away, was seated comfortably along the trail not twenty feet distant from the men of L Troop. You deployed G Troop under Captain Llewellen into the jungle at the right and sent K Troop after it, and Wood ordered Troops E and F into the field on our left. It must have been from ten to fifteen minutes after Capron and Wood had located the Spaniards before either side fired a shot. When the firing did come I went over to you and joined G Troop and a detachment of K Troop under Woodbury Kane, and we located more of the enemy on a ridge.

If it is to be ambushed when you find the enemy exactly where you went to find him, and your scouts see him soon enough to give you sufficient time to spread five troops in skirmish order to attack him, and you then drive him back out of three positions for a mile and a half, then most certainly, as Bonsal says, "L Troop of the Rough Riders was ambushed by the Spaniards on the morning of June 24th."

General Wood also writes me at length about Mr. Bonsal's book, stating that his account of the Guasimas fight is without foundation in fact. He says: "We had five troops completely deployed before the first shot was fired. Captain Capron was not wounded until the fight had been going on fully thirty-five minutes. The statement that Captain Capron's troop was ambushed is absolutely untrue. We had been informed, as you know, by Castillo's people that we should find the dead guerilla a few hundred yards on the Siboney side of the Spanish lines."

He then alludes to the waving of the guidon by K Troop as "the only means of communication with the regulars." He mentions that his orders did not come from General Wheeler, and that he had no instructions from General Wheeler directly or indirectly at any time previous to the fight.

General Wood does not think that I give quite enough credit to the Rough Riders as compared to the regulars in this Guasimas fight, and believes that I greatly underestimate the Spanish force and loss, and that Lieutenant Tejeiro is not to be trusted at all on these points. He states that we began the fight ten minutes before the regulars, and that the main attack was made and decided by us. This was the view that I and all the rest of us in the regiment took at the time; but as I had found since that the members of the First and Tenth Regiments held with equal sincerity the view that the main part was taken by their own commands, I have come to the conclusion that the way I have described the action is substantially correct. Owing to the fact that the Tenth Cavalry, which was originally in support, moved forward until it got mixed with the First, it is very difficult to get the exact relative position of the different troops of the First and Tenth in making the advance. Beck and Galbraith were on the left; apparently Wainwright was farthest over on the right. General Wood states that Leonardo Ros, the Civil Governor of Santiago at the time of the surrender, told him that the Spanish force at Guasimas consisted of not less than 2,600 men, and that there were nearly 300 of them killed and wounded. I do not myself see how it was possible for us, as we were the attacking party and were advancing against superior numbers well sheltered, to inflict five times as much damage as we received; but as we buried eleven dead Spaniards, and as they carried off some of their dead, I believe the loss to have been very much heavier than Lieutenant Tejeiro reports.

General Wood believes that in following Lieutenant Tejeiro I have greatly underestimated the number of Spanish troops who were defending Santiago on July 1st, and here I think he completely makes out his case, he taking the view that Lieutenant Tejeiro's statements were made for the purpose of saving Spanish honor. On this point his letter runs as follows:

A word in regard to the number of troops in Santiago. I have had, during my long association here, a good many opportunities to get information which you have not got and probably never will get; that is, information from parties who were actually in the fight, who are now residents of the city; also information which came to me as commanding officer of the city directly after the surrender.

To sum up briefly as follows: The Spanish surrendered in Santiago 12,000 men. We shipped from Santiago something over 14,000 men. The 2,000 additional were troops that came in from San Luis, Songo, and small up-country posts. The 12,000 in the city, minus the force of General Iscario, 3,300 infantry and 680 cavalry, or in round numbers 4,000 men (who entered the city just after the battles of San Juan and El Caney), leaves 8,000 regulars, plus the dead, plus Cervera's marines and blue-jackets, which he himself admits landing in the neighborhood of 1,200 (and reports here are that he landed 1,380), and plus the Spanish Volunteer Battalion, which was between 800 and 900 men (this statement I have from the lieutenant-colonel of this very battalion), gives us in round numbers, present for duty on the morning of July 1st, not less than 10,500 men. These men were distributed 890 at Caney, two companies of artillery at Morro, one at Socapa, and half a company at Puenta Gorda; in all, not over 500 or 600 men, but for the sake of argument we can say a thousand. In round numbers, then, we had immediately about the city 8,500 troops. These were scattered from the cemetery around to Aguadores. In front of us, actually in the trenches, there could not by any possible method of figuring have been less than 6,000 men. You can twist it any way you want to; the figures I have given you are absolutely correct, at least they are absolutely on the side of safety.

It is difficult for me to withstand the temptation to tell what has befallen some of my men since the regiment disbanded; how McGinty, after spending some weeks in Roosevelt Hospital in New York with an attack of fever, determined to call upon his captain, Woodbury Kane, when he got out, and procuring a horse rode until he found Kane's house, when he hitched the horse to a lamp-post and strolled in; how Cherokee Bill married a wife in Hoboken, and as that pleasant city ultimately proved an uncongenial field for his activities, how I had to send both himself and his wife out to the Territory; how Happy Jack, haunted by visions of the social methods obtaining in the best saloons of Arizona, applied for the position of "bouncer out" at the Executive Chamber when I was elected Governor, and how I got him a job at railroading instead, and finally had to ship him back to his own Territory also; how a valued friend from a cow ranch in the remote West accepted a pressing invitation to spend a few days at the home of another ex-trooper, a New Yorker of fastidious instincts, and arrived with an umbrella as his only baggage; how poor Holderman and Pollock both died and were buried with military honors, all of Pollock's tribesmen coming to the burial; how Tom Isbell joined Buffalo Bill's Wild West Show, and how, on the other hand, George Rowland scornfully refused to remain in the East at all, writing to a gallant young New Yorker who had been his bunkie: "Well, old boy, I am glad I didnt go home with you for them people to look at, because I aint a Buffalo or a rhinoceros or a giraffe, and I dont like to be Stared at, and you know we didnt do no hard fighting down there. I have been in closer places than that right here in Yunited States, that is Better men to fight than them dam Spaniards." In another letter Rowland tells of the fate of Tom Darnell, the rider, he who rode the sorrel horse of the Third Cavalry: "There aint much news to write of except poor old Tom Darnell got killed about a month ago. Tom and another fellow had a fight and he shot Tom through the heart and Tom was dead when he hit the floor. Tom was sure a good old boy, and I sure hated to hear of him going, and he had plenty of grit too. No man ever called on him for a fight that he didn't get it."

My men were children of the dragon's blood, and if they had no outland foe to fight and no outlet for their vigorous and daring energy, there was always the chance of their fighting one another: but the great majority, if given the chance to do hard or dangerous work, availed themselves of it with the utmost eagerness, and though fever sickened and weakened them so that many died from it during the few months following their return, yet, as a whole, they are now doing fairly well. A few have shot other men or been shot themselves; a few ran for office and got elected, like Llewellen and Luna in New Mexico, or defeated, like Brodie and Wilcox in Arizona; some have been trying hard to get to the Philippines; some have returned to college, or to the law, or the factory, or the counting-room; most of them have gone back to the mine, the ranch, and the hunting camp; and the great majority have taken up the threads of their lives where they dropped them when the *Maine* was blown up and the country called to arms.

# AN AUTOBIOGRAPHY

President Theodore Roosevelt in His Riding Costume.

# FOREWORD

NATURALLY, there are chapters of my autobiography which cannot now be written.

It seems to me that, for the nation as for the individual, what is most important is to insist on the vital need of combining certain sets of qualities, which separately are common enough, and, alas, useless enough. Practical efficiency is common, and lofty idealism not uncommon; it is the combination which is necessary, and the combination is rare. Love of peace is common among weak, short-sighted, timid, and lazy persons; and on the other hand courage is found among many men of evil temper and bad character. Neither quality shall by itself avail. Justice among the nations of mankind, and the uplifting of humanity, can be brought about only by those strong and daring men who with wisdom love peace, but who love righteousness more than peace. Facing the immense complexity of modern social and industrial conditions, there is need to use freely and unhesitatingly the collective power of all of us; and yet no exercise of collective power will ever avail if the average individual does not keep his or her sense of personal duty, initiative, and responsibility. There is need to develop all the virtues that have the state for their sphere of action; but these virtues are as dust in a windy street unless back of them lie the strong and tender virtues of a family life based on the love of the one man for the one woman and on their joyous and fearless acceptance of their common obligation to the children that are theirs. There must be the keenest sense of duty, and with it must go the joy of living; there must be shame at the thought of shirking the hard work of the world, and at the same time delight in the many-sided beauty of life. With soul of flame and temper of steel we must act as our coolest judgment bids us. We must exercise the largest charity towards the wrong-doer that is compatible with relentless war against the wrong-doing. We must be just to others, generous to others, and yet we must realize that it is a shameful and wicked thing not to withstand oppression with high heart and ready hand. With gentleness and tenderness there must go dauntless bravery and grim acceptance of labor and hardship and peril. All for each, and each for all, is a good motto; but only on condition that each works with might and main to so maintain himself as not to be a burden to others.

We of the great modern democracies must strive unceasingly to make our several countries lands in which a poor man who works hard can live comfortably and honestly, and in which a rich man cannot live dishonestly nor in slothful avoidance of duty; and yet we must judge rich man and poor man alike by a standard which rests on conduct and not on caste, and we must frown with the same stern severity on the mean and vicious envy which hates and would plunder a man because he is well off and on the brutal and selfish arrogance which looks down on and exploits the man with whom life has gone hard.

THEODORE ROOSEVELT.

Sagamore Hill, Oct. 1, 1913.

# CONTENTS

# ILLUSTRATIONS

# Chapter I

## BOYHOOD AND YOUTH

MY GRANDFATHER on my father's side was of almost purely Dutch blood. When he was young he still spoke some Dutch, and Dutch was last used in the services of the Dutch Reformed Church in New York while he was a small boy.

About 1644 his ancestor Klaes Martensen van Roosevelt came to New Amsterdam as a "settler" — the euphemistic name for an immigrant who came over in the steerage of a sailing ship in the seventeenth century instead of the steerage of a steamer in the nineteenth century. From that time for the next seven generations from father to son every one of us was born on Manhattan Island.

My father's paternal ancestors were of Holland stock; except that there was one named Waldron, a wheelwright, who was one of the Pilgrims who remained in Holland when the others came over to found Massachusetts, and who then accompanied the Dutch adventurers to New Amsterdam. My father's mother was a Pennsylvanian. Her forbears had come to Pennsylvania with William Penn, some in the same ship with him; they were of the usual type of the immigration of that particular place and time. They included Welsh and English Quakers, an Irishman, — with a Celtic name, and apparently not a Quaker, — and peace-loving Germans, who were among the founders of Germantown, having been driven from their Rhineland homes when the armies of Louis the Fourteenth ravaged the Palatinate; and, in addition, representatives of a by-no-means altogether peaceful people, the Scotch Irish, who came to Pennsylvania a little later, early in the eighteenth century. My grandmother was a woman of singular sweetness and strength, the keystone of the arch in her relations with her husband and sons. Although she was not herself Dutch, it was she who taught me the only Dutch I ever knew, a baby song of which the first line ran, "Trippe troppa tronjes." I always remembered this, and when I was in East Africa it proved a bond of union between me and the

Boer settlers, not a few of whom knew it, although at first they always had difficulty in understanding my pronunciation — at which I do not wonder. It was interesting to meet these men whose ancestors had gone to the Cape about the time that mine went to America two centuries and a half previously, and to find that the descendants of the two streams of emigrants still crooned to their children some at least of the same nursery songs.

Of my great-grandfather Roosevelt and his family life a century and over ago I know little beyond what is implied in some of his books that have come down to me — the Letters of Junius, a biography of John Paul Jones, Chief Justice Marshall's "Life of Washington." They seem to indicate that his library was less interesting than that of my wife's great-grandfather at the same time, which certainly included such volumes as the original *Edinburgh Review*, for we have them now on our own book-shelves. Of my grandfather Roosevelt my most vivid childish reminiscence is not something I saw, but a tale that was told me concerning him. In *his* boyhood Sunday was as dismal a day for small Calvinistic children of Dutch descent as if they had been of Puritan or Scotch Covenanting or French Huguenot descent — and I speak as one proud of his Holland, Huguenot, and Covenanting ancestors, and proud that the blood of that stark Puritan divine Jonathan Edwards flows in the veins of his children. One summer afternoon, after listening to an unusually long Dutch Reformed sermon for the second time that day, my grandfather, a small boy, running home before the congregation had dispersed, ran into a party of pigs, which then wandered free in New York's streets. He promptly mounted a big boar, which no less promptly bolted and carried him at full speed through the midst of the outraged congregation.

By the way, one of the Roosevelt documents which came down to me illustrates the change that has come over certain aspects of public life since the time which pessimists term "the earlier and better days of the Republic." Old Isaac Roosevelt was a member of an Auditing Committee which shortly after the close of the Revolution approved the following bill:

*The State of New York, to John Cape* Dr.

To a Dinner Given by His Excellency the Governor
and Council to their Excellencies the Minnister of
France and General Washington & Co.

1783
December

| | | |
|---|---|---|
| To 120 dinners at . . . . . . . . . | 48: | 0:0 |
| To 135 Bottles Madira . . . . . . | 54: | 0:0 |
| " 36 ditto Port . . . . . . . . . | 10:16:0 | |
| " 60 ditto English Beer . . . . . | 9: | 0:0 |
| " 30 Bouls Punch . . . . . . . . | 9: | 0:0 |
| " 8 dinners for Musick . . . . . | 1:12:0 | |
| " 10 ditto for Sarvts . . . . . . | 2: | 0:0 |
| " 60 Wine Glasses Broken . . . . | 4:10:0 | |
| " 8 Cutt decanters Broken . . . | 3: | 0:0 |
| " Coffee for 8 Gentlemen . . . | 1:12:0 | |
| " Music fees &ca . . . . . . . . | 8: | 0:0 |
| " Fruit & Nuts . . . . . . . . | 5: | 0:0 |

£156:10:0

By Cash . . . . . 100:16:0

55:14:0

WE a Committee of Council having examined the
above account do certify it (amounting to one
hundred and fifty-six Pounds ten Shillings) to
be just.

December 17th 1783.

ISAAC ROOSEVELT
JAS. DUANE
EGBT. BENSON
FRED. JAY

Received the above Contents in full
New York 17th December 1783

JOHN CAPE

Think of the Governor of New York now submitting such
a bill for such an entertainment of the French Ambassador and
the President of the United States! Falstaff's views of the
proper proportion between sack and bread are borne out by
the proportion between the number of bowls of punch and
bottles of port, Madeira, and beer consumed, and the "coffee
for eight gentlemen" — apparently the only ones who lasted
through to that stage of the dinner. Especially admirable is the
nonchalant manner in which, obviously as a result of the
drinking of said bottles of wine and bowls of punch, it is

recorded that eight cut-glass decanters and sixty wine-glasses were broken.

During the Revolution some of my forefathers, North and South, served respectably, but without distinction, in the army, and others rendered similar service in the Continental Congress or in various local legislatures. By that time those who dwelt in the North were for the most part merchants, and those who dwelt in the South, planters.

My mother's people were predominantly of Scotch, but also of Huguenot and English, descent. She was a Georgian, her people having come to Georgia from South Carolina before the Revolution. The original Bulloch was a lad from near Glasgow, who came hither a couple of centuries ago, just as hundreds of thousands of needy, enterprising Scotchmen have gone to the four quarters of the globe in the intervening two hundred years. My mother's great-grandfather, Archibald Bulloch, was the first Revolutionary "President" of Georgia. My grandfather, her father, spent the winters in Savannah and the summers at Roswell, in the Georgia uplands near Atlanta, finally making Roswell his permanent home. He used to travel thither with his family and their belongings in his own carriage, followed by a baggage wagon. I never saw Roswell until I was President, but my mother told me so much about the place that when I did see it I felt as if I already knew every nook and corner of it, and as if it were haunted by the ghosts of all the men and women who had lived there. I do not mean merely my own family, I mean the slaves. My mother and her sister, my aunt, used to tell us children all kinds of stories about the slaves. One of the most fascinating referred to a very old darky called Bear Bob, because in the early days of settlement he had been partially scalped by a black bear. Then there was Mom' Grace, who was for a time my mother's nurse, and whom I had supposed to be dead, but who greeted me when I did come to Roswell, very respectable, and apparently with years of life before her. The two chief personages of the drama that used to be repeated to us were Daddy Luke, the Negro overseer, and his wife, Mom' Charlotte. I never saw either Daddy Luke or Mom' Charlotte, but I inherited the care of them when my mother died. After the close of the war they resolutely refused to be emancipated or leave the place. The

"My father, Theodore Roosevelt, was the best man I ever knew."

only demand they made upon us was enough money annually to get a new "critter," that is, a mule. With a certain lack of ingenuity the mule was reported each Christmas as having passed away, or at least as having become so infirm as to necessitate a successor — a solemn fiction which neither deceived nor was intended to deceive, but which furnished a gauge for the size of the Christmas gift.

My maternal grandfather's house was on the line of Sherman's march to the sea, and pretty much everything in it that was portable was taken by the boys in blue, including most of the books in the library. When I was President the facts about my ancestry were published, and a former soldier in Sherman's army sent me back one of the books with my grandfather's name in it. It was a little copy of the poems of "Mr. Gray" — an eighteenth-century edition printed in Glasgow.

On October 27, 1858, I was born at No. 28 East Twentieth Street, New York City, in the house in which we lived during the time that my two sisters and my brother and I were small children. It was furnished in the canonical taste of the New York which George William Curtis described in the *Potiphar Papers*. The black haircloth furniture in the dining-room scratched the bare legs of the children when they sat on it. The middle room was a library, with tables, chairs, and bookcases of gloomy respectability. It was without windows, and so was available only at night. The front room, the parlor, seemed to us children to be a room of much splendor, but was open for general use only on Sunday evening or on rare occasions when there were parties. The Sunday evening family gathering was the redeeming feature in a day which otherwise we children did not enjoy — chiefly because we were all of us made to wear clean clothes and keep neat. The ornaments of that parlor I remember now, including the gas chandelier decorated with a great quantity of cut-glass prisms. These prisms struck me as possessing peculiar magnificence. One of them fell off one day, and I hastily grabbed it and stowed it away, passing several days of furtive delight in the treasure, a delight always alloyed with fear that I would be found out and convicted of larceny. There was a Swiss wood-carving representing a very big hunter on one side of an exceedingly small mountain, and a herd of chamois, disproportionately small for the hunter and large for the mountain, just across the ridge. This always fascinated us; but there was a small chamois kid for which we felt agonies lest the hunter might come on it and kill it. There was also a Russian moujik drawing a gilt sledge on a piece of malachite. Some one mentioned in my hearing that malachite was a valuable marble. This fixed in my mind that it was valuable exactly as diamonds are valuable. I accepted that moujik as a priceless work of art, and it was not until I was well in middle age that it occurred to me that I was mistaken.

Now and then we children were taken round to our grandfather's house; a big house for the New York of those days, on the corner of Fourteenth Street and Broadway, fronting Union Square. Inside there was a large hall running up to the roof; there was a tesselated black and white marble floor, and a circular staircase round the sides of the hall, from the top floor down. We children much admired both the tessellated floor and the circular staircase. I think we were right about the latter, but I am not so sure as to the tessellated floor.

The summers we spent in the country, now at one place, now at another. We children, of course, loved the country beyond anything. We disliked the city. We were always wildly eager to get to the country when spring came, and very sad when in the late fall the family moved back to town. In the country we of course had all kinds of pets — cats, dogs, rabbits, a coon, and a sorrel Shetland pony named General Grant. When my younger sister first heard of the real General Grant, by the way, she was much struck by the coincidence that some one should have given him the same name as the pony. (Thirty years later my own children had *their* pony Grant.) In the country we children ran barefoot much of the time, and the seasons went by in a round of uninterrupted and enthralling pleasures — supervising the haying and harvesting, picking apples, hunting frogs successfully and woodchucks unsuccessfully, gathering hickory-nuts and chestnuts for sale to patient parents, building wigwams in the woods, and sometimes playing Indians in too realistic manner by staining ourselves (and incidentally our clothes) in liberal fashion with poke-cherry juice. Thanksgiving was an appreciated festival, but it in no way came up to Christmas. Christmas was an occasion of literally delirious joy. In the evening we hung up our stockings — or rather the biggest stockings we could borrow from the grown-ups — and before dawn we trooped in to open them while sitting on father's and mother's bed; and the bigger presents were arranged, those for each child on its own table, in the drawing-room, the doors to which were thrown open after breakfast. I never knew any one else have what seemed to me such attractive Christmases, and in the next generation I tried to reproduce them exactly for my own children.

My father, Theodore Roosevelt, was the best man I ever knew. He combined strength and courage with gentleness, tenderness, and great unselfishness. He would not tolerate in us children selfishness or cruelty, idleness, cowardice, or untruthfulness. As we grew older he made us understand that the same standard of clean living was demanded for the boys as for the girls; that what was wrong in a woman could not be right in a man. With great love and patience, and the most understanding sympathy and consideration, he combined insistence on discipline. He never physically punished me but once, but he was the only man of whom I was ever really afraid. I do not mean that it was a wrong fear, for he was entirely just, and we children adored him. We used to wait in the library in the evening until we could hear his key rattling in the latch of the front hall, and then rush out to greet him; and we would troop into his room while he was dressing, to stay there as long as we were permitted, eagerly examining anything which came out of his pockets which could be regarded as an attractive novelty. Every child has fixed in his memory various details which strike it as of grave importance. The trinkets he used to keep in a little box on his dressing-table we children always used to speak of as "treasures." The word, and some of the trinkets themselves, passed on to the next generation. My own children, when small, used to troop into my room while I was dressing, and the gradually accumulating trinkets in the "ditty-box" — the gift of an enlisted man in the navy — always excited rapturous joy. On occasions of solemn festivity each child would receive a trinket for his or her "very own." My children, by the way, enjoyed one pleasure I do not remember enjoying myself. When I came back from riding, the child who brought the bootjack would

"My mother, Martha Bulloch, was a sweet, gracious, beautiful Southern woman, a delightful companion and beloved by everybody."

itself promptly get into the boots, and clump up and down the room with a delightful feeling of kinship with Jack of the seven-league strides.

The punishing incident I have referred to happened when I was four years old. I bit my elder sister's arm. I do not remember biting her arm, but I do remember running down to the yard, perfectly conscious that I had committed a crime. From the yard I went into the kitchen, got some dough from the cook, and crawled under the kitchen table. In a minute or two my father entered from the yard and asked where I was. The warm-hearted Irish cook had a characteristic contempt for "informers," but although she said nothing she compromised between informing and her conscience by casting a look under the table. My father immediately dropped on all fours and darted for me. I feebly heaved the dough at him, and, having the advantage of him because I could stand up under the table, got a fair start for the stairs, but was caught halfway up them. The punishment that ensued fitted the crime, and I hope — and believe — that it did me good.

I never knew any one who got greater joy out of living than did my father, or any one who more whole-heartedly performed every duty; and no one whom I have ever met approached his combination of enjoyment of life and performance of duty. He and my mother were given to a hospitality that at that time was associated more commonly with southern than northern households; and, especially in their later years when they had moved up town, in the neighborhood of Central Park, they kept a charming, open house.

My father worked hard at his business, for he died when he was forty-six, too early to have retired. He was interested in every social reform movement, and he did an immense amount of practical charitable work himself. He was a big, powerful man, with a leonine face, and his heart filled with gentleness for those who needed help or protection, and with the possibility of much wrath against a bully or an oppressor. He was very fond of riding both on the road and across the country, and was also a great whip. He usually drove four-in-hand, or else a spike team, that is, a pair with a third horse in the lead. I do not suppose that such a team exists now. The trap that he drove we always called the high phaëton. The

"I never saw Roswell until I was President."

wheels turned under in front. I have it yet. He drove long-tailed horses, harnessed loose in light American harness, so that the whole rig had no possible resemblance to anything that would be seen now. My father always excelled in improving every spare half-hour or three-quarters of an hour, whether for work or enjoyment. Much of his four-in-hand driving was done in the summer afternoons when he would come out on the train from his business in New York. My mother and one or perhaps two of us children might meet him at the station. I can see him now getting out of the car in his linen duster, jumping into the wagon, and instantly driving off at a rattling pace, the duster sometimes bagging like a balloon. The four-in-hand, as can be gathered from the above description, did not in any way in his eyes represent possible pageantry. He drove it because he liked it. He was always preaching caution to his boys, but in this respect he did not practice his preaching overmuch himself; and, being an excellent whip, he liked to take chances. Generally they came out all right. Occasionally they did not; but he was even better at getting out of a scrape than into it. Once when we were driving into New York late at night the leaders stopped. He flicked them, and the next moment we could dimly make out that they had jumped. It then appeared that the street was closed and that a board had been placed across it, resting on two barrels, but without a lantern. Over this board the leaders had jumped, and there was considerable excitement before we got the board taken off the barrels and resumed our way. When in the city on Thanksgiving or Christmas, my father was very apt to drive my mother and a couple of friends up to the racing park to take lunch. But he was always back in time to go to the dinner at the Newsboys' Lodging-House, and not infrequently also to Miss Sattery's Night School for little Italians. At a very early age we children were taken with him and were required to help. He was a stanch friend of Charles Loring Brace, and was particularly interested in the Newsboys' Lodging-Houses and in the night schools and in getting the children off the streets and out on farms in the West. When I was President, the Governor of Alaska under me, Governor Brady, was one of these ex-newsboys who had been sent from New York out West by Mr. Brace and my father. My father was greatly interested in the societies to prevent cruelty to children and cruelty to animals. On Sundays he had a mission class. On his way to it he used to drop us children at our Sunday-school in Dr. Adams's Presbyterian Church on Madison Square; I remember hearing my aunt, my mother's sister, saying that when he walked along with us children he always reminded her of Greatheart in Bunyan. Under the spur of his example I taught a mission class myself for three years before going to college and for all four years that I was in college. I do not think I made much of a success of it. But the other day on getting out of a taxi in New York the chauffeur spoke to me and told me that he was one of my old Sunday-school pupils. I remembered him well, and was much pleased to find that he was an ardent Bull Mooser!

"Her mother, my grandmother, one of the dearest old ladies, lived with us."

My mother, Martha Bulloch, was a sweet, gracious, beautiful Southern woman, a delightful companion and beloved by everybody. She was entirely "unreconstructed" to the day of her death. Her mother, my grandmother, one of the dearest of old ladies, lived with us, and was distinctly over-indulgent to us children, being quite unable to harden her heart towards us even when the occasion demanded it. Towards the close of the Civil War, although a very small boy, I grew to have a partial but alert understanding of the fact that the family were not one in their views about that conflict, my father being a strong Lincoln Republican; and once, when I felt that I had been wronged by maternal discipline during the day, I attempted a partial

vengeance by praying with loud fervor for the success of the
Union arms, when we all came to say our prayers before my
mother in the evening. She was not only a most devoted
mother, but was also blessed with a strong sense of humor,
and she was too much amused to punish me; but I was
warned not to repeat the offense, under penalty of my father's
being informed — he being the dispenser of serious punishment. Morning prayers were with my father. We used to
stand at the foot of the stairs, and when father came down
we called out, "I speak for you and the cubby-hole too!"
There were three of us young children, and we used to sit
with father on the sofa while he conducted morning prayers.
The place between father and the arm of the sofa we called
the "cubby-hole." The child who got that place we regarded
as especially favored both in comfort and somehow or other
in rank and title. The two who were left to sit on the much
wider expanse of sofa on the other side of father were outsiders for the time being.

My aunt Anna, my mother's sister, lived with us. She was
as devoted to us children as was my mother herself, and we
were equally devoted to her in return. She taught us our
lessons while we were little. She and my mother used to entertain us by the hour with tales of life on the Georgia plan-
tations; of hunting fox, deer, and wildcat; of the long-tailed
driving horses, Boone and Crockett, and of the riding horses,
one of which was named Buena Vista in a fit of patriotic exaltation during the Mexican War; and of the queer goings-on
in the Negro quarters. She knew all the "Br'er Rabbit" stories,
and I was brought up on them. One of my uncles, Robert
Roosevelt, was much struck with them, and took them down
from her dictation, publishing them in *Harper's*, where they
fell flat. This was a good many years before a genius arose who
in "Uncle Remus" made the stories immortal.

My mother's two brothers, James Dunwoodie Bulloch and
Irvine Bulloch, came to visit us shortly after the close of the
war. Both came under assumed names, as they were among
the Confederates who were at that time exempted from the
amnesty. "Uncle Jimmy" Bulloch was a dear old retired sea-
captain, utterly unable to "get on" in the worldly sense of that
phrase, as valiant and simple and upright a soul as ever lived,

a veritable Colonel Newcome. He was an Admiral in the Confederate navy, and was the builder of the famous Confederate war vessel *Alabama*. My uncle Irvine Bulloch was a midshipman on the *Alabama*, and fired the last gun discharged from her batteries in the fight with the *Kearsarge*. Both of these uncles lived in Liverpool after the war.

My uncle Jimmy Bulloch was forgiving and just in reference to the Union forces, and could discuss all phases of the Civil War with entire fairness and generosity. But in English politics he promptly became a Tory of the most ultra-conservative school. Lincoln and Grant he could admire, but he would not

"Two Georgia girls" — Martha Bulloch and Anna Bulloch.

listen to anything in favor of Mr. Gladstone. The only occasions on which I ever shook his faith in me were when I would venture meekly to suggest that some of the manifestly preposterous falsehoods about Mr. Gladstone could not be true. My uncle was one of the best men I have ever known, and when I have sometimes been tempted to wonder how good people can believe of me the unjust and impossible things they do believe, I have consoled myself by thinking of Uncle Jimmy Bulloch's perfectly sincere conviction that Gladstone was a man of quite exceptional and nameless infamy in both public and private life.

I was a sickly, delicate boy, suffered much from asthma, and frequently had to be taken away on trips to find a place where I could breathe. One of my memories is of my father walking up and down the room with me in his arms at night when I was a very small person, and of sitting up in bed gasping, with my father and mother trying to help me. I went very little to school. I never went to the public schools, as my own children later did, both at the "Cove school" at Oyster Bay and at the "Ford school" in Washington. For a few months I attended Professor McMullen's school in Twentieth Street near the house where I was born, but most of the time I had tutors. As I have already said, my aunt taught me when I was small. At one time we had a French governess, a loved and valued "mam'selle," in the household.

When I was ten years old I made my first journey to Europe. My birthday was spent in Cologne, and in order to give me a thoroughly "party" feeling I remember that my mother put on full dress for my birthday dinner. I do not think I gained anything from this particular trip abroad. I cordially hated it, as did my younger brother and sister. Practically all the enjoyment we had was in exploring any ruins or mountains when we could get away from our elders, and in playing in the different hotels. Our one desire was to get back to America, and we regarded Europe with the most ignorant chauvinism and contempt. Four years later, however, I made another journey to Europe, and was old enough to enjoy it thoroughly and profit by it.

While still a small boy I began to take an interest in natural history. I remember distinctly the first day that I started on my career as zoölogist. I was walking up Broadway, and as I passed the market to which I used sometimes to be sent before breakfast to get strawberries I suddenly saw a dead seal laid out on a slab of wood. That seal filled me with every possible feeling of romance and adventure. I asked where it was killed, and was informed in the harbor. I had already begun to read some of Mayne Reid's books and other boys' books of adventure, and I felt that this seal brought all these adventures in realistic fashion before me. As long as that seal remained there I haunted the neighborhood of the market day after day. I measured it, and I recall that, not having a tape measure, I had to do my best to get its girth with a folding pocket foot-rule, a difficult undertaking. I carefully made a record of the utterly useless measurements, and at once began to write a natural history of my own, on the strength of that seal. This, and subsequent natural histories, were written down in blank books in simplified spelling, wholly unpremeditated and unscientific. I had vague aspirations of in some way or another owning and preserving that seal, but they never got beyond the purely formless stage.

I think, however, I did get the seal's skull, and with two of my cousins promptly started what we ambitiously called the "Roosevelt Museum of Natural History." The collections were at first kept in my room, until a rebellion on the part of the chambermaid received the approval of the higher authorities of the household and the collection was moved up to a kind of bookcase in the back hall upstairs. It was the ordinary small boy's collection of curios, quite incongruous and entirely valueless except from the standpoint of the boy himself. My father and mother encouraged me warmly in this, as they always did in anything that could give me wholesome pleasure or help to develop me.

" 'My Uncle Jimmy' Bulloch was a dear old retired sea-captain — a veritable Colonel Newcome."

The adventure of the seal and the novels of Mayne Reid together strengthened my instinctive interest in natural history. I was too young to understand much of Mayne Reid, excepting the adventure part and the natural history part — these enthralled me. But of course my reading was not wholly confined to natural history. There was very little effort made to compel me to read books, my father and mother having the good sense not to try to get me to read anything I did not like, unless it was in the way of study. I was given the chance to read books that they thought I ought to read, but if I did not like them I was then given some other good book that I did like. There were certain books that were *taboo*. For instance, I was not allowed to read dime novels. I obtained some surreptitiously and did read them, but I do not think that the enjoyment compensated for the feeling of guilt. I was also forbidden to read the only one of Ouida's books which I wished to read — "Under Two Flags." I did read it, nevertheless, with greedy and fierce hope of coming on something unhealthy; but as a matter of fact all the parts that might have seemed unhealthy to an older person made no impression on me whatever. I simply enjoyed in a rather confused way the general adventures.

"My Uncle Irvine Bulloch was a midshipman on the *Alabama*, and fired the last gun discharged from her batteries in the fight with the *Kearsarge*."

I think there ought to be children's books. I think that the child will like grown-up books also, and I do not believe a child's book is really good unless grown-ups get something out of it. For instance, there is a book I did not have when I was a child because it was not written. It is Laura E. Richards's "Nursery Rhymes." My own children loved them dearly, and their mother and I loved them almost equally; the delightfully light-hearted "Man from New Mexico who Lost his Grandmother out in the Snow," the adventures of "The Owl, the Eel, and the Warming-Pan," and the extraordinary genealogy of the kangaroo whose "father was a whale with a feather in his tail who lived in the Greenland sea," while "his mother was a shark who kept very dark in the Gulf of Caribee."

As a small boy I had *Our Young Folks*, which I then firmly believed to be the very best magazine in the world — a belief, I may add, which I have kept to this day unchanged, for I seriously doubt if any magazine for old or young has ever surpassed it. Both my wife and I have the bound volumes of *Our Young Folks* which we preserved from our youth. I have tried to read again the Mayne Reid books which I so dearly loved as a boy, only to find, alas! that it is impossible. But I really believe that I enjoy going over *Our Young Folks* now nearly as much as ever. "Cast Away in the Cold," "Grandfather's Struggle for a Homestead," "The William Henry Letters" and a dozen others like them were first-class, good healthy stories, interesting in the first place, and in the next place teaching manliness, decency, and good conduct. At the cost of being deemed effeminate, I will add that I greatly liked the girls' stories — "Pussy Willow" and "A Summer in Leslie Goldthwaite's Life," just as I worshiped "Little Men" and "Little Women" and "An Old-Fashioned Girl."

This enjoyment of the gentler side of life did not prevent my reveling in such tales of adventure as Ballantyne's stories, or Marryat's "Midshipman Easy." I suppose everybody has kinks in him, and even as a child there were books which I ought to have liked and did not. For instance, I never cared at all for the first part of "Robinson Crusoe" (and although it is unquestionably the best part, I do not care for it now); whereas the second part, containing the adventures of Robinson Crusoe, with the wolves in the Pyrenees, and out in the Far East, simply fascinated me. What I did like in the first par° were the adventures before Crusoe finally reached his isl° the fight with the Sallee Rover, and the allusion to the s° beasts at night taking their improbable bath in th° Thanks to being already an embryo zoölogist, I d° "Swiss Family Robinson" because of the wholl° collection of animals met by that worthy ° ambled inland from the wreck. Even in po° lation of adventures that most appealed ° a pretty early age I began to read cer° notably Longfellow's poem, "The Sa°

absorbed me. This introduced me to Scandinavian literature; and I have never lost my interest in and affection for it.

Among my first books was a volume of a hopelessly unscientific kind by Mayne Reid, about mammals, illustrated with pictures no more artistic than but quite as thrilling as those in the typical school geography. When my father found how deeply interested I was in this not very accurate volume, he gave me a little book by J. G. Wood, the English writer of popular books on natural history, and then a larger one of his called "Homes Without Hands." Both of these were cherished possessions. They were studied eagerly; and they finally descended to my children. The "Homes Without Hands," by the way, grew to have an added association in connection with a pedagogical failure on my part. In accordance with what I believed was some kind of modern theory of making education interesting and not letting it become a task, I endeavored to teach my eldest small boy one or two of his letters from the title-page. As the letter "H" appeared in the title an unusual number of times, I selected that to begin on, my effort being to keep the small boy interested, not to let him realize that he was learning a lesson, and to convince him that he was merely having a good time. Whether it was the theory or my method of applying it that was defective I do not know, but I certainly absolutely eradicated from his brain any ability to learn what "H" was; and long after he had learned all the other letters of the alphabet in the old-fashioned way, he proved wholly unable to remember "H" under any circumstances.

Quite unknown to myself, I was, while a boy, under a hopeless disadvantage in studying nature. I was very near-sighted, so that the only things I could study were those I ran against or stumbled over. When I was about thirteen I was allowed to take lessons in taxidermy from a Mr. Bell, a tall, clean-shaven, white-haired old gentleman, as straight as an Indian, who had been a companion of Audubon's. He had a musty little shop, somewhat on the order of Mr. Venus's shop in "Our Mutual Friend," a little shop in which he had done very valuable work for science. This "vocational study," as I suppose it would be called by modern educators, spurred and directed my interest in collecting specimens for mounting and preservation. It was this summer that I got my first gun, and it puzzled me to find that my companions seemed to see things to shoot at which I could not see at all. One day they read aloud an advertisement in huge letters on a distant billboard, and I then realized that something was the matter, for not only was I unable to read the sign but I could not even see the letters. I spoke of this to my father, and soon afterwards got my first pair of spectacles, which literally opened an entirely new world to me. I had no idea how beautiful the world was until I got those spectacles. I had been a clumsy and awkward little boy, and while much of my clumsiness and awkwardness was doubtless due to general characteristics, a good deal of it was due to the fact that I could not see and yet was wholly ignorant that I was not seeing. The recollection of this experience gives me a keen sympathy with those who are trying in our public schools and elsewhere to remove the physical causes of deficiency in children, who are often unjustly blamed for being obstinate or unambitious, or mentally stupid.

This same summer, too, I obtained various new books on mammals and birds, including the publications of Spencer Baird, for instance, and made an industrious book-study of the subject. I did not accomplish much in outdoor study because I did not get spectacles until late in the fall, a short time before I started with the rest of the family for a second trip to Europe. We were living at Dobbs Ferry, on the Hudson. My gun was a breech-loading, pin-fire double-barrel, of French manufacture. It was an excellent gun for a clumsy and often absent-minded boy. There was no spring to open it, and if the mechanism became rusty it could be opened with a brick without serious damage. When the cartridges stuck they could be removed in the same fashion. If they were loaded, however, the result was not always happy, and I tattooed myself with partially unburned grains of powder more than once.

When I was fourteen years old, in the winter of '72 and '73, I visited Europe for the second time, and this trip formed a really useful part of my education. We went to Egypt, journeyed up the Nile, traveled through the Holy Land and part of Syria, visited Greece and Constantinople; and then we children spent the summer in a German family in Dresden. My first real collecting as a student of natural history was done in

Egypt during this journey. By this time I had a good working knowledge of American bird life from the superficially scientific standpoint. I had no knowledge of the ornithology of Egypt, but I picked up in Cairo a book by an English clergyman, whose name I have now forgotten, who described a trip up the Nile, and in an appendix to his volume gave an account of his bird collection. I wish I could remember the name of the author now, for I owe that book very much. Without it I should have been collecting entirely in the dark, whereas with its aid I could generally find out what the birds were. My first knowledge of Latin was obtained by learning the scientific names of the birds and mammals which I collected and classified by the aid of such books as this one.

The proprietor of the "Roosevelt Museum of Natural History."

*Theodore Roosevelt at the age of ten.*

The birds I obtained up the Nile and in Palestine represented merely the usual boy's collection. Some years afterward I gave them, together with the other ornithological specimens I had gathered, to the Smithsonian Institution in Washington, and I think some of them also to the American Museum of Natural History of New York. I am told that the skins are to be found yet in both places and in other public collections. I doubt whether they have my original labels on them. With great pride the directors of the "Roosevelt Museum," consisting of myself and the two cousins aforesaid, had printed a set of Roosevelt Museum labels in pink ink preliminary to what was regarded as my adventurous trip to Egypt. This bird-collecting gave what was really the chief zest to my Nile journey. I was old enough and had read enough to enjoy the temples and the desert scenery and the general feeling of romance; but this in time would have palled if I had not also had the serious work of collecting and preparing my specimens. Doubtless the family had their moments of suffering — especially on one occasion when a well-meaning maid extracted from my taxidermist's outfit the old tooth-brush with which I put on the skins the arsenical soap necessary for their preservation, partially washed it, and left it with the rest of my wash kit for my own personal use. I suppose that all growing boys tend to be grubby; but the ornithological small boy, or

"This, and subsequent natural histories, were written down in blank books in simplified spelling, wholly unpremeditated and unscientific."

indeed the boy with the taste for natural history of any kind, is generally the very grubbiest of all. An added element in my case was the fact that while in Egypt I suddenly started to grow. As there were no tailors up the Nile, when I got back to Cairo I needed a new outfit. But there was one suit of clothes too good to throw away, which we kept for a "change," and which was known as my "Smike suit," because it left my wrists and ankles as bare as those of poor Smike himself.

When we reached Dresden we younger children were left to spend the summer in the house of Herr Minckwitz, a member of either the Municipal or the Saxon Government — I have forgotten which. It was hoped that in this way we would acquire some knowledge of the German language and literature. They were the very kindest family imaginable. I shall never forget the unwearied patience of the two daughters. The father and mother, and a shy, thin, student cousin who was living in the flat, were no less kind. Whenever I could get out into the country I collected specimens industriously and enlivened the household with hedge-hogs and other small beasts and reptiles which persisted in escaping from partially closed bureau drawers. The two sons were fascinating students from the University of Leipsic, both of them belonging to dueling corps, and much scarred in consequence. One, a famous swordsman, was called *Der Rothe Herzog* (the Red Duke), and the other was nicknamed *Herr Nasehorn* (Sir Rhinoceros) because the tip of his nose had been cut off in a duel and sewn on again. I learned a good deal of German here, in spite of myself, and above all I became fascinated with the Nibelungenlied. German prose never became really easy to me in the sense that French prose did, but for German poetry I cared as much as for English poetry. Above all, I gained an impression of the German people which I never got over. From that time to this it would have been quite impossible to make me feel that the Germans were really foreigners. The affection, the *Gemüthlichkeit* (a quality which cannot be exactly expressed by any single English word), the capacity for hard work, the sense of duty, the delight in studying literature and science, the pride in the new Germany, the more than kind and friendly interest in three strange children — all these manifestations of the German character and of German family life made a subconscious impression upon me which I did not in the least define at the time, but which is very vivid still forty years later.

When I got back to America, at the age of fifteen, I began serious study to enter Harvard under Mr. Arthur Cutler, who later founded the Cutler School in New York. I could not go to school because I knew so much less than most boys of my age in some subjects and so much more in others. In science and history and geography and in unexpected parts of German and French I was strong, but lamentably weak in Latin and Greek and mathematics. My grandfather had made his summer home in Oyster Bay a number of years before, and my father now made Oyster Bay the summer home of his family also. Along with my college preparatory studies I carried on the work of a practical student of natural history. I worked with greater industry than either intelligence or success, and made very few additions to the sum of human knowledge; but to this day certain obscure ornithological publications may be found in which are recorded such items as, for instance, that on one occasion a fish-crow, and on another an Ipswich sparrow, were obtained by one Theodore Roosevelt, Jr., at Oyster Bay, on the shore of Long Island Sound.

In the fall of 1876 I entered Harvard, graduating in 1880. I thoroughly enjoyed Harvard, and I am sure it did me good, but only in the general effect, for there was very little in my actual studies which helped me in after life. More than one of my own sons have already profited by their friendship with certain of their masters in school or college. I certainly profited by my friendship with one of my tutors, Mr. Cutler; and in Harvard I owed much to the professor of English, Mr. A. S. Hill. Doubtless through my own fault, I saw almost nothing of President Eliot and very little of the professors. I ought to have gained much more than I did gain from writing the themes and forensics. My failure to do so may have been partly due to my taking no interest in the subjects. Before I left Harvard I was already writing one or two chapters of a book I afterwards published on the Naval War of 1812. Those chapters were so dry that they would have made a dictionary seem light reading by comparison. Still, they represented purpose and serious interest on my part, not the perfunctory effort to do well enough to get a certain mark; and corrections of them by a skilled older man would have impressed me and have commanded my respectful attention. But I was not sufficiently developed to make myself take an intelligent interest in some of the subjects assigned me — the character of the Gracchi, for instance. A very clever and studious lad would no doubt have done so, but I personally did not grow up to this particular subject until a good many years later. The frigate and sloop actions between the American and British sea-tigers of 1812 were much more within my grasp. I worked drearily at the Gracchi because I had to; my conscientious and much-to-be-pitied professor dragging me through the theme by main strength, with my feet firmly planted in dull and totally idea-proof resistance.

I had at the time no idea of going into public life, and I never studied elocution or practiced debating. This was a loss to me in one way. In another way it was not. Personally I have not the slightest sympathy with debating contests in which each side is arbitrarily assigned a given proposition and told to maintain it without the least reference to whether those maintaining it believe in it or not. I know that under our system this is necessary for lawyers, but I emphatically disbelieve in it as regards general discussion of political, social, and industrial matters. What we need is to turn out of our colleges young men with ardent convictions on the side of the right; not young men who can make a good argument for either right or wrong as their interest bids them. The present method of carrying on debates on such subjects as "Our Colonial Policy," or "The Need of a Navy," or "The Proper Position of the Courts in Constitutional Questions," encourages precisely the wrong attitude among those who take part in them. There is no effort to instill sincerity and intensity of conviction. On the contrary, the net result is to make the contestants feel that their convictions have nothing to do with their arguments. I am sorry I did not study elocution in college; but I am exceedingly glad that I did not take part in the type of debate in which stress is laid, not upon getting a speaker to think rightly, but on getting him to talk glibly on the side to which he is assigned, without regard either to what his convictions are or to what they ought to be.

I was a reasonably good student in college, standing just within the first tenth of my class, if I remember rightly; although I am not sure whether this means the tenth of the whole number that entered or of those that graduated. I was given a Phi Beta Kappa "key." My chief interests were scientific. When I entered college, I was devoted to out-of-doors natural history, and my ambition was to be a scientific man of the Audubon, or Wilson, or Baird, or Coues type — a man like Hart Merriam, or Frank Chapman, or Hornaday, to-day. My father had from the earliest days instilled into me the knowledge that I was to work and to make my own way in the world, and I had always supposed that this meant that I must enter business. But in my freshman year (he died when I was a sophomore) he told me that if I wished to become a scientific man I could do so. He explained that I must be sure that I really intensely desired to do scientific work, because if I went into it I must make it a serious career; that he had made enough money to enable me to take up such a career and do nonremunerative work of value *if I intended to do the very best work there was in me*; but that I must not dream of taking it up as a dilettante. He also gave me a piece of advice that I have always remembered, namely, that, if I was not going to earn money, I must even things up by not spending it. As he expressed it, I had to keep the fraction constant, and if I was not able to increase the numerator, then I must reduce the denominator. In other words, if I went into a scientific career, I must definitely abandon all thought of the enjoyment that could accompany a money-making career, and must find my pleasures elsewhere.

After this conversation I fully intended to make science my life-work. I did not, for the simple reason that at that time Harvard, and I suppose our other colleges, utterly ignored the possibilities of the faunal naturalist, the outdoor naturalist and observer of nature. They treated biology as purely a science of the laboratory and the microscope, a science whose adherents were to spend their time in the study of minute forms of marine life, or else in section-cutting and the study of the tissues of the higher organisms under the microscope. This attitude was, no doubt, in part due to the fact that in most colleges then there was a not always intelligent copying of what was done in the great German universities. The sound revolt against superficiality of study had been carried to an extreme; thoroughness in minutiæ as the only end of study had been erected into a fetish. There was a total failure to understand the great variety of kinds of work that could be done by naturalists, including what could be done by outdoor naturalists — the kind of work which Hart Merriam and his assistants in the Biological Survey have carried to such a high degree of perfection as regards North American mammals. In the entirely proper desire to be thorough and to avoid slipshod methods, the tendency was to treat as not serious, as unscientific, any kind of work that was not carried on with laborious minuteness in the laboratory. My taste was specialized in a totally different direction, and I had no more desire or ability to be a microscopist and section-cutter than to be a mathematician. Accordingly I abandoned all thought of becoming a scientist. Doubtless this meant that I really did not have the intense devotion to science which I thought I had; for, if I had possessed such devotion, I would have carved out a career for myself somehow without regard to discouragements.

As regards political economy, I was of course while in college taught the *laissez-faire* doctrines — one of them being free trade — then accepted as canonical. Most American boys of my age were taught both by their surroundings and by their studies certain principles which were very valuable from the standpoint of National interest, and certain others which were very much the reverse. The political economists were not especially to blame for this; it was the general attitude of the writers who wrote for us of that generation. Take my beloved *Our Young Folks*, the magazine of which I have already spoken, and which taught me much more than any of my text-books. Everything in this magazine instilled the individual virtues, and the necessity of character as the chief factor in any man's success — a teaching in which I now believe as sincerely as ever, for all the laws that the wit of man can devise will never make a man a worthy citizen unless he has within himself the right stuff, unless he has self-reliance, energy, courage, the power of insisting on his own rights and the sympathy that makes him regardful of the rights of others. All this individual morality I was taught by the books I read at home and the books I studied at Harvard. But there was almost no teaching of the need for collective action, and of the fact that in addition to, not as a substitute for, individual responsibility, there is a collective responsibility. Books such as Herbert Croly's "Promise of American Life" and Walter E. Weyl's "New Democracy" would generally at that time have been treated either as unintelligible or else as pure heresy.

The teaching which I received was genuinely democratic in one way. It was not so democratic in another. I grew into manhood thoroughly imbued with the feeling that a man must be respected for what he made of himself. But I had also, consciously or unconsciously, been taught that socially and industrially pretty much the whole duty of the man lay in thus making the best of himself; that he should be honest in his dealings with others and charitable in the old-fashioned way to the unfortunate; but that it was no part of his business to join with others in trying to make things better for the many by curbing the abnormal and excessive development of individualism in a few. Now I do not mean that this training was by any means all bad. On the contrary, the insistence upon individual responsibility was, and is, and always will be, a prime necessity. Teaching of the kind I absorbed from both my textbooks and my surroundings is a healthy anti-scorbutic to the sentimentality which by complacently excusing the individual for all his shortcomings would finally hopelessly weaken the spring of moral purpose. It also keeps alive that virile vigor for the lack of which in the average individual no possible perfection of law or of community action can ever atone. But such teaching, if not corrected by other teaching, means acquiescence in a riot of lawless business individualism which would be quite as destructive to real civilization as the lawless military individualism of the Dark Ages. I left college and entered the big world owing more than I can express to the training I had received, especially in my own home; but with much else also to learn if I were to become really fitted to do my part in the work that lay ahead for the generation of Americans to which I belonged.

# *Chapter II*

## THE VIGOR OF LIFE

Looking back, a man really has a more objective feeling about himself as a child than he has about his father or mother. He feels as if that child were not the present he, individually, but an ancestor; just as much an ancestor as either of his parents. The saying that the child is the father to the man may be taken in a sense almost the reverse of that usually given to it. The child is father to the man in the sense that his individuality is separate from the individuality of the grown-up into which he turns. This is perhaps one reason why a man can speak of his childhood and early youth with a sense of detachment.

Having been a sickly boy, with no natural bodily prowess, and having lived much at home, I was at first quite unable to hold my own when thrown into contact with other boys of rougher antecedents. I was nervous and timid. Yet from reading of the people I admired — ranging from the soldiers of Valley Forge, and Morgan's riflemen, to the heroes of my favorite stories — and from hearing of the feats performed by my Southern forefathers and kinsfolk, and from knowing my father, I felt a great admiration for men who were fearless and who could hold their own in the world, and I had a great desire to be like them. Until I was nearly fourteen I let this desire take no more definite shape than day-dreams. Then an incident happened that did me real good. Having an attack of asthma, I was sent off by myself to Moosehead Lake. On the stage-coach ride thither I encountered a couple of other boys who were about my own age, but very much more competent and also much more mischievous. I have no doubt they were good-hearted boys, but they were boys! They found that I was a foreordained and predestined victim, and industriously proceeded to make life miserable for me. The worst feature was that when I finally tried to fight them I discovered that either one singly could not only handle me with easy contempt, but handle me so as not to hurt me much and yet to prevent my doing any damage whatever in return.

Bronze Cougar, by Alexander P. Proctor.
Presented to Mr. Roosevelt by the "Tennis Cabinet."

The experience taught me what probably no amount of good advice could have taught me. I made up my mind that I must try to learn so that I would not again be put in such a helpless position; and having become quickly and bitterly conscious that I did not have the natural prowess to hold my own, I decided that I would try to supply its place by training. Accordingly, with my father's hearty approval, I started to learn to box. I was a painfully slow and awkward pupil, and certainly worked two or three years before I made any perceptible improvement whatever. My first boxing-master was John Long, an ex-prize-fighter. I can see his rooms now, with colored pictures of the fights between Tom Hyer and Yankee Sullivan, and Heenan and Sayers, and other great events in the annals of the squared circle. On one occasion, to excite interest among his patrons, he held a series of "championship" matches for the different weights, the prizes being, at least in my own class, pewter mugs of a value, I should suppose, approximating fifty cents. Neither he nor I had any idea that I could do anything, but I was entered in the lightweight contest, in which it happened that I was pitted in succession against a couple of reedy striplings who were even worse than I was. Equally to their surprise and to my own, and to John Long's, I won, and the pewter mug became one of my most prized possessions. I kept it, and alluded to it, and I fear bragged about it, for a number of years, and I only wish I knew where it was now. Years later I read an account of a little man who once in a fifth-rate handicap race won a worthless pewter medal and joyed in it ever after. Well, as soon as I read that story I felt that that little man and I were brothers.

This was, as far as I remember, the only one of my exceedingly rare athletic triumphs which would be worth relating. I did a good deal of boxing and wrestling in Harvard, but never attained to the first rank in either, even at my own weight. Once, in the big contests in the Gym, I got either into the finals or semi-finals, I forgot which; but aside from this the chief part I played was to act as trial horse for some friend or classmate who did have a chance of distinguishing himself in the championship contests.

I was fond of horseback-riding, but I took to it slowly and with difficulty, exactly as with boxing. It was a long time before I became even a respectable rider, and I never got much higher. I mean by this that I never became a first-flight man in the hunting field, and never even approached the bronco-busting class in the West. Any man, if he chooses, can gradually school himself to the requisite nerve, and gradually learn the requisite seat and hands, that will enable him to do respectably across country, or to perform the average work on a ranch. Of my ranch experiences I shall speak later. At intervals after leaving college I hunted on Long Island with the Meadowbrook hounds. Almost the only experience I ever had in this connection that was of any interest was on one occasion when I broke my arm. My purse did not permit me to own expensive horses. On this occasion I was riding an animal, a buggy horse originally, which its owner sold because now and then it insisted on thoughtfully lying down when in harness. It never did this under the saddle; and when he turned it out to grass it would solemnly hop over the fence and get somewhere where it did not belong. The last trait was what converted it into a hunter. It was a natural jumper, although without any speed. On the hunt in question I got along very well until the pace winded my ex-buggy horse, and it turned a somersault over a fence. When I got on it after the fall I found I could not use my left arm. I supposed it was merely a strain. The buggy horse was a sedate animal which I rode with a snaffle. So we pounded along at the tail of the hunt, and I did not appreciate that my arm was broken for three or four fences. Then we came to a big drop, and the jar made the bones slip past one another so as to throw the hand out of position. It did not hurt me at all, and

"Any man, if he chooses, can gradually school himself so as to do respectably across country."

as the horse was as easy to sit as a rocking-chair, I got in at the death.

I think August Belmont was master of the hunt when the above incident occurred. I know he was master on another occasion on which I met with a mild adventure. On one of the hunts when I was out a man was thrown, dragged by one stirrup, and killed. In consequence I bought a pair of safety stirrups, which I used the next time I went out. Within five minutes after the run began I found that the stirrups were so very "safe" that they would not stay in at all. First one went off at one jump, and then the other at another jump — with a fall for me on each occasion. I hated to give up the fun so early, and accordingly finished the run without any stirrups. My horse never went as fast as on that run. Doubtless a first-class horseman can ride as well without stirrups as with them. But I was not a first-class horseman. When anything unexpected happened, I was apt to clasp the solemn buggy horse firmly with my spurred heels, and the result was that he laid himself out to do his best in the way of galloping. He speedily found that, thanks to the snaffle bit, I could not pull him in, so when we came to a down grade he would usually put on steam. Then if there was a fence at the bottom and he checked at all, I was apt to shoot forward, and in such event we went over the fence in a way that reminded me of Leech's picture, in *Punch*, of Mr. Tom Noddy and his mare jumping a fence in the following order: Mr. Tom Noddy, I; his mare, II. However, I got in at the death this time also.

I was fond of walking and climbing. As a lad I used to go to the north woods, in Maine, both in fall and winter. There I made life friends of two men, Will Dow and Bill Sewall: I canoed with them, and tramped through the woods with them, visiting the winter logging camps on snow-shoes. Afterward they were with me in the West. Will Dow is dead. Bill Sewall was collector of customs under me, on the Aroostook border. Except when hunting I never did any mountaineering save for a couple of conventional trips up the Matterhorn and the Jungfrau on one occasion when I was in Switzerland.

I never did much with the shotgun, but I practiced a good deal with the rifle. I had a rifle range at Sagamore Hill, where I often took friends to shoot. Once or twice when I was vis-

ited by parties of released Boer prisoners, after the close of the
South African War, they and I held shooting matches together. The best man with both pistol and rifle who ever shot
there was Stewart Edward White. Among the many other
good men was a stanch friend, Baron Speck von Sternberg,
afterwards German Ambassador at Washington during my
Presidency. He was a capital shot, rider, and walker, a devoted
and most efficient servant of Germany, who had fought with
distinction in the Franco-German War when barely more
than a boy; he was the hero of the story of "the pig dog" in
Archibald Forbes's volume of reminiscences. It was he who
first talked over with me the raising of a regiment of horse riflemen from among the ranchmen and cowboys of the plains.
When Ambassador, the poor, gallant, tender-hearted fellow
was dying of a slow and painful disease, so that he could
not play with the rest of us, but the agony of his mortal illness never in the slightest degree interfered with his work.
Among the other men who shot and rode and walked with me
was Cecil Spring-Rice, who has just been appointed British
Ambassador to the United States. He was my groomsman,
my best man, when I was married — at St. George's, Hanover
Square, which made me feel as if I were living in one of
Thackeray's novels.

My own experience as regards marksmanship was much the
same as my experience as regards horsemanship. There are
men whose eye and hand are so quick and so sure that they
achieve a perfection of marksmanship to which no practice will
enable ordinary men to attain. There are other men who
cannot learn to shoot with any accuracy at all. In between
come the mass of men of ordinary abilities who, if they choose
resolutely to practice, can by sheer industry and judgment
make themselves fair rifle shots. The men who show this requisite industry and judgment can without special difficulty
raise themselves to the second class of respectable rifle shots;
and it is to this class that I belong. But to have reached
this point of marksmanship with the rifle at a target by no
means implies ability to hit game in the field, especially dangerous game. All kinds of other qualities, moral and physical,
enter into being a good hunter, and especially a good hunter
after dangerous game, just as all kinds of other qualities in

addition to skill with the rifle enter into being a good soldier. With dangerous game, after a fair degree of efficiency with the rifle has been attained, the prime requisites are cool judgment and that kind of nerve which consists in avoiding being rattled. Any beginner is apt to have "buck fever," and therefore no beginner should go at dangerous game.

Buck fever means a state of intense nervous excitement which may be entirely divorced from timidity. It may affect a man the first time he has to speak to a large audience just as it affects him the first time he sees a buck or goes into battle. What such a man needs is not courage but nerve control, cool-headedness. This he can get only by actual practice. He must, by custom and repeated exercise of self-mastery, get his nerves thoroughly under control. This is largely a matter of habit, in the sense of repeated effort and repeated exercise of will power. If the man has the right stuff in him, his will grows stronger and stronger with each exercise of it — and if he has not the right stuff in him he had better keep clear of dangerous game hunting, or indeed of any other form of sport or work in which there is bodily peril.

After he has achieved the ability to exercise wariness and judgment and the control over his nerves *which will make him shoot as well at the game as at a target*, he can begin his essays at dangerous game hunting, and he will then find that it does not demand such abnormal prowess as the outsider is apt to imagine. A man who can hit a soda-water bottle at the distance of a few yards can brain a lion or a bear or an elephant at that distance, and if he cannot brain it when it charges he can at least bring it to a standstill. All he has to do is to shoot as accurately as he would at a soda-water bottle; and to do this requires nerve, at least as much as it does physical address. Having reached this point, the hunter must not imagine that he is warranted in taking desperate chances. There are degrees in proficiency; and what is a warrantable and legitimate risk for a man to take when he has reached a certain grade of efficiency may be a foolish risk for him to take before he has reached that grade. A man who has reached the degree of proficiency indicated above is quite warranted in walking in at a lion at bay, in an open plain, to, say, within a hundred yards. If the lion has not charged, the man ought at that distance to knock him over and prevent his charging; and if the lion is already charging, the man ought at that distance to be able to stop him. But the amount of prowess which warrants a man in relying on his ability to perform this feat does not by any means justify him in thinking that, for instance, he can crawl after a wounded lion into thick cover. I have known men of indifferent prowess to perform this latter feat successfully, but at least as often they have been unsuccessful, and in these cases the result has been unpleasant. The man who habitually follows wounded lions into thick cover must be a hunter of the highest skill, or he can count with certainty on an ultimate mauling.

The first two or three bucks I ever saw gave me buck fever badly, but after I had gained experience with ordinary game I never had buck fever at all with dangerous game. In my case the overcoming of buck fever was the result of conscious effort and a deliberate determination to overcome it. More happily constituted men never have to make this determined effort at all — which may perhaps show that the average man can profit more from my experiences than he can from those of the exceptional man.

I have shot only five kinds of animals which can fairly be called dangerous game — that is, the lion, elephant, rhinoceros, and buffalo in Africa, and the big grizzly bear a quarter of a century ago in the Rockies. Taking into account not only my own personal experience, but the experiences of many veteran hunters, I regard all the four African animals, but especially the lion, elephant, and buffalo, as much more dangerous than the grizzly. As it happened, however, the only narrow escape I personally ever had was from a grizzly, and in Africa the animal killed closest to me as it was charging was a rhinoceros — all of which goes to show that a man must not generalize too broadly from his own personal experiences. On the whole, I think the lion the most dangerous of all these five animals; that is, I think that, if fairly hunted, there is a larger percentage of hunters killed or mauled for a given number of lions killed than for a given number of any one of the other animals. Yet I personally had no difficulties with lions. I twice killed lions which were at bay and just starting to charge, and I killed a heavy-maned male while it was in full charge. But in each instance I had plenty of leeway, the animal being so far off that even if my bullet had not been fatal I should have had time for a couple more shots. The African buffalo is undoubtedly a dangerous beast, but it happened that the few that I shot did not charge. A bull elephant, a vicious "rogue," which had been killing people in the native villages, did charge before being shot at. My son Kermit and I stopped it at forty yards. Another bull elephant, also unwounded, which charged, nearly got me, as I had just fired both cartridges from my heavy double-barreled rifle in killing the bull I was after — the first wild elephant I had ever seen. The second bull came through the thick brush to my left like a steam plow through a light snowdrift, everything snapping before his rush, and was so near that he could have hit me with his trunk. I slipped past him behind a tree. People have asked me how I felt on this occasion. My answer has always been that I suppose I felt as most men of like experience feel on such occasions. At such a moment a hunter is so very busy that he has no time to get frightened. He wants to get in his cartridges and try another shot.

Rhinoceros are truculent, blustering beasts, much the most stupid of all the dangerous game I know. Generally their attitude is one of mere stupidity and bluff. But on occasions they do charge wickedly, both when wounded and when entirely unprovoked. The first I ever shot I mortally wounded at a few rods' distance, and it charged with the utmost determination, whereat I and my companion both fired, and more by good luck than anything else brought it to the ground just thirteen paces from where we stood. Another rhinoceros may or may not have been meaning to charge me; I have never been certain which. It heard us and came at us through rather thick brush, snorting and tossing its head. I am by no means sure that it had fixedly hostile intentions, and indeed with my present experience I think it likely that if I had not fired it would have flinched at the last moment and either retreated or gone by me. But I am not a rhinoceros mind reader, and its actions were such as to warrant my regarding it as a suspicious character. I stopped it with a couple of bullets, and then followed it up and killed it. The skins of all these animals which I thus killed are in the National Museum at Washington.

But, as I said above, the only narrow escape I met with was not from one of these dangerous African animals, but from a grizzly bear. It was about twenty-four years ago. I had wounded the bear just at sunset, in a wood of lodge-pole pines, and, following him, I wounded him again, as he stood on the other side of a thicket. He then charged through the brush, coming with such speed and with such an irregular gait that, try as I would, I was not able to get the sight of my rifle on the brain-pan, though I hit him very hard with both the remaining barrels of my magazine Winchester. It was in the days of black powder, and the smoke hung. After my last shot, the first thing I saw was the bear's left paw as he struck at me, so close that I made a quick movement to one side. He was, however, practically already dead, and after another jump, and while in the very act of trying to turn to come at me, he collapsed like a shot rabbit.

By the way, I had a most exasperating time trying to bring in his skin. I was alone, traveling on foot with one very docile little mountain mare for a pack pony. The little mare cared nothing for bears or anything else, so there was no difficulty in packing her. But the man without experience can hardly realize the work it was to get that bearskin off the carcass and then to pack it, wet, slippery, and heavy, so that it would ride evenly on the pony. I was at the time fairly well versed in packing with a "diamond hitch," the standby of Rocky Mountain packers in my day; but the diamond hitch is a two-man job; and even working with a "squaw hitch," I got into endless trouble with that wet and slippery bearskin. With infinite labor I would get the skin on the pony and run the ropes over it until to all seeming it was fastened properly. Then off we would start, and after going about a hundred yards I would notice the hide beginning to bulge through between two ropes. I would shift one of them, and then the hide would bulge somewhere else. I would shift the rope again; and still the hide would flow slowly out as if it was lava. The first thing I knew it would come down on one side, and the little mare, with her feet planted resolutely, would wait for me to perform my part by getting that bearskin back in its proper place on the McClellan saddle which I was using as a makeshift pack saddle. The feat of killing the bear the previous day sank into nothing compared with the feat of making the bearskin ride properly as a pack on the following three days.

The reason why I was alone in the mountains on this occasion was because, for the only time in all my experience, I had a difficulty with my guide. He was a crippled old mountain man, with a profound contempt for "tenderfeet," a contempt that in my case was accentuated by the fact that I wore spectacles — which at that day and in that region were usually held to indicate a defective moral character in the wearer. He had never previously acted as guide, or, as he expressed it, "trundled a tenderfoot," and though a good hunter, who showed me much game, our experience together was not happy. He was very rheumatic and liked to lie abed late, so that I usually had to get breakfast, and, in fact, do most of the work around camp. Finally one day he declined to go out with me, saying that he had a pain. When, that afternoon, I got back to camp, I speedily found what the "pain" was. We were traveling very light indeed, I having practically nothing but my buffalo sleeping-bag, my wash kit, and a pair of socks. I had also taken a flask of whisky for emergencies — although, as I found that the emergencies never arose and that tea was better than whisky when a man was cold or done out, I abandoned the practice of taking whisky on hunting trips twenty years ago. When I got back to camp the old fellow was sitting on a tree-trunk, very erect, with his rifle across his knees, and in response to my nod of greeting he merely leered at me. I leaned my rifle against a tree, walked over to where my bed was lying, and, happening to rummage in it for something, I found the whisky flask was empty. I turned on him at once and accused him of having drunk it, to which he merely responded by asking what I was going to do about it. There did not seem much to do, so I said that we would part company — we were only four or five days from a settlement — and I would go in alone, taking one of the horses. He responded by cocking his rifle and saying that I could go alone and be damned to me, but I could not take any horse. I answered "all right," that if I could not I could not, and began to move around to get some flour and salt pork. He was misled by my quietness and by the fact that I had not in any way resented either his actions or his language during the days

The Tennis Cabinet.

The names of those standing behind Mr. Roosevelt are, from left to right: Captain Archibald Butt; William Phillips, Assistant Secretary of State; Herbert Knox Smith, Commissioner of Corporations; Beekman Winthrop, Assistant Secretary of the Treasury; Gifford Pinchot, Chief of the Forestry Service; Lawrence O. Murray, Comptroller; Henry L. Stimson, District Attorney; Herbert Satterlee, Assistant Secretary of the Navy; John J. McIlhenny, Civil Service Commissioner; Judge John C. Rose; Truman H. Newberry, Secretary of the Navy; Mr. George Woodruff, Counsel to the Forestry Service; M. Jusserand, French Ambassador; Mr. C. E. Heffelfinger; George von L. Meyer, Postmaster-General; Francis Leupp, Indian Commissioner; Mr. Justice Moody; James R. Garfield, Secretary of the Interior; Marshall Seth Bullock; Solicitor-General Hoyt; John C. Abernathy; Luther Kelly, Indian Agent; Robert Bacon, Secretary of State; C. P. Neill, Labor Commissioner; William D. Sewall, Collector of Customs; D. J. Keefe, Commissioner of Immigration; John C. O'Laughlin, Assistant Secretary of State; J. B. Reynolds; Dr. H. C. Pritchett; William Loeb, Jr., Secretary to the President.

we had been together, and did not watch me as closely as he ought to have done. He was sitting with the cocked rifle across his knees, the muzzle to the left. My rifle was leaning against a tree near the cooking things to his right. Managing to get near it, I whipped it up and threw the bead on him, calling, "Hands up!" He of course put up his hands, and then said, "Oh, come, I was only joking"; to which I answered, "Well, I am not. Now straighten your legs and let your rifle go to the ground." He remonstrated, saying the rifle would go off, and I told him to let it go off. However, he straightened his legs in such fashion that it came to the ground without a jar. I then made him move back, and picked up the rifle. By this time he was quite sober, and really did not seem angry, looking at me quizzically. He told me that if I would give him back his rifle, he would call it quits and we could go on together. I did not think it best to trust him, so I told him that our hunt was pretty well through, anyway, and that I would go home. There was a blasted pine on the trail, in plain view of the camp, about a mile off, and I told him that I would leave his rifle at that blasted pine if I could see him in camp, but that he must not come after me, for if he did I should assume that it was with hostile intent and would shoot. He said he had no intention of coming after me; and as he was very much crippled with rheumatism, I did not believe he would do so.

Accordingly I took the little mare, with nothing but some flour, bacon, and tea, and my bed-roll, and started off. At the blasted pine I looked round, and as I could see him in camp, I left his rifle there. I then traveled till dark, and that night, for the only time in my experience, I used in camping a trick of the old-time trappers in the Indian days. I did not believe I would be followed, but still it was not possible to be sure, so, after getting supper, while my pony fed round, I left the fire burning, repacked the mare and pushed ahead until it literally became so dark that I could not see. Then I picketed the mare, slept where I was without a fire until the first streak of dawn, and then pushed on for a couple of hours before halting to take breakfast and to let the little mare have a good feed. No plainsman needs to be told that a man should not lie near a fire if there is danger of an enemy creeping up on him, and that above all a man should not put himself in a position where he can be ambushed at dawn. On this second day I lost the trail, and toward nightfall gave up the effort to find it, camped where I was, and went out to shoot a grouse for supper. It was while hunting in vain for a grouse that I came on the bear and killed it as above described.

When I reached the settlement and went into the store, the storekeeper identified me by remarking: "You're the tenderfoot that old Hank was trundling, ain't you?" I admitted that I was. A good many years later, after I had been elected Vice-President, I went on a cougar hunt in northwestern Colorado with Johnny Goff, a famous hunter and mountain man. It was midwinter. I was rather proud of my achievements, and pictured myself as being known to the few settlers in the neighborhood as a successful mountain-lion hunter. I could not help grinning when I found out that they did not even allude to me as the Vice-President-elect, let alone as a hunter, but merely as "Johnny Goff's tourist."

Of course during the years when I was most busy at serious work I could do no hunting, and even my riding was of a decorous kind. But a man whose business is sedentary should get some kind of exercise if he wishes to keep himself in as good physical trim as his brethren who do manual labor. When I worked on a ranch, I needed no form of exercise except my work, but when I worked in an office the case was different. A couple of summers I played polo with some of my neighbors. I shall always believe we played polo in just the right way for middle-aged men with stables of the general utility order. Of course it was polo which was chiefly of interest to ourselves, the only onlookers being the members of our faithful families. My two ponies were the only occupants of my stable except a cart-horse. My wife and I rode and drove them, and they were used for household errands and for the children, and for two afternoons a week they served me as polo ponies. Polo is a good game, infinitely better for vigorous men than tennis or golf or anything of that kind. There is all the fun of football, with the horse thrown in; and if only people would be willing to play it in simple fashion it would be almost as much within their reach as golf. But at Oyster Bay our great and permanent amusements were rowing and sailing; I do not care for the latter, and am fond of the former.

I suppose it sounds archaic, but I cannot help thinking that the people with motor boats miss a great deal. If they would only keep to rowboats or canoes, and use oar or paddle themselves, they would get infinitely more benefit than by having their work done for them by gasoline. But I rarely took exercise merely as exercise. Primarily I took it because I liked it. Play should never be allowed to interfere with work; and a life devoted merely to play is, of all forms of existence, the most dismal. But the joy of life is a very good thing, and while work is the essential in it, play also has its place.

When obliged to live in cities, I for a long time found that boxing and wrestling enabled me to get a good deal of exercise in condensed and attractive form. I was reluctantly obliged to abandon both as I grew older. I dropped the wrestling earliest. When I became Governor, the champion middleweight wrestler of America happened to be in Albany, and I got him to come round three or four afternoons a week. Incidentally I may mention that his presence caused me a difficulty with the Comptroller, who refused to audit a bill I put in for a wrestling-mat, explaining that I could have a billiard-table, billiards being recognized as a proper Gubernatorial amusement, but that a wrestling-mat symbolized something unusual and unheard of and could not be permitted. The middleweight champion was of course so much better than I was that he could not only take care of himself but of me too and see that I was not hurt — for wrestling is a much more violent amusement than boxing. But after a couple of months he had to go away, and he left as a substitute a good-humored, stalwart professional oarsman. The oarsman turned out to know very little about wrestling. He could not even take care of himself, not to speak of me. By the end of our second afternoon one of his long ribs had been caved in and two of my short ribs badly damaged, and my left shoulder-blade so nearly shoved out of place that it creaked. He was nearly as pleased as I was when I told him I thought we would "vote the war a failure" and abandon wrestling. After that I took up boxing again. While President I used to box with some of the aides, as well as play single-stick with General Wood. After a few years I had to abandon boxing as well as wrestling, for in one bout a young captain of artillery cross-countered me on the eye, and the blow smashed the little blood-vessels. Fortunately it was my left eye, but the sight has been dim ever since, and if it had been the right eye I should have been entirely unable to shoot. Accordingly I thought it better to acknowledge that I had become an elderly man and would have to stop boxing. I then took up jiu-jitsu for a year or two.

When I was in the Legislature and was working very hard, with little chance of getting out of doors, all the exercise I got was boxing and wrestling. A young fellow turned up who was a second-rate prize-fighter, the son of one of my old boxing teachers. For several weeks I had him come round to my rooms in the morning to put on the gloves with me for half an hour. Then he suddenly stopped, and some days later I received a letter of woe from him from the jail. I found that he was by profession a burglar, and merely followed boxing as the amusement of his lighter moments, or when business was slack.

Naturally, being fond of boxing, I grew to know a good many prize-fighters, and to most of those I knew I grew genuinely attached. I have never been able to sympathize with the outcry against prize-fighters. The only objection I have to the prize ring is the crookedness that has attended its commercial development. Outside of this I regard boxing, whether professional or amateur, as a first-class sport, and I do not regard it as brutalizing. Of course matches can be conducted under conditions that make them brutalizing. But this is true of football games and of most other rough and vigorous sports. Most certainly prize-fighting is not half as brutalizing or demoralizing as many forms of big business and of the legal work carried on in connection with big business. Powerful, vigorous men of strong animal development must have some way in which their animal spirits can find vent. When I was Police Commissioner I found (and Jacob Riis will back me up in this) that the establishment of a boxing club in a tough neighborhood always tended to do away with knifing and gun-fighting among the young fellows who would otherwise have been in murderous gangs. Many of these young fellows were not naturally criminals at all, but they had to have some outlet for their activities. In the same way I have always regarded boxing as a first-class sport to encourage in the

Young Men's Christian Association. I do not like to see young Christians with shoulders that slope like a champagne bottle. Of course boxing should be encouraged in the army and navy. I was first drawn to two naval chaplains, Fathers Chidwick and Rainey, by finding that each of them had bought half a dozen sets of boxing-gloves and encouraged their crews in boxing.

When I was Police Commissioner, I heartily approved the effort to get boxing clubs started in New York on a clean basis. Later I was reluctantly obliged to come to the conclusion that the prize ring had become hopelessly debased and demoralized, and as Governor I aided in the passage of and signed the bill putting a stop to professional boxing for money. This was because some of the prize-fighters themselves were crooked, while the crowd of hangers-on who attended and made up and profited by the matches had placed the whole business on a basis of commercialism and brutality that was intolerable. I shall always maintain that boxing contests themselves make good, healthy sport. It is idle to compare them with bull-fighting; the torture and death of the wretched horses in bull-fighting is enough of itself to blast the sport, no matter how great the skill and prowess shown by the bull-fighters. Any sport in which the death and torture of animals is made to furnish pleasure to the spectators is debasing. There should always be the opportunity provided in a glove fight or bare-fist fight to stop it when one competitor is hopelessly outclassed or too badly hammered. But the men who take part in these fights are hard as nails, and it is not worth while to feel sentimental about their receiving punishment which as a matter of fact they do not mind. Of course the men who look on ought to be able to stand up with the gloves, or without them, themselves; I have scant use for the type of sportsmanship which consists merely in looking on at the feats of some one else.

Some as good citizens as I know are or were prize-fighters. Take Mike Donovan, of New York. He and his family represent a type of American citizenship of which we have a right to be proud. Mike is a devoted temperance man, and can be relied upon for every movement in the interest of good citizenship. I was first intimately thrown with him when I was

Police Commissioner. One evening he and I — both in dress suits — attended a temperance meeting of Catholic societies. It culminated in a lively set-to between myself and a Tammany Senator who was a very good fellow, but whose ideas of temperance differed radically from mine, and, as the event proved, from those of the majority of the meeting. Mike evidently regarded himself as my backer — he was sitting on the platform beside me — and I think felt as pleased and interested as if the set-to had been physical instead of merely verbal. Afterwards I grew to know him well both while I was Governor and while I was President, and many a time he came on and boxed with me.

Battling Nelson was another stanch friend, and he and I think alike on most questions of political and industrial life; although he once expressed to me some commiseration because, as President, I did not get anything like the money return for my services that he aggregated during the same term of years in the ring. Bob Fitzsimmons was another good friend of mine. He has never forgotten his early skill as a blacksmith, and among the things that I value and always keep in use is a penholder made by Bob out of a horseshoe, with an inscription saying that it is "Made for and presented to President Theodore Roosevelt by his friend and admirer, Robert Fitzsimmons." I have for a long time had the friendship of John L. Sullivan, than whom in his prime no better man ever stepped into the ring. He is now a Massachusetts farmer. John used occasionally to visit me at the White House, his advent always causing a distinct flutter among the waiting Senators and Congressmen. When I went to Africa he presented me with a gold-mounted rabbit's foot for luck. I carried it through my African trip; and I certainly had good luck.

On one occasion one of my prize-fighting friends called on me at the White House on business. He explained that he wished to see me alone, sat down opposite me, and put a very expensive cigar on the desk, saying, "Have a cigar." I thanked him and said I did not smoke, to which he responded, "Put it in your pocket." He then added, "Take another; put both in your pocket." This I accordingly did. Having thus shown at the outset the necessary formal courtesy, my visitor, an old and valued friend, proceeded to explain that a nephew of his had enlisted in the Marine Corps, but had been absent without leave, and was threatened with dishonorable discharge on the ground of desertion. My visitor, a good citizen and a patriotic American, was stung to the quick at the thought of such an incident occurring in his family, and he explained to me that it must not occur, that there must not be the disgrace to the family, although he would be delighted to have the offender "handled rough" to teach him a needed lesson; he added that he wished I would take him and handle him myself, for he knew that I would see that he "got all that was coming to him." Then a look of pathos came into his eyes, and he explained: "That boy I just cannot understand. He was my sister's favorite son, and I always took a special interest in him myself. I did my best to bring him up the way he ought to go. But there was just nothing to be done with him. His tastes were naturally low. He took to music!" What form this debasing taste for music assumed I did not inquire; and I was able to grant my friend's wish.

While in the White House I always tried to get a couple of hours' exercise in the afternoons — sometimes tennis, more often riding, or else a rough cross-country walk, perhaps down Rock Creek, which was then as wild as a stream in the White Mountains, or on the Virginia side along the Potomac. My companions at tennis or on these rides and walks we gradually grew to style the Tennis Cabinet; and then we extended the term to take in many of my old-time Western friends such as Ben Daniels, Seth Bullock, Luther Kelly, and others who had taken part with me in more serious outdoor adventures than walking and riding for pleasure. Most of the men who were oftenest with me on these trips — men like Major-General Leonard Wood; or Major-General Thomas Henry Barry; or Presley Marion Rixey, Surgeon-General of the Navy; or Robert Bacon, who was afterwards Secretary of State; or James Garfield, who was Secretary of the Interior; or Gifford Pinchot, who was chief of the Forest Service — were better men physically than I was; but I could ride and walk well enough for us all thoroughly to enjoy it. Often, especially in the winters and early springs, we would arrange for a point to point walk, not turning aside for anything — for instance, swimming Rock Creek or even the Potomac if it came

"Once I invited an entire class of officers who were attending lectures at
the War College, to come on one of these walks. I chose a route which
gave us the hardest climbing along the rocks and the deepest crossings
of the creek, and my army friends enjoyed it hugely — being the right
sort, to a man."

in our way. Of course under such circumstances we had to arrange that our return to Washington should be when it was dark, so that our appearance might scandalize no one. On several occasions we thus swam Rock Creek in the early spring when the ice was floating thick upon it. If we swam the Potomac, we usually took off our clothes. I remember one such occasion when the French Ambassador, Jusserand, who was a member of the Tennis Cabinet, was along, and, just as we were about to get in to swim, somebody said, "Mr. Ambassador, Mr. Ambassador, you haven't taken off your gloves," to which he promptly responded, "I think I will leave them on; we might meet ladies!"

We liked Rock Creek for these walks because we could do so much scrambling and climbing along the cliffs; there was almost as much climbing when we walked down the Potomac to Washington from the Virginia end of the Chain Bridge. I would occasionally take some big-game friend from abroad, Selous or St. George Littledale or Captain Radclyffe or Paul Niedicke, on these walks. Once I invited an entire class of officers who were attending lectures at the War College to come on one of these walks; I chose a route which gave us the hardest climbing along the rocks and the deepest crossings of the creek; and my army friends enjoyed it hugely — being the right sort, to a man.

On March 1, 1909, three days before leaving the Presidency, various members of the Tennis Cabinet lunched with me at the White House. "Tennis Cabinet" was an elastic term, and of course many who ought to have been at the lunch were, for one reason or another, away from Washington; but, to make up for this, a goodly number of out-of-town honorary members, so to speak, were present — for instance, Seth Bullock; Luther Kelly, better known as Yellowstone Kelly in the days when he was an army scout against the Sioux; and Abernathy, the wolf-hunter. At the end of the lunch Seth Bullock suddenly reached forward, swept aside a mass of flowers which made a centerpiece on the table, and revealed a bronze cougar by Proctor, which was a parting gift to me. The lunch party and the cougar were then photographed on the lawn.

Some of the younger officers who were my constant companions on these walks and rides pointed out to me the con-

dition of utter physical worthlessness into which certain of
the elder ones had permitted themselves to lapse, and the very
bad effect this would certainly have if ever the army were
called into service. I then looked into the matter for myself,
and was really shocked at what I found. Many of the older
officers were so unfit physically that their condition would
have excited laughter, had it not been so serious, to think that
they belonged to the military arm of the Government. A cavalry colonel proved unable to keep his horse at a smart trot for
even half a mile, when I visited his post; a Major-General
proved afraid even to let his horse canter, when he went on a
ride with us; and certain otherwise good men proved as
unable to walk as if they had been sedentary brokers. I consulted with men like Major-Generals Wood and Bell, who
were themselves of fine physique, with bodies fit to meet any
demand. It was late in my administration; and we deemed it
best only to make a beginning — experience teaches the most
inveterate reformer how hard it is to get a totally non-military
nation to accept seriously any military improvement. Accordingly, I merely issued directions that each officer should prove
his ability to walk fifty miles, or ride one hundred, in three
days. This is, of course, a test which many a healthy middle-
aged woman would be able to meet. But a large portion of
the press adopted the view that it was a bit of capricious
tyranny on my part; and a considerable number of elderly
officers, with desk rather than field experience, intrigued with
their friends in Congress to have the order annulled. So one
day I took a ride of a little over one hundred miles myself, in
company with Surgeon-General Rixey and two other officers.
The Virginia roads were frozen and in ruts, and in the afternoon and evening there was a storm of snow and sleet; and
when it had been thus experimentally shown, under unfavorable conditions, how easy it was to do in one day the task for
which the army officers were allowed three days, all open
objection ceased. But some bureau chiefs still did as much un-
derhanded work against the order as they dared, and it was
often difficult to reach them. In the Marine Corps Captain
Leonard, who had lost an arm at Tientsin, with two of his lieutenants did the fifty miles in one day; for they were vigorous
young men, who laughed at the idea of treating a fifty-mile

walk as over-fatiguing. Well, the Navy Department officials rebuked them, and made them take the walk over again in three days, on the ground that taking it in one day did not comply with the regulations! This seems unbelievable; but Leonard assures me it is true. He did not inform me at the time, being afraid to "get in wrong" with his permanent superiors. If I had known of the order, short work would have been made of the bureaucrat who issued it.*

*One of our best naval officers sent me the following letter, after the above had appeared: —

"I note in your Autobiography now being published in the *Outlook* that you refer to the reasons which led you to establish a physical test for the Army, and to the action you took (your 100-mile ride) to prevent the test being abolished. Doubtless you did not know the following facts:

"1. The first annual navy test of 50 miles in three days was subsequently reduced to 25 miles in two days in each quarter.

"2. This was further reduced to 10 miles each month, which is the present 'test,' and there is danger lest even this utterly insufficient test be abolished.

"I enclose a copy of a recent letter to the Surgeon General which will show our present deplorable condition and the worse condition into which we are slipping back.

"The original test of 50 miles in three days did a very great deal of good. It decreased by thousands of dollars the money expended on street car fare, and by a much greater sum the amount expended over the bar. It eliminated a number of the wholly unfit; it taught officers to walk; it forced them to learn the care of their feet and that of their men; and it improved their general health and was rapidly forming a taste for physical exercise."

The enclosed letter ran in part as follows: —

"I am returning under separate cover 'The Soldier's Foot and the Military Shoe.'

"The book contains knowledge of a practical character that is valuable for the men who HAVE TO MARCH, WHO HAVE SUFFERED FROM FOOT TROUBLES, AND WHO MUST AVOID THEM IN ORDER TO ATTAIN EFFICIENCY.

"The words in capitals express, according to my idea, the gist of the whole matter as regards military men.

"The army officer whose men break down on test gets a black eye. The one whose men show efficiency in this respect gets a bouquet.

"To such men the book is invaluable. There is no danger that they will neglect it. They will actually learn it, for exactly the same reasons that our fellows learn the gunnery instructions — or did learn them before they were withdrawn and burned.

"B U T, I have not been able to interest a single naval officer in this fine book. They will look at the pictures and say it is a good book, but they won't read it. The marine officers, on the contrary, are very much interested, be-

In no country with an army worth calling such is there a chance for a man physically unfit to stay in the service. Our countrymen should understand that every army officer — and every marine officer — ought to be summarily removed from the service unless he is able to undergo far severer tests than those which, as a beginning, I imposed. To follow any other course is to put a premium on slothful incapacity, and to do the gravest wrong to the Nation.

---

cause they have to teach their men to care for their feet and they must know how to care for their own. But the naval officers feel no such necessity, simply because their men do not have to demonstrate their efficiency by practice marches, and they themselves do not have to do a stunt that will show up their own ignorance and inefficiency in the matter.

"For example, some time ago I was talking with some chaps about shoes — the necessity of having them long enough and wide enough, etc., and one of them said: 'I have no use for such shoes, as I never walk except when I have to, and any old shoes do for the 10-mile-a-month stunt,' so there you are!

"When the first test was ordered, Edmonston (Washington shoe man) told me that he sold more real walking shoes to naval officers in three months than he had in the three preceding years. I know three officers who lost both big-toe nails after the first test, and another who walked nine miles in practice with a pair of heavy walking shoes that were too small and was laid up for three days — could not come to the office. I know plenty of men who after the first test had to borrow shoes from larger men until their feet 'went down' to their normal size.

"This test may have been a bit too strenuous for old hearts (of men who had never taken any exercise), but it was excellent as a matter of instruction and training of handling feet — and in an emergency (such as we soon may have in Mexico) sound hearts are not much good if the feet won't stand.

"However, the 25-mile test in two days each quarter answered the same purpose, for the reason that $12\frac{1}{2}$ miles will produce sore feet with bad shoes, and sore feet and lame muscles even with good shoes, if there has been no practice marching.

"It was the necessity of doing $12\frac{1}{2}$ MORE MILES ON THE SECOND DAY WITH SORE FEET AND LAME MUSCLES that made 'em sit up and take notice — made 'em practice walking, made 'em avoid street cars, buy proper shoes, show some curiosity about sox and the care of the feet in general.

"All this passed out with the introduction of the last test of 10 miles a month. As one fellow said: 'I can do that in sneakers' — but he couldn't if the second day involved a tramp on the sore feet.

"The point is that whereas formerly officers had to practice walking a bit and give some attention to proper footgear, now they don't have to, and the natural consequence is that they don't do it.

"There are plenty of officers who do not walk any more than is necessary

I have mentioned all these experiences, and I could mention scores of others, because out of them grew my philosophy — perhaps they were in part caused by my philosophy — of bodily vigor as a method of getting that vigor of soul without which vigor of the body counts for nothing. The dweller in cities has less chance than the dweller in the country to keep his body sound and vigorous. But he can do so, if only he will take the trouble. Any young lawyer, shopkeeper, or clerk, or shop-assistant can keep himself in good condition if he tries. Some of the best men who have ever served under me in the National Guard and in my regiment were former clerks or floor-walkers. Why, Johnny Hayes, the Marathon victor, and at one time world champion, one of my valued friends and supporters, was a floor-walker in Bloomingdale's big department store. Surely with Johnny Hayes as an example, any young man in a city can hope to make his body all that a vigorous man's body should be.

----

to reach a street car that will carry them from their residences to their offices. Some who have motors do not do so much. They take no exercise. They take cocktails instead and are getting beefy and 'ponchy,' and something should be done to remedy this state of affairs.

"It would not be necessary if service opinion required officers so to order their lives that it would be common knowledge that they were 'hard,' in order to avoid the danger of being selected out.

"We have no such service opinion, and it is not in process of formation. On the contrary, it is known that the 'Principal Dignitaries' unanimously advised the Secretary to abandon all physical tests. He, *a civilian*, was wise enough not to take the advice.

"I would like to see a test established that would oblige officers to take sufficient exercise to pass it without inconvenience. For the reasons given above, 20 miles in two days every other month would do the business, while 10 miles each month does not touch it, simply because nobody has to walk on 'next day' feet. As for the proposed test of so many hours 'exercise' a week, the flat foots of the pendulous belly muscles are delighted. They are looking into the question of pedometers, and will hang one of these on their wheezy chests and let it count every shuffling step they take out of doors.

"If we had an adequate test throughout 20 years, there would at the end of that time be few if any sacks of blubber at the upper end of the list; and service opinion against that sort of thing would be established."

These tests were kept during my administration. They were afterwards abandoned; not through perversity or viciousness; but through weakness, and inability to understand the need of preparedness in advance, if the emergencies of war are to be properly met, when, or if, they arrive.

I once made a speech to which I gave the title "The Strenuous Life." Afterwards I published a volume of essays with this for a title. There were two translations of it which always especially pleased me. One was by a Japanese officer who knew English well, and who had carried the essay all through the Manchurian campaign, and later translated it for the benefit of his countrymen. The other was by an Italian lady, whose brother, an officer in the Italian army who had died on duty in a foreign land, had also greatly liked the article and carried it round with him. In translating the title the lady rendered it in Italian as *Vigor di Vita*. I thought this translation a great improvement on the original, and have always wished that I had myself used "The Vigor of Life" as a heading to indicate what I was trying to preach, instead of the heading I actually did use.

There are two kinds of success, or rather two kinds of ability displayed in the achievement of success. There is, first, the success either in big things or small things which comes to the man who has in him the natural power to do what no one else can do, and what no amount of training, no perseverance or will power, will enable any ordinary man to do. This success, of course, like every other kind of success, may be on a very big scale or on a small scale. The quality which the man possesses may be that which enables him to run a hundred yards in nine and three-fifths seconds, or to play ten separate games of chess at the same time blindfolded, or to add five columns of figures at once without effort, or to write the "Ode to a Grecian Urn," or to deliver the Gettysburg speech, or to show the ability of Frederick at Leuthen or Nelson at Trafalgar. No amount of training of body or mind would enable any good ordinary man to perform any one of these feats. Of course the proper performance of each implies much previous study or training, but in no one of them is success to be attained save by the altogether exceptional man who has in him the something additional which the ordinary man does not have.

This is the most striking kind of success, and it can be attained only by the man who has in him the quality which separates him in kind no less than in degree from his fellows. But much the commoner type of success in every walk of life and in every species of effort is that which comes to the man who differs from his fellows not by the kind of quality which he possesses but by the degree of development which he has given that quality. This kind of success is open to a large number of persons, if only they seriously determine to achieve it. It is the kind of success which is open to the average man of sound body and fair mind, who has no remarkable mental or physical attributes, but who gets just as much as possible in the way of work out of the aptitudes that he does possess. It is the only kind of success that is open to most of us. Yet some of the greatest successes in history have been those of this second class — when I call it second class I am not running it down in the least, I am merely pointing out that it differs in kind from the first class. To the average man it is probably more useful to study this second type of success than to study the first. From the study of the first he can learn inspiration, he can get uplift and lofty enthusiasm. From the study of the second he can, if he chooses, find out how to win a similar success himself.

I need hardly say that all the successes I have ever won have been of the second type. I never won anything without hard labor and the exercise of my best judgment and careful planning and working long in advance. Having been a rather sickly and awkward boy, I was as a young man at first both nervous and distrustful of my own prowess. I had to train myself painfully and laboriously not merely as regards my body but as regards my soul and spirit.

When a boy I read a passage in one of Marryat's books which always impressed me. In this passage the captain of some small British man-of-war is explaining to the hero how to acquire the quality of fearlessness. He says that at the outset almost every man is frightened when he goes into action, but that the course to follow is for the man to keep such a grip on himself that he can act just as if he was not frightened. After this is kept up long enough it changes from pretense to reality, and the man does in very fact become fearless by sheer dint of practicing fearlessness when he does not feel it. (I am using my own language, not Marryat's.) This was the theory upon which I went. There were all kinds of things of which I was afraid at first, ranging from grizzly bears to "mean" horses and gun-fighters; but by acting as if I was not afraid I gradually ceased to be afraid. Most men can have the same experience if they choose. They will first learn to bear themselves well in trials which they anticipate and which they school themselves in advance to meet. After a while the habit will grow on them, and they will behave well in sudden and unexpected emergencies which come upon them unawares.

It is of course much pleasanter if one is naturally fearless, and I envy and respect the men who are naturally fearless. But it is a good thing to remember that the man who does not enjoy this advantage can nevertheless stand beside the man who does, and can do his duty with the like efficiency, *if he chooses to*. Of course he must not let his desire take the form merely of a day-dream. Let him dream about being a fearless man, and the more he dreams the better he will be, always provided he does his best to realize the dream in practice. He can do his part honorably and well provided only he sets fearlessness before himself as an ideal, schools himself to think of danger merely as something to be faced and overcome, and regards life itself as he should regard it, not as something to be thrown away, but as a pawn to be promptly hazarded whenever the hazard is warranted by the larger interests of the great game in which we are all engaged.

# Chapter III

## PRACTICAL POLITICS

W HEN I left Harvard, I took up the study of law. If I had been sufficiently fortunate to come under Professor Thayer, of the Harvard Law School, it may well be that I would have realized that the lawyer can do a great work for justice and against legalism.

But, doubtless chiefly through my own fault, some of the teaching of the law books and of the classroom seemed to me to be against justice. The *caveat emptor* side of the law, like the *caveat emptor* side of business, seemed to me repellent; it did not make for social fair dealing. The "let the buyer beware" maxim, when translated into actual practice, whether in law or business, tends to translate itself further into the seller making his profit at the expense of the buyer, instead of by a bargain which shall be to the profit of both. It did not seem to me that the law was framed to discourage as it should sharp practice, and all other kinds of bargains except those which are fair and of benefit to both sides. I was young; there was much in the judgment which I then formed on this matter which I should now revise; but, then as now, many of the big corporation lawyers, to whom the ordinary members of the bar then as now looked up, held certain standards which were difficult to recognize as compatible with the idealism I suppose every high-minded young man is apt to feel. If I had been obliged to earn every cent I spent, I should have gone wholeheartedly into the business of making both ends meet, and should have taken up the law or any other respectable occupation — for I then held, and now hold, the belief that a man's first duty is to pull his own weight and to take care of those dependent upon him; and I then believed, and now believe, that the greatest privilege and greatest duty for any man is to be happily married, and that no other form of success or service, for either man or woman, can be wisely accepted as a substitute or alternative. But it happened that I had been left enough money by my father not to make it necessary for me to think solely of earning bread for myself and my family. I had enough to get bread. What I had to do, if I wanted butter and jam, was to provide the butter and jam, but to count their cost as compared with other things. In other words, I made up my mind that, while I must earn money, I could afford to make earning money the secondary instead of the primary object of my career. If I had no money at all, then my first duty would have been to earn it in any honest fashion. As I had some money I felt that my need for more money was to be treated as a secondary need, and that while it was my business to make more money where I legitimately and properly could, yet that it was also my business to treat other kinds of work as more important than money-making.

Almost immediately after leaving Harvard in 1880 I began to take an interest in politics. I did not then believe, and I do not now believe, that any man should ever attempt to make politics his only career. It is a dreadful misfortune for a man to grow to feel that his whole livelihood and whole happiness depend upon his staying in office. Such a feeling prevents him from being of real service to the people while in office, and always puts him under the heaviest strain of pressure to barter his convictions for the sake of holding office. A man should have some other occupation — I had several other occupations — to which he can resort if at any time he is thrown out of office, or if at any time he finds it necessary to choose a course which will probably result in his being thrown out, unless he is willing to stay in at cost to his conscience.

At that day, in 1880, a young man of my bringing up and convictions could join only the Republican party, and join it I accordingly did. It was no simple thing to join it then. That was long before the era of ballot reform and the control of primaries; long before the era when we realized that the Government must take official notice of the deeds and acts of party organizations. The party was still treated as a private corporation, and in each district the organization formed a kind of social and political club. A man had to be regularly proposed for and elected into this club, just as into any other club. As a friend of mine picturesquely phrased it, I "had to break into the organization with a jimmy."

Under these circumstances there was some difficulty in joining the local organization, and considerable amusement and
excitement to be obtained out of it after I had joined.

It was over thirty-three years ago that I thus became a
member of the Twenty-first District Republican Association
in the city of New York. The men I knew best were the men
in the clubs of social pretension and the men of cultivated taste
and easy life. When I began to make inquiries as to the whereabouts of the local Republican Association and the means of
joining it, these men — and the big business men and lawyers
also — laughed at me, and told me that politics were "low";
that the organizations were not controlled by "gentlemen";
that I would find them run by saloon-keepers, horse-car conductors, and the like, and not by men with any of whom I
would come in contact outside; and, moreover, they assured
me that the men I met would be rough and brutal and unpleasant to deal with. I answered that if this were so it merely
meant that the people I knew did not belong to the governing class, and that the other people did — and that I intended
to be one of the governing class; that if they proved too hard-
bit for me I supposed I would have to quit, but that I certainly
would not quit until I had made the effort and found out
whether I really was too weak to hold my own in the rough
and tumble.

The Republican Association of which I became a member
held its meetings in Morton Hall, a large, barn-like room
over a saloon. Its furniture was of the canonical kind: dingy
benches, spittoons, a dais at one end with a table and chair
and a stout pitcher for iced water, and on the walls pictures
of General Grant, and of Levi P. Morton, to whose generosity we owed the room. We had regular meetings once or twice
a month, and between times the place was treated, at least on
certain nights, as a kind of club-room. I went around there
often enough to have the men get accustomed to me and to
have me get accustomed to them, so that we began to speak
the same language, and so that each could begin to live down
in the other's mind what Bret Harte has called "the defective
moral quality of being a stranger." It is not often that a man
can make opportunities for himself. But he can put himself
in such shape that when or if the opportunities come he is

ready to take advantage of them. This was what happened to me in connection with my experiences in Morton Hall. I soon became on good terms with a number of the ordinary "heelers" and even some of the minor leaders. The big leader was Jake Hess, who treated me with rather distant affability. There were prominent lawyers and business men who belonged, but they took little part in the actual meetings. What they did was done elsewhere. The running of the machine was left to Jake Hess and his captains of tens and of hundreds.

Among these lesser captains I soon struck up a friendship with Joe Murray, a friendship which is as strong now as it was thirty-three years ago. He had been born in Ireland, but brought to New York by his parents when he was three or four years old, and, as he expressed it, "raised as a barefooted boy on First Avenue." When not eighteen he had enlisted in the Army of the Potomac and taken part in the campaign that closed the Civil War. Then he came back to First Avenue, and, being a fearless, powerful, energetic young fellow, careless and reckless, speedily grew to some prominence as leader of a gang. In that district, and at that time, politics was a rough business, and Tammany Hall held unquestioned sway. The district was overwhelmingly Democratic, and Joe and his friends were Democrats who on election day performed the usual gang work for the local Democratic leader, whose business it was to favor and reward them in return. This same local leader, like many other greater leaders, became puffed up by prosperity, and forgot the instruments through which he had achieved prosperity. After one election he showed a callous indifference to the hard work of the gang and complete disregard of his before-election promises. He counted upon the resentment wearing itself out, as usual, in threats and bluster.

But Joe Murray was not a man who forgot. He explained to his gang his purposes and the necessity of being quiet. Accordingly they waited for their revenge until the next election day. They then, as Joe expressed it, decided "to vote furdest away from the leader" — I am using the language of Joe's youth — and the best way to do this was to vote the Republican ticket. In those days each party had a booth near the polling-place in each election district, where the party representative dispensed the party ballots. This had been a district in which, as a rule, very early in the day the Republican election leader had his hat knocked over his eyes and his booth kicked over and his ballots scattered; and then the size of the Democratic majority depended on an elastic appreciation of exactly how much was demanded from headquarters. But on this day things went differently. The gang, with a Roman sense of duty, took an active interest in seeing that the Republican was given his full rights. Moreover, they made the most energetic reprisals on their opponents, and as they were distinctly the tough and fighting element, justice came to her own with a whoop. Would-be repeaters were thrown out on their heads. Every person who could be cajoled or, I fear, intimidated, was given the Republican ticket, and the upshot was that at the end of the day a district which had never hitherto polled more than two or three per cent of its vote Republican broke about even between the two parties.

To Joe it had been merely an act of retribution in so far as it was not simply a spree. But the leaders at the Republican headquarters did not know this, and when they got over their paralyzed astonishment at the returns, they investigated to find out what it meant. Somebody told them that it represented the work of a young man named Joseph Murray. Accordingly they sent for him. The room in which they received him was doubtless some place like Morton Hall, and the men who received him were akin to those who had leadership in Morton Hall; but in Joe's eyes they stood for a higher civilization, for opportunity, for generous recognition of successful effort — in short, for all the things that an eager young man desires. He was received and patted on the back by a man who was a great man to the world in which he lived. He was introduced to the audience as a young man whose achievement was such as to promise much for the future, and moreover he was given a place in the post-office — as I have said, this was long before the day of Civil Service Reform.

Now, to the wrong kind of man all this might have meant nothing at all. But in Joe Murray's case it meant everything. He was by nature as straight a man, as fearless and as stanchly loyal, as any one whom I have ever met, a man to be trusted in any position demanding courage, integrity, and good faith. He did his duty in the public service, and became devotedly

Joseph Murray.

"By nature a straight man, as fearless and as
stanchly loyal as any one whom I have ever
met — a man to be trusted in any position
demanding courage, integrity, and good faith."

attached to the organization which he felt had given him his
chance in life. When I knew him he was already making his
way up; one of the proofs and evidences of which was that he
owned a first-class racing trotter — "Alice Lane" — behind
which he gave me more than one spin. During this first winter
I grew to like Joe and his particular cronies. But I had no idea
that they especially returned the liking, and in the first row we
had in the organization (which arose over a movement, that

I backed, to stand by a non-partisan method of street-cleaning) Joe and all his friends stood stiffly with the machine, and my side, the reform side, was left with only some half-dozen votes out of three or four hundred. I had expected no other outcome and took it good-humoredly, but without changing my attitude.

Next fall, as the elections drew near, Joe thought he would like to make a drive at Jake Hess, and after considerable planning decided that his best chance lay in the fight for the nomination to the Assembly, the lower house of the Legislature. He picked me as the candidate with whom he would be most likely to win; and win he did. It was not my fight, it was Joe's; and it was to him that I owe my entry into politics. I had at that time neither the reputation nor the ability to have won the nomination for myself, and indeed never would have thought of trying for it.

Jake Hess was entirely good-humored about it. In spite of my being anti-machine, my relations with him had been friendly and human, and when he was beaten he turned in to help Joe elect me. At first they thought they would take me on a personal canvass through the saloons along Sixth Avenue. The canvass, however, did not last beyond the first saloon. I was introduced with proper solemnity to the saloon-keeper — a very important personage, for this was before the days when saloon-keepers became merely the mortgaged chattels of the brewers — and he began to cross-examine me, a little too much in the tone of one who was dealing with a suppliant for his favor. He said he expected that I would of course treat the liquor business fairly; to which I answered, none too cordially, that I hoped I should treat all interests fairly. He then said that he regarded the licenses as too high; to which I responded that I believed they were really not high enough, and that I should try to have them made higher. The conversation threatened to become stormy. Messrs. Murray and Hess, on some hastily improvised plea, took me out into the street, and then Joe explained to me that it was not worth my while staying in Sixth Avenue any longer, that I had better go right back to Fifth Avenue and attend to my friends there, and that he would look after my interests on Sixth Avenue. I was triumphantly elected.

Once before Joe had interfered in similar fashion and secured the nomination of an Assemblyman; and shortly after
election he had grown to feel toward this Assemblyman that
he must have fed on the meat which rendered Cæsar proud,
as he became inaccessible to the ordinary mortals whose place
of resort was Morton Hall. He eyed me warily for a short time
to see if I was likely in this respect to follow in my predecessor's footsteps. Finding that I did not, he and all my other
friends and supporters assumed toward me the very pleasantest attitude that it was possible to assume. They did not ask
me for a thing. They accepted as a matter of course the view
that I was absolutely straight and was trying to do the best
I could in the Legislature. They desired nothing except that I
should make a success, and they supported me with hearty enthusiasm. I am a little at a loss to know quite how to express
the quality in my relationship with Joe Murray and my other
friends of this period which rendered that relationship so
beneficial to me. When I went into politics at this time I was
not conscious of going in with the set purpose to benefit other
people, but of getting for myself a privilege to which I was entitled in common with other people. So it was in my relationship with these men. If there had lurked in the innermost
recesses of my mind anywhere the thought that I was in some
way a patron or a benefactor, or was doing something noble
by taking part in politics, or that I expected the smallest consideration save what I could earn on my own merits, I am certain that somehow or other the existence of that feeling would
have been known and resented. As a matter of fact, there was
not the slightest temptation on my part to have any such feeling or any one of such feelings. I no more expected special
consideration in politics than I would have expected it in the
boxing ring. I wished to act squarely to others, and I wished
to be able to show that I could hold my own as against others.
The attitude of my new friends toward me was first one of
polite reserve, and then that of friendly alliance. Afterwards
I became admitted to comradeship, and then to leadership. I
need hardly say how earnestly I believe that men should have
a keen and lively sense of their obligations in politics, of their
duty to help forward great causes, and to struggle for the betterment of conditions that are unjust to their fellows, the men

and women who are less fortunate in life. But in addition to this feeling there must be a feeling of real fellowship with the other men and women engaged in the same task, fellowship of work, with fun to vary the work; for unless there is this feeling of fellowship, of common effort on an equal plane for a common end, it will be difficult to keep the relations wholesome and natural. To be patronized is as offensive as to be insulted. No one of us cares permanently to have some one else conscientiously striving to do him good; what we want is to work with that some one else for the good of both of us — any man will speedily find that other people can benefit him just as much as he can benefit them.

Neither Joe Murray nor I nor any of our associates at that time were alive to social and industrial needs which we now all of us recognize. But we then had very clearly before our minds the need of practically applying certain elemental virtues, the virtues of honesty and efficiency in politics, the virtue of efficiency side by side with honesty in private and public life alike, the virtues of consideration and fair dealing in business as between man and man, and especially as between the man who is an employer and the man who is an employee. On all fundamental questions Joe Murray and I thought alike. We never parted company excepting on the question of Civil Service Reform, where he sincerely felt that I showed doctrinaire affinities, that I sided with the pharisees. We got back again into close relations as soon as I became Police Commissioner under Mayor Strong, for Joe was then made Excise Commissioner, and was, I believe, the best Excise Commissioner the city of New York ever had. He is now a farmer, his boys have been through Columbia College, and he and I look at the questions, political, social, and industrial, which confront us in 1913 from practically the same standpoint, just as we once looked at the questions that confronted us in 1881.

There are many debts that I owe Joe Murray, and some for which he was only unconsciously responsible. I do not think that a man is fit to do good work in our American democracy unless he is able to have a genuine fellow-feeling for, understanding of, and sympathy with his fellow-Americans, whatever their creed or their birthplace, the section in which they live, or the work which they do, provided they possess the only kind of Americanism that really counts, the Americanism of the spirit. It was no small help to me, in the effort to make myself a good citizen and good American, that the political associate with whom I was on closest and most intimate terms during my early years was a man born in Ireland, by creed a Catholic, with Joe Murray's upbringing; just as it helped me greatly at a later period to work for certain vitally necessary public needs with Arthur von Briesen, in whom the spirit of the "Acht-und-Vierziger" idealists was embodied; just as my whole life was influenced by my long association with Jacob Riis, whom I am tempted to call the best American I ever knew, although he was already a young man when he came hither from Denmark.

I was elected to the Legislature in the fall of 1881, and found myself the youngest man in that body. I was reëlected the two following years. Like all young men and inexperienced members, I had considerable difficulty in teaching myself to speak. I profited much by the advice of a hard-headed old country-man — who was unconsciously paraphrasing the Duke of Wellington, who was himself doubtless paraphrasing somebody else. The advice ran: "Don't speak until you are sure you have something to say, and know just what it is; then say it, and sit down."

My first days in the Legislature were much like those of a boy in a strange school. My fellow-legislators and I eyed one another with mutual distrust. Each of us chose his seat, each began by following the lead of some veteran in the first routine matters, and then, in a week or two, we began to drift into groups according to our several affinities. The Legislature was Democratic. I was a Republican from the "silk stocking" district, the wealthiest district in New York, and I was put, as one of the minority members, on the Committee of Cities. It was a coveted position. I did not make any effort to get on, and, as far as I know, was put there merely because it was felt to be in accordance with the fitness of things.

A very short experience showed me that, as the Legislature was then constituted, the so-called party contests had no interest whatever for me. There was no real party division on most of the things that were of concern in State politics, both Republicans and Democrats being for and against them. My friendships were made, not with regard to party lines, but because I found, and my friends found, that we had the same convictions on questions of principle and questions of policy. The only difference was that there was a larger proportion of these men among the Republicans than among the Democrats, and that it was easier for me at the outset to scrape acquaintance, among the men who felt as I did, with the Republicans. They were for the most part from the country districts.

My closest friend for the three years I was there was Billy O'Neill, from the Adirondacks. He kept a small crossroads store. He was a young man, although a few years older than I was, and, like myself, had won his position without regard to the machine. He had thought he would like to be Assemblyman, so he had taken his buggy and had driven around Franklin County visiting everybody, had upset the local ring, and came to the Legislature as his own master. There is surely something in American traditions that does tend toward real democracy in spite of our faults and shortcomings. In most other countries two men of as different antecedents, ancestry, and surroundings as Billy O'Neill and I would have had far more difficulty in coming together. I came from the biggest city in America and from the wealthiest ward of that city, and he from a backwoods county where he kept a store at a crossroads. In all the unimportant things we seemed far apart. But in all the important things we were close together. We looked at all questions from substantially the same view-point, and we stood shoulder to shoulder in every legislative fight during those three years. He abhorred demagogy just as he abhorred corruption. He had thought much on political problems; he admired Alexander Hamilton as much as I did, being a strong believer in a powerful National government; and we both of us differed from Alexander Hamilton in being stout adherents of Abraham Lincoln's views wherever the rights of the people were concerned. Any man who has met with success, if he will be frank with himself, must admit that there has been a big element of fortune in the success. Fortune favored me, whereas her hand was heavy against Billy O'Neill. All his life he had to strive hard to wring his bread from harsh surroundings and a reluctant fate; if fate had been but a little kinder, I believe he would have had a great political career; and he would have done good service for the country in any position in which he might have been put.

There were other Republicans, like Isaac Hunt and Jonas van Duzer and Walter Howe and Henry Sprague, who were among my close friends and allies; and a gigantic one-eyed veteran of the Civil War, a gallant General, Curtis from St. Lawrence County; and a capital fellow, whom afterwards, when Governor, I put on the bench, Kruse, from Cattaraugus County. Kruse was a German by birth; as far as I know, the only German from Cattaraugus County at that time; and, besides being a German, he was also a Prohibitionist. Among the Democrats were Hamden Robb and Thomas Newbold, and Tom Welch of Niagara, who did a great service in getting the State to set aside Niagara Falls Park — after a discouraging experience with the first Governor before whom we brought the bill, who listened with austere patience to our arguments in favor of the State establishing a park, and then conclusively answered us by the question, "But, gentlemen, why should we spend the people's money when just as much water will run over the Falls without a park as with it?" Then there were a couple of members from New York and Brooklyn, Mike Costello and Pete Kelly.

Mike Costello had been elected as a Tammany man. He was as fearless as he was honest. He came from Ireland, and had accepted the Tammany Fourth of July orations as indicating the real attitude of that organization towards the rights of the people. A month or two in Albany converted him to a profound distrust of applied Tammany methods. He and I worked hand in hand with equal indifference to our local machines. His machine leaders warned him fairly that they would throw him out at the next election, which they did; but he possessed a seasoned-hickory toughness of ability to contend with adverse circumstances, and kept his head well above water. A better citizen does not exist; and our friendship has never faltered.

Peter Kelly's fate was a tragedy. He was a bright, well-educated young fellow, an ardent believer in Henry George. At the beginning he and I failed to understand each other or to get on together, for our theories of government were radically opposed. After a couple of months spent in active contests with men whose theories had nothing whatever to do with their practices, Kelly and I found in our turn that it really did not make much difference what our abstract theories were on questions that were not before the Legislature, in view of the fact that on the actual matters before the Legislature, the most important of which involved questions of elementary morality, we were heartily at one. We began to vote together and

Michael J. Costello.

act together, and by the end of the session found that in all practical matters that were up for action we thought together. Indeed, each of us was beginning to change his theories, so that even in theory we were coming closer together. He was ardent and generous; he was a young lawyer, with a wife and children, whose ambition had tempted him into politics, and who had been befriended by the local bosses under the belief that they could count upon him for anything they really wished. Unfortunately, what they really wished was often corrupt. Kelly defied them, fought the battles of the people with ardor and good faith, and when the bosses refused him a renomination, he appealed from them to the people. When we both came up for reëlection, I won easily in my district, where circumstances conspired to favor me; and Kelly, with exactly the same record that I had, except that it was more creditable because he took his stand against greater odds, was beaten in his district. Defeat to me would have meant merely chagrin; to Kelly it meant terrible material disaster. He had no money. Like every rigidly honest man, he had found that going into politics was expensive and that his salary as Assemblyman did not cover the financial outgo. He had lost his practice and he had incurred the ill will of the powerful, so that it was impossible at the moment to pick up his practice again; and the worry and disappointment affected him so much that shortly after election he was struck down by sickness. Just before Christmas some of us were informed that Kelly was in such financial straits that he and his family would be put out into the street before New Year. This was prevented by the action of some of his friends who had served with him in the Legislature, and he recovered, at least to a degree, and took up the practice of his profession. But he was a broken man. In the Legislature in which he served one of his fellow-Democrats from Brooklyn was the Speaker — Alfred C. Chapin, the leader and the foremost representative of the reform Democracy, whom Kelly zealously supported. A few years later Chapin, a very able man, was elected Mayor of Brooklyn on a reform Democratic ticket. Shortly after his election I was asked to speak at a meeting in a Brooklyn club at which various prominent citizens, including the Mayor, were present. I spoke on civic decency, and toward the close of my speech I sketched Kelly's career for my audience, told them how he had stood up for the rights of the people of Brooklyn, and how the people had failed to stand up for him, and the way he had been punished, precisely because he had been a good citizen who acted as a good citizen should act. I ended by saying that the reform Democracy had now come into power, that Mr. Chapin was Mayor, and that I very earnestly hoped recognition would at last be given to Kelly for the fight he had waged at such bitter cost to himself. My words created some impression, and Mayor Chapin at once said that he would take care of Kelly and see that justice was done him. I went home that evening much pleased. In the morning, at breakfast, I received a brief note from Chapin in these words: "It was nine last evening when you finished speaking of what Kelly had done, and when I said that I would take care of him. At ten last night Kelly died." He had been dying while I was making my speech, and he never knew that at last there was to be a tardy recognition of what he had done, a tardy justification for the sacrifices he had made. The man had fought, at heavy cost to himself and with entire disinterestedness, for popular rights; but no recognition for what he had done had come to him from the people, whose interest he had so manfully upheld.

Where there is no chance of statistical or mathematical measurement, it is very hard to tell just the degree to which conditions change from one period to another. This is peculiarly hard to do when we deal with such a matter as corruption. Personally I am inclined to think that in public life we are on the whole a little better and not a little worse than we were thirty years ago, when I was serving in the New York Legislature. I think the conditions are a little better in National, in State, and in municipal politics. Doubtless there are points in which they are worse, and there is an enormous amount that needs reformation. But it does seem to me as if, on the whole, things had slightly improved.

When I went into politics, New York City was under the control of Tammany, which was from time to time opposed by some other — and evanescent — city Democratic organization. The up-country Democrats had not yet fallen under Tammany sway, and were on the point of developing a big country political boss in the shape of David B. Hill. The Republican party was split into the Stalwart and Half-Breed factions. Accordingly neither party had one dominant boss, or one dominant machine, each being controlled by jarring and warring bosses and machines. The corruption was not what it had been in the days of Tweed, when outside individuals controlled the legislators like puppets. Nor was there any such centralization of the boss system as occurred later. Many of the members were under the control of local bosses or local machines. But the corrupt work was usually done through the members directly.

Of course I never had anything in the nature of legal proof of corruption, and the figures I am about to give are merely approximate. But three years' experience convinced me, in the first place, that there were a great many thoroughly corrupt men in the Legislature, perhaps a third of the whole number; and, in the next place, that the honest men outnumbered the corrupt men, and that, if it were ever possible to get an issue of right and wrong put vividly and unmistakably before them in a way that would arrest their attention and that would arrest the attention of their constituents, we could count on the triumph of the right. The trouble was that in most cases the issue was confused. To read some kinds of literature one would come to the conclusion that the only corruption in legislative circles was in the form of bribery by corporations, and that the line was sharp between the honest man who was always voting against corporations and the dishonest man who was always bribed to vote for them. My experience was the direct contrary of this. For every one bill introduced (not passed) corruptly to favor a corporation, there were at least ten introduced (not passed, and in this case not intended to be passed) to blackmail corporations. The majority of the corrupt members would be found voting for the blackmailing bills if they were not paid, and would also be found voting in the interests of the corporation if they were paid. The blackmailing, or, as they were always called, the "strike" bills, could themselves be roughly divided into two categories: bills which it would have been proper to pass, and those that it would not have been proper to pass. Some of the bills aimed at corporations were utterly wild and improper; and of these a proportion might be introduced by honest and foolish zealots, whereas most of them were introduced by men who had not the slightest intention of passing them, but who wished to be paid not to pass them. The most profitable type of bill to the accomplished blackmailer, however, was a bill aimed at a real corporate abuse which the corporation, either from wickedness or folly, was unwilling to remedy. Of the measures introduced in the interest of corporations there were also some that were proper and some that were improper. The corrupt legislators, the "black horse cavalry," as they were termed, would demand payment to vote as the corporations wished, no matter whether the bill was proper or improper. Sometimes, if the bill was a proper one, the corporation would have the virtue or the strength of mind to refuse to pay for its passage, and sometimes it would not.

A very slight consideration of the above state of affairs will show how difficult it was at times to keep the issue clear, for honest and dishonest men were continually found side by side voting now against and now for a corporation measure, the one set from proper and the other set from grossly improper motives. Of course part of the fault lay in the attitude of outsiders. It was very early borne in upon me that almost equal harm was done by indiscriminate defense of, and indiscriminate attack on, corporations. It was hard to say whether the man who prided himself upon always antagonizing the corporations, or the man who, on the plea that he was a good conservative, always stood up for them, was the more mischievous agent of corruption and demoralization.

In one fight in the House over a bill as to which there was a bitter contest between two New York City street railway organizations, I saw lobbyists come down on the floor itself and draw venal men out into the lobbies with almost no pretense of concealing what they were doing. In another case in which the elevated railway corporations of New York City, against the protest of the Mayor and the other local authorities, rushed through a bill remitting over half their taxes, some of the members who voted for the measure probably thought it was right; but every corrupt man in the House voted with them; and the man must indeed have been stupid who thought that these votes were given disinterestedly.

The effective fight against this bill for the revision of the elevated railway taxes — perhaps the most openly crooked measure which during my time was pushed at Albany — was waged by Mike Costello and myself. We used to spend a good deal of time in industrious research into the various bills introduced, so as to find out what their authors really had in mind; this research, by the way, being highly unappreciated and much resented by the authors. In the course of his researches Mike had been puzzled by an unimportant bill,

William O'Neill.   Mr. Spinney of the New York *Times*.   Theodore Roosevelt.
Isaac Hunt.   Walter Howe.

Theodore Roosevelt and a Group of his Friends, when he was a Member
of the New York Legislature.

seemingly related to a Constitutional amendment, introduced by a local saloon-keeper, whose interests, as far as we knew, were wholly remote from the Constitution, or from any form of abstract legal betterment. However, the measure seemed harmless; we did not interfere; and it passed the House. Mike, however, followed its career in the Senate, and at the last moment, almost by accident, discovered that it had been "amended" by the simple process of striking out everything after the enacting clause and unobtrusively substituting the proposal to remit the elevated railway taxes! The authors of the change wished to avoid unseemly publicity; their hope was to slip the measure through the Legislature and have it instantly signed by the Governor, before any public attention was excited. In the Senate their plan worked to perfection. There was in the Senate no fighting leadership of the forces of decency; and for such leadership of the non-fighting type the representatives of corruption cared absolutely nothing. By bold and adroit management the substitution in the Senate was effected without opposition or comment. The bill (in reality, of course, an absolutely new and undebated bill) then came back to the House nominally as a merely amended measure, which, under the rules, was not open to debate unless the amendment was first by vote rejected. This was the great bill of the session for the lobby; and the lobby was keenly alive to the need of quick, wise action. No public attention whatever had so far been excited. Every measure was taken to secure immediate and silent action. A powerful leader, whom the beneficiaries of the bill trusted, a fearless and unscrupulous man, of much force and great knowledge of parliamentary law, was put in the chair. Costello and I were watched; and when for a moment we were out of the House, the bill was brought over from the Senate, and the clerk began to read it, all the black horse cavalry, in expectant mood, being in their seats. But Mike Costello, who was in the clerk's room, happened to catch a few words of what was being read. In he rushed, despatched a messenger for me, and began a single-handed filibuster. The Speaker pro tem called him to order. Mike continued to speak and protest; the Speaker hammered him down; Mike continued his protests; the sergeant-at-arms was sent to arrest and remove him; and then I bounced in, and continued the protest, and refused to sit down or be silent. Amid wild confusion the amendment was declared adopted, and the bill was ordered engrossed and sent to the Governor. But we had carried our point. The next morning the whole press rang with what had happened; every detail of the bill, and every detail of the way it had been slipped through the Legislature, were made public. All the slow and cautious men in the House, who had been afraid of taking sides, now came forward in support of us. Another debate was held on the proposal to rescind the vote; the city authorities waked up to protest; the Governor refused to sign the bill. Two or three years later, after much litigation, the taxes are paid; in the newspapers it was stated that the amount was over $1,500,000. It was Mike Costello to whom primarily was due the fact that this sum was saved the public, and that the forces of corruption received a stinging rebuff. He did not expect recognition or reward for his services; and he got none. The public, if it knew of what he had done, promptly forgot it. The machine did not forget it, and turned him down at the next election.

One of the stand-by "strikes" was a bill for reducing the elevated railway fare, which at that time was ten cents, to five cents. In one Legislature the men responsible for the introduction of the bill suffered such an extraordinary change of heart that when the bill came up — being pushed by zealous radicals who really were honest — the introducers actually voted against it! A number of us who had been very doubtful about the principle of the bill voted for it simply because we were convinced that money was being used to stop it, and we hated to seem to side with the corruptionists. Then there came a wave of popular feeling in its favor, the bill was reintroduced at the next session, the railways very wisely decided that they would simply fight it on its merits, and the entire black horse cavalry contingent, together with all the former friends of the measure, voted against it. Some of us, who in our anger at the methods formerly resorted to for killing the bill had voted for it the previous year, with much heart-searching again voted for it, as I now think unwisely; and the bill was vetoed by the then Governor, Grover Cleveland. I believe the veto was proper, and those who felt as I did supported the veto; for although it was entirely right that the fare should be reduced to five cents, which was soon afterwards done, the method was unwise, and would have set a mischievous precedent.

An instance of an opposite kind occurred in connection with a great railway corporation which wished to increase its terminal facilities in one of our great cities. The representatives of the railway brought the bill to me and asked me to look into it, saying that they were well aware that it was the kind of bill that lent itself to blackmail, and that they wished to get it through on its merits, and invited the most careful examination. I looked carefully into it, found that the municipal authorities and the property-owners whose property was to be taken favored it, and also found that it was an absolute necessity from the standpoint of the city no less than from the standpoint of the railway. So I said I would take charge of it if I had guarantees that no money should be used and nothing improper done in order to push it. This was agreed to. I was then acting as chairman of the committee before which the bill went.

A very brief experience proved what I had already been practically sure of, that there was a secret combination of the majority of the committee on a crooked basis. On one pretext or another the crooked members of the committee held the bill up, refusing to report it either favorably or unfavorably. There were one or two members of the committee who were pretty rough characters, and when I decided to force matters I was not sure that we would not have trouble. There was a broken chair in the room, and I got a leg of it loose and put it down beside me where it was not visible, but where I might get at it in a hurry if necessary. I moved that the bill be reported favorably. This was voted down without debate by the "combine," some of whom kept a wooden stolidity of look, while others leered at me with sneering insolence. I then moved that it be reported unfavorably, and again the motion was voted down by the same majority and in the same fashion. I then put the bill in my pocket and announced that I would report it anyhow. This almost precipitated a riot, especially when I explained, in answer to statements that my conduct would be exposed on the floor of the Legislature, that in that case I should give the Legislature the reasons why I suspected that the men holding up all report of the bill were holding it up for purposes of blackmail. The riot did not come off; partly, I think, because the opportune production of the chair-leg had a sedative effect, and partly owing to wise counsels from one or two of my opponents.

Accordingly I got the bill reported to the Legislature and put on the calendar. But here it came to a dead halt. I think this was chiefly because most of the newspapers which noticed the matter at all treated it in such a cynical spirit as to encourage the men who wished to blackmail. These papers reported the introduction of the bill, and said that "all the hungry legislators were clamoring for their share of the pie"; and they accepted as certain the fact that there was going to be a division of "pie." This succeeded in frightening honest men, and also in relieving the rogues; the former were afraid they would be suspected of receiving money if they voted for the bill, and the latter were given a shield behind which to stand until they were paid. I was wholly unable to move the bill forward in the Legislature, and finally a representative of the railway told me that he thought he would like to take the bill out of my hands, that I did not seem able to get it through, and that perhaps some "older and more experienced" leader could be more successful. I was pretty certain what this meant, but of course I had no kind of proof, and moreover I was not in a position to say that I could promise success. Accordingly, the bill was given into the charge of a veteran, whom I believe to have been a personally honest man, but who was not inquisitive about the motives influencing his colleagues. This gentleman, who went by a nickname which I shall incorrectly call "the bald eagle of Weehawken," was efficient and knew his job. After a couple of weeks a motion to put the bill through was made by "the bald eagle"; the "black horse cavalry," whose feelings had undergone a complete change in the intervening time, voted unanimously for it, in company with all the decent members; and that was the end. Now here was a bit of work in the interest of a corporation and in the interest of a community, which the corporation at first tried honestly to have put through on its merits. The blame for the failure lay primarily in the supine indifference of the community to legislative wrong-doing, so long as only the corporations were blackmailed.

Except as above mentioned, I was not brought in contact with big business, save in the effort to impeach a certain judge. This judge had been used as an instrument in their business by certain of the men connected with the elevated railways and other great corporations at that time. We got hold of his correspondence with one of these men, and it showed a shocking willingness to use the judicial office in any way that one of the kings of finance of that day desired. He had actually held court in one of that financier's rooms. One expression in one of the judge's letters to this financier I shall always remember: "I am willing to go to the very verge of judicial discretion to serve your vast interests." The curious thing was that I was by no means certain that the judge himself was corrupt. He may have been; but I am inclined to think that, aside from his being a man of coarse moral fiber, the trouble lay chiefly in the fact that he had a genuine — if I had not so often seen it, I would say a wholly inexplicable — reverence for the possessor of a great fortune as such. He sincerely believed that business was the end of existence, and that judge and legislator alike should do whatever was necessary to favor it; and the bigger the business the more he desired to favor it. Big business of the kind that is allied with politics thoroughly appreciated the usefulness of such a judge, and every effort was strained to protect him. We fought hard — by "we" I mean some thirty or forty legislators, both Republicans and Democrats — but the "black horse cavalry," and the timid good men, and the dull conservative men, were all against us; and the vote in the Legislature was heavily against impeachment. The minority of the committee that investigated him, with Chapin at its head, recommended impeachment; the argument for impeachment before the committee was made by Francis Lynde Stetson.

It was my first experience of the kind. Various men whom I had known well socially and had been taught to look up to, prominent business men and lawyers, acted in a way which not only astounded me, but which I was quite unable to reconcile with the theories I had formed as to their high standing — I was little more than a year out of college at the time. Generally, as has been always the case since, they were careful to avoid any direct conversation with me on a concrete case of what we now call "privilege" in business and in politics, that is, of the alliance between business and politics which represents improper favors rendered to some men in return for improper conduct on the part of others being ignored or permitted.

One member of a prominent law firm, an old family friend, did, however, take me out to lunch one day, evidently for the purpose of seeing just what it was that I wished and intended to do. I believe he had a genuine personal liking for me. He explained that I had done well in the Legislature, that it was a good thing to have made the "reform play," that I had shown that I possessed ability such as would make me useful in the right kind of law office or business concern; but that I must not overplay my hand; that I had gone far enough, and that now was the time to leave politics and identify myself with the right kind of people, the people who would always in the long run control others and obtain the real rewards which were worth having. I asked him if that meant that I was to yield to the ring in politics. He answered somewhat impatiently that I was entirely mistaken (as in fact I was) about there being merely a political ring, of the kind of which the papers were fond of talking; that the "ring," if it could be called such — that is, the inner circle — included certain big business men, and the politicians, lawyers, and judges who were in alliance with and to a certain extent dependent upon them, and that the successful man had to win his success by the backing of the same forces, whether in law, business, or politics.

This conversation not only interested me, but made such an impression that I always remembered it, for it was the first glimpse I had of that combination between business and politics which I was in after years so often to oppose. In the America of that day, and especially among the people whom I knew, the successful business man was regarded by everybody as preëminently *the* good citizen. The orthodox books on political economy, not only in America but in England, were written for his especial glorification. The tangible rewards came to him, the admiration of his fellow-citizens of the respectable type was apt to be his, and the severe newspaper moralists who were never tired of denouncing politicians and political methods were wont to hold up "business methods" as the ideal which we were to strive to introduce into political life. Herbert Croly, in "The Promise of American Life," has set forth the reasons why our individualistic democracy — which taught that each man was to rely exclusively on himself, was in no way to be interfered with by others, and was to devote himself to his own personal welfare — necessarily produced the type of business man who sincerely believed, as did the rest of the community, that the individual who amassed a big fortune was the man who was the best and most typical American.

In the Legislature the problems with which I dealt were mainly problems of honesty and decency and of legislative and administrative efficiency. They represented the effort, the wise, the vitally necessary effort, to get efficient and honest government. But as yet I understood little of the effort which was already beginning, for the most part under very bad leadership, to secure a more genuine social and industrial justice. Nor was I especially to blame for this. The good citizens I then knew best, even when themselves men of limited means — men like my colleague Billy O'Neill, and my backwoods friends Sewall and Dow — were no more awake than I was to the changing needs the changing times were bringing. Their outlook was as narrow as my own, and, within its limits, as fundamentally sound.

I wish to dwell on the soundness of our outlook on life, even though as yet it was not broad enough. We were no respecters of persons. Where our vision was developed to a degree that enabled us to see crookedness, we opposed it whether in great or small. As a matter of fact, we found that it needed much more courage to stand up *openly* against labor men when they were wrong than against capitalists when they were wrong. The sins against labor are usually committed, and the improper services to capitalists are usually rendered, behind closed doors. Very often the man with the moral courage to speak in the open against labor when it is wrong is the only man anxious to do effective work for labor when labor is right.

The only kinds of courage and honesty which are permanently useful to good institutions anywhere are those shown by men who decide all cases with impartial justice on grounds of conduct and not on grounds of class. We found that in the long run the men who in public blatantly insisted that labor was never wrong were the very men who in private could not be trusted to stand for labor when it was right. We grew heartily to distrust the reformer who never denounced wickedness unless it was embodied in a rich man. Human nature does not change; and that type of "reformer" is as noxious now as he ever was. The loud-mouthed upholder of popular rights who attacks wickedness only when it is allied with wealth, and who never publicly assails any misdeed, no matter how flagrant, if committed nominally in the interest of labor, has either a warped mind or a tainted soul, and should be trusted by no honest man. It was largely the indignant and contemptuous dislike aroused in our minds by the demagogues of this class which then prevented those of us whose instincts at bottom were sound from going as far as we ought to have gone along the lines of governmental control of corporations and governmental interference on behalf of labor.

I did, however, have one exceedingly useful experience. A bill was introduced by the Cigar-Makers' Union to prohibit the manufacture of cigars in tenement-houses. I was appointed one of a committee of three to investigate conditions in the tenement-houses and see if legislation should be had. Of my two colleagues on the committee, one took no interest in the measure and privately said he did not think it was right, but that he had to vote for it because the labor unions were strong in his district and he was pledged to support the bill. The other, a sporting Tammany man who afterwards abandoned politics for the race-track, was a very good fellow. He told me frankly that he had to be against the bill because certain interests which were all-powerful and with which he had dealings required him to be against it, but that I was a free agent, and that if I would look into the matter he believed I would favor the legislation. As a matter of fact, I had supposed I would be against the legislation, and I rather think that I was put on the committee with that idea, for the respectable people I knew were against it; it was contrary to the principles of political economy of the *laissez faire* kind; and the business men who spoke to me about it shook their heads and said that it was designed to prevent a man doing as he wished and as he had a right to do with what was his own.

However, my first visits to the tenement-house districts in question made me feel that, whatever the theories might be, as a matter of practical common sense I could not conscientiously vote for the continuance of the conditions which I saw. These conditions rendered it impossible for the families of the tenement-house workers to live so that the children might grow up fitted for the exacting duties of American citizenship. I visited the tenement-houses once with my colleagues of the committee, once with some of the labor union representatives, and once or twice by myself. In a few of the tenement-houses there were suites of rooms ample in number where the work on the tobacco was done in rooms not occupied for cooking or sleeping or living. In the overwhelming majority of cases, however, there were one, two, or three room apartments, and the work of manufacturing the tobacco by men, women, and children went on day and night in the eating, living, and sleeping rooms — sometimes in one room. I have always remembered one room in which two families were living. On my inquiry as to who the third adult male was I was told that he was a boarder with one of the families. There were several children, three men, and two women in this room. The tobacco was stowed about everywhere, alongside the foul bedding, and in a corner where there were scraps of food. The men, women, and children in this room worked by day and far on into the evening, and they slept and ate there. They were Bohemians, unable to speak English, except that one of the children knew enough to act as interpreter.

Instead of opposing the bill I ardently championed it. It was a poorly drawn measure, and the Governor, Grover Cleveland, was at first doubtful about signing it. The Cigar-Makers' Union then asked me to appear before the Governor and argue for it. I accordingly did so, acting as spokesman for the battered, undersized foreigners who represented the Union and the workers. The Governor signed the bill. Afterwards this tenement-house cigar legislation was declared invalid by the Court of Appeals in the Jacobs decision. Jacobs was one of the rare tenement-house manufacturers of cigars who occupied quite a suite of rooms, so that in his case the living conditions were altogether exceptional. What the reason was which influenced those bringing the suit to select the exceptional instead of the average worker I do not know; of course such action was precisely the action which those most interested in having the law broken down were anxious to see taken. The Court of Appeals declared the law unconstitutional, and in their decision the judges reprobated the law as an assault upon the "hallowed" influences of "home." It was this case which first waked me to a dim and partial understanding of the fact that the courts were not necessarily the best judges of what should be done to better social and industrial conditions. The judges who rendered this decision were well-meaning men. They knew nothing whatever of tenement-house conditions; they knew nothing whatever of the needs, or of the life and labor, of three-fourths of their fellow-citizens in great cities. They knew legalism, but not life. Their choice of the words "hallowed" and "home," as applicable to the revolting conditions attending the manufacture of cigars in tenement-houses, showed that they had no idea what it was that they were deciding. Imagine the "hallowed" associations of a "home" consisting of one room where two families, one of them with a boarder, live, eat, and work! This decision completely blocked tenement-house reform legislation in New York for a score of years, and hampers it to this day. It was one of the most serious setbacks which the cause of industrial and social progress and reform ever received.

I had been brought up to hold the courts in especial reverence. The people with whom I was most intimate were apt to praise the courts for just such decisions as this, and to speak of them as bulwarks against disorder and barriers against demagogic legislation. These were the same people with whom the judges who rendered these decisions were apt to foregather at social clubs, or dinners, or in private life. Very naturally they all tended to look at things from the same standpoint. Of course it took more than one experience such as this Tenement Cigar Case to shake me out of the attitude in which I was brought up. But various decisions, not only of the New York court but of certain other State courts and even of the United States Supreme Court, during the quarter of a century following the passage of this tenement-house legislation, did at last thoroughly wake me to the actual fact. I grew to realize that all that Abraham Lincoln had said about the Dred

"Reform without Bloodshed."

A cartoon by Thomas Nast in *Harper's Weekly*, of April 19, 1884, entitled
"Governor Cleveland and Theodore Roosevelt at their work."

Scott decision could be said with equal truth and justice about the numerous decisions which in our own day were erected as bars across the path of social reform, and which brought to naught so much of the effort to secure justice and fair dealing for workingmen and workingwomen, and for plain citizens generally.

Some of the wickedness and inefficiency in public life was then displayed in simpler fashion than would probably now be the case. Once or twice I was a member of committees which looked into gross and widely ramifying governmental abuses. On the whole, the most important part I played was in the third Legislature in which I served, when I acted as chairman of a committee which investigated various phases of New York City official life.

The most important of the reform measures our committee recommended was the bill taking away from the Aldermen their power of confirmation over the Mayor's appointments. We found that it was possible to get citizens interested in the character and capacity of the head of the city, so that they would exercise some intelligent interest in his conduct and qualifications. But we found that as a matter of fact it was impossible to get them interested in the Aldermen and other subordinate officers. In actual practice the Aldermen were merely the creatures of the local ward bosses or of the big municipal bosses, and where they controlled the appointments the citizens at large had no chance whatever to make their will felt. Accordingly we fought for the principle, which I believe to be of universal application, that what is needed in our popular government is to give plenty of power to a few officials, and to make these few officials genuinely and readily responsible to the people for the exercise of that power. Taking away the confirming power of the Board of Aldermen did not give the citizens of New York good government. We knew that if they chose to elect the wrong kind of Mayor they would have bad government, no matter what the form of the law was. But we did secure to them the chance to get good government if they desired, and this was impossible as long as the old system remained. The change was fought in the way in which all similar changes always are fought. The corrupt and interested politicians were against it, and the battle-cries they used, which rallied to them most of the unthinking conservatives, were that we were changing the old constitutional system, that we were defacing the monuments of the wisdom of the founders of the government, that we were destroying that distinction between legislative and executive power which was the bulwark of our liberties, and that we were violent and unscrupulous radicals with no reverence for the past.

Of course the investigations, disclosures, and proceedings of the investigating committee of which I was chairman brought me into bitter personal conflict with very powerful financiers, very powerful politicians, and with certain newspapers which these financiers and politicians controlled. A number of able and unscrupulous men were fighting, some for their financial lives, and others to keep out of unpleasantly close neighborhood to State's prison. This meant that there were blows to be taken as well as given. In such political struggles, those who went in for the kind of thing that I did speedily excited animosities among strong and cunning men who would stop at little to gratify their animosity. Any man engaged in this particular type of militant and practical reform movement was soon made to feel that he had better not undertake to push matters home unless his own character was unassailable. On one of the investigating committees on which I served there was a countryman, a very able man, who, when he reached New York City, felt as certain Americans do when they go to Paris — that the moral restraints of his native place no longer applied. With all his ability, he was not shrewd enough to realize that the Police Department was having him as well as the rest of us carefully shadowed. He was caught red-handed by a plain-clothes man doing what he had no business to do; and from that time on he dared not act save as those who held his secret permitted him to act. Thenceforth those officials who stood behind the Police Department had one man on the committee on whom they could count. I never saw terror more ghastly on a strong man's face than on the face of this man on one or two occasions when he feared that events in the committee might take such a course as to force him into a position where his colleagues would expose him even if the city officials did not. However, he escaped, for we were never able to get the kind of proof which would warrant our asking for the action in which this man could not have joined.

Traps were set for more than one of us, and if we had walked into these traps our public careers would have ended, at least so far as following them under the conditions which alone make it worth while to be in public life at all. A man can of course hold public office, and many a man does hold public office, and lead a public career of a sort, even if there are other men who possess secrets about him which he cannot afford to have divulged. But no man can lead a public career really worth leading, no man can act with rugged independence in serious crises, nor strike at great abuses, nor afford to make powerful and unscrupulous foes, if he is himself vulnerable in his private character. Nor will clean conduct by itself enable a man to render good service. I have always been fond of Josh Billings's remark that "it is much easier to be a harmless dove than a wise serpent." There are plenty of decent legislators, and plenty of able legislators; but the blamelessness and the fighting edge are not always combined. Both qualities are necessary for the man who is to wage active battle against the powers that prey. He must be clean of life, so that he can laugh when his public or his private record is searched; and yet being clean of life will not avail him if he is either foolish or timid. He must walk warily and fearlessly, and while he should never brawl if he can avoid it, he must be ready to hit hard if the need arises. Let him remember, by the way, that the unforgivable crime is soft hitting. Do not hit at all if it can be avoided; but *never* hit softly.

Like most young men in politics, I went through various oscillations of feeling before I "found myself." At one period I became so impressed with the virtue of complete independence that I proceeded to act on each case purely as I personally viewed it, without paying any heed to the principles and prejudices of others. The result was that I speedily and deservedly lost all power of accomplishing anything at all; and I thereby learned the invaluable lesson that in the practical activities of life no man can render the highest service unless he can act in combination with his fellows, which means a certain amount of give-and-take between him and them. Again, I at one period began to believe that I had a future before me, and that it behooved me to be very far-sighted and scan each action carefully with a view to its possible effect on that future. This speedily made me useless to the public and an object of aversion to myself; and I then made up my mind that I would try not to think of the future at all, but would proceed on the assumption that each office I held would be the last I ever should hold, and that I would confine myself to trying to do my work as well as possible while I held that office. I found that for me personally this was the only way in which I could either enjoy myself or render good service to the country, and I never afterwards deviated from this plan.

As regards political advancement the bosses could of course do a good deal. At that time the warring Stalwart and Half-Breed factions of the Republican party were supporting respectively President Arthur and Senator Miller. Neither side cared for me. The first year in the Legislature I rose to a position of leadership, so that in the second year, when the Republicans were in a minority, I received the minority nomination for Speaker, although I was still the youngest man in the House, being twenty-four years old. The third year the Republicans carried the Legislature, and the bosses at once took a hand in the Speakership contest. I made a stout fight for the nomination, but the bosses of the two factions, the Stalwarts and the Half-Breeds, combined and I was beaten. I was much chagrined for the moment. But the fact that I had fought hard and efficiently, even though defeated, and that I had made the fight single-handed, with no machine back of me, assured my standing as floor leader. My defeat in the end materially strengthened my position, and enabled me to accomplish far more than I could have accomplished as Speaker. As so often, I found that the titular position was of no consequence; what counted was the combination of the opportunity with the ability to accomplish results. The achievement was the all-important thing; the position, whether titularly high or low, was of consequence only in so far as it widened the chance for achievement. After the session closed four of us who looked at politics from the same standpoint and were known as Independent or Anti-Machine Republicans were sent by the State Convention as delegates-at-large to the Republican National Convention of 1884, where I advocated, as vigorously as I knew how, the nomination of Senator George F. Edmunds. Mr. Edmunds was defeated and Mr. Blaine nominated. Mr. Blaine was clearly the choice of the rank and file of the party; his nomination was won in fair and aboveboard fashion, because the rank and file of the party stood back of him; and I supported him to the best of my ability in the ensuing campaign.

The Speakership contest enlightened me as regards more things than the attitude of the bosses. I had already had some exasperating experiences with the "silk stocking" reformer type, as Abraham Lincoln called it, the gentlemen who were very nice, very refined, who shook their heads over political corruption and discussed it in drawing-rooms and parlors, but who were wholly unable to grapple with real men in real life. They were apt vociferously to demand "reform" as if it were some concrete substance, like cake, which could be handed out at will, in tangible masses, if only the demand were urgent enough. These parlor reformers made up for inefficiency in action by zeal in criticising; and they delighted in criticising the men who really were doing the things which they said ought to be done, but which they lacked the sinewy power to do. They often upheld ideals which were not merely impossible but highly undesirable, and thereby played into the hands of the very politicians to whom they professed to be most hostile. Moreover, if they believed that their own interests, individually or as a class, were jeoparded, they were apt to show no higher standards than did the men they usually denounced.

One of their shibboleths was that the office should seek the man and not the man the office. This is entirely true of certain offices at certain times. It is entirely untrue when the circumstances are different. It would have been unnecessary and undesirable for Washington to have sought the Presidency. But if Abraham Lincoln had not sought the Presidency he never would have been nominated. The objection in such a case as this lies not to seeking the office, but to seeking it in any but an honorable and proper manner. The effect of the shibboleth in question is usually merely to put a premium on hypocrisy, and therefore to favor the creature who is willing to rise by hypocrisy. When I ran for Speaker, the whole body of machine politicians was against me, and my only chance lay in arousing the people in the different districts. To do this I had to visit the districts, put the case fairly before the men whom I saw, and make them understand that I was really making a fight and would stay in the fight to the end. Yet there were reformers who shook their heads and deplored my "activity" in the canvass. Of course the one thing which corrupt machine politicians most desire is to have decent men frown on the activity, that is, on the efficiency, of the honest man who genuinely wishes to reform politics.

If efficiency is left solely to bad men, and if virtue is confined solely to inefficient men, the result cannot be happy. When I entered politics there were, as there always had been — and as there always will be — any number of bad men in politics who were thoroughly efficient, and any number of good men who would like to have done lofty things in politics but who were thoroughly inefficient. If I wished to accomplish anything for the country, my business was to combine decency and efficiency; to be a thoroughly practical man of high ideals who did his best to reduce those ideals to actual practice. This was my ideal, and to the best of my ability I strove to live up to it.

To a young man, life in the New York Legislature was always interesting and often entertaining. There was always a struggle of some kind on hand. Sometimes it was on a naked question of right and wrong. Sometimes it was on a question of real constructive statesmanship. Moreover, there were all kinds of humorous incidents, the humor being usually of the unconscious kind. In one session of the Legislature the New York City Democratic representatives were split into two camps, and there were two rivals for leadership. One of these was a thoroughly good-hearted, happy-go-lucky person who was afterwards for several years in Congress. He had been a local magistrate and was called Judge. Generally he and I were friendly, but occasionally I did something that irritated him. He was always willing to vote for any other member's bill himself, and he regarded it as narrow-minded for any one to oppose one of his bills, especially if the opposition was upon the ground that it was unconstitutional — for his views of the Constitution were so excessively liberal as to make even me feel as if I belonged to the straitest sect of strict constructionists.

On one occasion he had a bill to appropriate money, with obvious impropriety, for the relief of some miscreant whom he styled "one of the honest yeomanry of the State." When I explained to him that it was clearly unconstitutional, he answered, "Me friend, the Constitution don't touch little things like that," and then added, with an ingratiating smile, "Anyhow, I'd never allow the Constitution to come between friends." At the time I was looking over the proofs of Mr. Bryce's "American Commonwealth," and I told him the incident. He put it into the first edition of the "Commonwealth"; whether it is in the last edition or not, I cannot say.

On another occasion the same gentleman came to an issue with me in a debate, and wound up his speech by explaining that I occupied what "lawyers would call a quasi position on the bill." His rival was a man of totally different type, a man of great natural dignity, also born in Ireland. He had served with gallantry in the Civil War. After the close of the war he organized an expedition to conquer Canada. The expedition, however, got so drunk before reaching Albany that it was there incarcerated in jail, whereupon its leader abandoned it and went into New York politics instead. He was a man of influence, and later occupied in the Police Department the same position as Commissioner which I myself at one time occupied. He felt that his rival had gained too much glory at my expense, and, walking over with ceremonious solemnity to where the said rival was sitting close beside me, he said to him: "I would like you to know, Mr. Cameron [Cameron, of course, was not the real name], that Mr. Roosevelt knows more law in a wake than you do in a month; and, more than that, Michael Cameron, what do you mane by quoting Latin on the floor of this House when you don't know the alpha and omayga of the language?"

There was in the Legislature, during the deadlock above mentioned, a man whom I will call Brogan. He looked like a serious elderly frog. I never heard him speak more than once. It was before the Legislature was organized, or had adopted any rules; and each day the only business was for the clerk to call the roll. One day Brogan suddenly rose, and the following dialogue occurred:

*Brogan.* Misther Clu-r-r-k!

*The Clerk.* The gentleman from New York.

*Brogan.* I rise to a point of ordher under the rules!

*The Clerk.* There are no rules.

*Brogan.* Thin I object to them!

*The Clerk.* There are no rules to object to.

*Brogan.* Oh! [nonplussed; but immediately recovering himself]. Thin I move that they be amended until there ar-r-re!

The deadlock was tedious; and we hailed with joy such enlivening incidents as the above.

During my three years' service in the Legislature I worked on a very simple philosophy of government. It was that personal character and initiative are the prime requisites in political and social life. It was not only a good but an absolutely indispensable theory as far as it went; but it was defective in that it did not sufficiently allow for the need of collective action. I shall never forget the men with whom I worked hand in hand in these legislative struggles, not only my fellow-legislators, but some of the newspaper reporters, such as Spinney and Cunningham; and then in addition the men in the various districts who helped us. We had made up our minds that we must not fight fire with fire, that on the contrary the way to win out was to equal our foes in practical efficiency and yet to stand at the opposite plane from them in applied morality.

It was not always easy to keep the just middle, especially when it happened that on one side there were corrupt and unscrupulous demagogues, and on the other side corrupt and unscrupulous reactionaries. Our effort was to hold the scales even between both. We tried to stand with the cause of righteousness even though its advocates were anything but righteous. We endeavored to cut out the abuses of property, even though good men of property were misled into upholding those abuses. We refused to be frightened into sanctioning improper assaults upon property, although we knew that the champions of property themselves did things that were wicked and corrupt. We were as yet by no means as thoroughly awake as we ought to have been to the need of controlling big business and to the damage done by the combination of politics with big business. In this matter I was not behind the rest of my friends; indeed, I was ahead of them, for no serious leader in political life then appreciated the prime need of grappling with these questions. One partial reason — not an excuse or a justification, but a partial reason — for my slowness in grasping the importance of action in these matters was the corrupt and unattractive nature of so many of the men who championed popular reforms, their insincerity, and the folly of so many of the actions which they advocated. Even at that date I had neither sympathy with nor admiration for the man who was merely a money king, and I did not regard the "money touch," when divorced from other qualities, as entitling a man to either respect or consideration. As recited above, we did on more than one occasion fight battles, in which we neither took nor gave quarter, against the most prominent and powerful financiers and financial interests of the day. But most of the fights in which we were engaged were for pure honesty and decency, and they were more apt to be against that form of corruption which found its expression in demagogy than against that form of corruption which defended or advocated privilege. Fundamentally, our fight was part of the eternal war against the Powers that Prey; and we cared not a whit in what rank of life these powers were found.

To play the demagogue for purposes of self-interest is a cardinal sin against the people in a democracy, exactly as to play the courtier for such purposes is a cardinal sin against the people under other forms of government. A man who stays long in our American political life, if he has in his soul the generous desire to do effective service for great causes, inevitably grows to regard himself merely as one of many instruments, all of which it may be necessary to use, one at one time, one at another, in achieving the triumph of those causes; and whenever the usefulness of any one has been exhausted, it is to be thrown aside. If such a man is wise, he will gladly do the thing that is next, when the time and the need come together, without asking what the future holds for him. Let the half-god play his part well and manfully, and then be content to draw aside when the god appears. Nor should he feel vain regrets that to another it is given to render greater services and reap a greater reward. Let it be enough for him that he too has served, and that by doing well he has prepared the way for the other man who can do better.

# Chapter IV

## IN COWBOY LAND

THOUGH I had previously made a trip into the then Territory of Dakota, beyond the Red River, it was not until 1883 that I went to the Little Missouri, and there took hold of two cattle ranches, the Chimney Butte and the Elkhorn.

It was still the Wild West in those days, the Far West, the West of Owen Wister's stories and Frederic Remington's drawings, the West of the Indian and the buffalo-hunter, the soldier and the cow-puncher. That land of the West has gone now, "gone, gone with lost Atlantis," gone to the isle of ghosts and of strange dead memories. It was a land of vast silent spaces, of lonely rivers, and of plains where the wild game stared at the passing horseman. It was a land of scattered ranches, of herds of long-horned cattle, and of reckless riders who unmoved looked in the eyes of life or of death. In that land we led a free and hardy life, with horse and with rifle. We worked under the scorching midsummer sun, when the wide plains shimmered and wavered in the heat; and we knew the freezing misery of riding night guard round the cattle in the late fall round-up. In the soft springtime the stars were glorious in our eyes each night before we fell asleep; and in the winter we rode through blinding blizzards, when the driven snow-dust burnt our faces. There were monotonous days, as we guided the trail cattle or the beef herds, hour after hour, at the slowest of walks; and minutes or hours teeming with excitement as we stopped stampedes or swam the herds across rivers treacherous with quicksands or brimmed with running ice. We knew toil and hardship and hunger and thirst; and we saw men die violent deaths as they worked among the horses and cattle, or fought in evil feuds with one another; but we felt the beat of hardy life in our veins, and ours was the glory of work and the joy of living.

It was right and necessary that this life should pass, for the safety of our country lies in its being made the country of the small home-maker. The great unfenced ranches, in the days of "free grass," necessarily represented a temporary stage in our

President Roosevelt returning from the Bear Hunt,
Newcastle, Colorado, in 1905.

history. The large migratory flocks of sheep, each guarded by the hired shepherds of absentee owners, were the first enemies of the cattlemen; and owing to the way they ate out the grass and destroyed all other vegetation, these roving sheep bands represented little of permanent good to the country. But the homesteaders, the permanent settlers, the men who took up each his own farm on which he lived and brought up his family, these represented from the National standpoint the most desirable of all possible users of, and dwellers on, the soil. Their advent meant the breaking up of the big ranches; and the change was a National gain, although to some of us an individual loss.

I first reached the Little Missouri on a Northern Pacific train about three in the morning of a cool September day in 1883. Aside from the station, the only building was a ramshackle structure called the Pyramid Park Hotel. I dragged my dufflebag thither, and hammered at the door until the frowsy proprietor appeared, muttering oaths. He ushered me upstairs, where I was given one of the fourteen beds in the room which by itself constituted the entire upper floor. Next day I walked over to the abandoned army post, and, after some hours among the gray log shacks, a ranchman who had driven into the station agreed to take me out to his ranch, the Chimney Butte ranch, where he was living with his brother and their partner.

The ranch was a log structure with a dirt roof, a corral for the horses near by, and a chicken-house jabbed against the rear of the ranch house. Inside there was only one room, with a table, three or four chairs, a cooking-stove, and three bunks. The owners were Sylvane and Joe Ferris and William J. Merrifield. Later all three of them held my commissions while I was President. Merrifield was Marshal of Montana, and as Presidential elector cast the vote of that State for me in 1904; Sylvane Ferris was Land Officer in North Dakota, and Joe Ferris Postmaster at Medora. There was a fourth man, George Meyer, who also worked for me later. That evening we all played old sledge round the table, and at one period the game was interrupted by a frightful squawking outside which told us that a bobcat had made a raid on the chicken-house.

After a buffalo hunt with my original friend, Joe Ferris, I

A Reunion.

"Twenty-nine years later my four friends of that night (of bobcats and old sledge) were delegates to the First Progressive National Convention at Chicago." — Mr. Roosevelt, seated. From left to right, J. A. Ferris, S. M. Ferris, W. J. Merrifield, G. W. Meyer.

entered into partnership with Merrifield and Sylva,
and we started a cow ranch, with the maltese cross [
always known as "maltee cross," by the way, as the gen
pression along the Little Missouri was that "maltese" m
a plural. Twenty-nine years later my four friends of that
were delegates to the First Progressive National Conven
at Chicago. They were among my most constant compani
for the few years next succeeding the evening when the bobc
interrupted the game of old sledge. I lived and worked with
them on the ranch, and with them and many others like them
on the round-up; and I brought out from Maine, in order to
start the Elkhorn ranch lower down the river, my two backwoods friends Sewall and Dow. My brands for the lower
ranch were the elkhorn and triangle.

I do not believe there ever was any life more attractive to a
vigorous young fellow than life on a cattle ranch in those days.
It was a fine, healthy life, too; it taught a man self-reliance,
hardihood, and the value of instant decision — in short, the
virtues that ought to come from life in the open country. I enjoyed the life to the full. After the first year I built on the
Elkhorn ranch a long, low ranch house of hewn logs, with a
veranda, and with, in addition to the other rooms, a bedroom
for myself, and a sitting-room with a big fire-place. I got out
a rocking-chair — I am very fond of rocking-chairs — and
enough books to fill two or three shelves, and a rubber bath-
tub so that I could get a bath. And then I do not see how any
one could have lived more comfortably. We had buffalo robes
and bearskins of our own killing. We always kept the house
clean — using the word in a rather large sense. There were at
least two rooms that were always warm, even in the bitterest
weather; and we had plenty to eat. Commonly the mainstay
of every meal was game of our own killing, usually antelope
or deer, sometimes grouse or ducks, and occasionally, in the
earlier days, buffalo or elk. We also had flour and bacon, sugar,
salt, and canned tomatoes. And later, when some of the men
married and brought out their wives, we had all kinds of good
things, such as jams and jellies made from the wild plums and
the buffalo berries, and potatoes from the forlorn little garden
patch. Moreover, we had milk. Most ranchmen at that time
never had milk. I knew more than one ranch with ten thou-

sand head of cattle where there was not a cow that could be milked. We made up our minds that we would be more enterprising. Accordingly, we started to domesticate some of the cows. Our first effort was not successful, chiefly because we did not devote the needed time and patience to the matter. And we found that to race a cow two miles at full speed on horseback, then rope her, throw her, and turn her upside down to milk her, while exhilarating as a pastime, was not productive of results. Gradually we accumulated tame cows, and, after we had thinned out the bobcats and coyotes, more chickens.

The ranch house stood on the brink of a low bluff overlooking the broad, shallow bed of the Little Missouri, through which at most seasons there ran only a trickle of water, while in times of freshet it was filled brimful with the boiling, foaming, muddy torrent. There was no neighbor for ten or fifteen miles on either side of me. The river twisted down in long curves between narrow bottoms bordered by sheer cliff walls, for the Bad Lands, a chaos of peaks, plateaus, and ridges, rose abruptly from the edges of the level, tree-clad, or grassy, alluvial meadows. In front of the ranch-house veranda was a row of cottonwood trees with gray-green leaves which quivered all day long if there was a breath of air. From these trees came the far-away, melancholy cooing of mourning doves, and little owls perched in them and called tremulously at night. In the long summer afternoons we would sometimes sit on the piazza, when there was no work to be done, for an hour or two at a time, watching the cattle on the sand-bars, and the sharply channeled and strangely carved amphitheater of cliffs across the bottom opposite; while the vultures wheeled overhead, their black shadows gliding across the glaring white of the dry river-bed. Sometimes from the ranch we saw deer, and once when we needed meat I shot one across the river as I stood on the piazza. In the winter, in the days of iron cold, when everything was white under the snow, the river lay in its bed fixed and immovable as a bar of bent steel, and then at night wolves and lynxes traveled up and down it as if it had been a highway passing in front of the ranch house. Often in the late fall or early winter, after a hard day's hunting, or when returning from one of the winter line camps, we did not reach the ranch until hours after sunset; and after the weary tramping in the cold it was keen pleasure to catch the first red gleam of the fire-lit windows across the snowy wastes.

The Elkhorn ranch house was built mainly by Sewall and Dow, who, like most men from the Maine woods, were mighty with the ax. I could chop fairly well for an amateur, but I could not do one-third the work they could. One day when we were cutting down the cottonwood trees, to begin our building operations, I heard some one ask Dow what the total cut had been, and Dow, not realizing that I was within hearing, answered: "Well, Bill cut down fifty-three, I cut forty-nine, and the boss he beavered down seventeen." Those who have seen the stump of a tree which has been gnawed down by a beaver will understand the exact force of the comparison.

In those days on a cow ranch the men were apt to be away on the various round-ups at least half the time. It was interesting and exciting work, and except for the lack of sleep on the spring and summer round-ups it was not exhausting work; compared to lumbering or mining or blacksmithing, to sit in the saddle is an easy form of labor. The ponies were of course grass-fed and unshod. Each man had his own string of nine or ten. One pony would be used for the morning work, one for the afternoon, and neither would again be used for the next three days. A separate pony was kept for night riding.

The spring and early summer round-ups were especially for the branding of calves. There was much hard work and some risk on a round-up, but also much fun. The meeting-place was appointed weeks beforehand, and all the ranchmen of the territory to be covered by the round-up sent their representatives. There were no fences in the West that I knew, and their place was taken by the cowboy and the branding-iron. The cattle wandered free. Each calf was branded with the brand of the cow it was following. Sometimes in winter there was what we called line riding; that is, camps were established and the line riders traveled a definite beat across the desolate wastes of snow, to and fro from one camp to another, to prevent the cattle from drifting. But as a rule nothing was done to keep the cattle in any one place. In the spring there was a general round-up in each locality. Each outfit took part in its own round-up, and all the outfits of a given region combined to

send representatives to the two or three round-ups that covered the neighborhoods near by into which their cattle might
drift. For example, our Little Missouri round-up generally
worked down the river from a distance of some fifty or sixty
miles above my ranch towards the Kildeer Mountains, about
the same distance below. In addition we would usually send
representatives to the Yellowstone round-up, and to the
round-up along the upper Little Missouri; and, moreover, if
we heard that cattle had drifted, perhaps toward the Indian
reservation southeast of us, we would send a wagon and rider
after them.

At the meeting-point, which might be in the valley of a half-
dry stream, or in some broad bottom of the river itself, or per-
chance by a couple of ponds under some queerly shaped butte
that was a landmark for the region round about, we would all
gather on the appointed day. The chuck-wagons, containing
the bedding and food, each drawn by four horses and driven
by the teamster cook, would come jolting and rattling over
the uneven sward. Accompanying each wagon were eight or
ten riders, the cow-punchers, while their horses, a band of a
hundred or so, were driven by the two herders, one of whom
was known as the day wrangler and one as the night wrangler.
The men were lean, sinewy fellows, accustomed to riding half-
broken horses at any speed over any country by day or by
night. They wore flannel shirts, with loose handkerchiefs knotted round their necks, broad hats, high-heeled boots with
jingling spurs, and sometimes leather shaps, although often
they merely had their trousers tucked into the tops of their
high boots. There was a good deal of rough horse-play, and,
as with any other gathering of men or boys of high animal
spirits, the horse-play sometimes became very rough indeed;
and as the men usually carried revolvers, and as there were occasionally one or two noted gun-fighters among them, there
was now and then a shooting affray. A man who was a coward
or who shirked his work had a bad time, of course; a man
could not afford to let himself be bullied or treated as a butt;
and, on the other hand, if he was "looking for a fight," he was
certain to find it. But my own experience was that if a man did
not talk until his associates knew him well and liked him, and
if he did his work, he never had any difficulty in getting on.

In my own round-up district I speedily grew to be friends with most of the men. When I went among strangers I always had to spend twenty-four hours in living down the fact that I wore spectacles, remaining as long as I could judiciously deaf to any side remarks about "four eyes," unless it became evident that my being quiet was misconstrued and that it was better to bring matters to a head at once.

If, for instance, I was sent off to represent the Little Missouri brands on some neighboring round-up, such as the Yellowstone, I usually showed that kind of diplomacy which consists in not uttering one word that can be avoided. I would probably have a couple of days' solitary ride, mounted on one horse and driving eight or ten others before me, one of them carrying my bedding. Loose horses drive best at a trot, or canter, and if a man is traveling alone in this fashion it is a good thing to have them reach the camp ground sufficiently late to make them desire to feed and sleep where they are until morning. In consequence I never spent more than two days on the journey from whatever the point was at which I left the Little Missouri, sleeping the one night for as limited a number of hours as possible.

As soon as I reached the meeting-place I would find out the wagon to which I was assigned. Riding to it, I turned my horses into the saddle-band and reported to the wagon boss, or, in his absence, to the cook — always a privileged character, who was allowed and expected to order men around. He would usually grumble savagely and profanely about my having been put with his wagon, but this was merely conventional on his part; and if I sat down and said nothing he would probably soon ask me if I wanted anything to eat, to which the correct answer was that I was not hungry and would wait until meal-time. The bedding rolls of the riders would be strewn round the grass, and I would put mine down a little outside the ring, where I would not be in any one's way, with my six or eight branding-irons beside it. The men would ride in, laughing and talking with one another, and perhaps nodding to me. One of their number, usually the wagon foreman, might put some question to me as to what brands I represented, but no other word would be addressed to me, nor would I be expected to volunteer any conversation. Supper

The Elkhorn Ranch House and the Deeds of Purchase.

would consist of bacon, Dutch oven bread, and possibly beef; once I won the good graces of my companions at the outset by appearing with two antelope which I had shot. After supper I would roll up in my bedding as soon as possible, and the others would follow suit at their pleasure.

At three in the morning or thereabouts, at a yell from the cook, all hands would turn hurriedly out. Dressing was a simple affair. Then each man rolled and corded his bedding — if he did not, the cook would leave it behind and he would go without any for the rest of the trip — and came to the fire, where he picked out a tin cup, tin plate, and knife and fork, helped himself to coffee and to whatever food there was, and ate it standing or squatting as best suited him. Dawn was probably breaking by this time, and the trampling of unshod hoofs showed that the night wrangler was bringing in the pony herd. Two of the men would then run ropes from the wagon at right angles to one another, and into this as a corral the horses would be driven. Each man might rope one of his own horses, or more often point it out to the most skillful roper of the outfit, who would rope it for him — for if the man was an unskillful roper and roped the wrong horse or roped the horse in the wrong place there was a chance of the whole herd stampeding. Each man then saddled and bridled his horse. This was usually followed by some resolute bucking on the part of two or three of the horses, especially in the early days of each round-up. The bucking was always a source of amusement to all the men whose horses did not buck, and these fortunate ones would gather round giving ironical advice, and especially adjuring the rider not to "go to leather" — that is, not to steady himself in the saddle by catching hold of the saddle-horn.

As soon as the men had mounted, the whole outfit started on the long circle, the morning circle. Usually the ranch foreman who bossed a given wagon was put in charge of the men of one group by the round-up foreman; he might keep his men together until they had gone some ten or fifteen miles from camp, and then drop them in couples at different points. Each couple made its way toward the wagon, gathering all the cattle it could find. The morning's ride might last six or eight hours, and it was still longer before some of the men got in.

Singly and in twos and threes they appeared from every quarter of the horizon, the dust rising from the hoofs of the steers
and bulls, the cows and calves, they had collected. Two or
three of the men were left to take care of the herd while the
others changed horses, ate a hasty dinner, and then came out
to the afternoon work. This consisted of each man in succession being sent into the herd, usually with a companion, to
cut out the cows of his brand or brands which were followed

The Cow-punchers.
"The men were lean, sinewy fellows, accustomed to riding half-broken
horses, at any speed, over any country, by day or by night."

by unbranded calves, and also to cut out any mavericks or
unbranded yearlings. We worked each animal gently out to
the edge of the herd, and then with a sudden dash took it off
at a run. It was always desperately anxious to break back and
rejoin the herd. There was much breakneck galloping and
twisting and turning before its desire was thwarted and it was
driven to join the rest of the cut — that is, the other animals
which had been cut out, and which were being held by one or
two other men. Cattle hate being alone, and it was no easy

matter to hold the first one or two that were cut out; but soon they got a little herd of their own, and then they were contented. When the cutting out had all been done, the calves were branded, and all misadventures of the "calf wrestlers," the men who seized, threw, and held each calf when roped by the mounted roper, were hailed with yelling laughter. Then the animals which for one reason or another it was desired to drive along with the round-up were put into one herd and left in charge of a couple of night guards, and the rest of us would loaf back to the wagon for supper and bed.

By this time I would have been accepted as one of the rest of the outfit, and all strangeness would have passed off, the attitude of my fellow cow-punchers being one of friendly forgiveness even toward my spectacles. Night guards for the cattle herd were then assigned by the captain of the wagon, or perhaps by the round-up foreman, according to the needs of the case, the guards standing for two hours at a time from eight in the evening till four in the morning. The first and last watches were preferable, because sleep was not broken as in both of the other two. If things went well, the cattle would soon bed down and nothing further would occur until morning, when there was a repetition of the work, the wagon moving each day eight or ten miles to some appointed camping-place.

Each man would picket his night horse near the wagon, usually choosing the quietest animal in his string for that purpose, because to saddle and mount a "mean" horse at night is not pleasant. When utterly tired, it was hard to have to get up for one's trick at night herd. Nevertheless, on ordinary nights the two hours round the cattle in the still darkness were pleasant. The loneliness, under the vast empty sky, and the silence, in which the breathing of the cattle sounded loud, and the alert readiness to meet any emergency which might suddenly arise out of the formless night, all combined to give one a sense of subdued interest. Then, one soon got to know the cattle of marked individuality, the ones that led the others into mischief; and one also grew to recognize the traits they all possessed in common, and the impulses which, for instance, made a whole herd get up towards midnight, each beast turning round and then lying down again. But by the end of the watch each rider had studied the cattle until it grew monotonous, and heartily welcomed his relief guard. A newcomer, of course, had any amount to learn, and sometimes the simplest things were those which brought him to grief.

One night early in my career I failed satisfactorily to identify the direction in which I was to go in order to reach the night herd. It was a pitch-dark night. I managed to get started wrong, and I never found either the herd or the wagon again until sunrise, when I was greeted with withering scorn by the injured cow-puncher, who had been obliged to stand double guard because I failed to relieve him.

There were other misadventures that I met with where the excuse was greater. The punchers on night guard usually rode round the cattle in reverse directions; calling and singing to them if the beasts seemed restless, to keep them quiet. On rare occasions something happened that made the cattle stampede, and then the duty of the riders was to keep with them as long as possible and try gradually to get control of them.

One night there was a heavy storm, and all of us who were at the wagons were obliged to turn out hastily to help the night herders. After a while there was a terrific peal of thunder, the lightning struck right by the herd, and away all the beasts went, heads and horns and tails in the air. For a minute or two I could make out nothing except the dark forms of the beasts running on every side of me, and I should have been very sorry if my horses had stumbled, for those behind would have trodden me down. Then the herd split, part going to one side, while the other part seemingly kept straight ahead, and I galloped as hard as ever beside them. I was trying to reach the point — the leading animals — in order to turn them, when suddenly there was a tremendous splashing in front. I could dimly make out that the cattle immediately ahead and to one side of me were disappearing, and the next moment the horse and I went off a cut bank into the Little Missouri. I bent away back in the saddle, and though the horse almost went down he just recovered himself, and, plunging and struggling through water and quicksand, we made the other side. Here I discovered that there was another cowboy with the same part of the herd that I was with; but almost immediately we separated. I galloped hard through a bottom covered with big cottonwood trees, and stopped the part of the herd that I was with, but very soon they broke on me again, and repeated this twice. Finally toward morning the few I had left came to a halt.

It had been raining hard for some time. I got off my horse and leaned against a tree, but before long the infernal cattle started on again, and I had to ride after them. Dawn came soon after this, and I was able to make out where I was and head the cattle back, collecting other little bunches as I went. After a while I came on a cowboy on foot carrying his saddle on his head. He was my companion of the previous night. His horse had gone full speed into a tree and killed itself, the man, however, not being hurt. I could not help him, as I had all I could do to handle the cattle. When I got them to the wagon, most of the other men had already come in and the riders were just starting on the long circle. One of the men changed my horse for me while I ate a hasty breakfast, and then we were off for the day's work.

As only about half of the night herd had been brought back, the circle riding was particularly heavy, and it was ten hours before we were back at the wagon. We then changed horses again and worked the whole herd until after sunset, finishing just as it grew too dark to do anything more. By this time I had been nearly forty hours in the saddle, changing horses five times, and my clothes had thoroughly dried on me, and I fell asleep as soon as I touched the bedding. Fortunately some men who had gotten in late in the morning had had their sleep during the daytime, so that the rest of us escaped night guard and were not called until four next morning. Nobody ever gets enough sleep on a round-up.

The above was the longest number of consecutive hours I ever had to be in the saddle. But, as I have said, I changed horses five times, and it is a great lightening of labor for a rider to have a fresh horse. Once when with Sylvane Ferris I spent about sixteen hours on one horse, riding seventy or eighty miles. The round-up had reached a place called the ox-bow of the Little Missouri, and we had to ride there, do some work around the cattle, and ride back.

Another time I was twenty-four hours on horseback in company with Merrifield without changing horses. On this occasion we did not travel fast. We had been coming back with the wagon from a hunting trip in the Big Horn Mountains. The team was fagged out, and we were tired of walking at a snail's pace beside it. When we reached country that the driver thoroughly knew, we thought it safe to leave him, and we loped in one night across a distance which it took the wagon the three following days to cover. It was a beautiful moonlight night, and the ride was delightful. All day long we had plodded at a walk, weary and hot. At supper time we had rested two or three hours, and the tough little riding horses seemed as fresh as ever. It was in September. As we rode out of the circle of the firelight, the air was cool in our faces. Under the bright moonlight, and then under the starlight, we loped and cantered mile after mile over the high prairie. We passed bands of antelope and herds of long-horn Texas cattle, and at last, just as the first red beams of the sun flamed over the bluffs in front of us, we rode down into the valley of the Little Missouri, where our ranch house stood.

I never became a good roper, nor more than an average rider, according to ranch standards. Of course a man on a ranch has to ride a good many bad horses, and is bound to encounter a certain number of accidents, and of these I had my share, at one time cracking a rib, and on another occasion the point of my shoulder. We were hundreds of miles from a doctor, and each time, as I was on the round-up, I had to get through my work for the next few weeks as best I could, until the injury healed of itself. When I had the opportunity I broke my own horses, doing it gently and gradually and spending much time over it, and choosing the horses that seemed gentle to begin with. With these horses I never had any difficulty. But frequently there was neither time nor opportunity to handle our mounts so elaborately. We might get a band of horses, each having been bridled and saddled two or three times, but none of them having been broken beyond the extent implied in this bridling and saddling. Then each of us in succession would choose a horse (for his string), I as owner of the ranch being given the first choice on each round, so to speak. The first time I was ever on a round-up Sylvane Ferris, Merrifield, Meyer, and I each chose his string in this fashion. Three or four of the animals I got were not easy to ride. The effort both to ride them and to look as if I enjoyed doing so, on some cool morning when my grinning cowboy friends had gathered round "to see whether the high-headed bay could buck the boss off," doubtless was of benefit to me, but lacked much of being enjoyable. The time I smashed my rib I was bucked off on a stone. The time I hurt the point of my shoulder I was riding a big, sulky horse named Ben Butler, which went over backwards with me. When we got up it still refused to go anywhere; so, while I sat it, Sylvane Ferris and George Meyer got their ropes on its neck and dragged it a few hundred yards, choking but stubborn, all four feet firmly planted and plowing the ground. When they released the ropes it lay down and wouldn't get up. The round-up had started; so Sylvane gave me his horse, Baldy, which sometimes bucked but never went over backwards, and he got on the now rearisen Ben Butler. To my discomfiture Ben started quietly beside us, while Sylvane remarked, "Why, there's nothing the matter with this horse; he's a plumb gentle horse." Then Ben fell slightly behind and I heard Sylvane again, "That's all right! Come alone! Here, you! Go on, you! Hi, hi, fellows, help me out! he's lying on me!" Sure enough, he was; and when we dragged Sylvane from under him the first thing the rescued Sylvane did was to execute a war-dance, spurs and all, on the iniquitous Ben. We could do nothing with him that day; subsequently we got him so that we could ride him; but he never became a nice saddle-horse.

As with all other forms of work, so on the round-up, a man of ordinary power, who nevertheless does not shirk things merely because they are disagreeable or irksome, soon earns his place. There were crack riders and ropers who, just because they felt such overweening pride in their own prowess, were not really very valuable men. Continually on the circles a cow or a calf would get into some thick patch of bulberry bush and refuse to come out; or when it was getting late we would pass some bad lands that would probably not contain cattle, but might; or a steer would turn fighting mad, or a calf grow tired and want to lie down. If in such a case the man steadily persists in doing the unattractive thing, and after two hours of exasperation and harassment does finally get the cow out, and keep her out, of the bulberry bushes, and drives her to the wagon, or finds some animals that have been passed by in the fourth or fifth patch of bad lands he hunts through, or gets the calf up on his saddle and takes it in anyhow, the foreman soon grows to treat him as having his uses and as being an asset of worth in the round-up, even though neither a fancy roper nor a fancy rider.

When at the Progressive Convention last August, I met George Meyer for the first time in many years, and he recalled to me an incident on one round-up where we happened to be thrown together while driving some cows and calves to camp.

On the Long Circle.

When the camp was only just across the river, two of the calves positively refused to go any further. He took one of them in his arms, and after some hazardous maneuvering managed to get on his horse, in spite of the objections of the latter, and rode into the river. My calf was too big for such treatment, so in despair I roped it, intending to drag it over. However, as soon as I roped it, the calf started bouncing and bleating, and, owing to some lack of dexterity on my part, suddenly swung round the rear of the horse, bringing the rope under his tail. Down went the tail tight, and the horse "went into figures," as the cow-puncher phrase of that day was. There was a cut bank about four feet high on the hither side of the river, and over this the horse bucked. We went into the water with a splash. With a "pluck" the calf followed, described a parabola in the air, and landed beside us. Fortunately, this took the rope out from under the horse's tail, but left him thoroughly frightened. He could not do much bucking in the stream, for there were one or two places where we had to swim, and the shallows were either sandy or muddy; but across we went, at speed, and the calf made a wake like Pharaoh's army in the Red Sea.

On several occasions we had to fight fire. In the geography books of my youth prairie fires were always portrayed as taking place in long grass, and all living things ran before them. On the Northern cattle plains the grass was never long enough to be a source of danger to man or beast. The fires were nothing like the forest fires in the Northern woods. But they destroyed large quantities of feed, and we had to stop them where possible. The process we usually followed was to kill a steer, split it in two lengthwise, and then have two riders drag each half-steer, the rope of one running from his saddle-horn to the front leg, and that of the other to the hind leg. One of the men would spur this horse over or through the line of fire, and the two would then ride forward, dragging the steer bloody side downward along the line of flame, men following on foot with slickers or wet horse-blankets to beat out any flickering blaze that was still left. It was exciting work, for the fire and the twitching and plucking of the ox carcass over the uneven ground maddened the fierce little horses so that it was necessary to do some riding in order to keep them to their work. After a while it also became very exhausting, the thirst and fatigue being great, as, with parched lips and blackened from head to foot, we toiled at our task.

In those years the Stockman's Association of Montana was a powerful body. I was the delegate to it from the Little Missouri. The meetings that I attended were held in Miles City, at that time a typical cow town. Stockmen of all kinds attended, including the biggest men in the stock business, men like old Conrad Kohrs, who was and is the finest type of pioneer in all the Rocky Mountain country; and Granville

Stewart, who was afterwards appointed Minister by Cleveland, I think to the Argentine; and "Hashknife" Simpson, a
Texan who had brought his cattle, the Hashknife brand, up
the trail into our country. He and I grew to be great friends.
I can see him now the first time we met, grinning at me as,
none too comfortable, I sat a half-broken horse at the edge of
a cattle herd we were working. His son Sloan Simpson went
to Harvard, was one of the first-class men in my regiment, and
afterwards held my commission as Postmaster at Dallas.

At the stockmen's meeting in Miles City, in addition to the
big stockmen, there were always hundreds of cowboys galloping up and down the wide dusty streets at every hour of
the day and night. It was a picturesque sight during the three
days the meetings lasted. There was always at least one big
dance at the hotel. There were few dress suits, but there was
perfect decorum at the dance, and in the square dances most
of the men knew the figures far better than I did. With such
a crowd in town, sleeping accommodations of any sort were
at a premium, and in the hotel there were two men in every
bed. On one occasion I had a roommate whom I never saw,
because he always went to bed much later than I did and I
always got up much earlier than he did. On the last day, however, he rose at the same time and I saw that he was a man I
knew named Carter, and nicknamed "Modesty" Carter. He
was a stalwart, good-looking fellow, and I was sorry when
later I heard that he had been killed in a shooting row.

When I went West, the last great Indian wars had just come
to an end, but there were still sporadic outbreaks here and
there, and occasionally bands of marauding young braves were
a menace to outlying and lonely settlements. Many of the
white men were themselves lawless and brutal, and prone to
commit outrages on the Indians. Unfortunately, each race
tended to hold all the members of the other race responsible
for the misdeeds of a few, so that the crime of the miscreant,
red or white, who committed the original outrage too often
invited retaliation upon entirely innocent people, and this
action would in its turn arouse bitter feeling which found
vent in still more indiscriminate retaliation. The first year I
was on the Little Missouri some Sioux bucks ran off all the
horses of a buffalo-hunter's outfit. One of the buffalo-hunters

tried to get even by stealing the horses of a Cheyenne hunting party, and when pursued made for a cow camp, with, as a result, a long-range skirmish between the cowboys and the Cheyennes. One of the latter was wounded; but this particular wounded man seemed to have more sense than the other participants in the chain of wrong-doing, and discriminated among the whites. He came into our camp and had his wound dressed.

A year later I was at a desolate little mud road ranch on the Deadwood trail. It was kept by a very capable and very forceful woman, with sound ideas of justice and abundantly well able to hold her own. Her husband was a worthless devil, who finally got drunk on some whisky he obtained from an outfit of Missouri bull-whackers — that is, freighters, driving ox wagons. Under the stimulus of the whisky he picked a quarrel with his wife and attempted to beat her. She knocked him down with a stove-lid lifter, and the admiring bull whackers bore him off, leaving the lady in full possession of the ranch. When I visited her she had a man named Crow Joe working for her, a slab-sided, shifty-eyed person who later, as I heard my foreman explain, "skipped the country with a bunch of horses." The mistress of the ranch made first-class buckskin shirts of great durability. The one she made for me, and which I used for years, was used by one of my sons in Arizona a couple of winters ago. I had ridden down into the country after some lost horses, and visited the ranch to get her to make me the buckskin shirt in question. There were, at the moment, three Indians there, Sioux, well behaved and self-respecting, and she explained to me that they had been resting there waiting for dinner, and that a white man had come along and tried to run off their horses. The Indians were on the lookout, however, and, running out, they caught the man; but, after retaking their horses and depriving him of his gun, they let him go. "I don't see why they let him go," exclaimed my hostess. "I don't believe in stealing Indians' horses any more than white folks'; so I told 'em they could go along and hang him — I'd never cheep. Anyhow, I won't charge them anything for their dinner," concluded my hostess. She was in advance of the usual morality of the time and place, which drew a sharp line between stealing citizens' horses and stealing horses from the Government or the Indians.

A fairly decent citizen, Jap Hunt, who long ago met a violent death, exemplified this attitude towards Indians in some remarks I once heard him make. He had started a horse ranch, and had quite honestly purchased a number of broken-down horses of different brands, with the view of doctoring them and selling them again. About this time there had been much horse-stealing and cattle-killing in our Territory and in Montana, and under the direction of some of the big cattle-growers a committee of vigilantes had been organized to take action against the rustlers, as the horse thieves and cattle thieves were called. The vigilantes, or stranglers, as they were locally known, did their work thoroughly; but, as always happens with bodies of the kind, toward the end they grew reckless in their actions, paid off private grudges, and hung men on slight provocation. Riding into Jap Hunt's ranch, they nearly hung him because he had so many horses of different brands. He was finally let off. He was much upset by the incident, and explained again and again, "The idea of saying that I was a horse thief! Why, I never stole a horse in my life — leastways from a white man. I don't count Indians nor the Government, of course." Jap had been reared among men still in the stage of tribal morality, and while they recognized their obligations to one another, both the Government and the Indians seemed alien bodies, in regard to which the laws of morality did not apply.

On the other hand, parties of savage young bucks would treat lonely settlers just as badly, and in addition sometimes murder them. Such a party was generally composed of young fellows burning to distinguish themselves. Some one of their number would have obtained a pass from the Indian Agent allowing him to travel off the reservation, which pass would be flourished whenever their action was questioned by bodies of whites of equal strength. I once had a trifling encounter with such a band. I was making my way along the edge of the bad lands, northward from my lower ranch, and was just crossing a plateau when five Indians rode up over the further rim. The instant they saw me they whipped out their guns and raced full speed at me, yelling and flogging their horses. I was on a favorite horse, Manitou, who was a wise old fellow, with nerves not to be shaken by anything. I at once leaped off him and stood with my rifle ready.

It was possible that the Indians were merely making a bluff and intended no mischief. But I did not like their actions, and I thought it likely that if I allowed them to get hold of me they would at least take my horse and rifle, and possibly kill me. So I waited until they were a hundred yards off and then drew a bead on the first. Indians — and, for the matter of that, white men — do not like to ride in on a man who is cool and means shooting, and in a twinkling every man was lying over the side of his horse, and all five had turned and were galloping backwards, having altered their course as quickly as so many teal ducks.

After this one of them made the peace sign, with his blanket first, and then, as he rode toward me, with his open hand. I halted him at a fair distance and asked him what he wanted. He exclaimed, "How! Me good Injun, me good Injun," and tried to show me the dirty piece of paper on which his agency pass was written. I told him with sincerity that I was glad that he was a good Indian, but that he must not come any closer. He then asked for sugar and tobacco. I told him I had none. Another Indian began slowly drifting toward me in spite of my calling out to keep back, so I once more aimed with my rifle, whereupon both Indians slipped to the other side of their horses and galloped off, with oaths that did credit to at least one side of their acquaintance with English. I now mounted and pushed over the plateau on to the open prairie. In those days an Indian, although not as good a shot as a white man, was infinitely better at crawling under and taking advantage of cover; and the worst thing a white man could do was to get into cover, whereas out in the open if he kept his head he had a good chance of standing off even half a dozen assailants. The Indians accompanied me for a couple of miles. Then I reached the open prairie, and resumed my northward ride, not being further molested.

In the old days in the ranch country we depended upon game for fresh meat. Nobody liked to kill a beef, and although now and then a maverick yearling might be killed on the round-up, most of us looked askance at the deed, because if the practice of beef-killing was ever allowed to start, the rustlers — the horse thieves and cattle thieves — would be sure to seize on it as an excuse for general slaughter. Getting meat for the ranch usually devolved upon me. I almost always carried a rifle when I rode, either in a scabbard under my thigh, or across the pommel. Often I would pick up a deer or antelope while about my regular work, when visiting a line camp or riding after the cattle. At other times I would make a day's trip after them. In the fall we sometimes took a wagon and made a week's hunt, returning with eight or ten deer carcasses, and perhaps an elk or a mountain sheep as well. I never became more than a fair hunter, and at times I had most exasperating experiences, either failing to see game which I ought to have seen, or committing some blunder in the stalk, or failing to kill when I fired. Looking back, I am inclined to say that if I had any good quality as a hunter it was that of perseverance. "It is dogged that does it" in hunting as in many other things. Unless in wholly exceptional cases, when we were very hungry, I never killed anything but bucks.

Occasionally I made long trips away from the ranch and among the Rocky Mountains with my ranch foreman Merrifield; or in later years with Tazewell Woody, John Willis, or John Goff. We hunted bears, both the black and the grizzly, cougars and wolves, and moose, wapiti, and white goat. On one of these trips I killed a bison bull, and I also killed a bison bull on the Little Missouri some fifty miles south of my ranch on a trip which Joe Ferris and I took together. It was rather a rough trip. Each of us carried only his slicker behind him on the saddle, with some flour and bacon done up in it. We met with all kinds of misadventures. Finally one night, when we were sleeping by a slimy little prairie pool where there was not a stick of wood, we had to tie the horses to the horns of our saddles; and then we went to sleep with our heads on the saddles. In the middle of the night something stampeded the horses, and away they went, with the saddles after them. As we jumped to our feet Joe eyes me with an evident suspicion that I was the Jonah of the party, and said: "O Lord! *I've* never done anything to deserve this. Did *you* ever do anything to deserve this?"

In addition to my private duties, I sometimes served as deputy sheriff for the northern end of our county. The sheriff and I crisscrossed in our public and private relations. He often worked for me as a hired hand at the same time that I was his deputy. His name, or at least the name he went by, was Bill Jones, and as there were in the neighborhood several Bill Joneses — Three Seven Bill Jones, Texas Bill Jones, and the like — the sheriff was known as Hell Roaring Bill Jones. He

Sheriff Duty.
"When I served as deputy sheriff for the northern end of our county."

was a thorough frontiersman, excellent in all kinds of emergencies, and a very game man. I became much attached to him. He was a thoroughly good citizen when sober, but he was a little wild when drunk. Unfortunately, toward the end of his life he got to drinking very heavily. When, in 1905, John Burroughs and I visited the Yellowstone Park, poor Bill Jones, very much down in the world, was driving a team in Gardiner outside the park. I had looked forward to seeing him, and he was equally anxious to see me. He kept telling his cronies of our intimacy and of what we were going to do together, and then got drinking; and the result was that by the time I reached Gardiner he had to be carried out and left in the sage-brush. When I came out of the park, I sent on in advance to tell them to be sure to keep him sober, and they did so. But it was a rather sad interview. The old fellow had gone to pieces, and soon after I left he got lost in a blizzard and was dead when they found him.

Bill Jones was a gun-fighter and also a good man with his fists. On one occasion there was an election in town. There had been many threats that the party of disorder would import section hands from the neighboring railway stations to down our side. I did not reach Medora, the forlorn little cattle town which was our county seat, until the election was well under way. I then asked one of my friends if there had been any disorder. Bill Jones was standing by. "Disorder hell!" said my friend. "Bill Jones just stood there with one hand on his gun and the other pointing over toward the new jail whenever any man who didn't have a right to vote came near the polls. There was only one of them tried to vote, and Bill knocked him down. Lord!" added my friend, medita-tively, "the way that man fell!" "Well," struck in Bill Jones, "if he hadn't fell I'd have walked round behind him to see what was propping him up!"

In the days when I lived on the ranch I usually spent most of the winter in the East, and when I returned in the early spring I was always interested in finding out what had hap-pened since my departure. On one occasion I was met by Bill Jones and Sylvane Ferris, and in the course of our conversa-tion they mentioned "the lunatic." This led to a question on my part, and Sylvane Ferris began the story: "Well, you see, he was on a train and he shot the newsboy. At first they weren't going to do anything to him, for they thought he just had it in for the newsboy. But then somebody said, 'Why, he's plumb crazy, and he's liable to shoot any of *us*!' and then they threw him off the train. It was here at Medora, and they asked if any-body would take care of him, and Bill Jones said he would, be-cause he was the sheriff and the jail had two rooms, and he was living in one and would put the lunatic in the other." Here Bill Jones interrupted: "Yes, and more fool me! I wouldn't take charge of another lunatic if the whole county asked me. Why" (with the air of a man announcing an astounding discovery), "that lunatic didn't have his right senses! He wouldn't eat, till me and Snyder got him down on the shavings and *made* him eat." Snyder was a huge, happy-go-lucky, kind-hearted Pennsylvania Dutchman, and was Bill Jones's chief deputy. Bill continued: "You know, Snyder's soft-hearted, he is. Well, he'd think that lunatic looked peaked, and he'd take him out for an airing. Then the boys would get joshing him as to how much start he could give him over the prairie and catch him again." Apparently the amount of the start given the lunatic depended upon the amount of the bet to which the joshing led up. I asked Bill what he would have done if Snyder hadn't caught the lunatic. This was evidently a new idea, and he responded that Snyder always did catch him. "Well, but suppose he hadn't caught him?" "Well," said Bill Jones, "if Snyder hadn't caught the lunatic, I'd have whaled hell out of Snyder!"

Under these circumstances Snyder ran his best and always did catch the patient. It must not be gathered from this that the lunatic was badly treated. He was well treated. He became greatly attached to both Bill Jones and Snyder, and he objected strongly when, after the frontier theory of treatment of the insane had received a full trial, he was finally sent off to the territorial capital. It was merely that all the relations of life in that place and day were so managed as to give ample opportunity for the expression of individuality, whether in sheriff or ranchman. The local practical joker once attempted to have some fun at the expense of the lunatic, and Bill Jones described the result. "You know Bixby, don't you? Well," with deep disapproval, "Bixby thinks he is funny, he does. He'd come and he'd wake that lunatic up at night, and I'd have to get up and soothe him. I fixed Bixby all right, though. I fastened a rope on the latch, and next time Bixby came I let the lunatic out on him. He 'most bit Bixby's nose off. I learned Bixby!"

Bill Jones had been unconventional in other relations besides that of sheriff. He once casually mentioned to me that he had served on the police force of Bismarck, but he had left because he "beat the Mayor over the head with his gun one day." He added: "The Mayor, he didn't mind it, but the Superintendent of Police said he guessed I'd better resign." His feeling, obviously, was that the Superintendent of Police was a martinet, unfit to take large views of life.

It was while with Bill Jones that I first made acquaintance with Seth Bullock. Seth was at that time sheriff in the Black Hills district, and a man he had wanted — a horse thief — I finally got, I being at the time deputy sheriff two or three hundred miles to the north. The man went by a nickname which I will call "Crazy Steve"; a year or two afterwards I received a letter asking about him from his uncle, a thoroughly respectable man in a Western State; and later this uncle and I met at Washington when I was President and he a United States Senator. It was some time after "Steve's" capture that I went down to Deadwood on business, Sylvane Ferris and I on horseback, while Bill Jones drove the wagon. At a little town, Spearfish, I think, after crossing the last eighty or ninety miles of gumbo prairie, we met Seth Bullock. We had had rather a rough trip, and had lain out for a fortnight, so I suppose we looked somewhat unkempt. Seth received us with rather distant courtesy at first, but unbent when he found out who we were, remarking, "You see, by your looks I thought you were some kind of a tin-horn gambling outfit, and that I might have to keep an eye on you!" He then inquired after the capture of "Steve" — with a little of the air of one sportsman when another has shot a quail that either might have claimed — "My bird, I believe?" Later Seth Bullock became, and has ever since remained, one of my stanchest and most valued friends. He served as Marshal for South Dakota under me as President. When, after the close of my term, I went to Africa, on getting back to Europe I cabled Seth Bullock to bring over Mrs. Bullock and meet me in London, which he did; by that time I felt that I just had to meet my own people, who spoke my neighborhood dialect.

When serving as deputy sheriff I was impressed with the advantage the officer of the law has over ordinary wrong-doers, provided he thoroughly knows his own mind. There are exceptional outlaws, men with a price on their heads and of remarkable prowess, who are utterly indifferent to taking life, and whose warfare against society is as open as that of a savage on the war-path. The law officer has no advantage whatever over these men save what his own prowess may — or may not — give him. Such a man was Billy the Kid, the notorious man-killer and desperado of New Mexico, who was himself finally slain by a friend of mine, Pat Garrett, whom, when I was President, I made collector of customs at El Paso. But the ordinary criminal, even when murderously inclined, feels just a moment's hesitation as to whether he cares to kill an officer of the law engaged in his duty. I took in more than one man who was probably a better man than I was with both rifle and revolver; but in each case I knew just what I wanted to do, and, like David Harum, I "did it first," whereas the fraction of a second that the other man hesitated put him in a position where it was useless for him to resist.

I owe more than I can ever express to the West, which of course means to the men and women I met in the West. There were a few people of bad type in my neighborhood — that would be true of every group of men, even in a theological seminary — but I could not speak with too great affection and respect of the great majority of my friends, the hard-working men and women who dwelt for a space of perhaps a hundred and fifty miles along the Little Missouri. I was always as welcome at their houses as they were at mine. Everybody worked, everybody was willing to help everybody else, and yet nobody asked any favors. The same thing was true of the people whom I got to know fifty miles east and fifty miles west of my own range, and of the men I met on the round-ups. They soon accepted me as a friend and fellow-worker who stood on an equal footing with them, and I believe that most of them have kept their feeling for me ever since. No guests were ever more welcome at the White House than these old friends of the cattle ranches and the cow camps — the men with whom I had ridden the long circle and eaten at the tail-board of a chuck-wagon — whenever they turned up at Washington during my Presidency. I remember one of them who appeared at Washington one day just before lunch, a huge, powerful man who, when I knew him, had been distinctly a fighting character. It happened that on that day another old friend, the British Ambassador, Mr. Bryce, was among those coming to lunch. Just before we went in I turned to my cow-puncher friend and said to him with great solemnity, "Remember, Jim, that if you shot at the feet of the British Ambassador to make him dance, it would be likely to cause international complications"; to which Jim responded with unaffected horror, "Why, Colonel, I shouldn't think of it, I shouldn't think of it!"

Not only did the men and women whom I met in the cow country quite unconsciously help me, by the insight which working and living with them enabled me to get into the mind and soul of the average American of the right type, but they helped me in another way. I made up my mind that the men were of just the kind whom it would be well to have with me if ever it became necessary to go to war. When the Spanish War came, I gave this thought practical realization.

Fortunately, Wister and Remington, with pen and pencil, have made these men live as long as our literature lives. I have sometimes been asked if Wister's "Virginian" is not overdrawn; why, one of the men I have mentioned in this chapter was in all essentials the Virginian in real life, not only in his force but in his charm. Half of the men I worked with or played with and half of the men who soldiered with me afterwards in my regiment might have walked out of Wister's stories or Remington's pictures.

There were bad characters in the Western country at that time, of course, and under the conditions of life they were probably more dangerous than they would have been elsewhere. I hardly ever had any difficulty, however. I never went into a saloon, and in the little hotels I kept out of the bar-room unless, as sometimes happened, the bar-room was the only room on the lower floor except the dining-room. I always endeavored to keep out of a quarrel until self-respect forbade my making any further effort to avoid it, and I very rarely had even the semblance of trouble.

Of course amusing incidents occurred now and then. Usually these took place when I was hunting lost horses, for in hunting lost horses I was ordinarily alone, and occasionally had to travel a hundred or a hundred and fifty miles away from my own country. On one such occasion I reached a little cow town long after dark, stabled my horse in an empty outbuilding, and when I reached the hotel was informed in response to my request for a bed that I could have the last one left, as there was only one other man in it. The room to which I was shown contained two double beds; one contained two men fast asleep, and the other only one man, also asleep. This man proved to be a friend, one of the Bill Joneses whom I have previously mentioned. I undressed according to the fashion of the day and place, that is, I put my trousers, boots, shaps, and gun down beside the bed, and turned in. A couple of hours later I was awakened by the door being thrown open and a lantern flashed in my face, the light gleaming on the muzzle of a cocked .45. Another man said to the lantern-bearer, "It ain't him"; the next moment my bedfellow was covered with

"Seth Bullock became, and has ever since remained, one of my stanchest and most valued friends."

two guns, and addressed, "Now, Bill, don't make a fuss, but come along quiet." "I'm not thinking of making a fuss," said Bill. "That's right," was the answer; "we're your friends; we don't want to hurt you; we just want you to come along, you know why." And Bill pulled on his trousers and boots and walked out with them. Up to this time there had not been a sound from the other bed. Now a match was scratched, a candle lit, and one of the men in the other bed looked round the room. At this point I committed the breach of etiquette of asking questions. "I wonder why they took Bill," I said. There was no answer, and I repeated "I wonder why they took Bill." "Well," said the man with the candle, dryly, "I reckon they wanted him," and with that he blew out the candle and conversation ceased. Later I discovered that Bill in a fit of playfulness had held up the Northern Pacific train at a near-by station by shooting at the feet of the conductor to make him dance. This was purely a joke on Bill's part, but the Northern Pacific people possessed a less robust sense of humor, and on their complaint the United States Marshal was sent after Bill, on the ground that by delaying the train he had interfered with the mails.

The only time I ever had serious trouble was at an even more primitive little hotel than the one in question. It was also on an occasion when I was out after lost horses. Below the hotel had merely a bar-room, a dining-room, and a lean-to kitchen; above was a loft with fifteen or twenty beds in it. It was late in the evening when I reached the place. I heard one or two shots in the bar-room as I came up, and I disliked going in. But there was nowhere else to go, and it was a cold night. Inside the room were several men, who, including the bartender, were wearing the kind of smile worn by men who are making believe to like what they don't like. A shabby individual in a broad hat with a cocked gun in each hand was walking up and down the floor talking with strident profanity. He had evidently been shooting at the clock, which had two or three holes in its face.

He was not a "bad man" of the really dangerous type, the true man-killer type, but he was an objectionable creature, a would-be bad man, a bully who for the moment was having things all his own way. As soon as he saw me he hailed me as "Four eyes," in reference to my spectacles, and said, "Four eyes is going to treat." I joined in the laugh and got behind the stove and sat down, thinking to escape notice. He followed me, however, and though I tried to pass it off as a jest this merely made him more offensive, and he stood leaning over me, a gun in each hand, using very foul language. He was foolish to stand so near, and, moreover, his heels were close together, so that his position was unstable. Accordingly, in response to his reiterated command that I should set up the drinks, I said, "Well, if I've got to, I've got to," and rose, looking past him.

As I rose, I struck quick and hard with my right just to one side of the point of his jaw, hitting with my left as I straightened out, and then again with my right. He fired the guns, but I do not know whether this was merely a convulsive action of his hands or whether he was trying to shoot at me. When he went down he struck the corner of the bar with his head. It was not a case in which one could afford to take chances, and if he had moved I was about to drop on his ribs with my knees; but he was senseless. I took away his guns, and the other people in the room, who were now loud in their denunciation of him, hustled him out and put him in a shed. I got dinner as soon as possible, sitting in a corner of the dining-room away from the windows, and then went upstairs to bed where it was dark so that there would be no chance of any one shooting at me from the outside. However, nothing happened. When my assailant came to, he went down to the station and left on a freight.

As I have said, most of the men of my regiment were just such men as those I knew in the ranch country; indeed, some of my ranch friends were in the regiment — Fred Herrig, the forest ranger, for instance, in whose company I shot my biggest mountain ram. After the regiment was disbanded the careers of certain of the men were diversified by odd incidents. Our relations were of the friendliest, and, as they explained, they felt "as if I was a father" to them. The manifestations of this feeling were sometimes less attractive than the phrase sounded, as it was chiefly used by the few who were behaving like very bad children indeed. The great majority of the men when the regiment disbanded took up the business of their lives where they had dropped it a few months previously, and these men merely tried to help me or help one another as the occasion arose; no man ever had more cause to be proud of his regiment than I had of mine, both in war and in peace. But there was a minority among them who in certain ways were unsuited for a life of peaceful regularity, although often enough they had been first-class soldiers.

It was from these men that letters came with a stereotyped opening which always caused my heart to sink — "Dear Colonel: I write you because I am in trouble." The trouble might take almost any form. One correspondent continued: "I did not take the horse, but they say I did." Another complained that his mother-in-law had put him in jail for bigamy. In the case of another the incident was more markworthy. I will call him Gritto. He wrote me a letter beginning: "Dear Colonel: I write you because I am in trouble. I have shot a lady in the eye. But, Colonel, I was not shooting at the lady. I was shooting at my wife," which he apparently regarded as a sufficient excuse as between men of the world. I answered that I drew the line at shooting at ladies, and did not hear any more of the incident for several years.

Then, while I was President, a member of the regiment, Major Llewellyn, who was Federal District Attorney under me in New Mexico, wrote me a letter filled, as his letters usually were, with bits of interesting gossip about the comrades. It ran in part as follows: "Since I last wrote you Comrade Ritchie has killed a man in Colorado. I understand that the comrade was playing a poker game, and the man sat into the game and used such language that Comrade Ritchie had to shoot. Comrade Webb has killed two men in Beaver, Arizona. Comrade Webb is in the Forest Service, and the killing was in the line of professional duty. I was out at the penitentiary the other day and saw Comrade Gritto, who, you may remember, was put there for shooting his sister-in-law [this was the first information I had had as to the identity of the lady who was shot in the eye]. Since he was in there Comrade Boyne has run off to old Mexico with his (Gritto's) wife, and the people of Grant County think he ought to be let out." Evidently the sporting instincts of the people of Grant County had been roused, and they felt that, as Comrade Boyne had had a fair start, the other comrade should be let out in order to see what would happen.

The men of the regiment always enthusiastically helped me when I was running for office. On one occasion Buck Taylor, of Texas, accompanied me on a trip and made a speech for me. The crowd took to his speech from the beginning and so did I, until the peroration, which ran as follows: "My fellow-citizens, vote for my Colonel! vote for my Colonel! *and he will lead you, as he led us, like sheep to the slaughter!*" This hardly seemed a tribute to my military skill; but it delighted the crowd, and as far as I could tell did me nothing but good.

On another tour, when I was running for Vice-President, a member of the regiment who was along on the train got into a discussion with a Populist editor who had expressed an unfavorable estimate of my character, and in the course of the discussion shot the editor — not fatally. We had to leave him to be tried, and as he had no money I left him $150 to hire counsel — having borrowed the money from Senator Wolcott, of Colorado, who was also with me. After election I received from my friend a letter running: "Dear Colonel: I find I will not have to use that $150 you lent me, as we have elected our candidate for District Attorney. So I have used it to settle a horse transaction in which I unfortunately became involved." A few weeks later, however, I received a heartbroken letter setting forth the fact that the District Attorney — whom he evidently felt to be a cold-blooded formalist — had put him in jail. Then the affair dropped out of sight until two or three years later, when as President I visited a town in another State, and the leaders of the delegation which received me included both my correspondent and the editor, now fast friends, and both of them ardent supporters of mine.

At one of the regimental reunions a man, who had been an excellent soldier, in greeting me mentioned how glad he was that the judge had let him out in time to get to the reunion. I asked what was the matter, and he replied with some surprise: "Why, Colonel, don't you know I had a difficulty with a gentleman, and . . . er . . . well, I killed the gentleman. But you can see that the judge thought it was all right or he wouldn't have let me go." Waiving the latter point, I said: "How did it happen? How did you do it?" Misinterpreting my question as showing an interest only in the technique of the performance, the ex-puncher replied: "With a .38 on a .45 frame, Colonel." I chuckled over the answer, and it became proverbial with my family and some of my friends, including Seth Bullock. When I was shot at Milwaukee, Seth Bullock wired an inquiry to which I responded that it was all right, that the weapon was merely "a .38 on a .45 frame." The telegram in some way became public, and puzzled outsiders.

By the way, both the men of my regiment and the friends I
had made in the old days in the West were themselves a little
puzzled at the interest shown in my making my speech after
being shot. This was what they expected, what they accepted
as the right thing for a man to do under the circumstances, a

The Broncho Buster, by Frederic Remington.

Presented to Colonel Roosevelt on September 15, 1898, by his regiment at
Camp Wikoff, Montauk Point, where the Rough Riders were disbanded
at the close of the Spanish-American War.

thing the non-performance of which would have been discreditable rather than the performance being creditable. They
would not have expected a man to leave a battle, for instance,
because of being wounded in such fashion; and they saw
no reason why he should abandon a less important and less
risky duty.

One of the best soldiers of my regiment was a huge man whom I made marshal of a Rocky Mountain State. He had spent his hot and lusty youth on the frontier during its viking age, and at that time had naturally taken part in incidents which seemed queer to men "accustomed to die decently of zymotic diseases." I told him that an effort would doubtless be made to prevent his confirmation by the Senate, and therefore that I wanted to know all the facts in his case. Had he played faro? He had; but it was when everybody played faro, and he had never played a brace game. Had he killed anybody? Yes, but it was in Dodge City on occasions when he was deputy marshal or town marshal, at a time when Dodge City, now the most peaceful of communities, was the toughest town on the continent, and crowded with man-killing outlaws and road agents; and he produced telegrams from judges of high character testifying to the need of the actions he had taken. Finally I said: "Now, Ben, how did you lose that half of your ear?" To which, looking rather shy, he responded: "Well, Colonel, it was bit off." "How did it happen, Ben?" "Well, you see, I was sent to arrest a gentleman, and him and me mixed it up, and he bit off my ear." "What did you do to the gentleman, Ben?" And Ben, looking more coy than ever, responded: "Well, Colonel, we broke about even!" I forebore to inquire what variety of mayhem he had committed on the "gentleman." After considerable struggle I got him confirmed by the Senate, and he made one of the best marshals in the entire service, exactly as he had already made one of the best soldiers in the regiment; and I never wish to see a better citizen, nor a man in whom I would more implicitly trust in every way.

When, in 1900, I was nominated for Vice-President, I was sent by the National Committee on a trip into the States of the high plains and the Rocky Mountains. These had all gone overwhelmingly for Mr. Bryan on the free-silver issue four years previously, and it was thought that I, because of my knowledge of and acquaintanceship with the people, might accomplish something towards bringing them back into line. It was an interesting trip, and the monotony usually attendant upon such a campaign of political speaking was diversified in vivid fashion by occasional hostile audiences. One or two of the meetings ended in riots. One meeting was finally broken up by a mob; everybody fought so that the speaking had to stop. Soon after this we reached another town where we were told there might be trouble. Here the local committee included an old and valued friend, a "two-gun" man of repute, who was not in the least quarrelsome, but who always kept his word. We marched round to the local opera-house, which was packed with a mass of men, many of them rather rough-looking. My friend the two-gun man sat immediately behind me, a gun on each hip, his arms folded, looking at the audience; fixing his gaze with instant intentness on any section of the house from which there came so much as a whisper. The audience listened to me with rapt attention. At the end, with a pride in my rhetorical powers which proceeded from a misunderstanding of the situation, I remarked to the chairman: "I held that audience well; there wasn't an interruption." To which the chairman replied: "Interruption? Well, I guess not! Seth had sent round word that if any son of a gun peeped he'd kill him!"

There was one bit of frontier philosophy which I should like to see imitated in more advanced communities. Certain crimes of revolting baseness and cruelty were never forgiven. But in the case of ordinary offenses, the man who had served his term and who then tried to make good was given a fair chance; and of course this was equally true of the women. Every one who has studied the subject at all is only too well aware that the world offsets the readiness with which it condones a crime for which a man escapes punishment, by its unforgiving relentlessness to the often far less guilty man who *is* punished, and who therefore has made his atonement. On the frontier, if the man honestly tried to behave himself there was generally a disposition to give him fair play and a decent show. Several of the men I knew and whom I particularly liked came in this class. There was one such man in my regiment, a man who had served a term for robbery under arms, and who had atoned for it by many years of fine performance of duty. I put him in a high official position, and no man under me rendered better service to the State, nor was there any man whom, as soldier, as civil officer, as citizen, and as friend, I valued and respected — and now value and respect — more.

Now I suppose some good people will gather from this that I favor men who commit crimes. I certainly do not favor them. I have not a particle of sympathy with the sentimentality — as I deem it, the mawkishness — which overflows with foolish pity for the criminal and cares not at all for the victim of the criminal. I am glad to see wrong-doers punished. The punishment is an absolute necessity from the standpoint of society; and I put the reformation of the criminal second to the welfare of society. But I do desire to see the man or woman who has paid the penalty and who wishes to reform given a helping hand — surely every one of us who knows his own heart must know that he too may stumble, and should be anxious to help his brother or sister who has stumbled. When the criminal has been punished, if he then shows a sincere desire to lead a decent and upright life, he should be given the chance, he should be helped and not hindered; and if he makes good, he should receive that respect from others which so often aids in creating self-respect — the most invaluable of all possessions.

## Chapter V

### APPLIED IDEALISM

In the spring of 1889 I was appointed by President Harrison Civil Service Commissioner. For nearly five years I had not been very active in political life; although I had done some routine work in the organization and had made campaign speeches, and in 1886 had run for Mayor of New York against Abram S. Hewitt, Democrat, and Henry George, Independent, and had been defeated.

I served six years as Civil Service Commissioner — four years under President Harrison and then two years under President Cleveland. I was treated by both Presidents with the utmost consideration. Among my fellow-Commissioners there was at one time ex-Governor Hugh Thompson, of South Carolina, and at another time John R. Proctor, of Kentucky. They were Democrats and ex-Confederate soldiers. I became deeply attached to both, and we stood shoulder to shoulder in every contest in which the Commission was forced to take part.

Civil Service Reform had two sides. There was, first, the effort to secure a more efficient administration of the public service, and, second, the even more important

Theodore Roosevelt.
Civil Service Commissioner.

effort to withdraw the administrative offices of the Government from the domain of spoils politics, and thereby cut out of American political life a fruitful source of corruption and degradation. The spoils theory of politics is that public office is so much plunder which the victorious political party is entitled to appropriate to the use of its adherents. Under this system the work of the Government was often done well even in those days, when Civil Service Reform was only an experiment, because the man running an office if himself an able and far-sighted man, knew that inefficiency in administration would be visited on his head in the long run, and therefore insisted upon most of his subordinates doing good work; and, moreover, the men appointed under the spoils system were necessarily men of a certain initiative and power, because those who lacked these qualities were not able to shoulder themselves to the front. Yet there were many flagrant instances of inefficiency, where a powerful chief quartered friend, adherent, or kinsman upon the Government. Moreover, the necessarily haphazard nature of the employment, the need of obtaining and holding the office by service wholly unconnected with official duty, inevitably tended to lower the standard of public morality, alike among the office-holders and among the politicians who rendered party service with the hope of reward in office. Indeed, the doctrine that "To the victor belong the spoils," the cynical battle-cry of the spoils politician in America for the sixty years preceding my own entrance into public life, is so nakedly vicious that few right-thinking men of trained mind defend it. To appoint, promote, reduce, and expel from the public service, letter-carriers, stenographers, women typewriters, clerks, because of the politics of themselves or their friends, without regard to their own service, is, from the standpoint of the people at large, as foolish and degrading as it is wicked.

Such being the case, it would seem at first sight extraordinary that it should be so difficult to uproot the system. Unfortunately, it was permitted to become habitual and traditional in American life, so that the conception of public office as something to be used primarily for the good of the dominant political party became ingrained in the mind of the average American, and he grew so accustomed to the whole process that it seemed part of the order of nature. Not merely the politicians but the bulk of the people accepted this in a matter-of-course way as the only proper attitude. There were plenty of communities where the citizens themselves did not think it natural, or indeed proper, that the Post-Office should be held by a man belonging to the defeated party. Moreover, unless both sides were forbidden to use the offices for purposes of political reward, the side that did use them possessed such an advantage over the other that in the long run it was out of the question for the other not to follow the bad example that had been set. Each party profited by the offices when in power, and when in opposition each party insincerely denounced its opponents for doing exactly what it itself had done and intended again to do.

It was necessary, in order to remedy the evil, both gradually to change the average citizen's mental attitude toward the question, and also to secure proper laws and proper administration of the laws. The work is far from finished even yet. There are still masses of office-holders who can be used by an unscrupulous Administration to debauch political conventions and fraudulently overcome public sentiment, especially in the "rotten borough" districts — those where the party is not strong, and where the office-holders in consequence have a disproportionate influence. This was done by the Republican Administration in 1912, to the ruin of the Republican party. Moreover, there are numbers of States and municipalities where very little has as yet been done to do away with the spoils system. But in the National Government scores of thousands of offices have been put under the merit system, chiefly through the action of the National Civil Service Commission.

The use of Government office as patronage is a handicap difficult to overestimate from the standpoint of those who strive to get good government. Any effort for reform of any sort, National, State, or municipal, results in the reformers immediately finding themselves face to face with an organized band of drilled mercenaries who are paid out of the public chest to train themselves with such skill that ordinary good citizens when they meet them at the polls are in much the position of militia matched against regular troops. Yet these citizens themselves support and pay their opponents in such a way that they are drilled to overthrow the very men who support them. Civil Service Reform is designed primarily to give the average American citizen a fair chance in politics, to give to this citizen the same weight in politics that the "ward heeler" has.

Patronage does not really help a party. It helps the bosses to get control of the machinery of the party — as in 1912 was true of the Republican party — but it does not help the party.

On the average, the most sweeping party victories in our history have been won when the patronage was against the victors. All that the patronage does is to help the worst element in the party retain control of the party organization. Two of the evil elements in our Government against which good citizens have to contend are, 1, the lack of continuous activity on the part of these good citizens themselves, and, 2, the ever-present activity of those who have only an evil self-interest in political life. It is difficult to interest the average citizen in any particular movement to the degree of getting him to take an efficient part in it. He wishes the movement well, but he will not, or often cannot, take the time and the trouble to serve it efficiently; and this whether he happens to be a mechanic or a banker, a telegraph operator or a storekeeper. He has his own interests, his own business, and it is difficult for him to spare the time to go around to the primaries, to see to the organization, to see to getting out the vote — in short, to attend to all the thousand details of political management.

On the other hand, the spoils system breeds a class of men whose financial interest it is to take this necessary time and trouble. They are paid for so doing, and they are paid out of the public chest. Under the spoils system a man is appointed to an ordinary clerical or ministerial position in the municipal, Federal, or State government, not primarily because he is expected to be a good servant, but because he has rendered help to some big boss or to the henchman of some big boss. His stay in office depends not upon how he performs service, but upon how he retains his influence in the party. This necessarily means that his attention to the interests of the public at large, even though real, is secondary to his devotion to his organization, or to the interest of the ward leader who put him in his place. So he and his fellows attend to politics, not once a year, not two or three times a year, like the average citizen, but every day in the year. It is the one thing that they talk of, for it is their bread and butter. They plan about it and they scheme about it. They do it because it is their business. I do not blame them in the least. I blame us, the people, for we ought to make it clear as a bell that the business of serving the people in one of the ordinary ministerial Government positions, which have nothing to do with deciding the policy of the Government, should have no necessary connection with the management of primaries, of caucuses, and of nominating conventions. As a result of our wrong thinking and supineness, we American citizens tend to breed a mass of men whose interests in governmental matters are often adverse to ours, who are thoroughly drilled, thoroughly organized, who make their livelihood out of politics, and who frequently make their livelihood out of bad politics. They know every little twist and turn, no matter how intricate, in the politics of their several wards, and when election day comes the ordinary citizen who has merely the interest that all good men, all decent citizens, should have in political life, finds himself as helpless before these men as if he were a solitary volunteer in the presence of a band of drilled mercenaries on a field of battle. There are a couple of hundred thousand Federal offices, not to speak of State and municipal offices. The men who fill these offices, and the men who wish to fill them, within and without the dominant party for the time being, make a regular army, whose interest it is that the system of bread-and-butter politics shall continue. Against their concrete interest we have merely the generally unorganized sentiment of the community in favor of putting things on a decent basis. The large number of men who believe vaguely in good are pitted against the smaller but still larger number of men whose interest it often becomes to act very concretely and actively for evil; and it is small wonder that the struggle is doubtful.

During my six years' service as Commissioner the field of the merit system was extended at the expense of the spoils system so as to include several times the number of offices that had originally been included. Generally this was done by the introduction of competitive entrance examinations; sometimes, as in the Navy-Yards, by a system of registration. This of itself was good work.

Even better work was making the law efficient and genuine where it applied. As was inevitable in the introduction of such a system, there was at first only partial success in its application. For instance, it applied to the ordinary employees in the big custom-houses and post-offices, but not to the heads of these offices. A number of the heads of the offices were slippery politicians of a low moral grade, themselves appointed under the spoils system, and anxious, directly or indirectly, to break down the merit system and to pay their own political debts by appointing their henchmen and supporters to the positions under them. Occasionally these men acted with open and naked brutality. Ordinarily they sought by cunning to evade the law. The Civil Service Reformers, on the other hand, were in most cases not much used to practical politics, and were often well-nigh helpless when pitted against veteran professional politicians. In consequence I found at the beginning of my experiences that there were many offices in which the execution of the law was a sham. This was very damaging, because it encouraged the politicians to assault the law everywhere, and, on the other hand, made good people feel that the law was not worth while defending.

The first effort of myself and my colleagues was to secure the genuine enforcement of the law. In this we succeeded after a number of lively fights. But of course in these fights we were obliged to strike a large number of influential politicians, some of them in Congress, some of them the supporters and backers of men who were in Congress. Accordingly we soon found ourselves engaged in a series of contests with prominent Senators and Congressmen. There were a number of Senators and Congressmen — men like Congressman (afterwards Senator) H. C. Lodge, of Massachusetts; Senator Cushman K. Davis, of Minnesota; Senator Orville H. Platt, of Connecticut; Senator Cockrell, of Missouri; Congressman (afterwards President) McKinley, of Ohio, and Congressman Dargan, of South Carolina — who abhorred the business of the spoilsman, who efficiently and resolutely championed the reform at every turn, and without whom the whole reform would certainly have failed. But there were plenty of other Senators and Congressmen who hated the whole reform and everything concerned with it and everybody who championed it; and sometimes, to use a legal phrase, their hatred was for cause, and sometimes it was peremptory — that is, sometimes the Commission interfered with their most efficient, and incidentally most corrupt and unscrupulous, supporters, and at other times, where there was no such interference, a man nevertheless had an innate dislike of anything that tended to decency in government. These men were always waging war against us, and they usually had the more or less open support of a certain number of Government officials, from Cabinet officers down. The Senators and Congressmen in question opposed us in many different ways. Sometimes, for instance, they had committees appointed to investigate us — during my public career without and within office I grew accustomed to accept appearances before investigating committees as part of the natural order of things. Sometimes they tried to cut off the appropriation for the Commission.

Occasionally we would bring to terms these Senators or Congressmen who fought the Commission by the simple expedient of not holding examinations in their districts. This always brought frantic appeals from their constituents, and we would explain that unfortunately the appropriations had been cut, so that we could not hold examinations in every district, and that obviously we could not neglect the districts of those Congressmen who believed in the reform and therefore in the examination. The constituents then turned their attention to the Congressman, and the result was that in the long run we obtained sufficient money to enable us to do our work. On the whole, the most prominent leaders favored us. Any man who is the head of a big department, if he has any fitness at all, wishes to see that department run well; and a very little practical experience shows him that it cannot be run well if he must make his appointments to please spoilsmongering politicians. As with almost every reform that I have ever undertaken, most of the opposition took the guise of shrewd slander. Our opponents relied chiefly on downright misrepresentation of what it was that we were trying to accomplish, and of our methods, acts, and personalities. I had more than one lively encounter with the authors and sponsors of these misrepresentations, which at the time were full of interest to me. But it would be a dreary thing now to go over the record of exploded mendacity, or to expose the meanness and malice shown by some men of high official position. A favorite argument was to call the reform Chinese, because the Chinese had constructed an inefficient governmental system based in part on the theory of written competitive examinations. The argument was simple. There had been written examinations in China; it was proposed to establish written examinations in the United States; therefore the proposed system was Chinese. The argument might have been applied still further. For instance, the Chinese had used gunpowder for centuries; gunpowder is used in Springfield rifles; therefore Springfield rifles were Chinese. One argument is quite as logical as the other. It was impossible to answer every falsehood about the system. But it was possible to answer certain falsehoods, especially when uttered by some Senator or Congressman of note. Usually these false statements took the form of assertions that we had asked preposterous questions of applicants. At times they also included the assertion that we credited people to districts where they did not live; this simply meaning that these persons were not known to the active ward politicians of those districts.

One opponent with whom we had a rather lively tilt was a Republican Congressman from Ohio, Mr. Grosvenor, one of the floor leaders. Mr. Grosvenor made his attack in the House, and enumerated our sins in picturesque rather than accurate fashion. There was a Congressional committee investigating us at the time, and on my next appearance before them I asked that Mr. Grosvenor be requested to meet me before the committee. Mr. Grosvenor did not take up the challenge for several weeks, until it was announced that I was leaving for my ranch in Dakota; whereupon, deeming it safe, he wrote me a letter expressing his ardent wish that I should appear before the committee to meet him. I promptly canceled my ticket, waited, and met him. He proved to be a person of happily treacherous memory, so that the simple expedient of arranging his statements in pairs was sufficient to reduce him to confusion. For instance, he had been trapped into making the unwary remark, "I do not want to repeal the Civil Service Law, and I never said so." I produced the following extract from one of his speeches: "I will vote not only to strike out this provision, but I will vote to repeal the whole law." To this he merely replied that there was "no inconsistency between those two statements." He asserted that "Rufus P. Putnam, fraudulently credited to Washington County, Ohio, never lived in Washington County, Ohio, or in my Congressional district, or in Ohio as far as I know." We produced a letter which, thanks to a beneficent Providence, he had himself writ-

ten about Mr. Rufus P. Putnam, in which he said: "Mr. Rufus
P. Putnam is a legal resident of my district and has relatives
living there now." He explained, first, that he had not written
the letter; second, that he had forgotten he had written the
letter; and, third, that he was grossly deceived when he wrote
it. He said: "I have not been informed of one applicant who
has found a place in the classified service from my district."
We confronted him with the names of eight. He looked them
over and said, "Yes, the eight men are living in my district as
now constituted," but added that his district had been gerry-
mandered so that he could no longer tell who did and who
didn't live in it. When I started further to question him, he accused me of a lack of humor in not appreciating that his statements were made "in a jesting way," and then announced that
"a Congressman making a speech on the floor of the House
of Representatives was perhaps in a little different position
from a witness on the witness stand" — a frank admission that
he did not consider exactitude of statement necessary when
he was speaking as a Congressman. Finally he rose with great
dignity and said that it was his "constitutional right" not to
be questioned elsewhere as to what he said on the floor of
the House of Representatives; and accordingly he left the delighted committee to pursue its investigations without further
aid from him.

A more important opponent was the then Democratic
leader of the Senate, Mr. Gorman. In a speech attacking the
Commission Mr. Gorman described with moving pathos
how a friend of his, "a bright young man from Baltimore," a
Sunday-school scholar, well recommended by his pastor,
wished to be a letter-carrier; and how he went before us to
be examined. The first question we asked him, said Mr.
Gorman, was the shortest route from Baltimore to China, to
which the "bright young man" responded that he didn't want
to go to China, and had never studied up that route. Thereupon, said Mr. Gorman, we asked him all about the steamship
lines from the United States to Europe, then branched him
off into geology, tried him in chemistry, and finally turned
him down.

Apparently Mr. Gorman did not know that we kept full
records of our examinations. I at once wrote to him stating

that I had carefully looked through all our examination papers and had not been able to find one question even remotely resembling any of these questions which he alleged had been asked, and that I would be greatly obliged if he would give me the name of the "bright young man" who had deceived him.

However, that "bright young man" remained permanently without a name. I also asked Mr. Gorman, if he did not wish to give us the name of his informant, to give us the date of the examination in which he was supposed to have taken part; and I offered, if he would send down a representative to look through our files, to give him all the aid we could in his effort to discover any such questions. But Mr. Gorman, not hitherto known as a sensitive soul, expressed himself as so shocked at the thought that the veracity of the "bright young man" should be doubted that he could not bring himself to answer my letter. So I made a public statement to the effect that no such questions had ever been asked. Mr. Gorman brooded over this; and during the next session of Congress he rose and complained that he had received a very "impudent" letter from me (my letter was a respectful note calling attention to the fact that, if he wished, he could by personal examination satisfy himself that his statements had no foundation in fact). He further stated that he had been "cruelly" called to account by me because he had been endeavoring to right a "great wrong" that the Civil Service Commission had committed; but he never, then or afterwards, furnished any clue to the identity of that child of his fondest fancy, the bright young man without a name.*

The incident is of note chiefly as shedding light on the mental make-up of the man who at the time was one of the two or three most influential leaders of the Democratic party. Mr. Gorman had been Mr. Cleveland's party manager in the Presidential campaign, and was the Democratic leader in Congress. It seemed extraordinary that he should be so reckless as to make statements with no foundation in fact, which he might have known that I would not permit to pass unchallenged.

*This is a condensation of a speech I at the time made to the St. Louis Civil Service Reform Association. Senator Gorman was then the Senate leader of the party that had just been victorious in the Congressional elections.

Then, as now, the ordinary newspaper, in New York and else-where, was quite as reckless in its misstatements of fact about public men and measures; but for a man in Mr. Gorman's position of responsible leadership such action seemed hardly worth while. However, it is at least to be said for Mr. Gorman that he was not trying by falsehood to take away any man's character. It would be well for writers and speakers to bear in mind the remark of Pudd'nhead Wilson to the effect that while there are nine hundred and ninety-nine kinds of falsehood, the only kind specifically condemned in Scripture, just as murder, theft, and adultery are condemned, is bearing false witness against one's neighbor.

One of the worst features of the old spoils system was the ruthless cruelty and brutality it so often bred in the treatment of faithful public servants without political influence. Life is hard enough and cruel enough at best, and this is as true of public service as of private service. Under no system will it be possible to do away with all favoritism and brutality and meanness and malice. But at least we can try to minimize the exhibition of these qualities. I once came across a case in Washington which very keenly excited my sympathy. Under an Administration prior to the one with which I was connected a lady had been ousted from a Government position. She came to me to see if she could be reinstated. (This was not possible, but by active work I did get her put back in a somewhat lower position, and this only by an appeal to the sympathy of a certain official.) She was so pallid and so care-worn that she excited my sympathy and I made inquiries about her. She was a poor woman with two children, a widow. She and her two children were in actual want. She could barely keep the two children decently clad, and she could not give them the food growing children need. Three years before she had been employed in a bureau in a department of Washington, doing her work faithfully, at a salary of about $800. It was enough to keep her and her two children in clothing, food, and shelter. One day the chief of the bureau called her up and told her he was very sorry that he had to dismiss her. In great distress she asked him why; she thought that she had been doing her work satisfactorily. He answered her that she had been doing well, and that he wished very much that he could keep her, that he would do so if he possibly could, but that he could not; for a certain Senator, giving his name, a very influential member of the Senate, had demanded her place for a friend of his who had influence. The woman told the bureau chief that it meant turning her out to starve. She

Mark Hanna.

"A man of rugged sincerity of purpose, of great courage and loyalty, and of unswerving devotion to the interests of the Nation and the people as he saw those interests."

had been thirteen or fourteen years in the public service; she had lost all touch with her friends in her native State; dismissal meant absolute want for her and her children. On this the chief, who was a kind man, said he would not have her turned out, and sent her back to her work.

But three weeks afterwards he called her up again and told her he could not say how sorry he was, but the thing had to be done. The Senator had been around in person to know why the change had not been made, and had told the chief that he would be himself removed if the place were not given him. The Senator was an extremely influential man. His wants had to be attended to, and the woman had to go. And go she did, and turned out she was, to suffer with her children and to starve outright, or to live in semi-starvation, just as might befall. I do not blame the bureau chief, who hated to do what he did, although he lacked the courage to refuse; I do not even very much blame the Senator, who did not know the hardship that he was causing, and who had been calloused by long training in the spoils system; but this system, a system which permits and encourages such deeds, is a system of brutal iniquity.

Any man accustomed to dealing with practical politics can with difficulty keep a straight face when he reads or listens to some of the arguments advanced against Civil Service Reform. One of these arguments, a favorite with machine politicians, takes the form of an appeal to "party loyalty" in filling minor offices. Why, again and again these very same machine politicians take just as good care of henchmen of the opposite party as of those of their own party. In the underworld of politics the closest ties are sometimes those which knit together the active professional workers of opposite political parties. A friend of mine in the New York Legislature — the hero of the alpha and omega incident — once remarked to me: "When you have been in public life a little longer, Mr. Roosevelt, you will understand that there are no politics in politics." In the politics to which he was referring this remark could be taken literally.

Another illustration of this truth was incidentally given me, at about the same time, by an acquaintance, a Tammany man named Costigan, a good fellow according to his lights. I had been speaking to him of a fight in one of the New York downtown districts, a Democratic district in which the Republican party was in a hopeless minority, and, moreover, was split into the Half-Breed and Stalwart factions. It had been an interesting fight in more than one way. For instance, the Republican party, at the general election, polled something like five hundred and fifty votes, and yet at the primary the two factions polled seven hundred and twenty-five all told. The sum of the parts was thus considerably greater than the whole. There had been other little details that made the contest worthy of note. The hall in which the primary was held had been hired by the Stalwarts from a conscientious gentleman. To him the Half-Breeds applied to know whether they could not hire the hall away from their opponents, and offered him a substantial money advance. The conscientious gentleman replied that his word was as good as his bond, that he had hired the hall to the Stalwarts, and that it must be theirs. But he added that he was willing to hire the doorway to the Half-Breeds if they paid him the additional sum of money they had mentioned. The bargain was struck, and the meeting of the hostile hosts was spirited, when the men who had rented the doorway sought to bar the path of the men who had rented the hall. I was asking my friend Costigan about the details of the struggle, as he seemed thoroughly acquainted with them, and he smiled good-naturedly over my surprise at there having been more votes cast than there were members of the party in the whole district. Said I, "Mr. Costigan, you seem to have a great deal of knowledge about this; how did it happen?" To which he replied, "Come now, Mr. Roosevelt, you know it's the same gang that votes in *all* the primaries."

So much for most of the opposition to the reform. There was, however, some honest and at least partially justifiable opposition both to certain of the methods advocated by Civil Service Reformers and to certain of the Civil Service Reformers themselves. The pet shibboleths of the opponents of the reform were that the system we proposed to introduce would give rise to mere red-tape bureaucracy, and that the reformers were pharisees. Neither statement was true. Each statement contained some truth.

If men are not to be appointed by favoritism, wise or unwise, honest or dishonest, they must be appointed in some automatic way, which generally means by competitive examination. The easiest kind of competitive examination is an examination in writing. This is entirely appropriate for certain classes of work, for lawyers, stenographers, typewriters, clerks, mathematicians, and assistants in an astronomical observatory, for instance. It is utterly inappropriate for carpenters, detectives, and mounted cattle inspectors along the Rio Grande — to instance three types of employment as to which I had to do battle to prevent well-meaning bureaucrats from insisting on written competitive entrance examinations. It would be quite possible to hold a very good competitive examination for mounted cattle inspectors by means of practical tests in brand reading and shooting with rifle and revolver, in riding "mean" horses and in roping and throwing steers. I did my best to have examinations of this kind instituted, but my proposal was of precisely the type which most shocks the routine official mind, and I was never able to get it put into practical effect.

The important point, and the point most often forgotten by zealous Civil Service Reformers, was to remember that the routine competitive examination was merely a means to an end. It did not always produce ideal results. But it was normally better than a system of appointments for spoils purposes; it sometimes worked out very well indeed; and in most big governmental offices it not only gave satisfactory results, but was the only system under which good results could be obtained. For instance, when I was Police Commissioner we appointed some two thousand policemen at one time. It was utterly impossible for the Commissioners each to examine personally the six or eight thousand applicants. Therefore they had to be appointed either on the recommendation of outsiders or else by written competitive examination. The latter method — the one we adopted — was infinitely preferable. We held a rigid physical and moral pass examination, and then, among those who passed, we held a written competitive examination, requiring only the knowledge that any good primary common school education would meet — that is, a test of ordinary intelligence and simple mental training. Occasionally a man who would have been a good officer failed, and occasionally a man who turned out to be a bad officer passed; but, as a rule, the men with intelligence sufficient to enable them to answer the questions were of a type very distinctly above that of those who failed.

The answers returned to some of the questions gave an

illuminating idea of the intelligence of those answering them. For instance, one of our questions in a given examination was a request to name five of the New England States. One competitor, obviously of foreign birth, answered: "England, Ireland, Scotland, Whales, and Cork." His neighbor, who had probably looked over his shoulder but who had North of Ireland prejudices, made the same answer except that he substituted Belfast for Cork. A request for a statement as to the life of Abraham Lincoln elicited, among other less startling pieces of information, the fact that many of the applicants thought that he was a general in the Civil War; several thought that he was President of the Confederate States; three thought he had been assassinated by Jefferson Davis, one by Thomas Jefferson, one by Garfield, several by Guiteau, and one by Ballington Booth — the last representing a memory of the fact that he had been shot by a man named Booth, to whose surname the writer added the name with which he was most familiar in connection therewith. A request to name five of the States that seceded in 1861 received answers that included almost every State in the Union. It happened to be at the time of the silver agitation in the West, and the Rocky Mountain States accordingly figured in a large percentage of the answers. Some of the men thought that Chicago was on the Pacific Ocean. Others, in answer to a query as to who was the head of the United States Government, wavered between myself and Recorder Goff; one brilliant genius, for inscrutable reasons, placed the leadership in the New York Fire Department. Now of course some of the men who answered these questions wrong were nevertheless quite capable of making good policemen; but it is fair to assume that on the average the candidate who has a rudimentary knowledge of the government, geography, and history of his country is a little better fitted, in point of intelligence, to be a policeman than the one who has not.

Therefore I felt convinced, after full experience, that as regards very large classes of public servants by far the best way to choose the men for appointment was by means of written competitive examination. But I absolutely split off from the bulk of my professional Civil Service Reform friends when they advocated written competitive examinations for promotion. In the Police Department I found these examinations a serious handicap in the way of getting the best men promoted, and never in any office did I find that the written competitive promotion examination did any good. The reason for a written competitive entrance examination is that it is impossible for the head of the office, or the candidate's prospective immediate superior, himself to know the average candidate or to test his ability. But when once in office the best way to test any man's ability is by long experience in seeing him actually at work. His promotion should depend upon the judgment formed of him by his superiors.

So much for the objections to the examinations. Now for the objections to the men who advocated the reform. As a rule these men were high-minded and disinterested. Certain of them, men like the leaders in the Maryland and Indiana Reform Associations, for instances, Messrs. Bonaparte and Rose, Foulke and Swift, added common sense, broad sympathy, and practical efficiency to their high-mindedness. But in New York, Philadelphia, and Boston there really was a certain mental and moral thinness among very many of the leaders in the Civil Service Reform movement. It was this quality which made them so profoundly antipathetic to vigorous and intensely human people of the stamp of my friend Joe Murray — who, as I have said, always felt that my Civil Service Reform affiliations formed the one blot on an otherwise excellent public record. The Civil Service Reform movement was one from above downwards, and the men who took the lead in it were not men who as a rule possessed a very profound sympathy with or understanding of the ways of thought and life of their average fellow-citizen. They were not men who themselves desired to be letter-carriers or clerks or policemen, or to have their friends appointed to these positions. Having no temptation themselves in this direction, they were eagerly anxious to prevent other people getting such appointments as a reward for political services. In this they were quite right. It would be impossible to run any big public office to advantage save along the lines of the strictest application of Civil Service Reform principles; and the system should be extended throughout our governmental service far more widely than is now the case.

But there are other and more vital reforms than this. Too many Civil Service Reformers, when the trial came, proved tepidly indifferent or actively hostile to reforms that were of profound and far-reaching social and industrial consequence. Many of them were at best lukewarm about movements for the improvement of the conditions of toil and life among men and women who labor under hard surroundings, and were positively hostile to movements which curbed the power of the great corporation magnates and directed into useful instead of pernicious channels the activities of the great corporation lawyers who advised them.

Most of the newspapers which regarded themselves as the especial champions of Civil Service Reform and as the highest exponents of civic virtue, and which distrusted the average citizen and shuddered over the "coarseness" of the professional politicians, were, nevertheless, given to vices even more contemptible than, although not so gross as, those they denounced and derided. Their editors were refined men of cultivated tastes, whose pet temptations were backbiting, mean slander, and the snobbish worship of anything clothed in wealth and the outward appearances of conventional respectability. They were not robust or powerful men; they felt ill at ease in the company of rough, strong men; often they had in them a vein of physical timidity. They avenged themselves to themselves for an uneasy subconsciousness of their own shortcomings by sitting in cloistered — or, rather, pleasantly upholstered — seclusion, and sneering at and lying about men who made them feel uncomfortable. Sometimes these were bad men, who made them feel uncomfortable by the exhibition of coarse and repellent vice; and sometimes they were men of high character, who held ideals of courage and of service to others, and who looked down and warred against the shortcomings of swollen wealth, and the effortless, easy lives of those whose horizon is bounded by a sheltered and timid respectability. These newspapers, owned and edited by these men, although free from the repulsive vulgarity of the yellow press, were susceptible to influence by the privileged interests, and were almost or quite as hostile to manliness as they were to unrefined vice — and were much more hostile to it than to the typical shortcomings of wealth and refinement. They favored Civil Service Reform; they favored copyright laws, and the removal of the tariff on works of art; they favored all the proper (and even more strongly all the improper) movements for international peace and arbitration; in short, they favored all good, and many goody-goody, measures so long as they did not cut deep into social wrong or make demands on National and individual virility. They opposed, or were lukewarm about, efforts to build up the army and the navy, for they were not sensitive concerning National honor; and, above all, they opposed every non-milk-and-water effort, however sane, to change our social and economic system in such a fashion as to substitute the ideal of justice towards all for the ideal of kindly charity from the favored few to the possibly grateful many.

Some of the men foremost in the struggle for Civil Service Reform have taken a position of honorable leadership in the battle for those other and more vital reforms. But many of them promptly abandoned the field of effort for decency when the battle took the form, not of a fight against the petty grafting of small bosses and small politicians — a vitally necessary battle, be it remembered — but of a fight against the great intrenched powers of privilege, a fight to secure justice through the law for ordinary men and women, instead of leaving them to suffer cruel injustice either because the law failed to protect them or because it was twisted from its legitimate purposes into a means for oppressing them.

One of the reasons why the boss so often keeps his hold, especially in municipal matters, is, or at least has been in the past, because so many of the men who claim to be reformers have been blind to the need of working in human fashion for social and industrial betterment. Such words as "boss" and "machine" now imply evil, but both the implication the words carry and the definition of the words themselves are somewhat vague. A leader is necessary; but his opponents always call him a boss. An organization is necessary; but the men in opposition always call it a machine. Nevertheless, there is a real and deep distinction between the leader and the boss, between organizations and machines. A political leader who fights openly for principles, and who keeps his position of leadership by stirring the consciences and convincing the intellects of his followers, so that they have confidence in him and will follow him because they can achieve greater results under him than under any one else, is doing work which is indispensable in a democracy. The boss, on the other hand, is a man who does not gain his power by open means, but by secret means, and usually by corrupt means. Some of the worst and most powerful bosses in our political history either held no public office or else some unimportant public office. They made no appeal either to intellect or conscience. Their work was done behind closed doors, and consisted chiefly in the use of that greed which gives in order that in return it may get. A boss of this kind can pull wires in conventions, can manipulate members of the Legislature, can control the giving or withholding of office, and serves as the intermediary for bringing together the powers of corrupt politics and corrupt business. If he is at one end of the social scale, he may through his agents traffic in the most brutal forms of vice and give protection to the purveyors of shame and sin in return for money bribes. If at the other end of the scale, he may be the means of securing favors from high public officials, legislative or executive, to great industrial interests; the transaction being sometimes a naked matter of bargain and sale, and sometimes being carried on in such manner that both parties thereto can more or less successfully disguise it to their consciences as in the public interest. The machine is simply another name for the kind of organization which is certain to grow up in a party or section of a party controlled by such bosses as these and by their henchmen, whereas, of course, an effective organization of decent men is essential in order to secure decent politics.

If these bosses were responsible for nothing but pure wickedness, they would probably last but a short time in any community. And, in any event, if the men who are horrified by their wickedness were themselves as practical and as thoroughly in touch with human nature, the bosses would have a short shrift. The trouble is that the boss does understand human nature, and that he fills a place which the reformer cannot fill unless he likewise understands human nature. Sometimes the boss is a man who cares for political power purely for its own sake, as he might care for any other hobby; more often he has in view some definitely selfish object such as political or financial advancement. He can rarely accomplish much unless he has another side to him. A successful boss is very apt to be a man who, in addition to committing wickedness in his own interest, also does look after the interests of others, even if not from good motives. There are some communities so fortunate that there are very few men who have private interests to be served, and in these the power of the boss is at a minimum. There are many country communities of this type. But in communities where there is poverty and ignorance, the conditions are ripe for the growth of a boss. Moreover, wherever big business interests are liable either to be improperly favored or improperly discriminated against and blackmailed by public officials — and the result is just as vicious in one case as in the other — the boss is almost certain to develop. The best way of getting at this type of boss is by keeping the public conscience aroused and alert, so that it will tolerate neither improper attack upon, nor improper favoritism towards, these corporations, and will quickly punish any public servant guilty of either.

There is often much good in the type of boss, especially common in big cities, who fulfills towards the people of his district in rough and ready fashion the position of friend and protector. He uses his influence to get jobs for young men who need them. He goes into court for a wild young fellow who has gotten into trouble. He helps out with cash or credit the widow who is in straits, or the breadwinner who is crippled or for some other cause temporarily out of work. He organizes clambakes and chowder parties and picnics, and is consulted by the local labor leaders when a cut in wages is threatened. For some of his constituents he does proper favors, and for others wholly improper favors; but he preserves human relations with all. He may be a very bad and very corrupt man, a man whose action in blackmailing and protecting vice is of far-reaching damage to his constituents. But these constituents are for the most part men and women who struggle hard against poverty and with whom the problem of living is very real and very close. They would prefer clean and honest government, if this clean and honest government is accompanied by human sympathy, human understanding. But an appeal made to them for virtue in the abstract, an appeal made by good men who do not really understand their needs, will often pass quite unheeded, if on the other side stands the boss, the friend and benefactor, who may have been guilty of much wrong-doing in things that they are hardly aware concern them, but who appeals to them, not only for the sake of favors to come, but in the name of gratitude and loyalty, and above all of understanding and fellow-feeling. They have a feeling of clan-loyalty to him; his and their relations may be substantially those which are right and proper among primitive people still in the clan stage of moral development. The successful fight against this type of vicious boss, and the type of vicious politics which produces it, can be made only by men who have a genuine fellow-feeling for and understanding of the people for and with whom they are to work, and who in practical fashion seek their social and industrial benefit.

There are communities of poor men, whose lives are hard, in which the boss, though he would be out of place in a more advanced community, if fundamentally an honest man, meets a real need which would otherwise not be met. Because of his limitations in other than purely local matters it may be our duty to fight such a boss; but it may also be our duty to recognize, within his limitations, both his sincerity and his usefulness.

Yet again even the boss who really is evil, like the business man who really is evil, may on certain points be sound, and be doing good work. It may be the highest duty of the patriotic public servant to work with the big boss or the big business man on these points, while refusing to work with him on others. In the same way there are many self-styled reformers whose conduct is such as to warrant Tom Reed's bitter remark, that when Dr. Johnson defined patriotism as the last refuge of a scoundrel he was ignorant of the infinite possibilities contained in the word reform. Yet, none the less, it is our duty to work for the reforms these men champion, without regard to the misconduct of the men themselves on other points. I have known in my life many big business men and many big political bosses who often or even generally did evil, but who on some occasions and on certain issues were right. I never hesitated to do battle against these men when they were wrong; and, on the other hand, as long as they were

going my way I was glad to have them do so. To have repudiated their aid when they were right and were striving for a
right end, and for what was of benefit to the people — no
matter what their motives may have been — would have been
childish, and moreover would have itself been misconduct
against the people.

My duty was to stand with every one while he was right,
and to stand against him when he went wrong; and this I have
tried to do as regards individuals and as regards groups of individuals. When a business man or labor leader, politician or
reformer, is right, I support him; when he goes wrong, I leave
him. When Mr. Lorimer upheld the war for the liberation
of Cuba, I supported him; when he became United States Senator by improper methods, I opposed him. The principles or
methods which the Socialists advocate and which I believe to
be in the interest of the people I support, and those which I
believe to be against the interest of the people I oppose. Moreover, when a man has done evil, but changes, and works for
decency and righteousness, and when, as far as I can see, the
change is real and the man's conduct sincere, then I welcome
him and work heartily with him, as an equal with an equal.
For thirty years after the Civil War the creed of mere materialism was rampant in both American politics and American
business, and many, many strong men, in accordance with the
prevailing commercial and political morality, did things for
which they deserve blame and condemnation; but if they now
sincerely change, and strive for better things, it is unwise and
unjust to bar them from fellowship. So long as they work for
evil, smite them with the sword of the Lord and of Gideon!
When they change and show their faith by their works, remember the words of Ezekiel: "If the wicked will turn from
all the sins he has committed, and keep all my statutes, and do
that which is lawful and right, he shall surely live, he shall not
die. All his transgressions that he hath committed, they shall
not be mentioned unto him: in his righteousness that he hath
done he shall live. Have I any pleasure at all that the wicked
should die? saith the Lord God; and not that he should return
from his ways and live?"

Every man who has been in practical politics grows to realize that politicians, big and little, are no more all of them bad

than they are all of them good. Many of these men are very bad men indeed, but there are others among them — and some among those held up to special obloquy, too — who, even although they may have done much that is evil, also show traits of sterling worth which many of their critics wholly lack. There are few men for whom I have ever felt a more cordial and contemptuous dislike than for some of the bosses and big professional politicians with whom I have been brought into contact. On the other hand, in the case of some political leaders who were most bitterly attacked as bosses, I grew to know certain sides of their characters which inspired in me a very genuine regard and respect.

To read much of the assault on Senator Hanna, one would have thought that he was a man incapable of patriotism or of far-sighted devotion to the country's good. I was brought into intimate contact with him only during the two and a half years immediately preceding his death. I was then President, and perforce watched all his actions at close range. During that time he showed himself to be a man of rugged sincerity of purpose, of great courage and loyalty, and of unswerving devotion to the interests of the Nation and the people as he saw those interests. He was as sincerely desirous of helping laboring men as of helping capitalists. His ideals were in many ways not my ideas, and there were points where both by temperament and by conviction we were far apart. Before this time he had always been unfriendly to me; and I do not think he ever grew to like me, at any rate not until the very end of his life. Moreover, I came to the Presidency under circumstances which, if he had been a smaller man, would inevitably have thrown him into violent antagonism to me. He was the close and intimate friend of President McKinley. He was McKinley's devoted ally and follower, and his trusted adviser, who was in complete sympathy with him. Partly because of this friendship, his position in the Senate and in the country was unique.

With McKinley's sudden death Senator Hanna found himself bereft of his dearest friend, while I, who had just come to the Presidency, was in his view an untried man, whose trustworthiness on many public questions was at least doubtful. Ordinarily, as has been shown, not only in our history, but in the history of all other countries, in countless instances, over and over again, this situation would have meant suspicion, ill will, and, at the last, open and violent antagonism. Such was not the result, in this case, primarily because Senator Hanna had in him the quality that enabled him to meet a serious crisis with dignity, with power, and with disinterested desire to work for the common good. Within a few days of my accession he called on me, and with entire friendliness and obvious sincerity, but also with entire self-respect, explained that he mourned McKinley as probably no other man did; that he had not been especially my friend, but that he wished me to understand that thenceforward, on every question where he could conscientiously support me, I could count upon his giving me as loyal aid as it was in his power to render. He added that this must not be understood as committing him to favor me for nomination and election, because that matter must be left to take care of itself as events should decide; but that, aside from this, what he said was to be taken literally; in other words, he would do his best to make my Administration a success by supporting me heartily on every point on which he conscientiously could, and that this I could count upon. He kept his word absolutely. He never became especially favorable to my nomination; and most of his close friends became bitterly opposed to me and used every effort to persuade him to try to bring about my downfall. Most men in his position would have been tempted to try to make capital at my expense by antagonizing me and discrediting me so as to make my policies fail, just for the sake of making them fail. Senator Hanna, on the contrary, did everything possible to make them succeed. He kept his word in the letter and the spirit, and on every point on which he felt conscientiously able to support me he gave me the heartiest and most effective support, and did all in his power to make my Administration a success; and this with no hope of any reward for himself, of any gratitude from me, or of any appreciation by the public at large, but solely because he deemed such action necessary for the well-being of the country as a whole.

My experience with Senator Quay was similar. I had no personal relations with him before I was President, and knew nothing of him save by hearsay. Soon after I became

President, Senator Quay called upon me, told me he had known me very slightly, that he thought most men who claimed to be reformers were hypocrites, but that he deemed me sincere, that he thought conditions had become such that aggressive courage and honesty were necessary in order to remedy them, that he believed I intended to be a good and efficient President, and that to the best of his ability he would support me in making my Administration a success. He kept his word with absolute good faith. He had been in the Civil War, and was a medal of honor man; and I think my having been in the Spanish War gave him at the outset a kindly feeling toward me. He was also a very well-read man — I owe to him, for instance, my acquaintance with the writings of the Finnish novelist Topelius. Not only did he support me on almost every public question in which I was most interested — including, I am convinced, every one on which he felt he conscientiously could do so — but he also at the time of his death gave a striking proof of his disinterested desire to render a service to certain poor people, and this under conditions in which not only would he never know if the service were rendered but in which he had no reason to expect that his part in it would ever be made known to any other man.

Quay was descended from a French voyageur who had some Indian blood in him. He was proud of this Indian blood, took an especial interest in Indians, and whenever Indians came to Washington they always called on him. Once during my Administration a delegation of Iroquois came over from Canada to call on me at the White House. Their visit had in it something that was pathetic as well as amusing. They represented the descendants of the Six Nations, who fled to Canada after Sullivan harried their towns in the Revolutionary War. Now, a century and a quarter later, their people thought that they would like to come back into the United States; and these representatives had called upon me with the dim hope that perhaps I could give their tribes land on which they could settle. As soon as they reached Washington they asked Quay to bring them to call on me, which he did, telling me that of course their errand was hopeless and that he had explained as much to them, but that they would like me to extend the courtesy of an interview. At the close of the interview, which had been conducted with all the solemnities of calumet and wampum, the Indians filed out. Quay, before following them, turned to me with his usual emotionless face and said, "Good-by, Mr. President; this reminds one of the Flight of a Tartar Tribe, doesn't it?" I answered, "So you're fond of De Quincey, Senator?" to which Quay responded, "Yes; always liked De Quincey; good-by." And away he went with the tribesmen, who seemed to have walked out of a remote past.

Quay had become particularly concerned about the Delawares in the Indian Territory. He felt that the Interior Department did not do them justice. He also felt that his colleagues of the Senate took no interest in them. When in the spring of 1904, he lay in his house mortally sick, he sent me word that he had something important to say to me, and would have himself carried round to see me. I sent back word not to think of doing so, and that on my way back from church next Sunday I would stop in and call on him. This I accordingly did. He was lying in his bed, death written on his face. He thanked me for coming, and then explained that, as he was on the point of death and knew he would never return to Washington — it was late spring and he was about to leave — he wished to see me to get my personal promise that, after he died, I would myself look after the interests of the Delaware Indians. He added that he did not trust the Interior Department — although he knew that I did not share his views on this point — and that still less did he believe that any of his colleagues in the Senate would exert themselves in the interests of the Delawares, and that therefore he wished my personal assurance that I would personally see that no injustice was done them. I told him I would do so, and then added, in rather perfunctory fashion, that he must not take such a gloomy view of himself, that when he got away for the summer I hoped he would recover and be back all right when Congress opened. A gleam came into the old fighter's eyes and he answered: "No, I am dying, and you know it. I don't mind dying; but I do wish it were possible for me to get off into the great north woods and crawl out on a rock in the sun and die like a wolf!"

I never saw him again. When he died I sent a telegram of sympathy to his wife. A paper which constantly preached reform, and which kept up its circulation by the no less constant practice of slander, a paper which in theory condemned all public men who violated the eighth commandment, and in practice subsisted by incessant violation of the ninth, assailed me for sending my message to the dead man's wife. I knew the editors of this paper, and the editor who was their predecessor. They had led lives of bodily ease and the avoidance of bodily risk; they earned their livelihood by the practice of

Matthew Stanley Quay.

"In his youth he freely risked his life for a great ideal, and when death was already clutching his breast he spent almost his last breath in serving humble and friendless people whom he had served with disinterested loyalty."

mendacity for profit; and they delivered malignant judgment on a dead man who, whatever his faults, had in his youth freely risked his life for a great ideal, and who when death was already clutching his breast had spent almost his last breath on behalf of humble and friendless people whom he had served with disinterested loyalty.

There is no greater duty than to war on the corrupt and unprincipled boss, and on the corrupt and unprincipled business

man; and for the matter of that, on the corrupt and unprincipled labor leader also, and on the corrupt and unprincipled editor, and on any one else who is corrupt and unprincipled.
But where the conditions are such, whether in politics or in
business, that the great majority of men have behaved in a
way which is gradually seen to be improper, but which at one
time did not conflict with the generally accepted morality,
then the warfare on the system should not include warfare on
the men themselves, unless they decline to amend their ways
and to dissociate themselves from the system. There are many
good, unimaginative citizens who in politics or in business
act in accordance with accepted standards, in a matter-of-
course way, without questioning these standards; until something happens which sharply arouses them to the situation,
whereupon they try to work for better things. The proper
course in such event is to let bygones be bygones, and if the
men prove by their actions the sincerity of their conversion,
heartily to work with them for the betterment of business and
political conditions.

By the time that I was ending my career as Civil Service
Commissioner I was already growing to understand that
mere improvement in political conditions by itself was not
enough. I dimly realized that an even greater fight must be
waged to improve economic conditions, and to secure social
and industrial justice, justice as between individuals and justice as between classes. I began to see that political effort was
largely valuable as it found expression and resulted in such
social and industrial betterment. I was gradually puzzling out,
or trying to puzzle out, the answers to various questions —
some as yet unsolvable to any of us, but for the solution of
which it is the bounden duty of all of us to work. I had grown
to realize very keenly that the duty of the Government to protect women and children must be extended to include the
protection of all the crushable elements of labor. I saw that
it was the affair of all our people to see that justice obtained
between the big corporation and its employees, and between
the big corporation and its smaller rivals, as well as its customers and the general public. I saw that it was the affair of
all of us, and not only of the employer, if dividends went up
and wages went down; that it was to the interest of all of us

that a full share of the benefit of improved machinery should go to the workman who used the machinery; and also that it was to the interest of all of us that each man, whether brain worker or hand worker, should do the best work of which he was capable, and that there should be some correspondence between the value of the work and the value of the reward. It is these and many similar questions which in their sum make up the great social and industrial problems of to-day, the most interesting and important of the problems with which our public life must deal.

In handling these problems I believe that much can be done by the Government. Furthermore, I believe that, after all that the Government can do has been done, there will remain as the most vital of all factors the individual character of the average man and the average woman. No governmental action can do more than supplement individual action. Moreover, there must be collective action of kinds distinct from governmental action. A body of public opinion must be formed, must make itself felt, and in the end transform, and be transformed by, the gradual raising of individual standards of conduct.

It is curious to see how difficult it is to make some men understand that insistence upon one factor does not and must not mean failure fully to recognize other factors. The selfish individual needs to be taught that we must now shackle cunning by law exactly as a few centuries back we shackled force by law. Unrestricted individualism spells ruin to the individual himself. But so does the elimination of individualism, whether by law or custom. It is a capital error to fail to recognize the vital need of good laws. It is also a capital error to believe that good laws will accomplish anything unless the average man has the right stuff in him. The toiler, the manual laborer, has received less than justice, and he must be protected, both by law, by custom, and by the exercise of his right to increase his wage; and yet to decrease the quantity and quality of his work will work only evil. There must be a far greater meed of respect and reward for the hand worker than we now give him, if our society is to be put on a sound basis; and this respect and reward cannot be given him unless he is as ambitious to do the best possible work as is the highest type of brain worker, whether doctor or writer or artist. There must be a raising of standards, and not a leveling down to the standard of the poorest and most inefficient. There is urgent need of intelligent governmental action to assist in making the life of the man who tills the soil all that it should be, and to see that the manual worker gets his full share of the reward for what he helps produce; but if either farmer, mechanic, or day laborer is shiftless or lazy, if he shirks downright hard work, if he is stupid or self-indulgent, then no law can save him, and he must give way to a better type.

I suppose that some good people will misunderstand what I say, and will insist on taking only half of it as representing the whole. Let me repeat. When I say, that, even after we have all the good laws necessary, the chief factor in any given man's success or failure must be that man's own character, it must not be inferred that I am in the least minimizing the importance of these laws, the real and vital need for them. The struggle for individual advancement and development can be brought to naught, or indefinitely retarded, by the absence of law or by bad law. It can be immeasurably aided by organized effort on the part of the State. Collective action and individual action, public law and private character, are both necessary. It is only by a slow and patient inward transformation such as these laws aid in bringing about that men are really helped upward in their struggle for a higher and a fuller life. Recognition of individual character as the most important of all factors does not mean failure fully to recognize that we must have good laws, and that we must have our best men in office to enforce these laws. The Nation collectively will in this way be able to be of real and genuine service to each of us individually; and, on the other hand, the wisdom of the collective action will mainly depend on the high individual average of citizenship.

The relationship of man and woman is the fundamental relationship that stands at the base of the whole social structure. Much can be done by law towards putting women on a footing of complete and entire equal rights with man — including the right to vote, the right to hold and use property, and the right to enter any profession she desires on the same terms as the man. Yet when this has been done it will amount to little unless on the one hand the man himself realizes his duty to the woman, and unless on the other hand the woman realizes that she has no claim to rights unless she performs the duties that go with those rights and that alone justify her in appealing to them. A cruel, selfish, or licentious man is an abhorrent member of the community; but, after all, his actions are no worse in the long run than those of the woman who is content to be a parasite on others, who is cold, selfish, caring for nothing but frivolous pleasure and ignoble ease. The law of worthy effort, the law of service for a worthy end, without regard to whether it brings pleasure or pain, is the only right law of life, whether for man or for woman. The man must not be selfish; nor, if the woman is wise, will she let the man grow selfish, and this not only for her own sake but for his. One of the prime needs is to remember that almost every duty is composed of two seemingly conflicting elements, and that over-insistence on one, to the exclusion of the other, may defeat its own end. Any man who studies the statistics of the birth-rate among the native Americans of New England, or among the native French of France, needs not to be told that when prudence and forethought are carried to the point of cold selfishness and self-indulgence, the race is bound to disappear. Taking into account the women who for good reasons do not marry, or who when married are childless or are able to have but one or two children, it is evident that the married woman able to have children must on an average have four or the race will not perpetuate itself. This is the mere statement of a self-evident truth. Yet foolish and self-indulgent people often resent this statement as if it were in some way possible by denunciation to reverse the facts of nature; and, on the other hand, improvident and shiftless people, inconsiderate and brutal people, treat the statement as if it justified heads of families in having enormous numbers of badly nourished, badly brought up, and badly cared for children for whom they make no effort to provide. A man must think well before he marries. He must be a tender and considerate husband and realize that there is no other human being to whom he owes so much of love and regard and consideration as he does to the woman who with pain bears and with labor rears the children that are his. No words can paint the scorn and contempt which must be felt by all right-thinking men, not only for the brutal husband, but for the husband who fails to show full loyalty and consideration to his wife. Moreover, he must work, he must do his part in the world. On the other hand, the woman must realize that she has no more right to shirk the business of wifehood and motherhood than the man has to shirk his business as breadwinner for the household. Women should have free access to every field of labor which they care to enter, and when their work is as valuable as that of a man it should be paid as highly. Yet normally for the man and the woman whose welfare is more important than the welfare of any other human beings, the woman must remain the house-mother, the homekeeper, and the man must remain the bread-winner, the provider for the wife who bears his children and for the children she brings into the world. No other work is as valuable or as exacting for either man or woman; it must always, in every healthy society, be for both man and woman the prime work, the most important work; normally all other work is of secondary importance, and must come as an addition to, not a substitute for, this primary work. The partnership should be one of equal rights, one of love, of self-respect and unselfishness, above all a partnership for the performance of the most vitally important of all duties. The performance of duty, and not an indulgence in vapid ease and vapid pleasure, is all that makes life worth while.

Suffrage for women should be looked on from this standpoint. Personally I feel that it is exactly as much a "right" of women as of men to vote. But the important point with both men and women is to treat the exercise of the suffrage as a duty, which, in the long run, must be well performed to be of the slightest value. I always favored woman's suffrage, but only tepidly, until my association with women like Jane Addams and Frances Kellor, who desired it as one means of enabling them to render better and more efficient service, changed me into a zealous instead of a lukewarm adherent of the cause — in spite of the fact that a few of the best women of the same type, women like Mary Antin, did not favor the movement. A vote is like a rifle: its usefulness depends upon the character of the user. The mere possession of the vote will no more benefit men and women not sufficiently developed to use it than the possession of rifles will turn untrained

Jane Addams.

Mary Antin.

Frances Kellor.

"I always favored Woman's Suffrage, but only tepidly, until my association with women like Jane Addams and Frances Kellor, who desired it as one means of enabling them to render better and more efficient service, changed me into a zealous instead of a lukewarm adherent of the cause, in spite of the fact that a few of the best women of the same type, women like Mary Antin, did not favor the movement."

Egyptian fellaheen into soldiers. This is as true of woman as of man — and no more true. Universal suffrage in Hayti has not made the Haytians able to govern themselves in any true sense; and woman suffrage in Utah in no shape or way affected the problem of polygamy. I believe in suffrage for women in America, because I think they are fit for it. I believe for women, as for men, more in the duty of fitting one's self to do well and wisely with the ballot than in the naked right to cast the ballot.

I wish that people would read books like the novels and stories, at once strong and charming, of Henry Bordeaux, books like Kathleen Norris's "Mother," and Cornelia Comer's "Preliminaries," and would use these, and other such books, as tracts, now and then! Perhaps the following correspondence will give a better idea than I can otherwise give of the problems that in everyday life come before men and women, and of the need that the man shall show himself unselfish and considerate, and do his full share of the joint duty:

January 3, 1913.

*Colonel Theodore Roosevelt:*

Dear Sir — I suppose you are willing to stand sponsor for the assertion that the women of the country are not doing their duty unless they have large families. I wonder if you know the real reason, after all. Society and clubs are held largely to blame, but society really takes in so few people, after all. I thought, when I got married at twenty, that it was the proper thing to have a family, and, as we had very little of this world's goods, also thought it the thing to do all the necessary work for them. I have had nine children, did all my own work, including washing, ironing, house-cleaning, and the care of the little ones as they came along, which was about every two years; also sewed everything they wore, including trousers for the boys and caps and jackets for the girls while little. I also helped them all in their school work, and started them in music, etc. But as they grew older I got behind the times. I never belonged to a club or a society or lodge, nor went to any one's house scarcely; there wasn't time. In consequence, I knew nothing that was going on in the town, much less the events of the country, and at the same time my husband kept growing in wisdom and knowledge, from mixing with men and hearing topics of the times discussed. At the beginning of our married life I had just as quick a mind to grasp things as he did, and had more school education, having graduated from a three years' high

school. My husband more and more declined to discuss things with
me; as he said, "I didn't know anything about it." When I'd ask, he'd
say, "Oh, you wouldn't understand if I'd tell you." So here I am, at
forty-five years, hopelessly dull and uninteresting, while he can mix
with the brightest minds in the country as an equal. He's a strong
Progressive man, took very active part in the late campaign, etc. I am
also Progressive, and tried my best, after so many years of shut-in
life, to grasp the ideas you stood for, and read everything I could find
during the summer and fall. But I've been out of touch with people
too long now, and my husband would much rather go and talk to
some woman who hasn't had any children, because she *knows things*
(I am not specifying any particular woman). I simply bore him to
death because I'm not interesting. Now, tell me, how was it my fault?
I was only doing what I thought was my duty. No woman can keep
up with things who never talks with any one but young children. As
soon as my children grew up they took the same attitude as their
father, and frequently say, "Oh, mother doesn't know." They look
up to and admire their father because he's a man of the world and
knows how to act when he goes out. How can I urge my daughters
now to go and raise large families? It means by the time you have
lost your figure and charm for them they are all ashamed of you.
Now, as a believer in woman's rights, do a little talking to the men
as to their duties to their wives, or else refrain from urging us women
to have children. I am only one of thousands of middle-class respectable women who give their lives to raise a nice family, and then
who become bitter from the injustice done us. Don't let this go into
the waste-basket, but think it over.

                                                    Yours respectfully,

                                                    —— ——.


                                                New York, January 11, 1913.
*My Dear Mrs. —— :*
    Most certainly your letter will not go into the waste-paper basket.
I shall think it over and show it to Mrs. Roosevelt. Will you let me
say, in the first place, that a woman who can write such a letter is certainly not "hopelessly dull and uninteresting"! If the facts are as you
state, then I do not wonder that you feel bitterly and that you feel
that the gravest kind of injustice has been done you. I have always
tried to insist to men that they should do their duty to the women
even more than the women to them. Now I hardly like to write specifically about your husband, because you might not like it yourself. It
seems to me almost incredible that any man who is the husband of
a woman who has borne him nine children should not feel that they

and he are lastingly her debtors. You say that you have had nine children, that you did all your own work, including washing, ironing,
house-cleaning, and the care of the little ones as they came along;
that you sewed everything they wore, including trousers for the boys
and caps and jackets for the girls while little; that you helped them
all in their school work and started them in music; but that as they
grew older you got behind the times, that you never belonged to a
club or society or lodge, nor went to any one's house, as you hardly
had time to do so; and that in consequence your husband outgrew
you, and that your children look up to him and not to you and feel
that they have outgrown you. If these facts are so, you have done a
great and wonderful work, and the only explanation I can possibly
give of the attitude you describe on the part of your husband and
children is that they do not understand what it is that you have done.
I emphatically believe in unselfishness, but I also believe that it is a
mistake to let other people grow selfish, even when the other people
are husband and children.

Now, I suggest that you take your letter to me, of which I send
you back a copy, and this letter, and then select out of your family
the one with whom you feel most sympathy, whether it is your husband or one of your children. Show the two letters to him or her,
and then have a frank talk about the matter. If any man, as you say,
becomes ashamed of his wife because she has lost her figure in bearing his children, then that man is a hound and has every cause to be
ashamed of himself. I am sending you a little book called "Mother,"
by Kathleen Norris, which will give you my views on the matter.
Of course there are base and selfish men, just as there are, although
I believe in smaller number, base and selfish women. Man and
woman alike should profit by the teachings in such a story as this of
"Mother."

Sincerely yours,

THEODORE ROOSEVELT.

January 21, 1913.

*Colonel Theodore Roosevelt:*

My dear Sir — Your letter came as a surprise, for I wasn't expecting an answer. The next day the book came, and I thank you for your
ready sympathy and understanding. I feel as though you and Mrs.
Roosevelt would think I was hardly loyal to my husband and children; but knowing of no other way to bring the idea which was so
strong in my mind to your notice, I told my personal story. If it will,
in a small measure, be the means of helping some one else by mold-
ing public opinion, through you, I shall be content. You have helped

me more than you know. Just having you interested is as good as a tonic, and braces me up till I feel as though I shall refuse to be "laid on the shelf." . . . To think that you'd bother to send me a book. I shall always treasure it both for the text of the book and the sender. I read it with absorbing interest. The mother was so splendid. She was ideal. The situations are so startlingly real, just like what happens here every day with variations.

—— —— .

A narrative of facts is often more convincing than a homily; and these two letters of my correspondent carry their own lesson.

Parenthetically, let me remark that whenever a man thinks that he has outgrown the woman who is his mate, he will do well carefully to consider whether his growth has not been downward instead of upward, whether the facts are not merely that he has fallen away from his wife's standard of refinement and of duty.

## Chapter VI

## THE NEW YORK POLICE

I N THE SPRING of 1895 I was appointed by Mayor Strong Police Commissioner, and I served as President of the Police Commission of New York for the two following years. Mayor Strong had been elected Mayor the preceding fall, when the general anti-Democratic wave of that year coincided with one of the city's occasional insurrections of virtue and consequent turning out of Tammany from municipal control. He had been elected on a non-partisan ticket — usually (although not always) the right kind of ticket in municipal affairs, provided it represents not a bargain among factions but genuine non-partisanship with the genuine purpose to get the right men in control of the city government on a platform which deals with the needs of the average men and women, the men and women who work hard and who too often live hard. I was appointed with the distinct understanding that I was to administer the Police Department with entire disregard of partisan politics, and only from the standpoint of a good citizen interested in promoting the welfare of all good citizens. My task, therefore, was really simple. Mayor Strong had already offered me the Street-Cleaning Department. For this work I did not feel that I had any especial fitness. I resolutely refused to accept the position, and the Mayor ultimately got a far better man for his purpose in Colonel George F. Waring. The work of the Police Department, however, was in my line, and I was glad to undertake it.

The man who was closest to me throughout my two years in the Police Department was Jacob Riis. By this time, as I have said, I was getting our social, industrial, and political needs into pretty fair perspective. I was still ignorant of the extent to which big men of great wealth played a mischievous part in our industrial and social life, but I was well awake to the need of making ours in good faith both an economic and an industrial as well as a political democracy. I already knew Jake Riis, because his book "How the Other Half Lives" had been to me both an enlightenment and an inspiration for which I felt I could never be too grateful. Soon after it was written I had called at his office to tell him how deeply impressed I was by the book, and that I wished to help him in any practical way to try to make things a little better. I have

Jacob A. Riis.

"He and I looked at life and its problems from substantially the same standpoint. Our ideals and principles and purposes, and our beliefs as to the methods necessary to realize them, were alike."

always had a horror of words that are not translated into deeds, of speech that does not result in action — in other words, I believe in realizable ideals and in realizing them, in preaching what can be practiced and then in practicing it. Jacob Riis had drawn an indictment of the things that were wrong, pitifully and dreadfully wrong, with the tenement homes and the tenement lives of our wage-workers. In his book he had pointed out how the city government, and especially those connected with the departments of police and health, could aid in remedying some of the wrongs.

As President of the Police Board I was also a member of the Health Board. In both positions I felt that with Jacob Riis's guidance I would be able to put a goodly number of his principles into actual effect. He and I looked at life and its problems from substantially the same standpoint. Our ideals and principles and purposes, and our beliefs as to the methods necessary to realize them, were alike. After the election in 1894 I had written him a letter which ran in part as follows:

It is very important to the city to have a business man's Mayor, but it is more important to have a workingman's Mayor; and I want Mr. Strong to be that also. . . . It is an excellent thing to have rapid transit, but it is a good deal more important, if you look at matters with a proper perspective, to have ample playgrounds in the poorer quarters of the city, and to take the children off the streets so as to prevent them growing up toughs. In the same way it is an admirable thing to have clean streets; indeed, it is an essential thing to have them; but it would be a better thing to have our schools large enough to give ample accommodation to all who should be pupils and to provide them with proper playgrounds.

And I added, while expressing my regret that I had not been able to accept the street-cleaning commissionership, that "I would have been delighted to smash up the corrupt contractors and put the street-cleaning force absolutely out of the domain of politics."

This was nineteen years ago, but it makes a pretty good platform in municipal politics even to-day — smash corruption, take the municipal service out of the domain of politics, insist upon having a Mayor who shall be a workingman's Mayor even more than a business man's Mayor, and devote all the attention possible to the welfare of the children.

Therefore, as I viewed it, there were two sides to the work: first, the actual handling of the Police Department; second, using my position to help in making the city a better place in which to live and work for those to whom the conditions of life and labor were hardest. The two problems were closely connected; for one thing never to be forgotten in striving to better the conditions of the New York police force is the connection between the standard of morals and behavior in that force and the general standard of morals and behavior in the city at large. The form of government of the Police Department at that time was such as to make it a matter of extreme difficulty to get good results. It represented that device of old-school American political thought, the desire to establish checks and balances so elaborate that no man shall have power enough to do anything very bad. In practice this always means that no man has power enough to do anything good, and that what is bad is done anyhow.

In most positions the "division of powers" theory works unmitigated mischief. The only way to get good service is to give somebody power to render it, facing the fact that power which will enable a man to do a job well will also necessarily enable him to do it ill if he is the wrong kind of man. What is normally needed is the concentration in the hands of one man, or of a very small body of men, of ample power to enable him or them to do the work that is necessary; and then the devising of means to hold these men fully responsible for the exercise of that power by the people. This of course means that, if the people are willing to see power misused, it will be misused. But it also means that if, as we hold, the people are fit for self-government — if, in other words, our talk and our institutions are not shams — we will get good government. I do not contend that my theory will automatically bring good government. I do contend that it will enable us to get as good government as we deserve, and that the other way will not.

The then government of the Police Department was so devised as to render it most difficult to accomplish anything good, while the field for intrigue and conspiracy was limitless. There were four Commissioners, two supposed to belong to one party and two to the other, although, as a matter of fact, they never divided on party lines. There was a Chief, appointed by the Commissioners, but whom they could not remove without a regular trial subject to review by the courts of law. This Chief and any one Commissioner had power to hold up most of the acts of the other three Commissioners. It was made easy for the four Commissioners to come to a dead-lock among themselves; and if this danger was avoided, it was easy for one Commissioner, by intriguing with the Chief, to bring the other three to a standstill. The Commissioners were appointed by the Mayor, but he could not remove them with-out the assent of the Governor, who was usually politically opposed to him. In the same way the Commissioners could appoint the patrolmen, but they could not remove them, save after a trial which went up for review to the courts.

As was inevitable under our system of law procedure, this meant that the action of the court was apt to be determined by legal technicalities. It was possible to dismiss a man from the service for quite insufficient reasons, and to provide against the reversal of the sentence, if the technicalities of procedure were observed. But the worst criminals were apt to be adroit men, against whom it was impossible to get legal evidence which a court could properly consider in a criminal trial (and the mood of the court might be to treat the case as if it were a criminal trial), although it was easy to get evidence which would render it not merely justifiable but necessary for a man to remove them from his private employ — and surely the public should be as well treated as a private employer. Accordingly, most of the worst men put out were reinstated by the courts; and when the Mayor attempted to remove one of my colleagues who made it his business to try to nullify the work done by the rest of us, the Governor sided with the recalcitrant Commissioner and refused to permit his removal.

Nevertheless, an astounding quantity of work was done in reforming the force. We had a good deal of power, anyhow; we exercised it to the full; and we accomplished some things by assuming the appearance of a power which we did not really possess.

The first fight I made was to keep politics absolutely out of the force; and not only politics, but every kind of improper favoritism. Doubtless in making thousands of appointments and hundreds of promotions there were men who contrived to use influence of which I was ignorant. But these cases must have been few and far between. As far as was humanly possi-ble, the appointments and promotions were made without regard to any question except the fitness of the man and the needs of the service. As Civil Service Commissioner I had been instructing heads of departments and bureaus how to get men appointed without regard to politics, and assuring them that by following our methods they would obtain first-class results. As Police Commissioner I was able practically to apply my own teachings.

The appointments to the police force were made as I have described in the last chapter. We paid not the slightest attention to a man's politics or creed, or where he was born, so long as he was an American citizen; and on an average we obtained far and away the best men that had ever come into the Police Department. It was of course very difficult at first to convince both the politicians and the people that we really meant what we said, and that every one really would have a fair trial. There had been in previous years the most widespread and gross corruption in connection with every activity in the Police Department, and there had been a regular tariff for appointments and promotions. Many powerful politicians and many corrupt outsiders believed that in some way or other it would still be possible to secure appointments by corrupt and improper methods, and many good citizens felt the same conviction. I endeavored to remove the impression from the minds of both sets of people by giving the widest publicity to what we were doing and how we were doing it, by making the whole process open and aboveboard, and by making it evident that we would probe to the bottom every charge of corruption.

For instance, I received visits at one time from a Catholic priest, and at another time from a Methodist clergyman, who had parishioners who wished to enter the police force, but who did not believe they could get in save by the payment of money or through political pressure. The priest was running a temperance lyceum in connection with his church, and he wished to know if there would be a chance for some of the young men who belonged to that lyceum. The Methodist clergyman came from a little patch of old native America which by a recent extension had been taken within the limits of the huge, polyglot, pleasure-loving city. His was a small church, most of the members being shipwrights, mechanics, and sailormen from the local coasters. In each case I assured my visitor that we wanted on the force men of the exact type which he said he could furnish. I also told him that I was as anxious as he was to find out if there was any improper work being done in connection with the examinations, and that I would like him to get four or five of his men to take the examinations without letting me know their names. Then, whether the men failed or succeeded, he and I would take their papers and follow them through every stage so that we could tell at once whether they had been either improperly favored or improperly discriminated against. This was accordingly done, and in each case my visitor turned up a few weeks later, his face wreathed in smiles, to say that his candidates had passed and that everything was evidently all straight. During my two years as President of the Commission I think I appointed a dozen or fifteen members of that little Methodist congregation, and certainly twice that number of men from the temperance lyceum of the Catholic church in question. They were all men of the very type I most wished to see on the force — men of strong physique and resolute temper, sober, self-respecting, self-reliant, with a strong wish to improve themselves.

Occasionally I would myself pick out a man and tell him to take the examination. Thus one evening I went down to speak in the Bowery at the Young Men's Institute, a branch of the Young Men's Christian Association, at the request of Mr. Cleveland H. Dodge. While there he told me he wished to show me a young Jew who had recently, by an exhibition of marked pluck and bodily prowess, saved some women and children from a burning building. The young Jew, whose name was Otto Raphael, was brought up to see me; a powerful fellow, with good-humored, intelligent face. I asked him about his education, and told him to try the examination. He did, passed, was appointed, and made an admirable officer; and he and all his family, wherever they may dwell, have been close friends of mine ever since. Otto Raphael was a genuine East Sider. He and I were both "straight New York," to use the vernacular of our native city. To show our community of feeling and our grasp of the facts of life, I may mention that we were almost the only men in the Police Department who picked Fitzsimmons as a winner against Corbett. Otto's parents had come over from Russia, and not only in social standing but in pay a policeman's position meant everything to him. It enabled Otto to educate his little brothers and sisters who had been born in this country, and to bring over from Russia two or three kinsfolk who had perforce been left behind.

Otto Raphael.
"A young Jew who had recently, by an exhibition of marked pluck and bodily prowess, saved some women and children from a burning building."

Rather curiously, it was by no means as easy to keep politics and corruption out of the promotions as out of the entrance examinations. This was because I could take complete charge of the entrance examinations myself; and, moreover, they were largely automatic. In promotions, on the other hand, the prime element was the record and capacity of the officer, and for this we had largely to rely upon the judgment of the man's immediate superiors. This doubtless meant that in certain cases that judgment was given for improper reasons.

However, there were cases where I could act on personal knowledge. One thing that we did was to endeavor to recognize gallantry. We did not have to work a revolution in the force as to courage in the way that we had to work a revolution in honesty. They had always been brave in dealing with riotous and violent criminals. But they had gradually become very corrupt. Our great work, therefore, was the stamping out of dishonesty, and this work we did thoroughly, so far as the ridiculous bi-partisan law under which the Department was administered would permit. But we were anxious that, while stamping out what was evil in the force, we should keep and improve what was good. While warring on dishonesty, we made very effort to increase efficiency. It has unfortunately been shown by sad experience that at times a police organization which is free from the taint of corruption may yet show itself weak in some great crisis or unable to deal with the more dangerous kinds of criminals. This we were determined to prevent.

Our efforts were crowned with entire success. The improvement in the efficiency of the force went hand in hand with the improvement in its honesty. The men in uniform and the men in plain clothes — the detectives — did better work than ever before. The aggregate of crimes where punishment followed the commission of the crime increased, while the aggregate of crimes where the criminal escaped punishment decreased. Every discredited politician, every sensational newspaper, and every timid fool who could be scared by clamor was against us. All three classes strove by every means in their power to show that in making the force honest we had impaired its efficiency; and by their utterances they tended to bring about the very condition of things against which they professed to protest. But we went steadily along the path we had marked out. The fight was hard, and there was plenty of worry and anxiety, but we won. I was appointed in May, 1895. In February, 1897, three months before I resigned to become Assistant Secretary of the Navy, the Judge who charged the

Grand Jury of New York County was able to congratulate them on the phenomenal decrease in crime, especially of the violent sort. This decrease was steady during the two years. The police, after the reform policy was thoroughly tried, proved more successful than ever before in protecting life and property and in putting down crime and criminal vice.

The part played by the recognition and reward of actual personal prowess among the members of the police force in producing this state of affairs was appreciable, though there were many other factors that combined to bring about the betterment. The immense improvement in discipline by punishing all offenders without mercy, no matter how great their political or personal influence; the resolute warfare against every kind of criminal who had hitherto been able corruptly to purchase protection; the prompt recognition of ability even where it was entirely unconnected with personal prowess — all these were elements which had enormous weight in producing the change. Mere courage and daring, and the rewarding of courage and daring, cannot supply the lack of discipline, of ability, of honesty. But they are of vital consequence, nevertheless. No police force is worth anything if its members are not intelligent and honest; but neither is it worth anything unless its members are brave, hardy, and well disciplined.

We showed recognition of daring and of personal prowess in two ways: first, by awarding a medal or a certificate in remembrance of the deed; and, second, by giving it weight in making any promotion, especially to the lower grades. In the higher grades — in all promotions above that of sergeant, for instance — resolute and daring courage cannot normally be considered as a factor of determining weight in making promotions; rather is it a quality the lack of which unfits a man for promotion. For in the higher places we must assume the existence of such a quality in any fit candidate, and must make the promotion with a view to the man's energy, executive capacity, and power of command. In the lower grades, however, marked gallantry should always be taken into account in deciding among different candidates for any given place.

During our two years' service we found it necessary over a hundred times to single out men for special mention because of some feat of heroism. The heroism usually took one of four forms; saving somebody from drowning, saving somebody from a burning building, stopping a runaway team, or arresting some violent lawbreaker under exceptional circumstances. To illustrate our method of action, I will take two of the first promotions made after I became Commissioner. One case was that of an old fellow, a veteran of the Civil War, who was at the time a roundsman. I happened to notice one day that he had saved a woman from drowning, and had him summoned so that I might look into the matter. The old fellow brought up his record before me, and showed not a little nervousness and agitation; for it appeared that he had grown gray in the service, had performed feat after feat of heroism, but had no political backing of any account. No heed had ever been paid him. He was one of the quiet men who attend solely to duty, and although a Grand Army man, he had never sought to use influence of any kind. Now, at last, he thought there was a chance for him. He had been twenty-two years on the force, and during that time had saved some twenty-five persons from death by drowning, varying the performance two or three times by saving persons from burning buildings. Twice Congress had passed laws especially to empower the then Secretary of the Treasury, John Sherman, to give him a medal for distinguished gallantry in saving life. The Life-Saving Society had also given him its medal, and so had the Police Department. There was not a complaint in all his record against him for any infraction of duty, and he was sober and trustworthy. He was entitled to his promotion; and he got it, there and then. It may be worth mentioning that he kept on saving life after he was given his sergeantcy. On October 21, 1896, he again rescued a man from drowning. It was at night, nobody else was in the neighborhood, and the dock from which he jumped was in absolute darkness, and he was ten minutes in the water, which was very cold. He was fifty-five years old when he saved this man. It was the twenty-ninth person whose life he had saved during his twenty-three years' service in the Department.

The other man was a patrolman whom we promoted to roundsman for activity in catching a burglar under rather peculiar circumstances. I happened to note his getting a burglar one week. Apparently he had fallen into the habit, for he got another next week. In the latter case the burglar escaped from the house soon after midnight, and ran away toward Park Avenue, with the policeman in hot chase. The New York Central Railroad runs under Park Avenue, and there is a succession of openings in the top of the tunnel. Finding that the policeman was gaining on him, the burglar took a desperate chance and leaped down one of these openings, at the risk of breaking his neck. Now the burglar was running for his liberty, and it was the part of wisdom for him to imperil life or limb; but the policeman was merely doing his duty, and nobody could have blamed him for not taking the jump. However, he jumped; and in this particular case the hand of the Lord was heavy upon the unrighteous. The burglar had the breath knocked out of him, and the "cop" didn't. When his victim could walk, the officer trotted him around to the station-house; and a week after I had the officer up and promoted him, for he was sober, trustworthy, and strictly attentive to duty.

Now I think that any decent man of reasonable intelligence will agree that we were quite right in promoting men in cases like these, and quite right in excluding politics from promotions. Yet it was because of our consistently acting in this manner, resolutely warring on dishonesty and on that peculiar form of baseness which masquerades as "practical" politics, and steadily refusing to pay heed to any consideration except the good of the service and the city, and the merits of the men themselves, that we drew down upon our heads the bitter and malignant animosity of the bread-and-butter spoils politicians. They secured the repeal of the Civil Service Law by the State Legislature. They attempted and almost succeeded in the effort to legislate us out of office. They joined with the baser portion of the sensational press in every species of foul, indecent falsehood and slander as to what we were doing. They attempted to seduce or frighten us by every species of intrigue and cajolery, of promise of political reward and threat of political punishment. They failed in their purpose. I believe in political organizations, and I believe in practical politics. If a man is not practical, he is of no use anywhere. But when politicians treat practical politics as foul politics, and when they turn what ought to be a necessary and useful political organization into a machine run by professional spoilsmen of low morality in their own interest, then it is time to drive the politician from public life, and either to mend or destroy the machine, according as the necessity may determine.

We promoted to roundsman a patrolman, with an already excellent record, for gallantry shown in a fray which resulted in the death of his antagonist. He was after a gang of toughs who had just waylaid, robbed, and beaten a man. They scattered and he pursued the ringleader. Running hard, he gained on his man, whereupon the latter suddenly turned and fired full in his face. The officer already had his revolver drawn, and the two shots rang out almost together. The policeman was within a fraction of death, for the bullet from his opponent's pistol went through his helmet and just broke the skin of his head. His own aim was truer, and the man he was after fell dead, shot through the heart. I may explain that I have not the slightest sympathy with any policy which tends to put the policeman at the mercy of a tough, or which deprives him of efficient weapons. While Police Commissioner we punished any brutality by the police with such immediate severity that all cases of brutality practically came to an end. No decent citizen had anything to fear from the police during the two years of my service. But we consistently encouraged the police to prove that the violent criminal who endeavored to molest them or to resist arrest, or to interfere with them in the discharge of their duty, was himself in grave jeopardy; and we had every "gang" broken up and the members punished with whatever severity was necessary. Of course where possible the officer merely crippled the criminal who was violent.

One of the things that we did while in office was to train the men in the use of the pistol. A school of pistol practice was established, and the marksmanship of the force was wonderfully improved. The man in charge of the school was a roundsman, Petty, whom we promoted to sergeant. He was one of the champion revolver shots of the country, and could hit just about where he aimed. Twice he was forced to fire at criminals who resisted arrest, and in each case he hit his man in the arm or leg, simply stopping him without danger to his life.

In May, 1896, a number of burglaries occurred far uptown, in the neighborhood of One Hundred and Fifty-sixth Street and Union Avenue. Two officers were sent out each night to patrol the streets in plain clothes. About two o'clock on the morning of May 8 they caught a glimpse of two men loitering about a large corner house, and determined to make them explain their actions. In order to cut off their escape, one officer went down one street and one the other. The first officer, whose name was Ryan, found the two men at the gateway of the side entrance of the house, and hailed to know what they were doing. Without answering, they turned and ran toward Prospect Avenue, with Ryan in close pursuit. After running about one hundred feet, one of them turned and fired three shots at Ryan, but failed to hit him. The two then separated, and the man who had done the shooting escaped. The other man, whose name proved to be O'Connor, again took to his heels, with Ryan still after him; they turned the corner and met the other officer, whose name was Reid, running as hard as he could toward the shooting. When O'Connor saw himself cut off by Reid, he fired at his new foe, the bullet cutting Reid's overcoat on the left shoulder. Reid promptly fired in return, his bullet going into O'Connor's neck and causing him to turn a complete somersault. The two officers then cared for their prisoner until the ambulance arrived, when he was taken to the hospital and pronounced mortally wounded. His companion was afterward caught, and they turned out to be the very burglars for whom Reid and Ryan had been on the lookout.

In December, 1896, one of our officers was shot. A row occurred in a restaurant, which ended in two young toughs drawing their revolvers and literally running amuck, shooting two or three men. A policeman, attracted by the noise, ran up and seized one of them, whereupon the other shot him in the mouth, wounding him badly. Nevertheless, the officer kept his prisoner and carried him to the station-house. The tough who had done the shooting ran out and was seized by another officer. The tough fired at him, the bullet passing through the officer's overcoat, but he was promptly knocked down, disarmed, and brought to the station-house. In this case neither policeman used his revolver, and each brought in

A Squad of Mounted Police.

his man, although the latter was armed and resisted arrest, one of the officers taking in his prisoner after having been himself severely wounded. A lamentable feature of the case was that this same officer was a man who, though capable of great gallantry, was also given to shirking his work, and we were finally obliged to dismiss him from the force, after passing over two or three glaring misdeeds in view of his record for courage.

We promoted another man on account of finding out accidentally that he had performed a notable feat, which he had forborne even to mention, so that his name never came on the roll of honor. Late at night, while patrolling a lonely part of his post, he came upon three young toughs who had turned highwaymen and were robbing a peddler. He ran in at once with his night-stick, whereupon the toughs showed fight, and one of them struck at him with a bludgeon, breaking his left hand. The officer, however, made such good use of his night-stick that he knocked down two of his assailants, whereupon the third ran away, and he brought both of his prisoners to the station-house. Then he went round to the hospital, had his broken hand set in plaster, and actually reported for duty at the next tour, without losing one hour. He was a quiet fellow, with a record free from complaints, and we made him roundsman.

The mounted squad have, of course, many opportunities to distinguish themselves in stopping runaways. In May, 1895, a mounted policeman named Heyer succeeded in stopping a runaway at Kingsbridge under rather noteworthy circumstances. Two men were driving in a buggy, when the horse stumbled, and in recovering himself broke the headstall, so that the bridle fell off. The horse was a spirited trotter, and at once ran away at full speed. Heyer saw the occurrence, and followed at a run. When he got alongside the runaway he seized him by the forelock, guided him dexterously over the bridge, preventing him from running into the numerous wagons that were on the road, and finally forced him up a hill and into a wagon-shed. Three months later this same officer saved a man from drowning.

The members of the bicycle squad, which was established shortly after we took office, soon grew to show not only extraordinary proficiency on the wheel, but extraordinary daring.

They frequently stopped runaways, wheeling alongside of them, and grasping the horses while going at full speed; and, what was even more remarkable, they managed not only to overtake but to jump into the vehicle and capture, on two or three different occasions, men who were guilty of reckless driving, and who fought violently in resisting arrest. They were picked men, being young and active, and any feat of daring which could be accomplished on the wheel they were certain to accomplish.

Three of the best riders of the bicycle squad, whose names and records happen to occur to me, were men of the three ethnic strains most strongly represented in the New York police force, being respectively of native American, German, and Irish parentage.

The German was a man of enormous power, and he was able to stop each of the many runaways he tackled without losing his wheel. Choosing his time, he would get alongside the horse and seize the bit in his left hand, keeping his right on the crossbar of the wheel. By degrees he then got the animal under control. He never failed to stop it, and he never lost his wheel. He also never failed to overtake any "scorcher," although many of these were professional riders who deliberately violated the law to see if they could not get away from him; for the wheelmen soon get to know the officers whose beats they cross.

The Yankee, though a tall, powerful man and a very good rider, scarcely came up to the German in either respect; he possessed exceptional ability, however, as well as exceptional nerve and coolness, and he also won his promotion. He stopped about as many runaways; but when the horse was really panic-stricken he usually had to turn his wheel loose, getting a firm grip on the horse's reins and then kicking his wheel so that it would fall out of the way of injury from the wagon. On one occasion he had a fight with a drunken and reckless driver who was urging to top speed a spirited horse. He first got hold of the horse, whereupon the driver lashed both him and the beast, and the animal, already mad with terror, could not be stopped. The officer had of course kicked away his wheel at the beginning, and after being dragged along for some distance he let go the beast and made a grab at the wagon. The driver hit him with his whip, but he managed to get in, and after a vigorous tussle overcame his man, and disposed of him by getting him down and sitting on him. This left his hands free for the reins. By degrees he got the horse under control, and drove the wagon round to the station-house, still sitting on his victim. "I jounced up and down on him to keep him quiet when he turned ugly," he remarked to me parenthetically. Having disposed of the wagon, he took the man round to the court, and on the way the prisoner suddenly sprang on him and tried to throttle him. Convinced at last that patience had ceased to be a virtue, he quieted his assailant with a smash on the head that took all the fight out of him until he was brought before the judge and fined. Like the other "bicycle cops," this office made a number of arrests of criminals, such as thieves, highwaymen, and the like, in addition to his natural prey — scorcher, runaway, and reckless drivers.

The third member of the trio, a tall, sinewy man with flaming red hair, which rather added to the terror he inspired in evil-doers, was usually stationed in a tough part of the city, where there was a tendency to crimes of violence, and incidentally an occasional desire to harass wheelmen. The officer was as good off his wheel as on it, and he speedily established perfect order on his beat, being always willing to "take chances" in getting his man. He was no respecter of persons, and when it became his duty to arrest a wealthy man for persistently refusing to have his carriage lamps lighted after nightfall, he brought him in with the same indifference that he displayed in arresting a street-corner tough who had thrown a brick at a wheelman.

Occasionally a policeman would perform work which ordinarily comes within the domain of the fireman. In November, 1896, an officer who had previously saved a man from death by drowning added to his record by saving five persons from burning. He was at the time asleep, when he was aroused by a fire in a house a few doors away. Running over the roofs of the adjoining houses until he reached the burning building, he found that on the fourth floor the flames had cut off all exit from an apartment in which there were four women, two of them over fifty, and one of the others with a six-months-old baby. The officer ran down to the adjoining house, broke open the door of the apartment on the same floor — the fourth — and crept out on the coping, less than three inches wide, that ran from one house to the other. Being a large and very powerful and active man, he managed to keep hold of the casing of the window with one hand, and with the other to reach to the window of the apartment where the women and child were. The firemen appeared, and stretched a net underneath. The crowd that was looking on suddenly became motionless and silent. Then, one by one, he drew the women out of their window, and, holding them tight against the wall, passed them into the other window. The exertion in such an attitude was great, and he strained himself badly; but he possessed a practical mind, and as soon as the women were saved he began a prompt investigation of the cause of the fire, and arrested two men whose carelessness, as was afterward proved, caused it.

Now and then a man, though a brave man, proved to be slack or stupid or vicious, and we could make nothing out of him; but hardihood and courage were qualities upon which we insisted and which we rewarded. Whenever I see the police force attacked and vilified, I always remember my association with it. The cases I have given above are merely instances chosen almost at random among hundreds of others. Men such as those I have mentioned have the right stuff in them! If they go wrong, the trouble is with the system, and therefore with us, the citizens, for permitting the system to go unchanged. The conditions of New York life are such as to make the police problem therein more difficult than in any other of the world's great capitals. I am often asked if policemen are honest. I believe that the great majority of them want to be honest and will be honest whenever they are given the chance. The New York police force is a body thoroughly representative of the great city itself. As I have said above, the predominant ethnic strains in it are, first, the men of Irish birth or parentage, and, following these, the native Americans, usually from the Country districts, and the men of German birth or parentage. There are also Jews, Scandinavians, Italians, Slavs, and men of other nationalities. All soon become welded into one body. They are physically a fine lot. Moreover, their instincts are right; they are game, they are alert and self-reliant, they prefer to act squarely if they are allowed so to act. All that they need is to be given the chance to prove themselves honest, brave, and self-respecting.

The law at present is much better than in our day, so far as governing the force is concerned. There is now a single Commissioner, and the Mayor has complete power over him. The Mayor, through his Commissioner, now has power to keep the police force on a good level of conduct if with resolution and common sense he insists on absolute honesty within the force and at the same time heartily supports it against the criminal classes. To weaken the force in its dealings with gangs and toughs and criminals generally is as damaging as to permit dishonesty, and, moreover, works towards dishonesty. But while under the present law very much improvement can be worked, there is need of change of the law which will make the Police Commissioner a permanent, non-partisan official, holding office so long as he proves thoroughly fit for the job, completely independent of the politicians and privileged interests, and with complete power over the force. This means that there must be the right law, and the right public opinion back of the law.

The many-sided ethnic character of the force now and then gives rise to, or affords opportunity for, queer happenings. Occasionally it enables one to meet emergencies in the best possible fashion. While I was Police Commissioner an anti-Semitic preacher from Berlin, Rector Ahlwardt, came over to New York to preach a crusade against the Jews. Many of the New York Jews were much excited and asked me to prevent him from speaking and not to give him police protection. This, I told them, was impossible; and if possible would have been undesirable because it would have made him a martyr. The proper thing to do was to make him ridiculous. Accordingly I detailed for his protection a Jew sergeant and a score or two of Jew policemen. He made his harangue against the Jews under the active protection of some forty policemen, every one of them a Jew! It was the most effective possible answer; and incidentally it was an object-lesson to our people, whose greatest need it is to learn that there must be no division by class hatred, whether this hatred be that of creed against creed, nationality against nationality, section against section, or men of one social or industrial condition against men of another social and industrial condition. We must ever judge each individual on his own conduct and merits, and not on his membership in any class, whether that class be based on theological, social, or industrial considerations.

Among my political opponents when I was Police Commissioner was the head of a very influential local Democratic organization. He was a State Senator usually known as Big Tim Sullivan. Big Tim represented the morals of another era; that is, his principles and actions were very much those of a Norman noble in the years immediately succeeding the Battle of Hastings. (This will seem flattery only to those who are not acquainted with the real histories and antecedents of the Norman nobles of the epoch in question.) His application of these eleventh-century theories to our nineteenth-century municipal democratic conditions brought him into sharp contact with me, and with one of my right-hand men in the Department, Inspector John McCullough. Under the old dispensation this would have meant that his friends and kinsfolk were under the ban.

Now it happened that in the Department at that time there was a nephew or cousin of his, Jerry D. Sullivan. I found that Jerry was an uncommonly good man, a conscientious, capable officer, and I promoted him. I do not know whether Jerry or Jerry's cousin (Senator Sullivan) was more astonished. The Senator called upon me to express what I am sure was a very genuine feeling of appreciation. Poor Jerry died, I think of consumption, a year or two after I left the Department. He was promoted again after I left, and he then showed that he possessed the very rare quality of gratitude, for he sent me a telegram dated January 15, 1898, running as follows: "Was made sergeant to-day. I thank you for all in my first advancement." And in a letter written to me he said: "In the future, as in the past, I will endeavor at all times to perform my duty honestly and fearlessly, and never cause you to feel that you were mistaken in me, so that you will be justly proud of my record." The Senator, though politically opposed to me, always kept a feeling of friendship for me after this incident. He served in Congress while I was President.

The police can be used to help all kinds of good purposes. When I was Police Commissioner much difficulty had been encountered in locating illegal and fraudulent practitioners of medicine. Dr. Maurice Lewi called on me, with a letter from James Russell Parsons, the Secretary of the Board of Regents at Albany, and asked me if I could not help. After questioning him I found that the local authorities were eager to prosecute these men, but could not locate them; and I made up my mind I would try my hand at it. Accordingly, a sealed order was sent to the commanding officer of each police precinct in New York, not to be opened until just before the morning roll call, previous to the police squad going on duty. This order required that, immediately upon reaching post, each patrolman should go over his beat and enter upon a sheet of paper, provided for that purpose, the full name and address of every doctor sign there appearing. Immediately upon securing this information, the patrolman was instructed to return the sheet to the officer in charge of the precinct. The latter in turn was instructed to collect and place in one large envelope and to return to Police Headquarters all the data thus received. As a result of this procedure, within two hours the prosecuting officials of the city of New York were in possession of the name and address of every person in New York who announced himself as a physician; and scores of pretended physicians were brought to book or driven from the city.

One of the perennially serious and difficult problems, and one of the chief reasons for police blackmail and corruption, is to be found in the excise situation in New York. When I was Police Commissioner, New York was a city with twelve or fifteen thousand saloons, with a State law which said they should be closed on Sundays, and with a local sentiment which put a premium on violating the law by making Sunday the most profitable day in the week to the saloon-keeper who was willing to take chances. It was this willingness to take chances that furnished to the corrupt politician and the corrupt police officer their opportunities.

There was in New York City a strong sentiment in favor of honesty in politics; there was also a strong sentiment in favor of opening the saloons on Sundays; and, finally, there was a strong sentiment in favor of keeping the saloons closed on

Sunday. Unfortunately, many of the men who favored honest government nevertheless preferred keeping the saloons open to having honest government; and many others among the men who favored honest government put it second to keeping the saloons closed. Moreover, among the people who wished the law obeyed and the saloons closed there were plenty who objected strongly to every step necessary to accomplish the result, although they also insisted that the result should be accomplished.

Meanwhile the politicians found an incredible profit in using the law as a club to keep the saloons in line; all except the biggest, the owners of which, or the owners of the breweries back of which, sat in the inner councils of Tammany, or controlled Tammany's allies in the Republican organization. The police used the partial and spasmodic enforcement of the law as a means of collecting blackmail. The result was that the officers of the law, the politicians, and the saloon-keepers became inextricably tangled in a network of crime and connivance at crime. The most powerful saloon-keepers controlled the politicians and the police, while the latter in turn terrorized and blackmailed all the other saloon-keepers. It was not a case of non-enforcement of the law. The law was very actively enforced, but it was enforced with corrupt discrimination.

It is difficult for men who have not been brought into contact with that side of political life which deals with the underworld to understand the brazen openness with which this blackmailing of lawbreakers was carried out. A further very dark fact was that many of the men responsible for putting the law on the statute-books in order to please one element of their constituents, also connived at or even profited by the corrupt and partial non-enforcement of the law in order to please another set of their constituents, or to secure profit for themselves. The organ of the liquor-sellers at that time was the *Wine and Spirit Gazette*. The editor of this paper believed in selling liquor on Sunday, and felt that it was an outrage to forbid it. But he also felt that corruption and blackmail made too big a price to pay for the partial non-enforcement of the law. He made in his paper a statement, the correctness of which was never questioned, which offers a startling commentary on

New York politics of that period. In this statement he recited the fact that the system of blackmail had been brought to such a state of perfection, and had become so oppressive to the liquor dealers themselves, that they communicated at length on the subject with Governor Hill (the State Democratic boss) and then with Mr. Croker (the city Democratic boss). Finally the matter was formally taken up by a committee of the Central Association of Liquor Dealers in an interview they held with Mr. Martin, my Tammany predecessor as President of the police force. In matter-of-course way the editor's statement continues: "An agreement was made between the leaders of Tammany Hall and the liquor dealers according to which the monthly blackmail paid to the force should be discontinued in return for political support." Not only did the big bosses, State and local, treat this agreement, and the corruption to which it was due, as normal and proper, but they never even took the trouble to deny what had been done when it was made public. Tammany and the police, however, did not fully live up to the agreement; and much discrimination of a very corrupt kind, and of a very exasperating kind to liquor-sellers who wished to be honest, continued in connection with the enforcing of the law.

In short, the agreement was kept only with those who had "pull." These men with "pull" were benefited when their rivals were bullied and blackmailed by the police. The police, meanwhile, who had bought appointment or promotion, and the politicians back of them, extended the blackmailing to include about everything from the pushcart peddler and the big or small merchant who wished to use the sidewalk illegally for his goods, up to the keepers of the brothel, the gambling-house, and the policy-shop. The total blackmail ran into millions of dollars. New York was a wide-open town. The big bosses rolled in wealth, and the corrupt policemen who ran the force lost all sense of decency and justice. Nevertheless, I wish to insist on the fact that the honest men on the patrol posts, "the men with the night-sticks," remained desirous to see honesty obtain, although they were losing courage and hope.

This was the situation that confronted me when I came to Mulberry Street. The saloon was the chief source of mischief.

It was with the saloon that I had to deal, and there was only one way to deal with it. That was to enforce the law. The howl that rose was deafening. The professional politicians raved. The yellow press surpassed themselves in clamor and mendacity. A favorite assertion was that I was enforcing a "blue" law, an obsolete law that had never before been enforced. As a matter of fact, I was only enforcing honestly a law that had hitherto been enforced dishonestly. There was very little increase in the number of arrests made for violating the Sunday law. Indeed, there were weeks when the number of arrests went down. The only difference was that there was no protected class. Everybody was arrested alike, and I took especial pains to see that there was no discrimination, and that the big men and the men with political influence were treated like every one else. The immediate effect was wholly good. I had been told that it was not possible to close the saloons on Sunday and that I could not succeed. However, I did succeed. The warden of Bellevue Hospital reported, two or three weeks after we had begun, that for the first time in its existence there had not been a case due to a drunken brawl in the hospital all Monday. The police courts gave the same testimony, while savings banks recorded increased deposits and pawnshops hard times. The most touching of all things was the fact that we received letters, literally by the hundred, from mothers in tenement-houses who had never been allowed to take their children to the country in the wide-open days, and who now found their husbands willing to take them and their families for an outing on Sunday. Jake Riis and I spent one Sunday from morning till night in the tenement districts, seeing for ourselves what had happened.

During the two years that we were in office things never slipped back to anything like what they had been before. But we did not succeed in keeping them quite as highly keyed as during these first weeks. As regards the Sunday-closing law, this was partly because public sentiment was not really with us. The people who had demanded honesty, but who did not like to pay for it by the loss of illegal pleasure, joined the openly dishonest in attacking us. Moreover, all kinds of ways of evading the law were tried, and some of them were successful. The statute, for instance, permitted any man to take liquor with meals. After two or three months a magistrate was found who decided judicially that seventeen beers and one pretzel made a meal — after which decision joy again became unconfined in at least some of the saloons, and the yellow press gleefully announced that my "tyranny" had been curbed. But my prime object, that of stopping blackmail, was largely attained.

All kinds of incidents occurred in connection with this crusade. One of them introduced me to a friend who remains a friend yet. His name was Edward J. Bourke. He was one of the men who entered the police force through our examinations shortly after I took office. I had summoned twenty or thirty of the successful applicants to let me look over them; and as I walked into the hall, one of them, a well-set-up man, called out sharply to the others, "Gangway," making them move to one side. I found he had served in the United States navy. The incident was sufficient to make me keep him in mind. A month later I was notified by a police reporter, a very good fellow, that Bourke was in difficulties, and that he thought I had better look into the matter myself, as Bourke was being accused by certain very influential men of grave misconduct in an arrest he had made the night before. Accordingly, I took the matter up personally. I found that on the new patrolman's beat the preceding night — a new beat — there was a big saloon run by a man of great influence in political circles known as "King" Calahan. After midnight the saloon was still running in full blast, and Bourke, stepping inside, told Calahan to close up. It was at the time filled with "friends of personal liberty," as Governor Hill used at that time, in moments of pathos, to term everybody who regarded as tyranny any restriction on the sale of liquor. Calahan's saloon had never before in its history been closed, and to have a green cop tell him to close it seemed to him so incredible that he regarded it merely as a bad jest. On his next round Bourke stepped in and repeated the order. Calahan felt that the jest had gone too far, and by way of protest knocked Bourke down. This was an error of judgment on his part, for when Bourke arose he knocked down Calahan. The two then grappled and fell on the floor, while the "friends of personal liberty" danced around the fight and endeavored to stamp on everything they thought wasn't Calahan. However, Bourke, though pretty roughly handled, got his man and shut the saloon. When he appeared against the lawbreaker in court next day, he found the court-room crowded with influential Tammany Hall politicians, backed by one or two Republican leaders of the same type; for Calahan was a baron of the underworld, and both his feudal superiors and his feudal inferiors gathered to the rescue. His backers in court included a

Captain Edward J. Bourke.

" 'King' Calahan's saloon had never before in its history been closed, and to have a green cop tell him to close seemed to him so incredible that he regarded it merely as a bad jest."

Congressman and a State Senator, and so deep-rooted was the police belief in "pull" that his own superiors had turned against Bourke and were preparing to sacrifice him. Just at this time I acted on the information given me by my newspaper friend by starting in person for the court. The knowledge that I knew what was going on, that I meant what I said, and that I intended to make the affair personal, was all that was necessary. Before I reached the court all effort to defend Calahan had promptly ceased, and Bourke had come forth triumphant. I immediately promoted him to roundsman. He is a captain now. He has been on the force ever since, save that when the Spanish War came he obtained a holiday without pay for six months and reëntered the navy, serving as gun captain in one of the gunboats, and doing his work, as was to be expected, in first-rate fashion, especially when under fire.

Let me again say that when men tell me that the police are irredeemably bad I remember scores and hundreds of cases like this of Bourke, like the case I have already mentioned of Raphael, like the other cases I have given above. It is useless to tell me that these men are bad. They are naturally first-rate men. There are no better men anywhere than the men of the New York police force; and when they go bad it is because the system is wrong, and because they are not given the chance to do the good work they can do and would rather do. I never coddled these men. I punished them severely whenever I thought their conduct required it. All I did was to try to be just; to reward them when they did well; in short, to act squarely by them. I believe that, as a whole, they liked me. When, in 1912, I ran for President on the Progressive ticket, I received a number of unsigned letters inclosing sums of money for the campaign. One of these inclosed twenty dollars. The writer, who did not give his name, said that he was a policeman, that I had once had him before me on charges, and had fined him twenty dollars; that, as a matter of fact, he had not committed the offense for which I fined him, but that the evidence was such that he did not wonder that I had been misled, and never blamed me for it, because I had acted squarely and had given honest and decent men a chance in the Police Department; and that now he inclosed a twenty-dollar bill, the amount of the fine inflicted on him so many years before. I have always wished I knew who the man was.

The disciplinary courts were very interesting. But it was extraordinary difficult to get at the facts in the more complicated cases — as must always be true under similar circumstances; for ordinarily it is necessary to back up the superior officer who makes the charge, and yet it is always possible that this superior officer is consciously or unconsciously biased against his subordinate.

In the courts the charges were sometimes brought by police officers and sometimes by private citizens. In the latter case we would get queer insights into twilight phases of New York life. It was necessary to be always on our guard. Often an accusation would be brought against the policeman because he had been guilty of misconduct. Much more often the accusation merely meant that the officer had incurred animosity by doing his duty. I remember one amusing case where the officer was wholly to blame but had acted in entire good faith.

One of the favorite and most demoralizing forms of gambling in New York was policy-playing. The policy slips consisted of papers with three rows of figures written on them. The officer in question was a huge pithecoid lout of a creature, with a wooden face and a receding forehead, and his accuser whom he had arrested the preceding evening was a little grig of a red-headed man, obviously respectable, and almost incoherent with rage. The anger of the little red-headed man was but natural, for he had just come out from a night in the station-house. He had been arrested late in the evening on suspicion that he was a policy-player, because of the rows of figures on a piece of paper which he had held in his hand, and because at the time of his arrest he had just stepped into the entrance of the hall of a tenement-house in order to read by lamplight. The paper was produced in evidence. There were the three rows of figures all right, but, as the accuser explained, hopping up and down with rage and excitement, they were all of them the numbers of hymns. He was the superintendent of a small Sunday-school. He had written down the hymns for several future services, one under the other, and on the way home was stopping to look at them, under convenient lamp-posts, and finally by the light of the lamp in a tenement-house hallway; and it was this conduct which struck the sagacious man in uniform as "suspicious."

One of the saddest features of police work is dealing with the social evil, with prostitutes and houses of ill fame. In so far as the law gave me power, I always treated the men taken in any raid on these houses precisely as the women were treated. My experience brought me to the very strong conviction that there ought not to be any toleration by law of the vice. I do not know of any method which will put a complete stop to the evil, but I do know certain things that ought to be done to minimize it. One of these is treating men and women on an exact equality for the same act. Another is the establishment of night courts and of special commissions to deal with this special class of cases. Another is that suggested by the Rev. Charles Stelzle, of the Labor Temple — to publish conspicuously the name of the owner of any property used for immoral purposes, after said owner has been notified of the use and has failed to prevent it. Another is to prosecute the keepers and backers of brothels, men and women, as relentlessly and punish them as severely as pickpockets and common thieves. They should never be fined; they should be imprisoned. As for the girls, the very young ones and first offenders should be put in the charge of probation officers or sent to reformatories, and the large percentage of feeble-minded girls and of incorrigible girls and women should be sent to institutions created for them. We would thus remove from this hideous commerce the articles of commerce. Moreover, the Federal Government must in ever-increasing measure proceed against the degraded promoters of this commercialism, for their activities are inter-State, and the Nation can often deal with them more effectively than the States; although, as public sentiment becomes aroused, Nation, State, and municipality will all cooperate towards the same end of rooting out the traffic. But the prime need is to raise the level of individual morality; and, moreover, to encourage early marriages, the single standard of sex-morality, and a strict sense of reciprocal conjugal obligation. The women who preach late marriages are by just so much making it difficult to better the standard of chastity.

As regards the white slave traffic, the men engaged in it, and the women too, are far worse criminals than any ordinary murderers can be. For them there is need of such a law as that recently adopted in England through the efforts of Arthur Lee, M.P., a law which includes whipping for the male offenders. There are brutes so low, so infamous, so degraded and bestial in their cruelty and brutality, that the only way to get at them is through their skins. Sentimentality on behalf of such men is really almost as unhealthy and wicked as the criminality of the men themselves. My experience is that there should be no toleration of any "tenderloin" or "red light" district, and that, above all, there should be the most relentless war on commercialized vice. The men who profit and make their living by the depravity and the awful misery of other human beings stand far below any ordinary criminals, and no measures taken against them can be too severe.

As for the wretched girls who follow the dreadful trade in question, a good deal can be done by a change in economic conditions. This ought to be done. When girls are paid wages inadequate to keep them from starvation, or to permit them to live decently, a certain proportion are forced by their economic misery into lives of vice. The employers and all others responsible for these conditions stand on a moral level not far above the white slavers themselves. But it is a mistake to suppose that either the correction of these economic conditions or the abolition of the white slave trade will wholly correct the evil or will even reach the major part of it. The economic factor is very far from being the chief factor in inducing girls to go into this dreadful life. As with so many other problems, while there must be governmental action, there must also be strengthening of the average individual character in order to achieve the desired end. Even where economic conditions are bad, girls who are both strong and pure will remain unaffected by temptations to which girls of weak character or lax standards readily yield. Any man who knows the wide variation in the proportions of the different races and nationalities engaged in prostitution must come to the conclusion that it is out of the question to treat economic conditions as the sole conditions or even as the chief conditions that determine this question. There are certain races — the Irish are honorably conspicuous among them — which, no matter what the economic pressure, furnish relatively few inmates of houses of ill fame. I do not believe that the differences are due to permanent race characteristics; this is shown by the fact that the best settlement houses find that practically all their "long-term graduates," so to speak, all the girls that come for a long period under their influence, no matter what their race or national origin, remain pure. In every race there are some naturally vicious individuals and some weak individuals who readily succumb under economic pressure. A girl who is lazy and hates hard work, a girl whose mind is rather feeble, who is of "subnormal intelligence," as the phrase now goes, or a girl who craves cheap finery and vapid pleasure, is always in danger. A high ideal of personal purity is essential. Where the same pressure under the same economic conditions has tenfold the effect on one set of people that it has on another, it is evident that the question of moral standards is even more important than the question of economic standards, very important though this question is. It is important for us to remember that the girl ought to have the chance, not only for the necessaries of life, but for innocent pleasure; and that even more than the man she must not be broken by overwork, by excessive toil. Moreover, public opinion and the law should combine to hunt down the "flagrant man swine" who himself hunts down poor or silly or unprotected girls. But we must not, in foolish sentimentality, excuse the girl from her duty to keep herself pure. Our duty to achieve the same moral level for the two sexes must be performed by raising the level for the man, not by lowering it for the woman; and the fact that society must recognize its duty in no shape or way relieves, not even to the smallest degree, the individual from doing his or her duty. Sentimentality which grows maudlin on behalf of the willful prostitute is a curse; to confound her with the entrapped or coerced girl, the real white slave, is both foolish and wicked. There are evil women just as there are evil men, naturally depraved girls just as there are naturally depraved young men; and the right and wise thing, the just thing, to them, and the generous thing to innocent girls and decent men, is to wage stern war against the evil creatures of both sexes.

In company with Jacob Riis, I did much work that was not connected with the actual discipline of the force or indeed with the actual work of the force. There was one thing which he and I abolished — police lodging-houses, which were simply tramp lodging-houses, and a fruitful encouragement to vagrancy. Those who read Mr. Riis's story of his own life will remember the incidents that gave him from actual personal experience his horror of these tramp lodging-houses. As member of the Health Board I was brought into very close relations with the conditions of life in the tenement-house districts.

Here again I used to visit the different tenement-house regions, usually in company with Riis, to see for myself what the conditions were. It was largely this personal experience that enabled me while on the Health Board to struggle not only zealously, but with reasonable efficiency and success, to improve conditions. We did our share in making forward strides in the matter of housing the working people of the city with some regard to decency and comfort.

The midnight trips that Riis and I took enabled me to see what the Police Department was doing, and also gave me

Theodore Roosevelt and the Children of the Tenement.

personal insight into some of the problems of city life. It is one thing to listen in perfunctory fashion to tales of overcrowded tenements, and it is quite another actually to see what that overcrowding means, some hot summer night, by even a single inspection during the hours of darkness. There was a very hot spell one midsummer while I was Police Commissioner, and most of each night I spent walking through the tenement-house districts and visiting police stations to see what was being done. It was a tragic week. We did everything possible to alleviate the suffering. Much of it was heartbreaking, especially the gasping misery of the little children and of the worn-out mothers. Every resource of the Health Department, of the Police Department, and even the Fire Department (which flooded the hot streets) was taxed in the effort to render service. The heat killed such multitudes of horses that the means at our disposal for removing the poor dead beasts proved quite inadequate, although every nerve was strained to the limit. In consequence we received scores of complaints from persons before whose doors dead horses had remained, festering in the heat, for two or three days. One irascible man sent us furious denunciations, until we were at last able to send a big dray to drag away the horse that lay dead before his shop door. The huge dray already contained eleven other dead horses, and when it reached this particular door it broke down, and it was hours before it could be moved. The unfortunate man who had thus been cursed with a granted wish closed his doors in despair and wrote us a final pathetic letter in which he requested us to remove either the horses or his shop, he didn't care which.

I have spoken before of my experience with the tenement-house cigar factory law which the highest court of New York State declared unconstitutional. My experience in the Police Department taught me that not a few of the worst tenement-houses were owned by wealthy individuals, who hired the best and most expensive lawyers to persuade the courts that it was "unconstitutional" to insist on the betterment of conditions. These business men and lawyers were very adroit in using a word with fine and noble associations to cloak their opposition to vitally necessary movements for industrial fair play and decency. They made it evident that they valued the Constitution, not as a help to righteousness, but as a means for thwarting movements against unrighteousness. After my experience with them I became more set than ever in my distrust of those men, whether business men or lawyers, judges, legislators, or executive officers, who seek to make of the Constitution a fetich for the prevention of the work of social reform, for the prevention of work in the interest of those men, women, and children on whose behalf we should be at liberty to employ freely every governmental agency.

Occasionally during the two years we had to put a stop to

riotous violence, and now and then on these occasions some
of the labor union leaders protested against the actions of the
police. By this time I was becoming a strong believer in labor
unions, a strong believer in the rights of labor. For that very
reason I was all the more bound to see that lawlessness and
disorder were put down, and that no rioter was permitted to
masquerade under the guise of being a friend of labor or a
sympathizer with labor. I was scrupulous to see that the labor
men had fair play; that, for instance, they were allowed to
picket just so far as under the law picketing could be permitted, so that the strikers had ample opportunity peacefully to
persuade other labor men not to take their places. But I made
it clearly and definitely understood that under no circumstances would I permit violence or fail to insist upon the keeping of order. If there were wrongs, I would join with a full
heart in striving to have them corrected. But where there was
violence all other questions had to drop until order was restored. This is a democracy, and the people have the power,
if they choose to exercise it, to make conditions as they ought
to be made, and to do this strictly within the law; and therefore the first duty of the true democrat, of the man really loyal
to the principles of popular government, is to see that law is
enforced and order upheld. It was a peculiar gratification to
me that so many of the labor leaders with whom I was thrown
in contact grew cordially to accept this view. When I left the
Department, several called upon me to say how sorry they
were that I was not to continue in office. One, the Secretary
of the Journeyman Bakers' and Confectioners' International
Union, Henry Weismann, wrote me expressing his regret that
I was going, and his appreciation as a citizen of what I had
done as Police Commissioner; he added: "I am particularly
grateful for your liberal attitude toward organized labor, your
cordial championship of those speaking in behalf of the toil-
ers, and your evident desire to do the right thing as you saw
it at whatever cost."

Some of the letters I received on leaving the Department
were from unexpected sources. Mr. E. L. Godkin, an editor
who in international matters was not a patriotic man, wrote
protesting against my taking the Assistant-Secretaryship of
the Navy, and adding: "I have a concern, as the Quakers say,

to put on record my earnest belief that in New York you are doing the greatest work of which any American to-day is capable, and exhibiting to the young men of the country the spectacle of a very important office administered by a man of high character in the most efficient way amid a thousand difficulties. As a lesson in politics I cannot think of anything more instructive."

About the same time I had a letter from Mr. (afterwards Ambassador) James Bryce, also expressing regret that I was leaving the Police Department, but naturally with much more appreciation of the work that was to be done in the Navy Department. This letter I quote, with his permission, because it conveys a lesson to those who are inclined always to think that the conditions of the present time are very bad. It was written July 7, 1897. Mr. Bryce spoke of the possibility of coming to America in a month or so, and continued: "I hope I may have a chance of seeing you if I do get over, and of drawing some comfort from you as regards your political phenomena, which, so far as I can gather from those of your countrymen I have lately seen, furnish some good opportunities for a persistent optimist like myself to show that he is not to be lightly discouraged. Don't suppose that things are specially 'nice,' as a lady would say, in Europe either. They are not." Mr. Bryce was a very friendly and extraordinarily competent observer of things American; and there was this distinct note of discouragement about our future in the intimate letter he was thus sending. Yet this was at the very time when the United States was entering on a dozen years during which our people accomplished more good, and came nearer realizing the possibilities of a great, free, and conscientious democracy, than during any other dozen years in our history, save only the years of Lincoln's Presidency and the period during which the Nation was founded.

# Chapter VII

## THE WAR OF AMERICA THE UNREADY

I SUPPOSE the United States will always be unready for war, and in consequence will always be exposed to great expense, and to the possibility of the gravest calamity, when the Nation goes to war. This is no new thing. Americans learn only from catastrophes and not from experience.

There would have been no war in 1812 if, in the previous decade, America, instead of announcing that "peace was her passion," instead of acting on the theory that unpreparedness averts war, had been willing to go to the expense of providing a fleet of a score of ships of the line. However, in that case, doubtless the very men who in the actual event deplored the loss of life and waste of capital which their own supineness had brought about would have loudly inveighed against the "excessive and improper cost of armaments"; so it all came to about the same thing in the end.

There is no more thoroughgoing international Mrs. Gummidge, and no more utterly useless and often utterly mischievous citizen, than the peace-at-any-price, universal-arbitration type of being, who is always complaining either about war or else about the cost of the armaments which act as the insurance against war. There is every reason why we should try to limit the cost of armaments, as these tend to grow excessive, but there is also every reason to remember that in the present stage of civilization a proper armament is the surest guarantee of peace — and is the only guarantee that war, if it does come, will not mean irreparable and overwhelming disaster.

In the spring of 1897 President McKinley appointed me Assistant Secretary of

A Spanish Cannon on the Lawn at Sagamore.

the Navy. I owed the appointment chiefly to the efforts of Senator H. C. Lodge of Massachusetts, who doubtless was actuated mainly by his long and close friendship for me, but also — I like to believe — by his keen interest in the navy. The first book I had ever published, fifteen years previously, was "The History of the Naval War of 1812"; and I have always taken the interest in the navy which every good American ought to take. At the time I wrote the book, in the early eighties, the navy had reached its nadir, and we were then utterly incompetent to fight Spain or any other power that had a navy at all. Shortly afterwards we began timidly and hesitatingly to build up a fleet. It is amusing to recall the roundabout steps we took to accomplish our purpose. In the reaction after the colossal struggle of the Civil War our strongest and most capable men had thrown their whole energy into business, into money-making, into the development, and above all the exploitation and exhaustion at the most rapid rate possible, of our natural resources — mines, forests, soil, and rivers. These men were not weak men, but they permitted themselves to grow shortsighted and selfish; and while many of them down at the bottom possessed the fundamental virtues, including the fighting virtues, others were purely of the glorified huckster or glorified pawnbroker type — which when developed to the exclusion of everything else makes about as poor a national type as the world has seen. This unadulterated huckster or pawnbroker type is rarely keenly sympathetic in matters of social and industrial justice, and is usually physically timid and likes to cover an unworthy fear of the most just war under high-sounding names.

It was reënforced by the large mollycoddle vote — the people who are soft physically and morally, or who have a twist in them which makes them acidly cantankerous and unpleasant as long as they can be so with safety to their bodies. In addition there are the good people with no imagination and no foresight, who think war will not come, but that if it does come armies and navies can be improvised — a very large element, typified by a Senator I knew personally who, in a public speech, in answer to a question as to what we would do if America were suddenly assailed by a first-class military power, answered that "we would build a battle-ship in every creek." Then, among the wise and high-minded people who in self-respecting and genuine fashion strive earnestly for peace, there are the foolish fanatics always to be found in such a movement and always discrediting it — the men who form the lunatic fringe in all reform movements.

All these elements taken together made a body of public opinion so important during the decades immediately succeeding the Civil War as to put a stop to any serious effort to keep the Nation in a condition of reasonable military preparedness. The representatives of this opinion then voted just as they now do when they vote against battle-ships or against fortifying the Panama Canal. It would have been bad enough if we had been content to be weak, and, in view of our weakness, not to bluster. But we were not content with such a policy. We wished to enjoy the incompatible luxuries of an unbridled tongue and an unready hand. There was a very large element which was ignorant of our military weakness, or, naturally enough, unable to understand it; and another large element which liked to please its own vanity by listening to offensive talk about foreign nations. Accordingly, too many of our politicians, especially in Congress, found that the cheap and easy thing to do was to please the foolish peace people by keeping us weak, and to please the foolish violent people by passing denunciatory resolutions about international matters — resolutions which would have been improper even if we had been strong. Their idea was to please both the mollycoddle vote and the vote of the international tail-twisters by upholding, with pretended ardor and mean intelligence, a National policy of peace with insult.

I abhor unjust war. I abhor injustice and bullying by the strong at the expense of the weak, whether among nations or individuals. I abhor violence and bloodshed. I believe that war should never be resorted to when, or so long as, it is honorably possible to avoid it. I respect all men and women who from high motives and with sanity and self-respect do all they can to avert war. I advocate preparation for war in order to avert war; and I should never advocate war unless it were the only alternative to dishonor. I describe the folly of which so many of our people were formerly guilty, in order that we may in our own day be on our guard against similar folly.

We did not at the time of which I write take our foreign duties seriously, and as we combined bluster in speech with refusal to make any preparation whatsoever for action, we were not taken seriously in return. Gradually a slight change for the better occurred, the writings of Captain Mahan playing no small part therein. We built some modern cruisers to start with; the people who felt that battle-ships were wicked compromising with their misguided consciences by saying that the cruisers could be used "to protect our commerce" — which they could not be, unless they had battle-ships to back them. Then we attempted to build more powerful fighting vessels, and as there was a section of the public which regarded battle-ships as possessing a name immorally suggestive of violence, we compromised by calling the new ships armored cruisers, and making them combine with exquisite nicety all the defects and none of the virtues of both types. Then we got to the point of building battle-ships. But there still remained a public opinion, as old as the time of Jefferson, which thought that in the event of war all our problem ought to be one of coast defense, that we should do nothing except repel attack; an attitude about as sensible as that of a prize-fighter who expected to win by merely parrying instead of hitting. To meet the susceptibilities of this large class of well-meaning people, we provided for the battle-ships under the name of "coast defense battle-ships"; meaning thereby that we did not make them quite as seaworthy as they ought to have been, or with quite as much coal capacity as they ought to have had. Then we decided to build real battle-ships. But there still remained a lingering remnant of public opinion that clung to the coast defense theory, and we met this in beautiful fashion by providing for "sea-going coast defense battle-ships" — the fact that the name was a contradiction in terms being of very small consequence compared to the fact that we did thereby get real battle-ships.

Our men had to be trained to handle the ships singly and in fleet formation, and they had to be trained to use the new weapons of precision with which the ships were armed. Not a few of the older officers, kept in the service under our foolish rule of pure seniority promotion, were not competent for the task; but a proportion of the older officers were excellent, and this was true of almost all the younger officers. They were naturally first-class men, trained in the admirable naval school at Annapolis. They were overjoyed that at last they were given proper instruments to work with, and they speedily grew to handle these ships individually in the best fashion. They were fast learning to handle them in squadron and fleet formation; but when the war with Spain broke out, they had as yet hardly grasped the principles of modern scientific naval gunnery.

Soon after I began work as Assistant Secretary of the Navy I became convinced that the war would come. The revolt in Cuba had dragged its weary length until conditions in the island had become so dreadful as to be a standing disgrace to us for permitting them to exist. There is much that I sincerely admire about the Spanish character; and there are few men for whom I have felt greater respect than for certain gentlemen of Spain whom I have known. But Spain attempted to govern her colonies on archaic principles which rendered her control of them incompatible with the advance of humanity and intolerable to the conscience of mankind. In 1898 the so-called war in Cuba had dragged along for years with unspeakable horror, degradation, and misery. It was not "war" at all, but murderous oppression. Cuba was devastated.

During those years, while we continued at "peace," several hundred times as many lives were lost, lives of men, women, and children, as were lost during the three months' "war" which put an end to this slaughter and opened a career of peaceful progress to the Cubans. Yet there were misguided professional philanthropists who cared so much more for names than for facts that they preferred a "peace" of continuous murder to a "war" which stopped the murder and brought real peace. Spain's humiliation was certain, anyhow; indeed, it was more certain without war than with it, for she could not permanently keep the island, and she minded yielding to the Cubans more than yielding to us. Our own direct interests were great, because of the Cuban tobacco and sugar, and especially because of Cuba's relation to the projected Isthmian canal. But even greater were our interests from the standpoint of humanity. Cuba was at our very doors. It was a dreadful thing for us to sit supinely and watch her death agony. It was our duty, even more from the standpoint of National honor than from the standpoint of National interest, to stop the devastation and destruction. Because of these considerations I favored war; and to-day, when in retrospect it is easier to see things clearly, there are few humane and honorable men who do not believe that the war was both just and necessary.

The big financiers and the men generally who were susceptible to touch on the money nerve, and who cared nothing for National honor if it conflicted even temporarily with business prosperity, were against the war. The more fatuous type of philanthropist agreed with them. The newspapers controlled by, or run in the interests of, these two classes deprecated war, and did everything in their power to prevent any preparation for war. As a whole the people in Congress were at that time (and are now) a shortsighted set as regards international matters. There were a few men, Senators Cushman K. Davis,* for instance, and John Morgan, who did look ahead; and Senator H. C. Lodge, who throughout his quarter of a century of service in the Senate and House has ever stood foremost among those who uphold with farsighted fearlessness and strict justice to others our national honor and interest; but most of the Congressmen were content to follow the worst of all possible courses, that is, to pass resolutions which made war more

---

*In a letter written me just before I became Assistant Secretary, Senator Davis unburdened his mind about one of the foolish "peace" proposals of that period; his letter running in part: "I left the Senate Chamber about three o'clock this afternoon when there was going on a deal of mowing and chattering over the treaty by which the United States is to be bound to arbitrate its sovereign functions — for policies are matters of sovereignty. . . . The aberrations of the social movement are neither progress nor retrogression. They represent merely a local and temporary sagging of the line of the great orbit. Tennyson knew this when he wrote that fine and noble 'Maud.' I often read it, for to do so does me good." After quoting one of Poe's stories the letter continues: "The world will come out all right. Let him who believes in the decline of the military spirit observe the boys of a common school during the recess or the noon hour. Of course when American patriotism speaks out from its rank and file and demands action or expression, and when, thereupon, the 'business man,' so called, places his hand on his stack of reds as if he feared a policeman were about to disturb the game, and protests until American patriotism ceases to continue to speak as it had started to do — why, you and I get mad, and I swear. I hope you will be with us here after March 4. We can then pass judgment together on the things we don't like, and together indulge in hopes that I believe are prophetic."

Mr. Roosevelt at his Desk when Assistant Secretary of the Navy.

likely, and yet to decline to take measures which would enable us to meet the war if it did come.

However, in the Navy Department we were able to do a good deal, thanks to the energy and ability of some of the bureau chiefs, and to the general good tone of the service. I soon found my natural friends and allies in such men as Evans, Taylor, Sampson, Wainwright, Brownson, Schroeder, Bradford, Cowles, Cameron Winslow, O'Neil, and others like them. I used all the power there was in my office to aid these men in getting the material ready. I also tried to gather from every source information as to who the best men were to occupy the fighting positions.

Sound naval opinion was overwhelmingly in favor of Dewey to command one squadron. I was already watching him, for I had been struck by an incident in his past career. It was at a time when there was threat of trouble with Chile. Dewey was off the Argentine, and was told to get ready to move to the other coast of South America. If the move became necessary, he would have to have coal, and yet if he did not make the move, the coal would not be needed. In such a case a man afraid of responsibility always acts rigidly by the regulations and communicates with the Department at home to get authority for everything he does; and therefore he usually accomplishes nothing whatever, but is able to satisfy all individuals with red-tape minds by triumphantly pointing out his compliance with the regulations. In a crisis, the man worth his salt is the man who meets the needs of the situation in whatever way is necessary. Dewey purchased the coal and was ready to move at once if need arose. The affair blew over; the need to move did not occur; and for some time there seemed to be a chance that Dewey would get into trouble over having purchased the coal, for our people are like almost all other peoples in requiring responsible officers under such conditions to decide at their own personal peril, no matter which course they follow. However, the people higher up ultimately stood by Dewey.

The incident made me feel that here was a man who could be relied upon to prepare in advance, and to act promptly, fearlessly, and on his own responsibility when the emergency arose. Accordingly I did my best to get him put in command of the Asiatic fleet, the fleet where it was most essential to have a man who would act without referring things back to the home authorities. An officer senior to him, of the respectable commonplace type, was being pushed by certain politicians who I knew had influence with the Navy Department and with the President. I would have preferred to see Dewey get the appointment without appealing to any politician at all. But while this was my preference, the essential thing was to get him the appointment. For a naval officer to bring pressure to get himself a soft and easy place is unpardonable; but a large leniency should be observed toward the man who uses influence only to get himself a place in the picture near the flashing of the guns. There was a Senator, Proctor of Vermont, who I knew was close to McKinley, and who was very ardent for the war, and desirous to have it fought in the most efficient fashion. I suggested to Dewey that he should enlist the services of Senator Proctor, which was accordingly done. In a fortunate hour for the Nation, Dewey was given command of the Asiatic squadron.

When the Maine was blown up in Havana Harbor, war became inevitable. A number of the peace-at-any-price men of course promptly assumed the position that she had blown herself up; but investigation showed that the explosion was from outside. And, in any event, it would have been impossible to prevent war. The enlisted men of the navy, who often grew bored to the point of desertion in peace, became keyed up to a high pitch of efficiency, and crowds of fine young fellows, from the interior as well as from the seacoast, thronged to enlist. The navy officers showed alert ability and unwearied industry in getting things ready. There was one deficiency, however, which there was no time to remedy, and of the very existence of which, strange to say, most of our best men were ignorant. Our navy had no idea how low our standard of marksmanship was. We had not realized that the modern battle-ship had become such a complicated piece of mechanism that the old methods of training in marksmanship were as obsolete as the old muzzle-loading broadside guns themselves. Almost the only man in the navy who fully realized this was our naval attaché at Paris, Lieutenant Sims. He wrote letter after letter pointing out how frightfully backward we were in marksmanship. I was much impressed by his letters; but Wainwright was about the only other man who was. And as Sims proved to be mistaken in his belief that the French had taught the Spaniards how to shoot, and as the Spaniards proved to be much worse even than we were, in the service generally Sims was treated as an alarmist. But although I at first partly acquiesced in this view, I grew uneasy when I studied the small proportion of hits to shots made by our vessels in battle. When I was President I took up the matter, and speedily became convinced that we needed to revolutionize our whole training in marksmanship. Sims was given the lead in organizing and introducing the new system; and to him more than to any other one man was due the astonishing progress made by our fleet in this respect, a progress which made the fleet, gun for gun, at least three times as effective, in point of fighting efficiency, in 1908, as it was in 1902. The shots that hit are the shots that count!

Like the people, the Government was for a long time unwilling to prepare for war, because so many honest but misguided men believed that the preparation itself tended to bring on the war. I did not in the least share this feeling, and whenever I was left as Acting Secretary I did everything in my power to put us in readiness. I knew that in the event of war Dewey could be slipped like a wolf-hound from a leash; I was sure that if he were given half a chance he would strike instantly and with telling effect; and I made up my mind that all I could do to give him that half-chance should be done. I was in the closest touch with Senator Lodge throughout this period, and either consulted him about or notified him of all the moves I was taking. By the end of February I felt it was vital to send Dewey (as well as each of our other commanders who were not in home waters) instructions that would enable him to be in readiness for immediate action. On the afternoon of Saturday, February 25, when I was Acting Secretary, Lodge called on me just as I was preparing the order, which (as it was addressed to a man of the right stamp) was of much importance to the subsequent operations. Admiral Dewey speaks of the incident as follows, in his autobiography:

"The first real step [as regards active naval preparations] was taken on February 25, when telegraphic instructions were sent to the Asiatic, European, and South Atlantic squadrons to rendezvous at certain convenient points where, should war break out, they would be most available.

"The message to the Asiatic squadron bore the signature of that Assistant Secretary who had seized the opportunity while Acting Secretary to hasten preparations for a conflict which was inevitable. As Mr. Roosevelt reasoned, precautions for readiness would cost little in time of peace, and yet would be invaluable in case of war. His cablegram was as follows:

"'Washington, February 25, '98.

" '*Dewey, Hong Kong:*

" 'Order the squadron, except the Monocacy, to Hong Kong. Keep full of coal. In the event of declaration of war Spain, your duty will be to see that the Spanish squadron does not leave the Asiatic coast, and then offensive operations in Philippine Islands. Keep Olympia until further orders.

ROOSEVELT.'

"(The reference to keeping the Olympia until further orders was due to the fact that I had been notified that she would soon be recalled to the United States.)"

All that was needed with Dewey was to give him the chance to get ready, and then to strike, without being hampered by orders from those not on the ground. Success in war depends very largely upon choosing a man fit to exercise such powers, and then giving him the powers.

It would be instructive to remember, if only we were willing to do so, the fairly comic panic which swept in waves over our seacoast, first when it became evident that war was about to be declared, and then when it was declared. The public waked up to the sufficiently obvious fact that the Government was in its usual state — perennial unreadiness for war. Thereupon the people of the seaboard district passed at one bound from unreasoning confidence that war never could come to unreasoning fear as to what might happen now that it had come. That acute philosopher Mr. Dooley proclaimed that in the Spanish War we were in a dream, but that the Spaniards were in a trance. This just about summed up the facts. Our people had for decades scoffed at the thought of making ready for possible war. Now, when it was too late, they not only backed every measure, wise and unwise, that offered a chance of supplying a need that ought to have been met before, but they also fell into a condition of panic apprehension as to what the foe might do.

For years we had been saying, just as any number of our people now say, that no nation would venture to attack us. Then when we did go to war with an exceedingly feeble nation, we, for the time being, rushed to the other extreme of feeling, and attributed to this feeble nation plans of offensive warfare which it never dreamed of making, and which, if made, it would have been wholly unable to execute. Some of my readers doubtless remember the sinister intentions and unlimited potentialities for destruction with which the fertile imagination of the yellow press endowed the armored cruiser Viscaya when she appeared in American waters just before war was declared. The state of nervousness along much of the sea-coast was funny in view of the lack of foundation for it; but it offered food for serious thought as to what would happen if we ever became engaged with a serious foe.

The Governor of one State actually announced that he would not permit the National Guard of that State to leave its borders, the idea being to retain it against a possible Spanish invasion. So many of the business men of the city of Boston took their securities inland to Worcester that the safe deposit companies of Worcester proved unable to take care of them. In my own neighborhood on Long Island clauses were gravely put into leases to the effect that if the property were destroyed by the Spaniards the lease should lapse. As Assistant Secretary of the Navy I had every conceivable impossible request made to me. Members of Congress who had actively opposed build-ing any navy came clamorously around to ask each for a ship for some special purpose of protection connected with his dis-trict. It seems incredible, but it is true, that not only these Congressmen but the Chambers of Commerce and Boards of Trade of different coast cities all lost their heads for the time being, and raised a deafening clamor and brought every species of pressure to bear on the Administration to get it to adopt the one most fatal course — that is, to distribute the navy, ship by ship, at all kinds of points and in all kinds of ports with the idea of protecting everything everywhere, and thereby rendering it absolutely certain that even the Spanish fleet, poor though it was, would be able to pick up our own navy ship by ship in detail. One Congressman besought me for a ship to protect Jekyll Island, off the coast of Georgia, an island which derived its sole consequence because it contained the winter homes of certain millionaires. A lady whose husband occupied a very influential position, and who was normally a most admirable and sensible woman, came to insist that a ship should be anchored off a huge seaside hotel because she had a house in the neighborhood.

There were many such instances. One stood out above the others. A certain seaboard State contained in its Congressional delegation one of the most influential men in the Senate, and one of the most influential men in the lower house. These two men had been worse than lukewarm about building up the navy, and had scoffed at the idea of there ever being any danger from any foreign power. With the advent of war the feelings of their constituents, and therefore their own feelings, suffered an immediate change, and they demanded that a ship be anchored in the harbor of their city as a protection. Getting no comfort from me, they went "higher up," and became a kind of permanent committee in attendance upon the President. They were very influential men in the Houses, with whom it was important for the Administration to keep on good terms; and, moreover, they possessed a pertinacity as great as the widow who won her case from the unjust judge. Finally the President gave in and notified me to see that a ship was sent to the city in question. I was bound that, as long as a ship had to be sent, it should not be a ship worth anything. Accordingly a Civil War Monitor, with one smoothbore gun, manned by a crew of about twenty-one naval militia, was sent to the city in question, under convoy of a tug. It was a hazardous trip for the unfortunate naval militiamen, but it was safely accomplished; and joy and peace descended upon the Senator and the Congressman, and upon the President whom they had jointly harassed. Incidentally, the fact that the protecting war-vessel would not have been a formidable foe to any antagonists of much more modern construction than the galleys of Alcibiades seemed to disturb nobody.

This was one side of the picture. The other side was that the crisis at once brought to the front any amount of latent fighting strength. There were plenty of Congressmen who showed cool-headed wisdom and resolution. The plain people, the men and women back of the persons who lost their heads, set seriously to work to see that we did whatever was necessary, and made the job a thorough one. The young men swarmed to enlist. In time of peace it had been difficult to fill the scanty regular army and navy, and there were innumerable desertions; now the ships and regiments were over-enlisted, and so many deserters returned in order to fight that it became difficult to decide what to do with them. England, and to a less degree Japan, were friendly. The great powers of Continental Europe were all unfriendly. They jeered at our ships and men, and with fatuous partisanship insisted that the Spaniards would prove too much for our "mercenaries" because we were a commercial people of low ideals who could not fight, while the men whom we attempted to hire for that purpose were certain to run on the day of battle.

Among my friends was the then Army Surgeon Leonard Wood. He was a surgeon. Not having an income, he had to earn his own living. He had gone through the Harvard Medical School, and had then joined the army in the Southwest as a contract doctor. He had every physical, moral, and mental quality which fitted him for a soldier's life and for the exercise of command. In the inconceivably wearing and harassing campaigns against the Apaches he had served nominally as a surgeon, really in command of troops, on more than one expedition. He was as anxious as I was that if there were war we should both have our part in it. I had always felt that if there were a serious war I wished to be in a position to explain to my children why I did take part in it, and not why I did not take part in it. Moreover, I had very deeply felt that it was our duty to free Cuba, and I had publicly expressed this feeling; and when a man takes such a position, he ought to be willing to make his words good by his deeds unless there is some very strong reason to the contrary. He should pay with his body.

As soon as war was upon us, Wood and I began to try for a chance to go to the front. Congress had authorized the raising of three National Volunteer Cavalry regiments, wholly apart from the State contingents. Secretary Alger of the War Department was fond of me personally, and Wood was his family doctor. Alger had been a gallant soldier in the Civil War, and was almost the only member of the Administration who felt all along that we would have to go to war with Spain over Cuba. He liked my attitude in the matter, and because of his remembrance of his own experiences he sympathized with my desire to go to the front. Accordingly he offered me the command of one of the regiments. I told him that after six weeks' service in the field I would feel competent to handle the regiment, but that I would not know how to equip it or how to get it into the first action; but that Wood was entirely competent at once to take command, and that if he would make Wood colonel I would accept the lieutenant-colonelcy. General Alger thought this an act of foolish self-abnegation on my part — instead of its being, what it was, the wisest act I could have performed. He told me to accept the colonelcy, and that he would make Wood lieutenant-colonel, and that Wood would do the work anyway; but I answered that I did not wish to rise on any man's shoulders; that I hoped to be given every chance that my deeds and abilities warranted; but that I did not wish what I did not earn, and that above all I did not wish to hold any position where any one else did the work. He laughed at me a little and said I was foolish, but I do not think he really minded, and he promised to do as I wished. True to his word, he secured the appointment of Wood as colonel and of myself as lieutenant-colonel of the First United States Volunteer Cavalry. This was soon nicknamed, both by the public and by the rest of the army, the Rough Riders, doubtless because the bulk of the men were from the Southwestern ranch country and were skilled in the wild horsemanship of the great plains.

Wood instantly began the work of raising the regiment. He first assembled several old non-commissioned officers of experience, put them in office, and gave them blanks for requisitions for the full equipment of a cavalry regiment. He selected San Antonio as the gathering-place, as it was in a good horse country, near the Gulf from some port on which we would have to embark, and near an old arsenal and an old

The Colonel of the Rough Riders.

army post from which we got a good deal of stuff — some of it practically condemned, but which we found serviceable at a pinch, and much better than nothing. He organized a horse board in Texas, and began purchasing all horses that were not too big and were sound. A day or two after he commissioned he wrote out in the office of the Secretary of War, under his authority, telegrams to the Governors of Arizona, New Mexico, Oklahoma, and Indian Territory, in substance as follows:

The President desires to raise —— volunteers in your Territory to form part of a regiment of mounted riflemen to be commanded by Leonard Wood, Colonel; Theodore Roosevelt, Lieutenant-Colonel. He desires that the men selected should be young, sound, good shots and good riders, and that you expedite by all means in your power the enrollment of these men.

(Signed) R. A. ALGER, Secretary of War.

As soon as he had attended to a few more odds and ends he left Washington, and the day after his arrival in San Antonio the troops began to arrive.

For several weeks before I joined the regiment, to which Wood went ahead of me, I continued as Assistant Secretary of the Navy, trying to get some coherence of plan between the War Department and the Navy Department; and also being used by Wood to finish getting the equipment for the regiment. As regards finding out what the plans of the War Department were, the task was simple. They had no plans. Even during the final months before the outbreak of hostilities very little was done in the way of efficient preparation. On one occasion, when every one knew that the declaration of war was sure to come in a few days, I went on military business to the office of one of the highest line generals of the army, a man who at that moment ought to have been working eighteen hours out of the twenty-four on the vital problems ahead of him. What he was actually doing was trying on a new type of smart-looking uniform on certain enlisted men; and he called me in to ask my advice as to the position of the pockets in the blouse, with a view to making it look attractive. An aide of this general — funnily enough a good fighting man in actual service — when I consulted him as to what my uniform for the campaign should be, laid special stress upon my purchasing a pair of black top boots for full dress, explaining that they were very effective on hotel piazzas and in parlors. I did not intend to be in any hotel if it could possibly be avoided; and as things turned out, I had no full-dress uniform, nothing but my service uniform, during my brief experience in the army.

I suppose that war always does bring out what is highest and lowest in human nature. The contractors who furnish poor materials to the army or the navy in time of war stand on a level of infamy only one degree above that of the participants in the white slave traffic themselves. But there is conduct far short of this which yet seems inexplicable to any man who has in him any spirit of disinterested patriotism combined with any power of imagination. Respectable men, who I suppose lack the imagination thoroughly to realize what they are doing, try to make money out of the Nation's necessities in war at the very time that other men are making every sacrifice, financial and personal, for the cause. In the closing weeks of my service as Assistant Secretary of the Navy we were collecting ships for auxiliary purposes. Some men, at cost to their own purses, helped us freely and with efficiency; others treated the affair as an ordinary business transaction; and yet others endeavored, at some given crisis when our need was great, to sell us inferior vessels at exorbitant prices, and used every pressure, through Senators and Congressmen, to accomplish their ends. In one or two cases they did accomplish them too, until we got a really first-class board established to superintend such purchases. A more curious experience was in connection with the point chosen for the starting for the expedition against Cuba. I had not supposed that any human being could consider this matter save from the standpoint of military need. But one morning a very wealthy and influential man, a respectable and upright man according to his own lights, called on me to protest against our choice of Tampa, and to put in a plea for a certain other port, *on the ground that his railroad was entitled to its share of the profit for hauling the army and equipment!* I happened to know that at this time this very man had kinsfolk with the army, who served gallantly, and the circumstances of his coming to me were such as to show that he was not acting secretly, and had no idea that there was anything out of the way in his proposal. I think the facts were merely that he had been trained to regard business as the sole object in life, and that he lacked the imagination to enable him to understand the real nature of the request that he was making; and, moreover, he had good reason to believe that one of his business competitors had been unduly favored.

The War Department was in far worse shape than the Navy Department. The young officers turned out from West Point are precisely as good as the young officers turned out from Annapolis, and this always has been true. But at that time (something has been done to remedy the worst conditions since), and ever since the close of the Civil War, the conditions were such that after a few years the army officer stagnated so far as his profession was concerned. When the Spanish War broke out the navy really was largely on a war footing, as any navy which is even respectably cared for in time of peace must be. The admirals, captains, and lieutenants were continually practicing their profession in almost precisely the way that it has to be practiced in time of war. Except actually shooting at a foe, most of the men on board ship went through in time of peace practically all that they would have to go through in time of war. The heads of bureaus in the Navy Department were for the most part men who had seen sea service, who expected to return to sea service, and who were preparing for needs which they themselves knew by experience. Moreover, the civilian head of the navy had to provide for keeping the ships in a state of reasonable efficiency, and Congress could not hopelessly misbehave itself about the navy without the fact at once becoming evident.

All this was changed so far as the army was concerned. Not only was it possible to decrease the efficiency of the army without being called to account for it, but the only way in which the Secretary of War could gain credit for himself or the Administration was by economy, and the easiest way to economize was in connection with something that would not be felt unless war should arise. The people took no interest whatever in the army; demagogues clamored against it, and, inadequate though it was in size, insisted that it should be still further reduced. Popular orators always appealed to the volunteers;

the regulars had no votes and there was no point in politicians thinking of them. The chief activity shown by Congressmen about the army was in getting special army posts built in places where there was no need for them. Even the work of the army in its campaigns against the Indians was of such a character that it was generally performed by small bodies of fifty or a hundred men. Until a man ceased being a lieutenant he usually had plenty of professional work to attend to and was employed in the field, and, in short, had the same kind of practice that his brother in the navy had, and he did his work as well. But once past this stage he had almost no opportunity to perform any work corresponding to his rank, and but little opportunity to do any military work whatsoever. The very best men, men like Lawton, Young, Chaffee, Hawkins, and Sumner, to mention only men under or beside whom I served, remained good soldiers, soldiers of the best stamp, in spite of the disheartening conditions. But it was not to be expected that the average man could continue to grow when every influence was against him. Accordingly, when the Spanish War suddenly burst upon us, a number of inert elderly captains and field officers were, much against their own wishes, suddenly pitchforked into the command of regiments, brigades, and even divisions and army corps. Often these men failed painfully. This was not their fault; it was the fault of the Nation, that is, the fault of all of us, of you, my reader, and of myself, and of those like us, because we had permitted conditions to be such as to render these men unfit for command. Take a stout captain of an out-of-the-way two-company post, where nothing in the world ever occurred even resembling military action, and where the only military problem that really convulsed the post to its foundations was the quarrel between the captain and the quartermaster as to how high a mule's tail ought to be shaved (I am speaking of an actual incident). What could be expected of such a man, even though thirty-five years before he had been a gallant second lieutenant in the Civil War, if, after this intervening do-nothing period, he was suddenly put in command of raw troops in a midsummer campaign in the tropics?

The bureau chiefs were for the most part elderly incompetents, whose idea was to do their routine duties in such way as to escape the censure of routine bureaucratic superiors and to avoid a Congressional investigation. They had not the slightest conception of preparing the army for war. It was impossible that they could have any such conception. The people and the Congress did not wish the army prepared for war; and those editors and philanthropists and peace advocates who felt vaguely that if the army were incompetent their principles were safe, always inveighed against any proposal to make it efficient, on the ground that this showed a natural bloodthirstiness in the proposer. When such were the conditions, it was absolutely impossible that either the War Department or the army could do well in the event of war. Secretary Alger happened to be Secretary when war broke out, and all the responsibility for the shortcomings of the Department were visited upon his devoted head. He was made the scapegoat for our National shortcomings. The fault was not his; the fault and responsibility lay with us, the people, who for thirty-three years had permitted our representatives in Congress and in National executive office to bear themselves so that it was absolutely impossible to avoid the great bulk of all the trouble that occurred, and of all the shortcomings of which our people complained, during the Spanish War. The chief immediate cause was the condition of red-tape bureaucracy which existed in the War Department at Washington, which had prevented any good organization or the preparation of any good plan of operation for using our men and supplies. The recurrence of these conditions, even though in somewhat less aggravated form, in any future emergency is as certain as sunrise unless we bring about the principle of a four years' detail in the staff corps — a principle which Congress has now for years stubbornly refused to grant.

There are nations who only need to have peaceful ideals inculcated, and to whom militarism is a curse and a misfortune. There are other nations, like our own, so happily situated that the thought of war is never present to their minds. They are wholly free from any tendency improperly to exalt or to practice militarism. These nations should never forget that there must be military ideals no less than peaceful ideals. The exaltation of Nogi's career, set forth so strikingly in Stanley Washburn's little volume on the great Japanese warrior, contains much that is especially needed for us of America, prone as we are to regard the exigencies of a purely commercial and industrial civilization as excusing us from the need of admiring and practicing the heroic and warlike virtues.

Our people are not military. We need normally only a small standing army; but there should be behind it a reserve of instructed men big enough to fill it up to full war strength, which is over twice the peace strength. Moreover, the young men of the country should realize that it is the duty of every one of them to prepare himself so that in time of need he may speedily become an efficient soldier — a duty now generally forgotten, but which should be recognized as one of the vitally essential parts of every man's training.

In endeavoring to get the "Rough Riders" equipped I met with some experiences which were both odd and instructive. There were not enough arms and other necessaries to go round, and there was keen rivalry among the intelligent and zealous commanders of the volunteer organizations as to who should get first choice. Wood's experience was what enabled us to equip ourselves in short order. There was another cavalry organization whose commander was at the War Department about this time, and we had been eyeing him with much alertness as a rival. One day I asked him what his plans were about arming and drilling his troops, who were of precisely the type of our own men. He answered that he expected "to give each of the boys two revolvers and a lariat, and then just turn them loose." I reported the conversation to Wood, with the remark that we might feel ourselves safe from rivalry in that quarter; and safe we were.

In trying to get the equipment I met with checks and rebuffs, and in return was the cause of worry and concern to various bureau chiefs who were unquestionably estimable men in their private and domestic relations, and who doubtless had been good officers thirty years before, but who were as unfit for modern war as if they were so many smoothbores. One fine old fellow did his best to persuade us to take black powder rifles, explaining with paternal indulgence that no one yet really knew just what smokeless powder might do, and that there was a good deal to be said in favor of having smoke to conceal us from the enemy. I saw this pleasing theory actually worked out in practice later on, for the National Guard regiments with us at Santiago had black powder muskets, and the regular artillery black powder guns, and they really might almost as well have replaced these weapons by crossbows and mangonels. We succeeded, thanks to Wood, in getting the same cavalry carbines that were used by the regulars. We were determined to do this, not only because the weapons were good, but because this would in all probability mean that we were brigaded with the regular cavalry, which it was certain would be sent immediately to the front for the fighting.

Colonel Theodore Roosevelt and a Group of Rough Riders.

There was one worthy bureau chief who was continually refusing applications of mine as irregular. In each case I would appeal to Secretary Alger — who helped me in every way — and get an order from him countenancing the irregularity. For instance, I found out that as we were nearer the July date than the January date for the issuance of clothing, and as it had long been customary to issue the winter clothing in July, so as to give ample leisure for getting it to all the various posts, it was therefore solemnly proposed to issue this same winter clothing to us who were about to start for a summer campaign in the tropics. This would seem incredible to those who have never dealt with an inert officialdom, a red-tape bureaucracy, but such is the fact. I rectified this and got an order for khaki clothing. We were then told we would have to advertise thirty days for horses. This meant that we would have missed the Santiago expedition. So I made another successful appeal to the Secretary. Other difficulties came up about wagons, and various articles, and in each case the same result followed. On the last occasion, when I came up in triumph with the needed order, the worried office head, who bore me no animosity, but who did feel that fate had been very unkind, threw himself back in his chair and exclaimed with a sigh: "Oh, dear! I had this office running in such good shape — and then along came the war and upset everything!" His feeling was that war was an illegitimate interruption to the work of the War Department.

There were of course department heads and bureau chiefs and assistants who, in spite of the worthlessness of the system, and of the paralyzing conditions that had prevailed, remained first-class men. An example of these was Commissary-General Weston. His energy, activity, administrative efficiency, and common sense were supplemented by an eager desire to help everybody do the best that could be done. Both in Washington and again down at Santiago we owed him very much. When I was President, it was my good fortune to repay him in part our debt, which means the debt of the people of the country, by making him a major-general.

The regiment assembled at San Antonio. When I reached there, the men, rifles, and horses, which were the essentials, were coming in fast, and the saddles, blankets, and the like were also accumulating. Thanks to Wood's exertions, when we reached Tampa we were rather better equipped than most of the regular regiments. We adhered strictly to field equipment, allowing no luxuries or anything else unnecessary, and so we were able to move off the field when ordered, with our own transportation, leaving nothing behind.

I suppose every man tends to brag about his regiment; but it does seem to me that there never was a regiment better worth bragging about than ours. Wood was an exceptional commander, of great power, with a remarkable gift for organization. The rank and file were as fine natural fighting men as ever carried a rifle or rode a horse in any country or any age. We had a number of first-class young fellows from the East, most of them from colleges like Harvard, Yale, and Princeton; but the great majority of the men were South-westerners, from the then territories of Oklahoma, Indian Territory, Arizona, and New Mexico. They were accustomed to the use of firearms, accustomed to taking care of themselves in the open; they were intelligent and self-reliant; they possessed hardihood and endurance and physical prowess; and, above all, they had the fighting edge, the cool and resolute fighting temper. They went into the war with full knowledge, having deliberately counted the cost. In the great majority of cases each man was chiefly anxious to find out what he should do to make the regiment a success. They bought, first and last, about 800 copies of the cavalry drill regulations and studied them industriously. Such men were practically soldiers to start with, in all the essentials. It is small wonder that with them as material to work upon the regiment was raised, armed, equipped, drilled, sent on trains to Tampa, embarked, disembarked, and put through two victorious offensive — not defensive — fights in which a third of the officers and one-fifth of the men were killed or wounded, all within sixty days. It is a good record, and it speaks well for the men of the regiment; and it speaks well for Wood.*

Wood was so busy getting the regiment ready that when I reached San Antonio he turned most of the drilling of it over

*To counterbalance the newspapers which ignorantly and indiscriminately praised all the volunteers there were others whose blame was of the same intelligent quality. The New York *Evening Post*, on June 18, gave expression to the following gloomy foreboding: "Competent observers have remarked that nothing more extraordinary has been done than the sending to Cuba of the First United States Volunteer Cavalry, known as the 'rough riders.' Organized but four weeks, barely given their full complement of officers, and only a week of regular drill, these men have been sent to the front before they have learned the first elements of soldiering and discipline, or have even become acquainted with their officers. In addition to all this, like the regular cavalry, they have been sent with only their carbines and revolvers to meet an enemy armed with long-range rifles. There have been few cases of such military cruelty in our military annals." A week or so after this not wholly happy prophecy was promulgated, the "cruelty" was consummated, first at Las Guasimas and then in the San Juan fighting.

to me. This was a piece of great good fortune for me, and I drilled the men industriously, mounted and unmounted. I had plenty to learn, and the men and the officers even more; but we went at our work with the heartiest good will. We speedily made it evident that there was no room and no mercy for any man who shirked any duty, and we accomplished good results. The fact is that the essentials of drill and work for a cavalry or an infantry regiment are easy to learn, which of course is not true for the artillery or the engineers or for the navy. The reason why it takes so long to turn the average civilized man into a good infantryman or cavalryman is because it takes a long while to teach the average untrained man how to shoot, to ride, to march, to take care of himself in the open, to be alert, resourceful, cool, daring, and resolute, to obey quickly, as well as to be willing, and to fit himself, to act on his own responsibility. If he already possesses these qualities, there is very little difficulty in making him a solider; all the drill that is necessary to enable him to march and to fight is of a simple character. Parade ground and barrack square maneuvers are of no earthly consequence in real war. When men can readily change from line to column, and column to line, can form front in any direction, and assemble and scatter, and can do these things with speed and precision, they have a fairly good grasp of the essentials. When our regiment reached Tampa it could already be handled creditably at fast gaits, and both in mass and extended formations, mounted and dismounted.

I had served three years in the New York National Guard, finally becoming a captain. This experience was invaluable to me. It enabled me at once to train the men in the simple drill without which they would have been a mob; for although the drill requirements are simple, they are also absolutely indispensable. But if I had believed that my experience in the National Guard had taught me all that there was to teach about a soldier's career, it would have been better for me not to have been in it at all. There were in the regiment a number of men who had served in the National Guard, and a number of others who had served in the Regular Army. Some of these latter had served in the field in the West under campaign conditions, and were accustomed to long marches, privation, risk, and unexpected emergencies. These men were of the utmost benefit to the regiment. They already knew their profession, and could teach and help the others. But if the man had merely served in a National Guard regiment, or in the Regular Army at some post in a civilized country where he learned nothing except what could be picked up on the parade ground, in the barracks, and in practice marches of a few miles along good roads, then it depended purely upon his own good sense whether he had been helped or hurt by the experience. If he realized that he had learned only five per cent of his profession, that there remained ninety-five per cent to accomplish before he would be a good soldier, why, he had profited immensely.

To start with five per cent handicap was a very great advantage; and if the man was really a good man, he could not be overtaken. But if the man thought that he had learned all about the profession of a soldier because he had been in the National Guard or in the Regular Army under the conditions I have described, then he was actually of less use than if he had never had any military experience at all. Such a man was apt to think that nicety of alignment, precision in wheeling, and correctness in the manual of arms were the ends of training and the guarantees of good soldiership, and that from guard mounting to sentry duty everything in war was to be done in accordance with what he had learned in peace. As a matter of fact, most of what he had learned was never used at all, and some of it had to be unlearned. The one thing, for instance, that a sentry ought never to do in an actual campaign is to walk up and down a line where he will be conspicuous. His business is to lie down somewhere off a ridge crest where he can see any one approaching, but where a man approaching cannot see him. As for the ceremonies, during the really hard part of a campaign only the barest essentials are kept.

Almost all of the junior regular officers, and many of the senior regular officers, were fine men. But, through no fault of their own, had been forced to lead lives that fairly paralyzed their efficiency when the strain of modern war came on them. The routine elderly regular officer who knew nothing whatever of modern war was in most respects nearly as worthless as a raw recruit. The positions and commands prescribed in the text-books were made into fetishes by some of these men, and treated as if they were the ends, instead of the not always important means by which the ends were to be achieved. In the Cuban fighting, for instance, it would have been folly for me to have taken my place in the rear of the regiment, the canonical text-book position. My business was to be where I could keep most command over the regiment, and, in a rough-and-tumble, scrambling fight in thick jungle, this had to depend upon the course of events, and usually meant that I had to be at the front. I saw in that fighting more than one elderly regimental commander who unwittingly rendered the only service he could render to his regiment by taking up his proper position several hundred yards in the rear when the fighting began; for then the regiment disappeared in the jungle, and for its good fortune the commanding officer never saw it again until long after the fight was over.

After one Cuban fight a lieutenant-colonel of the regulars, in command of a regiment, who had met with just such an experience and had rejoined us at the front several hours after the close of the fighting, asked me what my men were doing when the fight began. I answered that they were following in trace in column of twos, and that the instant the shooting began I deployed them as skirmishers on both sides of the trail. He answered triumphantly, "You can't deploy men as skirmishers from column formation"; to which I responded, "Well, I did, and, what is more, if any captain had made any difficulty about it, I would have sent him to the rear." My critic was quite correct from the parade ground standpoint. The prescribed orders at that time were to deploy the column first into a line of squads at correct intervals, and then to give an order which, if my memory serves correctly, ran: "As skirmishers, by the right and left flanks, at six yards, take intervals, march." The order I really gave ran more like this: "Scatter out to the right there, quick, you! scatter to the left! look alive, look alive!" And they looked alive, and they scattered, and each took advantage of cover, and forward went the line.

Now I do not wish what I have said to be misunderstood. If ever we have a great war, the bulk of our soldiers will not be men who have had any opportunity to train soul and mind and body so as to meet the iron needs of an actual campaign. Long continued and faithful drill will alone put these men in shape to begin to do their duty, and failure to recognize this on the part of the average man will mean laziness and folly and not the possession of efficiency. Moreover, if men have been trained to believe, for instance, that they can "arbitrate questions of vital interest and national honor," if they have been brought up with flabbiness of moral fiber as well as flabbiness of physique, then there will be need of long and laborious and faithful work to give the needed tone to mind and body. But if the men have in them the right stuff, it is not so very difficult.

At San Antonio we entrained for Tampa. In various sociological books by authors of Continental Europe, there are jeremiads as to the way in which service in the great European armies, with their minute and machine-like efficiency and regularity, tends to dwarf the capacity for individual initiative among the officers and men. There is no such danger for any officer or man of a volunteer organization in America when our country, with playful light-heartedness, has pranced into war without making any preparation for it. I know no larger or finer field for the display of an advanced individualism than that which opened before us as we went from San Antonio to Tampa, camped there, and embarked on a transport for Cuba. Nobody ever had any definite information to give us, and whatever information we unearthed on our own account was usually wrong. Each of us had to show an alert and not over-scrupulous self-reliance in order to obtain food for his men, provender for his horses, or transportation of any kind for any object. One lesson early impressed on me was that if I wanted anything to eat it was wise to carry it with me; and if any new war should arise, I would earnestly advise the men of every volunteer organization always to proceed upon the belief that their supplies will not turn up, and to take every opportunity of getting food for themselves.

Tampa was a scene of the wildest confusion. There were miles of tracks loaded with cars of the contents of which nobody seemed to have any definite knowledge. General Miles, who was supposed to have supervision over everything, and General Shafter, who had charge of the expedition, were both there. But, thanks to the fact that nobody had had any experience in handling even such a small force as ours — about

17,000 men — there was no semblance of order. Wood and I were bound that we should not be left behind when the expedition started. When we were finally informed that it was to leave next morning, we were ordered to go to a certain track to meet a train. We went to the track, but the train never came. Then we were sent to another track to meet another train. Again it never came. However, we found a coal train, of which we took possession, and the conductor, partly under duress and partly in a spirit of friendly helpfulness, took us down to the quay.

All kinds of other organizations, infantry and cavalry, regular and volunteer, were arriving at the quay and wandering around it, and there was no place where we could get any specific information as to what transport we were to have. Finally Wood was told to "get any ship you can get which is not already assigned." He borrowed without leave a small motor boat, and commandeered the transport Yucatan. When asked by the captain what his authority was, he reported that he was acting "by orders of General Shafter," and directed the ship to be brought to the dock. He had already sent me word to be ready, as soon as the ship touched the pier, to put the regiment aboard her. I found that she had already been assigned to a regular regiment, and to another volunteer regiment, and as it was evident that not more than half of the men assigned to her could possibly get on, I was determined that we should not be among the men left off. The volunteer regiment offered a comparatively easy problem. I simply marched my men past them to the allotted place and held the gangway. With the regulars I had to be a little more diplomatic, because their commander, a lieutenant-colonel, was my superior in rank, and also doubtless knew his rights. He sent word to me to make way, to draw my regiment off to one side, and let his take possession of the gangway. I could see the transport coming in, and could dimly make out Wood's figure thereon. Accordingly I played for time. I sent respectful requests through his officers to the commander of the regulars, entered into parleys, and made protestations, until the transport got near enough so that by yelling at the top of my vice I was able to get into a — highly constructive — communication with Wood. What he was saying I had no idea, but he was evidently speaking, and on my own responsibility I translated it into directions to hold the gangway, and so informed the regulars that I was under the orders of my superior and of a ranking officer, and — to my great regret, etc., etc. — could not give way as they desired. As soon as the transport was fast we put our men aboard at the double. Half of the regular regiment got on, and the other half and the other volunteer regiment went somewhere else.

We were kept several days on the transport, which was jammed with men, so that it was hard to move about on the deck. Then the fleet got under way, and we steamed slowly down to Santiago. Here we disembarked, higgledy-piggledy, just as we had embarked. Different parts of different outfits were jumbled together, and it was no light labor afterwards to assemble the various batteries. For instance, one transport had guns, and another the locks for the guns; the two not getting together for several days after one of them had been landed. Soldiers went here, provisions there; and who got ashore first largely depended upon individual activity. Fortunately for us, my former naval aide, when I had been Assistant Secretary of the Navy, Lieutenant-Commander Sharp, a first-class fellow, was there in command of a little ship to which I had succeeded in getting him appointed before I left the Navy Department. He gave us a black pilot, who took our transport right in shore, the others following like a flock of sheep; and we disembarked with our rifles, ammunition belts, and not much else. In theory it was out of our turn, but if we had not disembarked then, Heaven only knows when our turn would have come, and we did not intend to be out of the fighting if we could help it. I carried some food in my pockets, and a light waterproof coat, which was my sole camp equipment for the next two or three days. Twenty-four hours after getting ashore we marched from Daiquiri, where we had landed, to Siboney, also on the coast, reaching it during a terrific downpour of rain. When this was over, we built a fire, dried our clothes, and ate whatever we had brought with us.

We were brigaded with the First and Tenth Regular Cavalry, under Brigadier-General Sam Young. He was a fine type of the American regular. Like General Chaffee, another of the same type, he had entered the army in the Civil War as a private. Later, when I was President, it was my good fortune to make each of them in succession Lieutenant-General of the army of the United States. When General Young retired and General Chaffee was to take his place, the former sent to the latter his three stars to wear on his first official presentation, with a note that they were from "Private Young to Private Chaffee." The two fine old fellows had served in the ranks, one in the cavalry, one in the infantry, in their golden youth, in the days of the great war nearly half a century before; each had grown gray in a lifetime of honorable service under the flag, and each closed his active career in command of the army. General Young was one of the few men who had given and taken wounds with the saber. He was an old friend of mine, and when in Washington before starting for the front he told me that if we got in his brigade he would put us into the fighting all right. He kept his word.

General Young had actively superintended getting his two regular regiments, or at least a squadron of each, off the transports, and late that night he sent us word that he had received permission to move at dawn and strike the Spanish advance position. He directed us to move along a ridge trail with our two squadrons (one squadron having been left at Tampa), while with the two squadrons of regulars, one of the First and one of the Tenth, under his personal supervision, he marched up the valley trail. Accordingly Wood took us along the hill trail early next morning, till we struck the Spaniards, and began our fight just as the regulars began the fight in the valley trail.

It was a mountainous country covered with thick jungle, a most confusing country, and I had an awful time trying to get into the fight and trying to do what was right when in it; and all the while I was thinking that I was the only man who did not know what I was about, and that all the others did — whereas, as I found out later, pretty much everybody else was as much in the dark as I was. There was no surprise; we struck the Spaniards exactly where we had expected; then Wood halted us and put us into the fight deliberately and in order. He ordered us to deploy alternately by troops to the right and left of the trail, giving our senior major, Brodie, a West Pointer and as good a soldier as ever wore a uniform, the left wing, while I took the right wing. I was told if possible to connect with the regulars who were on the right. In theory this was excellent, but as the jungle was very dense the first troop that deployed to the right vanished forthwith, and I never saw it again until the fight was over — having a frightful feeling meanwhile that I might be court-martialed for losing it. The next troop deployed to the left under Brodie. Then the third came along, and I started to deploy it to the right as before.

By the time the first platoon had gotten into the jungle I realized that it likewise would disappear unless I kept hold of it. I managed to keep possession of the last platoon. One learns fast in a fight, and I marched this platoon and my next two troops in column through the jungle without any attempt to deploy until we got on the firing line. This sounds simple. But it was not. I did not know when I had gotten on the firing line! I could hear a good deal of firing, some over to my right at a good distance, and the rest to the left and ahead. I pushed on, expecting to strike the enemy somewhere between.

Soon we came to the brink of a deep valley. There was a good deal of cracking of rifles way off in front of us, but as they used smokeless powder we had no idea as to exactly where they were, or who they were shooting at. Then it dawned on us that we were the target. The bullets began to come overhead, making a sound like the ripping of a silk dress, with sometimes a kind of pop; a few of my men fell, and I deployed the rest, making them lie down and get behind trees. Richard Harding Davis was with us, and as we scanned the landscape with our glasses it was he who first pointed out to us some Spaniards in a trench some three-quarters of a mile off. It was difficult to make them out. There were not many of them. However, we finally did make them out, and we could see their conical hats, for the trench was a poor one. We advanced, firing at them, and drove them off.

What to do then I had not an idea. The country in front fell away into a very difficult jungle-filled valley. There was nothing but jungle all around, and if I advanced I was afraid I might get out of touch with everybody and not be going in the right direction. Moreover, as far as I could see, there was now nobody in front who was shooting at us, although some of the men on my left insisted that our own men had fired into us — an allegation which I soon found was almost always made in such a fight, and which in this case was not true. At this moment some of the regulars appeared across the ravine on our right. The first thing they did was to fire a volley at us, but one of our first sergeants went up a tree and waved a guidon at them and they stopped. Firing was still going on to our left, however, and I was never more puzzled to know what to do. I did not wish to take my men out of their position without orders, for fear that I might thereby be leaving a gap if there was a Spanish force which meditated an offensive return. On the other hand, it did not seem to me that I had been doing enough fighting to justify my existence, and there was obviously fighting going on to the left. I remember that I kept thinking of the refrain of the fox-hunting song, "Here's to every friend who struggled to the end"; in the hunting field I had always acted on this theory, and, no matter how discouraging appearances might be, had never stopped trying to get in at the death until the hunt was actually over; and now that there was work, and not play, on hand, I intended to struggle as hard as I knew how not to be left out of any fighting into which I could, with any possible propriety, get.

So I left my men where they were and started off at a trot toward where the firing was, with a couple of orderlies to send back for the men in case that proved advisable. Like most tyros, I was wearing my sword, which in thick jungle now and then got between my legs — from that day on it always went corded in the baggage. I struck the trail, and began to pass occasional dead men. Pretty soon I reached Wood and found, much to my pleasure, that I had done the right thing, for as I came up word was brought to him that Brodie had been shot, and he at once sent me to take charge of the left wing. It was more open country here, and at least I was able to get a glimpse of my own men and exercise some control over them. There was much firing going on, but for the life of me I could not see any Spaniards, and neither could any one else. Finally we made up our minds that they were shooting at us from a set of red-tiled ranch buildings a good way in front, and these I assaulted, finally charging them. Before we came anywhere near, the Spaniards, who, as it proved, really were inside and around them, abandoned them, leaving a few dead men.

By the time I had taken possession of these buildings all firing had ceased everywhere. I had not the faintest idea what had happened: whether the fight was over; or whether this was merely a lull in the fight; or where the Spaniards were; or whether we might be attacked again; or whether we ought ourselves to attack somebody somewhere else. I got my men in order and sent out small parties to explore the ground in front, who returned without finding any foe. (By this time, as a matter of fact, the Spaniards were in full retreat.) Meanwhile I was extending my line so as to get into touch with our people on the right. Word was brought to me that Wood had been shot — which fortunately proved not to be true — and as, if this were so, it meant that I must take charge of the regiment, I moved over personally to inquire. Soon I learned that he was all right, that the Spaniards had retreated along the main road, and that Colonel Wood and two or three other officers were a short distance away. Before I reached them I encountered a captain of the Ninth Cavalry, very glum because his troopers had not been up in time to take part in the fight, and he congratulated me — with visible effort! — upon my share in our first victory. I thanked him cordially, not confiding in him that till that moment I myself knew exceeding little about the victory; and proceeded to where Generals Wheeler, Lawton, and Chaffee, who had just come up, in company with Wood, were seated on a bank. They expressed appreciation of the way that I had handled my troops, first on the right wing and then on the left! As I was quite prepared to find I had committed some awful sin, I did my best to accept this in a nonchalant manner, and not to look as relieved as I felt. As throughout the morning I had preserved a specious aspect of wisdom, and had commanded first one and then the other wing, the fight was really a capital thing for me, for practically all the men had served under my actual command, and thenceforth felt an enthusiastic belief that I would lead them aright.

It was a week after this skirmish before the army made the advance on Santiago. Just before this occurred General Young was stricken down with fever. General Wheeler, who had commanded the Cavalry Division, was put in general charge of the left wing of the army, which fought before the city itself. Brigadier-General Sam Sumner, an excellent officer, who had the second cavalry brigade, took command of the cavalry division, and Wood took command of our brigade, while, to my intense delight, I got my regiment. I therefore had command of the regiment before the stiffest fighting occurred.

General Joseph Wheeler, in the Foreground, Commander of the Left Wing of the Army before San Juan Hill. From Left to Right: Major George M. Dunn, Colonel Brodie, Chaplain Brown, Leonard Wood, and Colonel Theodore Roosevelt.

Later, when Wood was put in command in Santiago, I became the brigade commander.

Late in the evening we camped at El Poso. There were two regular officers, the brigade commander's aides, Lieutenants A. L. Mills and W. E. Shipp, who were camped by our regiment. Each of my men had food in his haversack, but I had none, and I would have gone supperless to bed if Mills and Shipp had not given me out of their scanty stores a big sandwich, which I shared with my orderly, who also had nothing. Next morning my body servant Marshall, an ex-soldier of the Ninth (Colored) Cavalry, a fine and faithful fellow, had turned up and I was able in my turn to ask Mills and Shipp, who had eaten all their food the preceding evening, to take breakfast with me. A few hours later gallant Shipp was dead, and Mills, an exceptionally able officer, had been shot through the head from side to side, just back of the eyes; yet he lived, although one eye was blinded, and before I left the Presidency I gave him his commission as Brigadier-General.

Early in the morning our artillery began firing from the hill-crest immediately in front of where our men were camped. Several of the regiment were killed and wounded by the shrapnel of the return fire of the Spaniards. One of the shrapnel bullets fell on my wrist and raised a bump as big as a hickory nut, but did not even break the skin. Then we were marched down from the hill on a muddy road through thick jungle towards Santiago. The heat was great, and we strolled into the fight with no definite idea on the part of any one as to what we were to do or what would happen. There was no plan that our left wing was to make a serious fight that day; and as there were no plans, it was naturally exceedingly hard to get orders, and each of us had to act largely on his own responsibility.

Lawton's infantry division attacked the little village of El Caney, some miles to the right. Kent's infantry division and Sumner's dismounted cavalry division were supposed to retain the Spanish army in Santiago until Lawton had captured El Caney. Spanish towns and villages, however, with their massive buildings, are natural fortifications, as the French found in the Peninsular War, and as both the French and our people found in Mexico. The Spanish troops in El Caney fought very bravely, as did the Spanish troops in front of us, and it was late in the afternoon before Lawton accomplished his task.

Meanwhile we of the left wing had by degrees become involved in a fight which toward the end became not even a colonel's fight, but a squad leader's fight. The cavalry division was put at the head of the line. We were told to march forward, cross a little river in front, and then, turning to the right, march up alongside the stream until we connected with Lawton. Incidentally, this movement would not have brought us into touch with Lawton in any event. But we speedily had to abandon any thought of carrying it out. The maneuver brought us within fair range of the Spanish intrenchments along the line of hills which we called the San Juan Hills, because on one of them was the San Juan blockhouse. On that day my regiment had the lead of the second brigade, and we marched down the trail following in trace behind the first brigade. Apparently the Spaniards could not make up their minds what to do as the three regular regiments of the first brigade crossed and defiled along the other bank of the stream, but when our regiment was crossing they began to fire at us.

Under this flank fire it soon became impossible to continue the march. The first brigade halted, deployed, and finally began to fire back. Then our brigade was halted. From time to time some of our men would fall, and I sent repeated word to the rear to try to get authority to attack the hills in front. Finally General Sumner, who was fighting the division in fine shape, sent word to advance. The word was brought to me by Mills, who said that my orders were to support the regulars in the assault on the hills, and that my objective would be the red-tiled ranch-house in front, on a hill which we afterwards christened Kettle Hill. I mention Mills saying this because it was exactly the kind of definite order the giving of which does so much to insure success in a fight, as it prevents all obscurity as to what is to be done. The order to attack did not reach the first brigade until after we ourselves reached it, so that at first there was doubt on the part of their officers whether they were at liberty to join in the advance.

I had not enjoyed the Guasimas fight at all, because I had been so uncertain as to what I ought to do. But the San Juan fight was entirely different. The Spaniards had a hard position to attack, it is true, but we could see them, and I knew exactly how to proceed. I kept on horseback, merely because I found it difficult to convey orders along the line, as the men were lying down; and it is always hard to get men to start when they cannot see whether their comrades are also going. So I rode up and down the lines, keeping them straightened out, and gradually worked through line after line until I found myself at the head of the regiment. By the time I had reached the lines of the regulars of the first brigade I had come to the conclusion that it was silly to stay in the valley firing at the hills, because that was really where we were most exposed, and that the thing to do was to try to rush the intrenchments. Where I struck the regulars there was no one of superior rank to mine, and after asking why they did not charge, and being answered that they had no orders, I said I would give the order. There was naturally a little reluctance shown by the elderly officer in command to accept my order, so I said, "Then let my men through, sir," and I marched through, followed by my grinning men. The younger officers and the enlisted men of the regulars jumped up and joined us. I waved my hat, and we went up the hill with a rush. Having taken it, we looked across at the Spaniards in the trenches under the San Juan blockhouse to our left, which Hawkins's brigade was assaulting. I ordered our men to open fire on the Spaniards in the trenches.

Memory plays funny tricks in such a fight, where things happen quickly, and all kinds of mental images succeed one another in a detached kind of way, while the work goes on. As I gave the order in question there slipped through my mind Mahan's account of Nelson's orders that each ship as it sailed forward, if it saw another ship engaged with an enemy's ship, should rake the latter as it passed. When Hawkins's soldiers captured the blockhouse, I, very much elated, ordered a charge on my own hook to a line of hills still farther on. Hardly anybody heard this order, however; only four men started with me, three of whom were shot. I gave one of them, who was only wounded, my canteen of water, and ran back, much irritated that I had not been followed — which was quite unjustifiable, because I found that nobody had heard my orders. General Sumner had come up by this time, and I asked his permission to lead the charge. He ordered me to do so, and this time away we went, and stormed the Spanish intrenchments. There was some close fighting, and we took a few prisoners. We also captured the Spanish provisions, and ate them that night with great relish. One of the items was salted flying-fish, by the way. There were also bottles of wine, and jugs of fiery spirit, and as soon as possible I had these broken, although not before one or two of my men had taken too much liquor. Lieutenant Howze, of the regulars, an aide of General Sumner's, brought me an order to halt where I was; he could not make up his mind to return until he had spent an hour or two with us under fire. The Spaniards attempted a counter-attack in the middle of the afternoon, but were driven back without effort, our men laughing and cheering as they rose to fire; because hitherto they had been assaulting breastworks, or lying still under artillery fire, and they were glad to get a chance to shoot at the Spaniards in the open. We lay on our arms that night and as we were drenched with sweat, and had no blankets save a few we took from the dead Spaniards, we found even the tropic night chilly before morning came.

During the afternoon's fighting, while I was the highest officer at our immediate part of the front, Captains Boughton and Morton of the regular cavalry, two as fine officers as any man could wish to have beside him in battle, came along the firing line to tell me that they had heard a rumor that we might fall back, and that they wished to record their emphatic protest against any such course. I did not believe there was any truth in the rumor, for the Spaniards were utterly incapable of any effective counter-attack. However, late in the evening, after the fight, General Wheeler visited us at the front, and he told me to keep myself in readiness, as at any moment it might be decided to fall back. Jack Greenway was beside me when General Wheeler was speaking. I answered, "Well, General, I really don't know whether we would obey an order to fall back. We can take that city by a rush, and if we have to move out of here at all I should be inclined to make the rush in the right direction." Greenway nodded an eager assent. The old General, after a moment's pause, expressed his hearty agreement, and said that he would see that there was no falling back. He had been very sick for a couple of days, but, sick as he was, he managed to get into the fight. He was a gamecock if ever there was one, but he was in very bad physical shape on the day of the fight. If there had been any one in high command to supervise and press the attack that afternoon, we would have gone right into Santiago. In my part of the line the advance was halted only because we received orders not to move forward, but to stay on the crest of the captured hill and hold it.

We are always told that three-o'clock-in-the-morning courage is the most desirable kind. Well, my men and the regulars of the cavalry had just that brand of courage. At about three o'clock on the morning after the first fight, shooting began in our front and there was an alarm of a Spanish advance. I was never more pleased than to see the way in which the hungry, tired, shabby men all jumped up and ran forward to the hill-crest, so as to be ready for the attack; which, however, did not come. As soon as the sun rose the Spaniards again opened upon us with artillery. A shell burst between Dave Goodrich and myself, blacking us with powder, and killing and wounding several of the men immediately behind us.

Next day the fight turned into a siege; there were some stirring incidents; but for the most part it was trench work. A fortnight later Santiago surrendered. Wood won his brigadier-generalship by the capital way in which he handled his brigade in the fight, and in the following siege. He was put in command of the captured city; and in a few days I succeeded to the command of the brigade.

The health of the troops was not good, and speedily became very bad. There was some dysentery, and a little yellow fever; but most of the trouble was from a severe form of malarial fever. The Washington authorities had behaved better than those in actual command of the expedition at one crisis. Immediately after the first days' fighting around Santiago the latter had hinted by cable to Washington that they might like to withdraw, and Washington had emphatically vetoed the proposal. I record this all the more gladly because there were not too many gleams of good sense shown in the home management of the war; although I wish to repeat that the real blame for this rested primarily with us ourselves, the people of the United States, who had for years pursued in military matters a policy that rendered it certain that there would be ineptitude and failure in high places if ever a crisis came. After the siege the people in Washington showed no knowledge whatever of the conditions around Santiago, and proposed to keep the army there. This would have meant that at least three-fourths of the men would either have died or have been permanently invalided, as a virulent form of malaria was widespread, and there was a steady growth of dysentery and other complaints. No object of any kind was to be gained by keeping the army in or near the captured city. General Shafter tried his best to get the Washington authorities to order the army home. As he failed to accomplish anything, he called a council of the division and brigade commanders and the chief medical officers to consult over the situation.

Although I had command of a brigade, I was only a colonel, and so I did not intend to attend, but the General informed me that I was particularly wanted, and accordingly I went. At the council General Shafter asked the medical authorities as to conditions, and they united in informing him that they were very bad, and were certain to grow much worse; and that in order to avoid frightful ravages from disease, chiefly due to malaria, the army should be sent back at once to some part of the northern United States. The General then explained that he could not get the War Department to understand the situation; that he could not get the attention of the public; and that he felt that there should be some authoritative publication which would make the War Department take action before it was too late to avert the ruin of the army. All who were in the room expressed their agreement.

Then the reason for my being present came out. It was explained to me by General Shafter, and by others, that as I was a volunteer officer and intended immediately to return to civil life, I could afford to take risks which the regular army men could not afford to take and ought not to be expected to take, and that therefore I ought to make the publication in question; because to incur the hostility of the War Department would not make any difference to me, whereas it would be destructive to the men in the regular army, or to those who hoped to get into the regular army. I thought this true, and said I would write a letter or make a statement which could then be published. Brigadier-General Ames, who was in the same position that I was, also announced that he would make a statement.

When I left the meeting it was understood that I was to make my statement as an interview in the press; but Wood, who was by that time Brigadier-General commanding the city of Santiago, gave me a quiet hint to put my statement in the form of a letter to General Shafter, and this I accordingly did. When I had written my letter, the correspondent of the Associated Press, who had been informed by others of what had occurred, accompanied me to General Shafter. I presented the letter to General Shafter, who waved it away and said: "I don't want to take it; do whatever you wish with it." I, however, insisted on handing it to him, whereupon he shoved it toward the correspondent of the Associated Press, who took hold of it, and I released my hold. General Ames made a statement direct to the correspondent, and also sent a cable to the Assistant Secretary of the Navy at Washington, a copy of which he gave to the correspondent. By this time the other division and brigade commanders who were present felt that they had better take action themselves. They united in a round robin to General Shafter, which General Wood dictated, and which was signed by Generals Kent, Bates, Chaffee, Sumner, Ludlow, Ames, and Wood, and by myself. General Wood handed this to General Shafter, and it was made public by General Shafter precisely as mine was made public.* Later I was much amused when General Shafter stated that he could not imagine how my letter and the round robin got out! When I saw this statement, I appreciated how wise Wood had been in hinting to me not to act on the suggestion of the General that I should make a statement to the newspapers, but to put my statement in the form of a letter to him as my superior officer, a letter which I delivered to him. Both the letter and the round robin were written at General Shafter's wish, and at the unanimous suggestion of all the commanding and medical officers of the Fifth Army Corps, and both were published by General Shafter.

*General Wood writes me: "The representative of the Associated Press was very anxious to get a copy of this despatch or see it, and I told him it was impossible for him to have it or see it. I then went in to General Shafter and stated the case to him, handing him the despatch, saying, 'The matter is now in your hands.' He, General Shafter, then said, 'I don't care whether this gentleman has it or not,' and I left then. When I went back the General told me he had given the Press representative a copy of the despatch, and that he had gone to the office with it."

In a regiment the prime need is to have fighting men; the prime virtue is to be able and eager to fight with the utmost effectiveness. I have never believed that this was incompatible with other virtues. On the contrary, while there are of course exceptions, I believe that on the average the best fighting men are also the best citizens. I do not believe that a finer set of natural soldiers than the men of my regiment could have been found anywhere, and they were first-class citizens in civil life also. One fact may perhaps be worthy of note. Whenever we were in camp and so fixed that we could have regular meals, we used to have a general officers' mess, over which I of course presided. During our entire service there was never a foul or indecent word uttered at the officers' mess — I mean this literally; and there was very little swearing — although now and then in the fighting, if there was a moment when swearing seemed to be the best method of reaching the heart of the matter, it was resorted to.

The men I cared for most in the regiment were the men who did the best work; and therefore my liking for them was obliged to take the shape of exposing them to most fatigue and hardship, of demanding from them the greatest service, and of making them incur the greatest risk. Once I kept Greenway and Goodrich at work for forty-eight hours, without sleeping, and with very little food, fighting and digging trenches. I freely sent the men for whom I cared most, to where death might smite them; and death often smote them — as it did the two best officers in my regiment, Allyn Capron and Bucky O'Neil. My men would not have respected me had I acted otherwise. Their creed was my creed. The life even of the most useful man, of the best citizen, is not to be hoarded if there be need to spend it. I felt, and feel, this about others; and of course also about myself. This is one reason why I have always felt impatient contempt for the effort to abolish the death penalty on account of sympathy with criminals. I am willing to listen to arguments in favor of abolishing the death penalty so far as they are based purely on grounds of public expediency, although these arguments have never convinced me. But inasmuch as, without hesitation, in the performance of duty, I have again and again sent good and gallant and upright men to die, it seems to me the height of a folly both mischievous and mawkish to contend that criminals who have deserved death should nevertheless be allowed to shirk it. No brave and good man can properly shirk death; and no criminal who has earned death should be allowed to shirk it.

One of the best men with our regiment was the British military attaché, Captain Arthur Lee, an old friend. The other military attachés were herded together at headquarters and saw little. Captain Lee, who had known me in Washington, escaped and stayed with the regiment. We grew to feel that he was one of us, and made him an honorary member. There were two other honorary members. One was Richard Harding Davis, who was with us continually and who performed valuable service on the fighting line. The other was a regular officer, Lieutenant Parker, who had a battery of gatlings. We were with this battery throughout the San Juan fighting, and we grew to have the strongest admiration for Parker as a soldier and the strongest liking for him as a man. During our brief campaign we were closely and intimately thrown with various regular officers of the type of Mills, Howze, and Parker. We felt not merely fondness for them as officers and gentlemen, but pride in them as Americans. It is a fine thing to feel that we have in the army and in the navy modest, efficient, gallant gentlemen of this type, doing such disinterested work for the honor of the flag and of the Nation. No American can overpay the debt of gratitude we all of us owe to the officers and enlisted men of the army and of the navy.

Of course with a regiment of our type there was much to learn both among the officers and the men. There were all kinds of funny incidents. One of my men, an ex-cow-puncher and former round-up cook, a very good shot and rider, got into trouble on the way down on the transport. He understood entirely that he had to obey the officers of his own regiment, but, like so many volunteers, or at least like so many volunteers of my regiment, he did not understand that this obligation extended to officers of other regiments. One of the regular officers on the transport ordered him to do something which he declined to do. When the officer told him to consider himself under arrest, he responded by offering to fight him for a trifling consideration. He was brought before a court martial which sentenced him to a year's imprisonment at hard labor with dishonorable discharge, and the major-general commanding the division approved the sentence.

We were on the transport. There was no hard labor to do; and the prison consisted of another cow-puncher who kept guard over him with his carbine, evidently divided in his feelings as to whether he would like most to shoot him or to let him go. When we landed, somebody told the prisoner that I intended to punish him by keeping him with the baggage. He at once came to me in great agitation, saying: "Colonel, they say you're going to leave me with the baggage when the fight is on. Colonel, if you do that, I will never show my face in Arizona again. Colonel, if you will let me go to the front, I promise I will obey any one you say; any one you say, Colonel," with the evident feeling that, after this concession, I could not, as a gentleman, refuse his request. Accordingly I answered: "Shields, there is no one in this regiment more entitled to be shot than you are, and you shall go to the front." His gratitude was great, and he kept repeating, "I'll never forget this, Colonel, never." Nor did he. When we got very hard up, he would now and then manage to get hold of some flour and sugar, and would cook a doughnut and bring it round to me, and watch me with a delighted smile as I ate it. He behaved extremely well in both fights, and after the second one I had him formally before me and remitted his sentence — something which of course I had not the slightest power to do, although at the time it seemed natural and proper to me.

When we came to be mustered out, the regular officer who was doing the mustering, after all the men had been discharged, finally asked me where the prisoner was. I said, "What prisoner?" He said, "The prisoner, the man who was sentenced to a year's imprisonment with hard labor and dishonorable discharge." I said, "Oh! I pardoned him"; to which he responded, "I beg your pardon; you did what?" This made me grasp the fact that I had exceeded authority, and I could only answer, "Well, I did pardon him, anyhow, and he has gone with the rest"; whereupon the mustering-out officer sank back in his chair and remarked, "He was sentenced by a court martial, and the sentence was approved by the major-general commanding the division. You were a lieutenant-colonel, and you pardoned him. Well, it was nervy, that's all I'll say."

The simple fact was that under the circumstances it was necessary for me to enforce discipline and control the regiment, and therefore to reward and punish individuals in whatever way the exigencies demanded. I often explained to the men what the reasons for an order were, the first time it was issued, if there was any trouble on their part in understanding what they were required to do. They were very intelligent and very eager to do their duty, and I hardly ever had any difficulty the second time with them. If, however, there was the slightest willful shirking of duty or insubordination, I punished instantly and mercilessly, and the whole regiment cordially

On the Firing Line.

backed me up. To have punished men for faults and short-comings which they had no opportunity to know were such would have been as unwise as to have permitted any of the occasional bad characters to exercise the slightest license. It was a regiment which was sensitive about its dignity and was very keenly alive to justice and to courtesy, but which cordially approved absence of mollycoddling, insistence upon the performance of duty, and summary punishment of wrong-doing.

In the final fighting at San Juan, when we captured one of the trenches, Jack Greenway had seized a Spaniard, and shortly afterwards I found Jack leading his captive round with a string. I told him to turn him over to a man who had two or three other captives, so that they should all be taken to the rear. It was the only time I ever saw Jack look aggrieved. "Why, Colonel, can't I keep him for myself?" he asked, plaintively. I think he had an idea that as a trophy of his bow and spear the Spaniard would make a fine body servant.

One reason that we never had the slightest trouble in the regiment was because, when we got down to hard pan, officers and men shared exactly alike. It is all right to have differences in food and the like in times of peace and plenty, when everybody is comfortable. But in really hard times officers and men must share alike if the best work is to be done. As long as I had nothing but two hardtacks, which was the allowance to each man on the morning after the San Juan fight, no one could complain; but if I had had any private little luxuries the men would very naturally have realized keenly their own shortages.

Soon after the Guasimas fight we were put on short commons; and as I knew that a good deal of food had been landed and was on the beach at Siboney, I marched thirty or forty of the men down to see if I could not get some and bring it up. I finally found a commissary officer, and he asked me what I wanted, and I answered, anything he had. So he told me to look about for myself. I found a number of sacks of beans, I think about eleven hundred pounds, on the beach; and told the officer that I wanted eleven hundred pounds of beans. He produced a book of regulations, and showed me the appropriate section and subdivision which announced that beans were issued only for the officers' mess. This did me no good, and I told him so. He said he was sorry, and I answered that he was not as sorry as I was. I then "studied on it," as Br'er Rabbit would say, and came back with a request for eleven hundred pounds of beans for the officers' mess. He said, "Why, Colonel, your officers can't eat eleven hundred pounds of beans," to which I responded, "You don't know what appetites my officers have." He then said he would send the requisition to Washington. I told him I was quite willing, so long as he gave me the beans. He was a good fellow, so we finally effected a working compromise — he got the requisition and I got the beans, although he warned me that the price would probably be deducted from my salary.

Under some regulation or other only the regular supply trains were allowed to act, and we were supposed not to have any horses or mules in the regiment itself. This was very pretty in theory; but, as a matter of fact, the supply trains were not numerous enough. My men had a natural genius for acquiring horseflesh in odd ways, and I continually found that they had staked out in the brush various captured Spanish cavalry horses and Cuban ponies and abandoned commissary mules. Putting these together, I would organize a small pack train and work it industriously for a day or two, until they learned about it at headquarters and confiscated it. Then I would have to wait for a week or so until my men had accumulated some more ponies, horses, and mules, the regiment meanwhile living in plenty on what we had got before the train was confiscated.

All of our men were good at accumulating horses, but within our own ranks I think we were inclined to award the palm to our chaplain. There was not a better man in the regiment than the chaplain, and there could not have been a better chaplain for our men. He took care of the sick and the wounded, he never spared himself, and he did every duty. In addition, he had a natural aptitude for acquiring mules, which made some admirer, when the regiment was disbanded, propose that we should have a special medal struck for him, with, on the obverse, "A Mule passant and Chaplain regardant." After the surrender of Santiago, a Philadelphia clergyman whom I knew came down to General Wheeler's headquarters, and after visiting him announced that he intended to call on the Rough Riders, because he knew their colonel. One of General Wheeler's aides, Lieutenant Steele, who liked us both individually and as a regiment, and who appreciated some of our ways, asked the clergyman, after he had announced that he knew Colonel Roosevelt, "But do you know Colonel Roosevelt's regiment?" "No," said the clergyman. "Very well, then, let me give you a piece of advice. When you go down to see the Colonel, don't let your horse out of your sight; and if the chaplain is there, don't get off the horse!"

We came back to Montauk Point and soon after were disbanded. We had been in the service only a little over four months. There are no four months of my life to which I look back with more pride and satisfaction. I believe most earnestly and sincerely in peace, but as things are yet in this world the nation that cannot fight, the people that have lost the fighting edge, that have lost the virile virtues, occupy a position as dangerous as it is ignoble. The future greatness of America in no small degree depends upon the possession by the average American citizen of the qualities which my men showed when they served under me at Santiago.

Moreover, there is one thing in connection with this war which it is well that our people should remember, our people who genuinely love the peace of righteousness, the peace of justice — and I would be ashamed to be other than a lover of the peace of righteousness and of justice. The true preachers of peace, who strive earnestly to bring nearer the day when peace shall obtain among all peoples, and who really do help forward the cause, are men who never hesitate to choose righteous war when it is the only alternative to unrighteous peace. These are the men who, like Dr. Lyman Abbott, have backed every genuine movement for peace in this country, and who nevertheless recognized our clear duty to war for the freedom of Cuba.

But there are other men who put peace ahead of righteousness, and who care so little for facts that they treat fantastic declarations for immediate universal arbitration as being valuable, instead of detrimental, to the cause they profess to champion, and who seek to make the United States impotent for international good under the pretense of making us impotent for international evil. All the men of this kind, and all of the organizations they have controlled, since we began our career as a nation, all put together, have not accomplished one hundredth part as much for both peace and righteousness, have not done one hundredth part as much either for ourselves or for other peoples, as was accomplished by the people of the United States when they fought the war with Spain and with resolute good faith and common sense worked out the solution of the problems which sprang from the war.

Our army and navy, and above all our people, learned some lessons from the Spanish War, and applied them to our own uses. During the following decade the improvement in our navy and army was very great; not in material only, but also in personnel, and, above all, in the ability to handle our forces in good-sized units. By 1908, when our battle fleet steamed round the world, the navy had become in every respect as fit a fighting instrument as any other navy in the world, fleet for fleet. Even in size there was but one nation, England, which was completely out of our class; and in view of our relations with England and all the English-speaking peoples, this was of no consequence. Of our army, of course, as much could not be said. Nevertheless the improvement in efficiency was marked. Our artillery was still very inferior in training and practice to the artillery arm of any one of the great Powers such as Germany, France, or Japan — a condition which we only then began to remedy. But the workmanlike speed and efficiency with which the expedition of some 6000 troops of all arms was mobilized and transported to Cuba during the revolution of 1908 showed that, as regards our cavalry and infantry, we had at least reached the point where we could assemble and handle in first-rate fashion expeditionary forces. This is mighty little to boast of, for a Nation of our wealth and population; it is not pleasant to compare it with the extraordinary feats of contemporary Japan and the Balkan peoples; but, such as it is, it represents a long stride in advance over conditions as they were in 1898.

# APPENDIX A

There was a sequel to the "round robin" incident which caused a little stir at the moment; Secretary Alger had asked me to write him freely from time to time. Accordingly, after the surrender of Santiago, I wrote him begging that the cavalry division might be put into the Porto Rican fighting, preparatory to what we supposed would be the big campaign against Havana in the fall. In the letter I extolled the merits of the Rough Riders and of the Regulars, announcing with much complacency that each of our regiments was worth "three of the National Guard regiments, armed with their archaic black powder rifles."* Secretary Alger believed, mistakenly, that I had made public the round robin, and was naturally irritated, and I suddenly received from him a published telegram, not alluding to the round robin incident, but quoting my reference to the comparative merits of the cavalry regiments and the National Guard regiments and rebuking me for it. The publication of the extract from my letter was not calculated to help me secure the votes of the National Guard if I ever became a candidate for office. However, I did not mind the matter much, for I had at the time no idea of being a candidate for anything — while in the campaign I ate and drank and thought and dreamed regiment and nothing but regiment, until I got the brigade, and then I devoted all my thoughts to handling the brigade. Anyhow, there was nothing I could do about the matter.

When our transport reached Montauk Point, an army officer came aboard and before doing anything else handed me a sealed letter from the Secretary of War which ran as follows: —

WAR DEPARTMENT, WASHINGTON,
August 10, 1898.

DEAR COL. ROOSEVELT:

You have been a most gallant officer and in the battle before Santiago showed superb soldierly qualities. I would rather add to, then detract from, the honors you have so fairly won, and I wish you all good things. In a moment of aggravation under great stress of feeling, first because I thought you spoke in a disparaging manner of the volunteers (probably without intent, but because of your great enthusiasm for your own men) and second that I believed your published letter would embarrass the Department I sent you a telegram which with an extract from a private letter of yours I gave to the

*I quote this sentence from memory; it is substantially correct.

press. I would gladly recall both if I could, but unable to do that I write you this letter which I hope you will receive in the same friendly spirit in which I sent it. Come and see me at a very early day. No one will welcome you more heartily than I.

Yours very truly,
(Signed) R. A. Alger.

I thought this a manly letter, and paid no more heed to the incident; and when I was President, and General Alger was Senator from Michigan, he was my stanch friend and on most matters my supporter.

# APPENDIX B

## THE SAN JUAN FIGHT

The San Juan fight took its name from the San Juan Hill or hills — I do not know whether the name properly belonged to a line of hills or to only one hill.

To compare small things with large things, this was precisely as the Battle of Gettysburg took its name from the village of Gettysburg, where only a small part of the fighting was done; and the Battle of Waterloo from the village of Waterloo, where none of the fighting was done. When it became the political interest of certain people to endeavor to minimize my part in the Santiago fighting (which was merely like that of various other squadron, battalion and regimental commanders) some of my opponents laid great stress on the alleged fact that the cavalry did not charge up San Juan Hill. We certainly charged some hills; but I did not ask their names before charging them. To say that the Rough Riders and the cavalry division, and among other people myself, were not in the San Juan fight is precisely like saying that the men who made Pickett's Charge, or the men who fought at Little Round Top and Culps Hill, were not at Gettysburg; or that Picton and the Scotch Greys and the French and English guards were not at Waterloo. The present Vice-President of the United States in the campaign last year was reported in the press as repeatedly saying that I was not in the San Juan fight. The documents following herewith have been printed for many years, and were accessible to him had he cared to know or to tell the truth.

These documents speak for themselves. The first is the official report issued by the War Department. From this it will be seen that there were in the Santiago fighting thirty infantry and cavalry regiments represented. Six of these were volunteer, of which one was the Rough Riders. The other twenty-four were regular regiments. The percentage of loss of our regiment was about seven times as great as that of the other five volunteer regiments. Of the twenty-four regular regiments, twenty-two suffered a smaller percentage of loss than we suffered. Two, the Sixth United States Infantry and the Thirteenth United States Infantry, suffered a slightly greater percentage of loss — twenty-six per cent and twenty-three per cent as against twenty-two per cent.

(Congressional Record, 55th Congress, Third Session,
Volume 32, Part II, Page 1250)

## NOMINATIONS BY THE PRESIDENT

*To be Colonel by Brevet*
Lieutenant-Colonel Theodore Roosevelt, First Volunteer Cavalry, for gallantry in battle, La Guasima, Cuba, June 24, 1898.

*To be Brigadier-General by Brevet*
Lieutenant-Colonel Theodore Roosevelt, First Volunteer Cavalry, for gallantry in battle, Santiago de Cuba, July 1, 1898. (Nominated for brevet colonel, to rank from June 24, 1898.)

Fort San Juan, Cuba,
July 17, 1898.

The Adjutant-General United States Army,
    Washington, D.C.
        (Through military channels)
    Sir: I have the honor to invite attention to the following list of officers and enlisted men who specially distinguished themselves in the action at Las Guasimas, Cuba, June 24, 1898.

These officers and men have been recommended for favorable consideration by their immediate commanding officers in their respective reports, and I would respectfully urge that favorable action be taken.

## OFFICERS

. . . . . . .

In First United States Volunteer Cavalry — Colonel Leonard Wood, Lieutenant-Colonel Roosevelt.

. . . . . . .

Respectfully,
JOSEPH WHEELER,
*Major-General United States Volunteers, Commanding.*

HEADQUARTERS SECOND CAVALRY BRIGADE,
CAMP NEAR SANTIAGO DE CUBA, CUBA,
June 29, 1898.

THE ADJUTANT-GENERAL CAVALRY DIVISION.

SIR: By direction of the major-general commanding the Cavalry Division, I have the honor to submit the following report of the engagement of a part of this brigade with the enemy at Guasimas, Cuba, on June 24th, accompanied by detailed reports from the regimental and other commanders engaged, and a list of the killed and wounded:

. . . . . . .

I cannot speak too highly of the efficient manner in which Colonel Wood handled his regiment, and of his magnificent behavior on the field. The conduct of Lieutenant-Colonel Roosevelt, as reported to me by my two aides, deserves my highest commendation. Both Colonel Wood and Lieutenant-Colonel Roosevelt disdained to take advantage of shelter or cover from the enemy's fire while any of their men remained exposed to it — an error of judgment, but happily on the heroic side.

. . . . . . .

Very respectfully,
S. B. M. YOUNG,
*Brigadier General United States Volunteers, Commanding.*

HEADQUARTERS FIRST DIVISION SECOND ARMY CORPS
CAMP MACKENZIE, GA.,
December 30, 1898.

ADJUTANT-GENERAL,
Washington, D.C.

SIR: I have the honor to recommend Hon. Theodore Roosevelt, late Colonel First United States Volunteer Cavalry, for a medal of honor, as a reward for conspicuous gallantry at the battle of San Juan, Cuba, on July 1, 1898.

# CASUALTIES IN THE 5TH CORPS IN THE OPERATIONS AGAINST SANTIAGO, JUNE 22 TO JULY 17, 1898.

| Command. | Las Guasimas, June 24. Killed Officers | Killed Enlisted men | Wounded Officers | Wounded Enlisted men | El Caney, July 1. Killed Officers | Killed Enlisted men | Wounded Officers | Wounded Enlisted men | San Juan, July 1–3. Killed Officers | Killed Enlisted men | Wounded Officers | Wounded Enlisted men | Aguadores, July 1–2. Killed Officers | Killed Enlisted men | Wounded Officers | Wounded Enlisted men | Around Santiago, July 10–12. Killed Officers | Killed Enlisted men | Wounded Officers | Wounded Enlisted men | Total. Killed Officers | Killed Enlisted men | Wounded Officers | Wounded Enlisted men | Aggregate. | Present for duty equipped June 30. Officers | Enlisted men |
|---|---|---|---|---|---|---|---|---|---|---|---|---|---|---|---|---|---|---|---|---|---|---|---|---|---|---|---|
| Maj. Gen. W. R. Shafter, headquarters and staff |  |  |  |  |  |  |  |  |  |  |  |  |  |  |  |  |  |  |  |  |  |  |  |  |  | 17 | 81 |
| Signal Corps |  |  |  |  |  |  |  |  |  |  |  |  |  |  |  |  |  |  |  |  |  |  |  | 1 | 1 | 7 |  |
| Hospital corps |  |  |  |  |  |  |  |  |  |  |  |  |  |  |  |  |  |  |  |  |  |  |  | 3 | 3 |  | 275 |
| C and E, Engineer Battalion |  |  |  |  |  |  |  |  |  |  |  |  |  |  |  |  |  |  |  |  |  |  |  | 1 | 1 | 8 | 192 |
| Second U. S. Cavalry |  |  |  |  |  |  |  |  |  |  |  | 1 |  |  |  |  |  |  |  |  |  |  |  | 1 | 1 | 9 | 257 |
| First Division, Brig. Gen. J. F. Kent |  |  |  |  |  |  |  |  |  |  |  |  |  |  |  |  |  |  |  |  |  |  |  |  |  | 11 |  |
| First Brigade, Brig. Gen. H. S. Hawkins |  |  |  |  |  |  |  |  | 2 |  | 1 |  |  |  |  |  |  |  |  |  | 2 |  | 1 |  | 3 | 6 | 6 |
| Sixteenth U. S. Infantry |  |  |  |  |  |  |  |  | 1 | 13 | 6 | 109 |  |  |  |  |  |  |  |  | 1 | 13 | 6 | 109 | 129 | 24 | 655 |
| Sixth U. S. Infantry |  |  |  |  |  |  |  |  | 2 | 10 | 8 | 106 |  |  |  |  |  |  |  | 1 | 2 | 10 | 8 | 107 | 127 | 31 | 461 |
| Seventy-first New York Infantry |  |  |  |  |  |  |  |  |  | 12 | 1 | 67 |  |  |  |  |  |  |  |  |  | 12 | 1 | 67 | 80 | 47 | 922 |
| Second Brigade, Col. E. P. Pearson, 5th Infantry |  |  |  |  |  |  |  |  |  |  |  |  |  |  |  |  |  |  |  |  |  |  |  |  |  | 6 | 8 |
| Second U. S. Infantry |  |  |  |  |  |  |  |  | 1 | 7 | 4 | 49 |  |  |  |  |  |  | 1 | 3 | 1 | 7 | 5 | 52 | 65 | 20 | 618 |
| Tenth U. S. Infantry |  |  |  |  |  |  |  |  | 1 | 4 | 5 | 35 |  |  |  |  |  |  |  |  | 1 | 4 | 5 | 35 | 45 | 23 | 432 |
| Twenty-first U. S. Infantry |  |  |  |  |  |  |  |  |  | 6 | 1 | 30 |  |  |  |  |  |  |  | 1 |  | 6 | 1 | 31 | 38 | 26 | 441 |
| Third Brigade, Col. C. A. Wikoff, 2d Infantry |  |  |  |  |  |  |  |  |  |  |  |  |  |  |  |  |  |  |  |  |  |  |  |  |  | 5 |  |
| Ninth U. S. Infantry |  |  |  |  |  |  |  |  | 1 | 4 |  | 27 |  |  |  |  |  |  |  |  | 1 | 4 |  | 27 | 32 | 21 | 445 |
| Thirteenth U. S. Infantry |  |  |  |  |  |  |  |  | 1 | 17 | 6 | 85 |  |  |  |  |  |  |  |  | 1 | 17 | 6 | 85 | 109 | 24 | 441 |
| Twenty-fourth U. S. Infantry |  |  |  |  |  |  |  |  | 1 | 6 | 7 | 76 |  |  |  |  |  |  |  |  | 1 | 6 | 7 | 76 | 90 | 23 | 516 |
| Second Division, Brig. Gen. H. W. Lawton |  |  |  |  |  |  |  |  |  |  |  |  |  |  |  |  |  |  |  |  |  |  |  |  |  | 8 |  |
| First Brigade, Brig. Gen. W. Ludlow |  |  |  |  |  |  |  |  |  |  |  |  |  |  |  |  |  |  |  |  |  |  |  |  |  | 4 | 7 |
| Eighth U. S. Infantry |  |  |  |  |  | 6 | 1 | 45 |  |  |  |  |  |  |  |  |  |  |  |  |  | 6 | 1 | 45 | 52 | 19 | 487 |
| Twenty-second U. S. Infantry |  |  |  |  |  | 7 | 6 | 36 |  | 2 |  | 3 |  |  |  |  |  |  |  |  |  | 9 | 6 | 39 | 54 | 29 | 467 |
| Second Massachusetts Infantry |  |  |  |  | 1 | 4 | 3 | 37 |  |  |  | 4 |  |  |  |  |  |  |  |  | 1 | 4 | 3 | 41 | 49 | 44 | 863 |

| Command | Total |
|---|---|
| Second Brigade, Col. Evan Miles, 1st Infantry | 8 |
| First U. S. Infantry | 438 |
| Fourth U. S. Infantry | 444 |
| Twenty-fifth U. S. Infantry | 509 |
| Third Brigade, Brig. Gen. A. R. Chaffee | 16 |
| Seventh U. S. Infantry | 891 |
| Twelfth U. S. Infantry | 564 |
| Seventeenth U. S. Infantry | 482 |
| Independent Brigade, Brig. Gen. J. C. Bates | 6 |
| Third U. S. Infantry | 464 |
| Twentieth U. S. Infantry | 573 |
| Cavalry Division, Maj. Gen. J. Wheeler | 6 |
| First Brigade, Brig. Gen. S. S. Sumner | 6 |
| Third U. S. Cavalry | 433 |
| Sixth U. S. Cavalry | 435 |
| Ninth U. S. Cavalry | 207 |
| Second Brigade, Brig. Gen. S. B. M. Young | 3 |
| First U. S. Cavalry | 503 |
| Tenth U. S. Cavalry | 453 |
| First U. S. Volunteer Cavalry | 557 |
| Artillery Battalion, Maj. J. W. Dillenback | 1 |
| E, 1st Artillery | 79 |
| K, 1st Artillery | 78 |
| A, 2d Artillery | 79 |
| F, 2d Artillery | 77 |
| G, 4th Artillery | 53 |
| H, 4th Artillery | 65 |
| Brig. Gen. H. M. Duffield's Brigade | 4 |
| Ninth Massachusetts Infantry | 800* |
| Thirty-third Michigan Infantry | 958 |
| Thirty-fourth Michigan Infantry | 612 |
| Total | 17,349 |

*Estimated — no return.

ADJUTANT GENERAL'S OFFICE, *April 23, 1900.*

H. C. CORBIN,
*Adjutant General, U. S. A.*

Colonel Roosevelt by his example and fearlessness inspired his men, and both at Kettle Hill and the ridge known as San Juan he led his command in person. I was an eye-witness of Colonel Roosevelt's action.

As Colonel Roosevelt has left the service, a Brevet Commission is of no particular value in his case.

Very respectfully,<br>
SAMUEL S. SUMNER,<br>
*Major-General United States Volunteers.*

WEST POINT, N.Y.,<br>
December 17, 1898.

MY DEAR COLONEL: I saw you lead the line up the first hill — you were certainly the first officer to reach the top — and through your efforts, and your personally jumping to the front, a line more or less thin, but strong enough to take it, was led by you to the San Juan or first hill. In this your life was placed in extreme jeopardy, as you may recall, and as it proved by the number of dead left in that vicinity. Captain Stevens, then of the Ninth Cavalry, now of the Second Cavalry, was with you, and I am sure he recalls your gallant conduct. After the line started on the advance from the first hill, I did not see you until our line was halted, under a most galling fire, at the extreme front, where you afterwards entrenched. I spoke to you there and gave instructions from General Sumner that the position was to be held and that there would be no further advance till further orders. You were the senior officer there, took charge of the line, scolded me for having my horse so high upon the ridge; at the same time you were exposing yourself most conspicuously, while adjusting the line, for the example was necessary, as was proved when several colored soldiers — about eight or ten, Twenty-fourth Infantry, I think — started at a run to the rear to assist a wounded colored soldier, and you drew your revolver and put a short and effective stop to such apparent stampede — it quieted them. That position was hot, and now I marvel at your escaping there. . . .

Very sincerely yours,<br>
ROBERT L. HOWZE.

WEST POINT, N.Y.,<br>
December 17, 1898.

I hereby certify that on July 1, 1898, Colonel (then Lieutenant-Colonel) Theodore Roosevelt, First Volunteer Cavalry, distinguished himself through the action, and on two occasions during the battle when I was an eye-witness, his conduct was most conspicuous and clearly distinguished above other men, as follows:

1. At the base of San Juan, or first hill, there was a strong wire fence, or entanglement, at which the line hesitated under a galling fire, and where the losses were severe. Colonel Roosevelt jumped through the fence and by his enthusiasm, his example and courage succeeded in leading to the crest of the hill a line sufficiently strong to capture it. In this charge the Cavalry Brigade suffered its greatest loss, and the Colonel's life was placed in extreme jeopardy, owing to the conspicuous position he took in leading the line, and being the first to reach the crest of that hill, while under heavy fire of the enemy at close range.

2. At the extreme advanced position occupied by our lines, Colonel Roosevelt found himself the senior, and under his instructions from General Sumner to hold that position. He displayed the greatest bravery and placed his life in extreme jeopardy by unavoidable exposure to severe fire while adjusting and strengthening the line, placing the men in positions which afforded best protection, etc., etc. His conduct and example steadied the men, and on one occasion by severe but necessary measures prevented a small detachment from stampeding to the rear. He displayed the most conspicuous gallantry, courage and coolness, in performing extraordinarily hazardous duty.

ROBERT L. HOWZE,
*Captain A. A. G., U. S. V.*
(*First Lieutenant Sixth United States Cavalry*)

TO THE ADJUTANT-GENERAL UNITED STATES ARMY,
Washington, D.C.

HEADQUARTERS UNITED STATES MILITARY ACADEMY,
WEST POINT, N.Y.,
April 5, 1899.

LIEUTENANT-COLONEL W. H. CARTER,
*Assistant Adjutant-General United States Army,*
Washington, D.C.

SIR: In compliance with the request, contained in your letter of April 30th, of the Board convened to consider the awarding of brevets, medals of honor, etc., for the Santiago Campaign, that I state any facts, within my knowledge as Adjutant-General of the Brigade in which Colonel Theodore Roosevelt served, to aid the Board in determining, in connection with Colonel Roosevelt's application for a medal of honor, whether his conduct at Santiago was such as to distinguish him above others, I have the honor to submit the following:

My duties on July 1, 1898, brought me in constant observation of and contact with Colonel Roosevelt from early morning until shortly before the climax of the assault of the Cavalry Division on the San Juan Hill — the so-called Kettle Hill. During this time, while under the enemy's artillery fire at El Poso, and while on the march from El Poso by the San Juan ford to the point from which his regiment moved to the assault — about two miles, the greater part under fire — Colonel Roosevelt was conspicuous above any others I observed in his regiment in the zealous performance of duty, in total disregard of his personal danger and in his eagerness to meet the enemy. At El Poso, when the enemy opened on that place with artillery fire, a shrapnel bullet grazed and bruised one of Colonel Roosevelt's wrists. The incident did not lessen his hazardous exposure, but he continued so exposed until he had placed his command under cover. In moving to the assault of San Juan Hill, Colonel Roosevelt was most conspicuously brave, gallant and indifferent to his own safety. He, in the open, led his regiment; no officer could have set a more striking example to his men or displayed greater intrepidity.

Very respectfully,
Your obedient servant,
A. L. MILLS,
*Colonel United States Army, Superintendent.*

HEADQUARTERS DEPARTMENT OF SANTIAGO DE CUBA,
SANTIAGO DE CUBA,
December 30, 1898.
TO THE ADJUTANT-GENERAL, UNITED STATES ARMY,
Washington, D.C.

SIR: I have the honor to make the following statement relative to the conduct of Colonel Theodore Roosevelt, late First United States Volunteer Cavalry, during the assault upon San Juan Hill, July 1, 1898.

I have already recommended this officer for a medal of honor, which I understand has been denied him, upon the ground that my previous letter was too indefinite. I based my recommendation upon the fact that Colonel Roosevelt, accompanied only by four or five men, led a very desperate and extremely gallant charge on San Juan Hill, thereby setting a splendid example to the troops and encouraging them to pass over the open country intervening between their position and the trenches of the enemy. In leading this charge, he started off first, as he supposed, with quite a following of men, but soon discovered that he was alone. He then returned and gathered up a few men and led them to the charge, as above stated. The charge in itself was an extremely gallant one, and the example set a most inspiring one to the troops in that part of the line, and while it is perfectly true that everybody finally went up the hill in good style, yet there is no doubt that the magnificent example set by Colonel Roosevelt had a very encouraging effect and had great weight in bringing up the troops behind him. During the assault, Colonel Roosevelt was the first to reach the trenches in his part of the line and killed one of the enemy with his own hand.

I earnestly recommend that the medal be conferred upon Colonel Roosevelt, for I believe that he in every way deserves it, and that his services on the day in question were of great value and of a most distinguished character.

Very respectfully,
LEONARD WOOD,
*Major-General, United States Volunteers.*
*Commanding Department of Santiago de Cuba.*

HUNTSVILLE, ALA.,
January 4, 1899.

THE ADJUTANT-GENERAL, UNITED STATES ARMY,
Washington, D.C.

SIR: I have the honor to recommend that a "Congressional Medal of Honor" be given to Theodore Roosevelt (late Colonel First Volunteer Cavalry), for distinguished conduct and conspicuous bravery in command of his regiment in the charge on San Juan Hill, Cuba, July 1, 1898.

In compliance with G. O. 135, A. G. O. 1898, I enclose my certificate showing my personal knowledge of Colonel Roosevelt's conduct.

Very respectfully,
C. J. STEVENS,
*Captain Second Cavalry.*

I hereby certify that on July 1, 1898, at the battle of San Juan, Cuba, I witnessed Colonel (then Lieutenant-Colonel) Roosevelt, First Volunteer Cavalry, United States of America, mounted, leading his regiment in the charge on San Juan. By his gallantry and strong personality he contributed most materially to the success of the charge of the Cavalry Division up San Juan Hill.

Colonel Roosevelt was among the first to reach the crest of the hill, and his dashing example, his absolute fearlessness and gallant leading rendered his conduct conspicuous and clearly distinguished above other men.

C. J. STEVENS,
*Captain Second Cavalry.*
(*Late First Lieutenant Ninth Cavalry*)

YOUNG'S ISLAND, S.C.,
December 28, 1898.

TO THE ADJUTANT-GENERAL, UNITED STATES ARMY.

   Washington, D.C.

   SIR: Believing that information relating to superior conduct on the part of any of the higher officers who participated in the Spanish-American War (and which information may not have been given) would be appreciated by the Department over which you preside, I have the honor to call your attention to the part borne by Colonel Theodore Roosevelt, of the late First United States Volunteer Cavalry, in the battle of July 1st last. I do this not only because I think you ought to know, but because his regiment as a whole were very proud of his splendid actions that day and believe they call for that most coveted distinction of the American officer, the Medal of Honor. Held in support, he brought his regiment, at exactly the right time, not only up to the line of regulars, but went through them and headed, on horseback, the charge on Kettle Hill; this being done on his own initiative, the regulars as well as his own men following. He then headed the charge on the next hill, both regulars and the First United States Volunteer Cavalry following. He was so near the intrenchments on the second hill, that he shot and killed with a revolver one of the enemy before they broke completely. He then led the cavalry on the chain of hills overlooking Santiago, where he remained in charge of all the cavalry that was at the extreme front for the rest of that day and night. His unhesitating gallantry in taking the initiative against intrenchments lined by men armed with rapid fire guns certainly won him the highest consideration and admiration of all who witnessed his conduct throughout that day.

   What I here write I can bear witness to from personally having seen.

Very respectfully,
M. J. JENKINS,
*Major Late First United States Cavalry.*

PRESCOTT, A. T.,
December 25, 1898.

   I was Colonel Roosevelt's orderly at the battle of San Juan Hill, and from that time on until our return to Montauk Point. I was with him all through the fighting, and believe I was the only man who was always with him, though during part of the time Lieutenants Ferguson and Greenwald were also close to him. He led our regiment forward on horseback until he came to the men of the Ninth Cavalry lying down. He led us through these and they got up and joined us. He gave the order to charge on Kettle Hill, and led us on horseback up the hill, both Rough Riders and the Ninth Cavalry. He was the first on the hill, I being very nearly alongside of him. Some Spanish riflemen were coming out of the intrenchments and he killed one with his revolver. He took the men on to the crest of the hill and bade them begin firing on the blockhouse on the hill to our left, the one the infantry were attacking. When we took it, he gave the order to charge, and led the troops on Kettle Hill forward against the blockhouse on our front. He then had charge of all the cavalry on the hills overlooking Santiago, where we afterwards dug our trenches. He had command that afternoon and night, and for the rest of the time commanded our regiment at this point.

> Yours very truly,
> H. P. BARDSHAR.

CAMBRIDGE, MD.,
March 27, 1902.

Theodore Roosevelt, *President of the United States.*
    Washington, D.C.

DEAR SIR: At your request, I send you the following extracts from my diary, and from notes taken on the day of the assault on San Juan. I kept in my pocket a small pad on which incidents were noted daily from the landing until the surrender. On the day of the fight notes were taken just before Grimes fired his first gun, just after the third reply from the enemy — when we were massed in the road about seventy paces from Grimes' guns, and when I was beginning to get scared and to think I would be killed — at the halt just before you advanced, and under the shelter of the hills in the evening. Each time that notes were taken, the page was put in an envelope addressed to my wife. At the first chance they were mailed to her, and on my arrival in the United States the story of the fight, taken from these notes, was entered in the diary I keep in a book. I make this lengthy explanation that you may see that everything put down was fresh in my memory.

I quote from my diary: "The tension on the men was great. Suddenly a line of men appeared coming from our right. They were advancing through the long grass, deployed as skirmishers and were under fire. At their head, or rather in front of them and leading them, rode Colonel Roosevelt. He was very conspicuous, mounted as he was. The men were the 'Rough Riders,' so-called. I heard some one calling to them not to fire into us, and seeing Colonel Carrol, reported to him, and was told to go out and meet them, and caution them as to our position, we being between them and the enemy. I did so, speaking to Colonel Roosevelt. I also told him we were under orders not to advance, and asked him if he had received any orders.

He replied that he was going to charge the Spanish trenches. I told this to Colonel Carrol, and to Captain Dimmick, our squadron commander. A few moments after the word passed down that our left (Captain Taylor) was about to charge. Captain McBlain called out, 'we must go in with those troops; we must support Taylor.' I called this to Captain Dimmick, and he gave the order to assault."

"The cheer was taken up and taken up again, on the left, and in the distance it rolled on and on. And so we started. Colonel Roosevelt, of the Rough Riders, started the whole movement on the left, which was the first advance of the assault."

The following is taken from my notes and was hastily jotted down on the field: "The Rough Riders came in line — Colonel Roosevelt said he would assault — Taylor joined them with his troop — McBlain called to Dimmick, 'let us go, we must go to support them.' Dimmick said all right — and so, with no orders, we went in."

I find many of my notes are illegible from perspiration. My authority for saying Taylor went in with you, "joined with his troop" was the word passed to me and repeated to Captain Dimmick that Taylor was about to charge with you. I could not see his troop. I have not put it in my diary, but in another place I have noted that Colonel Carrol, who was acting as brigade commander, told me to ask you if you had any orders.

I have the honor to be,

Very respectfully,
Your obedient servant,
HENRY ANSON BARBER,
*Captain Twenty-Eighth Infantry,*
*(formerly of Ninth Cavalry)*

HEADQUARTERS PACIFIC DIVISION,
SAN FRANCISCO, CAL.,
May 11, 1905.

DEAR MR. PRESIDENT: As some discussion has arisen in the public prints regarding the battle of San Juan, Cuba, July 1, 1898, and your personal movements during that day have been the subject of comment, it may not be amiss in me to state some facts coming under my personal observation as Commanding General of the Cavalry Division, of which your regiment formed a part. It will, perhaps, be advisable to show first how I came to be in command, in order that my statement may have due weight as an authoritative statement of facts: I was placed in command of the Cavalry Division on the afternoon of June 30th by General Shafter; the assignment was made owing to the severe illness of General Wheeler, who was the permanent commander of said Division. Brigadier General Young, who commanded the Second Cavalry Brigade, of which your regiment — the First Volunteer Cavalry — formed a part, was also very ill, and I found it necessary to relieve him from command and place Colonel Wood, of the Rough Riders, in command of the Brigade; this change placed you in command of your regiment.

The Division moved from its camp on the evening of June 30th, and bivouacked at and about El Poso. I saw you personally in the vicinity of El Poso, about 8 A.M., July 1st. I saw you again on the road leading from El Poso to the San Juan River; you were at the head of your regiment, which was leading the Second Brigade, and immediately behind the rear regiment of the First Brigade. My orders were to turn to the right at San Juan River and take up a line along that stream and try and connect with General Lawton, who was to engage the enemy at El Caney. On reaching the river we came under the fire of the Spanish forces posted on San Juan Ridge and Kettle Hill. The First Brigade was faced to the front in line as soon as it had cleared the road, and the Second Brigade was ordered to pass in rear of the first and face to the front when clear of the First Brigade. This movement was very difficult, owing to the heavy undergrowth, and the regiments became more or less tangled up, but eventually the formation was accomplished, and the Division stood in an irregular line along the San Juan River, the Second Brigade on the right. We were subjected to a heavy fire from the forces on San Juan Ridge and Kettle Hill; our position was untenable, and it became necessary to assault the enemy or fall back. Kettle Hill was immediately in front of the Cavalry, and it was determined to assault that hill. The First Brigade was ordered forward, and the Second Brigade was ordered to support the attack; personally, I accompanied a portion of the Tenth Cavalry, Second Brigade, and the Rough Riders were to the right. This brought your regiment to the right of the house which was at the summit of the hill. Shortly after I reached the crest of the hill you came to me, accompanied, I think, by Captain C. J. Stevens, of the Ninth Cavalry. We were then in a position to see the line of intrenchments along San Juan Ridge, and could see Kent's Infantry Division engaged on our left, and Hawkins' assault against Fort San Juan. You asked me for permission to move forward and assault San Juan Ridge. I gave you the order in person to move forward, and I saw you move forward and assault San Juan Ridge with your regiment and portions of the First and Tenth Cavalry belonging to your Brigade. I held a portion of the Second Brigade as a reserve on Kettle Hill, not knowing what force the enemy might have in reserve behind the ridge. The First Brigade also moved forward and assaulted the ridge to the right of Fort San Juan. There was a small lake between Kettle Hill and San Juan Ridge, and in moving forward your command passed to the right of this lake. This brought you opposite a house on San Juan Ridge — not Fort San Juan proper, but a frame house surrounded by an earthwork. The enemy lost a number of men at this point, whose bodies lay in the trenches. Later in the day I rode along the line, and, as I recall it, a portion of the Tenth Cavalry was immediately about this house, and your regiment occupied an irregular semi-circular position along the ridge and immediately to the right of the house. You had pickets out to your front; and several hundred yards to your front the Spaniards had a heavy outpost occupying a house, with rifle pits surrounding it. Later in the day, and during the following day, the various regiments forming the Division were rearranged and brought into tactical formation, the First Brigade on the left and immediately to the right of Fort San Juan, and the Second Brigade on the right of the First.

This was the position occupied by the Cavalry Division until the final surrender of the Spanish forces, on July 17, 1898.

In conclusion allow me to say, that I saw you, personally, at about 8 A.M., at El Poso; later, on the road to San Juan River; later, on the summit of Kettle Hill, immediately after its capture by the Cavalry Division. I saw you move forward with your command to assault San Juan Ridge, and I saw you on San Juan Ridge, where we visited your line together, and you explained to me the disposition of your command.

> I am, sir, with much respect,
> Your obedient servant,
> SAMUEL S. SUMNER,
> *Major-General United States Army.*

# Chapter VIII

## THE NEW YORK GOVERNORSHIP

IN SEPTEMBER, 1898, the First Volunteer Cavalry, in company with most of the rest of the Fifth Army Corps, was disembarked at Montauk Point. Shortly after it was disbanded, and a few days later, I was nominated for Governor of New York by the Republican party. Timothy L. Woodruff was nominated for Lieutenant-Governor. He was my stanch friend throughout the term of our joint service.

The previous year, the machine or standpat Republicans, who were under the domination of Senator Platt, had come to a complete break with the anti-machine element over the New York mayoralty. This had brought the Republican party to a smash, not only in New York City, but in the State, where the Democratic candidate for Chief Judge of the Court of Appeals, Alton B. Parker, was elected by sixty or eighty thousand majority. Mr. Parker was an able man, a lieutenant of Mr. Hill's, standing close to the conservative Democrats of the Wall Street type. These conservative Democrats were planning how to wrest the Democratic party from the control of Mr. Bryan. They hailed Judge Parker's victory as a godsend. The Judge at once loomed up as a Presidential possibility, and was carefully groomed for the position by the New York Democratic machine, and its financial allies in the New York business world.

The Republicans realized that the chances were very much against them. Accordingly the leaders were in a chastened mood and ready to nominate any candidate with whom they thought there was a chance of winning. I was the only possibility, and, accordingly, under pressure from certain of the leaders who recognized this fact, and who responded to popular pressure, Senator Platt picked me for the nomination. He was entirely frank in the matter. He made no pretense that he liked me personally; but he deferred to the judgment of those who insisted that I was the only man who could be elected, and that therefore I had to be nominated.

Foremost among the leaders who pressed me on Mr. Platt (who "pestered" him about me, to use his own words) were

Mr. Quigg, Mr. Odell — then State Chairman of the Republican organization, and afterwards Governor — and Mr. Hazel, now United States Judge. Judge Hazel did not know me personally, but felt that the sentiment in his city, Buffalo, demanded my nomination, and that the then Republican Governor, Mr. Black, could not be reëlected. Mr. Odell, who hardly knew me personally, felt the same way about Mr. Black's chances, and, as he had just taken the State Chairmanship, he was very anxious to win a victory. Mr. Quigg knew me quite well personally; he had been in touch with me for years, while he was a reporter on the *Tribune*, and also when he edited a paper in Montana; he had been on good terms with me while he was in Congress and I was Civil Service Commissioner, meeting me often in company with my especial cronies in Congress — men like Lodge, Speaker Tom Reed, Greenhalge, Butterworth, and Dolliver — and he had urged my appointment as Police Commissioner on Mayor Strong.

It was Mr. Quigg who called on me at Montauk Point to sound me about the Governorship; Mr. Platt being by no means enthusiastic over Mr. Quigg's mission, largely because he disapproved of the Spanish War and of my part in bringing it about. Mr. Quigg saw me in my tent, in which he spent a couple of hours with me, my brother-in-law, Douglas Robinson, being also present. Quigg spoke very frankly to me, stating that he earnestly desired to see me nominated and believed that the great body of Republican voters in the State so desired, but that the organization and the State Convention would finally do what Senator Platt desired. He said that county leaders were already coming to Senator Platt, hinting at a close election, expressing doubt of Governor Black's availability for reëlection, and asking why it would not be a good thing to nominate me; that now that I had returned to the United States this would go on more and more all the time, and that he (Quigg) did not wish that these men should be discouraged and be sent back to their localities to suppress a rising sentiment in my favor. For this reason he said that he wanted from me a plain statement as to whether or not I wanted the nomination, and as to what would be my attitude toward the organization in the event of my nomination and election, whether or not I would "make war" on Mr. Platt and his friends, or whether I would confer with them and with the organization leaders generally, and give fair consideration to their point of view as to party policy and public interest. He said he had not come to make me any offer of the nomination,

Theodore Roosevelt, Governor of New York State.

and had not authority to do so, nor to get any pledges or promises. He simply wanted a frank definition of my attitude towards existing party conditions.

To this I replied that I should like to be nominated, and if nominated would promise to throw myself into the campaign with all possible energy. I said that I should not make war on Mr. Platt or anybody else if war could be avoided; that what I wanted was to be Governor and not a faction leader; that I certainly would confer with the organization men, as with everybody else who seemed to me to have knowledge of and interest in public affairs, and that as to Mr. Platt and the organization leaders, I would do so in the sincere hope that there might always result harmony of opinion and purpose; but that while I would try to get on well with the organization, the organization must with equal sincerity strive to do what I regarded as essential for the public good; and that in every case, after full consideration of what everybody had to say who might possess real knowledge of the matter, I should have to act finally as my own judgment and conscience dictated and administer the State government as I thought it ought to be administered. Quigg said that this was precisely what he supposed I would say, that it was all anybody could expect, and that he would state it to Senator Platt precisely as I had put it to him, which he accordingly did; and, throughout my term as Governor, Quigg lived loyally up to our understanding.*

After being nominated, I made a hard and aggressive campaign through the State. My opponent was a respectable man, a judge, behind whom stood Mr. Croker, the boss of Tammany Hall. My object was to make the people understand that it was Croker, and not the nominal candidate, who was my real opponent; that the choice lay between Crokerism and myself. Croker was a powerful and truculent man, the autocrat of his organization, and of a domineering nature. For his own reasons he insisted upon Tammany's turning down an excellent Democratic judge who was a candidate for reëlection. This gave me my chance. Under my attack, Croker, who was a stalwart fighting man and who would not take an attack tamely, himself came to the front. I was able to fix the contest in the public mind as one between himself and myself; and,

---

*In a letter to me Mr. Quigg states, what I had forgotten, that I told him to tell the Senator that while I would talk freely with him, and had no intention of becoming a factional leader with a personal organization, yet that I must have direct personal relations with everybody, and get their views at first hand whenever I so desired, because I could not have one man speaking for all.

against all probabilities, I won by the rather narrow margin of eighteen thousand plurality.

As I have already said, there is a lunatic fringe to every reform movement. At least nine-tenths of all the sincere reformers supported me; but the ultra-pacificists, the so-called anti-imperialists, or anti-militarists, or peace-at-any-price men, preferred Croker to me; and another knot of extremists who had at first ardently insisted that I must be "forced" on Platt, as soon as Platt supported me themselves opposed me *because* he supported me. After election John Hay wrote me as follows: "While you are Governor, I believe the party can be made solid as never before. You have already shown that a man may be absolutely honest and yet practical; a reformer by instinct and a wise politician; brave, bold, and uncompromising, and yet not a wild ass of the desert. The exhibition made by the professional independents in voting against you for no reason on earth except that somebody else was voting for you, is a lesson that is worth its cost."

At that time boss rule was at its very zenith. Mr. Bryan's candidacy in 1896 on a free silver platform had threatened such frightful business disaster as to make the business men, the wage-workers, and the professional classes generally, turn eagerly to the Republican party. East of the Mississippi the Republican vote for Mr. McKinley was larger by far than it had been for Abraham Lincoln in the days when the life of the Nation was at stake. Mr. Bryan championed many sorely needed reforms in the interest of the plain people; but many of his platform proposals, economic and otherwise, were of such a character that to have put them into practice would have meant to plunge all our people into conditions far worse than any of those for which he sought a remedy. The free silver advocates included sincere and upright men who were able to make a strong case for their position; but with them and dominating them were all the believers in the complete or partial repudiation of National, State, and private debts; and not only the business men but the workingmen grew to feel that under these circumstances too heavy a price could not be paid to avert the Democratic triumph. The fear of Mr. Bryan threw almost all the leading men of all classes into the arms of whoever opposed him.

The Republican bosses, who were already very powerful, and who were already in fairly close alliance with the privileged interests, now found everything working to their advantage. Good and high-minded men of conservative temperament in their panic played into the hands of the ultra-reactionaries of business and politics. The alliance between the two kinds of privilege, political and financial, was closely cemented; and wherever there was any attempt to break it up, the cry was at once raised that this merely represented another phase of the assault on National honesty and individual and mercantile integrity. As so often happens, the excesses and threats of an unwise and extreme radicalism had resulted in immensely strengthening the position of the beneficiaries of reaction. This was the era when the Standard Oil Company achieved a mastery of Pennsylvania politics so far-reaching and so corrupt that it is difficult to describe it without seeming to exaggerate.

In New York State, United States Senator Platt was the absolute boss of the Republican party. "Big business" was back of him; yet at the time this, the most important element in his strength, was only imperfectly understood. It was not until I was elected Governor that I myself came to understand it. We were still accustomed to talking of the "machine" as if it were something merely political, with which business had nothing to do. Senator Platt did not use his political position to advance his private fortunes — therein differing absolutely from many other political bosses. He lived in hotels and had few extravagant tastes. Indeed, I could not find that he had any tastes at all except for politics, and on rare occasions for a very dry theology wholly divorced from moral implications. But big business men contributed to him large sums of money, which enabled him to keep his grip on the machine and secured for them the help of the machine if they were threatened with adverse legislation. The contributions were given in the guise of contributions for campaign purposes, of money for the good of the party; when the money was contributed there was rarely talk of specific favors in return.* It was simply

---

*Each nation has its own pet sins to which it is merciful and also sins which it treats as most abhorrent. In America we are peculiarly sensitive

put into Mr. Platt's hands and treated by him as in the campaign chest. Then he distributed it in the districts where it was most needed by the candidates and organization leaders. Ordinarily no pledge was required from the latter to the bosses, any more than it was required by the business men from Mr. Platt or his lieutenants. No pledge was needed. It was all a "gentlemen's understanding." As the Senator once said to me, if a man's character was such that it was necessary to get a promise from him, it was clear proof that his character was such that the promise would not be worth anything after it was made.

It must not be forgotten that some of the worst practices of the machine in dealings of this kind represented merely virtues in the wrong place, virtues wrenched out of proper relation to their surroundings. A man in a doubtful district might win only because of the help Mr. Platt gave him; he might be a decent young fellow without money enough to finance his own campaign, who was able to finance it only because Platt of his own accord found out or was apprised of his need and advanced the money. Such a man felt grateful, and, because of his good qualities, joined with the purely sordid and corrupt heelers and crooked politicians to become part of the Platt machine. In his turn Mr. Platt was recognized by the business men, the big contributors, as an honorable man; not only a man of his word, but a man who, whenever he received a favor, could be trusted to do his best to repay it on any occasion that arose. I believe that usually the contributors, and the recipient, sincerely felt that the transaction was proper and subserved the cause of good politics and good business; and, indeed, as regards the major part of the contributions, it is probable that this was the fact, and that the only criticism that could properly be made about the contributions was that they were not made with publicity — and at that time neither

---

about big money contributions for which the donors expect any reward. In England, where in some ways the standard is higher than here, such contributions are accepted as a matter of course, nay, as one of the methods by which wealthy men obtain peerages. It would be well-nigh an impossibility for a man to secure a seat in the United States Senate by mere campaign contributions, in the way that seats in the British House of Lords have often been secured without any scandal being caused thereby.

the parties nor the public had any realization that publicity was necessary, or any adequate understanding of the dangers of the "invisible empire" which throve by what was done in secrecy. Many, probably most, of the contributors of this type never wished anything personal in exchange for their contributions, and made them with sincere patriotism, desiring in return only that the Government should be conducted on a proper basis. Unfortunately, it was, in practice, exceedingly difficult to distinguish these men from the others who contributed big sums to the various party bosses with the expectation of gaining concrete and personal advantages (in which the bosses shared) at the expense of the general public. It was very hard to draw the line between these two types of contributions.

There was but one kind of money contribution as to which it seemed to me absolutely impossible for either the contributor or the recipient to disguise to themselves the evil meaning of the contribution. This was where a big corporation contributed to both political parties. I knew of one such case where in a State campaign a big corporation which had many dealings with public officials frankly contributed in the neighborhood of a hundred thousand dollars to one campaign fund and fifty thousand dollars to the campaign fund of the other side — and, I believe, made some further substantial contributions in the same ratio of two dollars to one side for every one dollar given to the other. The contributors were Democrats, and the big contributions went to the Democratic managers. The Republican was elected, and after his election, when a matter came up affecting the company, in which its interests were hostile to those of the general public, the successful candidate, then holding a high State office, was approached by his campaign managers and the situation put frankly before him. He was less disturbed than astonished, and remarked, "Why, I thought So-and-so and his associates were Democrats and subscribed to the Democratic campaign fund." "So they did," was the answer; "they subscribed to them twice as much as they subscribed to us, but if they had had any idea that you intended doing what you now say you will do, they would have subscribed it all to the other side, and more too." The State official in his turn answered that he was very sorry if any one had subscribed under a misapprehension, that it was no fault of his, for he had stated definitely and clearly his position, that he of course had no money wherewith himself to return what without his knowledge had been contributed, and that all he could say was that any man who had subscribed to his campaign fund under the impression that the receipt of the subscription would be a bar to the performance of public duty was sadly mistaken.

The control by Mr. Platt and his lieutenants over the organization was well-nigh complete. There were splits among the bosses, and insurgent movements now and then, but the ordinary citizens had no control over the political machinery except in a very few districts. There were, however, plenty of good men in politics, men who either came from districts where there was popular control, or who represented a genuine aspiration towards good citizenship on the part of some boss or group of bosses, or else who had been nominated frankly for reasons of expediency by bosses whose attitude towards good citizenship was at best one of Gallio-like indifference. At the time when I was nominated for Governor, as later when Mr. Hughes was nominated and renominated for Governor, there was no possibility of securing the nomination unless the bosses permitted it. In each case the bosses, the machine leaders, took a man for whom they did not care, because he was the only man with whom they could win. In the case of Mr. Hughes there was of course also the fact of pressure from the National Administration. But the bosses were never overcome in a fair fight, when they had made up their minds to fight, until the Saratoga Convention in 1910, when Mr. Stimson was nominated for Governor.

Senator Platt had the same inborn capacity for the kind of politics which he liked that many big Wall Street men have shown for not wholly dissimilar types of finance. It was his chief interest, and he applied himself to it unremittingly. He handled his private business successfully; but it was politics in which he was absorbed, and he concerned himself therewith every day in the year. He had built up an excellent system of organization, and the necessary funds came from corporations and men of wealth who contributed as I have described above. The majority of the men with a natural capacity for organization leadership of the type which has generally been prevalent in New York politics turned to Senator Platt as their natural chief and helped build up the organization, until under his leadership it became more powerful and in a position of greater control than any other Republican machine in the country, excepting in Pennsylvania. The Democratic machines in some of the big cities, as in New York and Boston, and the country Democratic machine of New York under David B. Hill, were probably even more efficient, representing an even more complete mastery by the bosses, and an even greater degree of drilled obedience among the henchmen. It would be an entire mistake to suppose that Mr. Platt's lieutenants were either all bad men or all influenced by unworthy motives. He was constantly doing favors for men. He had won the gratitude of many good men. In the country districts especially, there were many places where his machine included the majority of the best citizens, the leading and substantial citizens, among the inhabitants. Some of his strongest and most efficient lieutenants were disinterested men of high character.

There had always been a good deal of opposition to Mr. Platt and the machine, but the leadership of this opposition was apt to be found only among those whom Abraham Lincoln called the "silk stockings," and much of it excited almost as much derision among the plain people as the machine itself excited anger or dislike. Very many of Mr. Platt's opponents really disliked him and his methods, for æsthetic rather than for moral reasons, and the bulk of the people half-consciously felt this and refused to submit to their leadership. The men who opposed him in this manner were good citizens according to their lights, prominent in the social clubs and in philanthropic circles, men of means and often men of business standing. They disliked coarse and vulgar politicians, and they sincerely reprobated all the shortcomings that were recognized by, and were offensive to, people of their own caste. They had not the slightest understanding of the needs, interests, ways of thought, and convictions of the average small man; and the small man felt this, although he could not express it, and sensed that they were really not concerned with his welfare, and that they did not offer him anything materially better from his point of view than the machine.

When reformers of this type attempted to oppose Mr. Platt, they usually put up either some rather inefficient, well-meaning person, who bathed every day, and didn't steal, but whose only good point was "respectability," and who knew nothing of the great fundamental questions looming before us; or else they put up some big business man or corporation lawyer who was wedded to the gross wrong and injustice of our economic system, and who neither by personality nor by programme gave the ordinary plain people any belief that there was promise of vital good to them in the change. The correctness of their view was proved by the fact that as soon as fundamental economic and social reforms were at stake the æsthetic, as distinguished from the genuinely moral, reformers, for the most part sided with the bosses against the people.

When I became Governor, the conscience of the people was in no way or shape aroused, as it has since become roused. The people accepted and practiced in a matter-of-course way as quite proper things which they would not now tolerate. They had no definite and clearly outlined conception of what they wished in the way of reform. They on the whole tolerated, and indeed approved of, the machine; and there had been no development on any considerable scale of reformers with the vision to see what the needs of the people were, and the high purpose sanely to achieve what was necessary in order to meet these needs. I knew both the machine and the silk-stocking reformers fairly well, from many years' close association with them. The machine as such had no ideals at all, although many of the men composing it did have. On the other hand, the ideals of very many of the silk-stocking reformers did not relate to the questions of real and vital interest to our people; and, singularly enough, in international matters, these same silk-stockings were no more to be trusted than the average ignorant demagogue or shortsighted spoils politicians. I felt that these men would be broken reeds to which to trust in any vital contest for betterment of social and industrial conditions.

I had neither the training nor the capacity that would have enabled me to match Mr. Platt and his machine people on their own ground. Nor did I believe that the effort to build up a machine of my own under the then existing conditions would meet the needs of the situation so far as the people were concerned. I therefore made no effort to create a machine of my own, and consistently adopted the plan of going over the heads of the men holding public office and of the men in control of the organization, and appealing directly to the people behind them. The machine, for instance, had a more or less strong control over the great bulk of the members of the State Legislature; but in the last resort the people behind these legislators had a still greater control over them. I made up my mind that the only way I could beat the bosses whenever the need to do so arose (and unless there was such need I did not wish to try) was, not by attempting to manipulate the machinery, and not by trusting merely to the professional reformers, but my making my appeal as directly and as emphatically as I knew how to the mass of voters themselves, to the people, to the men who if waked up would be able to impose their will on their representatives. My success depended upon getting the people in the different districts to look at matters in my way, and getting them to take such an active interest in affairs as to enable them to exercise control over their representatives.

There were a few of the Senators and Assemblymen whom I could reach by seeing them personally and putting before them my arguments; but most of them were too much under the control of the machine for me to shake them loose unless they knew that the people were actively behind me. In making my appeal to the people as a whole I was dealing with an entirely different constituency from that which, especially in the big cities, liked to think of itself as the "better element," the particular exponent of reform and good citizenship. I was dealing with shrewd, hard-headed, kindly men and women, chiefly concerned with the absorbing work of earning their own living, and impatient of fads, who had grown to feel that the associations with the word "reformer" were not much better than the associations with the word "politician." I had to convince these men and women of my good faith, and, moreover, of my common sense and efficiency. They were most of them strong partisans, and an outrage had to be very real and very great to shake them even partially loose from their party affiliations. Moreover, they took little interest in any fight of mere personalities. They were not influenced in the least by the silk-stocking reform view of Mr. Platt. I knew that if they were persuaded that I was engaged in a mere faction fight against him, that it was a mere issue between his ambition and mine, they would at once become indifferent, and my fight would be lost.

But I felt that I could count on their support wherever I could show them that the fight was not made just for the sake of the row, that it was not made merely as a factional contest against Senator Platt and the organization, but was waged from a sense of duty for real and tangible causes such as the promotion of governmental efficiency and honesty, and forcing powerful moneyed men to take the proper attitude toward the community at large. They stood by me when I insisted upon having the canal department, the insurance department, and the various departments of the State Government run with efficiency and honesty; they stood by me when I insisted upon making wealthy men who owned franchises pay the State what they properly ought to pay; they stood by me when, in connection with the strikes on the Croton Aqueduct and in Buffalo, I promptly used the military power of the State to put a stop to rioting and violence.

In the latter case my chief opponents and critics were local politicians who were truckling to the labor vote; but in all cases coming under the first two categories I had serious trouble with the State leaders of the machine. I always did my best, in good faith, to get Mr. Platt and the other heads of the machine to accept my views, and to convince them, by repeated private conversations, that I was right. I never wantonly antagonized or humiliated them. I did not wish to humiliate them or to seem victorious over them; what I wished was to secure the things that I thought it essential to the men and women of the State to secure. If I could finally persuade them to support me, well and good; in such case I continued to work with them in the friendliest manner.

If after repeated and persistent effort I failed to get them to support me, then I made a fair fight in the open, and in a majority of cases I carried my point and succeeded in getting through the legislation which I wished. In theory the Executive has nothing to do with legislation. In practice, as things

now are, the Executive is or ought to be peculiarly representative of the people as a whole. As often as not the action of
the Executive offers the only means by which the people can
get the legislation they demand and ought to have. Therefore
a good executive under the present conditions of American
political life must take a very active interest in getting the right
kind of legislation, in addition to performing his executive
duties with an eye single to the public welfare. More than half
of my work as Governor was in the direction of getting
needed and important legislation. I accomplished this only by
arousing the people, and riveting their attention on what was
done.

Gradually the people began to wake up more and more to
the fact that the machine politicians were not giving them the
kind of government which they wished. As this waking up
grew more general, not merely in New York or any other
one State, but throughout most of the Nation, the power of
the bosses waned. Then a curious thing happened. The professional reformers who had most loudly criticized these
bosses began to change toward them. Newspaper editors, college presidents, corporation lawyers, and big business men, all
alike, had denounced the bosses and had taken part in reform
movements against them so long as these reforms dealt only
with things that were superficial, or with fundamental things
that did not affect themselves and their associates. But the majority of these men turned to the support of the bosses when
the great new movement began clearly to make itself evident
as one against privilege in business no less than against privilege in politics, as one for social and industrial no less than for
political righteousness and fair dealing. The big corporation
lawyer who had antagonized the boss in matters which he regarded as purely political stood shoulder to shoulder with the
boss when the movement for betterment took shape in direct
attack on the combination of business with politics and with
the judiciary which has done so much to enthrone privilege in
the economic world.

The reformers who denounced political corruption and
fraud when shown at the expense of their own candidates by
machine ward heelers of a low type hysterically applauded similar corrupt trickery when practiced by these same politicians

against men with whose political and industrial programme the reformers were not in sympathy. I had always been instinctively and by nature a democrat, but if I had needed conversion to the democratic ideal here in America the stimulus would have been supplied by what I saw of the attitude, not merely of the bulk of the men of greatest wealth, but of the bulk of the men who most prided themselves upon their education and culture, when we began in good faith to grapple with the wrong and injustice of our social and industrial system, and to hit at the men responsible for the wrong, no matter how high they stood in business or in politics, at the bar or on the bench. It was while I was Governor, and especially in connection with the franchise tax legislation, that I first became thoroughly aware of the real causes of this attitude among the men of great wealth and among the men who took their tone from the men of great wealth.

Very soon after my victory in the race for Governor I had one or two experiences with Senator Platt which showed in amusing fashion how absolute the rule of the boss was in the politics of that day. Senator Platt, who was always most kind and friendly in his personal relations with me, asked me in one day to talk over what was to be done at Albany. He had the two or three nominal heads of the organization with him. They were his lieutenants, who counseled and influenced him, whose advice he often followed, but who, when he had finally made up his mind, merely registered and carried out his decrees. After a little conversation the Senator asked if I had any member of the Assembly whom I wished to have put on any committee, explaining that the committees were being arranged. I answered no, and expressed my surprise at what he had said, because I had not understood the Speaker who appointed the committees had himself been agreed upon by the members-elect. "Oh!" responded the Senator, with a tolerant smile, "He has not been chosen yet, but of course whoever we choose as Speaker will agree beforehand to make the appointments we wish." I made a mental note to the effect that if they attempted the same process with the Governor-elect they would find themselves mistaken.

In a few days the opportunity to prove this arrived. Under the preceding Administration there had been grave scandals about the Erie Canal, the trans-State Canal, and these scandals had been one of the chief issues in the campaign for the Governorship. The construction of this work was under the control of the Superintendent of Public Works. In the actual state of affairs his office was by far the most important office under me, and I intended to appoint to it some man of high character and capacity who could be trusted to do the work not merely honestly and efficiently, but without regard to politics. A week or so after the Speakership incident Senator Platt asked me to come and see him (he was an old and physically feeble man, able to move about only with extreme difficulty).

On arrival I found the Lieutenant-Governor elect, Mr. Woodruff, who had also been asked to come. The Senator informed me that he was glad to say that I would have a most admirable man as Superintendent of Public Works, as he had just received a telegram from a certain gentleman, whom he named, saying that he would accept the position! He handed me the telegram. The man in question was a man I liked; later I appointed him to an important office in which he did well. But he came from a city along the line of the canal, so that I did not think it best that he should be appointed anyhow; and, moreover, what was far more important, it was necessary to have it understood at the very outset that the Administration was my Administration and was no one else's but mine. So I told the Senator very politely that I was sorry, but that I could not appoint his man. This produced an explosion, but I declined to lose my temper, merely repeating that I must decline to accept any man chosen for me, and that I must choose the man myself. Although I was very polite, I was also very firm, and Mr. Platt and his friends finally abandoned their position.

I appointed an engineer from Brooklyn, a veteran of the Civil War, Colonel Partridge, who had served in Mayor Low's administration. He was an excellent man in every way. He chose as his assistant, actively to superintend the work, a Cornell graduate named Elon Hooker, a man with no political backing at all, picked simply because he was the best equipped man for the place. The office, the most important office under me, was run in admirable fashion throughout my Administration; I doubt if there ever was an important department of the New York State Government run with a higher standard of efficiency and integrity.

But this was not all that had to be done about the canals. Evidently the whole policy hitherto pursued had been foolish and inadequate. I appointed a first-class non-partisan commission of business men and expert engineers who went into the matter exhaustively, and their report served as the basis upon which our entire present canal system is based. There remained the question of determining whether the canal officials who were in office before I became Governor, and whom I had declined to reappoint, had been guilty of any action because of which it would be possible to proceed against them criminally or otherwise under the law. Such criminal action had been freely charged against them during the campaign by the Democratic (including the so-called mugwump) press. To determine this matter I appointed two Democratic lawyers, Messrs. Fox and MacFarlane (the latter Federal District Attorney for New York under President Cleveland), and put the whole investigation in their hands. These gentlemen made an exhaustive investigation lasting several months. They reported that there had been grave delinquency in the prosecution of the work, delinquency which justified public condemnation of those responsible for it (who were out of office), but that there was no ground for criminal prosecution. I laid their report before the Legislature with a message in which I said: "There is probably no lawyer of high standing in the State who, after studying the report of counsel in this case and the testimony taken by the investigating commission, would disagree with them as to the impracticability of a successful prosecution. Under such circumstances the one remedy was a thorough change in the methods and management. This change has been made."

When my successor in the Governorship took office, Colonel Partridge retired, and Elon Hooker, finding that he could no longer act with entire disregard of politics and with an eye single to the efficiency of the work, also left. A dozen years later — having in the meantime made a marked success in a business career — he became the Treasurer of the National Progressive party.

My action in regard to the canals, and the management of his office, the most important office under me, by Colonel Partridge, established my relations with Mr. Platt from the outset on pretty nearly the right basis. But, besides various small difficulties, we had one or two serious bits of trouble before my duties as Governor ceased. It must be remembered that Mr. Platt was to all intents and purposes a large part of, and sometimes a majority of, the Legislature. There were a few entirely independent men such as Nathaniel Elsberg, Regis Post, and Alford Cooley, in each of the two houses; the remainder were under the control of the Republican and Democratic bosses, but could also be more or less influenced by an aroused public opinion. The two machines were apt to make common cause if their vital interests were touched. It was my business to devise methods by which either the two machines could be kept apart or else overthrown if they came together.

My desire was to achieve results, and not merely to issue manifestoes of virtue. It is very easy to be efficient if the efficiency is based on unscrupulousness, and it is still easier to be virtuous if one is content with the purely negative virtue which consists in not doing anything wrong, but being wholly unable to accomplish anything positive for good. My favorite quotation from Josh Billings again applies: It is so much easier to be a harmless dove than a wise serpent. My duty was to combine both idealism and efficiency. At that time the public conscience was still dormant as regards many species of political and business misconduct, as to which during the next decade it became sensitive. I had to work with the tools at hand and to take into account the feeling of the people, which I have already described. My aim was persistently to refuse to be put in a position where what I did would seem to be a mere faction struggle against Senator Platt. My aim was to make a fight only when I could so manage it that there could be no question in the minds of honest men that my prime purpose was not to attack Mr. Platt or any one else except as a necessary incident to securing clean and efficient government.

In each case I did my best to persuade Mr. Platt not to oppose me. I endeavored to make it clear to him that I was not trying to wrest the organization from him; and I always gave him in detail the reasons why I felt I had to take the position I intended to adopt. It was only after I had exhausted all the resources of my patience that I would finally, if he still proved obstinate, tell him that I intended to make the fight anyhow. As I have said, the Senator was an old and feeble man in physique, and it was possible for him to go about very little. Until Friday evening he would be kept at his duties at Washington, while I was in Albany. If I wished to see him it generally had to be at his hotel in New York on Saturday, and usually I would go there to breakfast with him. The one thing I would not permit was anything in the nature of a secret or clandestine meeting. I always insisted on going openly. Solemn reformers of the tom-fool variety, who, according to their custom, paid attention to the name and not the thing, were much exercised over my "breakfasting with Platt." Whenever I breakfasted with him they became sure that the fact carried with it some sinister significance. The worthy creatures never took the trouble to follow the sequence of facts and events for themselves. If they had done so they would have seen that any series

William Loeb, Jr.

"Mr. Loeb gave me much information about various improper practices in the insurance business."

of breakfasts with Platt always meant that I was going to do something he did not like, and that I was trying, courteously and frankly, to reconcile him to it. My object was to make it as easy as possible for him to come with me. As long as there was no clash between us there was no object in my seeing him; it was only when the clash came or was imminent that I had to see him. A series of breakfasts was always the prelude to some active warfare.* In every instance I substantially carried my point, although in some cases not in exactly the way in which I had originally hoped.

There were various measures to which he gave a grudging and querulous assent without any break being threatened. I secured the reënactment of the Civil Service Law, which under my predecessor had very foolishly been repealed. I secured a mass of labor legislation, including the enactment of laws to increase the number of factory inspectors, to create a Tenement-House Commission (whose findings resulted in further and excellent legislation to improve housing conditions), to regulate and improve sweatshop labor, to make the eight-hour and prevailing rate of wages law effective, to secure the genuine enforcement of the act relating to the hours of railway workers, to compel railways to equip freight trains with air-brakes, to regulate the working hours of women and protect both women and children from dangerous machinery, to enforce good scaffolding provisions for workmen on buildings, to provide seats for the use of waitresses in hotels and restaurants, to reduce the hours of labor for drug-store clerks, to provide for the registration of laborers for municipal employment. I tried hard but failed to secure an employers' liability law and the state control of employment offices. There was hard fighting over some of these bills, and, what was much more serious, there was effort to get round the law by trickery and by securing its inefficient enforcement. I was continually helped by men with whom I had gotten in touch while in the Police Department; men such as James Bronson Reynolds, through whom I first became interested in settlement work on the East Side. Once or twice I went suddenly down to New York City without warning any one and traversed the tenement-house quarters, visiting various sweat-

*To illustrate my meaning I quote from a letter of mine to Senator Platt of December 13, 1899. He had been trying to get me to promote a certain Judge X over the head of another Judge Y. I wrote: "There is a strong feeling among the judges and the leading members of the bar that Judge Y ought not to have Judge X jumped over his head, and I do not see my way clear to doing it. I am inclined to thing that the solution I mentioned to you is the solution I shall have to adopt. Remember the breakfast at Douglas Robinson's at 8:30."

shops picked at random. Jake Riis accompanied me; and as a result of our inspection we got not only an improvement in the law but a still more marked improvement in its administration. Thanks chiefly to the activity and good sense of Dr. John H. Pryor, of Buffalo, and by the use of every pound of pressure which as Governor I could bring to bear in legitimate fashion — including a special emergency message — we succeeded in getting through a bill providing for the first State hospital for incipient tuberculosis. We got valuable laws for the farmer; laws preventing the adulteration of food products (which laws were equally valuable to the consumer), and laws helping the dairyman. In addition to labor legislation I was able to do a good deal for forest preservation and the protection of our wild life. All that later I strove for in the Nation in connection with Conservation was foreshadowed by what I strove to obtain for New York State when I was Governor; and I was already working in connection with Gifford Pinchot and Newell. I secured better administration, and some improvement in the laws themselves. The improvement in administration, and in the character of the game and forest wardens, was secured partly as the result of a conference in the executive chamber which I held with forty of the best guides and woodsmen of the Adirondacks.

As regards most legislation, even that affecting labor and the forests, I got on fairly well with the machine. But on the two issues in which "big business" and the kind of politics which is allied to big business were most involved we clashed hard — and clashing with Senator Platt meant clashing with the entire Republican organization, and with the organized majority in each house of the Legislature. One clash was in connection with the Superintendent of Insurance, a man whose office made him a factor of immense importance in the big business circles of New York. The then incumbent of the office was an efficient man, the boss of an up-State county, a veteran politician and one of Mr. Platt's right-hand men. Certain investigations which I made — in the course of the fight — showed that this Superintendent of Insurance had been engaged in large business operations in New York City. These operations had thrown him into a peculiarly intimate business contact of one sort and another with various financiers with whom I did not deem it expedient that the Superintendent of Insurance, while such, should have any intimate and secret money-making relations. Moreover, the gentleman in question represented the straitest sect of the old-time spoils politicians. I therefore determined not to reappoint him. Unless I could get his successor confirmed, however, he would stay in under the law, and the Republican machine, with the assistance of Tammany, expected to control far more than a majority of all the Senators.

Mr. Platt issued an ultimatum to me that the incumbent must be reappointed or else that he would fight, and that if he chose to fight the man would stay in anyhow because I could not oust him — for under the New York Constitution the assent of the Senate was necessary not only to appoint a man to office but to remove him from office. As always with Mr. Platt, I persistently refused to lose my temper, no matter what he said — he was much too old and physically feeble for there to be any point of honor in taking up any of his remarks — and I merely explained good-humoredly that I had made up my mind and that the gentleman in question would not be retained. As for not being able to get his successor confirmed, I pointed out that as soon as the Legislature adjourned I could and would appoint another man temporarily. Mr. Platt then said that the incumbent would be put back as soon as the Legislature reconvened; I admitted that this was possible, but added cheerfully that I would remove him again just as soon as that Legislature adjourned, and that even though I had an uncomfortable time myself, I would guarantee to make my opponents more uncomfortable still. We parted without any sign of reaching an agreement.

There remained some weeks before final action could be taken, and the Senator was confident that I would have to yield. His most efficient allies were the pretended reformers, most of them my open or covert enemies, who loudly insisted that I must make an open fight on the Senator himself and on the Republican organization. This was what he wished, for at that time there was no way of upsetting him within the Republican party; and, as I have said, if I had permitted the contest to assume the shape of a mere faction fight between the Governor and the United States Senator, I would have insured the victory of the machine. So I blandly refused to let the thing become a personal fight, explaining again and again that I was perfectly willing to appoint an organization man, and naming two or three whom I was willing to appoint, but also explaining that I would not retain the incumbent, and would not appoint any man of his type. Meanwhile pressure on behalf of the said incumbent began to come from the business men of New York.

The Superintendent of Insurance was not a man whose ill will the big life insurance companies cared to incur, and company after company passed resolutions asking me to reappoint him, although in private some of the men who signed these resolutions nervously explained that they did not mean what they had written, and hoped I would remove the man. A citizen prominent in reform circles, marked by the Cato-like austerity of his reform professions, had a son who was a counsel for one of the insurance companies. The father was engaged in writing letters to the papers demanding in the name of uncompromising virtue that I should not only get rid of the Superintendent of Insurance, but in his place should appoint somebody or other personally offensive to Senator Platt — which last proposition, if adopted, would have meant that the Superintendent of Insurance would have stayed in, for the reasons I have already given. Meanwhile the son came to see me on behalf of the insurance company he represented and told me that the company was anxious that there should be a change in the superintendency; that if I really meant to fight, they thought they had influence with four of the State Senators, Democrats and Republicans, whom they could get to vote to confirm the man I nominated, but that they wished to be sure that I would not abandon the fight, because it would be a very bad thing for them if I started the fight and then backed down. I told my visitor that he need be under no apprehensions, that I would certainly see the fight through. A man who has much to do with that kind of politics which concerns both New York politicians and New York business men and lawyers is not easily surprised, and therefore I felt no other emotion than a rather sardonic amusement when thirty-six hours later I read in the morning paper an open letter from the officials of the very company who had been

communicating with me in which they enthusiastically advocated the renomination of the Superintendent. Shortly afterwards my visitor, the young lawyer, called me up on the
telephone and explained that the officials did not mean what
they had said in this letter, that they had been obliged to write
it for fear of the Superintendent, but that if they got the
chance they intended to help me get rid of him. I thanked him
and said I thought I could manage the fight by myself. I did
not hear from him again, though his father continued to
write public demands that I should practice pure virtue, un-
defiled and offensive.

Meanwhile Senator Platt declined to yield. I had picked out
a man, a friend of his, who I believed would make an honest
and competent official, and whose position in the organization was such that I did not believe the Senate would venture
to reject him. However, up to the day before the appointment
was to go to the Senate, Mr. Platt remained unyielding. I saw
him that afternoon and tried to get him to yield, but he said
No, that if I insisted, it would be war to the knife, and my destruction, and perhaps the destruction of the party. I said I
was very sorry, that I could not yield, and if the war came it
would have to come, and that next morning I should send in
the name of the Superintendent's successor. We parted, and
soon afterwards I received from the man who was at the
moment Mr. Platt's right-hand lieutenant a request to know
where he could see me that evening. I appointed the Union
League Club. My visitor went over the old ground, explained
that the Senator would under no circumstances yield, that he
was certain to win in the fight, that my reputation would be
destroyed, and that he wished to save me from such a lamentable smash-up as an ending to my career. I could only repeat
what I had already said, and after half an hour of futile argument I rose and said that nothing was to be gained by further
talk and that I might as well go. My visitor repeated that I had
this last chance, and that ruin was ahead of me if I refused
it; whereas, if I accepted, everything would be made easy. I
shook my head and answered, "There is nothing to add to
what I have already said." He responded, "You have made up
your mind?" and I said, "I have." He then said, "You know it
means your ruin?" and I answered, "Well, we will see about

that," and walked toward the door. He said, "You understand, the fight will begin to-morrow and will be carried on to the bitter end." I said, "Yes," and added, as I reached the door, "Good night." Then, as the door opened, my opponent, or visitor, whichever one chooses to call him, whose face was as impassive and as inscrutable as that of Mr. John Hamlin in a poker game, said: "Hold on! We accept. Send in So-and-so [the man I had named]. The Senator is very sorry, but he will make no further opposition!" I never saw a bluff carried more resolutely through to the final limit. My success in the affair, coupled with the appointment of Messrs. Partridge and Hooker, secured me against further effort to interfere with my handling of the executive departments.

It was in connection with the insurance business that I first met Mr. George W. Perkins. He came to me with a letter of introduction from the then Speaker of the National House of Representatives, Tom Reed, which ran: "Mr. Perkins is a personal friend of mine, whose straightforwardness and intelligence will commend to you whatever he has to say. If you will give him proper opportunity to explain his business, I have no doubt that what he will say will be worthy of your attention." Mr. Perkins wished to see me with reference to a bill that had just been introduced in the Legislature, which aimed to limit the aggregate volume of insurance that any New York State company could assume. There were then three big insurance companies in New York — the Mutual Life, Equitable, and New York Life. Mr. Perkins was a Vice-President of the New York Life Insurance Company and Mr. John A. McCall was its President. I had just finished my fight against the Superintendent of Insurance, whom I refused to continue in office. Mr. McCall had written me a very strong letter urging that he be retained, and had done everything he could to aid Senator Platt in securing his retention. The Mutual Life and Equitable people had openly followed the same course, but in private had hedged. They were both backing the proposed bill. Mr. McCall was opposed to it; he was in California, and just before starting thither he had been told by the Mutual Life and Equitable that the Limitation Bill was favored by me and would be put through if such a thing were possible. Mr. McCall did not know me, and on leaving for

California told Mr. Perkins that from all he could learn he was sure I was bent on putting this bill through, and that nothing he could say to me would change my view; in fact, because he had fought so hard to retain the old Insurance Superintendent, he felt that I would be particularly opposed to anything he might wish done.

As a matter of fact, I had no such feeling. I had been carefully studying the question. I had talked with the Mutual Life and Equitable people about it, but was not committed to any particular course, and had grave doubts as to whether it was well to draw the line on size instead of on conduct. I was therefore very glad to see Perkins and get a new point of view. I went over the matter with a great deal of care and at considerable length, and after we had thrashed the matter out pretty fully and Perkins had laid before me in detail the methods employed by Austria, Germany, Switzerland, and other European countries to handle their large insurance companies, I took the position that there undoubtedly were evils in the insurance business, but that they did not consist in insuring people's lives, for that certainly was not an evil; and I did not see how the real evils could be eradicated by limiting or suppressing a company's ability to protect an additional number of lives with insurance. I therefore announced that I would not favor a bill that limited volume of business, and would not sign it if it were passed; but that I favored legislation that would make it impossible to place, through agents, policies that were ambiguous and misleading, or to pay exorbitant prices to agents for business, or to invest policy-holders' money in improper securities, or to give power to officers to use the company's funds for their own personal profit. In reaching this determination I was helped by Mr. Loeb, then merely a stenographer in my office, but who had already attracted my attention both by his efficiency and by his loyalty to his former employers, who were for the most part my political opponents. Mr. Loeb gave me much information about various improper practices in the insurance business. I began to gather data on the subject, with the intention of bringing about corrective legislation, for at that time I expected to continue in office as Governor. But in a few weeks I was nominated as Vice-President, and my successor did nothing about the matter.

So far as I remember, this was the first time the question of correcting evils in a business by limiting the volume of business to be done was ever presented to me, and my decision in the matter was on all fours with the position I have always since taken when any similar principle was involved. At the time when I made my decision about the Limitation Bill, I was on friendly terms with the Mutual and Equitable people who were back of it, whereas I did not know Mr. McCall at all, and Mr. Perkins only from hearing him discuss the bill.

An interesting feature of the matter developed subsequently. Five years later, after the insurance investigations took place, the Mutual Life strongly urged the passage of a Limitation Bill, and, because of the popular feeling developed by the exposure of the improper practices of the companies, this bill was generally approved. Governor Hughes adopted the suggestion, such a bill was passed by the Legislature, and Governor Hughes signed it. This bill caused the three great New York companies to reduce markedly the volume of busi-

George Perkins.

"I got Mr. Perkins to serve on the Palisade Park Commission . . . to save the Palisades from vandalism."

ness they were doing; it threw a great many agents out of employment, and materially curtailed the foreign business of the companies — which business was bringing annually a considerable sum of money to this country for investment. In short, the experiment worked so badly that before Governor Hughes went out of office one of the very last bills he signed was one that permitted the life insurance companies to increase their business each year by an amount representing a certain percentage of the business they had previously done. This in practice, within a few years, practically annulled the

Limitation Bill that had been previously passed. The experiment of limiting the size of business, of legislating against it merely because it was big, had been tried, and had failed so completely that the authors of the bill had themselves in effect repealed it. My action in refusing to try the experiment had been completely justified.

As a sequel to this incident I got Mr. Perkins to serve on the Palisade Park Commission. At the time I was taking active part in the effort to save the Palisades from vandalism and destruction by getting the States of New York and New Jersey jointly to include them in a public park. It is not easy to get a responsible and capable man of business to undertake such a task, which is unpaid, which calls on his part for an immense expenditure of time, money, and energy, which offers no reward of any kind, and which entails the certainty of abuse and misrepresentation. Mr. Perkins accepted the position, and has filled it for the last thirteen years, doing as disinterested, efficient, and useful a bit of public service as any man in the State has done throughout these thirteen years.

The case of most importance in which I clashed with Senator Platt related to a matter of fundamental governmental policy, and was the first step I ever took toward bringing big corporations under effective governmental control. In this case I had to fight the Democratic machine as well as the Republican machine, for Senator Hill and Senator Platt were equally opposed to my action, and the big corporation men, the big business men back of both of them, took precisely the same view of these matters without regard to their party feelings on other points. What I did convulsed people at that time, and marked the beginning of the effort, at least in the Eastern states, to make the great corporations really responsible to popular wish and governmental command. But we have gone so far past the stage in which we then were that now it seems well-nigh incredible that there should have been any opposition at all to what I at that time proposed.

The substitution of electric power for horse power in the street car lines of New York offered a fruitful chance for the most noxious type of dealing between business men and politicians. The franchises granted by New York were granted without any attempt to secure from the grantees returns, in the way of taxation or otherwise, for the value received. The fact that they were thus granted by improper favoritism, a favoritism which in many cases was unquestionably secured by downright bribery, led to all kinds of trouble. In return for the continuance of these improper favors to the corporations the politicians expected improper favors in the way of excessive campaign contributions, often contributed by the same corporation at the same time to two opposing parties. Before I became Governor a bill had been introduced into the New York Legislature to tax the franchises of these street railways. It affected a large number of corporations, but particularly those in New York and Buffalo. It had been suffered to slumber undisturbed, as none of the people in power dreamed of taking it seriously, and both the Republican and Democratic machines were hostile to it. Under the rules of the New York Legislature a bill could always be taken up out of its turn and passed if the Governor sent in a special emergency message on its behalf.

After I was elected Governor I had my attention directed to the franchise tax matter, looked into the subject, and came to the conclusion that it was a matter of plain decency and honesty that these companies should pay a tax on their franchises, inasmuch as they did nothing that could be considered as service rendered the public in lieu of a tax. This seemed to me so evidently the common-sense and decent thing to do that I was hardly prepared for the storm of protest and anger which my proposal aroused. Senator Platt and the other machine leaders did everything to get me to abandon my intention. As usual, I saw them, talked the matter all over with them, and did my best to convert them to my way of thinking. Senator Platt, I believe, was quite sincere in his opposition. He did not believe in popular rule, and he did believe that the big business men were entitled to have things their way. He profoundly distrusted the people — naturally enough, for the kind of human nature with which a boss comes in contact is not of an exalted type. He felt that anarchy would come if there was any interference with a system by which the people in mass were, under various necessary cloaks, controlled by the leaders in the political and business worlds. He wrote me a very strong letter of protest against my attitude, expressed in dignified, friendly, and temperate language, but using one word in a curious way. This was the word "altruistic." He stated in his letter that he had not objected to my being independent in politics, because he had been sure that I had the good of the party at heart, and meant to act fairly and honorably; but that he had been warned, before I became a candidate, by a number of his business friends that I was a dangerous man because I was "altruistic," and that he now feared that my conduct would justify the alarm thus expressed. I was interested in this, not only because Senator Platt was obviously sincere, but because of the way in which he used "altruistic" as a term of reproach, as if it was Communistic or Socialistic — the last being a word he did use to me when, as now and then happened, he thought that my proposals warranted fairly reckless vituperation.

Senator Platt's letter ran in part as follows:

"When the subject of your nomination was under consideration, there was one matter that gave me real anxiety. I think you will have no trouble in appreciating the fact that it was *not* the matter of your independence. I think we have got far enough along in our political acquaintance for you to see that my support in a convention does not imply subsequent 'demands,' nor any other relation that may not reasonably exist for the welfare of the party. . . . The thing that did bother me was this: I had heard from a good many sources that you were a little loose on the relations of capital and labor, on trusts and combinations, and, indeed, on those numerous questions which have recently arisen in politics affecting the security of earnings and the right of a man to run his own business in his own way, with due respect of course to the Ten Commandments and the Penal Code. Or, to get at it even more clearly, I understood from a number of business men, and among them many of your own personal friends, that you entertained various altruistic ideas, all very well in their way, but which before they could safely be put into law needed very profound consideration. . . . You have just adjourned a Legislature which created a good opinion throughout the State. I congratulate you heartily upon this fact because I sincerely believe, as everybody else does, that this good impression exists very largely as a result of your personal influence in the Legislative chambers. But at the last moment, and to my very great surprise, you did a thing which has caused the business community of New York to wonder how far the notions of Populism, as laid down in Kansas and Nebraska, have taken hold upon the Republican party of the State of New York."

In my answer I pointed out to the Senator that I had as Governor unhesitatingly acted, at Buffalo and elsewhere, to put down mobs, without regard to the fact that the professed leaders of labor furiously denounced me for so doing; but that I could no more tolerate wrong committed in the name of property than wrong committed against property. My letter ran in part as follows: "I knew that you had just the feelings that you describe; that is, apart from my 'impulsiveness,' you felt that there was a justifiable anxiety among men of means, and especially men representing large corporate interests, lest I might feel too strongly on what you term the 'altruistic' side in matters of labor and capital and as regards the relations of the State to great corporations. . . . I know that when parties divide on such issues [as Bryanism] the tendency is to force everybody into one of two camps, and to throw out entirely men like myself, who are as strongly opposed to Populism in every stage as the greatest representative of corporate wealth, but who also feel strongly that many of these representatives of enormous corporate wealth have themselves been responsible for a portion of the conditions against which Bryanism is in ignorant revolt. I do not believe that it is wise or safe for us as a party to take refuge in mere negation and to say that there are no evils to be corrected. It seems to me that our attitude should be one of correcting the evils and thereby showing that, whereas the Populists, Socialists, and others really do not correct the evils at all, or else only do so at the expense of producing others in aggravated form, on the contrary we Republicans hold the just balance and set ourselves as resolutely against improper corporate influence on the one hand as against demagogy and mob rule on the other. I understand perfectly that such an attitude of moderation is apt to be misunderstood when passions are greatly excited and when victory is apt to rest with the extremists on one side or the other; yet I think it is in the long run the only wise attitude. . . . I appreciate absolutely [what Mr. Platt had said] that any applause I get will be too evanescent for a moment's consideration. I appreciate absolutely that the people who now loudly approve of my action in the franchise tax bill will forget all about it in a fortnight, and that, on the other hand, the very powerful interests adversely affected will always remember it. . . . [The leaders] urged upon me that I personally could not afford to take this action, for under no circumstances could I ever again be nominated for any public office, as no corporation would subscribe to a campaign fund if I was on the ticket, and that they would subscribe most heavily to beat me; and when I asked if this were true of Republican corporations, the cynical answer was made that the corporations that subscribed most heavily to the campaign funds subscribed impartially to both party organizations. Under all these circumstances, it seemed to me there was no alternative but to do what I could to secure the passage of the bill."

These two letters, written in the spring of 1899, express clearly the views of the two elements of the Republican party, whose hostility gradually grew until it culminated, thirteen years later. In 1912 the political and financial forces of which Mr. Platt had once been the spokesman, usurped the control of the party machinery and drove out of the party the men who were loyally endeavoring to apply the principles of the founders of the party to the needs and issues of their own day.

I had made up my mind that if I could get a show in the Legislature the bill would pass, because the people had become interested and the representatives would scarcely dare to vote the wrong way. Accordingly, on April 27, 1899, I sent a special message to the Assembly, certifying that the emergency demanded the immediate passage of the bill. The machine leaders were bitterly angry, and the Speaker actually tore up the message without reading it to the Assembly. That night they were busy trying to arrange some device for the defeat of the bill — which was not difficult, as the session was about to close. At seven the next morning I was informed of what had occurred. At eight I was in the Capitol at the Executive chamber, and sent in another special message, which opened as follows: "I learn that the emergency message which I sent last evening to the Assembly on behalf of the Franchise Tax Bill has not been read. I therefore send hereby another message on the subject. I need not impress upon the Assembly the need of passing this bill at once." I sent this message to the Assembly, by my secretary, William J. Youngs, afterwards United States District Attorney of Kings, with an intimation that if this were not promptly read I should come up in person and read it. Then, as so often happens, the opposition collapsed and the bill went through both houses with a rush. I had in the House stanch friends, such as Regis Post and Alford Cooley, men of character and courage, who would have fought to a finish had the need arisen.

My troubles were not at an end, however. The bill put the taxation in the hands of the local county boards, and as the railways sometimes passed through several different counties, this was inadvisable. It was the end of the session, and the Legislature adjourned. The corporations affected, through various counsel, and the different party leaders of both organizations, urged me not to sign the bill, laying especial stress on this feature, and asking that I wait until the following year, when a good measure could be put through with this obnoxious feature struck out. I had thirty days under the law in which to sign the bill. If I did not sign it by the end of that time it would not become a law. I answered my political and corporation friends by telling them that I agreed with them that this feature was wrong, but that I would rather have the bill with this feature than not have it at all; and that I was not willing to trust to what might be done a year later. Therefore, I explained, I would reconvene the Legislature in special session, and if the legislators chose to amend the bill by placing the power of taxation in the State instead of in the county or municipality, I would be glad; but that if they failed to amend it, or amended it improperly, I would sign the original bill and let it become law as it was.

When the representatives of Mr. Platt and of the corporations affected found they could do no better, they assented to this proposition. Efforts were tentatively made to outwit me, by inserting amendments that would nullify the effect of the law, or by withdrawing the law when the Legislature convened; which would at once have deprived me of the whip hand. On May 12 I wrote Senator Platt, outlining the amendments I desired, and said: "Of course it must be understood that I will sign the present bill if the proposed bill containing the changes outlined above fails to pass." On May 18 I notified the Senate leader, John Raines, by telegram: "Legislature has no power to withdraw the Ford bill. If attempt is made to do so, I will sign the bill at once." On the same day, by telegram, I wired Mr. Odell concerning the bill the leaders were preparing: "Some provisions of bill very objectionable. I am at work on bill to show you to-morrow. The bill must not contain greater changes than those outlined in my message." My wishes were heeded, and when I had reconvened the Legislature it amended the bill as I outlined in my message; and in its amended form the bill became law.

There promptly followed something which afforded an index of the good faith of the corporations that had been protesting to me. As soon as the change for which they had begged was inserted in the law, and the law was signed, they turned round and refused to pay the taxes; and in the lawsuit that followed, they claimed that the law was unconstitutional, because it contained the very clause which they had so clamorously demanded. Senator David B. Hill had appeared before me on behalf of the corporations to argue for the change; and he then appeared before the courts to make the argument on the other side. The suit was carried through to the Supreme Court of the United States, which declared the law constitutional during the time that I was President.

One of the painful duties of the chief executive in States like New York, as well as in the Nation, is the refusing of pardons. Yet I can imagine nothing more necessary from the standpoint of good citizenship than the ability to steel one's heart in this matter of granting pardons. The pressure is always greatest in two classes of cases: first, that where capital punishment is inflicted; second, that where the man is prominent socially and in the business world, and where in consequence his crime is apt to have been one concerned in some way with finance.

As regards capital cases, the trouble is that emotional men and women always see only the individual whose fate is up at the moment, and neither his victim nor the many millions of unknown individuals who would in the long run be harmed by what they ask. Moreover, almost any criminal, however brutal, has usually some person, often a person whom he has greatly wronged, who will plead for him. If the mother is alive she will always come, and she cannot help feeling that the case in which she is so concerned is peculiar, that in this case a pardon should be granted. It was really heartrending to have to see the kinfolk and friends of murderers who were condemned to death, and among the very rare occasions when anything governmental or official caused me to lose sleep were the times when I had to listen to some poor mother making a plea for a criminal so wicked, so utterly brutal and depraved, that it would have been a crime on my part to remit his punishment.

On the other hand, there were certain crimes where requests for leniency merely made me angry. Such crimes were, for instance, rape, or the circulation of indecent literature, or anything connected with what would now be called the "white slave" traffic, or wife murder, or gross cruelty to women and children, or seduction and abandonment, or the action of some man in getting a girl whom he had seduced to commit abortion. I am speaking in each instance of cases that actually came before me, either while I was Governor or while I was President. In an astonishing number of these cases men of high standing signed petitions or wrote letters asking me to show leniency to the criminal. In two or three of the cases — one where some young roughs had committed rape on a helpless immigrant girl, and another in which a physician of wealth and high standing had seduced a girl and then induced her to commit abortion — I rather lost my temper, and wrote to the individuals who had asked for the pardon, saying that I extremely regretted that it was not in my power to increase the sentence. I then let the facts be made public, for I thought that my petitioners deserved public censure. Whether they received this public censure or not I did not know, but that my action made them very angry I do know, and their anger gave me real satisfaction. The list of these petitioners was a fairly long one, and included two United States Senators, a Governor of a State, two judges, an editor, and some eminent lawyers and business men.

In the class of cases where the offense was one involving the misuse of large sums of money the reason for the pressure was different. Cases of this kind more frequently came before me when I was President, but they also came before me when I was Governor, chiefly in the cases of county treasurers who had embezzled funds. A big bank president, a railway magnate, an official connected with some big corporation, or a Government official in a responsible fiduciary position, necessarily belongs among the men who have succeeded in life. This means that his family are living in comfort, and perhaps luxury and refinement, and that his sons and daughters have been well educated. In such a case the misdeed of the father comes as a crushing disaster to the wife and children, and the people of the community, however bitter originally against the man, grow to feel the most intense sympathy for the bowed-down women and children who suffer for the man's fault. It is a dreadful thing in life that so much of atonement for wrong-doing is vicarious. If it were possible in such a case to think only of the banker's or county treasurer's wife and children, any man would pardon the offender at once. Unfortunately, it is not right to think only of the women and children. The very fact that in cases of this class there is certain to be pressure from high sources, pressure sometimes by men who have been beneficially, even though remotely, interested in the man's criminality, no less than pressure because of honest sympathy with the wife and children, makes it necessary that the good public servant shall, no matter how deep his sympathy and regret, steel his heart and do his duty by refusing to let the wrong-doer out. My experience of the way in which pardons are often granted is one of the reasons why I do not believe that life imprisonment for murder and rape is a proper substitute for the death penalty. The average term of so-called life imprisonment in this country is only about fourteen years.

Of course there were cases where I either commuted sentences or pardoned offenders with very real pleasure. For instance, when President, I frequently commuted sentences for horse stealing in the Indian Territory because the penalty for stealing a horse was disproportionate to the penalty for many other crimes, and the offense was usually committed by some ignorant young fellow who found a half-wild horse, and really did not commit anything like as serious an offense as the penalty indicated. The judges would be obliged to give the minimum penalty, but would forward me memoranda stating that if there had been a less penalty they would have inflicted it, and I would then commute the sentence to the penalty thus indicated.

In one case in New York I pardoned outright a man convicted of murder in the second degree, and I did this on the recommendation of a friend, Father Doyle of the Paulist Fathers. I had become intimate with the Paulist Fathers while I was Police Commissioner, and I had grown to feel confidence in their judgment, for I had found that they always told me exactly what the facts were about any man, whether he belonged to their church or not. In this case the convicted man was a strongly built, respectable old Irishman employed as a watchman around some big cattle-killing establishments.

The young roughs of the neighborhood, which was then of a rather lawless type, used to try to destroy the property of the companies. In a conflict with a watchman a member of one of the gangs was slain. The watchman was acquitted, but the neighborhood was much wrought up over the acquittal. Shortly afterwards, a gang of the same roughs attacked another watchman, the old Irishman in question, and finally, to save his own life, he was obliged in self-defense to kill one of his assailants. The feeling in the community, however, was strongly against him, and some of the men high up in the corporation became

Father Doyle of the Paulist Fathers.

"I had become very intimate with the Paulist Fathers while I was Police Commissioner."

frightened and thought that it would be better to throw over the watchman. He was convicted. Father Doyle came to me, told me that he knew the man well, that he was one of the best members of his church, admirable in every way, that he had simply been forced to fight for his life while loyally doing his duty, and that the conviction represented the triumph of the tough element of the district and the abandonment of this man, by those who should have stood by him, under the influence of an unworthy fear. I looked into the case, came to the conclusion that Father Doyle was right, and gave the man a full pardon before he had served thirty days.

The various clashes between myself and the machine, my triumph in them, and the fact that the people were getting more and more interested and aroused, brought on a curious situation in the Republican National Convention at Philadelphia in June, 1900. Senator Platt and the New York machine leaders had become very anxious to get me out of the Governorship, chiefly because of the hostility of the big corporation men towards me; but they had also become convinced that there was such popular feeling on my behalf that it would be difficult to refuse me a renomination if I demanded it. They accordingly decided to push me for Vice-President, taking advantage of the fact that there was at that time a good deal of feeling for me in the country at large.* I myself did not appreciate that there was any such feeling, and as I greatly disliked the office of Vice-President and was much interested in the Governorship, I announced that I would not accept the Vice-Presidency. I was one of the delegates to Philadelphia. On reaching there I found that the situation was complicated. Senator Hanna appeared on the surface to have control of the Convention. He was anxious that I should not be nominated as Vice-President. Senator Platt was anxious that I should be nominated as Vice-President, in order to get me out of the New York Governorship. Each took a position opposite to that of the other, but each at that time cordially sympathized with the other's feelings about me — it was the manifestations and not the feelings that differed. My supporters in New York State did not wish me nominated for Vice-President because they wished me to continue as Governor; but in every other State all the people who admired me were bound that I should be nominated as Vice-President. These people were almost all desirous of seeing Mr. McKinley renominated as President, but they became angry at Senator Hanna's opposition to me as Vice-President. He in his turn suddenly became aware that if he persisted he might find that in their anger these men would oppose Mr. McKinley's renomination, and although

*See Appendix B to this chapter.

they could not have prevented the nomination, such opposition would have been a serious blow in the campaign which was to follow. Senator Hanna, therefore, began to waver.

Meanwhile a meeting of the New York delegation was called. Most of the delegates were under the control of Senator Platt. The Senator notified me that if I refused to accept the nomination for Vice-President I would be beaten for the nomination for Governor. I answered that I would accept the challenge, that we would have a straight-out fight on the proposition, and that I would begin it at once by telling the assembled delegates of the threat, and giving fair warning that I intended to fight for the Governorship nomination, and, moreover, that I intended to get it. This brought Senator Platt to terms. The effort to instruct the New York delegation for me was abandoned, and Lieutenant-Governor Woodruff was presented for nomination in my place.

I supposed that this closed the incident, and that no further effort would be made to nominate me for the Vice-Presidency. On the contrary, the effect was directly the reverse. The upset of the New York machine increased the feeling of the delegates from other States that it was necessary to draft me for the nomination. By next day Senator Hanna himself concluded that this was a necessity, and acquiesced in the movement. As New York was already committed against me, and as I was not willing that there should be any chance of supposing that the New Yorkers had nominated me to get rid of me, the result was that I was nominated and seconded from outside States. No other candidate was placed in the field.

By this time the Legislature had adjourned, and most of my work as Governor of New York was over. One unexpected bit of business arose, however. It was the year of the Presidential campaign. Tammany, which had been lukewarm about Bryan in 1896, cordially supported him in 1900; and when Tammany heartily supports a candidate it is well for the opposing candidate to keep a sharp lookout for election frauds. The city government was in the hands of Tammany; but I had power to remove the Mayor, the Sheriff, and the District Attorney for malfeasance or misfeasance in office. Such power had not been exercised by any previous Governor, as far as I knew; but it existed, and if the misfeasance or malfeasance warranted it, and if the Governor possessed the requisite determination, the power could be, and ought to be, exercised.

By an Act of the Legislature, a State Bureau of Elections had been created in New York City, and a Superintendent of Elections appointed by the Governor. The Chief of the State Bureau of Elections was John McCullagh, formerly in the Police Department when I was Police Commissioner. The Chief of Police for the city was William F. Devery, one of the Tammany leaders, who represented in the Police Department all that I had warred against while Commissioner. On November 4 Devery directed his subordinates in the Police Department to disregard the orders which McCullagh had given to his deputies, orders which were essential if we were to secure an honest election in the city. I had just returned from a Western campaign trip, and was at Sagamore Hill. I had no direct power over Devery; but the Mayor had; and I had power over the Mayor. Accordingly, I at once wrote to the Mayor of New York, to the Sheriff of New York, and to the District Attorney of New York County the following letters:

STATE OF NEW YORK

OYSTER BAY, November 5, 1900.

*To the Mayor of the City of New York.*

SIR: My attention has been called to the official order issued by Chief of Police Devery, in which he directs his subordinates to disregard the Chief of the State Election Bureau, John McCullagh, and his deputies. Unless you have already taken steps to secure the recall of this order, it is necessary for me to point out that I shall be obliged to hold you responsible as the head of the city government for the action of the Chief of Police, if it should result in any breach of the peace and intimidation or any crime whatever against the election laws. The State and city authorities should work together. I will not fail to call to summary account either State or city authority in the event of either being guilty of intimidation or connivance at fraud or of failure to protect every legal voter in his rights. I therefore hereby notify you that in the event of any wrongdoing following upon the failure immediately to recall Chief Devery's order, or upon any action or inaction on the part of Chief Devery, I must necessarily call you to account.

Yours, etc.,<br>THEODORE ROOSEVELT.

STATE OF NEW YORK

OYSTER BAY, November 5, 1990.

*To the Sheriff of the County of New York.*

SIR: My attention has been called to the official order issued by Chief of Police Devery in which he directs his subordinates to disregard the Chief of the State Election Bureau, John McCullagh, and his deputies.

It is your duty to assist in the orderly enforcement of the law, and I shall hold you strictly responsible for any breach of the public peace within your county, or for any failure on your part to do your full duty in connection with the election to-morrow.

Yours truly,
THEODORE ROOSEVELT.

STATE OF NEW YORK

OYSTER BAY, November 5, 1900.

*To the District Attorney of the County of New York.*

SIR: My attention has been called to the official order issued by Chief of Police Devery, in which he directs his subordinates to disregard the Chief of the State Election Bureau, John McCullagh, and his deputies.

In view of this order I call your attention to the fact that it is your duty to assist in the orderly enforcement of the law, and there must be no failure on your part to do your full duty in the matter.

Yours truly,
THEODORE ROOSEVELT.

These letters had the desired effect. The Mayor promptly required Chief Devery to rescind the obnoxious order, which was as promptly done. The Sheriff also took prompt action. The District Attorney refused to heed my letter, and assumed an attitude of defiance, and I removed him from office. On election day there was no clash between the city and State authorities; the election was orderly and honest.

# APPENDIX A

## CONSERVATION

As foreshadowing the course I later, as President, followed in this matter, I give extracts from one of my letters to the Commission, and from my second (and last) Annual Message. I spent the first months of my term in investigations to find out just what the situation was.

On November 28, 1899, I wrote to the Commission as follows:

". . . I have had very many complaints before this as to the inefficiency of the game wardens and game protectors, the complaints usually taking the form that the men have been appointed and are retained without due regard to the duties to be performed. I do not wish a man to be retained or appointed who is not thoroughly fit to perform the duties of game protector. The Adirondacks are entitled to a peculiar share of the Commission's attention, both from the standpoint of forestry, and from the less important, but still very important, standpoint of game and fish protection. The men who do duty as game protectors in the Adirondacks should, by preference, be appointed from the locality itself, and should in all cases be thorough woodsmen. The mere fact that a game protector has to hire a guide to pilot him through the woods is enough to show his unfitness for the position. I want as game protectors men of courage, resolution, and hardihood, who can handle the rifle, ax, and paddle; who can camp out in summer or winter; who can go on snow-shoes, if necessary; who can go through the woods by day or by night without regard to trails.

"I should like full information about all your employees, as to their capacities, as to the labor they perform, as to their distribution from and where they do their work."

Many of the men hitherto appointed owed their positions principally to political preference. The changes I recommended were promptly made, and much to the good of the public service. In my Annual Message, in January, 1900, I said:

"Great progress has been made through the fish hatcheries in the propagation of valuable food and sporting fish. The laws for the protection of deer have resulted in their increase. Nevertheless, as railroads tend to encroach on the wilderness, the temptation to illegal hunting becomes greater, and the danger from forest fires increases. There is need of great improvement both in our laws and in their administration. The game wardens have been too few in number. More should be provided. None save fit men must be appointed; and their retention in office must depend purely upon the zeal, ability, and efficiency with which they perform their duties. The game wardens in the forests must be woodsmen; and they should have no outside business. In short, there should be a thorough reorganization of the work of the Commission. A careful study of the resources and condition of the forests on State land must be made. It is certainly not too much to expect that the State forests should be managed as efficiently as the forests on private lands in the same neighborhoods. And the measure of difference in efficiency of management must be the measure of condemnation or praise of the way the public forests have been managed.

"The subject of forest preservation is of the utmost importance to the State. The Adirondacks and Catskills should be great parks kept in perpetuity for the benefit and enjoyment of our people. Much has been done of late years towards their perservation, but very much remains to be done. The provisions of law in reference to sawmills and wood-pulp mills are defective and should be changed so as to prohibit dumping dye-stuff, sawdust, or tanbark, in any amount whatsoever, into the streams. Reservoirs should be made, but not where they will tend to destroy large sections of the forest, and only after a careful and scientific study of the water resources of the region. The people of the forest regions are themselves growing more and more to realize the necessity of preserving both the trees and the game. A live deer in the woods will attract to the neighborhood ten times the money that could be obtained for the deer's dead carcass. Timber theft on the State lands is, of course, a grave offense against the whole public.

"Hardy outdoor sports, like hunting, are in themselves of no small value to the National character and should be encouraged in every way. Men who go into the wilderness, indeed, men who take part in any field sports with horse or rifle, receive a benefit which can hardly be given by even the most vigorous athletic games.

"There is a further and more immediate and practical end in view. A primeval forest is a great sponge which absorbs and distills the rain water. And when it is destroyed the result is apt to be an alternation of flood and drought. Forest fires ultimately make the land a desert, and are a detriment to all that portion of the State tributary to the streams through the woods where they occur. Every effort should be made to minimize their destructive influence. We need to have our system of forestry gradually developed and conducted along scientific principles. When this has been done it will be possible to allow marketable lumber to be cut everywhere without damage to the forests — indeed, with positive advantage to them.

But until lumbering is thus conducted, on strictly scientific principles no less than upon principles of the strictest honesty toward the State, we cannot afford to suffer it at all in the State forests. Unrestrained greed means the ruin of the great woods and the drying up of the sources of the rivers.

"Ultimately the administration of the State lands must be so centralized as to enable us definitely to place responsibility in respect to everything concerning them, and to demand the highest degree of trained intelligence in their use.

"The State should not permit within its limits factories to make bird skins or bird feathers into articles of ornament or wearing apparel. Ordinary birds, and especially song birds, should be rigidly protected. Game birds should never be shot to a greater extent than will offset the natural rate of increase. . . . Care should be taken not to encourage the use of cold storage or other market systems which are a benefit to no one but the wealthy epicure who can afford to pay a heavy price for luxuries. These systems tend to the destruction of the game, which would bear most severely upon the very men whose rapacity has been appealed to in order to secure its extermination. . . ."

I reorganized the Commission, putting Austin Wadsworth at its head.

## APPENDIX B

### THE POLITICAL SITUATION IN 1900

My general scheme of action as Governor was given in a letter I wrote one of my supporters among the independent district organization leaders, Norton Goddard, on April 16, 1900. It runs in part as follows: "Nobody can tell, and least of all the machine itself, whether the machine intends to renominate me next fall or not. If for some reason I should be weak, whether on account of faults or virtues, doubtless the machine will throw me over, and I think I am not uncharitable when I say they would feel no acute grief at so doing. It would be very strange if they did feel such grief. If, for instance, we had strikes which led to riots, I would of course be obliged to preserve order and stop the riots. Decent citizens would demand that I should do it, and in any event I should do it wholly without regard to their demands. But, once it was done, they would forget all about it, while a great many laboring men, honest but ignorant and prejudiced, would bear a grudge against me for doing it. This might put me out of the running as a candidate. Again, the big corporations undoubtedly want to beat me. They prefer the chance of being black-mailed to the certainty that they will not be allowed any more than their due. Of course they will try to beat me on some entirely different issue, and, as they are very able and very unscrupulous, nobody can tell that they won't succeed. . . . I have been trying to stay in with the organization. I did not do it with the idea that they would renominate me. I did it with the idea of getting things done, and in that I have been absolutely successful. Whether Senator Platt and Mr. Odell endeavor to beat me, or do beat me, for the renomination next fall, is of very small importance compared to the fact that for my two years I have been able to make a Republican majority in the Legislature do good and decent work and have prevented any split within the party. The task was one of great difficulty, because, on the one hand, I had to keep clearly before me the fact that it was better to have a split than to permit *bad* work to be done, and, on the other hand, the fact that to have that split would absolutely prevent all *good* work. The result has been that I have avoided a split and that as a net result of my two years and the two sessions of the Legislature, there has been an enormous improvement in the administration of the Government, and there has also been a great advance in legislation."

To show my reading of the situation at the time I quote from a letter of mine to Joseph B. Bishop, then editor of the *Commercial Advertiser*, with whom towards the end of my term I had grown into very close relations, and who, together with two other old friends, Albert Shaw, of the *Review of Reviews*, and Silas McBee, now editor of the *Constructive Quarterly*, knew the inside of every movement, so far as I knew it myself. The letter, which is dated April 11, 1900, runs in part as follows: "The dangerous element as far as I am concerned comes from the corporations. The [naming certain men] crowd and those like them have been greatly exasperated by the franchise tax. They would like to get me out of politics for good, but at the moment they think the best thing to do is to put me into the Vice-Presidency. Naturally I will not be opposed openly on the ground of the corporations' grievance; but every kind of false statement will continually be made, and men like [naming the editors of certain newspapers] will attack me, not as the enemy of corporations, but as their tool! There is no question whatever that if the leaders can they will upset me."

One position which as Governor (and as President) I consistently took, seems to me to represent what ought to be a fundamental principle in American legislative work. I steadfastly refused to advocate any law, no matter how admirable in theory, if there was good reason to believe that in practice it would not be executed. I have always sympathized with the view set forth by Pelatiah Webster in 1783 — quoted by Hannis Taylor in his *Genesis of the Supreme Court* — "Laws or ordinances of any kind (especially of august bodies of high dignity and consequence) which fail of execution, are much worse than none. They weaken the government, expose it to contempt, destroy the confidence of all men, native and foreigners, in it, and expose both aggregate bodies and individuals who have placed confidence in it to many ruinous disappointments which they would have escaped had no such law or ordinance been made." This principle, by the way, not only applies to an internal law which cannot be executed; it applies even more to international action, such as a universal arbitration treaty which cannot and will not be kept; and most of all it applies to proposals to make such universal arbitration treaties at the very time that we are not keeping our solemn promise to execute limited arbitration treaties which we have already made. A general arbitration treaty is merely a promise; it represents merely a debt of honorable obligation; and nothing is more discreditable, for a nation or an individual, than to cover up the repudiation of a debt which can be and ought to be paid, by recklessly promising to incur a new and insecure debt which no wise man for one moment supposes ever will be paid.

# Chapter IX

## OUTDOORS AND INDOORS

THERE ARE men who love out-of-doors who yet never open a book; and other men who love books but to whom the great book of nature is a sealed volume, and the lines written therein blurred and illegible. Nevertheless among those men whom I have known the love of books and the love of outdoors, in their highest expressions, have usually gone hand in hand. It is an affectation for the man who is praising outdoors to sneer at books. Usually the keenest appreciation of what is seen in nature is to be found in those who have also profited by the hoarded and recorded wisdom of their fellowmen. Love of outdoor life, love of simple and hardy pastimes, can be gratified by men and women who do not possess large means, and who work hard; and so can love of good books — not of good bindings and of first editions, excellent enough in their way but sheer luxuries — I mean love of reading books, owning them if possible of course, but, if that is not possible, getting them from a circulating library.

Sagamore Hill takes its name from the old Sagamore Mohannis, who, as chief of his little tribe, signed away his rights to the land two centuries and a half ago. The house stands right on the top of the hill, separated by fields and belts of woodland from all other houses, and looks out over the bay and the Sound. We see the sun go down beyond long reaches of land and of water. Many birds dwell in the trees round the house or in the pastures and the woods near by, and of course in winter gulls, loons, and wild fowl frequent the waters of the bay and the Sound. We love all the seasons; the snows and bare woods of winter; the rush of growing things and the blossom-spray of spring; the yellow grain, the ripening fruits and tasseled corn, and the deep, leafy shades that are heralded by "the green dance of summer"; and the sharp fall winds that tear the brilliant banners with which the trees greet the dying year.

The Sound is always lovely. In the summer nights we watch it from the piazza, and see the lights of the tall Fall River boats as they steam steadily by. Now and then we spend a day on it, the two of us together in the light rowing skiff, or perhaps with one of the boys to pull an extra pair of oars; we land for lunch at noon under wind-beaten oaks on the edge of a low bluff, or among the wild plum bushes on a spit of white sand, while the sails of the coasting schooners gleam in the sunlight, and the tolling of the bell-buoy comes landward across the waters.

Sagamore Hill.

Long Island is not as rich in flowers as the valley of the Hudson. Yet there are many. Early in April there is one hillside near us which glows like a tender flame with the white of the bloodroot. About the same time we find the shy mayflower, the trailing arbutus; and although we rarely pick wild flowers, one member of the household always plucks a little bunch of mayflowers to send to a friend working in Panama, whose soul hungers for the Northern spring. Then there are shadblow and delicate anemones, about the time of the cherry blossoms; the brief glory of the apple orchards follows; and then the thronging dogwoods fill the forests with their radiance; and so flowers follow flowers until the springtime splendor closes with the laurel and the evanescent, honey-sweet locust bloom. The late summer flowers follow, the flaunting lilies, and cardinal flowers, and marshmallows, and pale beach rosemary; and the goldenrod and the asters when the afternoons shorten and we again begin to think of fires in the wide fireplaces.

Most of the birds in our neighborhood are the ordinary home friends of the house and the barn, the wood lot and the pasture; but now and then the species make queer shifts. The cheery quail, alas! are rarely found near us now; and we no longer hear the whip-poor-wills at night. But some birds visit us now which formerly did not. When I was a boy neither the black-throated green warbler nor the purple finch nested around us, nor were bobolinks found in our fields. The black-throated green warbler is now one of our commonest summer warblers; there are plenty of purple finches; and, best of all, the bobolinks are far from infrequent. I had written about these new visitors to John Burroughs, and once when he came out to see me I was able to show them to him.

When I was President, we owned a little house in western Virginia; a delightful house, to us at least, although only a shell of rough boards. We used sometimes to go there in the fall, perhaps at Thanksgiving, and on these occasions we would have quail and rabbits of our own shooting, and once in a while a wild turkey. We also went there in the spring. Of course many of the birds were different from our Long Island friends. There were mocking-birds, the most attractive of all birds, and blue grosbeaks, and cardinals and summer redbirds, instead of scarlet tanagers, and those wonderful singers the Bewick's wrens, and Carolina wrens. All these I was able to show John Burroughs when he came to visit us; although, by the way, he did not appreciate as much as we did one set of inmates of the cottage — the flying squirrels. We loved having the flying squirrels, father and mother and half-grown young, in their nest among the rafters; and at night we slept so soundly that we did not in the least mind the wild gambols of the little fellows through the rooms, even when, as sometimes happened, they would swoop down to the bed and scuttle across it.

From a painting by Gari Melchers.

Theodore Roosevelt in Winter Riding Costume.

One April I went to Yellowstone Park, when the snow was still very deep, and I took John Burroughs with me. I wished to show him the big game of the Park, the wild creatures that have become so astonishingly tame and tolerant of human presence. In the Yellowstone the animals seem always to behave as one wishes them to! It is always possible to see the sheep and deer and antelope, and also the great herds of elk, which are shyer than the smaller beasts. In April we found the elk weak after the short commons and hard living of winter. Once without much difficulty I regularly rounded up a big band of them, so that John Burroughs could look at them. I do not think, however, that he cared to see them as much as I did. The birds interested him more, especially a tiny owl the size of a robin which we saw perched on the top of a tree in mid-afternoon entirely uninfluenced by the sun and making a queer noise like a cork being pulled from a bottle. I was rather ashamed to find how much better his eyes were than mine in seeing the birds and grasping their differences.

When wolf-hunting in Texas, and when bear-hunting in Louisiana and Mississippi, I was not only enthralled by the sport, but also by the strange new birds and other creatures, and the trees and flowers I had not known before. By the way, there was one feast at the White House which stands above all others in my memory — even above the time when I lured Joel Chandler Harris thither for a night, a deed in which to triumph, as all who knew that inveterately shy recluse will testify. This was "the bear-hunters' dinner." I had been treated so kindly by my friends on these hunts, and they were such fine fellows, men whom I was so proud to think of as Americans, that I set my heart on having them at a hunters' dinner at the White House. One December I succeeded; there were twenty or thirty of them, all told, as good hunters, as daring riders, as first-class citizens as could be found anywhere; no finer set of guests ever sat at meat in the White House; and among other game on the table was a black bear, itself contributed by one of these same guests.

When I first visited California, it was my good fortune to see the "big trees," the Sequoias, and then to travel down into the Yosemite, with John Muir. Of course of all people in the world he was the one with whom it was best worth while thus to see the Yosemite. He told me that when Emerson came to California he tried to get him to come out and camp with him, for that was the only way in which to see at their best the majesty and charm of the Sierras. But at the time Emerson was getting old and could not go. John Muir met me with a couple of packers and two mules to carry our tent, bedding, and food for a three days' trip. The first night was clear, and we lay down in the darkening aisles of the great Sequoia grove. The majestic trunks, beautiful in color and in symmetry, rose

Under the Porch at Sagamore.

round us like the pillars of a mightier cathedral than ever was conceived even by the fervor of the Middle Ages. Hermit thrushes sang beautifully in the evening, and again, with a burst of wonderful music, at dawn. I was interested and a little surprised to find that, unlike John Burroughs, John Muir cared little for birds or bird songs, and knew little about them. The hermit thrushes meant nothing to him, the trees and the flowers and the cliffs everything. The only birds he noticed or cared for were some that were very conspicuous, such as the water-ousels — always particular favorites of mine too. The second night we camped in a snow-storm, on the edge of the cañon walls, under the spreading limbs of a grove of mighty silver fir; and next day we went down into the wonderland of the valley itself. I shall always be glad that I was in the Yosemite with John Muir and in the Yellowstone with John Burroughs.

Like most Americans interested in birds and books, I know a good deal about English birds as they appear in books. I know the lark of Shakespeare and Shelley and the Ettrick

Shepherd; I know the nightingale of Milton and Keats; I know Wordsworth's cuckoo; I know mavis and merle singing in the merry green wood of the old ballads; I know Jenny Wren and Cock Robin of the nursery books. Therefore I had always much desired to hear the birds in real life; and the

Before the Morning Ride at Sagamore.

opportunity offered in June, 1910, when I spent two or three weeks in England. As I could snatch but a few hours from a very exacting round of pleasures and duties, it was necessary for me to be with some companion who could identify both song and singer. In Sir Edward Grey, a keen lover of outdoor life in all its phases, and a delightful companion, who knows the songs and ways of English birds as very few do know them, I found the best possible guide.

We left London on the morning of June 9, twenty-four hours before I sailed from Southampton. Getting off the train at Basingstoke, we drove to the pretty, smiling valley of the Itchen. Here were tramped for three or four hours, then again drove, this time to the edge of the New Forest, where we first took tea at an inn, and then tramped through the forest to an inn on its other side, at Brockenhurst. At the conclusion of our walk my companion made a list of the birds we had seen, putting an asterisk (*) opposite those which we had heard sing. There were forty-one of the former and twenty-three of the latter, as follows:

*Thrush, *blackbird, *lark, *yellowhammer, *robin, *wren, *golden-crested wren, *goldfinch, *chaffinch, *greenfinch, pied wagtail, sparrow, *dunnock (hedge, accentor), missel thrush, starling, rook, jackdaw, *blackcap, *garden warbler, *willow warbler, *chiffchaff, *wood warbler, tree-creeper, *reed bunting, *sedge warbler, coot, water hen, little grebe (dabchick), tufted duck, wood pigeon, stock dove, *turtle dove, peewit, tit (? coal tit), *cuckoo, *nightjar, *swallow, martin, swift, pheasant, partridge.

The valley of the Itchen is typically the England that we know from novel and story and essay. It is very beautiful in every way, with a rich, civilized, fertile beauty — the rapid brook twisting among its reed beds, the rich green of trees and grass, the stately woods, the gardens and fields, the exceedingly picturesque cottages, the great handsome houses standing in their parks. Birds were plentiful; I know but few places in America where one would see such an abundance of individuals, and I was struck by seeing such large birds as coots, water hens, grebes, tufted ducks, pigeons, and peewits. In places in America as thickly settled as the valley of the Itchen, I should not expect to see any like number of birds of this size; but I hope that the efforts of the Audubon societies and kindred organizations will gradually make themselves felt until it becomes a point of honor not only with the American man, but with the American small boy, to shield and protect all forms of harmless wild life. True sportsmen should take the lead in such a movement, for if there is to be any shooting there must be something to shoot; the prime necessity is to keep, and not kill out, even the birds which in legitimate numbers may be shot.

The New Forest is a wild, uninhabited stretch of heath and woodland, many of the trees gnarled and aged, and its very wildness, the lack of cultivation, the ruggedness, made it strongly attractive in my eyes, and suggested my own country. The birds of course were much less plentiful than beside the Itchen.

The bird that most impressed me on my walk was the blackbird. I had already heard nightingales in abundance near Lake Como, and had also listened to larks, but I had never heard either the blackbird, the song thrush, or the blackcap warbler; and while I knew that all three were good singers, I did not know what really beautiful singers they were. Blackbirds were very abundant, and they played a prominent part in the chorus which we heard throughout the day on every hand, though perhaps loudest the following morning at dawn. In its habits and manners the blackbird strikingly resembles our American robin, and indeed looks exactly like a robin, with a yellow bill and coal-black plumage. It hops everywhere over the lawns, just as our robin does, and it lives and nests in the gardens in the same fashion. Its song has a general resemblance to that of our robin, but many of the notes are far more musical, more like those of our wood thrush. Indeed, there were individuals among those we heard certain of whose notes seemed to me almost to equal in point of melody the chimes of the wood thrush; and the highest possible praise for any song-bird is to liken its song to that of the wood thrush or hermit thrush. I certainly do not think that the blackbird has received full justice in the books. I knew that he was a singer, but I really had no idea how fine a singer he was. I suppose one of his troubles has been his name, just as with our own catbird. When he appears in the ballads as the merle, bracketed with his cousin the mavis, the song thrush, it is far easier to recognize him as the master singer that he is. It is a fine thing for England to have such an asset of the countryside, a bird so common, so much in evidence, so fearless, and such a really beautiful singer.

The thrush is a fine singer too, a better singer than our American robin, but to my mind not at the best quite as good as the blackbird at his best; although often I found difficulty in telling the song of one from the song of the other, especially if I only heard two or three notes.

The larks were, of course, exceedingly attractive. It was fascinating to see them spring from the grass, circle upwards, steadily singing and soaring for several minutes, and then return to the point whence they had started. As my companion pointed out, they exactly fulfilled Wordsworth's description; they soared but did not roam. It is quite impossible wholly to differentiate a bird's voice from its habits and surroundings. Although in the lark's song there are occasional musical notes, the song as a whole is not very musical; but it is so joyous, buoyant and unbroken, and uttered under such conditions as fully to entitle the bird to the place he occupies with both poet and prose writer.

The most musical singer we heard was the blackcap warbler. To my ear its song seemed more musical than that of the nightingale. It was astonishingly powerful for so small a bird; in volume and continuity it does not come up to the songs of the thrushes and of certain other birds, but in quality, as an isolated bit of melody, it can hardly be surpassed.

Among the minor singers the robin was noticeable. We all know this pretty little bird from the books, and I was prepared to find him as friendly and attractive as he proved to be, but I had not realized how well he sang. It is not a loud song, but very musical and attractive, and the bird is said to sing practically all through the year. The song of the wren interested me much, because it was not in the least like that of our house wren, but, on the contrary, like that of our winter wren. The theme is the same as the winter wren's, but the song did not seem to me to be as brilliantly musical as that of the tiny singer of the North Woods. The sedge warbler sang in the thick reeds a mocking ventriloquial lay, which reminded me at times of the less pronounced parts of our yellow-breasted chat's song. The cuckoo's cry was singularly attractive and musical, far more so than the rolling, many times repeated, note of our rain-crow.

We did not reach the inn at Brockenhurst until about nine

o'clock, just at nightfall, and a few minutes before that we heard a nightjar. It did not sound in the least like either our whip-poor-will or our night-hawk, uttering a long-continued call of one or two syllables, repeated over and over. The chaffinch was very much in evidence, continually chaunting its unimportant little ditty. I was pleased to see the bold, masterful missel thrush, the stormcock as it is often called; but this bird breeds and sings in the early spring, when the weather is still tempestuous, and had long been silent when we saw it. The starlings, rooks, and jackdaws did not sing, and their calls were attractive merely as the calls of our grakles are attractive;

From the Summer House at Sagamore.

and the other birds that we heard sing, though they played their part in the general chorus, were performers of no especial note, like our tree-creepers, pine warblers, and chipping sparrows. The great spring chorus had already begun to subside, but the woods and fields were still vocal with beautiful bird music, the country was very lovely, the inn as comfortable as possible, and the bath and supper very enjoyable after our tramp; and altogether I passed no pleasanter twenty-four hours during my entire European trip.

Ten days later, at Sagamore Hill, I was among my own birds, and was much interested as I listened to and looked at them in remembering the notes and actions of the birds I had seen in England. On the evening of the first day I sat in my rocking-chair on the broad veranda, looking across the Sound towards the glory of the sunset. The thickly grassed hillside sloped down in front of me to a belt of forest from which rose the golden, leisurely chiming of the wood thrushes, chanting their vespers; through the still air came the warble of vireo and tanager; and after nightfall we heard the flight song of an ovenbird from the same belt of timber. Overhead an oriole sang in the weeping elm, now and then breaking his song to scold like an overgrown wren. Song-sparrows and catbirds sang in the shrubbery; one robin had built its nest over the front and one over the back door, and there was a chippy's nest in the wistaria vine by the stoop. During the next twenty-four hours I saw and heard, either right around the house or while walking down to bathe, through the woods, the following forty-two birds:

Little green heron, night heron, red-tailed hawk, yellow-billed cuckoo, kingfisher, flicker, humming-bird, swift, meadow-lark, red-winged blackbird, sharp-tailed finch, song sparrow, chipping sparrow, bush sparrow, purple finch, Baltimore oriole, cowbunting, robin, wood thrush, thrasher, catbird, scarlet tanager, red-eyed vireo, yellow warbler, black-throated green warbler, kingbird, wood peewee, crow, blue jay, cedar-bird, Maryland yellowthroat, chickadee, black and white creeper, barn swallow, white-breasted swallow, ovenbird, thistlefinch, vesperfinch, indigo bunting, towhee, grasshopper-sparrow, and screech owl.

The birds were still in full song, for on Long Island there is little abatement in the chorus until about the second week of July, when the blossoming of the chestnut trees patches the woodland with frothy greenish-yellow.*

Our most beautiful singers are the wood thrushes; they sing not only in the early morning but throughout the long hot June afternoons. Sometimes they sing in the trees immediately around the house, and if the air is still we can always hear them from among the tall trees at the foot of the hill.

---

*Alas! the blight has now destroyed the chestnut trees, and robbed our woods of one of their distinctive beauties.

The thrashers sing in the hedgerows beyond the garden, the catbirds everywhere. The catbirds have such an attractive song that it is extremely irritating to know that at any moment they may interrupt it to mew and squeal. The bold, cheery music of the robins always seems typical of the bold, cheery birds themselves. The Baltimore orioles nest in the young elms around the house, and the orchard orioles in the apple trees near the garden and outbuildings. Among the earliest sounds of spring is the cheerful, simple, homely song of the song-sparrow; and in March we also hear the piercing cadence of the meadow-lark — to us one of the most attractive of all bird calls. Of late years now and then we hear the rollicking, bubbling melody of the bobolink in the pastures back of the barn; and when the full chorus of these and of many other of the singers of spring is dying down, there are some true hot-weather songsters, such as the brightly hued indigo buntings and thistlefinches. Among the finches one of the most musical and plaintive songs is that of the bush-sparrow — I do not know why the books call it field-sparrow, for it does not dwell in the open fields like the vesperfinch, the savannah-sparrow, and grasshopper-sparrow, but among the cedars and bayberry bushes and young locusts in the same places where the prairie warbler is found. Nor is it only the true songs that delight us. We love to hear the flickers call, and we readily pardon any one of their number which, as occasionally happens, is bold enough to wake us in the early morning by drumming on the shingles of the roof. In our ears the red-winged blackbirds have a very attractive note. We love the screaming of the red-tailed hawks as they soar high overhead, and even the calls of the night heron that nest in the tall water maples by one of the wood ponds on our place, and the little green herons that nest beside the salt marsh. It is hard to tell just how much of the attraction in any bird-note lies in the music itself and how much in the associations. This is what makes it so useless to try to compare the bird songs of one country with those of another. A man who is worth anything can no more be entirely impartial in speaking of the bird songs with which from his earliest childhood he has been familiar than he can be entirely impartial in speaking of his own family.

At Sagamore Hill we love a great many thing — birds and trees and books, and all things beautiful, and horses and rifles and children and hard work and the joy of life. We have great fireplaces, and in them the logs roar and crackle during the long winter evenings. The big piazza is for the hot, still afternoons of summer. As in every house, there are things that appeal to the householder because of their associations, but which would not mean much to others. Naturally, any man who has been President, and filled other positions, accumulates such things, with scant regard to his own personal merits. Perhaps our most cherished possessions are a Remington bronze, "The Bronco Buster," given me by my men when the regiment was mustered out, and a big Tiffany silver vase given to Mrs. Roosevelt by the enlisted men of the battleship Louisiana after we returned from a cruise on her to Panama. It was a real surprise gift, presented to her in the White House, on behalf of the whole crew, by four as strapping man-of-war's-men as ever swung a turret or pointed a twelve-inch gun. The enlisted men of the army I already knew well — of course I knew well the officers of both army and navy. But the enlisted men of the navy I only grew to know well when I was President. On the Louisiana Mrs. Roosevelt and I once dined at the chief petty officers' mess, and on another battleship, the Missouri (when I was in company with Admiral Evans and Captain Cowles), and again on the Sylph and on the Mayflower, we also dined as guests of the crew. When we finished our trip on the Louisiana I made a short speech to the assembled crew, and at its close one of the petty officers, the very picture of what a man-of-war's-man should look like, proposed three cheers for me in terms that struck me as curiously illustrative of America at her best; he said, "Now, then, men, three cheers for Theodore Roosevelt, the typical American citizen!" That was the way in which they thought of the American President — and a very good way, too. It was an expression that would have come naturally only to men in whom the American principles of government and life were ingrained, just as they were ingrained in the men of my regiment. I need scarcely add, but I will add for the benefit of those who do not know, that this attitude of self-respecting identification of interest and purpose is not only compatible with but can only exist when there is fine and real discipline, as thorough and genuine as the discipline that has always obtained in the most formidable fighting fleets and armies. The discipline and the mutual respect are complementary, not antagonistic. During the Presidency all of us, but especially the children, became close friends with many of the sailor men. The four bearers of the vase to Mrs. Roosevelt were promptly hailed as delightful big brothers by our two smallest boys, who at once took them to see the sights of Washington in the landau — "the President's land-ho!" as, with seafaring humor, our guests immediately styled it. Once, after we were in private life again, Mrs. Roosevelt was in a railway station and had some difficulty with her ticket. A fine-looking, quiet man stepped up and asked if he could be of help; he remarked that he had been one of the Mayflower's crew, and knew us well; and in answer to a question explained that he had left the navy in order to study dentistry, and added — a delicious touch — that while thus preparing himself to be a dentist he was earning the necessary money to go on with his studies by practicing the profession of a prize-fighter, being a good man in the ring.

Jack and his Master.

There are various bronzes in the house: Saint-Gaudens's "Puritan," a token from my staff officers when I was Governor; Proctor's cougar, the gift of the Tennis Cabinet — who also gave us a beautiful silver bowl, which is always lovingly pronounced to rhyme with "owl" because that was the pronunciation used at the time of the giving by the valued friend who acted as spokesman for his fellow-members, and who was himself the only non-American member of the said Cabinet. There is a horseman by Macmonnies, and a big bronze vase by Kemys, an adaptation or development of the pottery vases of the Southwestern Indians. Mixed with all of these are gifts from varied sources, ranging from a brazen Buddha sent me by the Dalai Lama and a wonderful psalter from the Emperor Menelik to a priceless ancient Samurai sword, coming from Japan in remembrance of the peace of Portsmouth, and a beautifully inlaid miniature suit of Japanese armor, given me by a favorite hero of mine, Admiral Togo, when he visited Sagamore Hill. There are things from European friends; a mosaic picture of Pope Leo XIII in his garden; a huge, very handsome edition of the Nibelungenlied; a striking miniature of John Hampden from Windsor Castle; editions of Dante, and the campaigns of "Eugenio von Savoy" (another of my heroes, a dead hero this time); a Viking cup; the state sword of a Uganda king; the gold box in which the "freedom of the city of London" was given me; a beautiful head of Abraham Lincoln given me by the French authorities after my speech at the Sorbonne; and many other things from sources as diverse as the Sultan of Turkey and the Dowager Empress of China. Then there are things from home friends: a Polar bear skin from Peary; a Sioux buffalo robe with, on it, painted by some long-dead Sioux artist, the picture story of Custer's fight; a bronze portrait plaque of Joel Chandler Harris; the candlestick used in sealing the Treaty of Portsmouth, sent me by Captain Cameron Winslow; a shoe worn by Dan Patch when he paced a mile in 1.59, sent me by his owner. There is a picture of a bull moose by Carl Rungius, which seems to me as spirited an animal painting as I have ever seen. In the north room, with its tables and mantelpiece and desks and chests made of woods sent from the Philippines by army friends, or by other friends for other reasons; with its bison and wapiti heads; there are three paintings by Marcus Symonds — "Where Light and Shadow Meet," "The Porcelain Towers," and "The Seats of the Mighty"; he is dead now, and he had scant recognition while he lived, yet surely he was a great imaginative artist, a wonderful colorist, and a man with a vision more wonderful still. There is one of Lungren's pictures of the Western plains; and a picture of the Grand Canyon; and one by a Scandinavian artist who could see the fierce picturesqueness of workaday Pittsburgh; and sketches of the White House by Sargent and by Hopkinson Smith.

The books are everywhere. There are as many in the north room and in the parlor — is drawing-room a more appropriate name than parlor? — as in the library; the gun-room at the top of the house, which incidentally has the loveliest view of all, contains more books than any of the other rooms; and they are particularly delightful books to browse among, just because they have not much relevance to one another, this being one of the reasons why they are relegated to their pres-

The North Room at Sagamore.

ent abode. But the books have overflowed into all the other rooms too.

I could not name any principle upon which the books have been gathered. Books are almost as individual as friends. There is no earthly use in laying down general laws about them. Some meet the needs of one person, and some of another; and each person should beware of the booklover's besetting sin, of what Mr. Edgar Allan Poe calls "the mad pride of intellectuality," taking the shape of arrogant pity for the man who does not like the same kind of books. Of course there are books which a man or woman uses as instruments of a profession — law books, medical books, cookery books, and the like. I am not speaking of these, for they are not properly "books" at all; they come in the category of time-tables, telephone directories, and other useful agencies of civilized life. I am speaking of books that are meant to be read. Personally, granted that these books are decent and healthy, the one test to which I demand that they all submit is that of being interesting. If the book is not interesting to the reader, then in all but an infinitesimal number of cases it gives scant benefit to the reader. Of course any reader ought to cultivate his or her taste so that good books will appeal to it, and that trash won't. But after this point has once been reached, the needs of each reader must be met in a fashion that will appeal to those needs. Personally the books by which I have profited infinitely more than by any others have been those in which profit was a by-product of the pleasure; that is, I read them because I enjoyed them, because I liked reading them, and the profit came in as part of the enjoyment.

Of course each individual is apt to have some special tastes in which he cannot expect that any but a few friends will share. Now, I am very proud of my big-game library. I suppose there must be many big-game libraries in Continental Europe, and possibly in England, more extensive than mine, but I have not happened to come across any such library in this country. Some of the originals go back to the sixteenth century, and there are copies or reproductions of the two or three most famous hunting books of the Middle Ages, such as the Duke of York's translation of Gaston Phœbus, and the queer book of the Emperor Maximilian. It is only very occasionally that I meet any one who cares for any of these books. On the other hand, I expect to find many friends who will turn naturally to some of the old or the new books of poetry or romance or history to which we of the household habitually turn. Let me add that ours is in no sense a collector's library. Each book was procured because some one of the family wished to read it. We could never afford to take overmuch thought for the outsides of books; we were too much interested in their insides.

Now and then I am asked as to "what books a statesman should read," and my answer is, poetry and novels —

including short stories under the head of novels. I don't mean that he should read only novels and modern poetry. If he cannot also enjoy the Hebrew prophets and the Greek dramatists, he should be sorry. He ought to read interesting books on history and government, and books of science and philosophy; and really good books on these subjects are as enthralling as any fiction ever written in prose or verse. Gibbon and Macaulay, Herodotus, Thucydides and Tacitus, the Heimskringla, Froissart, Joinville and Villehardouin, Parkman and Mahan, Mommsen and Ranke — why! there are scores and scores of solid histories, the best in the world, which are as absorbing as the best of all the novels, and of as permanent value. The same thing is true of Darwin and Huxley and Carlyle and Emerson, and parts of Kant, and of volumes like Sutherland's "Growth of the Moral Instinct," or Acton's Essays and Lounsbury's studies — here again I am not trying to class books together, or measure one by another, or enumerate one in a thousand of those worth reading, but just to indicate that any man or woman of some intelligence and some cultivation can in some line or other of serious thought, scientific or historical or philosophical or economic or governmental, find any number of books which are charming to read, and which in addition give that for which his or her soul hungers. I do not for a minute mean that the statesman ought not to read a great many different books of this character, just as every one else should read them. But, in the final event, the statesman, and the publicist, and the reformer, and the agitator for new things, and the upholder of what is good in old things, all need more than anything else to know human nature, to know the needs of the human soul; and they will find this nature and these needs set forth as nowhere else by the great imaginative writers, whether of prose or of poetry.

The room for choice is so limitless that to my mind it seems absurd to try to make catalogues which shall be supposed to appeal to all the best thinkers. This is why I have no sympathy whatever with writing lists of *the* One Hundred Best Books, or *the* Five-Foot Library. It is all right for a man to amuse himself by composing *a* list of a hundred very good books; and if he is to go off for a year or so where he cannot get many books, it is an excellent thing to choose a five-foot library of particular books which in that particular year and on that particular trip he would like to read. But there is no such thing as a hundred books that are best for all men, or for the majority of men, or for one man at all times; and there is no such thing as a five-foot library which will satisfy the needs of even one particular man on different occasions extending over a number of years. Milton is best for one mood and Pope for another. Because a man likes Whitman or Browning or Lowell

The Mistress of Sagamore Hill.

he should not feel himself debarred from Tennyson or Kipling or Körner or Heine or the Bard of the Dimbovitza. Tolstoy's novels are good at one time and those of Sienkiewicz at another; and he is fortunate who can relish "Salammbo" and "Tom Brown" and the "Two Admirals" and "Quentin Durward" and "Artemus Ward" and the "Ingoldsby Legends" and "Pickwick" and "Vanity Fair." Why, there are hundreds of books like these, each one of which, if really read, really assimilated, by the person to whom it happens to appeal, will enable that person quite unconsciously to furnish himself with much ammunition which he will find of use in the battle of life.

A book must be interesting to the particular reader at that particular time. But there are tens of thousands of interesting books, and some of them are sealed to some men and some are sealed to others; and some stir the soul at some given point of a man's life and yet convey no message at other times. The reader, the booklover, must meet his own needs without paying too much attention to what his neighbors say those needs should be. He must not hypocritically pretend to like what he does not like. Yet at the same time he must avoid that most unpleasant of all the indications of puffed-up vanity which consists in treating mere individual, and perhaps unfortunate, idiosyncrasy as a matter of pride. I happen to be devoted to Macbeth, whereas I very seldom read Hamlet (though I like parts of it). Now I am humbly and sincerely conscious that this is a demerit in me and not in Hamlet; and yet it would not do me any good to pretend that I like Hamlet as much as Macbeth when, as a matter of fact, I don't. I am very fond of simple epics and of ballad poetry, from the Nibelungenlied and the Roland song through "Chevy Chase" and "Patrick Spens" and "Twa Corbies" to Scott's poems and Longfellow's "Saga of King Olaf" and "Othere." On the other hand, I don't care to read dramas as a rule; I cannot read them with enjoyment unless they appeal to me very strongly. They must almost be Æschylus or Euripides, Goethe or Molière, in order that I may not feel after finishing them a sense of virtuous pride in having achieved a task. Now I would be the first to deny that even the most delightful old English ballad should be put on a par with any one of scores of dramatic works by authors whom I have not mentioned; I know that each of these dramatists has written what is of more worth than the ballad; only, I enjoy the ballad, and I don't enjoy the drama; and therefore the ballad is better for me, and this fact is not altered by the other fact that my own shortcomings are to blame in the matter. I still read a number of Scott's novels over and over again, whereas if I finish anything by Miss Austen I have a feeling that duty performed is a rainbow to the soul. But other booklovers who are very close kin to me, and whose taste I know to be better than mine, read Miss Austen all the time — and, moreover, they are very kind, and never pity me in too offensive a manner for not reading her myself.

Aside from the masters of literature, there are all kinds of books which one person will find delightful, and which he certainly ought not to surrender just because nobody else is able to find as much in the beloved volume. There is on our bookshelves a little pre-Victorian novel or tale called "The Semi-Attached Couple." It is told with much humor; it is a story of gentlefolk who are really gentlefolk; and to me it is altogether delightful. But outside the members of my own family I have never met a human being who had even heard of it, and I don't suppose I ever shall meet one. I often enjoy a story by some living author so much that I write to tell him so — or to tell her so; and at least half the time I regret my action, because it encourages the writer to believe that the public shares my views, and he then finds that the public doesn't.

Books are all very well in their way, and we love them at Sagamore Hill; but children are better than books. Sagamore Hill is one of three neighboring houses in which small cousins spent very happy years of childhood. In the three houses there were at one time sixteen of these small cousins, all told, and once we ranged them in order of size and took their photograph. There are many kinds of success in life worth having. It is exceedingly interesting and attractive to be a successful business man, or railroad man, or farmer, or a successful lawyer or doctor; or a writer, or a President, or a ranchman, or the colonel of a fighting regiment, or to kill grizzly bears and lions. But for unflagging interest and enjoyment, a household of children, if things go reasonably well, certainly makes all other forms of success and achievement lose their importance by comparison. It may be true that he travels farthest who travels alone; but the goal thus reached is not worth reaching. And as for a life deliberately devoted to pleasure as an end — why, the greatest happiness is the happiness that comes as a by-product of striving to do what must be done, even though sorrow is met in the doing. There is a bit of homely philosophy, quoted by Squire Bill Widener, of Widener's Valley, Virginia, which sums up one's duty in life: "Do what you can, with what you've got, where you are."

The country is the place for children, and if not the country, a city small enough so that one can get out into the country. When our own children were little, we were for several winters in Washington, and each Sunday afternoon the whole family spent in Rock Creek Park, which was then very real country indeed. I would drag one of the children's wagons; and when the very smallest pairs of feet grew tired of trudging bravely after us, or of racing on rapturous side trips after flowers and other treasures, the owners would clamber into the wagon. One of these wagons, by the way, a gorgeous red one, had "Express" painted on it in gilt letters, and was known to the younger children as the " 'spress" wagon. They evidently associated the color with the term. Once while we were at Sagamore something happened to the cherished " 'spress" wagon to the distress of the children, and especially of the child who owned it. Their mother and I were just starting for a drive in the buggy, and we promised the bereaved owner that we would visit a store we knew in East Norwich, a village a few miles away, and bring back another " 'spress" wagon. When we reached the store, we found to our dismay that the wagon which we had seen had been sold. We could not bear to return without the promised gift, for we knew that

The Sixteen Cousins.

the brains of small persons are much puzzled when their elders seem to break promises. Fortunately, we saw in the store a delightful little bright-red chair and bright-red table, and these we brought home and handed solemnly over to the expectant recipient, explaining that as there unfortunately was not a " 'spress" wagon we had brought him back a " 'spress" chair and " 'spress" table. It worked beautifully! The " 'spress" chair and table were received with such rapture that we had to get duplicates for the other small member of the family who was the particular crony of the proprietor of the new treasures.

When their mother and I returned from a row, we would often see the children waiting for us, running like sand-spiders along the beach. They always liked to swim in company with a grown-up of buoyant temperament and inventive mind, and the float offered limitless opportunities for enjoyment while bathing. All dutiful parents know the game of "stage-coach"; each child is given a name, such as the whip, the nigh leader, the off wheeler, the old lady passenger, and, under penalty of paying a forfeit, must get up and turn round when the grown-up, who is improvising a thrilling story, mentions that particular object; and when the word "stage-coach" is mentioned, everybody has to get up and turn round. Well, we used to play stage-coach on the float while in swimming, and instead of tamely getting up and turning round, the child whose turn it was had to plunge overboard. When I mentioned "stage-coach," the water fairly foamed with vigorously kicking little legs; and then there was always a moment of interest while I counted, so as to be sure that the number of heads that came up corresponded with the number of children who had gone down.

Bubbles.

No man or woman will ever forget the time when some child lies sick of a disease that threatens its life. Moreover, much less serious sickness is unpleasant enough at the time. Looking back, however, there are elements of comedy in certain of the less serious cases. I well remember one such instance which occurred when we were living in Washington, in a small house, with barely enough room for everybody when all the chinks were filled. Measles descended on the household. In the effort to keep the children that were well and those that were sick apart, their mother and I had to camp out in improvised fashion. When the eldest small boy was getting well, and had recovered his spirits, I slept on a sofa beside his bed — the sofa being so short that my feet projected over anyhow. One afternoon the small boy was given a toy organ by a sympathetic friend. Next

morning early I was waked to find the small boy very viva-
cious and requesting a story. Having drowsily told the story,
I said, "Now, father's told you a story, so you amuse yourself
and let father go to sleep"; to which the small boy responded
most virtuously, "Yes, father will go to sleep and I'll play
the organ," which he did, at a distance of two feet from my
head. Later his sister, who had just come down with the
measles, was put into the same room. The small boy was con-
valescing, and was engaged in playing on the floor with some
tin ships, together with two or three pasteboard monitors and
rams of my own manufacture. He was giving a vivid rendering of Farragut at Mobile Bay, from memories of how I had
told the story. My pasteboard rams and monitors were fascinating — if a naval architect may be allowed to praise his own
work — and as property they were equally divided between
the little girl and the small boy. The little girl looked on with
alert suspicion from the bed, for she was not yet convalescent
enough to be allowed down on the floor. The small boy was
busily reciting the phases of the fight, which now approached
its climax, and the little girl evidently suspected that her monitor was destined to play the part of victim.

*Little boy.* "And then they steamed bang into the monitor."

*Little girl.* "Brother, don't you sink my monitor!"

*Little boy* (without heeding, and hurrying toward the climax).
"And the torpedo went at the monitor!"

*Little girl.* "My monitor is not to sink!"

*Little boy*, dramatically: "And bang the monitor sank!"

*Little girl.* "It didn't do any such thing. My monitor always
goes to bed at seven, and it's now quarter past. My monitor
was in bed and *couldn't* sink!"

When I was Assistant Secretary of the Navy, Leonard Wood
and I used often to combine forces and take both families of
children out to walk, and occasionally some of their playmates.
Leonard Wood's son, I found, attributed the paternity of all
of those not of his own family to me. Once we were taking
the children across Rock Creek on a fallen tree. I was standing on the middle of the log trying to prevent any of the children from falling off, and while making a clutch at one
peculiarly active and heedless child I fell off myself. As I
emerged from the water I heard the little Wood boy calling

frantically to the General: "Oh! oh! The father of all the children fell into the creek!" — which made me feel like an uncommonly moist patriarch.

Of course the children took much interest in the trophies I occasionally brought back from my hunts. When I started for my regiment, in '98, the stress of leaving home, which was naturally not pleasant, was somewhat lightened by the next to the youngest boy, whose ideas of what was about to happen were

Daisies.

hazy, clasping me round the legs with a beaming smile and saying, "And is my father going to the war? And will he bring me back a bear?" When, some five months later, I returned, of course in my uniform, this little boy was much puzzled as to my identity, although he greeted me affably with "Good afternoon, Colonel." Half an hour later somebody asked him, "Where's father?" to which he responded, "I don't know; but the Colonel is taking a bath."

Of course the children anthropomorphized — if that is the proper term — their friends of the animal world. Among these friends at one period was the baker's horse, and on a very rainy day I heard the little girl, who was looking out of the window, say, with a melancholy shake of her head, "Oh! there's poor Kraft's horse, all soppin' wet!"

While I was in the White House the youngest boy became an *habitué* of a small and rather noisome animal shop, and the good-natured owner would occasionally let him take pets home to play with. On one occasion I was holding a conversation with one of the leaders in Congress, Uncle Pete Hepburn, about the Railroad Rate Bill. The children were strictly trained not to interrupt business, but on this particular occasion the little boy's feelings overcame him. He had been loaned a king-snake, which, as all nature-lovers know, is not only a useful but a beautiful snake, very friendly to human beings; and he came rushing home to show the treasure. He was holding it inside his coat, and it contrived to wiggle partly down the sleeve. Uncle Pete Hepburn naturally did not understand the full import of what the little boy was saying to me as he endeavored to wriggle out of his jacket, and kindly started to help him — and then jumped back with alacrity as the small boy and the snake both popped out of the jacket.

There could be no healthier and pleasanter place in which to bring up children than in that nook of old-time America around Sagamore Hill. Certainly I never knew small people to have a better time or a better training for their work in after life than the three families of cousins at Sagamore Hill. It was real country, and — speaking from the somewhat detached point of view of the masculine parent — I should say there was just the proper mixture of freedom and control in the management of the children. They were never allowed to be disobedient or to shirk lessons or work; and they were encouraged to have all the fun possible. They often went barefoot, especially during the many hours passed in various enthralling pursuits along and in the waters of the bay. They swam, they tramped, they boated, they coasted and skated in winter, they were intimate friends with the cows, chickens, pigs, and other live stock. They had in succession two ponies, General Grant and, when the General's legs became such that he lay down too often and too unexpectedly in the road, a calico pony named Algonquin, who is still living a life of honorable leisure in the stable and in the pasture — where he has to be picketed, because otherwise he chases the cows. Sedate pony Grant used to draw the cart in which the children went driving when they were very small, the driver being their old nurse Mame, who had held their mother in her arms when she was born, and who was knit to them by a tie as close as any tie of blood. I doubt whether I ever saw Mame really offended with them except once when, out of pure but misunderstood affection, they named a pig after her. They loved pony Grant. Once I saw the then little boy of three hugging pony Grant's fore legs. As he leaned over, his broad straw hat tilted on end, and pony Grant meditatively munched the brim; whereupon the small boy looked up with a wail of anguish, evidently thinking the pony had decided to treat him like a radish.

The children had pets of their own, too, of course. Among them guinea pigs were the stand-bys — their highly unemotional nature fits them for companionship with adoring but over-enthusiastic young masters and mistresses. Then there were flying squirrels, and kangaroo rats, gentle and trustful, and a badger whose temper was short but whose nature was fundamentally friendly. The badger's name was Josiah; the particular little boy whose property he was used to carry

Josiah and his Master.

him about, clasped firmly around what would have been his waist if he had had any. Inasmuch as when on the ground the badger would play energetic games of tag with the little boy and nip his bare legs, I suggested that it would be uncommonly disagreeable if he took advantage of being held in the little boy's arms to bite his face; but this suggestion was repelled with scorn as an unworthy assault on the character of Josiah. "He bites legs sometimes, but he never bites faces," said the little boy. We also had a young black bear whom the children christened Jonathan Edwards, partly out of compliment to their mother, who was descended from that great Puritan divine, and partly because the bear possessed a temper in which gloom and strength were combined in what the children regarded as Calvinistic proportions. As for the dogs, of course there were many, and during their lives they were intimate and valued family friends, and their deaths were household tragedies. One of them, a large yellow animal of several good breeds and valuable rather because of psychical than physical traits, was named "Susan" by his small owners, in commemoration of another retainer, a white cow; the fact that the cow and the dog were not of the same sex being treated with indifference. Much the most individual of the dogs and the one with the strongest character was Sailor Boy, a Chesapeake Bay dog. He had a masterful temper and a strong sense of both dignity and duty. He would never let the other dogs fight, and he himself never fought unless circumstances imperatively demanded it; but he was a murderous animal when he did fight. He was not only exceedingly fond of the water, as was to be expected, but passionately devoted to gunpowder in every form, for he loved firearms and fairly reveled in the Fourth of July celebrations — the latter being rather hazardous occasions, as the children strongly objected to any "safe and sane" element being injected into them, and had the normal number of close shaves with rockets, Roman candles, and firecrackers.

One of the stand-bys for enjoyment, especially in rainy weather, was the old barn. This had been built nearly a century previously, and was as delightful as only the pleasantest kind of old barn can be. It stood at the meeting-spot of three fences. A favorite amusement used to be an obstacle race when the barn was full of hay. The contestants were timed and were started successively from outside the door. They rushed inside, clambered over or burrowed through the hay, as suited them best, dropped out of a place where a loose board had come off, got over, through, or under the three fences, and raced back to the starting-point. When they were little, their respective fathers were expected also to take part in the obstacle race, and when with the advance of years the fathers finally refused to be contestants, there was a general feeling of pained regret among the children at such a decline in the sporting spirit.

Another famous place for handicap races was Cooper's Bluff, a gigantic sand-bank rising from the edge of the bay, a mile from the house. If the tide was high there was an added thrill, for some of the contestants were sure to run into the water.

As soon as the little boys learned to swim they were allowed to go off by themselves in rowboats and camp out for the night along the Sound. Sometimes I would go along so as to take the smaller children. Once a schooner was wrecked on a point half a dozen miles away. She held together well for a season or two after having been cleared of everything down to the timbers, and this gave us the chance to make camping-out trips in which the girls could also be included, for we put them to sleep in the wreck, while the boys slept on the shore; squaw picnics, the children called them.

My children, when young, went to the public school near us, the little Cove School, as it is called. For nearly thirty years we have given the Christmas tree to the school. Before the

The Obstacle Race around the Old Barn.

gifts are distributed I am expected to make an address, which is always mercifully short, my own children having impressed upon me with frank sincerity the attitude of other children to addresses of this kind on such occasions. There are of course performances by the children themselves, while all of us parents look admiringly on, each sympathizing with his or her particular offspring in the somewhat wooden recital of "Darius Green and his Flying Machine" or "The Mountain and the Squirrel had a Quarrel." But the tree and the gifts make up for all shortcomings.

We had a sleigh for winter; but if, when there was much snow, the whole family desired to go somewhere, we would put the body of the farm wagon on runners and all bundle in together. We always liked snow at Christmas time, and the sleigh-ride down to the church on Christmas eve. One of the hymns always sung at this Christmas eve festival begins, "It's Christmas eve on the river, it's Christmas eve on the bay." All good natives of the village firmly believe that this hymn was written here, and with direct reference to Oyster Bay; although if such were the case the word "river" would have to be taken in a hyperbolic sense, as the nearest approach to a river is the village pond. I used to share this belief myself, until my faith was shaken by a Denver lady who wrote that she had sung that hymn when a child in Michigan, and that at the present time her little Denver babies also loved it, although in their case the river was not represented by even a village pond.

The Small Boy of the White House.

When we were in Washington, the children usually went with their mother to the Episcopal church, while I went to the Dutch Reformed. But if any child misbehaved itself, it was sometimes sent next Sunday to church with me, on the theory that my companionship would have a sedative effect — which it did, as I and the child walked along with rather constrained politeness, each eying the other with watchful readiness for the unexpected. On one occasion, when the child's conduct fell just short of warranting such extreme measures, his mother, as they were on the point of entering church, concluded a homily by a quotation which showed a certain haziness of memory concerning the marriage and baptismal services: "No, little boy, if this conduct continues, I shall think that you neither love, honor, nor obey me!" However, the culprit was much impressed with a sense of shortcoming as to the obligations he had undertaken; so the result was as satisfactory as if the quotation had been from the right service.

As for the education of the children, there was of course much of it that represented downright hard work and drudgery. There was also much training that came as a by-product and was perhaps almost as valuable — not as a substitute but as an addition. After their supper, the children, when little, would come trotting up to their mother's room to be read to, and it was always a surprise to me to notice the extremely varied reading which interested them, from Howard Pyle's "Robin Hood," Mary Alicia Owen's "Voodoo Tales," and Joel Chandler Harris's "Aaron in the Wild Woods," to "Lycidas" and "King John." If their mother was absent, I would try to act as vice-mother — a poor substitute, I fear — superintending the supper and reading aloud afterwards. The children did not wish me to read the books they desired their mother to read, and I usually took some such book as "Hereward the Wake," or "Guy Mannering," or "The Last of the Mohicans" or else some story about a man-eating tiger, or a man-eating lion, from one of the hunting books in my library. These latter stories were always favorites, and as the authors told them in the first person, my interested auditors grew to know them by the name of the "I" stories, and regarded them as adventures all of which happened to the same individual. When Selous, the African hunter, visited us, I had to get him to tell to the younger children two or three of the stories with which they were already familiar from my reading; and as Selous is a most graphic narrator, and always enters thoroughly into the feeling not only of himself but of the opposing lion or buffalo, my own rendering of the incidents was cast entirely into the shade.

Besides profiting by the more canonical books on education, we profited by certain essays and articles of a less orthodox type. I wish to express my warmest gratitude for such books — not of avowedly didactic purpose — as Laura Richards's books, Josephine Dodge Daskam's "Madness of Philip," Palmer Cox's "Queer People," the melodies of Father

Goose and Mother Wild Goose, Flandreau's "Mrs. White's," Myra Kelly's stories of her little East Side pupils, and Michelson's "Madigans." It is well to take duties, and life generally, seriously. It is also well to remember that a sense of humor is a healthy anti-scorbutic to that portentous seriousness which defeats its own purpose.

The First Grandchild at Sagamore Hill.

Occasionally bits of self-education proved of unexpected help to the children in later years. Like other children, they were apt to take to bed with them treasures which they particularly esteemed. One of the boys, just before his sixteenth birthday, went moose hunting with the family doctor, and close personal friend of the entire family, Alexander Lambert. Once night overtook them before they camped, and they had to lie down just where they were. Next morning Dr. Lambert rather enviously congratulated the boy on the fact that stones and roots evidently did not interfere with the soundness of his sleep; to which the boy responded, "Well, Doctor, you see it isn't very long since I used to take fourteen china animals to bed with me every night!"

As the children grew up, Sagamore Hill remained delightful for them. There were picnics and riding parties, there were dances in the north room — sometimes fancy dress dances — and open-air plays on the green tennis court of one of the cousin's houses. The children are no longer children now. Most of them are men and women, working out their own fates in the big world; some in our own land, others across the great oceans or where the Southern Cross blazes in the tropic nights. Some of them have children of their own; some are working at one thing, some at another; in cable ships, in business offices, in factories, in newspaper offices, building steel bridges, bossing gravel trains and steam shovels, or laying tracks and superintending freight traffic. They have had their share of accidents and escapes; as I write, word comes from a far-off land that one of them, whom Seth Bullock used to call "Kim" because he was the friend of all mankind, while bossing a dangerous but necessary steel structural job has had two ribs and two back teeth broken, and is back at work. They have known and they will know joy and sorrow, triumph and temporary defeat. But I believe they are all the better off because of their happy and healthy childhood.

It is impossible to win the great prizes of life without running risks, and the greatest of all prizes are those connected with the home. No father and mother can hope to escape sorrow and anxiety, and there are dreadful moments when death comes very near those we love, even if for the time being it passes by. But life is a great adventure, and the worst of all fears is the fear of living. There are many forms of success, many forms of triumph. But there is no other success that in any shape or way approaches that which is open to most of the many, many men and women who have the right ideals. These are the men and the women who see that it is the intimate and homely things that count most. They are the men and women who have the courage to strive for the happiness which comes only with labor and effort and self-sacrifice, and only to those whose joy in life springs in part from power of work and sense of duty.

# *Chapter X*

## THE PRESIDENCY; MAKING AN OLD PARTY PROGRESSIVE

O N SEPTEMBER 6, 1901, President McKinley was shot by an Anarchist in the city of Buffalo. I went to Buffalo at once. The President's condition seemed to be improving, and after a day or two we were told that he was practically out of danger. I then joined my family, who were in the Adirondacks, near the foot of Mount Tahawus. A day or two afterwards we took a long tramp through the forest, and in the afternoon I climbed Mount Tahawus. After reaching the top I had descended a few hundred feet to a shelf of land where there was a little lake, when I saw a guide coming out of the woods on our trail from below. I felt at once that he had bad news, and, sure enough, he handed me a telegram saying that the President's condition was much worse and that I must come to Buffalo immediately. It was late in the afternoon, and darkness had fallen by the time I reached the clubhouse where we were staying. It was some time afterwards before I could get a wagon to drive me out to the nearest railway station, North Creek, some forty or fifty miles distant. The roads were the ordinary wilderness roads and the night was dark. But we changed horses two or three times — when I say "we" I mean the driver and I, as there was no one else with us — and reached the station just at dawn, to learn from Mr. Loeb, who had a special train waiting, that the President was dead. That evening I took the oath of office, in the house of Ansley Wilcox, at Buffalo.

On three previous occasions the Vice-President had succeeded to the Presidency on the death of the President. In each case there had been a reversal of party policy, and a nearly immediate and nearly complete change in the personnel of the higher offices, especially the Cabinet. I had never felt that this was wise from any standpoint. If a man is fit to be President, he will speedily so impress himself in the office that the policies pursued will be his anyhow, and he will not have to bother as to whether he is changing them or not; while as regards the

President Roosevelt.
This portrait of Theodore Roosevelt, by John S. Sargent,
is at the White House.

offices under him, the important thing for him is that his subordinates shall make a success in handling their several departments. The subordinate is sure to desire to make a success of his department for his own sake, and if he is a fit man, whose views on public policy are sound, and whose abilities entitle him to his position, he will do excellently under almost any chief with the same purposes.

I at once announced that I would continue unchanged McKinley's policies for the honor and prosperity of the country, and I asked all the members of the Cabinet to stay. There were no changes made among them save as changes were made among their successors whom I myself appointed. I continued Mr. McKinley's policies, changing and developing them and adding new policies only as the questions before the public changed and as the needs of the public developed. Some of my friends shook their heads over this, telling me that the men I retained would not be "loyal to me," and that I would seem as if I were "a pale copy of McKinley." I told them that I was not nervous on this score, and that if the men I retained were loyal to their work they would be giving me the loyalty for which I most cared; and that if they were not, I would change them anyhow; and that as for being "a pale copy of McKinley," I was not primarily concerned with either following or not following in his footsteps, but in facing the new problems that arose; and that if I were competent I would find ample opportunity to show my competence by my deeds without worrying myself as to how to convince people of the fact.

For the reasons I have already given in my chapter on the Governorship of New York, the Republican party, which in the days of Abraham Lincoln was founded as the radical progressive party of the Nation, had been obliged during the last decade of the nineteenth century to uphold the interests of popular government against a foolish and illjudged mockradicalism. It remained the Nationalist as against the particularist or State's rights party, and in so far it remained absolutely sound; for little permanent good can be done by any party which worships the State's rights fetish or which fails to regard the State, like the county or the municipality, as merely a convenient unit for local self-government, while in all National matters, of importance to the whole people, the

Nation is to be supreme over State, county, and town alike. But the State's rights fetish, although still effectively used at certain times by both courts and Congress to block needed National legislation directed against the huge corporations or in the interests of workingmen, was not a prime issue at the time of which I speak. In 1896, 1898, and 1900 the campaigns were waged on two great moral issues: (1) the imperative need of a sound and honest currency; (2) the need, after 1898, of meeting in manful and straightforward fashion the extraterritorial problems arising from the Spanish War. On these great moral issues the Republican party was right, and the men who were opposed to it, and who claimed to be the radicals, and their allies among the sentimentalists, were utterly and hopelessly wrong. This had, regrettably but perhaps inevitably, tended to throw the party into the hands not merely of the conservatives but of the reactionaries; of men who, sometimes for personal and improper reasons, but more often with entire sincerity and uprightness of purpose, distrusted anything that was progressive and dreaded radicalism. These men still from force of habit applauded what Lincoln had done in the way of radical dealing with the abuses of his day; but they did not apply the spirit in which Lincoln worked to the abuses of their own day. Both houses of Congress were controlled by these men. Their leaders in the Senate were Messrs. Aldrich and Hale. The Speaker of the House when I became President was Mr. Henderson, but in a little over a year he was succeeded by Mr. Cannon, who, although widely differing from Senator Aldrich in matters of detail, represented the same type of public sentiment. There were many points on which I agreed with Mr. Cannon and Mr. Aldrich, and some points on which I agreed with Mr. Hale. I made a resolute effort to get on with all three and with their followers, and I have no question that they made an equally resolute effort to get on with me. We succeeded in working together, although with increasing friction, for some years, I pushing forward and they hanging back. Gradually, however, I was forced to abandon the effort to persuade them to come my way, and then I achieved results only by appealing over the heads of the Senate and House leaders to the people, who were the masters of both of us. I continued in this way to get results until almost the close of my term; and the Republican party became once more the progressive and indeed the fairly radical progressive party of the Nation. When my successor was chosen, however, the leaders of the House and Senate, or most of them, felt that it was safe to come to a break with me, and the last or short session of Congress, held between the election of my successor and his inauguration four months later, saw a series of contests between the majorities in the two houses of Congress and the President, — myself, — quite as bitter as if they and I had belonged to opposite political parties. However, I held my own. I was not able to push through the legislation I desired during these four months, but I was able to prevent them doing anything I did not desire, or undoing anything that I had already succeeded in getting done.

There were, of course, many Senators and members of the lower house with whom up to the very last I continued to work in hearty accord, and with a growing understanding. I have not the space to enumerate, as I would like to, these men. For many years Senator Lodge had been my close personal and political friend, with whom I discussed all public questions that arose, usually with agreement; and our intimately close relations were of course unchanged by my entry into the White House. He was of all our public men the man who had made the closest and wisest study of our foreign relations, and more clearly than almost any other man he understood the vital fact that the efficiency of our navy conditioned our national efficiency in foreign affairs. Anything relating to our international relations, from Panama and the navy to the Alaskan boundary question, the Algeciras negotiations, or the peace of Portsmouth, I was certain to discuss with Senator Lodge and also with certain other members of Congress, such as Senator Turner of Washington and Representative Hitt of Illinois. Anything relating to labor legislation and to measures for controlling big business or efficiently regulating the giant railway systems, I was certain to discuss with Senator Dolliver or Congressman Hepburn or Congressman Cooper. With men like Senator Beveridge, Congressman (afterwards Senator) Dixon, and Congressman Murdock, I was apt to discuss pretty nearly everything relating to either our internal or our external affairs. There were many, many others. The present President of the Senate, Senator Clark, of Arkansas, was as fearless and high-minded a representative of the people of the United States as I ever dealt with. He was one of the men who combined loyalty to his own State with an equally keen loyalty to the people of all the United States. He was politically opposed to me; but when the interests of the country were at stake, he was incapable of considering party differences; and this was especially his attitude in international matters — including certain treaties which most of his party colleagues, with narrow lack of patriotism, and complete subordination of National to factional interest, opposed. I have never anywhere met finer, more faithful, more disinterested, and more loyal public servants than Senator O. H. Platt, a Republican, from Connecticut, and Senator Cockrell, a Democrat, from Missouri. They were already old men when I came to the Presidency; and doubtless there were points on which I seemed to them to be extreme and radical; but eventually they found that our motives and beliefs were the same, and they did all in their power to help any movement that was for the interest of our people as a whole. I had met them when I was Civil Service Commissioner and Assistant Secretary of the Navy. All I ever had to do with either was to convince him that a given measure I championed was right, and he then at once did all he could to have it put into effect. If I could not convince them, why! that was my fault, or my misfortune; but if I could convince them, I never had to think again as to whether they would or would not support me. There were many other men of mark in both houses with whom I could work on some points, whereas on others we had to differ. There was one powerful leader — a burly, forceful man, of admirable traits — who had, however, been trained in the post-bellum school of business and politics, so that his attitude towards life, quite unconsciously, reminded me a little of Artemus Ward's view of the Tower of London — "If I like it, I'll buy it." There was a big governmental job in which this leader was much interested, and in reference to which he always wished me to consult a man whom he trusted, whom I will call Pitt Rodney. One day I answered him, "The trouble with Rodney is that he misestimates his relations to cosmos"; to which he responded, "Cosmos — Cosmos? Never heard of him. You stick to Rodney. He's your man!" Outside of the public servants there were multitudes of men, in newspaper offices, in magazine offices, in business or the professions or on farms or in shops, who actively supported the policies for which I stood and did work of genuine leadership which was quite as effective as any work done by men in public office. Without the active support of these men I would have been powerless. In particular, the leading newspaper correspondents at Washington were as a whole a singularly able, trustworthy, and public-spirited body of men, and the most useful of all agents in the fight for efficient and decent government.

As for the men under me in executive office, I could not overstate the debt of gratitude I owe them. From the heads of the departments, the Cabinet officers, down, the most striking feature of the Administration was the devoted, zealous, and efficient work that was done as soon as it became understood that the one bond of interest among all of us was the desire to make the Government the most effective instrument in advancing the interests of the people as a whole, the interests of the average men and women of the United States and of their children. I do not think I overstate the case when I say that most of the men who did the best work under me felt that ours was a partnership, that we all stood on the same level of purpose and service, and that it mattered not what position any one of us held so long as in that position he gave the very best that was in him. We worked very hard; but I made a point of getting a couple of hours off each day for equally vigorous play. The men with whom I then played, whom we laughingly grew to call the "Tennis Cabinet," have been mentioned in a previous chapter of this book in connection with the gift they gave me at the last breakfast which they took at the White House. There were many others in the public service under me with whom I happened not to play, but who did their share of our common work just as effectively as it was done by us who did play. Of course nothing could have been done in my Administration if it had not been for the zeal, intelligence, masterful ability, and downright hard labor of these men in countless positions under me. I was helpless to do anything except as my thoughts and orders were translated into action by them; and, moreover, each of them, as he grew specially fit for his job, used to suggest to me the right thought to have, and the right order to give, concerning that job. It is of course hard for me to speak with cold and dispassionate partiality of these men, who were as close to me as were the men of my regiment. But the outside observers best fitted to pass judgment about them felt as I did. At the end of my Administration Mr. Bryce, the British Ambassador, told me that in a long life, during which he had studied intimately the government of many different countries, he had never in any country seen a more eager, high-minded, and efficient set of public servants, men more useful and more creditable to their country, than the men then doing the work of the American Government in Washington and in the field. I repeat this statement with the permission of Mr. Bryce.

At about the same time, or a little before, in the spring of 1908, there appeared in the English *Fortnightly Review* an article, evidently by a competent eye witness, setting forth more in detail the same views to which the British Ambassador thus privately gave expression. It was in part as follows:

"Mr. Roosevelt has gathered around him a body of public servants who are nowhere surpassed, I question whether they are anywhere equaled, for efficiency, self-sacrifice, and an absolute devotion to their country's interests. Many of them are poor men, without private means, who have voluntarily abandoned high professional ambitions and turned their backs on the rewards of business to serve their country on salaries that are not merely inadequate, but indecently so. There is not one of them who is not constantly assailed by offers of positions in the world of commerce, finance, and the law that would satisfy every material ambition with which he began life. There is not one of them who could not, if he chose, earn outside Washington from ten to twenty times the income on which he economizes as a State official. But these men are as indifferent to money and to the power that money brings as to the allurements of Newport and New York, or to merely personal distinctions, or to the commercialized ideals which the great bulk of their fellow-countrymen accept without question. They are content, and more than content, to sink themselves in the National service without a thought of private advancement, and often at a heavy sacrifice of worldly honors, and to

The White House from the Garden.

toil on . . . sustained by their own native impulse to make of patriotism an efficient instrument of public betterment."

The American public rarely appreciate the high quality of the work done by some of our diplomats — work, usually entirely unnoticed and unrewarded, which redounds to the interest and the honor of all of us. The most useful man in the entire diplomatic service, during my presidency, and for many years before, was Henry White; and I say this having in mind the high quality of work done by such admirable ambassadors and ministers as Bacon, Meyer, Straus, O'Brien, Rockhill, and Egan, to name only a few among many. When I left the presidency White was Ambassador to France; shortly afterwards he was removed by Mr. Taft, for reasons unconnected with the good of the service.

The most important factor in getting the right spirit in my Administration, next to the insistence upon courage, honesty, and a genuine democracy of desire to serve the plain people, was my insistence upon the theory that the executive power was limited only by specific restrictions and prohibitions appearing in the Constitution or imposed by the Congress under its Constitutional powers. My view was that every executive officer, and above all every executive officer in high position, was a steward of the people bound actively and affirmatively to do all he could for the people, and not to content himself with the negative merit of keeping his talents undamaged in a napkin. I declined to adopt the view that what was imperatively necessary for the Nation could not be done by the President unless he could find some specific authorization to do it. My belief was that it was not only his right but his duty to do anything that the needs of the Nation demanded unless such action was forbidden by the Constitution or by the laws. Under this interpretation of executive power I did and caused to be done many things not previously done by the President and the heads of the departments. I did not usurp power, but I did greatly broaden the use of executive power. In other words, I acted for the public welfare, I acted for the common well-being of all our people, whenever and in whatever manner was necessary, unless prevented by direct constitutional or legislative prohibition. I did not care a rap for the mere form and show of power; I cared immensely for the use that could be made of the substance. The Senate at one time objected to my communicating with them in printing, preferring the expensive, foolish, and laborious practice of writing out the messages by hand. It was not possible to return to the outworn archaism of hand writing; but we endeavored to have the printing made as pretty as possible. Whether I communicated with the Congress in writing or by word of mouth, and whether the writing was by a machine, or a pen, were equally, and absolutely, unimportant matters. The importance lay in what I said and in the heed paid to what I said. So as to my meeting and consulting Senators, Congressmen, politicians, financiers, and labor men. I consulted all who wished to see me; and if I wished to see any one, I sent for him; and where the consultation took place was a matter of supreme unimportance. I consulted every man with the sincere hope that I could profit by and follow his advice; I consulted every member of Congress who wished to be consulted, hoping to be able to come to an agreement of action with him; and I always finally acted as my conscience and common sense bade me act.

About appointments I was obliged by the Constitution to consult the Senate; and the long-established custom of the Senate meant that in practice this consultation was with individual Senators and even with big politicians who stood behind the Senators. I was only one-half the appointing power; I nominated; but the Senate confirmed. In practice, by what was called "the courtesy of the Senate," the Senate normally refused to confirm any appointment if the Senator from the State objected to it. In exceptional cases, where I could arouse public attention, I could force through the appointment in spite of the opposition of the Senators; in all ordinary cases this was impossible. On the other hand, the Senator could of course do nothing for any man unless I chose to nominate him. In consequence the Constitution itself forced the President and the Senators from each State to come to a working agreement on the appointments in and from that State.

My course was to insist on absolute fitness, including honesty, as a prerequisite to every appointment; and to remove only for good cause, and, where there was such cause, to refuse even to discuss with the Senator in interest the unfit servant's retention. Subject to these considerations, I normally accepted each Senator's recommendations for offices of a routine kind, such as most post-offices and the like, but insisted on myself choosing the men for the more important positions. I was willing to take any good man for postmaster; but in the case of a Judge or District Attorney or Canal Commissioner or Ambassador, I was apt to insist either on a given man or else on any man with a given class of qualifications. If the Senator deceived me, I took care that he had no opportunity to repeat the deception.

I can perhaps best illustrate my theory of action by two specific examples. In New York Governor Odell and Senator Platt sometimes worked in agreement and sometimes were at swords' points, and both wished to be consulted. To a friendly Congressman, who was also their friend, I wrote as follows on July 22, 1903:

"I want to work with Platt. I want to work with Odell. I want to support both and take the advice of both. But of course ultimately I must be the judge as to acting on the advice given. When, as in the case of the judgeship, I am convinced that the advice of both is wrong, I shall act as I did when I appointed Holt. When I can find a friend of Odell's like Cooley, who is thoroughly fit for the position I desire to fill, it gives me the greatest pleasure to appoint him. When Platt proposes to me a man like Hamilton Fish, it is equally a pleasure to appoint him."

This was written in connection with events which led up to my refusing to accept Senator Platt's or Governor Odell's suggestions as to a Federal Judgeship and a Federal District Attorneyship, and insisting on the appointment, first of Judge Hough and later of District Attorney Stimson; because in each case I felt that the work to be done was of so high an order that I could not take an ordinary man.

The other case was that of Senator Fulton, of Oregon. Through Francis Heney I was prosecuting men who were implicated in a vast network of conspiracy against the law in connection with the theft of public land in Oregon. I had been acting on Senator Fulton's recommendations for office, in the usual manner. Heney had been insisting that Fulton was in league with the men we were prosecuting, and that he had recommended unfit men. Fulton had been protesting against my following Heney's advice, particularly as regards appointing Judge Wolverton as United States Judge. Finally Heney laid before me a report which convinced me of the truth of his

Mrs. Theodore Roosevelt.

statements. I then wrote to Fulton as follows, on November 20, 1905: "My dear Senator Fulton: I inclose you herewith a copy of the report made to me by Mr. Heney. I have seen the originals of the letters from you and Senator Mitchell quoted therein. I do not at this time desire to discuss the report itself, which of course I must submit to the Attorney-General. But

I have been obliged to reach the painful conclusion that your own letters as therein quoted tend to show that you recommended for the position of District Attorney B when you had good reason to believe that he had himself been guilty of fraudulent conduct; that you recommended C for the same position simply because it was for B's interest that he should be so recommended, and, as there is reason to believe, because he had agreed to divide the fees with B if he were appointed; and that you finally recommended the reappointment of H with the knowledge that if H were appointed he would abstain from prosecuting B for criminal misconduct, this being why B advocated H's claims for reappointment. If you care to make any statement in the matter, I shall of course be glad to hear it. As the District Judge of Oregon I shall appoint Judge Wolverton." In the letter I of course gave in full the names indicated above by initials. Senator Fulton gave no explanation. I therefore ceased to consult him about appointments under the Department of Justice and the Interior, the two departments in which the crookedness had occurred — there was no question of crookedness in the other offices in the State, and they could be handled in the ordinary manner. Legal proceedings were undertaken against his colleague in the Senate, and one of his colleagues in the lower house, and the former was convicted and sentenced to the penitentiary.

In a number of instances the legality of executive acts of my Administration was brought before the courts. They were uniformly sustained. For example, prior to 1907 statutes relating to the disposition of coal lands had been construed as fixing the flat price at $10 to $20 per acre. The result was that valuable coal lands were sold for wholly inadequate prices, chiefly to big corporations. By executive order the coal lands were withdrawn and not opened for entry until proper classification was placed thereon by Government agents. There was a great clamor that I was usurping legislative power; but the acts were not assailed in court until we brought suits to set aside entries made by persons and associations to obtain larger areas than the statutes authorized. This position was opposed on the ground that the restrictions imposed were illegal; that the executive orders were illegal. The Supreme Court sustained the Government. In the same way our attitude in the water power question was sustained, the Supreme Court holding that the Federal Government had the rights we claimed over streams that are or may be declared navigable by Congress. Again, when Oklahoma became a State we were obliged to use the executive power to protect Indian rights and property, for there had been an enormous amount of fraud in the obtaining of Indian lands by white men. Here we were denounced as usurping power over a State as well as usurping power that did not belong to the executive. The Supreme Court sustained our action.

In connection with the Indians, by the way, it was again and again necessary to assert the position of the President as steward of the whole people. I had a capital Indian Commissioner, Francis E. Leupp. I found that I could rely on his judgment not to get me into fights that were unnecessary, and therefore I always backed him to the limit when he told me that a fight was necessary. On one occasion, for example, Congress passed a bill to sell to settlers about half a million acres of Indian land in Oklahoma at one and a half dollars an acre. I refused to sign it, and turned the matter over to Leupp. The bill was accordingly withdrawn, amended so as to safeguard the welfare of the Indians, and the minimum price raised to five dollars an acre. Then I signed the bill. We sold that land under sealed bids, and realized for the Kiowa, Comanche, and Apache Indians more than four million dollars — three millions and a quarter more than they would have obtained if I had signed the bill in its original form. In another case, where there had been a division among the Sac and Fox Indians, part of the tribe removing to Iowa, the Iowa delegation in Congress, backed by two Iowans who were members of my Cabinet, passed a bill awarding a sum of nearly a half million dollars to the Iowa seceders. They had not consulted the Indian Bureau. Leupp protested against the bill, and I vetoed it. A subsequent bill was passed on the lines laid down by the Indian Bureau, referring the whole controversy to the courts, and the Supreme Court in the end justified our position by deciding against the Iowa seceders and awarding the money to the Oklahoma stay-at-homes.

As to all action of this kind there have long been two schools of political thought, upheld with equal sincerity. The

division has not normally been along political, but tempera-
mental, lines. The course I followed, of regarding the executive as subject only to the people, and, under the Constitution,
bound to serve the people affirmatively in cases where the
Constitution does not explicitly forbid him to render the service, was substantially the course followed by both Andrew
Jackson and Abraham Lincoln. Other honorable and well-
meaning Presidents, such as James Buchanan, took the opposite and, as it seems to me, narrowly legalistic view that the
President is the servant of Congress rather than of the people,
and can do nothing, no matter how necessary it be to act,
unless the Constitution explicitly commands the action. Most
able lawyers who are past middle age take this view, and so do
large numbers of well-meaning, respectable citizens. My successor in office took this, the Buchanan, view of the President's
powers and duties.

For example, under my Administration we found that one
of the favorite methods adopted by the men desirous of stealing the public domain was to carry the decision of the Secretary of the Interior into court. By vigorously opposing such
action, and only by so doing, we were able to carry out the
policy of properly protecting the public domain. My successor not only took the opposite view, but recommended to
Congress the passage of a bill which would have given the
courts direct appellate power over the Secretary of the Interior in these land matters. This bill was reported favorably
by Mr. Mondell, Chairman of the House Committee on public lands, a Congressman who took the lead in every measure to prevent the conservation of our natural resources and
the preservation of the National domain for the use of home-
seekers. Fortunately, Congress declined to pass the bill. Its
passage would have been a veritable calamity.

I acted on the theory that the President could at any time
in his discretion withdraw from entry any of the public lands
of the United States and reserve the same for forestry, for
water-power sites, for irrigation, and other public purposes.
Without such action it would have been impossible to stop
the activity of the land thieves. No one ventured to test its
legality by lawsuit. My successor, however, himself questioned it, and referred the matter to Congress. Again Congress

showed its wisdom by passing a law which gave the President the power which he had long exercised, and of which my successor had shorn himself.

Perhaps the sharp difference between what may be called the Lincoln-Jackson and the Buchanan-Taft schools, in their views of the power and duties of the President, may be best illustrated by comparing the attitude of my successor toward his Secretary of the Interior, Mr. Ballinger, when the latter was accused of gross misconduct in office, with my attitude towards my chiefs of department and other subordinate officers. More than once while I was President my officials were attacked by Congress, generally because these officials did their duty well and fearlessly. In every such case I stood by the official and refused to recognize the right of Congress to interfere with me excepting by impeachment or in other Constitutional manner. On the other hand, wherever I found the officer unfit for his position I promptly removed him, even although the most influential men in Congress fought for his retention. The Jackson-Lincoln view is that a President who is fit to do good work should be able to form his own judgment as to his own subordinates, and, above all, of the subordinates standing highest and in closest and most intimate touch with him. My secretaries and their subordinates were responsible to me, and I accepted the responsibility for all their deeds. As long as they were satisfactory to me I stood by them against every critic or assailant, within or without Congress; and as for getting Congress to make up my mind for me about them, the thought would have been inconceivable to me. My successor took the opposite, or Buchanan, view when he permitted and requested Congress to pass judgment on the charges made against Mr. Ballinger as an executive officer. These charges were made to the President; the President had the facts before him and could get at them at any time, and he alone had power to act if the charges were true. However, he permitted and requested Congress to investigate Mr. Ballinger. The party minority of the committee that investigated him, and one member of the majority, declared that the charges were well founded and that Mr. Ballinger should be removed. The other members of the majority declared the charges ill founded. The President abode by the view of the majority. Of course believers in the Jackson-Lincoln theory of the Presidency would not be content with this town meeting majority and minority method of determining by another branch of the Government what it seems the especial duty of the President himself to determine for himself in dealing with his own subordinate in his own department.

There are many worthy people who reprobate the Buchanan method as a matter of history, but who in actual life reprobate still more strongly the Jackson-Lincoln method when it is put into practice. These persons conscientiously believe that the President should solve every doubt in favor of inaction as against action, that he should construe strictly and narrowly the Constitutional grant of powers both to the National Government, and to the President within the National Government. In addition, however, to the men who conscientiously believe in this course from high, although as I hold misguided, motives, there are many men who affect to believe in it merely because it enables them to attack and to try to hamper, for partisan or personal reasons, an executive whom they dislike. There are other men in whom, especially when they are themselves in office, practical adherence to the Buchanan principle represents not well-thought-out devotion to an unwise course, but simple weakness of character and desire to avoid trouble and responsibility. Unfortunately, in practice it makes little difference which class of ideas actuates the President, who by his action sets a cramping precedent. Whether he is highminded and wrongheaded or merely infirm of purpose, whether he means well feebly or is bound by a mischievous misconception of the powers and duties of the National Government and of the President, the effect of his actions is the same. The President's duty is to act so that he himself and his subordinates shall be able to do efficient work for the people, and this efficient work he and they cannot do if Congress is permitted to undertake the task of making up his mind for him as to how he shall perfrom what is clearly his sole duty.

One of the ways in which by independent action of the executive we were able to accomplish an immense amount of work for the public was through volunteer unpaid commissions appointed by the President. It was possible to get the work done by these volunteer commissions only because of the

The Rough Rider.

*With Mr. Punch's best wishes to Colonel Roosevelt, President of the United States.*

*Punch's* congratulations when Colonel Roosevelt became President.

enthusiasm for the public service which, starting in the higher offices at Washington, made itself felt throughout the Government departments — as I have said, I never knew harder and more disinterested work done by any people than was done by the men and women of all ranks in the Government service. The contrast was really extraordinary between their live interest in their work and the traditional clerical apathy which has so often been the distinguishing note of governmental work in Washington. Most of the public service performed by these volunteer commissions, carried on without a cent of pay to the men themselves, and wholly without cost to the Government, was done by men the great majority of whom were already in the Government service and already charged with responsibilities amounting each to a full man's job.

The first of these Commissions was the Commission on the Organization of Government Scientific Work, whose Chairman was Charles D. Walcott. Appointed March 13, 1903, its duty was to report directly to the President "upon the organization, present condition, and needs of the Executive Government work wholly or partly scientific in character, and upon the steps which should be taken, if any, to prevent the duplication of such work, to co-ordinate its various branches, to increase its efficiency and economy, and to promote its usefulness to the Nation at large." This Commission spent four months in an examination which covered the work of about thirty of the larger scientific and executive bureaus of the Government, and prepared a report which furnished the basis for numerous improvements in the Government service.

Another Commission, appointed June 2, 1905, was that on Department Methods — Charles H. Keep, Chairman — whose task was to "find out what changes are needed to place the conduct of the executive business of the Government in all its branches on the most economical and effective basis in the light of the best modern business practice." The letter appointing this Commission laid down nine principles of effective Governmental work, the most striking of which was: "The existence of any method, standard, custom, or practice is not reason for its continuance when a better is offered." This Commission, composed like that just described, of men already charged with important work, performed its functions wholly without cost to the Government. It was assisted by a body of about seventy experts in the Government departments chosen for their special qualifications to carry forward a study of the best methods in business, and organized into assistant committees under the leadership of Overton W. Price, Secretary of the Commission. These assistant committees, all of whose members were still carrying on their regular work, made their reports during the last half of 1906. The Committee informed itself fully regarding the business methods of practically every individual branch of the business of the Government, and effected a marked improvement in general efficiency throughout the service. The conduct of the routine business of the Government had never been thoroughly overhauled before, and this examination of it resulted in the promulgation of a set of working principles for the transaction of public business which are as sound to-day as they were when the Committee finished its work. The somewhat elaborate and costly investigations of Government business methods since made have served merely to confirm the findings of the Committee on Departmental Methods, which were achieved without costing the Government a dollar. The actual saving in the conduct of the business of the Government through the better methods thus introduced amounted yearly to many hundreds of thousands of dollars; but a far more important gain was due to the remarkable success of the Commission in establishing a new point of view in public servants toward their work.

The need for improvement in the Governmental methods of transacting business may be illustrated by an actual case. An officer in charge of an Indian agency made a requisition in the autumn for a stove costing seven dollars, certifying at the same time that it was needed to keep the infirmary warm during the winter, because the old stove was worn out. Thereupon the customary papers went through the customary routine, without unusual delay at any point. The transaction moved like a glacier with dignity to its appointed end, and the stove reached the infirmary in good order in time for the Indian agent to acknowledge its arrival in these words: "The stove is here. So is spring."

The Civil Service Commission, under men like John McIlhenny and Garfield, rendered service without which the

Government could have been conducted with neither efficiency nor honesty. The politicians were not the only persons at fault; almost as much improper pressure for appointments is due to mere misplaced sympathy, and to the spiritless inefficiency which seeks a Government office as a haven for the incompetent. An amusing feature of office seeking is that each man desiring an office is apt to look down on all others with the same object as forming an objectionable class with which *he* has nothing in common. At the time of the eruption of Mt. Pelée, when among others the American Consul was killed, a man who had long been seeking an appointment promptly applied for the vacancy. He was a good man, of persistent nature, who felt I had been somewhat blind to his merits. The morning after the catastrophe he wrote, saying that as the consul was dead he would like his place, and that I could surely give it to him, because "even the office seekers could not have applied for it yet!"

The method of public service involved in the appointment and the work of the two commissions just described was applied also in the establishment of four other commissions, each of which performed its task without salary or expense for its members, and wholly without cost to the Government. The other four commissions were:

Commission on Public Lands;

Commission on Inland Waterways;

Commission on Country Life; and

Commission on National Conservation.

All of these commissions were suggested to me by Gifford Pinchot, who served upon them all. The work of the last four will be touched upon in connection with the chapter on Conservation. These commissions by their reports and findings directly interfered with many place-holders who were doing inefficient work, and their reports and the action taken thereon by the Administration strengthened the hands of those administrative officers who in the various departments, and especially in the Secret Service, were proceeding against land thieves and other corrupt wrong-doers. Moreover, the mere fact that they did efficient work for the public along lines new to veteran and cynical politicians of the old type created vehement hostility to them. Senators like Mr. Hale and Congressmen like Mr. Tawney were especially bitter against these commissions; and towards the end of my term they were followed by the majority of their fellows in both houses, who had gradually been sundered from me by the open or covert hostility of the financial or Wall Street leaders and of the newspaper editors and politicians who did their bidding in the interest of privilege. These Senators and Congressmen asserted that they had a right to forbid the President profiting by the unpaid advice of disinterested experts. Of course I declined to admit the existence of any such right, and continued the Commissions. My successor acknowledged the right, upheld the view of the politicians in question, and abandoned the commissions, to the lasting detriment of the people as a whole.

One thing is worth pointing out: During the seven and a half years of my Administration we greatly and usefully extended the sphere of Governmental action, and yet we reduced the burden of the taxpayers; for we reduced the interest-bearing debt by more than $90,000,000. To achieve a marked increase in efficiency and at the same time an increase in economy is not an easy feat; but we performed it.

There was one ugly and very necessary task. This was to discover and root out corruption wherever it was found in any of the departments. The first essential was to make it clearly understood that no political or business or social influence of any kind would for one moment be even considered when the honesty of a public official was at issue. It took a little time to get this fact thoroughly drilled into the heads both of the men within the service and of the political leaders without. The feat was accomplished so thoroughly that every effort to interfere in any shape or way with the course of justice was abandoned definitely and for good. Most, although not all, of the frauds occurred in connection with the Post-Office Department and the Land Office.

It was in the Post-Office Department that we first definitely established the rule of conduct which became universal throughout the whole service. Rumors of corruption in the department became rife, and finally I spoke of them to the then First Assistant Postmaster-General, afterwards Postmaster-General, Robert J. Wynne. He reported to me, after some investigation, that in his belief there was doubtless corruption, but that it was very difficult to get at it, and that the offenders were confident and defiant because of their great political and business backing and the ramifications of their crimes. Talking the matter over with him, I came to the conclusion that the right man to carry on the investigation was the then Fourth Assistant Postmaster-General, now a Senator from Kansas, Joseph L. Bristow, who possessed the iron fearlessness needful to front such a situation. Mr. Bristow had perforce seen a good deal of the seamy side of politics, and of the extent of the unscrupulousness with which powerful influence was brought to bear to shield offenders. Before undertaking the investigation he came to see me, and said that he did not wish to go into it unless he could be assured that I would stand personally behind him, and, no matter where his inquiries led him, would support him and prevent interference with him. I answered that I would certainly do so. He went into the investigation with relentless energy, dogged courage, and keen intelligence. His success was complete, and the extent of his services to the Nation are not easily to be exaggerated. He unearthed a really appalling amount of corruption, and he did his work with such absolute thoroughness that the corruption was completely eradicated.

We had, of course, the experience usual in all such investigations. At first there was popular incredulity and disbelief that there was much behind the charges, or that much could be unearthed. Then when the corruption was shown there followed a yell of anger from all directions, and a period during which any man accused was forthwith held guilty by the public; and violent demands were made by the newspapers for the prosecution not only of the men who could be prosecuted with a fair chance of securing conviction and imprisonment, but of other men whose misconduct had been such as to warrant my removing them from office, but against whom it was not possible to get the kind of evidence which would render likely conviction in a criminal case. Suits were brought against all the officials whom we thought we could convict; and the public complained bitterly that we did not bring further suits. We secured several convictions, including convictions of the most notable offenders. The trials consumed a good deal of time. Public attention was attracted to something else. Indifference succeeded to excitement, and in some subtle way the juries seemed to respond to the indifference. One of the worst offenders was acquitted by a jury; whereupon not a few of the same men who had insisted that the Government was derelict in not criminally prosecuting every man whose misconduct was established so as to make it necessary to turn him out of office, now turned round and, inasmuch as the jury had not found this man guilty of crime, demanded that he should be reinstated in office! It is needless to say that the demand was not granted. There were two or three other acquittals, of prominent outsiders. Nevertheless the net result was that the majority of the worst offenders were sent to prison, and the remainder dismissed from the Government service, if they were public officials, and if they were not public officials at least so advertised as to render it impossible that they should ever again have dealings with the Government. The department was absolutely cleaned and became one of the very best in the Government. Several Senators came to me — Mr. Garfield was present on the occasion — and said that they were glad I was putting a stop to corruption, but they hoped I would avoid all scandal; that if I would make an example of some one man and then let the others quietly resign, it would avoid a disturbance which might hurt the party. They were advising me in good faith, and I was as courteous as possible in my answer, but explained that I would have to act with the utmost rigor against the offenders, no matter what the effect on the party, and, moreover, that I did not believe it would hurt the party. It did not hurt the party. It helped the party. A favorite war-cry in American political life has always been, "Turn the rascals out." We made it evident that, as far as we were concerned, this war-cry was pointless; for we turned our own rascals out.

There were important and successful land fraud prosecutions in several Western States. Probably the most important were the cases prosecuted in Oregon by Francis J. Heney, with the assistance of William J. Burns, a secret service agent who at that time began his career as a great detective. It would be impossible to overstate the services rendered to the cause of decency and honesty by Messrs. Heney and Burns. Mr. Heney was my close and intimate adviser professionally and non-professionally, not only as regards putting a stop to frauds in the public lands, but in many other matters of vital interest to the Republic. No man in the country has waged the battle for National honesty with greater courage and success, with more whole-hearted devotion to the public good; and no man has been more traduced and maligned by the wrong-doing agents and representatives of the great sinister forces of evil. He secured the conviction of various men of high political and financial standing in connection with the Oregon prosecutions; he and Burns behaved with scrupulous fairness and propriety; but their services to the public caused them to incur the bitter hatred of those who had wronged the public, and after I left office the National Administration turned against them. One of the most conspicuous of the men whom they had succeeded in convicting was pardoned by President Taft — in spite of the fact that the presiding Judge, Judge Hunt, had held that the evidence amply warranted the conviction, and had sentenced the man to imprisonment. As was natural, the one hundred and forty-six land-fraud defendants in Oregon, who included the foremost machine political leaders in the State, furnished the backbone of the opposition to me in the Presidential contest of 1912. The opposition rallied behind Messrs. Taft and LaFollette; and although I carried the primaries handsomely, half of the delegates elected from Oregon under instructions to vote for me, sided with my opponents in the National Convention — and as regards some of them I became convinced that the mainspring of their motive lay in the intrigue for securing the pardon of certain of the men whose conviction Heney had secured.

Land fraud and post-office cases were not the only ones. We were especially zealous in prosecuting all of the "higher up" offenders in the realms of politics and finance who swindled on a large scale. Special assistants of the Attorney-General, such as Mr. Frank Kellogg, of St. Paul, and various first-class Federal district attorneys in different parts of the country secured notable results: Mr. Stimson and his assistants, Messrs. Wise, Denison, and Frankfurter, in New York, for instance, in connection with the prosecution of the Sugar Trust and of the banker Morse, and of a great metropolitan newspaper for opening its columns to obscene and immoral advertisements;

and in St. Louis Messrs. Dyer and Nortoni, who, among other services, secured the conviction and imprisonment of Senator Burton, of Kansas; and in Chicago Mr. Sims, who raised his office to the highest pitch of efficiency, secured the conviction of the banker Walsh and of the Beef Trust, and first broke through the armor of the Standard Oil Trust. It is not too much to say that these men, and others like them, worked a complete revolution in the enforcement of the Federal laws, and made their offices organized legal machines fit and ready to conduct smashing fights for the people's rights and to enforce the laws in aggressive fashion. When I took the Presidency, it was a common and bitter saying that a big man, a rich man, could not be put in jail. We put many big and rich men in jail; two United States Senators, for instance, and among others two great bankers, one in New York and one in Chicago. One of the United States Senators died, the other served his term. (One of the bankers was released from prison by executive order after I left office.) These were merely individual cases among many others like them. Moreover, we were just as relentless in dealing with crimes of violence among the disorderly and brutal classes as in dealing with the crimes of cunning and fraud of which certain wealthy men and big politicians were guilty. Mr. Sims in Chicago was particularly efficient in sending to the penitentiary numbers of the infamous men who batten on the "white slave" traffic, after July, 1908, when by proclamation I announced the adherence of our Government to the international agreement for the suppression of the traffic.

The views I then held and now hold were expressed in a memorandum made in the case of a Negro convicted of the rape of a young Negro girl, practically a child. A petition for his pardon had been sent me.

WHITE HOUSE, WASHINGTON, D.C.,
August 8, 1904.

The application for the commutation of sentence of John W. Burley is denied. This man committed the most hideous crime known to our laws, and twice before he has committed crimes of a similar, though less horrible, character. In my judgment there is no justification whatever for paying heed to the allegations that he is not of sound mind, allegations made after the trial and conviction.

Nobody would pretend that there has ever been any such degree of mental unsoundness shown as would make people even consider sending him to an asylum if he had not committed this crime. Under such circumstances he should certainly be esteemed sane enough to suffer the penalty for his monstrous deed. I have scant sympathy with the plea of insanity advanced to save a man from the consequences of crime, when unless that crime had been committed it would have been impossible to persuade any responsible authority to commit him to an asylum as insane. Among the most dangerous criminals, and especially among those prone to commit this particular kind of offense, there are plenty of a temper so fiendish or so brutal as to be incompatible with any other than a brutish order of intelligence; but these men are nevertheless responsible for their acts; and nothing more tends to encourage crime among such men than the belief that through the plea of insanity or any other method it is possible for them to escape paying the just penalty of their crimes. The crime in question is one to the existence of which we largely owe the existence of that spirit of lawlessness which takes form in lynching. It is a crime so revolting that the criminal is not entitled to one particle of sympathy from any human being. It is essential that the punishment for it should be not only as certain but as swift as possible. The jury in this case did their duty by recommending the infliction of the death penalty. It is to be regretted that we do not have special provision for more summary dealing with this type of cases. The more we do what in us lies to secure certain and swift justice in dealing with these cases, the more effectively do we work against the growth of that lynching spirit which is so full of evil omen for this people, because it seeks to avenge one infamous crime by the commission of another of equal infamy.

The application is denied and the sentence will be carried into effect.

(Signed) THEODORE ROOSEVELT.

One of the most curious incidents of lawlessness with which I had to deal affected an entire State. The State of Nevada in the year 1907 was gradually drifting into utter governmental impotence and downright anarchy. The people were at heart all right; but the forces of evil had been permitted to get the upper hand, and for the time being the decent citizens had become helpless to assert themselves either by controlling the greedy corporations on the one hand or repressing the murderous violence of certain lawless labor organizations on the other hand. The Governor of the State was a Democrat and a

Southern man, and in the abstract a strong believer in the doctrine of State's Rights. But his experience finally convinced him that he could obtain order only through the intervention of the National Government; and then he went over too far and wished to have the National Government do his police work for him. In the Rocky Mountain States there had existed for years what was practically a condition of almost constant war between the wealthy mine-owners and the Western Federation of Miners, at whose head stood Messrs. Haywood, Pettibone, and Moyer, who were about that time indicted for the murder of the Governor of Idaho. Much that was lawless, much that was indefensible, had been done by both sides. The Legislature of Nevada was in sympathy with, or at least was afraid of not expressing sympathy for, Messrs. Moyer, Haywood, Pettibone, and their associates. The State was practically without any police, and the Governor had recommended the establishment of a State Constabulary, along the lines of the Texas Rangers; but the Legislature rejected his request. The Governor reported to me the conditions as follows. During 1907 the Goldfield mining district became divided into two hostile camps. Half of the Western Federation of Miners were constantly armed, and arms and ammunition were purchased and kept by the union as a body, while the mine-owners on their side retained large numbers of watchmen and guards who were also armed and always on duty. In addition to these opposing forces there was, as the Governor reported, an unusually large number of the violent and criminal element, always attracted to a new and booming mining camp. Under such conditions the civil authorities were practically powerless, and the Governor, being helpless to avert civil war, called on me to keep order. I accordingly threw in a body of regular troops under General Funston. These kept order completely, and the Governor became so well satisfied that he thought he would like to have them there permanently! This seemed to me unhealthy, and on December 28, 1907, I notified him that while I would do my duty, the first need was that the State authorities should do theirs, and that the first step towards this was the assembling of the Legislature. I concluded my telegram: "If within five days from receipt of this telegram you shall have issued the necessary notice to convene

The Soap-and-Water Cure.

President Roosevelt: "As I recently remarked at Nashville, Tenn.: 'During the next sixteen months of my term of office this policy shall be persevered in unswervingly.' "

AMERICAN EAGLE: "JE-HOSAPHAT!"

the Legislature of Nevada, I shall continue the troops during a period of three weeks. If when the term of five days has elapsed the notice has not been issued, the troops will be immediately returned to their former stations." I had already investigated the situation through a committee, composed of the Chief of the Bureau of Corporations, Mr. H. K. Smith, the Chief of the Bureau of Labor, Mr. C. P. Neill, and the Comptroller of the Treasury, Mr. Lawrence Murray. These men I could thoroughly trust, and their report, which was not over-favorable to either side, had convinced me that the only permanent way to get good results was to insist on the people of the State themselves grappling with and solving their own troubles. The Governor summoned the Legislature, it met, and the constabulary bill was passed. The troops remained in Nevada until time had been given for the State authorities to organize their force so that violence could at once be checked. Then they were withdrawn.

Nor was it only as regards their own internal affairs that I sometimes had to get into active communication with the State authorities. There has always been a strong feeling in California against the immigration of Asiatic laborers, whether these are wage-workers or men who occupy and till the soil. I believe this to be fundamentally a sound and proper attitude, an attitude which must be insisted upon, and yet which can be insisted upon in such a manner and with such courtesy and such sense of mutual fairness and reciprocal obligation and respect as not to give any just cause of offense to Asiatic peoples. In the present state of the world's progress it is highly inadvisable that peoples in wholly different stages of civilization, or of wholly different types of civilization even although both equally high, shall be thrown into intimate contact. This is especially undesirable when there is a difference of both race and standard of living. In California the question became acute in connection with the admission of the Japanese. I then had and now have a hearty admiration for the Japanese people. I believe in them; I respect their great qualities; I wish that our American people had many of these qualities. Japanese and American students, travelers, scientific and literary men, merchants engaged in international trade, and the like can meet on terms of entire equality and should be given the freest access each to the country of the other. But the Japanese themselves would not tolerate the intrusion into their country of a mass of Americans who would displace Japanese in the business of the land. I think they are entirely right in this position. I would be the first to admit that Japan has the absolute right to declare on what terms foreigners shall be admitted to work in her country, or to own land in her country, or to become citizens of her country. America has and must insist upon the same right. The people of California were right in insisting that the Japanese should not come thither in mass, that there should be no influx of laborers, of agricultural workers, or small tradesmen — in short, no mass settlement or immigration.

Unfortunately, during the latter part of my term as President certain unwise and demagogic agitators in California, to show their disapproval of the Japanese coming into the State, adopted the very foolish procedure of trying to provide by law that the Japanese children should not be allowed to attend the schools with the white children, and offensive and injurious language was used in connection with the proposal. The Federal Administration promptly took up the matter with the California authorities, and I got into personal touch with them. At my request the Mayor of San Francisco and other leaders in the movement came on to see me. I explained that the duty of the National Government was twofold: in the first place, to meet every reasonable wish and every real need of the people of California or any other State in dealing with the people of a foreign power; and, in the next place, itself exclusively and fully to exercise the right of dealing with this foreign power.

Inasmuch as in the last resort, including that last of all resorts, war, the dealing of necessity had to be between the foreign power and the National Government, it was impossible to admit that the doctrine of State sovereignty could be invoked in such a matter. As soon as legislative or other action in any State affects a foreign nation, then the affair becomes one for the Nation, and the State should deal with the foreign power purely through the Nation.

I explained that I was in entire sympathy with the people of California as to the subject of immigration of the Japanese in mass; but that of course I wished to accomplish the object they had in view in the way that would be most courteous and most agreeable to the feelings of the Japanese; that all relations between the two peoples must be those of reciprocal justice, and that it was an intolerable outrage on the part of newspapers and public men to use offensive and insulting language about a high-spirited, sensitive, and friendly people; and that such action as was proposed about the schools could only have bad effects, and would in no shape or way achieve the purpose that the Californians had in mind. I also explained that I would use every resource of the National Government to protect the Japanese in their treaty rights, and would count upon the State authorities backing me up to the limit in such action. In short, I insisted upon the two points (1) that the Nation and not the individual States must deal with matters of such international significance and must treat foreign nations with entire courtesy and respect; and (2) that the Nation would at once, and in efficient and satisfactory manner, take action that would meet the needs of California. I both asserted the power of the Nation and offered a full remedy for the needs of the State. This is the right, and the only right, course. The worst possible course in such a case is to fail to insist on the right of the Nation, to offer no action of the Nation to remedy what is wrong, and yet to try to coax the State not to do what it is mistakenly encouraged to believe it has the power to do, when no other alternative is offered.

After a good deal of discussion, we came to an entirely satisfactory conclusion. The obnoxious school legislation was abandoned, and I secured an arrangement with Japan under which the Japanese themselves prevented any emigration to our country of their laboring people, it being distinctly understood that if there was such emigration the United States would at once pass an exclusion law. It was of course infinitely better that the Japanese should stop their own people from coming rather than that we should have to stop them; but it was necessary for us to hold this power in reserve.

Unfortunately, after I left office, a most mistaken and ill-advised policy was pursued towards Japan, combining irritation and inefficiency, which culminated in a treaty under which we surrendered this important and necessary right. It was alleged in excuse that the treaty provided for its own abrogation; but of course it is infinitely better to have a treaty under which the power to exercise a necessary right is explicitly retained rather than a treaty so drawn that recourse must be had to the extreme step of abrogating if it ever becomes necessary to exercise the right in question.

The arrangement we made worked admirably, and entirely achieved its purpose. No small part of our success was due to the fact that we succeeded in impressing on the Japanese that we sincerely admired and respected them, and desired to treat them with the utmost consideration. I cannot too strongly express my indignation with, and abhorrence of, reckless public writers and speakers who, with coarse and vulgar insolence, insult the Japanese people and thereby do the greatest wrong not only to Japan but to their own country.

Such conduct represents the nadir of underbreeding and folly. The Japanese are one of the great nations of the world, entitled to stand, and standing, on a footing of full equality with any nation of Europe or America. I have the heartiest admiration for them. They can teach us much. Their civilization is in some respects higher than our own. It is eminently undesirable that Japanese and Americans should attempt to live together in masses; any such attempt would be sure to result disastrously, and the far-seeing statesmen of both countries should join to prevent it.

But this is not because either nation is inferior to the other; it is because they are different. The two peoples represent two civilizations which, although in many respects equally high, are so totally distinct in their past history that it is idle to expect in one or two generations to overcome this difference. One civilization is as old as the other; and in neither case is the line of cultural descent coincident with that of ethnic descent. Unquestionably the ancestors of the great majority both of the modern Americans and the modern Japanese were barbarians in that remote past which saw the origins of the cultured peoples to which the Americans and the Japanese of to-day severally trace their civilizations. But the lines of development of these two civilizations, of the Orient and the Occident, have been separate and divergent since thousands of years before the Christian era; certainly since that hoary eld in which the Akkadian predecessors of the Chaldean Semites held sway in Mesopotamia. An effort to mix together, out of hand, the peoples representing the culminating points of two such lines of divergent cultural development would be fraught with peril; and this, I repeat, because the two are different, not because either is inferior to the other. Wise statesmen, looking to the future, will for the present endeavor to keep the two nations from mass contact and intermingling, precisely because they wish to keep each in relations of permanent good will and friendship with the other.

Exactly what was done in the particular crisis to which I refer is shown in the following letter which, after our policy had been successfully put into execution, I sent to the then Speaker of the California lower house of the Legislature:

THE WHITE HOUSE, WASHINGTON,
February 8, 1909.

HON. P. A. STANTON,
*Speaker of the Assembly,*
Sacramento, California:

I trust there will be no misunderstanding of the Federal Government's attitude. We are jealously endeavoring to guard the interests of California and of the entire West in accordance with the desires of our Western people. By friendly agreement with Japan, we are now carrying out a policy which, while meeting the interests and desires of the Pacific slope, is yet compatible, not merely with mutual self-respect, but with mutual esteem and admiration between the Americans and Japanese. The Japanese Government is loyally and in good faith doing its part to carry out this policy, precisely as the American Government is doing. The policy aims at mutuality of obligation and behavior. In accordance with it the purpose is that the Japanese shall come here exactly as Americans go to Japan, which is in effect that travelers, students, persons engaged in international business, men who sojourn for pleasure or study, and the like, shall have the freest access from one country to the other, and shall be sure of the best treatment, but that there shall be no settlement in mass by the people of either country in the other. During the last six months under this policy more Japanese have left the country than have come in, and the total number in the United States has diminished by over two thousand. These figures are absolutely accurate and cannot be impeached. In other words, if the present policy is consistently followed and works as well in the future as it is now working, all difficulties and causes of friction will disappear, while at the same time each nation will retain its self-respect and the good will of the other. But such a bill as this school bill accomplishes literally nothing whatever in the line of the object aimed at, and gives just and grave cause for irritation; while in addition the United States Government would be obliged immediately to take action in the Federal courts to test such legislation, as we hold it to be clearly a violation of the treaty. On this point I refer you to the numerous decisions of the United States Supreme Court in regard to State laws which violate treaty obligations of the United States. The legislation would accomplish nothing beneficial and would certainly cause some mischief, and might cause very grave mischief. In short, the policy of the Administration is to combine the maximum of efficiency in achieving the real object which the people of the Pacific Slope have at heart, with the minimum of friction and trouble, while the misguided men who advocate such action as this against which I protest are following a policy which combines the very minimum of efficiency with the maximum of insult, and which, while totally failing to achieve any real result for good, yet might accomplish an infinity of harm. If in the next year or two the action of the Federal Government fails to achieve what it is now achieving, then through the further action of the President and Congress it can be made entirely efficient. I am sure that the sound judgment of the people of California will support you, Mr. Speaker, in your effort. Let me repeat that at present we are actually doing the very thing which the people of California wish to be done, and to upset the arrangement under which this is being done cannot do good and may do great harm. If in the next year or two the figures of immigration prove that the arrangement which has worked so successfully during the last six months is no longer working successfully, then there would be ground for grievance and for the reversal by the National Government of its present policy. But at present the policy is working well, and until it works badly it would be a grave misfortune to change it, and when changed it can only be changed effectively by the National Government.

THEODORE ROOSEVELT.

In foreign and domestic affairs alike the policy pursued during my Administration was simple. In foreign affairs the principle from which we never deviated was to have the Nation behave toward other nations precisely as a strong, honorable, and upright man behaves in dealing with his fellow-men. There is no such thing as international law in the sense that there is municipal law or law within a nation. Within the nation there is always a judge, and a policeman who stands back of the judge. The whole system of law depends first upon

From a painting by John S. Sargent.

Rear Portico — The White House.

the fact that there is a judge competent to pass judgment, and second upon the fact that there is some competent officer whose duty it is to carry out this judgment, by force if necessary. In international law there is no judge, unless the parties in interest agree that one shall be constituted; and there is no policeman to carry out the judge's orders. In consequence, as yet each nation must depend upon itself for its own protection. The frightful calamities that have befallen China, solely because she has had no power of self-defense, ought to make it inexcusable in any wise American citizen to pretend to patriotic purpose, and yet to fail to insist that the United States shall keep in a condition of ability if necessary to assert its rights with a strong hand. It is folly of the criminal type for the Nation not to keep up its navy, not to fortify its vital strategic points, and not to provide an adequate army for its needs. On the other hand, it is wicked for the Nation to fail in either justice, courtesy, or consideration when dealing with any other power, big or little. John Hay was Secretary of State when I became President, and continued to serve under me until his death, and his and my views as to the attitude that the Nation should take in foreign affairs were identical, both as regards our duty to be able to protect ourselves against the strong and as regards our duty always to act not only justly but generously toward the weak.

John Hay was one of the most delightful of companions, one of the most charming of all men of cultivation and action. Our views on foreign affairs coincided absolutely; but, as was natural enough, in domestic matters he felt much more conservative than he did in the days when as a young man he was private secretary to the great radical democratic leader of the '60's, Abraham Lincoln. He was fond of jesting with me about my supposedly dangerous tendencies in favor of labor against capital. When I was inaugurated on March 4, 1905, I wore a ring he sent me the evening before, containing the hair of Abraham Lincoln. This ring was on my finger when the Chief Justice administered to me the oath of allegiance to the United States; I often thereafter told John Hay that when I wore such a ring on such an occasion I bound myself more than ever to treat the Constitution, after the manner of Abraham Lincoln, as a document which put human rights above property rights when the two conflicted. The last Christmas John Hay was alive he sent me the manuscript of a Norse saga by William Morris, with the following note:

Christmas Eve, 1904.

DEAR THEODORE: In your quality of Viking this Norse saga should belong to you, and in your character of Enemy of Property this Ms. of William Morris will appeal to you. Wishing you a Merry Christmas and many happy years, I am yours affectionately,

JOHN HAY.

In internal affairs I cannot say that I entered the Presidency with any deliberately planned and far-reaching scheme of social betterment. I had, however, certain strong convictions; and I was on the lookout for every opportunity of realizing those convictions. I was bent upon making the Government the most efficient possible instrument in helping the people of the United States to better themselves in every way, politically, socially, and industrially. I believed with all my heart in real and thoroughgoing democracy, and I wished to make this democracy industrial as well as political, although I had only partially formulated the methods I believed we should follow. I believed in the people's rights, and therefore in National rights and States' rights just exactly to the degree in which they severally secured popular rights. I believed in invoking the National power with absolute freedom for every National need; and I believed that the Constitution should be treated as the greatest document ever devised by the wit of man to aid a people in exercising every power necessary for its own betterment, and not as a straitjacket cunningly fashioned to strangle growth. As for the particular methods of realizing these various beliefs, I was content to wait and see what method might be necessary in each given case as it arose; and I was certain that the cases would arise fast enough.

As the time for the Presidential nomination of 1904 drew near, it became evident that I was strong with the rank and file of the party, but that there was much opposition to me among many of the big political leaders, and especially among many of the Wall Street men. A group of these men met in conference to organize this opposition. It was to be done with complete secrecy. But such secrets are very hard to keep. I speedily knew all about it, and took my measures accordingly. The big men in question, who possessed much power so long as they could work under cover, or so long as they were merely throwing their weight one way or the other between forces fairly evenly balanced, were quite helpless when fighting in the open by themselves. I never found out that anything practical was even attempted by most of the men who took part in the conference. Three or four of them, however, did attempt something. The head of one big business corporation attempted to start an effort to control the delegations from New Jersey, North Carolina, and certain Gulf States against me. The head of a great railway system made preparations for a more ambitious effort looking towards the control of the delegations from Iowa, Kansas, Nebraska, Colorado, and California against me. He was a very powerful man financially, but his power politically was much more limited, and he did not really understand his own limitations or the situation itself, whereas I did. He could not have secured a delegate against me from Iowa, Nebraska, or Kansas. In Colorado and California he could have made a fight, but even there I think he would have been completely beaten. However, long before the time for the Convention came round, it was recognized that it was hopeless to make any opposition to my nomination. The effort was abandoned, and I was nominated unanimously. Judge Parker was nominated by the Democrats against me. Practically all the metropolitan newspapers of largest circulation were against me; in New York City fifteen out of every sixteen copies of papers issued were hostile to me. I won by a popular majority of about two million and a half, and in the electoral college carried 330 votes against 136. It was by far the largest popular majority ever hitherto given any Presidential candidate.

My opponents during the campaign had laid much stress upon my supposed personal ambition and intention to use the office of President to perpetuate myself in power. I did not say anything on the subject prior to the election, as I did not wish to say anything that could be construed into a promise offered as a consideration in order to secure votes. But on election night, after the returns were in I issued the following statement: "The wise custom which limits the President to two terms regards the substance and not the form, and under no circumstances will I be a candidate for or accept another nomination."

The reason for my choice of the exact phraseology used was twofold. In the first place, many of my supporters were insisting that, as I had served only three and a half years of my first term, coming in from the Vice-Presidency when President McKinley was killed, I had really had only one elective term, so that the third term custom did not apply to me; and I wished to repudiate this suggestion. I believed then (and I believe now) the third term custom or tradition to be wholesome, and, therefore, I was determined to regard its substance, refusing to quibble over the words usually employed to express it. On the other hand, I did not wish simply and specifically to say that I would not be a candidate for the nomination in 1908, because if I had specified the year when I would not be a candidate, it would have been widely accepted as meaning that I intended to be a candidate some other year; and I had no such intention, and had no idea that I would ever be a candidate again. Certain newspaper men did ask me if I intended to apply my prohibition to 1912, and I answered that I was not thinking of 1912, nor of 1920, nor of 1940, and that I must decline to say anything whatever except what appeared in my statement.

The Presidency is a great office, and the power of the President can be effectively used to secure a renomination, especially if the President has the support of certain great political and financial interests. It is for this reason, and this reason alone, that the wholesome principle of continuing in office, so long as he is willing to serve, an incumbent who has proved capable, is not applicable to the Presidency. Therefore, the American people have wisely established a custom against allowing any man to hold that office for more than two consecutive terms. But every shred of power which a President exercises while in office vanishes absolutely when he has once left office. An ex-President stands precisely in the position of any other private citizen, and has not one particle more power to secure a nomination or election than if he had never held the office at all — indeed, he probably has less because of the very fact that he has held the office. Therefore the reasoning on which the anti-third term custom is based has no application

whatever to an ex-President, and no application whatever
to anything except consecutive terms. As a barrier of precaution against more than two consecutive terms the custom
embodies a valuable principle. Applied in any other way it becomes a mere formula, and like all formulas a potential source
of mischievous confusion. Having this in mind, I regarded the
custom as applying practically, if not just as much, to a President who had been seven and a half years in office as to one
who had been eight years in office, and therefore, in the teeth
of a practically unani-
mous demand from my
own party that I accept
another nomination,
and the reasonable cer-
tainty that the nomina-
tion would be ratified
at the polls, I felt that
the substance of the
custom applied to me
in 1908. On the other
hand, it had no ap-
plication whatever to
any human being save
where it was invoked
in the case of a man de-
siring a third consecu-
tive term. Having given
such substantial proof
of my own regard for
the custom, I deem it a
duty to add this com-

His Favorite Author.

"There was one cartoon made while I was
President, in which I appeared incidentally, that was always a great favorite of
mine. It pictured an old fellow with chin
whiskers, a farmer, in his shirt-sleeves,
with his boots off, sitting before the fire,
reading the President's message."

ment on it. I believe that it is well to have a custom of this
kind, to be generally observed, but that it would be very
unwise to have it definitely hardened into a Constitutional
prohibition. It is not desirable ordinarily that a man should
stay in office twelve consecutive years as President; but most
certainly the American people are fit to take care of themselves,
and stand in no need of an irrevocable self-denying ordinance.
They should not bind themselves never to take action which
under some quite conceivable circumstances it might be to

their great interest to take. It is obviously of the last importance to the safety of a democracy that in time of real peril it should be able to command the service of every one among its citizens in the precise position where the service rendered will be most valuable. It would be a benighted policy in such event to disqualify absolutely from the highest office a man who while holding it had actually shown the highest capacity to exercise its powers with the utmost effect for the public defense. If, for instance, a tremendous crisis occurred at the end of the second term of a man like Lincoln, as such a crisis occurred at the end of his first term, it would be a veritable calamity if the American people were forbidden to continue to use the services of the one man whom they knew, and did not merely guess, could carry them through the crisis. The third term tradition has no value whatever except as it applies to a third consecutive term. While it is well to keep it as a custom, it would be a mark both of weakness and unwisdom for the American people to embody it into a Constitutional provision which could not do them good and on some given occasion might work real harm.

There was one cartoon made while I was President, in which I appeared incidentally, that was always a great favorite of mine. It pictured an old fellow with chin whiskers, a farmer, in his shirt-sleeves, with his boots off, sitting before the fire, reading the President's Message. On his feet were stockings of the kind I have seen hung up by the dozen in Joe Ferris's store at Medora, in the days when I used to come in to town and sleep in one of the rooms over the store. The title of the picture was "His Favorite Author." This was the old fellow whom I always used to keep in my mind. He had probably been in the Civil War in his youth; he had worked hard ever since he left the army; he had been a good husband and father; he had brought up his boys and girls to work; he did not wish to do injustice to any one else, but he wanted justice done to himself and to others like him; and I was bound to secure that justice for him if it lay in my power to do so.*

*I believe I realized fairly well this ambition. I shall turn to my enemies to attest the truth of this statement. The New York *Sun*, shortly before the National Convention of 1904, spoke of me as follows:

"President Roosevelt holds that his nomination by the National Republican Convention of 1904 is an assured thing. He makes no concealment of his conviction, and it is unreservedly shared by his friends. We think President Roosevelt is right.

"There are strong and convincing reasons why the President should feel that success is within his grasp. He has used the opportunities that he found or created, and he has used them with consummate skill and undeniable success.

"The President has disarmed all his enemies. Every weapon they had, new or old, has been taken from them and added to the now unassailable Roosevelt arsenal. Why should people wonder that Mr. Bryan clings to silver? Has not Mr. Roosevelt absorbed and sequestered every vestige of the Kansas City platform that had a shred of practical value? Suppose that Mr. Bryan had been elected President. What could he have accomplished compared with what Mr. Roosevelt has accomplished? Will his most passionate followers pretend for one moment that Mr. Bryan could have conceived, much less enforced, any such pursuit of the trusts as that which Mr. Roosevelt has just brought to a triumphant issue? Will Mr. Bryan himself intimate that the Federal courts would have turned to his projects the friendly countenance which they have lent to those of Mr. Roosevelt?

"Where is 'government by injunction' gone to? The very emptiness of that once potent phrase is beyond description! A regiment of Bryans could not compete with Mr. Roosevelt in harrying the trusts, in bringing wealth to its knees, and in converting into the palpable actualities of action the wildest dreams of Bryan's campaign orators. He has outdone them all.

"And how utterly the President has routed the pretensions of Bryan, and of the whole Democratic horde in respect to organized labor! How empty were all their professions, their mouthings and their howlings in the face of the simple and unpretentious achievements of the President! In his own straightforward fashion he inflicted upon capital in one short hour of the coal strike a greater humiliation than Bryan could have visited upon it in a century. He is the leader of the labor unions of the United States. Mr. Roosevelt has put them above the law and above the Constitution, because for him they are the American people." [This last, I need hardly say, is merely a rhetorical method of saying that I gave the labor union precisely the same treatment as the corporation.]

Senator La Follette, in the issue of his magazine immediately following my leaving the Presidency in March, 1909, wrote as follows:

"Roosevelt steps from the stage gracefully. He has ruled his party to a large extent against its will. He has played a large part in the world's work, for the past seven years. The activities of his remarkably forceful personality have been so manifold that it will be long before his true rating will be fixed in the opinion of the race. He is said to think that the three great things done by him are the undertaking of the construction of the Panama Canal and its rapid and successful carrying forward, the making of peace between Russia and Japan, and the sending around the world of the fleet.

"These are important things, but many will be slow to think them his greatest services. The Panama Canal will surely serve mankind when in operation; and the manner of organizing this work seems to be fine. But no one can yet say whether this project will be a gigantic success or a gigantic failure; and the task is one which must, in the nature of things, have been undertaken and carried through some time soon, as historic periods go, anyhow. The Peace of Portsmouth was a great thing to be responsible for, and Roosevelt's good offices undoubtedly saved a great and bloody battle in Manchuria. But the war was fought out, and the parties ready to quit, and there is reason to think that it was only when this situation was arrived at that the good offices of the President of the United States were, more or less indirectly, invited. The fleet's cruise was a strong piece of diplomacy, by which we informed Japan that we will send our fleet wherever we please and whenever we please. It worked out well.

"But none of these things, it will seem to many, can compare with some of Roosevelt's other achievements. Perhaps he is loth to take credit as a reformer, for he is prone to spell the word with question marks, and to speak disparingly of 'reform.'

"But for all that, this contemner of 'reformers' made reform respectable in the United States, and this rebuker of 'muck-rakers' has been the chief agent in making the history of 'muck-raking' in the United States a National one, conceded to be useful. He has preached from the White House many doctrines; but among them he has left impressed on the American mind the one great truth of economic justice couched in the pithy and stinging phrase 'the square deal.' The task of making reform respectable in a commercialized world, and of giving the Nation a slogan in a phrase, is greater than the man who performed it is likely to think.

"And, then, there is the great and statesmanlike movement for the conservation of our National resources, into which Roosevelt so energetically threw himself at a time when the Nation as a whole knew not that we are ruining and bankrupting ourselves as fast as we can. This is probably the greatest thing Roosevelt did, undoubtedly. This globe is the capital stock of the race. It is just so much coal and oil and gas. This may be economized or wasted. The same thing is true of phosphates and other mineral resources. Our water resources are immense, and we are only just beginning to use them. Our forests have been destroyed; they must be restored. Our soils are being depleted; they must be built up and conserved.

"These questions are not of this day only or of this generation. They belong all to the future. Their consideration requires that high moral tone which regards the earth as the home of a posterity to whom we owe a sacred duty.

"This immense idea Roosevelt, with high statesmanship, dinned into the ears of the Nation until the Nation heeded. He held it so high that it attracted the attention of the neighboring nations of the continent, and will so spread and intensify that we will soon see the world's conferences devoted to it.

"Nothing can be greater or finer than this. It is so great and so fine that when the historian of the future shall speak of Theodore Roosevelt he is likely to say that he did many notable things, among them that of inaugurating the movement which finally resulted in the square deal, but that his greatest work was inspiring and actually beginning a world movement for staying terrestrial waste and saving for the human race the things upon which, and upon which alone, a great and peaceful and progressive and happy race life can be founded.

"What statesman in all history has done anything calling for so wide a view and for a purpose more lofty?"

# Chapter XI

## THE NATURAL RESOURCES
## OF THE NATION

WHEN Governor of New York, as I have already described, I had been in consultation with Gifford Pinchot and F. H. Newell, and had shaped my recommendations
about forestry largely in accordance with their suggestions.
Like other men who had thought about the national future at
all, I had been growing more and more concerned over the
destruction of the forests.

While I had lived in the West I had come to realize the vital
need of irrigation to the country, and I had been both amused
and irritated by the attitude of Eastern men who obtained
from Congress grants of National money to develop harbors
and yet fought the use of the Nation's power to develop the irrigation work of the West. Major John Wesley Powell, the explorer of the Grand Cañon, and Director of the Geological
Survey, was the first man who fought for irrigation, and he
lived to see the Reclamation Act passed and construction actually begun. Mr. F. H. Newell, the present Director of the
Reclamation Service, began his work as an assistant hydraulic
engineer under Major Powell; and, unlike Powell, he appreciated the need of saving the forests and the soil as well as
the need of irrigation. Between Powell and Newell came,
as Director of the Geological Survey, Charles D. Walcott,
who, after the Reclamation Act was passed, by his force, pertinacity, and tact, succeeded in putting the act into effect in
the best possible manner. Senator Francis G. Newlands, of
Nevada, fought hard for the cause of reclamation in Congress.
He attempted to get his State to act, and when that proved
hopeless to get the Nation to act; and was ably assisted by Mr.
G. H. Maxwell, a Californian, who had taken a deep interest
in irrigation matters. Dr. W. J. McGee was one of the leaders
in all the later stages of the movement. But Gifford Pinchot
is the man to whom the nation owes most for what has been
accomplished as regards the preservation of the natural resources of our country. He led, and indeed during its most

vital period embodied, the fight for the preservation through use of our forests. He played one of the leading parts in the effort to make the National Government the chief instrument in developing the irrigation of the arid West. He was the foremost leader in the great struggle to coördinate all our social and governmental forces in the effort to secure the adoption of a rational and farseeing policy for securing the conservation of all our national resources. He was already in the Government service as head of the Forestry Bureau when I became President; he continued throughout my term, not only as head of the Forest service, but as the moving and directing spirit in most of the conservation work, and as counsellor and assistant on most of the other work connected with the internal affairs of the country. Taking into account the varied nature of the work he did, its vital importance to the nation and the fact that as regards much of it he was practically breaking new ground, and taking into account also his tireless energy and activity, his fearlessness, his complete disinterestedness, his single-minded devotion to the interests of the plain people, and his extraordinary efficiency, I believe it is but just to say that among the many, many public officials who under my administration rendered literally invaluable service to the people of the United States, he, on the whole, stood first. A few months after I left the Presidency he was removed from office by President Taft.

The first work I took up when I became President was the work of reclamation. Immediately after I had come to Washington, after the assassination of President McKinley, while staying at the house of my sister, Mrs. Cowles, before going into the White House, Newell and Pinchot called upon me and laid before me their plans for National irrigation of the arid lands of the West, and for the consolidation of the forest work of the Government in the Bureau of Forestry.

At that time a narrowly legalistic point of view toward natural resources obtained in the Departments, and controlled the Governmental administrative machinery. Through the General Land Office and other Government bureaus, the public resources were being handled and disposed of in accordance with the small considerations of petty legal formalities, instead of for the large purposes of constructive development, and the

habit of deciding, whenever possible, in favor of private interests against the public welfare was firmly fixed. It was as
little customary to favor the bona-fide settler and home
builder, as against the strict construction of the law, as it was
to use the law in thwarting the operations of the land grabbers. A technical compliance with the letter of the law was all
that was required.

The idea that our natural resources were inexhaustible still
obtained, and there was as yet no real knowledge of their
extent and condition. The relation of the conservation of
natural resources to the problems of National welfare and
National efficiency had not yet dawned on the public mind.
The reclamation of arid public lands in the West was still a
matter for private enterprise alone; and our magnificent river
system, with its superb possibilities for public usefulness, was
dealt with by the National Government not as a unit, but as
a disconnected series of pork-barrel problems, whose only
real interest was in their effect on the reëlection or defeat of
a Congressman here and there — a theory which, I regret to
say, still obtains.

The place of the farmer in the National economy was still
regarded solely as that of a grower of food to be eaten by
others, while the human needs and interests of himself and his
wife and children still remained wholly outside the recognition of the Government.

All the forests which belonged to the United States were
held and administered in one Department, and all the foresters
in Government employ were in another Department. Forests
and foresters had nothing whatever to do with each other. The
National Forests in the West (then called forest reserves) were
wholly inadequate in area to meet the purposes for which they
were created, while the need for forest protection in the East
had not yet begun to enter the public mind.

Such was the condition of things when Newell and Pinchot
called on me. I was a warm believer in reclamation and in
forestry, and, after listening to my two guests, I asked them
to prepare material on the subject for me to use in my first
message to Congress, of December 3, 1901. This message laid
the foundation for the development of irrigation and forestry
during the next seven and one-half years. It set forth the new

attitude toward the natural resources in the words: "The Forest and water problems are perhaps the most vital internal problems in the United States."

On the day the message was read, a committee of Western Senators and Congressmen was organized to prepare a Reclamation Bill in accordance with the recommendations. By far the most effective of the Senators in drafting and pushing the bill, which became known by his name, was Newlands. The draft of the bill was worked over by me and others at several conferences and revised in important particulars; my active interference was necessary to prevent it from being made unworkable by an undue insistence upon States Rights, in accordance with the efforts of Mr. Mondell and other Congressmen, who consistently fought for local and private interests as against the interests of the people as a whole.

On June 17, 1902, the Reclamation Act was passed. It set aside the proceeds of the disposal of public lands for the purpose of reclaiming the waste areas of the arid West by irrigating lands otherwise worthless, and thus creating new homes upon the land. The money so appropriated was to be repaid to the Government by the settlers, and to be used again as a revolving fund continuously available for the work.

The impatience of the Western people to see immediate results from the Reclamation Act was so great that red tape was disregarded, and the work was pushed forward at a rate previously unknown in Government affairs. Later, as in almost all such cases, there followed the criticisms of alleged illegality and haste which are so easy to make after results have been accomplished and the need for the measures without which nothing could have been done has gone by. These criticisms were in character precisely the same as that made about the acquisition of Panama, the settlement of the anthracite coal strike, the suits against the big trusts, the stopping of the panic of 1907 by the action of the Executive concerning the Tennessee Coal and Iron Company; and, in short, about most of the best work done during my administration.

With the Reclamation work, as with much other work under me, the men in charge were given to understand that they must get into the water if they would learn to swim; and, furthermore, they learned to know that if they acted honestly, and boldly and fearlessly accepted responsibility, I would stand by them to the limit. In this, as in every other case, in the end the boldness of the action fully justified itself.

Every item of the whole great plan of Reclamation now in effect was undertaken between 1902 and 1906. By the spring of 1909 the work was an assured success, and the Government had become fully committed to its continuance. The work of Reclamation was at first under the United States Geological Survey, of which Charles D. Walcott was at that time Director. In the spring of 1908 the United States Reclamation Service was established to carry it on, under the direction of Frederick Hayes Newell, to whom the inception of the plan was due. Newell's single-minded devotion to this great task, the constructive imagination which enabled him to conceive it, and the executive power and high character through which he and his assistant, Arthur P. Davis, built up a model service — all these have made him a model servant. The final proof of his merit is supplied by the character and records of the men who later assailed him.

Although the gross expenditure under the Reclamation Act is not yet as large as that for the Panama Canal, the engineering obstacles to be overcome have been almost as great, and the political impediments many times greater. The Reclamation work had to be carried on at widely separated points, remote from railroads, under the most difficult pioneer conditions. The twenty-eight projects begun in the years 1902 to 1906 contemplated the irrigation of more than three million acres and the watering of more than thirty thousand farms. Many of the dams required for this huge task are higher than any previously built anywhere in the world. They feed mainline canals over seven thousand miles in total length, and involve minor constructions, such as culverts and bridges, tens of thousands in number.

What the Reclamation Act has done for the country is by no means limited to its material accomplishment. This Act and the results flowing from it have helped powerfully to prove to the Nation that it can handle its own resources and exercise direct and business-like control over them. The population which the Reclamation Act has brought into the arid West, while comparatively small when compared with that in the more closely inhabited East, has been a most effective contribution to the National life, for it has gone far to transform the social aspect of the West, making for the stability of the institutions upon which the welfare of the whole country rests: it has substituted actual homemakers, who have settled on the land with their families, for huge, migratory bands of sheep herded by the hired shepherds of absentee owners.

The recent attacks on the Reclamation Service, and on Mr. Newell, arise in large part, if not altogether, from an organized effort to repudiate the obligation of the settlers to repay the Government for what it has expended to reclaim the land. The repudiation of any debt can always find supporters, and in this case it has attracted the support not only of certain men among the settlers who hope to be relieved of paying what they owe, but also of a variety of unscrupulous politicians, some highly placed. It is unlikely that their efforts to deprive the West of the revolving Irrigation fund will succeed in doing anything but discrediting these politicians in the sight of all honest men.

When in the spring of 1911 I visited the Roosevelt Dam in Arizona, and opened the reservoir, I made a short speech to the assembled people. Among other things, I said to the engineers present that in the name of all good citizens I thanked them for their admirable work, as efficient as it was honest, and conducted according to the highest standards of public service. As I looked at the fine, strong, eager faces of those of the force who were present, and thought of the similar men in the service, in the higher positions, who were absent, and who were no less responsible for the work done, I felt a foreboding that they would never receive any real recognition for their achievement; and, only half humorously, I warned them not to expect any credit, or any satisfaction, except their own knowledge that they had done well a first-class job, for that probably the only attention Congress would ever pay them would be to investigate them. Well, a year later a Congressional Committee actually did investigate them. The investigation was instigated by some unscrupulous local politicians and by some settlers who wished to be relieved from paying their just obligations; and the members of the Committee joined in the attack on as fine and honorable a set of public

The Roosevelt Dam in Arizona.

Just before the Roosevelt party arrived to dedicate the dam.

servants as the Government has ever had; an attack made on them solely because they were honorable and efficient and loyal to the interests both of the Government and the settlers.

When I became President, the Bureau of Forestry (since 1905 the United States Forest Service) was a small but growing organization, under Gifford Pinchot, occupied mainly with laying the foundation of American forestry by scientific study of the forests, and with the promotion of forestry on private lands. It contained all the trained foresters in the Government service, but had charge of no public timberland whatsoever. The Government forest reserves of that day were in the care of a Division in the General Land Office, under the management of clerks wholly without knowledge of forestry, few if any of whom had ever seen a foot of the timberlands for which they were responsible. Thus the reserves were neither well protected nor well used. There were no foresters among the men who had charge of the National Forests, and no Government forests in charge of the Government foresters.

In my first message to Congress I strongly recommended the consolidation of the forest work in the hands of the trained men of the Bureau of Forestry. This recommendation was repeated in other messages, but Congress did not give effect to it until three years later. In the meantime, by thorough study of the Western public timberlands, the groundwork was laid for the responsibilities which were to fall upon the Bureau of Forestry when the care of the National Forests came to be transferred to it. It was evident that trained American Foresters would be needed in considerable numbers, and a forest school was established at Yale to supply them.

In 1901, at my suggestion as President, the Secretary of the Interior, Mr. Hitchcock, made a formal request for technical advice from the Bureau of Forestry in handling the National Forests, and an extensive examination of their condition and needs was accordingly taken up. The same year a study was begun of the proposed Appalachian National Forest, the plan of which, already formulated at that time, has since been carried out. A year later experimental planting on the National Forests was also begun, and studies preparatory to the applications of practical forestry to the Indian Reservations were undertaken. In 1903, so rapidly did the public work of the

Bureau of Forestry increase, that the examination of land for new forest reserves was added to the study of those already created, the forest lands of the various States were studied, and coöperation with several of them in the examination and handling of their forest lands was undertaken. While these practical tasks were pushed forward, a technical knowledge of American Forests was rapidly accumulated. The special knowledge gained was made public in printed bulletins; and at the same time the Bureau undertook, through the newspaper and periodical press, to make all the people of the United States acquainted with the needs and the purposes of practical forestry. It is doubtful whether there has ever been elsewhere under the Government such effective publicity — publicity purely in the interest of the people — at so low a cost. Before the educational work of the Forest Service was stopped by the Taft Administration, it was securing the publication of facts about forestry in fifty million copies of newspapers a month at a total expense of $6000 a year. Not one cent has ever been paid by the Forest Service to any publication of any kind for the printing of this material. It was given out freely, and published without cost because it was news. Without this publicity the Forest Service could not have survived the attacks made upon it by the representatives of the great special interests in Congress; nor could forestry in America have made the rapid progress it has.

The result of all the work outlined above was to bring together in the Bureau of Forestry, by the end of 1904, the only body of forest experts under the Government, and practically all of the first-hand information about the public forests which was then in existence. In 1905, the obvious foolishness of continuing to separate the foresters and the forests, reënforced by the action of the First National Forest Congress, held in Washington, brought about the Act of February 1, 1905, which transferred the National Forests from the care of the Interior Department to the Department of Agriculture, and resulted in the creation of the present United States Forest Service.

The men upon whom the responsibility of handling some sixty million acres of National Forest lands was thus thrown were ready for the work, both in the office and in the field, because they had been preparing for it for more than five years.

Without delay they proceeded, under the leadership of Pinchot, to apply to the new work the principles they had already
formulated. One of these was to open all the resources of the
National Forests to regulated use. Another was that of putting every part of the land to that use in which it would best
serve the public. Following this principle, the Act of June 11,
1906, was drawn, and its passage was secured from Congress.
This law throws open to settlement all land in the National
Forests that is found, on examination, to be chiefly valuable
for agriculture. Hitherto all such land had been closed to the
settler.

The principles thus formulated and applied may be summed
up in the statement that the rights of the public to the natural
resources outweigh private rights, and must be given its first
consideration. Until that time, in dealing with the National
Forests, and the public lands generally, private rights had
almost uniformly been allowed to over-balance public rights.
The change we made was right, and was vitally necessary; but,
of course, it created bitter opposition from private interests.

One of the principles whose application was the source of
much hostility was this: It is better for the Government to
help a poor man to make a living for his family than to help a
rich man make more profit for his company. This principle
was too sound to be fought openly. It is the kind of principle to which politicians delight to pay unctuous homage in
words. But we translated the words into deeds; and when
they found that this was the case, many rich men, especially
sheep owners, were stirred to hostility, and they used the
Congressmen they controlled to assault us — getting most aid
from certain demagogues, who were equally glad improperly
to denounce rich men in public and improperly to serve them
in private. The Forest Service established and enforced regulations which favored the settler as against the large stock
owner; required that necessary reductions in the stock grazed
on any National Forest should bear first on the big man,
before the few head of the small man, upon which the living
of his family depended, were reduced; and made grazing in
the National Forests a help, instead of a hindrance, to permanent settlement. As a result, the small settlers and their families became, on the whole, the best friends the Forest Service

has; although in places their ignorance was played on by demagogues to influence them against the policy that was primarily for their own interest.

Another principle which led to the bitterest antagonism of all was this — whoever (except a bona-fide settler) takes public property for private profit should pay for what he gets. In the effort to apply this principle, the Forest Service obtained a decision from the Attorney-General that it was legal to make the men who grazed sheep and cattle on the National Forests pay for what they got. Accordingly, in the summer of 1906, for the first time, such a charge was made; and, in the face of the bitterest opposition, it was collected.

Up to the time the National Forests were put under the charge of the Forest Service, the Interior Department had made no effort to establish public regulation and control of water powers. Upon the transfer, the Service immediately began its fight to handle the power resources of the National Forests so as to prevent speculation and monopoly and to yield a fair return to the Government. On May 1, 1906, an Act was passed granting the use of certain power sites in Southern California to the Edison Electric Power Company, which Act, at the suggestion of the Service, limited the period of the permit to forty years, and required the payment of an annual rental by the company, the same conditions which were thereafter adopted by the Service as the basis for all permits for power development. Then began a vigorous fight against the position of the Service by the water-power interests. The right to charge for water-power development was, however, sustained by the Attorney-General.

In 1907, the area of the National Forests was increased by Presidential proclamation more than forty-three million acres; the plant necessary for the full use of the Forests, such as roads, trails, and telephone lines, began to be provided on a large scale; the interchange of field and office men, so as to prevent the antagonism between them, which is so destructive of efficiency in most great businesses, was established as a permanent policy; and the really effective management of the enormous area of the National Forests began to be secured.

With all this activity in the field, the progress of technical forestry and popular education was not neglected. In 1907, for example, sixty-one publications on various phases of forestry, with a total of more than a million copies, were issued, as against three publications, with a total of eighty-two thousand copies, in 1901. By this time, also, the opposition of the servants of the special interests in Congress to the Forest Service had become strongly developed, and more time appeared to be spent in the yearly attacks upon it during the passage of the appropriation bills than on all other Government Bureaus put together. Every year the Forest Service had to fight for its life.

One incident in these attacks is worth recording. While the Agricultural Appropriation Bill was passing through the Senate, in 1907, Senator Fulton, of Oregon, secured an amendment providing that the President could not set aside any additional National Forests in the six Northwestern States. This meant retaining some sixteen million of acres to be exploited by land grabbers and by the representatives of the great special interests, at the expense of the public interest. But for four years the Forest Service had been gathering field notes as to what forests ought to be set aside in these States, and so was prepared to act. It was equally undesirable to veto the whole agricultural bill, and to sign it with this amendment effective. Accordingly, a plan to create the necessary National Forest in these States before the Agricultural Bill could be passed and signed was laid before me by Mr. Pinchot. I approved it. The necessary papers were immediately prepared. I signed the last proclamation a couple of days before, by my signature, the bill became law; and, when the friends of the special interests in the Senate got their amendment through and woke up, they discovered that sixteen million acres of timberland had been saved for the people by putting them in the National Forests before the land grabbers could get at them. The opponents of the Forest Service turned handsprings in their wrath; and dire were their threats against the Executive; but the threats could not be carried out, and were really only a tribute to the efficiency of our action.

By 1908, the fire prevention work of the Forest Service had become so successful that eighty-six per cent of the fires that did occur were held down to an area of five acres or less, and the timber sales, which yielded $60,000 in 1905, in 1908 produced $850,000. In the same year, in addition to the work on the National Forests, the responsibility for the proper handling of Indian timberlands was laid upon the Forest Service, where it remained with great benefit to the Indians until it was withdrawn, as a part of the attack on the Conservation policy made after I left office.

By March 4, 1909, nearly half a million acres of agricultural land in the National Forests had been opened to settlement under the Act of June 11, 1906. The business management of the Forest Service became so excellent, thanks to the remarkable executive capacity of the Associate Forester, Overton W. Price (removed after I left office), that it was declared by a well-known firm of business organizers to compare favorably with the best managed of the great private corporations, an opinion which was confirmed by the report of a Congressional investigation, and by the report of the Presidential Committee on Department Method. The area of the National Forests had increased from 43 to 194 million acres; the force from about 500 to more than 3000. There was saved for public use in the National Forests more Government timberland during the seven and a half years prior to March 4, 1909, than during all previous and succeeding years put together.

The idea that the Executive is the steward of the public welfare was first formulated and given practical effect in the Forest Service by its law officer, George Woodruff. The laws were often insufficient, and it became well nigh impossible to get them amended in the public interest when once the representatives of privilege in Congress grasped the fact that I would sign no amendment that contained anything not in the public interest. It was necessary to use what law was already in existence, and then further to supplement it by Executive action. The practice of examining every claim to public land before passing it into private ownership offers a good example of the policy in question. This practice, which has since become general, was first applied in the National Forests. Enormous areas of valuable public timberland were thereby saved from fraudulent acquisition; more than 250,000 acres were thus saved in a single case.

This theory of stewardship in the interest of the public was well illustrated by the establishment of a water-power policy.

The Roosevelt Dam irrigating a Young Orchard.

Until the Forest Service changed the plan, water-powers on the navigable streams, on the public domain, and in the National Forests were given away for nothing, and substantially without question, to whoever asked for them. At last, under the principle that public property should be paid for and should not be permanently granted away when such permanent grant is avoidable, the Forest Service established the policy of regulating the use of power in the National Forests in the public interest and making a charge for value received. This was the beginning of the water-power policy now substantially accepted by the public, and doubtless soon to be enacted into law. But there was at the outset violent opposition to it on the part of the water-power companies, and such representatives of their views in Congress as Messrs. Tawney and Bede.

Many bills were introduced in Congress aimed, in one way or another, at relieving the power companies of control and payment. When these bills reached me I refused to sign them; and the injury to the public interest which would follow their passage was brought sharply to public attention in my message of February 26, 1908. The bills made no further progress.

Under the same principle of stewardship, railroads and other corporations, which applied for and were given rights in the National Forests, were regulated in the use of those rights. In short, the public resources in charge of the Forest Service were handled frankly and openly for the public welfare under the clear-cut and clearly set forth principle that the public rights come first and private interest second.

The natural result of this new attitude was the assertion in every form by the representatives of special interests that the Forest Service was exceeding its legal powers and thwarting the intention of Congress. Suits were begun wherever the chance arose. It is worth recording that, in spite of the novelty and complexity of the legal questions it had to face, no court of last resort has ever decided against the Forest Service. This statement includes two unanimous decisions by the Supreme Court of the United States (U.S. *vs.* Grimaud, 220 U.S., 506, and Light *vs.* U.S., 220 U.S., 523).

In its administration of the National Forests, the Forest Service found that valuable coal lands were in danger of passing into private ownership without adequate money return to the

Government and without safeguard against monopoly; and that existing leglslation was insufficient to prevent this. When this condition was brought to my attention I withdrew from all forms of entry about sixty-eight million acres of coal land in the United States, including Alaska. The refusal of Congress to act in the public interest was solely responsible for keeping these lands from entry.

The Conservation movement was a direct outgrowth of the forest movement. It was nothing more than the application to our other natural resources of the principles which had been worked out in connection with the forests. Without the basis of public sentiment which had been built up for the protection of the forests, and without the example of public foresight in the protection of this, one of the great natural resources, the Conservation movement would have been impossible. The first formal step was the creation of the Inland Waterways Commission, appointed on March 14, 1907. In my letter appointing the Commission, I called attention to the value of our streams as great natural resources, and to the need for a progressive plan for their development and control, and said: "It is not possible to properly frame so large a plan as this for the control of our rivers without taking account of the orderly development of other natural resources. Therefore I ask that the Inland Waterways Commission shall consider the relations of the streams to the use of all the great permanent natural resources and their conservation for the making and maintenance of prosperous homes."

Over a year later, writing on the report of the Commission, I said:

"The preliminary Report of the Inland Waterways Commission was excellent in every way. It outlines a general plan of waterway improvement which when adopted will give assurance that the improvements will yield practical results in the way of increased navigation and water transportation. In every essential feature the plan recommended by the Commission is new. In the principle of coördinating all uses of the waters and treating each waterway system as a unit; in the principle of correlating water traffic with rail and other land traffic; in the principle of expert initiation of projects in accordance with commercial foresight and the needs of a growing country; and in the principle of coöperation between the States and the Federal Government in the administration and use of waterways, etc.; the general plan proposed by the Commission is new, and at the same time sane and simple. The plan deserves unqualified support. I regret that it has not yet been adopted by Congress, but I am confident that ultimately it will be adopted."

The most striking incident in the history of the Commission was the trip down the Mississippi River in October, 1907, when, as President of the United States, I was the chief guest. This excursion, with the meetings which were held and the wide public attention it attracted, gave the development of our inland waterways a new standing in public estimation. During the trip a letter was prepared and presented to me asking me to summon a conference on the conservation of natural resources. My intention to call such a conference was publicly announced at a great meeting at Memphis, Tenn.

In the November following I wrote to each of the Governors of the several States and to the Presidents of various important National Societies concerned with natural resources, inviting them to attend the conference, which took place May 13 to 15, 1908, in the East Room of the White House. It is doubtful whether, except in time of war, any new idea of like importance has ever been presented to a Nation and accepted by it with such effectiveness and rapidity, as was the case with this Conservation movement when it was introduced to the American people by the Conference of Governors. The first result was the unanimous declaration of the Governors of all the States and Territories upon the subject of Conservation, a document which ought to be hung in every schoolhouse throughout the land. A further result was the appointment of thirty-six State Conservation Commissions and, on June 8, 1908, of the National Conservation Commission. The task of this Commission was to prepare an inventory, the first ever made for any nation, of all the natural resources which underlay its property. The making of this inventory was made possible by an Executive order which placed the resources of the Government Departments at the command of the Commission, and made possible the organization of subsidiary committees by which the actual facts for the inventory were

Down the Mississippi.

prepared and digested. Gifford Pinchot was made chairman of the Commission.

The report of the National Conservation Commission was not only the first inventory of our resources, but was unique in the history of Government in the amount and variety of information brought together. It was completed in six months. It laid squarely before the American people the essential facts regarding our natural resources, when facts were greatly needed as the basis for constructive action. This report was presented to the Joint Conservation Congress in December, at which there were present Governors of twenty States, representatives of twenty-two State Conservation Commissions, and representatives of sixty National organizations previously represented at the White House conference. The report was unanimously approved, and transmitted to me, January 11, 1909. On January 22, 1909, I transmitted the report of the National Conservation Commission to Congress with a Special Message, in which it was accurately described as "one of the most fundamentally important documents ever laid before the American people."

The Joint Conservation Conference of December, 1908, suggested to me the practicability of holding a North American Conservation Conference. I selected Gifford Pinchot to convey this invitation in person to Lord Grey, Governor General of Canada; to Sir Wilfrid Laurier; and to President Diaz of Mexico; giving as reason for my action, in the letter in which this invitation was conveyed, the fact that: "It is evident that natural resources are not limited by the boundary lines which separate nations, and that the need for conserving them upon this continent is as wide as the area upon which they exist."

In response to this invitation, which included the colony of Newfoundland, the Commissioners assembled in the White House on February 18, 1909. The American Commissioners were Gifford Pinchot, Robert Bacon, and James R. Garfield. After a session continuing through five days, the Conference united in a declaration of principles, and suggested to the President of the United States "that all nations should be invited to join together in conference on the subject of world resources, and their inventory, conservation, and wise utilization." Accordingly, on February 19, 1909, Robert Bacon, Secretary of State, addressed to forty-five nations a letter of invitation "to send delegates to a conference to be held at The Hague at such date to be found convenient, there to meet and consult the like delegates of the other countries, with a view of considering a general plan for an inventory of the natural resources of the world and to devising a uniform scheme for the expression of the results of such inventory, to the end that there may be a general understanding and appreciation of the world's supply of the material elements which underlie the development of civilization and the welfare of the peoples of the earth." After I left the White House the project lapsed.

Throughout the early part of my Administration the public land policy was chiefly directed to the defense of the public lands against fraud and theft. Secretary Hitchcock's efforts along this line resulted in the Oregon land fraud cases, which led to the conviction of Senator Mitchell, and which made Francis J. Heney known to the American people as one of their best and most effective servants. These land fraud prosecutions under Mr. Heney, together with the study of the public lands which preceded the passage of the Reclamation Act in 1902, and the investigation of land titles in the National Forests by the Forest Service, all combined to create a clearer understanding of the need of land law reform, and thus led to the appointment of the Public Lands Commission. This Commission, appointed by me on October 22, 1903, was directed to report to the President: "Upon the condition, operation, and effect of the present land laws, and to recommend such changes as are needed to effect the largest practicable disposition of the public lands to actual settlers who will build permanent homes upon them, and to secure in permanence the fullest and most effective use of the resources of the public lands." It proceeded without loss of time to make a personal study on the ground of public land problems throughout the West, to confer with the Governors and other public men most concerned, and to assemble the information concerning the public lands, the laws and decisions which governed them, and the methods of defeating or evading those laws, which was already in existence, but which remained unformulated in the records of the General Land Office and in the minds of its employees. The Public Lands Commission made its first preliminary report on March 7, 1904. It found "that the present land laws do not fit the conditions of the remaining public lands," and recommended specific changes to meet the public needs. A year later the second report of the Commission recommended still further changes, and said "The fundamental fact that characterizes the situation under the present land laws is this, that the number of patents issued is increasing out of all proportion to the number of new homes." This report laid the foundation of the movement for Government control of the open range, and included by far the most complete statement ever made of the disposition of the public domain.

Among the most difficult topics considered by the Public Lands Commission was that of the mineral land laws. This subject was referred by the Commission to the American Institute of Mining Engineers, which reported upon it through a Committee. This Committee made the very important recommendation, among others, "that the Government of the United States should retain title to all minerals, including coal and oil, in the lands of unceded territory, and lease the same to individuals or corporations at a fixed rental." The necessity for this action has since come to be very generally recognized. Another recommendation, since partly carried into effect, was for the separation of the surface and the minerals in lands containing coal and oil.

Our land laws have of recent years proved inefficient; yet the land laws themselves have not been so much to blame as the lax, unintelligent, and often corrupt administration of these laws. The appointment on March 4, 1907, of James R. Garfield as Secretary of the Interior led to a new era in the interpretation and enforcement of the laws governing the public lands. His administration of the Interior Department was beyond comparison the best we have ever had. It was based primarily on the conception that it is as much the duty of public land officials to help the honest settler get title to his claim as it is to prevent the looting of the public lands. The essential fact about public land frauds is not merely that public property is stolen, but that every claim fraudulently acquired stands in the way of the making of a home or a livelihood by an honest man.

The First Governors' Conference at the White House.

As the study of the public land laws proceeded and their administration improved, a public land policy was formulated in which the saving of the resources on the public domain for public use became the leading principle. There followed the withdrawal of coal lands as already described, of oil lands and phosphate lands, and finally, just at the end of the Administration, of water-power sites on the public domain. These withdrawals were made by the Executive in order to afford to Congress the necessary opportunity to pass wise laws dealing with their use and disposal; and the great crooked special interests fought them with incredible bitterness.

Among the men of this Nation interested in the vital problems affecting the welfare of the ordinary hard-working men and women of the Nation, there is none whose interest has been more intense, and more wholly free from taint of thought of self, than that of Thomas Watson, of Georgia. While President I often discussed with him the condition of women on the small farms, and on the frontier, the hardship of their lives as compared with those of the men, and the need for taking their welfare into consideration in whatever was done for the improvement of life on the land. I also went over the matter with C. S. Barrett, of Georgia, a leader in the Southern farmers' movement, and with other men, such as Henry Wallace, Dean L. H. Bailey, of Cornell, and Kenyon Butterfield. One man from whose advice I especially profited was not an American, but an Irishman, Sir Horace Plunkett. In various conversations he described to me and my close associates the reconstruction of farm life which had been accomplished by the Agricultural Organization Society of Ireland, of which he was the founder and the controlling force; and he discussed the application of similar methods to the improvements of farm life in the United States. In the spring of 1908, at my request, Plunkett conferred on the subject with Garfield and Pinchot, and the latter suggested to him the appointment of a Commission on Country Life as a means for directing the attention of the Nation to the problems of the farm, and for securing the necessary knowledge of the actual conditions of life in the open country. After long discussion a plan for a Country Life Commission was laid before me and approved. The appointment of the Commission followed in August, 1908. In the letter of appointment the reasons for creating the Commission were set forth as follows: "I doubt if any other nation can bear comparison with our own in the amount of attention given by the Government, both Federal and State, to agricultural matters. But practically the whole of this effort has hitherto been directed toward increasing the production of crops. Our attention has been concentrated almost exclusively on getting better farming. In the beginning this was unquestionably the right thing to do. The farmer must first of all grow good crops in order to support himself and his family. But when this has been secured, the effort for better farming should cease to stand alone, and should be accompanied by the effort for better business and better living on the farm. It is at least as important that the farmer should get the largest possible return in money, comfort, and social advantages from the crops he grows, as that he should get the largest possible return in crops from the land he farms. Agriculture is not the whole of country life. The great rural interests are human interests, and good crops are of little value to the farmer unless they open the door to a good kind of life on the farm."

The Commission on Country Life did work of capital importance. By means of a widely circulated set of questions the Commission informed itself upon the status of country life throughout the Nation. Its trip through the East, South, and West brought it into contact with large numbers of practical farmers and their wives, secured for the Commissioners a most valuable body of first-hand information, and laid the foundation for the remarkable awakening of interest in country life which has since taken place throughout the Nation.

One of the most illuminating — and incidentally one of the most interesting and amusing — series of answers sent to the Commission was from a farmer in Missouri. He stated that he had a wife and 11 living children, he and his wife being each 52 years old; and that they owned 520 acres of land without any mortgage hanging over their heads. He had himself done well, and his views as to why many of his neighbors had done less well are entitled to consideration. These views are expressed in terse and vigorous English; they cannot always be quoted in full. He states that the farm homes in his neighborhood are not as good as they should be because too many of them are encumbered by mortgages; that the schools do not train boys and girls satisfactorily for life on the farm, because they allow them to get an idea in their heads that city life is better, and that to remedy this practical farming should be taught. To the question whether the farmers and their wives in his neighborhood are satisfactorily organized, he answers: "Oh, there is a little one-horse grange gang in our locality, and every darned one thinks they ought to be a king." To the question, "Are the renters of farms in your neighborhood making a satisfactory living?" he answers: "No; because they move about so much hunting a better job." To the question, "Is the supply of farm labor in your neighborhood satisfactory?" the answer is: "No; because the people have gone out of the baby business"; and when asked as to the remedy, he answers, "Give a pension to every mother who gives birth to seven living boys on American soil." To the question, "Are the conditions surrounding hired labor on the farm in your neighborhood satisfactory to the hired men?" he answers: "Yes, unless he is a drunken cuss," adding that he would like to blow up the stillhouses and root out whisky and beer. To the question, "Are the sanitary conditions on the farms in your neighborhood satisfactory?" he answers: "No; too careless about chicken yards, and the like, and poorly covered wells. In one well on neighbor's farm I counted seven snakes in the wall of the well, and they used the water daily: his wife dead now and he is looking for another." He ends by stating that the most important single thing to be done for the betterment of country life is "good roads"; but in his answers he shows very clearly that most important of all is the individual equation of the man or woman.

Like the rest of the Commissions described in this chapter, the Country Life Commission cost the Government not one cent, but laid before the President and the country a mass of information so accurate and so vitally important as to disturb the serenity of the advocates of things as they are; and therefore it incurred the bitter opposition of the reactionaries. The report of the Country Life Commission was transmitted to Congress by me on February 9, 1909. In the accompanying message I asked for $25,000 to print and circulate the report and to prepare for publication the immense amount of valuable material collected by the Commission but still unpublished. The reply made by Congress was not only a refusal to appropriate the money, but a positive prohibition against continuing the work. The Tawney amendment to the Sundry Civil bill forbade the President to appoint any further Commissions unless specifically authorized by Congress to do so. Had this prohibition been enacted earlier *and complied with*, it would have prevented the appointment of the six Roosevelt Commissions. But I would not have complied with it. Mr. Tawney, one of the most efficient representatives of the cause of special privilege as against public interest to be found in the House, was later, in conjunction with Senator Hale and others, able to induce my successor to accept their view. As what was almost my last official act, I replied to Congress that if I did not believe the Tawney amendment to be unconstitutional I would veto the Sundry Civil bill which contained it, and that if I were remaining in office I would refuse to obey it. The memorandum ran in part: "The chief object of this provision, however, is to prevent the Executive repeating what it has done within the last year in connection with the Conservation Commission and the Country Life Commission. It is for the people of the country to decide whether or not they believe in the work done by the Conservation Commission and by the Country Life Commission. * * *

"If they believe in improving our waterways, in preventing the waste of soil, in preserving the forests, in thrifty use of the mineral resources of the country for the nation as a whole rather than merely for private monopolies, in working for the betterment of the condition of the men and women who live on the farms, then they will unstintedly condemn the action of every man who is in any way responsible for inserting this provision, and will support those members of the legislative branch who opposed its adoption. I would not sign the bill at all if I thought the provision entirely effective. But the Congress cannot prevent the President from seeking advice. Any future President can do as I have done, and ask disinterested men who desire to serve the people to give this service free to the people through these commissions. * * *

"My successor, the President-elect, in a letter to the Senate Commission on Appropriations, asked for the continuance and support of the Conservation Commission. The Conservation Commission was appointed at the request of the Governors of over forty States, and almost all of these States have since appointed commissions to cooperate with the National Commission. Nearly all the great national organizations concerned with natural resources have been heartily coöperating with the commission.

"With all these facts before it, the Congress has refused to pass a law to continue and provide for the commission; and it now passes a law with the purpose of preventing the Executive from continuing the commission at all. The Executive, therefore, must now either abandon the work and reject the coöperation of the States, or else must continue the work personally and through executive officers whom he may select for that purpose."

The Chamber of Commerce of Spokane, Washington, a singularly energetic and far-seeing organization, itself published the report which Congress had thus discreditably refused to publish.

The work of the Bureau of Corporations, under Herbert Knox Smith, formed an important part of the Conservation movement almost from the beginning. Mr. Smith was a member of the Inland Waterways Commission and of the National Conservation Commission and his Bureau prepared material of importance for the reports of both. The investigation of standing timber in the United States by the Bureau of Corporations furnished for the first time a positive knowledge of the facts. Over nine hundred counties in timbered regions were covered by the Bureau, and the work took five years. The most important facts ascertained were that forty years ago three-fourths of the standing timber in the United States was publicly owned, while at the date of the report four-fifths of the timber in the country was in private hands. The concentration of private ownership had developed to such an amazing extent that about two hundred holders owned nearly one-half of all privately owned timber in the United States; and of this the three greatest holders, the Southern Pacific Railway, the Northern Pacific Railway, and the Weyerhaeuser

Timber Company, held over ten per cent. Of this work, Mr. Smith says:

"It was important, indeed, to know the facts so that we could take proper action toward saving the timber still left to the public. But of far more importance was the light that this history (and the history of our other resources) throws on the basic attitude, tradition and governmental beliefs of the American people. The whole standpoint of the people toward the proper aim of government, toward the relation of property to the citizen, and the relation of property to the government, were brought out first by this Conservation work."

The work of the Bureau of Corporations as to water power was equally striking. In addition to bringing the concentration of water-power control first prominently to public attention, through material furnished for my message in my veto of the James River Dam Bill, the work of the Bureau showed that ten great interests and their allies held nearly sixty per cent of the developed water power of the United States. Says Commissioner Smith: "Perhaps the most important thing in the whole work was its clear demonstration of the fact that the only effective place to control water power in the public interest is at the power sites; that as to powers now owned by the public it is absolutely essential that the public shall retain title. . . . The only way in which the public can get back to itself the margin of natural advantage in the water-power site is to rent that site at a rental which, added to the cost of power production there, will make the total cost of water power about the same as fuel power, and then let the two sell at the same price, *i.e.*, the price of fuel power."

Of the fight of the water-power men for States Rights at the St. Paul Conservation Congress in September, 1909, Commissioner Smith says:

"It was the first open sign of the shift of the special interests to the Democratic party for a logical political reason, namely, because of the availability of the States Rights idea for the purposes of the large corporations. It marked openly the turn of the tide."

Mr. Smith brought to the attention of the Inland Waterways Commission the overshadowing importance to waterways of their relation with railroad lines, the fact that the bulk

Palisades, looking toward Slao Rock in the Northeast Quadrant of Crater Lake, National Park, Oregon.

of the traffic is long distance traffic, that it cannot pass over the whole distance by water, while it can go anywhere by rail, and that therefore the power of the rail lines to pro-rate or not to pro-rate, with water lines really determines the practical value of a river channel. The controlling value of terminals and the fact that out of fifty of our leading ports, over half the active water frontage in twenty-one ports was controlled by the railroads, was also brought to the Commission's attention, and reports of great value were prepared both for the Inland Waterways Commission and for the National Conservation Commission. In addition to developing the basic facts about the available timber supply, about waterways, water power, and iron ore, Mr. Smith helped to develop and drive into the public conscience the idea that the people ought to retain title to our natural resources and handle them by the leasing system.

The things accomplished that have been enumerated above were of immediate consequence to the economic well-being of our people. In addition certain things were done of which the economic bearing was more remote, but which bore directly upon our welfare, because they add to the beauty of living and therefore to the joy of life. Securing a great artist, Saint-Gaudens, to give us the most beautiful coinage since the decay of Hellenistic Greece was one such act. In this case I had power myself to direct the Mint to employ Saint-Gaudens. The first, and most beautiful, of his coins were issued in thousands before Congress assembled or could intervene; and a great and permanent improvement was made in the beauty of the coinage. In the same way, on the advice and suggestion of Frank Millet, we got some really capital medals by sculptors of the first rank. Similarly, the new buildings in Washington were erected and placed in proper relation to one another, on plans provided by the best architects and landscape architects. I also appointed a Fine Arts Council, an unpaid body of the best architects, painters, and sculptors in the country, to advise the Government as to the erection and decoration of all new buildings. The "pork-barrel" Senators and Congressmen felt for this body an instinctive, and perhaps from their standpoint a natural, hostility; and my successor a couple of months after taking office revoked the appointment and disbanded the Council.

Even more important was the taking of steps to preserve from destruction beautiful and wonderful wild creatures whose existence was threatened by greed and wantonness. During the seven and a half years closing on March 4, 1909, more was accomplished for the protection of wild life in the United States than during all the previous years, excepting only the creation of the Yellowstone National Park. The record includes the creation of five National Parks — Crater Lake, Oregon; Wind Cave, South Dakota; Platt, Oklahoma; Sully Hill, North Dakota, and Mesa Verde, Colorado; four big game refuges in Oklahoma, Arizona, Montana, and Washington; fifty-one bird reservations; and the enactment of laws for the protection of wild life in Alaska, the District of Columbia, and on National bird reserves. These measures may be briefly enumerated as follows:

The enactment of the first game laws for the Territory of Alaska in 1902 and 1908, resulting in the regulation of the export of heads and trophies of big game and putting an end to the slaughter of deer for hides along the southern coast of the Territory.

The securing in 1902 of the first appropriation for the preservation of buffalo and the establishment in the Yellowstone National Park of the first and now the largest herd of buffalo belonging to the Government.

The passage of the Act of January 24, 1905, creating the Wichita Game Preserves, the first of the National game preserves. In 1907, 12,000 acres of this preserve were inclosed with a woven wire fence for the reception of the herd of fifteen buffalo donated by the New York Zoölogical Society.

The passage of the Act of June 29, 1906, providing for the establishment of the Grand Cañon Game Preserve of Arizona, now comprising 1,492,928 acres.

The passage of the National Monuments Act of June 8, 1906, under which a number of objects of scientific interest have been preserved for all time. Among the Monuments created are Muir Woods, Pinnacles National Monument in California and the Mount Olympus National Monument, Washington, which form important refuges for game.

The passage of the Act of June 30, 1906, regulating shooting in the District of Columbia and making three-fourths of the environs of the National Capital within the District in effect a National Refuge.

The passage of the Act of May 23, 1908, providing for the establishment of the National Bison Range in Montana. This range comprises about 18,000 acres of land formerly in the Flathead Indian Reservation, on which is now established a herd of eighty buffalo, the nucleus of which was donated to the Government by the American Bison Society.

The issue of the Order protecting birds on the Niobrara Military Reservation, Nebraska, in 1908, making this entire reservation in effect a bird reservation.

The establishment by Executive Order between March 14, 1903, and March 4, 1909, of fifty-one National Bird Reservations distributed in seventeen States and Territories from Porto Rico to Hawaii and Alaska. The creation of these reservations at once placed the United States in the front rank in the world work of bird protection. Among these reservations are the celebrated Pelican Island rookery in Indian River, Florida; The Mosquito Inlet Reservation, Florida, the northernmost home of the manatee; the extensive marshes bordering Klamath and Malheur Lakes in Oregon, formerly the scene of slaughter of ducks for market and ruthless destruction of plume birds for the millinery trade; the Tortugas Key, Florida, where, in connection with the Carnegie Institute, experiments have been made on the homing instinct of birds; and the great bird colonies on Laysan and sister islets in Hawaii, some of the greatest colonies of sea birds in the world.

# Chapter XII

## THE BIG STICK AND THE SQUARE DEAL

ONE OF the vital questions with which as President I had to deal was the attitude of the Nation toward the great corporations. Men who understand and practice the deep underlying philosophy of the Lincoln school of American political thought are necessarily Hamiltonian in their belief in a strong and efficient National Government and Jeffersonian in their belief in the people as the ultimate authority, and in the welfare of the people as the end of Government. The men who first applied the extreme Democratic theory in American life were, like Jefferson, ultra individualists, for at that time what was demanded by our people was the largest liberty for the individual. During the century that had elapsed since Jefferson became President the need had been exactly reversed. There had been in our country a riot of individualistic materialism, under which complete freedom for the individual — that ancient license which President Wilson a century after the term was excusable has called the "New" Freedom — turned out in practice to mean perfect freedom for the strong to wrong the weak. The total absence of governmental control had led to a portentous growth in the financial and industrial world both of natural individuals and of artificial individuals — that is, corporations. In no other country in the world had such enormous fortunes been gained. In no other country in the world was such power held by the men who had gained these fortunes; and these men almost always worked through, and by means of, the giant corporations which they controlled. The power of the mighty industrial overlords of the country had increased with giant strikes, while the methods of controlling them, or checking abuses by them, on the part of the people, through the Government, remained archaic and therefore practically impotent. The courts, not unnaturally, but most regrettably, and to the grave detriment of the people and of their own standing, had for a quarter of a century been on the whole the agents of reaction, and by conflicting decisions which, however, in their sum were hostile to the interests of the people, had left both the nation and the several States well-nigh impotent to deal with the great business combinations. Sometimes they forbade the Nation to interfere, because such interference trespassed on the rights of the States; sometimes they forbade the States to interfere (and often they were wise in this), because to do so would trespass on the rights of the Nation; but always, or well-nigh always, their action was negative action against the interests of the people, ingeniously devised to limit their power against wrong, instead of affirmative action giving to the people power to right wrong. They had rendered these decisions sometimes as upholders of property rights against human rights, being especially zealous in securing the rights of the very men who were most competent to take care of themselves; and sometimes in the name of liberty, in the name of the so-called "new freedom," in reality the old, old "freedom," which secured to the powerful the freedom to prey on the poor and the helpless.

One of the main troubles was the fact that the men who saw the evils and who tried to remedy them attempted to work in two wholly different ways, and the great majority of them in a way that offered little promise of real betterment. They tried (by the Sherman law method) to bolster up an individualism already proved to be both futile and mischievous; to remedy by more individualism the concentration that was the inevitable result of the already existing individualism. They saw the evil done by the big combinations, and sought to remedy it by destroying them and restoring the country to the economic conditions of the middle of the nineteenth century. This was a hopeless effort, and those who went into it, although they regarded themselves as radical progressives, really represented a form of sincere rural toryism. They confounded monopolies with big business combinations, and in the effort to prohibit both alike, instead of where possible prohibiting one and drastically controlling the other, they succeeded merely in preventing any effective control of either.

On the other hand, a few men recognized that corporations and combinations had become indispensable in the business world, that it was folly to try to prohibit them, but that it was also folly to leave them without thoroughgoing control. These men realized that the doctrines of the old *laissez faire* economists, of the believers in unlimited competition, unlimited individualism, were in the actual state of affairs false and mischievous. They realized that the Government must now interfere to protect labor, to subordinate the big corporation to the public welfare, and to shackle cunning and fraud exactly as centuries before it had interfered to shackle the physical force which does wrong by violence.

The big reactionaries of the business world and their allies and instruments among politicians and newspaper editors took advantage of this division of opinion, and especially of the fact that most of their opponents were on the wrong path; and fought to keep matters absolutely unchanged. These men demanded for themselves an immunity from governmental control which, if granted, would have been as wicked and as foolish as immunity to the barons of the twelfth century. Many of them were evil men. Many others were just as good men as were some of these same barons; but they were as utterly unable as any medieval castle-owner to understand what the public interest really was. There have been aristocracies which have played a great and beneficent part at stages in the growth of mankind; but we had come to the stage where for our people what was needed was a real democracy; and of all forms of tyranny the least attractive and the most vulgar is the tyranny of mere wealth, the tyranny of a plutocracy.

When I became President, the question as to the *method* by which the United States Government was to control the corporations was not yet important. The absolutely vital question was whether the Government had power to control them at all. This question had not yet been decided in favor of the United States Government. It was useless to discuss methods of controlling big business by the National Government until it was definitely settled that the National Government had the power to control it. A decision of the Supreme Court had, with seeming definiteness, settled that the National Government had not the power.

This decision I caused to be annulled by the court that had rendered it; and the present power of the National Government to deal effectively with the trusts is due solely to the success of the Administration in securing this reversal of its former decision by the Supreme Court.

The Constitution was formed very largely because it had become imperative to give to some central authority the power to regulate and control interstate commerce. At that time when corporations were in their infancy and big combinations unknown, there was no difficulty in exercising the power granted. In theory, the right of the Nation to exercise this power continued unquestioned. But changing conditions obscured the matter in the sight of the people as a whole; and the conscious and the unconscious advocates of an unlimited and uncontrollable capitalism gradually secured the whittling away of the National power to exercise this theoretical right of control until it practically vanished. After the Civil War, with the portentous growth of industrial combinations in this country, came a period of reactionary decisions by the courts which, as regards corporations, culminated in what is known as the Knight case.

The Sherman Anti-Trust Law was enacted in 1890 because the formation of the Tobacco Trust and the Sugar Trust, the only two great trusts then in the country (aside from the Standard Oil Trust, which was a gradual growth), had awakened a popular demand for legislation to destroy monopoly and curb industrial combinations. This demand the Anti-Trust Law was intended to satisfy. The Administrations of Mr. Harrison and Mr. Cleveland evidently construed this law as prohibiting such combinations in the future, not as condemning those which had been formed prior to its enactment. In 1895, however, the Sugar Trust, whose output originally was about fifty-five per cent of all sugar produced in the United States, obtained control of three other companies in Philadelphia by exchanging its stock for theirs, and thus increased its business until it controlled ninety-eight per cent of the entire product. Under Cleveland, the Government brought proceedings against the Sugar Trust, involving the Anti-Trust Law, to set aside the acquisition of these corporations. The test case was on the absorption of the Knight Company.* The Supreme Court of the United States, with but one dissenting vote, held adversely to the Government. They took the ground that the

*The case is known in the law books as U.S. *vs.* E. C. Knight, 156 U.S., Sept., p. 1.

power conferred by the Constitution to regulate and control interstate commerce did not extend to the production or manufacture of commodities within a State, and that nothing in the Sherman Anti-Trust Law prohibited a corporation from acquiring all the stock of other corporations through exchange of its stock for theirs, such exchange not being "commerce" in the opinion of the Court, even though by such acquisition the corporation was enabled to control the entire production of a commodity that was a necessary of life. The effect of this decision was not merely the absolute nullification of the Anti-Trust Law, so far as industrial corporations were concerned, but was also in effect a declaration that, under the Constitution, the National Government could pass no law really effective for the destruction or control of such combinations.

Oscar Straus.

This decision left the National Government, that is, the people of the Nation, practically helpless to deal with the large combinations of modern business. The courts in other cases asserted the power of the Federal Government to enforce the Anti-Trust Law so far as transportation rates by railways engaged in interstate commerce were concerned. But so long as the trusts were free to control the production of commodities without interference from the General Government, they were well content to let the transportation of commodities take care of itself — especially as the law against rebates was at that time a dead letter; and the Court by its decision in the Knight case had interdicted any interference by the President or by Congress with the production of commodities. It was on the authority of this case that practically all the big trusts in the United States, excepting those already mentioned, were formed. Usually they were organized as "holding" companies, each one acquiring control of its constituent corporations by exchanging its stock for theirs, an operation which the Supreme Court had thus decided could not be prohibited, controlled, regulated, or even questioned by the Federal Government.

Such was the condition of our laws when I acceded to the Presidency. Just before my accession, a small group of financiers desiring to profit by the governmental impotence to which we had been reduced by the Knight decision, had arranged to take control of practically the entire railway system in the Northwest — possibly as the first step toward controlling the entire railway system of the country. This control of the Northwestern railway systems was to be effected by organizing a new "holding" company, and exchanging its stock against the stock of the various corporations engaged in railway transportation throughout that vast territory, exactly as the Sugar Trust had acquired control of the Knight company and other concerns. This company was called the Northern Securities Company. Not long after I became President, on the advice of the Attorney-General, Mr. Knox, and through him, I ordered proceedings to be instituted for the dissolution of the company. As far as could be told by their utterances at the time, among all the great lawyers in the United States Mr. Knox was the only one who believed that this action could be sustained. The defense was based expressly on the ground that the Supreme Court in the Knight case had explicitly sanctioned the formation of such a company as the Northern Securities Company. The representatives of privilege intimated, and sometimes asserted outright, that in directing the action to be brought I had shown a lack of respect for the Supreme Court, which had already decided the question at issue by a vote of eight to one. Mr. Justice White, then on the Court and now Chief Justice, set forth the position that the two cases were in principle identical with incontrovertible logic. In giving the views of the dissenting minority on the action I had brought, he said:

"The parallel between the two cases [the Knight case and the Northern Securities case] is complete. The one corporation acquired the stock of other and competing corporations in exchange for its own. It was conceded for the purposes of the case, that in doing so monopoly had been brought about in the refining of sugar, that the sugar to be produced was likely to become the subject of interstate commerce, and indeed that part of it would certainly become so. But the power of Congress was decided not to extend to the subject, because the ownership of the stock in the corporations was not itself commerce."*

Mr. Justice White was entirely correct in this statement. The cases were parallel. It was necessary to reverse the Knight case in the interests of the people against monopoly and privilege just as it had been necessary to reverse the Dred Scott case in the interest of the people against slavery and privilege; just as later it became necessary to reverse the New York Bakeshop case in the interest of the people against that form of monopolistic privilege which put human rights below property rights where wage workers were concerned.

By a vote of five to four the Supreme Court reversed its decision in the Knight case, and in the Northern Securities case sustained the Government. The power to deal with industrial monopoly and suppress it and to control and regulate combinations, of which the Knight case had deprived the Federal Government, was thus restored to it by the Northern Securities case. After this later decision was rendered, suits were brought by my direction against the American Tobacco Company and the Standard Oil Company. Both were adjudged criminal conspiracies, and their dissolution ordered. The Knight case was finally overthrown. The vicious doctrine it embodied no longer remains as an obstacle to obstruct the pathway of justice when it assails monopoly. Messrs. Knox, Moody, and Bonaparte, who successively occupied the position of Attorney-General under me, were profound lawyers and fearless and able men; and they completely established the newer and more wholesome doctrine under which the Federal Government may now deal with monopolistic combinations and conspiracies.

The decisions rendered in these various cases brought under my direction constitute the entire authority upon which any

*Northern Securities Company et al. *vs.* U.S., 156 U.S., Sept., pp. 391–2.

action must rest that seeks through the exercise of national power to curb monopolistic control. The men who organized and directed the Northern Securities Company were also the controlling forces in the Steel Corporation, which has since been prosecuted under the act. The proceedings against the Sugar Trust for corruption in connection with the New York Custom House are sufficiently interesting to be considered separately.

From the standpoint of giving complete control to the National Government over big corporations engaged in inter-State business, it would be impossible to over-estimate the importance of the Northern Securities decision and of the decisions afterwards rendered in line with it in connection with the other trusts whose dissolution was ordered. The success of the Northern Securities case definitely established the power of the Government to deal with all great corporations. Without this success the National Government must have remained in the impotence to which it had been reduced by the Knight decision as regards the most important of its internal functions. But our success in establishing the power of the National Government to curb monopolies did not establish the right method of exercising that power. We had gained the power. We had not devised the proper method of exercising it.

Monopolies can, although in rather cumbrous fashion, be broken up by law suits. Great business combinations, however, cannot possibly be made useful instead of noxious industrial agencies merely by law suits, and especially by law suits supposed to be carried on for their destruction and not for their control and regulation. I at once began to urge upon Congress the need of laws supplementing the Anti-Trust Law — for this law struck at all big business, good and bad, alike, and as the event proved was very inefficient in checking bad big business, and yet was a constant threat against decent business men. I strongly urged the inauguration of a system of thoroughgoing and drastic Governmental regulation and control over all big business combinations engaged in inter-State industry.

Here I was able to accomplish only a small part of what I desired to accomplish. I was opposed both by the foolish radicals who desired to break up all big business, with the impossible ideal of returning to mid-nineteenth century industrial conditions; and also by the great privileged interests themselves, who used these ordinarily — but sometimes not entirely — well-meaning "stool pigeon progressives" to further their own cause. The worst representatives of big business encouraged the outcry for the total abolition of big business, because they knew that they could not be hurt in this way, and that such an outcry distracted the attention of the public from the really effi-cient method of controlling and supervising them, in just but masterly fashion, which was advocated by the sane representatives of reform. However, we suc-ceeded in making a good beginning by securing the passage of a law creating the Department of Com-merce and Labor, and with it the erection of the Bu-reau of Corporations. The first head of the Depart-ment of Commerce and Labor was Mr. Cortelyou, later Secretary of the Trea-sury. He was succeeded by Mr. Oscar Straus. The first head of the Bureau of Cor-

Herbert Knox Smith.

porations was Mr. Garfield, who was succeeded by Mr. Her-bert Knox Smith. No four better public servants from the standpoint of the people as a whole could have been found.

The Standard Oil Company took the lead in opposing all this legislation. This was natural, for it had been the worst offender in the amassing of enormous fortunes by improper methods of all kinds, at the expense of business rivals and of the public, including the corruption of public servants. If any man thinks this condemnation extreme, I refer him to the lan-guage officially used by the Supreme Court of the nation in its decision against the Standard Oil Company. Through their counsel, and by direct telegrams and letters to Senators and Congressmen from various heads of the Standard Oil organization, they did their best to kill the bill providing for the Bureau of Corporations. I got hold of one or two of these telegrams and letters, however, and promptly published them; and, as generally happens in such a case, the men who were all-powerful as long as they could work in secret and behind closed doors became powerless as soon as they were forced into the open. The bill went through without further difficulty.

The true way of dealing with monopoly is to prevent it by administrative action before it grows so powerful that even when courts condemn it they shrink from destroying it. The Supreme Court in the Tobacco and Standard Oil cases, for instance, used very vigorous language in condemning these trusts; but the net result of the decision was of positive advantage to the wrongdoers, and this has tended to bring the whole body of our law into disrepute in quarters where it is of the very highest importance that the law be held in respect and even in reverence. My effort was to secure the creation of a Federal Commission which should neither excuse nor tolerate monopoly, but prevent it when possible and uproot it when discovered; and which should in addition effectively control and regulate all big combinations, and should give honest business certainty as to what the law was and security as long as the law was obeyed. Such a Commission would furnish a steady expert control, a control adapted to the problem; and dissolution is neither control nor regulation, but is purely negative; and negative remedies are of little permanent avail. Such a Commission would have complete power to examine into every big corporation engaged or proposing to engage in business between the States. It would have the power to discriminate sharply between corporations that are doing well and those that are doing ill; and the distinction between those who do well and those who do ill would be defined in terms so clear and unmistakable that no one could misapprehend them. Where a company is found seeking its profits through serving the community by stimulating production, lowering prices or improving service, while scrupulously respecting the rights of others (including its rivals, its employees, its customers, and the general public), and strictly obeying the law, then no matter how large its capital, or how great the volume of its business it would be encouraged to still more abundant production, or better service, by the fullest protection that the Government could afford it. On the other hand, if a corporation were found seeking profit through injury or oppression of the community, by restricting production through trick or device, by plot or conspiracy against competitors, or by oppression of wage-workers, and then extorting high prices for the commodity it had made artificially scarce, it would be prevented from organizing if its nefarious purpose could be discovered in time, or pursued and suppressed by all the power of Government whenever found in actual operation. Such a commission, with the power I advocate, would put a stop to abuses of big corporations and small corporations alike; it would draw the line on conduct and not on size; it would destroy monopoly, and make the biggest business man in the country conform squarely to the principles laid down by the American people, while at the same time giving fair play to the little man and certainty of knowledge as to what was wrong and what was right both to big man and little man.

Although under the decision of the courts the National Government had power over the railways, I found, when I became President, that this power was either not exercised at all or exercised with utter inefficiency. The law against rebates was a dead letter. All the unscrupulous railway men had been allowed to violate it with impunity; and because of this, as was inevitable, the scrupulous and decent railway men had been forced to violate it themselves, under penalty of being beaten by their less scrupulous rivals. It was not the fault of these decent railway men. It was the fault of the Government.

Thanks to a first-class railway man, Paul Morton of the Santa Fé, son of Mr. Cleveland's Secretary of Agriculture, I was able completely to stop the practice. Mr. Morton volunteered to aid the Government in abolishing rebates. He frankly stated that he, like every one else, had been guilty in the matter; but he insisted that he uttered the sentiments of the decent railway men of the country when he said that he hoped the practice would be stopped, and that if I would really stop it, and not merely make believe to stop it, he would give the testimony which would put into the hands of the Government the power to put a complete check to the practice. Accordingly he testified, and on the information which he gave us we were able to take such action through the Inter-State Commerce Commission and the Department of Justice, supplemented by the necessary additional legislation, that the evil was absolutely eradicated. He thus rendered, of his own accord, at his own personal risk, and from purely disinterested motives, an invaluable service to the people, a service which no other man who was able to render was willing to render. As an immediate sequel, the world-old alliance between Blifil and Black George was immediately revived against Paul Morton. In giving rebates he had done only what every honest railway man in the country had been obliged to do because of the failure of the Government to enforce the prohibition as regards dishonest railway men. But unlike his fellows he had then shown the courage and sense of obligation to the public which made him come forward and without evasion or concealment state what he had done, in order that we might successfully put an end to the practice; and put an end to the practice we did, and we did it because of the courage and patriotism he had shown. The unscrupulous railway men, whose dishonest practices were thereby put a stop to, and the unscrupulous demagogues who were either under the influence of these men or desirous of gaining credit with thoughtless and ignorant people no matter who was hurt, joined in vindictive clamor against Mr. Morton. They actually wished me to prosecute him, although such prosecution would have been a piece of unpardonable ingratitude and treachery on the part of the public toward him — for I was merely acting as the steward of the public in this matter. I need hardly say that I stood by him; and later he served under me as Secretary of the Navy, and a capital Secretary he made too.

We not only secured the stopping of rebates, but in the Hepburn Rate Bill we were able to put through a measure which gave the Inter-State Commerce Commission for the first time real control over the railways. There were two or three amusing features in the contest over this bill. All of the great business interests which objected to Governmental control banded to fight it, and they were helped by the honest men of ultra-conservative type who always dread change, whether good or bad. We finally forced it through the House. In the Senate it was referred to a committee in which the Republican majority was under the control of Senator Aldrich, who took the lead in opposing the bill. There was one Republican on the committee, however, whom Senator Aldrich could not control — Senator Dolliver, of Iowa. The leading Democrat on the committee was Senator Tillman, of South Carolina, with whom I was not on good terms, because I had been obliged to cancel an invitation to him to dine at the White House on account of his having made a personal assault in the Senate Chamber on his colleague from South Carolina; and later I had to take action against him on account of his conduct in connection with certain land matters. Senator Tillman favored the bill. The Republican majority in the committee under Senator Aldrich, when they acted adversely on the bill, turned it over to Senator Tillman, thereby making him its sponsor. The object was to create what it was hoped would be an impossible situation in view of the relations between Senator Tillman and myself. I regarded the action as simply childish. It was a curious instance of how able and astute men sometimes commit blunders because of sheer inability to understand intensity of disinterested motive in others. I did not care a rap about Mr. Tillman's getting credit for the bill, or having charge of it. I was delighted to go with him or with any one else just so long as he was traveling my way — and no longer.

There was another amusing incident in connection with the passage of the bill. All the wise friends of the effort to secure Governmental control of corporations know that this Government control must be exercised through administrative and not judicial officers if it is to be effective. Everything possible should be done to minimize the chance of appealing from the decisions of the administrative officer to the courts. But it is not possible Constitutionally, and probably would not be desirable anyhow, completely to abolish the appeal. Unwise zealots wished to make the effort totally to abolish the appeal in connection with the Hepburn Bill. Representatives of the special interests wished to extend the appeal to include what it ought not to include. Between stood a number of men whose votes would mean the passage of, or the failure to pass, the bill, and who were not inclined towards either side. Three or four substantially identical amendments were proposed, and we then suddenly found ourselves face to face with an absurd situation. The good men who were willing to go with us but had conservative misgivings about the ultra-radicals would not accept a good amendment if one of the latter proposed it; and the radicals would not accept their own

William H. Moody.

amendment if one of the conservatives proposed it. Each side got so wrought up as to be utterly unable to get matters into proper perspective; each prepared to stand on unimportant trifles; each announced with hysterical emphasis — the reformers just as hysterically as the reactionaries — that the decision as regards each unimportant trifle determined the worth or worthlessness of the measure. Gradually we secured a measurable return to sane appreciation of the essentials. Finally both sides reluctantly agreed to accept the so-called Allison amendment which did not, as a matter of fact, work any change in the bill at all. The amendment was drawn by Attorney-General Moody after consultation with the Inter-State Commerce Commission, and was forwarded by me to Senator Dolliver; it was accepted, and the bill became law.

Thanks to this law and to the way in which the Inter-State Commerce Commission was backed by the Administration, the Commission, under men like Prouty, Lane, and Clark, became a most powerful force for good. Some of the good that we had accomplished was undone after the close of my

Administration by the unfortunate law creating a Commerce Court; but the major part of the immense advance we had made remained. There was one point on which I insisted, and upon which it is necessary always to insist. The Commission cannot do permanent good unless it does justice to the corporations precisely as it exacts justice from them. The public, the shippers, the stock and bondholders, and the employees, all have their rights, and none should be allowed unfair privileges at the expense of the others. Stock watering, and swindling of any kind should of course not only be stopped but punished. When, however, a road is managed fairly and honestly, and when it renders a real and needed service, then the Government must see that it is not so burdened as to make it impossible to run it at a profit. There is much wise legislation necessary for the safety of the public, or — like workmen's compensation — necessary to the well-being of the employee, which nevertheless imposes such a burden on the road that the burden must be distributed between the general public and the corporation, or there will be no dividends. In such a case it may be the highest duty of the commission to raise rates; and the commission, when satisfied that the necessity exists, in order to do justice to the owners of the road, should no more hesitate to raise rates, than under other circumstances to lower them.

So much for the "big stick" in dealing with the corporations when they went wrong. Now for a sample of the square deal.

In the fall of 1907 there were severe business disturbances and financial stringency, culminating in a panic which arose in New York and spread over the country. The damage actually done was great, and the damage threatened was incalculable. Thanks largely to the action of the Government, the panic was stopped before, instead of being merely a serious business check, it became a frightful and Nation-wide calamity, a disaster fraught with untold misery and woe to all our people. For several days the Nation trembled on the brink of such a calamity, of such a disaster.

During these days both the Secretary of the Treasury and I personally were in hourly communication with New York, following every change in the situation, and trying to anticipate every development. It was the obvious duty of the

Administration to take every step possible to prevent appalling disaster by checking the spread of the panic before it grew so that nothing could check it. And events moved with such speed that it was necessary to decide and to act on the instant, as each successive crisis arose, if the decision and action were to accomplish anything. The Secretary of the Treasury took various actions, some on his own initiative, some by my direction. Late one evening I was informed that two representatives of the Steel Corporation wished to see me early the following morning, the precise object not being named. Next morning, while at breakfast, I was informed that Messrs. Frick and Gary were waiting at the office. I at once went over, and, as the Attorney-General, Mr. Bonaparte, had not yet arrived from Baltimore, where he had been passing the night, I sent a message asking the Secretary of State, Mr. Root, who was also a lawyer, to join us, which he did. Before the close of the interview and in the presence of the three gentlemen named, I dictated a note to Mr. Bonaparte, setting forth exactly what Messrs. Frick and Gary had proposed, and exactly what I had answered — so that there might be no possibility of misunderstanding. This note was published in a Senate Document while I was still President. It runs as follows:

THE WHITE HOUSE, WASHINGTON,
November 4, 1907.

*My dear Mr. Attorney-General:*

Judge E. H. Gary and Mr. H. C. Frick, on behalf of the Steel Corporation, have just called upon me. They state that there is a certain business firm (the name of which I have not been told, but which is of real importance in New York business circles), which will undoubtedly fail this week if help is not given. Among its assets are a majority of the securities of the Tennessee Coal Company. Application has been urgently made to the Steel Corporation to purchase this stock as the only means of avoiding a failure. Judge Gary and Mr. Frick informed me that as a mere business transaction they do not care to purchase the stock; that under ordinary circumstances they would not consider purchasing the stock, because but little benefit will come to the Steel Corporation from the purchase; that they are aware that the purchase will be used as a handle for attack upon them on the ground that they are striving to secure a monopoly of the business and prevent competition — not that this would represent what could honestly be said, but what might recklessly and untruthfully be said.

They further informed me that, as a matter of fact, the policy of the company has been to decline to acquire more than sixty per cent of the steel properties, and that this purpose has been persevered in for several years past, with the object of preventing these accusations, and, as a matter of fact, their proportion of steel properties has slightly decreased, so that it is below this sixty per cent, and the acquisition of the property in question will not raise it above sixty per cent. But they feel that it is immensely to their interest, as to the interest of every responsible business man, to try to prevent a panic and general industrial smash-up at this time, and that they are willing to go into this transaction, which they would not otherwise go into, because it seems the opinion of those best fitted to express judgment in New York that it will be an important factor in preventing a break that might be ruinous; and that this has been urged upon them by the combination of the most responsible bankers in New York who are now thus engaged in endeavoring to save the situation. But they asserted that they did not wish to do this if I stated that it ought not to be done. I answered that, while of course I could not advise them to take the action proposed, I felt it no public duty of mine to interpose any objections.

Sincerely yours,<br>(Signed) THEODORE ROOSEVELT.

HON. CHARLES J. BONAPARTE,
   *Attorney-General.*

Mr. Bonaparte received this note in about an hour, and that same morning he came over, acknowledged its receipt, and said that my answer was the only proper answer that could have been made, having regard both to the law and to the needs of the situation. He stated that the legal situation had been in no way changed, and that no sufficient ground existed for prosecution of the Steel Corporation. But I acted purely on my own initiative, and the responsibility for the act was solely mine.

I was intimately acquainted with the situation in New York. The word "panic" means fear, unreasoning fear; to stop a panic it is necessary to restore confidence; and at the moment the so-called Morgan interests were the only interests which retained a full hold on the confidence of the people of New York — not only the business people, but the immense mass of men and women who owned small investments or had small savings in the banks and trust companies. Mr. Morgan and his associates were of course fighting hard to prevent the loss of confidence and the panic distrust from increasing to such a degree as to bring any other big financial institutions down; for this would probably have been followed by a general, and very likely a worldwide, crash. The Knickerbocker Trust Company had already failed, and runs had begun on, or were threatened as regards, two other big trust companies.

Charles J. Bonaparte.

These companies were now on the fighting line, and it was to the interest of everybody to strengthen them, in order that the situation might be saved. It was a matter of general knowledge and belief that they, or the individuals prominent in them, held the securities of the Tennessee Coal and Iron Company, which securities had no market value, and were useless as a source of strength in the emergency. The Steel Corporation securities, on the contrary, were immediately marketable, their great value being known and admitted all over the world —

as the event showed. The proposal of Messrs. Frick and Gary was that the Steel Corporation should at once acquire the Tennessee Coal and Iron Company, and thereby substitute, among the assets of the threatened institutions (which, by the way, they did not name to me), securities of great and immediate value for securities which at the moment were of no value. It was necessary for me to decide on the instant, before the Stock Exchange opened, for the situation in New York was such that any hour might be vital, and failure to act for even an hour might make all subsequent effort to act utterly useless. From the best information at my disposal, I believed (what was actually the fact) that the addition of the Tennessee Coal and Iron property would only increase the proportion of the Steel Company's holdings by about four per cent, making them about sixty-two per cent instead of about fifty-eight per cent of the total value in the country; an addition which, by itself, in my judgment (concurred in, not only by the Attorney-General but by every competent lawyer), worked no change in the legal status of the Steel corporation. The diminution in the percentage of holdings, and production, has gone on steadily, and the percentage is now about ten per cent less than it was ten years ago.

The action was emphatically for the general good. It offered the only chance for arresting the panic, and it did arrest the panic. I answered Messrs. Frick and Gary, as set forth in the letter quoted above, to the effect that I did not deem it my duty to interfere, that is, to forbid the action which more than anything else in actual fact saved the situation. The result justified my judgment. The panic was stopped, public confidence in the solvency of the threatened institution being at once restored.

Business was vitally helped by what I did. The benefit was not only for the moment. It was permanent. Particularly was this the case in the South. Three or four years afterwards I visited Birmingham. Every man I met, without exception, who was competent to testify, informed me voluntarily that the results of the action taken had been of the utmost benefit to Birmingham, and therefore to Alabama, the industry having profited to an extraordinary degree, not only from the standpoint of the business, but from the standpoint of the community at large and of the wage-workers, by the change in ownership. The results of the action I took were beneficial from every standpoint, and the action itself, at the time when it was taken, was vitally necessary to the welfare of the people of the United States.

I would have been derelict in my duty, I would have shown myself a timid and unworthy public servant, if in that extraordinary crisis I had not acted precisely as I did act. In every such crisis the temptation to indecision, to non-action, is great, for excuses can always be found for non-action, and action means risk and the certainty of blame to the man who acts. But if the man is worth his salt he will do his duty, he will give the people the benefit of the doubt, and act in any way which their interests demand and which is not affirmatively prohibited by law, unheeding the likelihood that he himself, when the crisis is over and the danger past, will be assailed for what he has done.

Every step I took in this matter was open as the day, and was known in detail at the moment to all people. The press contained full accounts of the visit to me of Messrs. Frick and Gary, and heralded widely and with acclamation the results of that visit. At the time the relief and rejoicing over what had been done were well-nigh universal. The danger was too imminent and too appalling for men to be willing to condemn those who were successful in saving them from it. But I fully understood and expected that when there was no longer danger, when the fear had been forgotten, attack would be made upon me; and as a matter of fact after a year had elapsed the attack was begun, and has continued at intervals ever since; my ordinary assailant being some politician of rather cheap type.

If I were on a sail-boat, I should not ordinarily meddle with any of the gear; but if a sudden squall struck us, and the main sheet jammed, so that the boat threatened to capsize, I would unhesitatingly cut the main sheet, even though I were sure that the owner, no matter how grateful to me at the moment for having saved his life, would a few weeks later, when he had forgotten his danger and his fear, decide to sue me for the value of the cut rope. But I would feel a hearty contempt for the owner who so acted.

There were many other things that we did in connection with corporations. One of the most important was the passage of the meat inspection law because of scandalous abuses shown to exist in the great packing-houses in Chicago and elsewhere. There was a curious result of this law, similar to what occurred in connection with the law providing for effective railway regulation. The big beef men bitterly opposed the law; just as the big railway men opposed the Hepburn Act. Yet three or four years after these laws had been put on the statute books every honest man both in the beef business and the railway business came to the conclusion that they worked good and not harm to the decent business concerns. They hurt only those who were not acting as they should have acted. The law providing for the inspection of packing-houses, and the Pure Food and Drugs Act, were also extremely important; and the way in which they were administered was even more important. It would be hard to overstate the value of the service rendered in all these cases by such cabinet officers as Moody and Bonaparte, and their outside assistants of the stamp of Frank Kellogg.

It would be useless to enumerate all the suits we brought. Some of them I have already touched upon. Others, such as the suits against the Harriman railway corporations, which were successful, and which had been rendered absolutely necessary by the grossly improper action of the corporations concerned, offered no special points of interest. The Sugar Trust proceedings, however, may be mentioned as showing just the kind of thing that was done and the kind of obstacle encountered and overcome in prosecutions of this character.

It was on the advice of my secretary, William Loeb, Jr., afterward head of the New York Custom-House, that the action was taken which started the uncovering of the frauds perpetrated by the Sugar Trust and other companies in connection with the importing of sugar. Loeb had from time to time told me that he was sure that there was fraud in connection with the importations by the Sugar Trust through the New York Custom-House. Finally, some time toward the end of 1904, he informed me that Richard Parr, a sampler at the New York Appraisers' Stores (whose duties took him almost continually on the docks in connection with the sampling of merchandise), had called on him, and had stated that in his belief the sugar companies were defrauding the Government in the matter of weights, and had stated that if he could be made an investigating officer of the Treasury Department, he was confident that he could show there was wrongdoing. Parr had been a former school fellow of Loeb in Albany, and Loeb believed him to be loyal, honest, and efficient. He thereupon laid the matter before me, and advised the appointment of Parr as a special employee of the Treasury Department, for the specific purpose of investigating the alleged sugar frauds. I instructed the Treasury Department accordingly, and was informed that there was no vacancy in the force of special employees, but that Parr would be given the first place that opened up. Early in the spring of 1905 Parr came to Loeb again, and said that he had received additional information about the sugar frauds, and was anxious to begin the investigation. Loeb again discussed the matter with me; and I notified the Treasury Department to appoint Parr immediately. On June 1, 1905, he received his appointment, and was assigned to the port of Boston for the purpose of gaining some experience as an investigating officer. During the month he was transferred to the Maine District, with headquarters at Portland, where he remained until March, 1907. During his service in Maine he uncovered extensive wool smuggling frauds. At the conclusion of the wool case, he appealed to Loeb to have him transferred to New York, so that he might undertake the investigation of the sugar underweighing frauds. I now called the attention of Secretary Cortelyou personally to the matter, so that he would be able to keep a check over any subordinates who might try to interfere with Parr, for the conspiracy was evidently widespread, the wealth of the offenders great, and the corruption in the service far-reaching — while moreover as always happens with "respectable" offenders, there were many good men who sincerely disbelieved in the possibility of corruption on the part of men of such high financial standing. Parr was assigned to New York early in March, 1907, and at once began an active investigation of the conditions existing on the sugar docks. This terminated in the discovery of a steel spring in one of the scales of the Havemeyer & Elder docks in Brooklyn, November 20, 1907, which enabled us to uncover what were probably the most colossal frauds ever perpetrated in the Customs Service. From the beginning of his active work in the investigation of the sugar frauds in March, 1907, to March 4, 1909, Parr, from time to time, personally reported to Loeb, at the White House, the progress of his investigations, and Loeb in his turn kept me personally advised. On one occasion there was an attempt made to shunt Parr off the investigation and substitute another agent of the Treasury, who was suspected of having some relations with the sugar companies under investigation; but Parr reported the facts to Loeb, I sent for Secretary Cortelyou, and Secretary Cortelyou promptly took charge of the matter himself, putting Parr back on the investigation.

During the investigation Parr was subjected to all sorts of harassments, including an attempt to bribe him by Spitzer, the dock superintendent of the Havemeyer & Elder Refinery, for which Spitzer was convicted and served a term in prison. Brzezinski, a special agent, who was assisting Parr, was convicted of perjury and also served a term in prison, he having changed his testimony, in the trial of Spitzer for the attempted bribery of Parr, from that which he gave before the Grand Jury. For his extraordinary services in connection with this investigation Parr was granted an award of $100,000 by the Treasury Department.

District-Attorney Stimson, of New York, assisted by Denison, Frankfurter, Wise, and other employees of the Department of Justice, took charge of the case, and carried on both civil and criminal proceedings. The trial in the action against the Sugar Trust, for the recovery of duties on the cargo of sugar, which was being sent over the scales at the time of the discovery of the steel spring by Parr, was begun in 1908; judgment was rendered against the defendants on March 5, 1909, the day after I left office. Over four million dollars were recovered and paid back into the United States Treasury by the sugar companies which had perpetrated the various forms of fraud. These frauds were unearthed by Parr, Loeb, Stimson, Frankfurter, and the other men mentioned and their associates, and it was to them that the people owed the refunding of the huge sum of money mentioned. We had already secured heavy fines from the Sugar Trust, and from various big railways, and private individuals, such as Edwin Earle, for unlawful rebates. In the case of the chief offender, the American Sugar Refining Company (the Sugar Trust), criminal prosecutions were carried on against every living man whose position was such that he would naturally know about the fraud. All of them were indicted, and the biggest and most responsible ones were convicted. The evidence showed that the president of the company, Henry O. Havemeyer, virtually ran the entire company, and was responsible for all the details of the management. He died two weeks after the fraud was discovered, just as proceedings were being begun. Next to him in importance was the secretary and treasurer, Charles R. Heike, who was convicted. Various other officials and employees of the Trust, and various Government employees, were indicted, and most of them convicted. Ernest W. Gerbracht, the superintendent of one of the refineries, was convicted, but his sentence was commuted to a short jail imprisonment, because he became a Government witness and greatly assisted the Government in the suits.

Paul Morton.

Heike's sentence was commuted so as to excuse him from going to the penitentiary; just as the penitentiary sentence of Morse, the big New York banker, who was convicted of gross fraud and misapplication of funds, was commuted. Both commutations were granted long after I left office. In each case the commutation was granted because, as was stated, of the prisoner's age and state of health. In Morse's case the President originally refused the request, saying that Morse had exhibited "fraudulent and criminal disregard of the trust imposed upon him," that "he was entirely unscrupulous as to the methods he adopted," and "that he seemed at times to be absolutely heartless with regard to the consequences to others, and he showed great shrewdness in obtaining large sums of money from the bank without adequate security and without making himself personally liable therefor." The two cases may be considered in connection with the announcement in the public press that on May 17, 1913, the President commuted the sentence of Lewis A. Banks, who was serving a very long term penitentiary sentence for an attack on a girl in the Indian Territory;

"the reason for the commutation which is set forth in the press being that 'Banks is in poor health.' "

It is no easy matter to balance the claims of justice and mercy in such cases. In these three cases, of all of which I had personal cognizance, I disagreed radically with the views my successors took, and with the views which many respectable men took who in these and similar cases, both while I was in office and afterward, urged me to show, or to ask others to show, clemency. It then seemed to me, and it now seems to me, that such clemency is from the larger standpoint a gross wrong to the men and women of the country.

One of the former special assistants of the district-attorney, Mr. W. Cleveland Runyon, in commenting bitterly on the release of Heike and Morse on account of their health, pointed out that their health apparently became good when once they themselves became free men, and added:

"The commutation of these sentences amounts to a direct interference with the administration of justice by the courts. Heike got a $25,000 salary and has escaped his imprisonment, but what about the six $18 a week checkers, who were sent to jail, one of them a man of more than sixty? It is cases like this that create discontent and anarchy. They make it seem plain that there is one law for the rich and another for the poor man, and I for one will protest."

In dealing with Heike the individual (or Morse or any other individual), it is necessary to emphasize the social aspects of his case. The moral of the Heike case, as has been well said, is "how easy it is for a man in modern corporate organization to drift into wrongdoing." The moral restraints are loosened in the case of a man like Heike by the insulation of himself from the sordid details of crime, through industrially coerced intervening agents. Professor Ross has made the penetrating observation that "distance disinfects dividends"; it also weakens individual responsibility, particularly on the part of the very managers of large business, who should feel it most acutely. One of the officers of the Department of Justice who conducted the suit, and who inclined to the side of mercy in the matter, nevertheless writes: "Heike is a beautiful illustration of mental and moral obscuration in the business life of an otherwise valuable member of society. Heike had an ample share in the guidance of the affairs of the American Sugar Company, and we are apt to have a foreshortened picture of his responsibility, because he operated from the easy coign of vantage of executive remoteness. It is difficult to say to what extent he did, directly or indirectly, profit by the sordid practices of his company. But the social damage of an individual in his position may be just as deep, whether merely the zest of the game or hard cash be his dominant motive."

James R. Garfield.

I have coupled the cases of the big banker and the Sugar Trust official and the case of the man convicted of a criminal assault on a woman. All of the criminals were released from penitentiary sentences on grounds of ill health. The offenses were typical of the worst crimes committed at the two ends of the social scale. One offense was a crime of brutal violence; the other offenses were crimes of astute corruption. All of them were offenses which in my judgment were of such a character that clemency towards the offender worked grave injustice to the community as a whole, injustice so grave that its effects might be far-reaching in their damage.

Every time that rape or criminal assault on a woman is pardoned, and anything less than the full penalty of the law exacted, a premium is put on the practice of lynching such offenders. Every time a big monied offender, who naturally excites interest and sympathy, and who has many friends, is excused from serving a sentence which a man of less prominence and fewer friends would have to serve, justice is discredited in the eyes of plain people — and to undermine faith in justice is to strike at the foundation of the Republic. As for ill health, it must be remembered that few people are as healthy in prison as they would be outside; and there should be no discrimination among criminals on this score; either all criminals who grow unhealthy should be let out, or none. Pardons must sometimes be given in order that the cause of justice may be served; but in cases such as these I am considering, while I know that many amiable people differ from me, I am obliged to say that in my judgment the pardons work far-reaching harm to the cause of justice.

Among the big corporations themselves, even where they did wrong, there was a wide difference in the moral obliquity indicated by the wrongdoer. There was a wide distinction between the offenses committed in the case of the Northern Securities Company, and the offenses because of which the Sugar Trust, the Tobacco Trust, and the Standard Oil Trust were successfully prosecuted under my Administration. It was vital to destroy the Northern Securities Company; but the men creating it had done so in open and above-board fashion, acting under what they, and most of the members of the bar, thought to be the law established by the Supreme Court in the Knight sugar case. But the Supreme Court in its decree dissolving the Standard Oil and Tobacco Trusts, condemned them in the severest language for moral turpitude; and an even severer meed of condemnation should be visited on the Sugar Trust.

However, all the trusts and big corporations against which we proceeded — which included in their directorates practically all the biggest financiers in the country — joined in making the bitterest assaults on me and on my Administration. Of their actions I wrote as follows to Attorney-General Bonaparte, who had been a peculiarly close friend and adviser through the period covered by my public life in high office and who, together with Attorney-General Moody, possessed the same understanding sympathy with my social and industrial program that was possessed by such officials as Straus, Garfield, H. K. Smith, and Pinchot. The letter runs:

January 2, 1908.

*My dear Bonaparte:*
    I must congratulate you on your admirable speech at Chicago. You said the very things it was good to say at this time. What you said

bore especial weight because it represented what you had done. You have shown by what you have actually accomplished that the law is enforced against the wealthiest corporation, and the richest and most powerful manager or manipulator of that corporation, just as resolutely and fearlessly as against the humblest citizen. The Department of Justice is now in very fact the Department of Justice, and justice is meted out with an even hand to great and small, rich and poor, weak and strong. Those who have denounced you and the action of the Department of Justice are either misled, or else are the very wrongdoers, and the agents of the very wrongdoers, who have for so many years gone scot-free and flouted the laws with impunity. Above all, you are to be congratulated upon the bitterness felt and expressed towards you by the representatives and agents of the great law-defying corporations of immense wealth, who, until within the last half-dozen years, have treated themselves and have expected others to treat them as being beyond and above all possible check from law.

It was time to say something, for the representatives of predatory wealth, of wealth accumulated on a giant scale by iniquity, by wrongdoing in many forms, by plain swindling, by oppressing wage-workers, by manipulating securities, by unfair and unwholesome competition and by stock-jobbing, — in short, by conduct abhorrent to every man of ordinarily decent conscience, have during the last few months made it evident that they are banded together to work for a reaction, to endeavor to overthrow and discredit all who honestly administer the law, and to secure a return to the days when every unscrupulous wrongdoer could do what he wished unchecked, provided he had enough money. They attack you because they know your honesty and fearlessness, and dread them. The enormous sums of money these men have at their control enable them to carry on an effective campaign. They find their tools in a portion of the public press, including especially certain of the great New York newspapers. They find their agents in some men in public life, — now and then occupying, or having occupied, positions as high as Senator or Governor, — in some men in the pulpit, and most melancholy of all, in a few men on the bench. By gifts to colleges and universities they are occasionally able to subsidize in their own interest some head of an educational body, who, save only a judge, should of all men be most careful to keep his skirts clear from the taint of such corruption. There are ample material rewards for those who serve with fidelity the Mammon of unrighteousness, but they are dearly paid for by that institution of learning whose head, by example and precept, teaches the scholars who sit under him that there is one law for the rich and another for the poor. The amount of money the representatives of the great monied interests are willing to spend can be gauged by their recent publication broadcast throughout the papers of this country from the Atlantic to the Pacific of huge advertisements, attacking with envenomed bitterness the Administration's policy of warring against successful dishonesty, advertisements that must have cost enormous sums of money. This advertisement, as also a pamphlet called "The Roosevelt Panic," and one or two similar books and pamphlets, are written especially in the interest of the Standard Oil and Harriman combinations, but also defend all the individuals and corporations of great wealth that have been guilty of wrongdoing. From the railroad rate law to the pure food law, every measure for honesty in business that has been pressed during the last six years, has been opposed by these men, on its passage and in its administration, with every resource that bitter and unscrupulous craft could suggest, and the command of almost unlimited money secure. These men do not themselves speak or write; they hire others to do their bidding. Their spirit and purpose are made clear alike by the editorials of the papers owned in, or whose policy is dictated by, Wall Street, and by the speeches of public men who, as Senators, Governors, or Mayors, have served these their masters to the cost of the plain people. At one time one of their writers or speakers attacks the rate law as the cause of the panic; he is, whether in public life or not, usually a clever corporation lawyer, and he is not so foolish a being as to believe in the truth of what he says; he has too closely represented the railroads not to know well that the Hepburn Rate Bill has helped every honest railroad, and has hurt only the railroads that regarded themselves as above the law. At another time, one of them assails the Administration for not imprisoning people under the Sherman Anti-Trust Law; for declining to make what he well knows, in view of the actual attitude of juries (as shown in the Tobacco Trust cases and in San Francisco in one or two of the cases brought against corrupt business men) would have been the futile endeavor to imprison defendants whom we are actually able to fine. He raises the usual clamor, raised by all who object to the enforcement of the law, that we are fining corporations instead of putting the heads of the corporations in jail; and he states that this does not really harm the chief offenders. Were this statement true, he himself would not be found attacking us. The extraordinary violence of the assault upon our policy contained in speeches like these, in the articles in the subsidized press, in such huge advertisements and pamphlets as those above referred to, and the enormous sums of money spent in these various ways, give a fairly accurate measure of the anger and terror which our actions have caused the corrupt men of vast wealth to feel in the very marrow of their being.

The man thus attacking us is usually, like so many of his fellows, either a great lawyer, or a paid editor who takes his commands from the financiers and his arguments from their attorneys. If the former, he has defended many malefactors, and he knows well that, thanks to the advice of lawyers like himself, a certain kind of modern corporation has been turned into an admirable instrument by which to render it well nigh impossible to get at the really guilty man, so that in most cases the only way of punishing the wrong is by fining the corporation or by proceeding personally against some of the minor agents. These lawyers and their employers are the men mainly responsible for this state of things, and their responsibility is shared with the legislators who ingeniously oppose the passing of just and effective laws, and with those judges whose one aim seems to be to construe such laws so that they cannot be executed. Nothing is sillier than this outcry on behalf of the "innocent stockholders" in the corporations. We are besought to pity the Standard Oil Company for a fine relatively far less great than the fines every day inflicted in the police courts upon multitudes of push cart peddlers and other petty offenders, whose woes never extort one word from the men whose withers are wrung by the woes of the mighty. The stockholders have the control of the corporation in their own hands. The corporation officials are elected by those holding the majority of the stock and can keep office only by having behind them the good-will of these majority stockholders. They are not entitled to the slightest pity if they deliberately choose to resign into the hands of great wrongdoers the control of the corporations in which they own the stock. Of course innocent people have become involved in these big corporations and suffer because of the misdeeds of their criminal associates. Let these innocent people be careful not to invest in corporations where those in control are not men of probity, men who respect the laws; above all let them avoid the men who make it their one effort to evade or defy the laws. But if these honest innocent people are in the majority in any corporation they can immediately resume control and throw out of the directory the men who misrepresent them. Does any man for a moment suppose that the majority stockholders of the Standard Oil are others than Mr. Rockefeller and his associates themselves and the beneficiaries of their wrongdoing? When the stock is watered so that the innocent investors suffer, a grave wrong is indeed done to these innocent investors as well as to the public; but the public men, lawyers and editors, to whom I refer, do not under these circumstances express sympathy for the innocent; on the contrary they are the first to protest with frantic vehemence against our efforts by law to put a stop to overcapitalization and stock-watering. The apologists of successful dishonesty always declaim against any effort to punish or prevent it on the ground that such effort will "unsettle business." It is they who by their acts have unsettled business; and the very men raising this cry spend hundreds of thousands of dollars in securing, by speech, editorial, book or pamphlet, the defense by misstatement of what they have done; and yet when we correct their misstatements by telling the truth, they declaim against us for breaking silence, lest "values be unsettled!" They have hurt honest business men, honest working men, honest farmers; and now they clamor against the truth being told.

The keynote of all these attacks upon the effort to secure honesty in business and in politics, is expressed in a recent speech, in which the speaker stated that prosperity had been checked by the effort for the "moral regeneration of the business world," an effort which he denounced as "unnatural, unwarranted and injurious" and for which he stated the panic was the penalty. The morality of such a plea is precisely as great as if made on behalf of the men caught in a gambling establishment when that gambling establishment is raided by the police. If such words mean anything they mean that those whose sentiments they represent stand against the effort to bring about a moral regeneration of business which will prevent a repetition of the insurance, banking and street railroad scandals in New York; a repetition of the Chicago and Alton deal; a repetition of the combination between certain professional politicians, certain professional labor leaders and certain big financiers from the disgrace of which San Francisco has just been rescued; a repetition of the successful efforts by the Standard Oil people to crush out every competitor, to overawe the common carriers, and to establish a monopoly which treats the public with the contempt which the public deserves so long as it permits men like the public men of whom I speak to represent it in politics, men like the heads of colleges to whom I refer to educate its youth. The outcry against stopping dishonest practices among the very wealthy is precisely similar to the outcry raised against every effort for cleanliness and decency in city government because, forsooth, it will "hurt business." The same outcry is made against the Department of Justice for prosecuting the heads of colossal corporations that is made against the men who in San Francisco are prosecuting with impartial severity the wrongdoers among business men, public officials, and labor leaders alike. The principle is the same in the two cases. Just as the blackmailer and the bribe giver stand on the same evil eminence of infamy, so the man who makes an enormous fortune by corrupting Legislatures and municipalities and fleecing his stockholders and the public stands on a level with the creature who fattens on the blood money of the gambling house, the saloon and the brothel. Moreover, both kinds of corruption in the last analysis are far more intimately connected than would at first sight appear; the wrong-doing is at bottom the same. Corrupt business and corrupt politics act and react, with ever increasing debasement, one on the other; the rebate-taker, the franchise-trafficker, the manipulator of securities, the purveyor and protector of vice, the black-mailing ward boss, the ballot box stuffer, the demagogue, the mob leader, the hired bully and mankiller, all alike work at the same web of corruption, and all alike should be abhorred by honest men.

Gifford Pinchot.

The "business" which is hurt by the movement for honesty is the kind of business which, in the long run, it pays the country to have hurt. It is the kind of business which has tended to make the very name "high finance" a term of scandal to which all honest American men of business should join in putting an end. One of the special pleaders for business dishonesty, in a recent speech, in denouncing the Administration for enforcing the law against the huge and corrupt corporations which have defied the law, also denounced it for endeavoring to secure a far-reaching law making employers liable for injuries to their employees. It is meet and fit that the apologists for corrupt wealth should oppose every effort to relieve weak and helpless people from crushing misfortune brought upon them by injury in the business from which they gain a bare livelihood and their employers fortunes. It is hypocritical baseness to speak of a girl who works in a factory where the dangerous machinery is unprotected as having the "right" freely to contract to expose herself to dangers to life and limb. She has no alternative but to suffer want or else to expose herself to such dangers, and when she loses a hand or is otherwise maimed or disfigured for life it is a moral wrong that the burden of the risk necessarily incidental to the business should be placed with crushing weight upon her weak shoulders and the man who has profited by her work escape scot-free. This is what our opponents advocate, and it is proper that they should advocate it, for it rounds out their advocacy of those most dangerous members of the criminal class, the criminals of vast wealth, the men who can afford best to pay for such championship in the press and on the stump.

It is difficult to speak about the judges, for it behooves us all to treat with the utmost respect the high office of judge; and our judges as a whole are brave and upright men. But there is need that those who go wrong should not be allowed to feel that there is no condemnation of their wrongdoing. A judge who on the bench either truckles to the mob or bows down before a corporation; or who, having left the bench to become a corporation lawyer, seeks to aid his clients by denouncing as enemies of property all those who seek to stop the abuses of the criminal rich; such a man performs an even worse service to the body politic than the Legislator or Executive who goes wrong. In no way can respect for the courts be so quickly undermined as by teaching the public through the action of a judge himself that there is reason for the loss of such respect. The judge who by word or deed makes it plain that the corrupt corporation, the law-defying corporation, the law-defying rich man, has in him a sure and trustworthy ally, the judge who by misuse of the process of injunction makes it plain that in him the wage-worker has a determined and unscrupulous enemy, the judge who when he decides in an employers' liability or a tenement house factory case shows that he has neither sympathy for nor understanding of those fellow-citizens of his who most need his sympathy and understanding; these judges work as much evil as if they pandered to the mob, as if they shrank from sternly repressing violence and disorder. The judge who does his full duty well stands higher, and renders a better service to the people, than any other public servant; he is entitled to greater respect; and if he is a true servant of the people, if he is upright, wise and fearless, he will unhesitatingly disregard even the wishes of the people if they conflict with the eternal principles of right as against wrong. He must serve the people; but he must serve his conscience first. All honor to such a judge; and all honor cannot be rendered him if it is rendered equally to his brethren who fall immeasurably below the high ideals for which he stands. There should be a sharp discrimination against such judges. They claim immunity from criticism, and the claim is heatedly advanced by men and newspapers like those of whom I speak. Most certainly they can claim immunity from untruthful criticism; and their champions, the newspapers and the public men I have mentioned, exquisitely illustrate by their own actions mendacious criticism in its most flagrant and iniquitous form.

But no servant of the people has a right to expect to be free from just and honest criticism. It is the newspapers, and the public men whose thoughts and deeds show them to be most alien to honesty and truth who themselves loudly object to truthful and honest criticism of their fellow-servants of the great monied interests.

We have no quarrel with the individuals, whether public men, lawyers or editors, to whom I refer. These men derive their sole power from the great, sinister offenders who stand behind them. They are but puppets who move as the strings are pulled by those who control the enormous masses of corporate wealth which if itself left uncontrolled threatens dire evil to the Republic. It is not the puppets, but the strong, cunning men and the mighty forces working for evil behind, and to a certain extent through, the puppets, with whom we have to deal. We seek to control law-defying wealth, in the first place to prevent its doing evil, and in the next place to avoid the vindictive and dreadful radicalism which if left uncontrolled it is certain in the end to arouse. Sweeping attacks upon all property, upon all men of means, without regard to whether they do well or ill, would sound the death knell of the Republic; and such attacks become inevitable if decent citizens permit rich men whose lives are corrupt and evil to domineer in swollen pride, unchecked and unhindered, over the destinies of this country. We act in no vindictive spirit, and we are no respecters of persons. If a labor union does what is wrong, we oppose it as fearlessly as we oppose a corporation that does wrong; and we stand with equal stoutness for the rights of the man of wealth and for the rights of the wage-workers; just as much so for one as for the other. We seek to stop wrongdoing; and we desire to punish the wrongdoer only so far as is necessary in order to achieve this end. We are the stanch upholders of every honest man, whether business man or wage-worker.

I do not for a moment believe that our actions have brought on business distress; so far as this is due to local and not world-wide causes, and to the actions of any particular individuals, it is due to the speculative folly and flagrant dishonesty of a few men of great wealth, who now seek to shield themselves from the effects of their own wrongdoings by ascribing its results to the actions of those who have sought to put a stop to the wrongdoing. But if it were true that to cut out rottenness from the body politic meant a momentary check to an unhealthy seeming prosperity, I should not for one moment hesitate to put the knife to the cancer. On behalf of all our people, on behalf no less of the honest man of means than of the honest man who earns each day's livelihood by that day's sweat of his brow, it is necessary to insist upon honesty in business and politics alike, in all walks of life, in big things and in little things; upon just and fair dealing as between man and man. We are striving for the right in the spirit of Abraham Lincoln when he said:

"Fondly do we hope— fervently do we pray— that this mighty scourge may speedily pass away. Yet, if God wills that it continue until all the wealth piled by the bondsmen's two hundred and fifty years of unrequited toil shall be sunk, and until every drop of blood drawn with the lash shall be paid by another drawn with the sword, as was said three thousand years ago, so still it must be said, 'The judgments of the Lord are true and righteous altogether.'

"With malice toward none; with charity for all; with firmness in the right, as God gives us to see the right, let us strive on to finish the work we are in."

Sincerely yours,
THEODORE ROOSEVELT.

HON. CHARLES J. BONAPARTE.
*Attorney-General*

# Chapter XIII

## SOCIAL AND INDUSTRIAL JUSTICE

BY THE TIME I became President I had grown to feel with deep intensity of conviction that governmental agencies must find their justification largely in the way in which they are used for the practical betterment of living and working conditions among the mass of the people. I felt that the fight was really for the abolition of privilege; and one of the first stages in the battle was necessarily to fight for the rights of the workingman. For this reason I felt most strongly that all that the government could do in the interest of labor should be done. The Federal Government can rarely act with the directness that the State governments act. It can, however, do a good deal. My purpose was to make the National Government itself a model employer of labor, the effort being to make the per diem employee just as much as the Cabinet officer regard himself as one of the partners employed in the service of the public, proud of his work, eager to do it in the best possible manner, and confident of just treatment. Our aim was also to secure good laws wherever the National Government had power, notably in the Territories, in the District of Columbia, and in connection with inter-State commerce. I found the eight-hour law a mere farce, the departments rarely enforcing it with any degree of efficiency. This I remedied by executive action. Unfortunately, thoroughly efficient government servants often proved to be the prime offenders so far as the enforcement of the eight-hour law was concerned, because in their zeal to get good work done for the Government they became harsh taskmasters, and declined to consider the needs of their fellow-employees who served under them. The more I had studied the subject the more strongly I had become convinced that an eight-hour day under the conditions of labor in the United States was all that could, with wisdom and propriety, be required either by the Government or by private employers; that more than this meant, on the average, a decrease in the qualities that tell for good citizenship. I finally solved the problem, as far as Government employees were concerned, by calling in Charles P. Neill, the head of the Labor Bureau; and, acting on his advice, I speedily made the eight-hour law really effective. Any man who shirked his work, who dawdled and idled, received no mercy; slackness is even worse than harshness; for exactly as in battle mercy to the coward is cruelty to the brave man, so in civil life slackness towards the vicious and idle is harshness towards the honest and hard-working.

We passed a good law protecting the lives and health of miners in the Territories, and other laws providing for the supervision of employment agencies in the District of Columbia, and protecting the health of motormen and conductors on street railways in the District. We practically started the Bureau of Mines. We provided for safeguarding factory employees in the District against accidents, and for the restriction of child labor therein. We passed a workmen's compensation law for the protection of Government employees; a law which did not go as far as I wished, but which was the best I could get, and which committed the Government to the right policy. We provided for an investigation of woman and child labor in the United States. We incorporated the National Child Labor Committee. Where we had most difficulty was with the railway companies engaged in inter-State business. We passed an act improving safety appliances on railway trains without much opposition, but we had more trouble with acts regulating the hours of labor of railway employees and making those railways which were engaged in inter-State commerce liable for injuries to or the death of their employees while on duty. One important step in connection with these latter laws was taken by Attorney-General Moody when, on behalf of the Government, he intervened in the case of a wronged employee. It is unjust that a law which has been declared public policy by the representatives of the people should be submitted to the possibility of nullification because the Government leaves the enforcement of it to the private initiative of poor people who have just suffered some crushing accident. It should be the business of the Government to enforce laws of this kind, and to appear in court to argue for their constitutionality and proper enforcement. Thanks to Moody, the Government assumed this position. The first employers' liability law affecting inter-State railroads was declared unconstitutional. We got through another, which stood the test of the courts.

The principle to which we especially strove to give expression, through these laws and through executive action, was that a right is valueless unless reduced from the abstract to the concrete. This sounds like a truism. So far from being such, the effort practically to apply it was almost revolutionary, and gave rise to the bitterest denunciation of us by all the big lawyers, and all the big newspaper editors, who, whether sincerely or for hire, gave expression to the views of the privileged classes. Ever since the Civil War very many of the decisions of the courts, not as regards ordinary actions between man and man, but as regards the application of great governmental policies for social and industrial justice, had been in reality nothing but ingenious justifications of the theory that these policies were mere high-sounding abstractions, and were not to be given practical effect. The tendency of the courts had been, in the majority of cases, jealously to exert their great power in protecting those who least needed protection and hardly to use their power at all in the interest of those who most needed protection. Our desire was to make the Federal Government efficient as an instrument for protecting the rights of labor within its province, and therefore to secure and enforce judicial decisions which would permit us to make this desire effective. Not only some of the Federal judges, but some of the State courts invoked the Constitution in a spirit of the narrowest legalistic obstruction to prevent the Government from acting in defense of labor on inter-State railways. In effect, these judges took the view that while Congress had complete power as regards the goods transported by the railways, and could protect wealthy or well-to-do owners of these goods, yet that it had no power to protect the lives of the men engaged in transporting the goods. Such judges freely issued injunctions to prevent the obstruction of traffic in the interest of the property owners, but declared unconstitutional the action of the Government in seeking to safeguard the men, and the families of the men, without whose labor the traffic could not take place. It was an instance of the largely unconscious way in which the courts had been twisted into the exaltation of property rights over human rights, and the subordination of the welfare of the laborer when compared with the profit of the man for whom he labored. By what I fear my conservative friends regarded as frightfully aggressive missionary work, which included some uncommonly plain speaking as to certain unjust and anti-social judicial decisions, we succeeded in largely, but by no means altogether, correcting this view, at least so far as the best and most enlightened judges were concerned.

Very much the most important action I took as regards labor had nothing to do with legislation, and represented executive action which was not required by the Constitution. It illustrated as well as anything that I did the theory which I have called the Jackson-Lincoln theory of the Presidency; that is, that occasionally great national crises arise which call for immediate and vigorous executive action, and that in such cases it is the duty of the President to act upon the theory that he is the steward of the people, and that the proper attitude for him to take is that he is bound to assume that he has the legal right to do whatever the needs of the people demand, unless the Constitution or the laws explicitly forbid him to do it.

Early in the spring of 1902 a universal strike began in the anthracite regions. The miners and the operators became deeply embittered, and the strike went on throughout the summer and the early fall without any sign of reaching an end, and with almost complete stoppage of mining. In many cities, especially in the East, the heating apparatus is designed for anthracite, so that the bituminous coal is only a very partial substitute. Moreover, in many regions, even in farmhouses, many of the provisions are for burning coal and not wood. In consequence, the coal famine became a National menace as the winter approached. In most big cities and many farming districts east of the Mississippi the shortage of anthracite threatened calamity. In the populous industrial States, from Ohio eastward, it was not merely calamity, but the direst disaster, that was threatened. Ordinarily conservative men, men very sensitive as to the rights of property under normal conditions, when faced by this crisis felt, quite rightly, that there must be some radical action. The Governor of Massachusetts and the Mayor of New York both notified me, as the cold weather came on, that if the coal famine continued the misery throughout the Northeast, and especially in the great cities, would become appalling, and the consequent public disorder so great that frightful consequences might follow. It is not too much to say that the situation which confronted Pennsylvania, New York, and New England, and to a less degree the States of the Middle West, in October, 1902, was quite as serious as if they had been threatened by the invasion of a hostile army of overwhelming force.

The big coal operators had banded together, and positively refused to take any steps looking toward an accommodation. They knew that the suffering among the miners was great; they were confident that if order were kept, and nothing further done by the Government, they would win; and they refused to consider that the public had any rights in the matter. They were, for the most part, men of unquestionably good private life, and they were merely taking the extreme individualistic view of the rights of property and the freedom of individual action upheld in the *laissez faire* political economies. The mines were in the State of Pennsylvania. There was no duty whatever laid upon me by the Constitution in the matter, and I had in theory no power to act directly unless the Governor of Pennsylvania or the Legislature, if it were in session, should notify me that Pennsylvania could not keep order, and request me as commander-in-chief of the army of the United States to intervene and keep order.

As long as I could avoid interfering I did so; but I directed the head of the Labor Bureau, Carroll Wright, to make a thorough investigation and lay the facts fully before me. As September passed without any sign of weakening either among the employers or the striking workmen, the situation became so grave that I felt I would have to try to do something. The thing most feasible was to get both sides to agree to a Commission of Arbitration, with a promise to accept its findings; the miners to go to work as soon as the commission was appointed, at the old rate of wages. To this proposition the miners, headed by John Mitchell, agreed, stipulating only that I should have power to name the Commission. The operators, however, positively refused. They insisted that all that was necessary to do was for the State to keep order, using the militia as a police force; although both they and the miners asked me to intervene under the Inter-State Commerce Law, each side requesting that I proceed against the other, and both requests being impossible.

Finally, on October 3, the representatives of both the operators and the miners met before me, in pursuance of my request. The representatives of the miners included as their head and spokesman John Mitchell, who kept his temper admirably and showed to much advantage. The representatives of the operators, on the contrary, came down in a most insolent frame of mind, refused to talk of arbitration or other accommodation of any kind, and used language that was insulting to the miners and offensive to me. They were curiously ignorant of the popular temper; and when they went away from the interview they, with much pride, gave their own account of it to the papers, exulting in the fact that they had "turned down" both the miners and the President.

I refused to accept the rebuff, however, and continued the effort to get an agreement between the operators and the miners. I was anxious to get this agreement, because it would prevent the necessity of taking the extremely drastic action I meditated, and which is hereinafter described.

Fortunately, this time we were successful. Yet we were on the verge of failure, because of self-willed obstinacy on the part of the operators. This obstinacy was utterly silly from their own standpoint, and well-nigh criminal from the standpoint of the people at large. The miners proposed that I should name the Commission, and that if I put on a representative of the employing class I should also put on a labor union man. The operators positively declined to accept the suggestion. They insisted upon my naming a Commission of only five men, and specified the qualifications these men should have, carefully choosing these qualifications so as to exclude those whom it had leaked out I was thinking of appointing, including ex-President Cleveland. They made the condition that I was to appoint one officer of the engineer corps of the army or navy, one man with experience of mining, one "man of prominence," "eminent as a sociologist," one Federal judge of the Eastern District of Pennsylvania, and one mining engineer.

They positively refused to have me appoint any representative of labor, or to put on an extra man. I was desirous of putting on the extra man, because Mitchell and the other leaders of the miners had urged me to appoint some high Catholic ecclesiastic. Most of the miners were Catholics, and Mitchell and the leaders were very anxious to secure peaceful acquiescence by the miners in any decision rendered, and they felt that their hands would be strengthened if such an appointment were made. They also, quite properly, insisted that there should be one representative of labor on the Commission, as all of the others represented the propertied classes. The operators, however, absolutely refused to acquiesce in the appointment of any representative of labor, and also announced that they would refuse to accept a sixth man on the Commission; although they spoke much less decidedly on this point. The labor men left everything in my hands.

The final conferences with the representatives of the operators took place in my rooms on the evening of October 15. Hour after hour went by while I endeavored to make the operators through their representatives see that the country would not tolerate their insisting upon such conditions; but in vain. The two representatives of the operators were Robert Bacon and George W. Perkins. They were entirely reasonable. But the operators themselves were entirely unreasonable. They had worked themselves into a frame of mind where they were prepared to sacrifice everything and see civil war in the country rather than back down and acquiesce in the appointment of a representative of labor. It looked as if a deadlock were inevitable.

Then, suddenly, after about two hours' argument, it dawned on me that they were not objecting to the thing, but to the name. I found that they did not mind my appointing any man, whether he was a labor man or not, so long as he was not appointed *as* a labor man, or *as* a representative of labor; they did not object to my exercising any latitude I chose in the appointments so long as they were made under the headings they had given. I shall never forget the mixture of relief and amusement I felt when I thoroughly grasped the fact that while they would heroically submit to anarchy rather than have Tweedledum, yet if I would call it Tweedledee they would accept it with rapture; it gave me an illuminating glimpse into one corner of the mighty brains of these "captains of industry." In order to carry the great and vital point and secure agreement by both parties, all that was necessary for me to do was to commit a technical and nominal absurdity with a solemn face. This I gladly did. I announced at once that I accepted the terms laid down. With this understanding, I appointed the labor man I had all along had in view, Mr. E. E. Clark, the head of the Brotherhood of Railway Conductors, calling him an "eminent sociologist" — a term which I doubt whether he had ever previously heard. He was a first-class man, whom I afterward put on the Inter-State Commerce Commission. I added to the Arbitration Commission, on my own authority, a sixth member, in the person of Bishop Spalding, a Catholic bishop, of Peoria, Ill., one of the very best men to be found in the entire country. The man whom the operators had expected me to appoint as the sociologist was Carroll Wright — who really was an eminent sociologist. I put him on as recorder of

Father Curran.

the Commission, and added him as a seventh member as soon as the Commission got fairly started. In publishing the list of the Commissioners, when I came to Clark's appointment, I added: "As a sociologist — the President assuming that for the purposes of such a Commission, the term sociologist means a man who has thought and studied deeply on social questions and has practically applied his knowledge."

The relief of the whole country was so great that the sudden appearance of the head of the Brotherhood of Railway Conductors as an "eminent sociologist" merely furnished material for puzzled comment on the part of the press. It was a most admirable Commission. It did a noteworthy work, and its report is a monument in the history of the relations of labor and capital in this country. The strike, by the way, brought me into contact with more than one man who was afterward a valued friend and fellow-worker. On the suggestion of Carroll Wright I appointed as assistant recorders to the Commission Charles P. Neill, whom I afterward made Labor Commissioner, to succeed Wright himself, and Mr. Edward A. Moseley. Wilkes-Barre was the center of the strike; and the man in Wilkes-Barre who helped me most was Father Curran; I grew to know and trust and believe in him, and throughout my term in office, and afterward, he was not only my stanch friend, but one of the men by whose advice and counsel I profited most in matters affecting the welfare of the miners and their families.

I was greatly relieved at the result, for more than one reason. Of course, first and foremost, my concern was to avert a frightful calamity to the United States. In the next place I was anxious to save the great coal operators and all of the class of big propertied men, of which they were members, from the dreadful punishment which their own folly would have brought on them if I had not acted; and one of the exasperating things was that they were so blinded that they could not see that I was trying to save them from themselves and to avert, not only for their sakes, but for the sake of the country, the excesses which would have been indulged in at their expense if they had longer persisted in their conduct.

The great Anthracite Strike of 1902 left an indelible impress upon the people of the United States. It showed clearly to all wise and far-seeing men that the labor problem in this country had entered upon a new phase. Industry had grown. Great financial corporations, doing a nation-wide and even a worldwide business, had taken the place of the smaller concerns of an earlier time. The old familiar, intimate relations between employer and employee were passing. A few generations before, the boss had known every man in his shop; he called his men Bill, Tom, Dick, John; he inquired after their wives and babies; he swapped jokes and stories and perhaps a bit of tobacco with them. In the small establishment there had been a friendly human relationship between employer and employee.

There was no such relation between the great railway magnates, who controlled the anthracite industry, and the one hundred and fifty thousand men who worked in their mines, or the half million women and children who were dependent upon these miners for their daily bread. Very few of these mine workers had ever seen, for instance, the president of the Reading Railroad. Had they seen him many of them could not have spoken to him, for tens of thousands of the mine workers were recent immigrants who did not understand the language which he spoke and who spoke a language which he could not understand.

Again, a few generations ago an American workman could have saved money, gone West and taken up a homestead. Now the free lands were gone. In earlier days a man who began with pick and shovel might have come to own a mine. That outlet too was now closed, as regards the immense majority, and few, if any, of the one hundred and fifty thousand mine workers could ever aspire to enter the small circle of men who held in their grasp the great anthracite industry. The majority of the men who earned wages in the coal industry, if they wished to progress at all, were compelled to progress not by ceasing to be wage-earners, but by improving the conditions under which all the wage-earners in all the industries of the country lived and worked, as well, of course, as improving their own individual efficiency.

Another change which had come about as a result of the foregoing was a crass inequality in the bargaining relation between the employer and the individual employee standing alone. The great coal-mining and coal-carrying companies, which employed their tens of thousands, could easily dispense with the services of any particular miner. The miner, on the other hand, however expert, could not dispense with the companies. He needed a job; his wife and children would starve if he did not get one. What the miner had to sell — his labor — was a perishable commodity; the labor of to-day — if not sold to-day — was lost forever. Moreover, his labor was not like most commodities — a mere thing; it was part of a living, breathing human being. The workman saw, and all citizens who gave earnest thought to the matter saw, that the labor problem was not only an economic, but also a moral, a human problem. Individually the miners were impotent when they sought to enter a wage-contract with the great companies; they could make fair terms only by uniting into trade unions to bargain collectively. The men were forced to coöperate to secure not only their economic, but their simple human rights. They, like other workmen, were compelled by the very conditions under which they lived to unite in unions of their industry or trade, and these unions were bound to grow in size, in strength, and in power for good and evil as the industries in which the men were employed grew larger and larger.

A democracy can be such in fact only if there is some rough approximation to similarity in stature among the men composing it. One of us can deal in our private lives with the grocer or the butcher or the carpenter or the chicken raiser, or if we are the grocer or carpenter or butcher or farmer, we can deal with our customers, because *we are all of about the same size*. Therefore a simple and poor society can exist as a democracy on a basis of sheer individualism. But a rich and complex industrial society cannot so exist; for some individuals, and especially those artificial individuals called corporations, become so very big that the ordinary individual is utterly dwarfed beside them, and cannot deal with them on terms of equality. It therefore becomes necessary for these ordinary individuals to combine in their turn, first in order to act in their collective capacity through that biggest of all combinations called the Government, and second, to act, also in their own self-defense, through private combinations, such as farmer's associations and trade unions.

This the great coal operators did not see. They did not see that their property rights, which they so stoutly defended, were of the same texture as were the human rights, which they so blindly and hotly denied. They did not see that the power which they exercised of representing their stockholders was of the same texture as the power which the union leaders demanded of representing the workmen, who had democratically elected them. They did not see that the right to use one's property as one will can be maintained only so long as it is consistent with the maintenance of certain fundamental human rights, of the rights to life, liberty and the pursuit of happiness, or, as we may restate them in these later days, of the rights of the worker to a living wage, to reasonable hours of labor, to decent working and living conditions, to freedom of thought and speech and industrial representation, — in short, to a measure of industrial democracy and, in return for his arduous toil, to a worthy and decent life according to American standards. Still another thing these great business leaders did not see. They did not see that both their interests and the interests of the workers must be accommodated, and if need be, subordinated, to the fundamental permanent interests of the whole community. No man and no group of men may so exercise their rights as to deprive the nation of the things which are necessary and vital to the common life. A strike which ties up the coal supplies of a whole section is a strike invested with a public interest.

So great was that public interest in the Coal Strike of 1902, so deeply and strongly did I feel the wave of indignation which swept over the whole country that had I not succeeded in my efforts to induce the operators to listen to reason, I should reluctantly but none the less decisively have taken a step which would have brought down upon my head the execrations of many of "the captains of industry," as well as of sundry "respectable" newspapers who dutifully take their cue from them. As a man should be judged by his intentions as well as by his actions, I will give here the story of the intervention that never happened.

While the coal operators were exulting over the fact that they had "turned down" the miners and the President, there arose in all parts of the country an outburst of wrath so universal that even so naturally conservative a man as Grover Cleveland wrote to me, expressing his sympathy with the course I was following, his indignation at the conduct of the operators, and his hope that I would devise some method of effective action. In my own mind I was already planning effective action; but it was of a very drastic character, and I did not wish to take it until the failure of all other expedients had rendered it necessary. Above all, I did not wish to talk about it until and unless I actually acted. I had definitely determined that somehow or other act I would, that somehow or other the coal famine should be broken. To accomplish this end it was necessary that the mines should be run, and, if I could get no voluntary agreement between the contending sides, that an Arbitration Commission should be appointed which would command such public confidence as to enable me, without too much difficulty, to enforce its terms upon both parties. Ex-President Cleveland's letter not merely gratified me, but gave me the chance to secure him as head of the Arbitration Commission. I at once wrote him, stating that I would very probably have to appoint an Arbitration Commission or Investigating Commission to look into the matter and decide on the rights of the case, whether or not the operators asked for or agreed to abide by the decisions of such a Commission; and that I would ask him to accept the chief place on the Commission. He answered that he would do so. I picked out several first-class men for other positions on the Commission.

Meanwhile the Governor of Pennsylvania had all the Pennsylvania militia in the anthracite region, although without any effect upon the resumption of mining. The method of action upon which I had determined in the last resort was to get the Governor of Pennsylvania to ask me to keep order. Then I would put in the army under the command of some first-rate general. I would instruct this general to keep absolute order, taking any steps whatever that were necessary to prevent interference by the strikers or their sympathizers with men who wanted to work. I would also instruct him to dispossess the operators and run the mines as a receiver until such time as the Commission might make its report, and until I, as President, might issue further orders in view of this report. I had to find a man who possessed the necessary good sense, judgment, and nerve to act in such event. He was ready to hand in the person of Major-General Schofield. I sent for him, telling him that if I had to make use of him it would be because the crisis was only less serious than that of the Civil War, that the action taken would be practically a war measure, and that if I sent him he must act in a purely military capacity under me as commander-in-chief, paying no heed to any authority, judicial or otherwise, except mine. He was a fine fellow — a most respectable-looking old boy, with side

whiskers and a black skull-cap, without any of the outward
aspect of the conventional military dictator; but in both nerve
and judgment he was all right, and he answered quietly that
if I gave the order he would take possession of the mines, and
would guarantee to open them and to run them without permitting any interference either by the owners or the strikers
or anybody else, so long as I told him to stay. I then saw Senator Quay, who, like every other responsible man in high position, was greatly wrought up over the condition of things. I
told him that he need be under no alarm as to the problem
not being solved, that I was going to make another effort to
get the operators and miners to come together, but that I
would solve the problem in any event and get coal; that, however, I did not wish to tell him anything of the details of my
intention, but merely to have him arrange that whenever I
gave the word the Governor of Pennsylvania should request
me to intervene; that when this was done I would be responsible for all that followed, and would guarantee that the coal
famine would end forthwith. The Senator made no inquiry or
comment, and merely told me that he in his turn would guarantee that the Governor would request my intervention the
minute I asked that the request be made.

These negotiations were conducted with the utmost secrecy, General Schofield being the only man who knew exactly
what my plan was, and Senator Quay, two members of my
Cabinet, and ex-President Cleveland and the other men whom
I proposed to put on the Commission, the only other men
who knew that I had a plan. As I have above outlined, my
efforts to bring about an agreement between the operators and
miners were finally successful. I was glad not to have to take
possession of the mines on my own initiative by means of
General Schofield and the regulars. I was all ready to act, and
would have done so without the slightest hesitation or a
moment's delay if the negotiations had fallen through. And
my action would have been entirely effective. But it is never
well to take drastic action if the result can be achieved with
equal efficiency in less drastic fashion; and, although this was
a minor consideration, I was personally saved a good deal of
future trouble by being able to avoid this drastic action. At
the time I should have been almost unanimously supported.

With the famine upon them the people would not have tolerated any conduct that would have thwarted what I was doing.
Probably no man in Congress, and no man in the Pennsylvania State Legislature, would have raised his voice against me.
Although there would have been plenty of muttering, nothing would have been done to interfere with the solution of
the problem which I had devised, *until the solution was accomplished and the problem ceased to be a problem*. Once this
was done, and when people were no longer afraid of a coal
famine, and began to forget that they ever had been afraid of
it, and to be indifferent as regards the consequences to those
who put an end to it, then my enemies would have plucked
up heart and begun a campaign against me. I doubt if they
could have accomplished much anyway, for the only effective
remedy against me would have been impeachment, and that
they would not have ventured to try.*

*One of my appointees on the Anthracite Strike Commission was Judge
George Gray, of Delaware, a Democrat whose standing in the country was
second only to that of Grover Cleveland. A year later he commented on my
action as follows:

"I have no hesitation in saying that the President of the United States was
confronted in October, 1902, by the existence of a crisis more grave and
threatening than any that had occurred since the Civil War. I mean that the
cessation of mining in the anthracite country, brought about by the dispute
between the miners and those who controlled the greatest natural monopoly
in this country and perhaps in the world, had brought upon more than one-
half of the American people a condition of deprivation of one of the necessaries of life, and the probable continuance of the dispute threatened not
only the comfort and health, but the safety and good order, of the nation. He
was without legal or constitutional power to interfere, but his position as
President of the United States gave him an influence, a leadership, as first citizen of the republic, that enabled him to appeal to the patriotism and good
sense of the parties to the controversy and to place upon them the moral co-
ercion of public opinion to agree to an arbitrament of the strike then existing and threatening consequences so direful to the whole country. He acted
promptly and courageously, and in so doing averted the dangers to which I
have alluded.

"So far from interfering or infringing upon property rights, the President's
action tended to conserve them. The peculiar situation, as regards the anthracite coal interest, was that they controlled a natural monopoly of a product necessary to the comfort and to the very life of a large portion of the
people. A prolonged deprivation of the enjoyment of this necessary of life
would have tended to precipitate an attack upon these property rights of
which you speak; for, after all, it is vain to deny that this property, so pecu-

They would doubtless have acted precisely as they acted as regards the acquisition of the Panama Canal Zone in 1903, and the stoppage of the panic of 1907 by my action in the Tennessee Coal and Iron Company matter. Nothing could have made the American people surrender the canal zone. But after it was an accomplished fact, and the canal was under way, then they settled down to comfortable acceptance of the accomplished fact, and as their own interests were no longer in jeopardy, they paid no heed to the men who attacked me because of what I had done — and also continue to attack me, although they are exceedingly careful not to propose to right the "wrong," in the only proper way if it really was a wrong, by replacing the old Republic of Panama under the tyranny of Colombia and giving Colombia sole or joint ownership of the canal itself. In the case of the panic of 1907 (as in the case of Panama), what I did was not only done openly, but depended for its effect upon being done openly and with the widest advertisement. Nobody in Congress ventured to make an objection at the time. No serious leader outside made any objection. The one concern of everybody was to stop the panic, and everybody was overjoyed that I was willing to take the responsibility of stopping it upon my own shoulders. But a few months afterward, the panic was a thing of the past. People forgot the frightful condition of alarm in which they had been. They no longer had a personal interest in preventing any interference with the stoppage of the panic. Then the men who had not dared to raise their voices until all danger was past came bravely forth from their hiding places and denounced the action which had saved them. They had kept a hushed silence when there was danger; they made clamorous outcry when there was safety in doing so.

Just the same course would have been followed in connection with the Anthracite Coal Strike if I had been obliged to act in the fashion I intended to act had I failed to secure a

---

liar in its conditions, and which is properly spoken of as a natural monopoly, is affected with a public interest.

"I do not think that any President ever acted more wisely, courageously or promptly in a national crisis. Mr. Roosevelt deserves unstinted praise for what he did."

voluntary agreement between the miners and the operators. Even as it was, my action was remembered with rancor by the heads of the great monied interests; and as time went by was assailed with constantly increasing vigor by the newspapers these men controlled. Had I been forced to take possession of the mines, these men and the politicians hostile to me would have waited until the popular alarm was over and the popular needs met, just as they waited in the case of the Tennessee Coal and Iron Company; and then they would have attacked me precisely as they did attack me as regards the Tennessee Coal and Iron Company.

Of course, in labor controversies it was not always possible to champion the cause of the workers, because in many cases strikes were called which were utterly unwarranted and were fought by methods which cannot be too harshly condemned. No straightforward man can believe, and no fearless man will assert, that a trade union is always right. That man is an unworthy public servant who by speech or silence, by direct statement or cowardly evasion, invariably throws the weight of his influence on the side of the trade union, whether it is right or wrong. It has occasionally been my duty to give utterance to the feelings of all right thinking men by expressing the most emphatic disapproval of unwise or even immoral actions by representatives of labor. The man is no true democrat, and if an American, is unworthy of the traditions of his country who, in problems calling for the exercise of a moral judgment, fails to take his stand on conduct and not on class. There are good and bad wage-workers just as there are good and bad employers, and good and bad men of small means and of large means alike.

But a willingness to do equal and exact justice to all citizens, irrespective of race, creed, section or economic interest and position, does not imply a failure to recognize the enormous economic, political and moral possibilities of the trade union. Just as democratic government cannot be condemned because of errors and even crimes committed by men democratically elected, so trade-unionism must not be condemned because of errors or crimes of occasional trade-union leaders. The problem lies deeper. While we must repress all illegalities and discourage all immoralities, whether of labor organizations or of corporations, we must recognize the fact that to-day the organization of labor into trade unions and federations is necessary, is beneficent, and is one of the greatest possible agencies in the attainment of a true industrial, as well as a true political, democracy in the United States.

This is a fact which many well-intentioned people even to-day do not understand. They do not understand that the labor problem is a human and a moral as well as an economic problem; that a fall in wages, an increase in hours, a deterioration of labor conditions mean wholesale moral as well as economic degeneration, and the needless sacrifice of human lives and human happiness, while a rise of wages, a lessening of hours, a bettering of conditions, mean an intellectual, moral and social uplift of millions of American men and women. There are employers to-day who, like the great coal operators, speak as though they were lords of these countless armies of Americans, who toil in factory, in shop, in mill and in the dark places under the earth. They fail to see that all these men have the right and the duty to combine to protect themselves and their families from want and degradation. They fail to see that the Nation and the Government, within the range of fair play and a just administration of the law, must inevitably sympathize with the men who have nothing but their wages, with the men who are struggling for a decent life, as opposed to men, however honorable, who are merely fighting for larger profits and an autocratic control of big business. Each man should have all he earns, whether by brain or body; and the director, the great industrial leader, is one of the greatest of earners, and should have a proportional reward; but no man should live on the earnings of another, and there should not be too gross inequality between service and reward.

There are many men to-day, men of integrity and intelligence, who honestly believe that we must go back to the labor conditions of half a century ago. They are opposed to trade unions, root and branch. They note the unworthy conduct of many labor leaders, they find instances of bad work by union men, of a voluntary restriction of output, of vexatious and violent strikes, of jurisdictional disputes between unions which often disastrously involve the best intentioned and fairest of employers. All these things occur and should be repressed. But the same critic of the trade union might find equal cause of complaint against individual employers of labor, or even against great associations of manufacturers. He might find many instances of an unwarranted cutting of wages, of flagrant violations of factory laws and tenement house laws, of the deliberate and systematic cheating of employees by means of truck stores, of the speeding up of work to a point which is fatal to the health of the workman, of the sweating of foreign-born workers, of the drafting of feeble little children into dusty workshops, of black-listing, of putting spies into union meetings and of the employment in strike times of vicious and desperate ruffians, who are neither better nor worse than are the thugs who are occasionally employed by unions under the sinister name, "entertainment committees." I believe that the overwhelming majority, both of workmen and of employers, are law-abiding, peaceful, and honorable citizens, and I do not think that it is just to lay up the errors and wrongs of individuals to the entire group to which they belong. I also think — and this is a belief which has been borne upon me through many years of practical experience — that the trade union is growing constantly in wisdom as well as in power, and is becoming one of the most efficient agencies toward the solution of our industrial problems, the elimination of poverty and of industrial disease and accidents, the lessening of unemployment, the achievement of industrial democracy and the attainment of a larger measure of social and industrial justice.

If I were a factory employee, a workman on the railroads or a wage-earner of any sort, I would undoubtedly join the union of my trade. If I disapproved of its policy, I would join in order to fight that policy; if the union leaders were dishonest, I would join in order to put them out. I believe in the union and I believe that all men who are benefited by the union are morally bound to help to the extent of their power in the common interests advanced by the union. Nevertheless, irrespective of whether a man should or should not, and does or does not, join the union of his trade, all the rights, privileges and immunities of that man as an American and as a citizen should be safeguarded and upheld by the law. We dare not make an outlaw of any individual or any group, whatever his or its opinions or professions. The non-unionist, like the unionist, must be protected in all his legal rights by the full weight and power of the law.

This question came up before me in the shape of the right of a non-union printer named Miller to hold his position in the Government Printing Office. As I said before, I believe in trade unions. I always prefer to see a union shop. But my private preferences cannot control my public actions. The Government can recognize neither union men nor non-union men as such, and is bound to treat both exactly alike. In the Government Printing Office not many months prior to the opening of the Presidential campaign of 1904, when I was up for reëlection, I discovered that a man had been dismissed because he did not belong to the union. I reinstated him. Mr. Gompers, the President of the American Federation of Labor, with various members of the executive council of that body, called upon me to protest on September 29, 1903, and I answered them as follows:

"I thank you and your committee for your courtesy, and I appreciate the opportunity to meet with you. It will always be a pleasure to see you or any representatives of your organizations or of your Federation as a whole.

"As regards the Miller case, I have little to add to what I have already said. In dealing with it I ask you to remember that I am dealing purely with the relation of the Government to its employees. I must govern my action by the laws of the land, which I am sworn to administer, and which differentiate any case in which the Government of the United States is a party from all other cases whatsoever. These laws are enacted for the benefit of the whole people, and cannot and must not be construed as permitting discrimination against some of the people. I am President of all the people of the United States, without regard to creed, color, birthplace, occupation or social condition. My aim is to do equal and exact justice as among them all. In the employment and dismissal of men in the Government service I can no more recognize the fact that a man does or does not belong to a union as being for or against him than I can recognize the fact that he is a Protestant or a Catholic, a Jew or a Gentile, as being for or against him.

"In the communications sent me by various labor organizations protesting against the retention of Miller in the

The Coal Miners.

Government Printing Office, the grounds alleged are twofold: 1, that he is a non-union man; 2, that he is not personally fit. The question of his personal fitness is one to be settled in the routine of administrative detail, and cannot be allowed to conflict with or to complicate the larger question of governmental discrimination for or against him or any other man because he is or is not a member of a union. This is the only question now before me for decision; and as to this my decision is final."

Because of things I have done on behalf of justice to the workingman, I have often been called a Socialist. Usually I have not taken the trouble even to notice the epithet. I am not afraid of names, and I am not one of those who fear to do what is right because some one else will confound me with partisans with whose principles I am not in accord. Moreover, I know that many American Socialists are high-minded and honorable citizens, who in reality are merely radical social reformers. They are oppressed by the brutalities and industrial injustices which we see everywhere about us. When I recall how often I have seen Socialists and ardent non-Socialists working side by side for some specific measure of social or industrial reform, and how I have found opposed to them on the side of privilege many shrill reactionaries who insist on calling all reformers Socialists, I refuse to be panic-stricken by having this title mistakenly applied to me.

None the less, without impugning their motives, I do disagree most emphatically with both the fundamental philosophy and the proposed remedies of the Marxian Socialists. These Socialists are unalterably opposed to our whole industrial system. They believe that the payment of wages means everywhere and inevitably an exploitation of the laborer by the employer, and that this leads inevitably to a class war between those two groups, or, as they would say, between the capitalists and the proletariat. They assert that this class war is already upon us and can only be ended when capitalism is entirely destroyed and all the machines, mills, mines, railroads and other private property used in production are confiscated, expropriated or taken over by the workers. They do not as a rule claim — although some of the sinister extremists among them do — that this class war is a war of blood and bullets, but they do claim that there is and must be a continual struggle between two great classes, whose interests are opposed and cannot be reconciled. In this war they insist that the whole government — National, State and local — is on the side of the employers and is used by them against the workmen, and that our law and even our common morality are class weapons, like a policeman's club or a Gatling gun.

I have never believed, and do not to-day believe, that such a class war is upon us, or need ever be upon us; nor do I believe that the interests of wage-earners and employers cannot be harmonized, compromised and adjusted. It would be idle to deny that wage-earners have certain different economic interests from, let us say, manufacturers or importers, just as farmers have different interests from sailors, and fishermen from bankers. There is no reason why any of these economic groups should not consult their group interests by any legitimate means and with due regard to the common, overlying interests of all. I do not even deny that the majority of wage-earners, because they have less property and less industrial security than others and because they do not own the machinery with which they work (as does the farmer) are perhaps in greater need of acting together than are other groups in the community. But I do insist (and I believe that the great majority of wage-earners take the same view) that employers and employees have overwhelming interests in common, both as partners in industry and as citizens of the Republic, and that where these interests are apart they can be adjusted by so altering our laws and their interpretation as to secure to all members of the community social and industrial justice.

I have always maintained that our worst revolutionaries to-day are those reactionaries who do not see and will not admit that there is any need for change. Such men seem to believe that the four and a half million Progressive voters, who in 1912 registered their solemn protest against our social and industrial injustices, are "anarchists," who are not willing to let ill enough alone. If these reactionaries had lived at an earlier time in our history, they would have advocated Sedition Laws, opposed free speech and free assembly, and voted against free schools, free access by settlers to the public lands, mechanics' lien laws, the prohibition of truck stores and the abolition of imprisonment for debt; and they are the men who to-day oppose minimum wage laws; insurance of workmen against the ills of industrial life and the reform of our legislatures and our courts, which can alone render such measures possible. Some of these reactionaries are not bad men, but merely short-sighted and belated. It is these reactionaries, however, who, by "standing pat" on industrial injustice, incite inevitably to industrial revolt, and it is only we who advocate political and industrial democracy who render possible the progress of our American industry on large constructive lines with a minimum of friction because with a maximum of justice.

Everything possible should be done to secure the wage-workers fair treatment. There should be an increased wage for the worker of increased productiveness. Everything possible should be done against the capitalist who strives, not to reward special efficiency, but to use it as an excuse for reducing the reward of moderate efficiency. The capitalist is an unworthy citizen who pays the efficient man no more than he has been content to pay the average man, and nevertheless reduces the wage of the average man; and effort should be made by the Government to check and punish him. When labor-saving machinery is introduced, special care should be taken — by the Government if necessary — to see that the wage-worker gets his share of the benefit, and that it is not all absorbed by the employer or capitalist. The following case, which has come to my knowledge, illustrates what I mean. A number of new machines were installed in a certain shoe factory, and as a result there was a heavy increase in production even though there was no increase in the labor force. Some of the workmen were instructed in the use of these machines by special demonstrators sent out by the makers of the machines. These men, by reason of their special aptitudes and the fact that they were not called upon to operate the machines continuously nine hours every day, week in and week out, but only for an hour or so at special times, were naturally able to run the machines at their maximum capacity. When these demonstrators had left the factory, and the company's own employees had become used to operating the machines at a fair rate of speed, the foreman of the establishment gradually speeded the machines and demanded a larger and still larger output, constantly endeavoring to drive the men on to greater exertions. Even with a slightly less maximum capacity, the introduction of this machinery resulted in a great increase over former production with the same amount of labor; and so great were the profits from the business in the following two years as to equal the total capitalized stock of the company. But not a cent got into the pay envelope of the workmen beyond what they had formerly been receiving before the introduction of this new machinery, notwithstanding that it had meant an added strain, physical and mental, upon their energies, and that they were forced to work harder than ever before. The whole of the increased profits remained with the company. Now this represented an "increase of efficiency," with a positive decrease of social and industrial justice. The increase of prosperity which came from increase of production in no way benefited the wage-workers. I hold that they were treated with gross injustice; and that society, acting if necessary through the Government, in such a case should bend its energies to remedy such injustice; and I will support any proper legislation that will aid in securing the desired end.

The wage-worker should not only receive fair treatment; he should give fair treatment. In order that prosperity may be passed around it is necessary that the prosperity exist. In order that labor shall receive its fair share in the division of reward it is necessary that there be a reward to divide. Any proposal to reduce efficiency by insisting that the most efficient shall be limited in their output to what the least efficient can do, is a proposal to limit by so much production, and therefore to impoverish by so much the public, and specifically to reduce the amount that can be divided among the producers. This is all wrong. Our protest must be against unfair division of the reward for production. Every encouragement should be given the business man, the employer, to make his business prosperous, and therefore to earn more money for himself; and in like fashion every encouragement should be given the efficient workman. We must always keep in mind that to reduce the amount of production serves merely to reduce the amount that is to be divided, is in no way permanently efficient as a protest against unequal distribution and is permanently detrimental to the entire community. But increased productiveness is not secured by excessive labor amid unhealthy surroundings. The contrary is true. Shorter hours, and healthful conditions, and opportunity for the wage-worker to make more money, and the chance for enjoyment as well as work, all add to efficiency. My contention is that there should be no penalization of efficient productiveness, brought about under healthy conditions; but that every increase of production brought about by an increase in efficiency should benefit all the parties to it, including wage-workers as well as employers or capitalists, men who work with their hands as well as men who work with their heads.

With the Western Federation of Miners I more than once had serious trouble. The leaders of this organization had preached anarchy, and certain of them were indicted for having practiced murder in the case of Governor Steunenberg, of Idaho. On one occasion in a letter or speech I coupled condemnation of these labor leaders and condemnation of certain big capitalists, describing them all alike as "undesirable citizens." This gave great offense to both sides. The open attack upon me was made for the most part either by the New York newspapers which were frankly representatives of Wall Street, or else by those so-called — and miscalled — Socialists who had anarchistic leanings. Many of the latter sent me open letters of denunciation, and to one of them I responded as follows:

THE WHITE HOUSE, WASHINGTON,
April 22, 1907.

*Dear Sir:*

I have received your letter of the 19th instant, in which you enclose the draft of the formal letter which is to follow. I have been notified that several delegations, bearing similar requests, are on the way hither. In the letter you, on behalf of the Cook County Moyer-Haywood conference, protest against certain language I used in a recent letter which you assert to be designed to influence the course of justice in the case of the trial for murder of Messrs. Moyer and Haywood. I entirely agree with you that it is improper to endeavor to influence the course of justice, whether by threats or in any similar manner. For this reason I have regretted most deeply the actions of such organizations as your own in undertaking to accomplish this very result in the very case of which you speak. For instance, your letter is headed "Cook County Moyer-Haywood-Pettibone

Conference," with the headlines: "*Death* — cannot — will not — and shall not claim our brothers!" This shows that you and your associates are not demanding a fair trial, or working for a fair trial, but are announcing in advance that the verdict shall only be one way and that you will not tolerate any other verdict. Such action is flagrant in its impropriety, and I join heartily in condemning it.

But it is a simple absurdity to suppose that because any man is on trial for a given offense he is therefore to be freed from all criticism upon his general conduct and manner of life. In my letter to which you object I referred to a certain prominent financier, Mr. Harriman, on the one hand, and to Messrs Moyer, Haywood and Debs on the other, as being equally undesirable citizens. It is as foolish to assert that this was designed to influence the trial of Moyer and Haywood as to assert that it was designed to influence the suits that have been brought against Mr. Harriman. I neither expressed nor indicated any opinion as to whether Messrs. Moyer and Haywood were guilty of the murder of Governor Steunenberg. If they are guilty, they certainly ought to be punished. If they are not guilty, they certainly ought not to be punished. But no possible outcome either of the trial or the suits can affect my judgment as to the undesirability of the type of citizenship of those whom I mentioned. Messrs. Moyer, Haywood, and Debs stand as representatives of those men who have done as much to discredit the labor movement as the worst speculative financiers or most unscrupulous employers of labor and debauchers of legislatures have done to discredit honest capitalists and fair-dealing business men. They stand as the representatives of those men who by their public utterances and manifestoes, by the utterances of the papers they control or inspire, and by the words and deeds of those associated with or subordinated to them, habitually appear as guilty of incitement to or apology for bloodshed and violence. If this does not constitute undesirable citizenship, then there can never be any undesirable citizens. The men whom I denounce represent the men who have abandoned that legitimate movement for the uplifting of labor, with which I have the most hearty sympathy; they have adopted practices which cut them off from those who lead this legitimate movement. In every way I shall support the law-abiding and upright representatives of labor; and in no way can I better support them than by drawing the sharpest possible line between them on the one hand, and, on the other hand, those preachers of violence who are themselves the worst foes of the honest laboring man.

Let me repeat my deep regret that any body of men should so far forget their duty to the country as to endeavor by the formation of societies and in other ways to influence the course of justice in this

Breaker Boys.

matter. I have received many such letters as yours. Accompanying them were newspaper clippings announcing demonstrations, parades, and mass-meetings designed to show that the representatives of labor, without regard to the facts, demand the acquittal of Messrs. Haywood and Moyer. Such meetings can, of course, be designed only to coerce court or jury in rendering a verdict, and they therefore deserve all the condemnation which you in your letters say should be awarded to those who endeavor improperly to influence the course of justice.

You would, of course, be entirely within your rights if you merely announced that you thought Messrs. Moyer and Haywood were "desirable citizens" — though in such case I should take frank issue with you and should say that, wholly without regard to whether or not they are guilty of the crime for which they are now being tried, they represent as thoroughly undesirable a type of citizenship as can be found in this country; a type which, in the letter to which you so unreasonably take exception, I showed not to be confined to any one class, but to exist among some representatives of great capitalists as well as among some representatives of wage-workers. In that letter I condemned both types. Certain representatives of the great capitalists in turn condemned me for including Mr. Harriman in my condemnation of Messrs. Moyer and Haywood. Certain of the representatives of labor in their turn condemned me because I included Messrs. Moyer and Haywood as undesirable citizens together with Mr. Harriman. I am as profoundly indifferent to the condemnation in one case as in the other. I challenge as a right the support of all good Americans, whether wage-workers or capitalists, whatever their occupation or creed, or in whatever portion of the country they live, when I condemn both the types of bad citizenship which I have held up to reprobation. It seems to be a mark of utter insincerity to fail thus to condemn both; and to apologize for either robs the man thus apologizing of all right to condemn any wrongdoing in any man, rich or poor, in public or in private life.

You say you ask for a "square deal" for Messrs. Moyer and Haywood. So do I. When I say "square deal," I mean a square deal to every one; it is equally a violation of the policy of the square deal for a capitalist to protest against denunciation of a capitalist who is guilty of wrongdoing and for a labor leader to protest against the denunciation of a labor leader who has been guilty of wrongdoing. I stand for equal justice to both; and so far as in my power lies I shall uphold justice, whether the man accused of guilt has behind him the wealthiest corporations, the greatest aggregations of riches in the country, or whether he has behind him the most influential labor organizations in the country.

I treated anarchists and the bomb-throwing and dynamiting gentry precisely as I treated other criminals. Murder is murder. It is not rendered one whit better by the allegation that it is committed on behalf of "a cause." It is true that law and order are not all-sufficient; but they are essential; lawlessness and murderous violence must be quelled before any permanence of reform can be obtained. Yet when they have been quelled, the beneficiaries of the enforcement of law must in their turn be taught that law is upheld as a means to the enforcement of justice, and that we will not tolerate its being turned into an engine of injustice and oppression. The fundamental need in dealing with our people, whether laboring men or others, is not charity but justice; we must all work in common for the common end of helping each and all, in a spirit of the sanest, broadest and deepest brotherhood.

It was not always easy to avoid feeling very deep anger with the selfishness and short-sightedness shown both by the representatives of certain employers' organizations and by certain great labor federations or unions. One such employers' association was called the National Association of Manufacturers. Extreme though the attacks sometimes made upon me by the extreme labor organizations were, they were not quite as extreme as the attacks made upon me by the head of the National Association of Manufacturers, and as regards their attitude toward legislation I came to the conclusion toward the end of my term that the latter had actually gone further the wrong way than did the former — and the former went a good distance also. The opposition of the National Association of Manufacturers to every rational and moderate measure for benefiting workingmen, such as measures abolishing child labor, or securing workmen's compensation, caused me real and grave concern; for I felt that it was ominous of evil for the whole country to have men who ought to stand high in wisdom and in guiding force take a course and use language of such reactionary type as directly to incite revolution — for this is what the extreme reactionary always does.

Often I was attacked by the two sides at once. In the spring of 1906 I received in the same mail a letter from a very good friend of mine who thought that I had been unduly hard on some labor men, and a letter from another friend, the head of a great corporation, who complained about me for both favoring labor and speaking against large fortunes. My answers ran as follows:

April 26, 1906.

"Personal.
*My dear Doctor:*

In one of my last letters to you I enclosed you a copy of a letter of mine, in which I quoted from [So and so's] advocacy of murder. You may be interested to know that he and his brother Socialists — in reality anarchists — of the frankly murderous type have been violently attacking my speech because of my allusion to the sympathy expressed for murder. In *The Socialist*, of Toledo, Ohio, of April 21st, for instance, the attack [on me] is based specifically on the following paragraph of my speech, to which he takes violent exception:

We can no more and no less afford to condone evil in the man of capital than evil in the man of no capital. The wealthy man who exults because there is a failure of justice in the effort to bring some trust magnate to an account for his misdeeds is as bad as, and no worse than, the so-called labor leader who clamorously strives to excite a foul class feeling on behalf of some other labor leader who is implicated in murder. One attitude is as bad as the other, and no worse; in each case the accused is entitled to exact justice; and in neither case is there need of action by others which can be construed into an expression of sympathy for crime.

Remember, that this crowd of labor leaders have done all in their power to overawe the executive and the courts of Idaho on behalf of men accused of murder, and beyond question inciters of murder in the past."

April 26, 1906.

"*My dear Judge:*

I wish the papers had given more prominence to what I said as to the murder part of my speech. But oh, my dear sir, I utterly and radically disagree with you in what you say about large fortunes. I wish it were in my power to devise some scheme to make it increasingly difficult to heap them up beyond a certain amount. As the difficulties in the way of such a scheme are very great, let us at least prevent their being bequeathed after death or given during life to any one man in excessive amount.

You and other capitalist friends, on one side, shy off at what I say against them. Have you seen the frantic articles against me by [the anarchists and] the Socialists of the bomb-throwing persuasion, on the other side, because of what I said in my speech in reference to whose who, in effect, advocate murder?"

On another occasion I was vehemently denounced in certain capitalistic papers because I had a number of labor leaders, including miners from Butte, lunch with me at the White House; and this at the very time that the Western Federation of Miners was most ferocious in its denunciation of me because of what it alleged to be my unfriendly attitude toward labor. To one of my critics I set forth my views in the following letter:

November 26, 1903.

"I have your letter of the 25th instant, with enclosure. These men, not all of whom were miners, by the way, came here and were at lunch with me, in company with Mr. Carroll D. Wright, Mr. Wayne MacVeagh, and Secretary Cortelyou. They are as decent a set of men as can be. They all agreed entirely with me in my denunciation of what had been done in the Cœur d'Alene country; and it appeared that some of them were on the platform with me when I denounced this type of outrage three years ago in Butte. There is not one man who was here, who, I believe, was in any way, shape or form responsible for such outrages. I find that the ultra-Socialistic members of the unions in Butte denounced these men for coming here, in a manner as violent — and I may say as irrational — as the denunciation [by the capitalistic writer] in the article you sent me. Doubtless the gentleman of whom you speak as your general manager is an admirable man. I, of course, was not alluding to him; but I most emphatically *was* alluding to men who write such articles as that you sent me. These articles are to be paralleled by the similar articles in the Populist and Socialist papers when two years ago I had at dinner at one time Pierpont Morgan, and at another time J. J. Hill, and at another, Harriman, and at another time Schiff. Furthermore, they could be paralleled by the articles in the same type of paper which at the time of the Miller incident in the Printing Office were in a condition of nervous anxiety because I met the labor leaders to discuss it. It would have been a great misfortune if I had not met them; and it would have been an even greater misfortune if after meeting them I had yielded to their protests in the matter.

You say in your letter that you know that I am "on record" as opposed to violence. Pardon my saying that this seems to me not the right way to put the matter, if by "record" you mean utterance and not action. Aside from what happened when I was Governor in connection, for instance, with the Croton dam strike riots, all you have to do is to turn back to what took place last June in Arizona — and you can find out about it from [Mr. X] of New York. The miners struck, violence followed, and the Arizona Territorial authorities notified me they could not grapple with the situation. Within twenty minutes of the receipt of the telegram, orders were issued to the nearest available troops, and twenty-four hours afterwards General Baldwin and his regulars were on the ground, and twenty-four hours later every vestige of disorder had disappeared. The Miners' Federation in their meeting, I think at Denver, a short while afterwards, passed resolutions denouncing me. I do not know whether the *Mining and Engineering Journal* paid any heed to this incident or knew of it. If the *Journal* did, I suppose it can hardly have failed to understand that to put an immediate stop to rioting by the use of the United States army is a fact of importance beside which the criticism of my having "labor leaders" to lunch, shrinks into the same insignificance as the criticism in a different type of paper about my having "trust magnates" to lunch. While I am President I wish the labor man to feel that he has the same right of access to me that the capitalist has; that the doors swing open as easily to the wage-worker as to the head of a big corporation — *and no easier*. Anything else seems to be not only un-American, but as symptomatic of an attitude which will cost grave trouble if persevered in. To discriminate against labor men from Butte because there is reason to believe that rioting has been excited in other districts by certain labor unions, or individuals in labor unions in Butte, would be to adopt precisely the attitude of those who desire me to discriminate against all capitalists in Wall Street because there are plenty of capitalists in Wall Street who have been guilty of bad financial practices and who have endeavored to override or evade the laws of the land. In my judgment, the only safe attitude for a private citizen, and still more for a public servant, to assume, is that he will draw the line on conduct, discriminating against neither corporation nor union as such, nor in favor of either as such, but endeavoring to make the decent member of the union and the upright capitalists alike feel that they are bound, not only by self-interest, but by every consideration of principle and duty to stand together on the matters of most moment to the nation."

On another of the various occasions when I had labor leaders to dine at the White House, my critics were rather shocked because I had John Morley to meet them. The labor leaders in question included the heads of the various railroad brotherhoods, men like Mr. Morrissey, in whose sound judgment and high standard of citizenship I had peculiar confidence; and I asked Mr. Morley to meet them because they represented the exact type of American citizen with whom I thought he ought to be brought in contact.

One of the devices sometimes used by big corporations to break down the law was to treat the passage of laws as an excuse for action on their part which they knew would be resented by the public, it being their purpose to turn this resentment against the law instead of against themselves. The heads of the Louisville and Nashville road were bitter opponents of everything done by the Government toward securing good treatment for their employees. In February, 1908, they and various other railways announced that they intended to reduce the wages of their employees. A general strike, with all the attendant disorder and trouble, was threatened in consequence. I accordingly sent the following open letter to the Inter-State Commerce Commission:

February 18, 1908.

*"To the Inter-State Commerce Commission:*

I am informed that a number of railroad companies have served notice of a proposed reduction of wages of their employees. One of them, the Louisville and Nashville, in announcing the reduction, states that "the drastic laws inimical to the interests of the railroads that have in the past year or two been enacted by Congress and the State Legislatures" are largely or chiefly responsible for the conditions requiring the reduction.

Under such circumstances it is possible that the public may soon be confronted by serious industrial disputes, and the law provides that in such case either party may demand the services of your Chairman and of the Commissioner of Labor as a Board of Mediation and Conciliation. These reductions in wages may be warranted, or they may not. As to this the public, which is a vitally interested party, can form no judgment without a more complete knowledge of the essential facts and real merits of the case than it now has or than it can possibly obtain from the special pleadings, certain to be put forth by each side in case their dispute should bring about serious interruption to traffic. If the reduction in wages is due to natural causes, the loss of business being such that the burden should be, and is, equitably distributed between capitalist and wage-worker, the public should know it. If it is caused by legislation, the public, and Congress, should know it; and if it is caused by misconduct in the past financial or other operations of any railroad, then everybody should know it, especially if the excuse of unfriendly legislation is advanced as a method of covering up past business misconduct by the railroad managers, or as a justification for failure to treat fairly the wage-earning employees of the company.

Moreover, an industrial conflict between a railroad corporation and its employees offers peculiar opportunities to any small number of evil-disposed persons to destroy life and property and foment public disorder. Of course, if life, property, and public order are endangered, prompt and drastic measures for their protection become the first plain duty. All other issues then become subordinate to the preservation of the public peace, and the real merits of the original controversy are necessarily lost from view. This vital consideration should be ever kept in mind by all law-abiding and far-sighted members of labor organizations.

It is sincerely to be hoped, therefore, that any wage controversy that may arise between the railroads and their employees may find a peaceful solution through the methods of conciliation and arbitration already provided by Congress, which have proven so effective during the past year. To this end the Commission should be in a position to have available for any Board of Conciliation or Arbitration relevant data pertaining to such carriers as may become involved in industrial disputes. Should conciliation fail to effect a settlement and arbitration be rejected, accurate information should be available in order to develop a properly informed public opinion.

I therefore ask you to make such investigations, both of your records and by any other means at your command, as will enable you to furnish data concerning such conditions obtaining on the Louisville and Nashville and any other roads, as may relate, directly or indirectly, to the real merits of the possibly impending controversy.

THEODORE ROOSEVELT."

This letter achieved its purpose, and the threatened reduction of wages was not made. It was an instance of what could be accomplished by governmental action. Let me add, however, with all the emphasis I possess, that this does not mean any failure on my part to recognize the fact that if governmental action places too heavy burdens on railways, it will be impossible for them to operate without doing injustice to somebody. Railways cannot pay proper wages and render proper service unless they make money. The investors must get a reasonable profit or they will not invest, and the public cannot be well served unless the investors are making reasonable profits. There is every reason why rates should not be too high, but they must be sufficiently high to allow the railways to pay good wages. Moreover, when laws like workmen's compensation laws, and the like are passed, it must always be kept in mind by the Legislature that the purpose is to distribute over the whole community a burden that should not be borne only by those least able to bear it — that is, by the injured man or the widow and orphans of the dead man. If the railway is already receiving a disproportionate return from the public, then the burden may, with propriety, bear purely on the railway; but if it is not earning a disproportionate return, then the public must bear its share of the burden of the increased service the railway is rendering. Dividends and wages should go up together; and the relation of rates to them should never be forgotten. This of course does not apply to dividends based on water; nor does it mean that if foolish people have built a road that renders no service, the public must nevertheless in some way guarantee a return on the investment; but it does mean that the interests of the honest investor are entitled to the same protection as the interests of the honest manager, the honest shipper and the honest wage earner. All these conflicting considerations should be carefully considered by Legislatures before passing laws. One of the great objects in creating commissions should be the provision of disinterested, fair-minded experts who will really and wisely consider all these matters, and will shape their actions accordingly. This is one reason why such matters as the regulation of rates, the provision for full crews on roads and the like should be left for treatment by railway commissions, and not be settled off hand by direct legislative action.

# APPENDIX

## SOCIALISM

As regards what I have said in this chapter concerning Socialism, I wish to call especial attention to the admirable book on "Marxism versus Socialism," which has just been published by Vladimir D. Simkhovitch. What I have, here and elsewhere, merely pointed out in rough and ready fashion from actual observation of the facts of life around me, Professor Simkhovitch in his book has discussed with keen practical insight, with profundity of learning, and with a wealth of applied philosophy. Crude thinkers in the United States, and moreover honest and intelligent men who are not crude thinkers, but who are oppressed by the sight of the misery around them and have not deeply studied what has been done elsewhere, are very apt to adopt as their own the theories of European Marxian Socialists of half a century ago, ignorant that the course of events has so completely falsified the prophecies contained in these theories that they have been abandoned even by the authors themselves. With quiet humor Professor Simkhovitch now and then makes an allusion which shows that he appreciates to perfection this rather curious quality of some of our fellow countrymen; as for example when he says that "A Socialist State with the farmer outside of it is a conception that can rest comfortably only in the head of an American Socialist," or as when he speaks of Marx and Engels as men "to whom thinking was not an irrelevant foreign tradition." Too many thoroughly well-meaning men and women in the America of to-day glibly repeat and accept — much as medieval schoolmen repeated and accepted authorized dogma in their day — various assumptions and speculations by Marx and others which by the lapse of time and by actual experiment have been shown to possess not one shred of value. Professor Simkhovitch possesses the gift of condensation as well as the gift of clear and logical statement, and it is not possible to give in brief any idea of his admirable work. Every social reformer who desires to face facts should study it — just as social reformers should study John Graham Brooks's "American Syndicalism." From Professor Simkhovitch's book we Americans should learn: First, to discard crude thinking; second, to realize that the orthodox or so-called scientific or purely economic or materialistic socialism of the type preached by Marx is an exploded theory; and, third, that many of the men who call themselves Socialists to-day are in reality merely radical social reformers, with whom on many points good citizens can and ought to work in hearty general agreement, and whom in many practical matters of government good citizens can well afford to follow.

# Chapter XIV

## THE MONROE DOCTRINE AND
## THE PANAMA CANAL

No NATION can claim rights without acknowledging the duties that go with the rights. It is a contemptible thing for a great nation to render itself impotent in international action, whether because of cowardice or sloth, or sheer inability or unwillingness to look into the future. It is a very wicked thing for a nation to do wrong to others. But the most contemptible and most wicked course of conduct is for a nation to use offensive language or be guilty of offensive actions toward other people and yet fail to hold its own if the other nation retaliates; and it is almost as bad to undertake responsibilities and then not fulfil them. During the seven and a half years that I was President, this Nation behaved in international matters toward all other nations precisely as an honorable man behaves to his fellow-men. We made no promise which we could not and did not keep. We made no threat which we did not carry out. We never failed to assert our rights in the face of the strong, and we never failed to treat both strong and weak with courtesy and justice; and against the weak when they misbehaved we were slower to assert our rights than we were against the strong.

As a legacy of the Spanish War we were left with peculiar relations to the Philippines, Cuba, and Porto Rico, and with an immensely added interest in Central America and the Caribbean Sea. As regards the Philippines my belief was that we should train them for self-government as rapidly as possible, and then leave them free to decide their own fate. I did not believe in setting the time-limit within which we would give them independence, because I did not believe it wise to try to forecast how soon they would be fit for self-government; and once having made the promise I would have felt that it was imperative to keep it. Within a few months of my assuming office we had stamped out the last armed resistance in the Philippines that was not of merely sporadic character; and as soon as peace was secured we turned our energies to developing the islands in the interests of the natives. We established schools everywhere; we built roads; we administered an even-handed justice; we did everything possible to encourage agriculture and industry; and in constantly increasing measure we employed natives to do their own governing, and finally provided a legislative chamber. No higher grade of public officials ever handled the affairs of any colony than the public officials who in succession governed the Philippines. With the possible exception of the Sudan, and not even excepting Algiers, I know of no country ruled and administered by men of the white race where that rule and that administration have been exercised so emphatically with an eye single to the welfare of the natives themselves. The English and Dutch administrators of Malaysia have done admirable work; but the profit to the Europeans in those States has always been one of the chief elements considered; whereas in the Philippines our whole attention was concentrated upon the welfare of the Filipinos themselves, if anything to the neglect of our own interests.

I do not believe that America has any special beneficial interest in retaining the Philippines. Our work there has benefited us only as any efficiently done work performed for the benefit of others does incidentally help the character of those who do it. The people of the islands have never developed so rapidly, from every standpoint, as during the years of the American occupation. The time will come when it will be wise to take their own judgment as to whether they wish to continue their association with America or not. There is, however, one consideration upon which we should insist. Either we should retain complete control of the islands, or absolve ourselves from all responsibility for them. Any half and half course would be both foolish and disastrous. We are governing and have been governing the islands in the interests of the Filipinos themselves. If after due time the Filipinos themselves decide that they do not wish to be thus governed, then I trust that we will leave; but when we do leave it must be distinctly understood that we retain no protectorate — and above all that we take part in no joint protectorate — over the islands, and give them no guarantee, of neutrality or otherwise; that, in short, we are absolutely quit of responsibility for them, of every kind and description.

The Filipinos were quite incapable of standing by themselves when we took possession of the islands, and we had made no promise concerning them. But we had explicitly promised to leave the island of Cuba, had explicitly promised that Cuba should be independent. Early in my administration that promise was redeemed. When the promise was made, I doubt if there was a single ruler or diplomat in Europe who believed that it would be kept. As far as I know, the United States was the first power which, having made such a promise, kept it in letter and spirit. England was unwise enough to make such a promise when she took Egypt. It would have been a capital misfortune to have kept the promise, and England has remained in Egypt for over thirty years, and will unquestionably remain indefinitely; but though it is necessary for her to do so, the fact of her doing so has meant the breaking of a positive promise and has been a real evil. Japan made the same guarantee about Korea, but as far as can be seen there was never even any thought of keeping the promise in this case; and Korea, which had shown herself utterly impotent either for self-government or self-defense, was in actual fact almost immediately annexed to Japan.

We made the promise to give Cuba independence; and we kept the promise. Leonard Wood was left in as Governor for two or three years, and evolved order out of chaos, raising the administration of the island to a level, moral and material, which it had never before achieved. We also by treaty gave the Cubans substantial advantages in our markets. Then we left the island, turning the government over to its own people. After four or five years a revolution broke out, during my administration, and we again had to intervene to restore order. We promptly sent thither a small army of pacification. Under General Barry, order was restored and kept, and absolute justice done. The American troops were then withdrawn and the Cubans reëstablished in complete possession of their own beautiful island, and they are in possession of it now. There are plenty of occasions in our history when we have shown weakness or inefficiency, and some occasions when we have not been as scrupulous as we should have been as regards the rights of others. But I know of no action by any other government in relation to a weaker power which showed such disinterested efficiency in rendering service as was true in connection with our intervention in Cuba.

In Cuba, as in the Philippines and as in Porto Rico, Santo Domingo, and later in Panama, no small part of our success was due to the fact that we put in the highest grade of men as public officials. This practice was inaugurated under President McKinley. I found admirable men in office, and I continued them and appointed men like them as their successors. The way that the custom-houses in Santo Domingo were administered by Colton definitely established the success of our experiment in securing peace for that island republic; and in Porto Rico, under the administration of affairs under such officials as Hunt, Winthrop, Post, Ward and Grahame, more substantial progress was achieved in a decade than in any previous century.

The Philippines, Cuba, and Porto Rico came within our own sphere of governmental action. In addition to this we asserted certain rights in the Western Hemisphere under the Monroe Doctrine. My endeavor was not only to assert these rights, but frankly and fully to acknowledge the duties that went with the rights.

The Monroe Doctrine lays down the rule that the Western Hemisphere is not hereafter to be treated as subject to settlement and occupation by Old World powers. It is not international law; but it is a cardinal principle of our foreign policy. There is no difficulty at the present day in maintaining this doctrine, save where the American power whose interest is threatened has shown itself in international matters both weak and delinquent. The great and prosperous civilized commonwealths, such as the Argentine, Brazil, and Chile, in the Southern half of South America, have advanced so far that they no longer stand in any position of tutelage toward the United States. They occupy toward us precisely the position that Canada occupies. Their friendship is the friendship of equals for equals. My view was that as regards these nations there was no more necessity for asserting the Monroe Doctrine than there was to assert it in regard to Canada. They were competent to assert it for themselves. Of course if one of these nations, or if Canada, should be overcome by some Old World power, which then proceeded to occupy its territory, we would undoubtedly, if the American Nation needed our help, give it in order to prevent such occupation from taking place. But the initiative would come from the Nation itself, and the United States would merely act as a friend whose help was invoked.

The case was (and is) widely different as regards certain — not all — of the tropical states in the neighborhood of the Caribbean Sea. Where these states are stable and prosperous, they stand on a footing of absolute equality with all other communities. But some of them have been a prey to such continuous revolutionary misrule as to have grown impotent either to do their duties to outsiders or to enforce their rights against outsiders. The United States has not the slightest desire to make aggressions on any one of these states. On the contrary, it will submit to much from them without showing resentment. If any great civilized power, Russia or Germany, for instance, had behaved toward us as Venezuela under Castro behaved, this country would have gone to war at once. We did not go to war with Venezuela merely because our people declined to be irritated by the actions of a weak opponent, and showed a forbearance which probably went beyond the limits of wisdom in refusing to take umbrage at what was done by the weak; although we would certainly have resented it had it been done by the strong. In the case of two states, however, affairs reached such a crisis that we had to act. These two states were Santo Domingo and the then owner of the Isthmus of Panama, Colombia.

Medal awarded by Mr. Roosevelt for two years' continuous service on the Panama Canal.

The Santo Domingan case was the less important; and yet it possessed a real importance, and moreover is instructive because the action there taken should serve as a precedent for American action in all similar cases. During the early years of my administration Santo Domingo was in its usual condition of chronic revolution. There was always fighting, always plundering; and the successful graspers for governmental power were always pawning ports and custom-houses, or trying to put them up as guarantees for loans. Of course the foreigners who made loans under such conditions demanded exorbitant interest, and if they were Europeans expected their governments to stand by them. So utter was the disorder that on one occasion when Admiral Dewey landed to pay a call of ceremony on the President, he and his party were shot at by revolutionists in crossing the square, and had to return to the ships, leaving the call unpaid. There was default on the interest due to the creditors; and finally the latter insisted upon their governments intervening. Two or three of the European powers were endeavoring to arrange for concerted action, and I was finally notified that these powers intended to take and hold several of the seaports which held custom-houses.

This meant that unless I acted at once I would find foreign powers in partial possession of Santo Domingo; in which event the very individuals who, in the actual event deprecated the precaution taken to prevent such action, would have advocated extreme and violent measures to undo the effect of their own supineness. Nine-tenths of wisdom is to be wise in time, and at the right time; and my whole foreign policy was based on the exercise of intelligent forethought and of decisive action sufficiently far in advance of any likely crisis to make it improbable that we would run into serious trouble.

Santo Domingo had fallen into such chaos that once for some weeks there were two rival governments in it, and a revolution was being carried on against each. At one period one government was at sea in a small gunboat, but still stoutly maintained that it was in possession of the island and entitled to make loans and declare peace or war. The situation had become intolerable by the time that I interfered. There was a naval commander in the waters whom I directed to prevent any fighting which might menace the custom-houses. He carried out his orders, both to his and my satisfaction, in thoroughgoing fashion. On one occasion, when an insurgent force threatened to attack a town in which Americans had interests, he notified the commanders on both sides that he would not permit any fighting in the town, but that he would appoint a certain place where they could meet and fight it out, and that the victors should have the town. They agreed to meet his wishes, the fight came off at the appointed place, and the victors, who if I remember rightly were the insurgents, were given the town.

It was the custom-houses that caused the trouble, for they offered the only means of raising money, and the revolutions were carried on to get possession of them. Accordingly I secured an agreement with the governmental authorities, who for the moment seemed best able to speak for the country, by which these custom-houses were placed under American control. The arrangement was that we should keep order and prevent any interference with the custom-houses or the places where they stood, and should collect the revenues. Forty-five per cent of the revenue was then turned over to the Santo Domingan Government, and fifty-five per cent put in a sinking fund in New York for the benefit of the creditors. The arrangement worked in capital style. On the forty-five per cent basis the Santo Domingan Government received from us a larger sum than it had ever received before when nominally all the revenue went to it. The creditors were entirely satisfied with the arrangement, and no excuse for interference by European powers remained. Occasional disturbances occurred in the island, of course, but on the whole there ensued a degree of peace and prosperity which the island had not known before for at least a century.

All this was done without the loss of a life, with the assent of all the parties in interest, and without subjecting the United States to any charge, while practically all of the interference, after the naval commander whom I have mentioned had taken the initial steps in preserving order, consisted in putting a first-class man trained in our insular service at the head of the Santo Domingan customs service. We secured peace, we protected the people of the islands against foreign foes, and we minimized the chance of domestic trouble. We satisfied the creditors and the foreign nations to which the creditors belonged; and our own part of the work was done with the utmost efficiency and with rigid honesty, so that not a particle of scandal was ever so much as hinted at.

Under these circumstances those who do not know the nature of the professional international philanthropists would suppose that these apostles of international peace would have been overjoyed with what we had done. As a matter of fact, when they took any notice of it at all it was to denounce it; and those American newspapers which are fondest of proclaiming themselves the foes of war and the friends of peace violently attacked me for averting war from, and bringing peace to, the island. They insisted I had no power to make the agreement, and demanded the rejection of the treaty which was to perpetuate the agreement. They were, of course, wholly unable to advance a single sound reason of any kind for their attitude. I suppose the real explanation was partly their dislike of me personally, and unwillingness to see peace come through or national honor upheld by me; and in the next place their sheer, simple devotion to prattle and dislike of efficiency. They liked to have people come together and talk about peace, or even sign bits of paper with something about peace or arbitration on them, but they took no interest whatever in the practical achievement of a peace that told for good government and decency and honesty. They were joined by the many moderately well-meaning men who always demand that a thing be done, but also always demand that it be not done in the only way in which it is, as a matter of fact, possible to do it. The men of this kind insisted that of course Santo Domingo must be protected and made to behave itself, and that of course the Panama Canal must be dug; but they insisted even more strongly that neither feat should be accomplished in the only way in which it was possible to accomplish it at all.

The Constitution did not explicitly give me power to bring about the necessary agreement with Santo Domingo. But the Constitution did not forbid my doing what I did. I put the agreement into effect, and I continued its execution for two years before the Senate acted; and I would have continued it until the end of my term, if necessary, without any action by Congress. But it was far preferable that there should be action by Congress, so that we might be proceeding under a treaty which was the law of the land and not merely by a direction of the Chief Executive which would lapse when that particular executive left office. I therefore did my best to get the Senate to ratify what I had done. There was a good deal of difficulty about it. With the exception of one or two men like

Clark of Arkansas, the Democratic Senators acted in that spirit of unworthy partisanship which subordinates national interest to some fancied partisan advantage, and they were cordially backed by all that portion of the press which took its inspiration from Wall Street, and was violently hostile to the Administration because of its attitude towards great corporations. Most of the Republican Senators under the lead of Senator Lodge stood by me; but some of them, of the more "conservative" or reactionary type, who were already growing hostile to me on the trust question, first proceeded to sneer at what had been done, and to raise all kinds of meticulous objections, which they themselves finally abandoned, but which furnished an excuse on which the opponents of the treaty could hang adverse action. Unfortunately the Senators who were most apt to speak of the dignity of the Senate, and to insist upon its importance, were the very ones who were also most apt to try to make display of this dignity and importance by thwarting the public business. This case was typical. The Republicans in question spoke against certain provisions of the proposed treaty. They then, having ingeniously provided ammunition for the foes of the treaty, abandoned their opposition to it, and the Democrats stepped into the position they had abandoned. Enough Republicans were absent to prevent the securing of a two-thirds vote for the treaty, and the Senate adjourned without any action at all, and with a feeling of entire self-satisfaction at having left the country in the position of assuming a responsibility and then failing to fulfil it. Apparently the Senators in question felt that in some way they had upheld their dignity. All that they had really done was to shirk their duty. Somebody had to do that duty, and accordingly I did it. I went ahead and administered the proposed treaty anyhow, considering it as a simple agreement on the part of the Executive which would be converted into a treaty whenever the Senate acted. After a couple of years the Senate did act, having previously made some utterly unimportant changes which I ratified and persuaded Santo Domingo to ratify. In all its history Santo Domingo has had nothing happen to it as fortunate as this treaty, and the passing of it saved the United States from having to face serious difficulties with one or more foreign powers.

It cannot in the long run prove possible for the United States to protect delinquent American nations from punishment for the non-performance of their duties unless she undertakes to make them perform their duties. People may theorize about this as much as they wish, but whenever a sufficiently strong outside nation becomes sufficiently aggrieved, then either that nation will act or the United States Government itself will have to act. We were face to face at one period of my administration with this condition of affairs in Venezuela, when Germany, rather feebly backed by England, undertook a blockade against Venezuela to make Venezuela adopt the German and English view about certain agreements. There was real danger that the blockade would finally result in Germany's taking possession of certain cities or customhouses. I succeeded, however, in getting all the parties in interest to submit their cases to the Hague Tribunal.

Colonel G. W. Goethals.

By far the most important action I took in foreign affairs during the time I was President related to the Panama Canal. Here again there was much accusation about my having acted in an "unconstitutional" manner — a position which can be upheld only if Jefferson's action in acquiring Louisiana be also treated as unconstitutional; and at different stages of the affair believers in a do-nothing policy denounced me as having "usurped authority" — which meant, that when nobody else could or would exercise efficient authority, I exercised it.

During the nearly four hundred years that had elapsed since Balboa crossed the Isthmus, there had been a good deal of talk about building an Isthmus canal, and there had been various discussions of the subject and negotiations about it in Washington for the previous half century. So far it had all resulted merely in conversation; and the time had come when unless somebody was prepared to act with decision we would have to resign ourselves to at least half a century of further conversation. Under the Hay-Pauncefote Treaty signed shortly after I became President, and thanks to our negotiations with the French Panama Company, the United States at last acquired a possession, so far as Europe was concerned, which warranted her in immediately undertaking the task. It remained to decide where the canal should be, whether along the line already pioneered by the French company in Panama, or in Nicaragua. Panama belonged to the Republic of Colombia. Nicaragua bid eagerly for the privilege of having the United States build the canal through her territory. As long as it was doubtful which route we would decide upon, Colombia extended every promise of friendly coöperation: at the Pan-American Congress in Mexico her delegate joined in the unanimous vote which requested the United States forthwith to build the canal; and at her eager request we negotiated the Hay-Herran Treaty with her, which gave us the right to build the canal across Panama. A board of experts sent to the Isthmus had reported that this route was better than the Nicaragua route, and that it would be well to build the canal over it provided we could purchase the rights of the French company for forty million dollars; but that otherwise they would advise taking the Nicaragua route. Ever since 1846 we had had a treaty with the power then in control of the Isthmus, the Republic of New Granada, the predecessor of the Republic of Colombia and of the present Republic of Panama, by which treaty the United States was guaranteed free and open right of way across the Isthmus of Panama by any mode of communication that might be constructed, while in return our Government guaranteed the perfect neutrality of the Isthmus with a view to the preservation of free transit.

For nearly fifty years we had asserted the right to prevent the closing of this highway of commerce. Secretary of State Cass in 1858 officially stated the American position as follows:

"Sovereignty has its duties as well as its rights, and none

of these local governments, even if administered with more regard to the just demands of other nations than they have been, would be permitted, in a spirit of Eastern isolation, to close the gates of intercourse of the great highways of the world, and justify the act by the pretension that these avenues of trade and travel belong to them and that they choose to shut them, or, what is almost equivalent, to encumber them with such unjust relations as would prevent their general use."

We had again and again been forced to intervene to protect the transit across the Isthmus, and the intervention was frequently at the request of Colombia herself. The effort to build a canal by private capital had been made under De Lesseps and had resulted in lamentable failure. Every serious proposal to build the canal in such manner had been abandoned. The United States had repeatedly announced that we would not permit it to be built or controlled by any old-world government. Colombia was utterly impotent to build it herself. Under these circumstances it had become a matter of imperative obligation that we should build it ourselves without further delay.

I took final action in 1903. During the preceding fifty-three years the Governments of New Granada and of its successor, Colombia, had been in a constant state of flux; and the State of Panama had sometimes been treated as almost independent, in a loose Federal league, and sometimes as the mere property of the Government at Bogota; and there had been innumerable appeals to arms, sometimes for adequate, sometimes for inadequate, reasons. The following is a partial list of the disturbances on the Isthmus of Panama during the period in question, as reported to us by our consuls. It is not possible to give a complete list, and some of the reports that speak of "revolutions" must mean unsuccessful revolutions:

May 22, 1850. — Outbreak; two Americans killed. War vessel demanded to quell outbreak.

October, 1850. — Revolutionary plot to bring about independence of the Isthmus.

July 22, 1851. — Revolution in four Southern provinces.

November 14, 1851. — Outbreak at Chagres. Man-of-war requested for Chagres.

June 27, 1853. — Insurrection at Bogota, and consequent disturbance on Isthmus. War vessel demanded.

May 23, 1854. — Political disturbances. War vessel requested.

June 28, 1854. — Attempted revolution.

October 24, 1854. — Independence of Isthmus demanded by provincial legislature.

April, 1856. — Riot, and massacre of Americans.

May 4, 1856. — Riot.

May 18, 1856. — Riot.

June 3, 1856. — Riot.

October 2, 1856. — Conflict between two native parties. United States force landed.

December 18, 1858. — Attempted secession of Panama.

April, 1859. — Riots.

September, 1860. — Outbreak.

October 4, 1860. — Landing of United States forces in consequence.

May 23, 1861. — Intervention of the United States forces required, by intendente.

October 2, 1861. — Insurrection and civil war.

April 4, 1862. — Measures to prevent rebels crossing Isthmus.

June 13, 1862. — Mosquera's troops refused admittance to Panama.

March, 1865. — Revolution, and United States troops landed.

August, 1865. — Riots; unsuccessful attempt to invade Panama.

March, 1866. — Unsuccessful revolution.

April, 1867. — Attempt to overthrow Government.

August, 1867. — Attempt at revolution.

July 5, 1868. — Revolution; provisional government inaugurated.

August 29, 1868. — Revolution; provisional government overthrown.

April, 1871. — Revolution; followed apparently by counter revolution.

April, 1873. — Revolution and civil war which lasted to October, 1875.

August, 1876. — Civil war which lasted until April, 1877.
July, 1878. — Rebellion.
December, 1878. — Revolt.
April, 1879. — Revolution.
June, 1879. — Revolution.
March, 1883. — Riot.
May, 1883. — Riot.
June, 1884. — Revolutionary attempt.
December, 1884. — Revolutionary attempt.
January, 1885. — Revolutionary disturbances.
March, 1885. — Revolution.
April, 1887. — Disturbance on Panama Railroad.
November, 1887. — Disturbance on line of canal.
January, 1889. — Riot.
January, 1895. — Revolution which lasted until April.
March, 1895. — Incendiary attempt.
October, 1899. — Revolution.
February, 1900, to July, 1900. — Revolution.
January, 1901. — Revolution.
July, 1901. — Revolutionary disturbances.
September, 1901. — City of Colon taken by rebels.
March, 1902. — Revolutionary disturbances.
July, 1902. — Revolution.

The above is only a partial list of the revolutions, rebellions, insurrections, riots, and other outbreaks that occurred during the period in question; yet they number fifty-three for the fifty-three years, and they showed a tendency to increase, rather than decrease, in numbers and intensity. One of them lasted for nearly three years before it was quelled; another for nearly a year. In short, the experience of over half a century had shown Colombia to be utterly incapable of keeping order on the Isthmus. Only the active interference of the United States had enabled her to preserve so much as a semblance of sovereignty. Had it not been for the exercise by the United States of the police power in her interest, her connection with the Isthmus would have been sundered long before it was. In 1856, in 1860, in 1873, in 1885, in 1901, and again in 1902, sailors and marines from United States warships were forced to land in order to patrol the Isthmus, to protect life and property, and to see that the transit across the Isthmus was kept open. In 1861, in 1862, in 1885, and in 1900, the Colombian Government asked that the United States Government would land troops to protect Colombian interests and maintain order on the Isthmus. The people of Panama during the preceding twenty years had three times sought to establish their independence by revolution or secession — in 1885, in 1895, and in 1899.

The peculiar relations of the United States toward the Isthmus, and the acquiescence by Colombia in acts which were quite incompatible with the theory of her having an absolute and unconditioned sovereignty on the Isthmus, are illustrated

"Kindred Spirits of the Strenuous Life."
(Kaiser Wilhelm II and President Roosevelt.)

by the following three telegrams between two of our naval officers whose ships were at the Isthmus, and the Secretary of the Navy on the occasion of the first outbreak that occurred on the Isthmus after I became President (a year before Panama became independent):

September 12, 1902.

*Ranger, Panama:*

United States guarantees perfect neutrality of Isthmus and that a free transit from sea to sea be not interrupted or embarrassed. . . . Any transportation of troops which might contravene these provisions of treaty should not be sanctioned by you, nor should use of road be permitted which might convert the line of transit into theater of hostility.

MOODY.

COLON, September 20, 1902.

*Secretary Navy, Washington:*

Everything is conceded. The United States guards and guarantees traffic and the line of transit. To-day I permitted the exchange of Colombian troops from Panama to Colon, about 1000 men each way, the troops without arms in trains guarded by American naval force in the same manner as other passengers; arms and ammunition in separate train, guarded also by naval force in the same manner as other freight.

MCLEAN.

PANAMA, October 3, 1902.

*Secretary Navy,*
    Washington, D.C.:

Have sent this communication to the American Consul at Panama:

"Inform Governor, while trains running under United States protection, I must decline transportation any combatants, ammunition, arms, which might cause interruption to traffic or convert line of transit into theater hostilities."

CASEY.

When the Government in nominal control of the Isthmus continually besought American interference to protect the "rights" it could not itself protect, and permitted our Government to transport Colombian troops unarmed, under protection of our own armed men, while the Colombian arms and ammunition came in a separate train, it is obvious that the Colombian "sovereignty" was of such a character as to warrant our insisting that inasmuch as it only existed because of our protection there should be in requital a sense of the obligations that the acceptance of this protection implied.

Meanwhile Colombia was under a dictatorship. In 1898 M. A. Sanclamente was elected President, and J. M. Maroquin Vice-President, of the Republic of Colombia. On July 31, 1900, the Vice-President, Maroquin, executed a "coup d'état" by seizing the person of the President, Sanclamente, and imprisoning him at a place a few miles out of Bogota. Maroquin thereupon declared himself possessed of the executive power because of "the absence of the President" — a delightful touch of unconscious humor. He then issued a decree that public order was disturbed, and, upon that ground, assumed to himself legislative power under another provision

of the constitution; that is, having himself disturbed the
public order, he alleged the disturbance as a justification for
seizing absolute power. Thenceforth Maroquin, without the
aid of any legislative body, ruled as a dictator, combining
the supreme executive, legislative, civil, and military authorities, in the so-called Republic of Colombia. The "absence"
of Sanclamente from the capital became permanent by his
death in prison in the year 1902. When the people of Panama
declared their independence in November, 1903, no Congress
had sat in Colombia since the year 1898, except the special
Congress called by Maroquin to reject the canal treaty, and
which did reject it by a unanimous vote, and adjourned without legislating on any other subject. The constitution of 1886
had taken away from Panama the power of self-government
and vested it in Colombia. The *coup d'état* of Maroquin took
away from Colombia herself the power of government and
vested it in an irresponsible dictator.

Consideration of the above facts ought to be enough to
show any human being that we were not dealing with normal
conditions on the Isthmus and in Colombia. We were dealing
with the government of an irresponsible alien dictator, and with
a condition of affairs on the Isthmus itself which was marked
by one uninterrupted series of outbreaks and revolutions. As
for the "consent of the governed" theory, that absolutely justified our action; the people on the Isthmus were the "governed";
they were governed by Colombia, without their consent, and
they unanimously repudiated the Colombian government,
and demanded that the United States build the canal.

I had done everything possible, personally and through Secretary Hay, to persuade the Colombian Government to keep
faith. Under the Hay-Pauncefote Treaty, it was explicitly provided that the United States should build the canal, should
control, police and protect it, and keep it open to the vessels
of all nations on equal terms. We had assumed the position of
guarantor of the canal, including, of course, the building
of the canal, and of its peaceful use by all the world. The enterprise was recognized everywhere as responding to an international need. It was a mere travesty on justice to treat
the government in possession of the Isthmus as having the
right — which Secretary Cass forty-five years before had so

emphatically repudiated — to close the gates of intercourse on one of the great highways of the world. When we submitted to Colombia the Hay-Herran Treaty, it had been settled that the time for delay, the time for permitting any government of anti-social character, or of imperfect development, to bar the work, had passed. The United States had assumed in connection with the canal certain responsibilities not only to its own people but to the civilized world which imperatively demanded that there should be no further delay in beginning the work. The Hay-Herran Treaty, if it erred at all, erred in being overgenerous toward Colombia. The people of Panama were delighted with the treaty, and the President of Colombia, who embodied in his own person the entire government of Colombia, had authorized the treaty to be made. But after the treaty had been made the Colombian Government thought it had the matter in its own hands; and the further thought, equally wicked and foolish, came into the heads of the people in control at Bogota that they would seize the French Company at the end of another year and take for themselves the forty million dollars which the United States had agreed to pay the Panama Canal Company.

President Maroquin, through his Minister, had agreed to the Hay-Herran Treaty in January, 1903. He had the absolute power of an unconstitutional dictator to keep his promise or break it. He determined to break it. To furnish himself an excuse for breaking it he devised the plan of summoning a Congress especially called to reject the canal treaty. This the Congress — a Congress of mere puppets — did, without a dissenting vote; and the puppets adjourned forthwith without legislating on any other subject. The fact that this was a mere sham, and that the President had entire power to confirm his own treaty and act on it if he desired, was shown as soon as the revolution took place, for on November 6 General Reyes of Colombia addressed the American Minister at Bogota, on behalf of President Maroquin, saying that "if the Government of the United States would land troops and restore the Colombian sovereignty" the Colombian President would "declare martial law; and, by virtue of vested constitutional authority, when public order is disturbed, would approve by decree the ratification of the canal treaty as signed; or, if the Government of the United States prefers, would call an extra session of the Congress — with new and friendly members — next May to approve the treaty." This, of course, is proof positive that the Colombian dictator had used his Congress as a mere shield, and a sham shield at that, and it shows how utterly useless it would have been further to trust his good faith in the matter.

Confiscated by the Berlin Police. What are they afraid of? Is it this?

The Berlin Police have confiscated from the numbers of *Punch* of Nov. 16, the page containing the caricature of the Emperor William and President Roosevelt entitled "Kindred Spirits of the Strenuous Life."

When, in August, 1903, I became convinced that Colombia intended to repudiate the treaty made the preceding January, under cover of securing its rejection by the Colombian Legislature, I began carefully to consider what should be done. By my direction Secretary Hay, personally and through the Minister at Bogota, repeatedly warned Colombia that grave consequences might follow her rejection of the treaty. The possibility of ratification did not wholly pass away until the close of the session of the Colombian Congress on the last day of October. There would then be two possibilities. One was that Panama would remain quiet. In that case I was prepared to recommend to Congress that we should at once occupy the Isthmus anyhow, and proceed to dig the canal; and I had drawn out a draft of my message to this effect.* But from the information I received, I deemed it likely that there would be a revolution in Panama as soon as the Colombian Congress adjourned without ratifying the treaty, for the entire population of Panama felt that the immediate building of the canal was of vital concern to their well-being. Correspondents of the different newspapers on the Isthmus had sent to their respective papers widely published forecasts indicating that there would be a revolution in such event.

Moreover, on October 16, at the request of Lieutenant-General Young, Captain Humphrey and Lieutenant Murphy, two army officers who had returned from the Isthmus, saw me and told me that there would unquestionably be a revolution on the Isthmus, that the people were unanimous in their criticism of the Bogota Government and their disgust over the failure of that Government to ratify the treaty; and that the revolution would probably take place immediately after the adjournment of the Colombian Congress. They did not believe that it would be before October 20, but they were confident that it would certainly come at the end of October or immediately afterwards, when the Colombian Congress had adjourned. Accordingly I directed the Navy Department to station various ships within easy reach of the Isthmus, to be ready to act in the event of need arising.

These ships were barely in time. On November 3 the revolution occurred. Practically everybody on the Isthmus, including all the Colombian troops that were already stationed there, joined in the revolution, and there was no bloodshed. But on that same day four hundred new Colombian troops were landed at Colon. Fortunately, the gunboat *Nashville*, under Commander Hubbard, reached Colon almost immediately afterwards, and when the commander of the Colombian forces threatened the lives and property of the American citizens, including women and children, in Colon, Commander

*See appendix at end of this chapter.

Hubbard landed a few score sailors and marines to protect them. By a mixture of firmness and tact he not only prevented any assault on our citizens, but persuaded the Colombian commander to reëmbark his troops for Cartagena. On the Pacific side a Colombian gunboat shelled the City of Panama, with the result of killing one Chinaman — the only life lost in the whole affair.

No one connected with the American Government had any part in preparing, inciting, or encouraging the revolution, and except for the reports of our military and naval officers, which I forwarded to Congress, no one connected with the Government had any previous knowledge concerning the proposed revolution, except such as was accessible to any person who read the newspapers and kept abreast of current questions and current affairs. By the unanimous action of its people, and without the firing of a shot, the state of Panama declared themselves an independent republic. The time for hesitation on our part had passed.

My belief then was, and the events that have occurred since have more than justified it, that from the standpoint of the United States it was imperative, not only for civil but for military reasons, that there should be the immediate establishment of easy and speedy communication by sea between the Atlantic and the Pacific. These reasons were not of convenience only, but of vital necessity, and did not admit of indefinite delay. The action of Colombia had shown not only that the delay would be indefinite, but that she intended to confiscate the property and rights of the French Panama Canal Company. The report of the Panama Canal Committee of the Colombian Senate on October 14, 1903, on the proposed treaty with the United States, proposed that all consideration of the matter should be postponed until October 31, 1904, when the next Colombian Congress would have convened, because by that time the new Congress would be in condition to determine whether through lapse of time the French company had not forfeited its property and rights. "When that time arrives," the report significantly declared, "the Republic, without any impediment, will be able to contract and will be in more clear, more definite and more advantageous possession, both legally and materially." The naked meaning of this

was that Colombia proposed to wait a year, and then enforce
a forfeiture of the rights and property of the French Panama
Company, so as to secure the forty million dollars our Government had authorized as payment to this company. If we
had sat supine, this would doubtless have meant that France
would have interfered to protect the company, and we should
then have had on the Isthmus, not the company, but France;
and the gravest international complications might have ensued. Every consideration of international morality and expediency, of duty to the Panama people, and of satisfaction of
our own national interests and honor, bade us take immediate action. I recognized Panama forthwith on behalf of the
United States, and practically all the countries of the world
immediately followed suit. The State Department immediately
negotiated a canal treaty with the new Republic. One of the
foremost men in securing the independence of Panama, and
the treaty which authorized the United States forthwith to
build the canal, was M. Philippe Bunau-Varilla, an eminent
French engineer formerly associated with De Lesseps and then
living on the Isthmus; his services to civilization were notable,
and deserve the fullest recognition.

From the beginning to the end our course was straightforward and in absolute accord with the highest of standards of
international morality. Criticism of it can come only from mis-
information, or else from a sentimentality which represents
both mental weakness and a moral twist. To have acted otherwise than I did would have been on my part betrayal of the
interests of the United States, indifference to the interests of
Panama, and recreancy to the interests of the world at large.
Colombia had forfeited every claim to consideration; indeed,
this is not stating the case strongly enough: she had so acted
that yielding to her would have meant on our part that cul-
pable form of weakness which stands on a level with wickedness. As for me personally, if I had hesitated to act, and had
not in advance discounted the clamor of those Americans who
have made a fetish of disloyalty to their country, I should have
esteemed myself as deserving a place in Dante's inferno beside
the faint-hearted cleric who was guilty of "il gran rifiuto." The
facts I have given above are mere bald statements from the
record. They show that from the beginning there had been

acceptance of our right to insist on free transit, in whatever form was best, across the Isthmus; and that towards the end there had been a no less universal feeling that it was our duty to the world to provide this transit in the shape of a canal — the resolution of the Pan-American Congress was practically a mandate to this effect. Colombia was then under a one-man government, a dictatorship, founded on usurpation of absolute and irresponsible power. She eagerly pressed us to enter into an agreement with her, as long as there was any chance of our going to the alternative route through Nicaragua. When she thought we were committed, she refused to fulfil the agreement, with the avowed hope of seizing the French company's property for nothing and thereby holding us up. This was a bit of pure bandit morality. It would have achieved its purpose had I possessed as weak moral fiber as those of my critics who announced that I ought to have confined my action to feeble scolding and temporizing until the opportunity for action passed. I did not lift my finger to incite the revolutionists. The right simile to use is totally different. I simply ceased to stamp out the different revolutionary fuses that were already burning. When Colombia committed flagrant wrong against us, I considered it no part of my duty to aid and abet her in her wrongdoing at our expense, and also at the expense of Panama, of the French company, and of the world generally. There had been fifty years of continuous bloodshed and civil strife in Panama; because of my action Panama has now known ten years of such peace and prosperity as she never before saw during the four centuries of her existence — for in Panama, as in Cuba and Santo Domingo, it was the action of the American people, against the outcries of the professed apostles of peace, which alone brought peace. We gave to the people of Panama self-government, and freed them from subjection to alien oppressors. We did our best to get Colombia to let us treat her with a more than generous justice; we exercised patience to beyond the verge of proper forbearance. When we did act and recognize Panama, Colombia at once acknowledged her own guilt by promptly offering to do what we had demanded, and what she had protested it was not in her power to do. But the offer came too late. What we would gladly have done before, it had by that time become impossible for us honorably to do; for it would have necessitated our abandoning the people of Panama, our friends, and turning them over to their and our foes, who would have wreaked vengeance on them precisely because they had shown friendship to us. Colombia was solely responsible for her own humiliation; and she had not then, and has not now, one shadow of claim upon us, moral or legal; all the wrong that was done was done by her. If, as representing the American people, I had not acted precisely as I did, I would have been an unfaithful or incompetent representative; and inaction at that crisis would have meant not only indefinite delay in building the canal, but also practical admission on our part that we were not fit to play the part on the Isthmus which we had arrogated to ourselves. I acted on my own responsibility in the Panama matter. John Hay spoke of this action as follows: "The action of the President in the Panama matter is not only in the strictest accordance with the principles of justice and equity, and in line with all the best precedents of our public policy, but it was the only course he could have taken in compliance with our treaty rights and obligations."

I deeply regretted, and now deeply regret, the fact that the Colombian Government rendered it imperative for me to take the action I took; but I had no alternative, consistent with the full performance of my duty to my own people, and to the nations of mankind. (For, be it remembered, that certain other nations, Chile for example, will probably benefit even more by our action than will the United States itself.) I am well aware that the Colombian people have many fine traits; that there is among them a circle of high-bred men and women which would reflect honor on the social life of any country; and that there has been an intellectual and literary development within this small circle which partially atones for the stagnation and illiteracy of the mass of the people; and I also know that even the illiterate mass possesses many sterling qualities. But unfortunately in international matters every nation must be judged by the action of its Government. The good people in Colombia apparently made no effort, certainly no successful effort, to cause the Government to act with reasonable good faith towards the United States; and Colombia had to take the consequences. If Brazil, or the Argentine, or

A Gate at the Upper Lock at Gatun.

Chile, had been in possession of the Isthmus, doubtless the canal would have been built under the governmental control of the nation thus controlling the Isthmus, with the hearty acquiescence of the United States and of all other powers. But in the actual fact the canal would not have been built at all save for the action I took. If men choose to say that it would have been better not to build it, than to build it as the result of such action, their position, although foolish, is compatible with belief in their wrongheaded sincerity. But it is hypocrisy, alike odious and contemptible, for any man to say both that we ought to have built the canal and that we ought not to have acted in the way we did act.

After a sufficient period of wrangling, the Senate ratified the treaty with Panama, and work on the canal was begun. The first thing that was necessary was to decide the type of canal. I summoned a board of engineering experts, foreign and native. They divided on their report. The majority of the members, including all the foreign members, approved a sea-level canal. The minority, including most of the American members, approved a lock canal. Studying these conclusions, I came to the belief that the minority was right. The two great traffic canals of the world were the Suez and the Soo. The Suez Canal is a sea-level canal, and it was the one best known to European engineers. The Soo Canal, through which an even greater volume of traffic passes every year, is a lock canal, and the American engineers were thoroughly familiar with it; whereas, in my judgment, the European engineers had failed to pay proper heed to the lessons taught by its operation and management. Moreover, the engineers who were to do the work at Panama all favored a lock canal. I came to the conclusion that a sea-level canal would be slightly less exposed to damage in the event of war; that the running expenses, apart from the heavy cost of interest on the amount necessary to build it, would be less; and that for small ships the time of transit would be less. But I also came to the conclusion that the lock canal at the proposed level would cost only about half as much to build and would be built in half the time, with much less risk; that for large ships the transit would be quicker, and that, taking into account the interest saved, the cost of maintenance would be less. Accordingly I recommended to

Congress, on February 19, 1906, that a lock canal should be built, and my recommendation was adopted. Congress insisted upon having it built by a commission of several men. I tried faithfully to get good work out of the commission, and found it quite impossible; for a many-headed commission is an extremely poor executive instrument. At last I put Colonel Goethals in as head of the commission. Then, when Congress still refused to make the commission single-headed, I solved the difficulty by an executive order of January 6, 1908, which practically accomplished the object by enlarging the powers of the chairman, making all the other members of the commission dependent upon him, and thereby placing the work under one-man control. Dr. Gorgas had already performed an inestimable service by caring for the sanitary conditions so thoroughly as to make the Isthmus as safe as a health resort. Colonel Goethals proved to be the man of all others to do the job. It would be impossible to overstate what he has done. It is the greatest task of any kind that any man in the world has accomplished during the years that Colonel Goethals has been at work. It is the greatest task of its own kind that has ever been performed in the world at all. Colonel Goethals has succeeded in instilling into the men under him a spirit which elsewhere has been found only in a few victorious armies. It is proper and appropriate that, like the soldiers of such armies, they should receive medals which are allotted each man who has served for a sufficient length of time. A finer body of men has never been gathered by any nation than the men who have done the work of building the Panama Canal; the conditions under which they have lived and have done their work have been better than in any similar work ever undertaken in the tropics; they have all felt an eager pride in their work; and they have made not only America but the whole world their debtors by what they have accomplished.

# APPENDIX

## COLOMBIA: THE PROPOSED
## MESSAGE TO CONGRESS

The rough draft of the message I had proposed to send Congress ran as follows:

"The Colombian Government, through its representative here, and directly in communication with our representative at Colombia, has refused to come to any agreement with us, and has delayed action so as to make it evident that it intends to make extortionate and improper terms with us. The Isthmian Canal bill was, of course, passed upon the assumption that whatever route was used, the benefit to the particular section of the Isthmus through which it passed would be so great that the country controlling this part would be eager to facilitate the building of the canal. It is out of the question to submit to extortion on the part of a beneficiary of the scheme. All the labor, all the expense, all the risk are to be assumed by us and all the skill shown by us. Those controlling the ground through which the canal is to be put are wholly incapable of building it.

"Yet the interest of international commerce generally and the interest of this country generally demands that the canal should be begun with no needless delay. The refusal of Colombia properly to respond to our sincere and earnest efforts to come to an agreement, or to pay heed to the many concessions we have made, renders it in my judgment necessary that the United States should take immediate action on one of two lines: either we should drop the Panama canal project and immediately begin work on the Nicaraguan canal, or else we should purchase all the rights of the French company, and, without any further parley with Colombia, enter upon the completion of the canal which the French company has begun. I feel that the latter course is the one demanded by the interests of this Nation, and I therefore bring the matter to your attention for such action in the premises as you may deem wise. If in your judgment it is better not to take such action, then I shall proceed at once with the Nicaraguan canal.

"The reason that I advocate the action above outlined in regard to the Panama canal is, in the first place, the strong testimony of the experts that this route is the most feasible; and in the next place, the impropriety from an international standpoint of permitting such conduct as that to which Colombia seems to incline. The testimony of the experts is very strong, not only that the Panama route is feasible, but that in the Nicaragua route we may encounter some unpleasant surprises, and that it is far more difficult to forecast the result with any certainty as regards this latter route. As for Colombia's attitude, it is incomprehensible upon any theory of desire to see the canal built upon the basis of mutual advantage alike to those building it and to Colombia herself. All we desire to do is to take up the work begun by the French Government and to finish it. Obviously it is Colombia's duty to help towards such completion. We are most anxious to come to an agreement with her in which most scrupulous care should be taken to guard her interests and ours. But we cannot consent to permit her to block the performance of the work which it is so greatly to our interest immediately to begin and carry through."

Shortly after this rough draft was dictated the Panama revolution came, and I never thought of the rough draft again until I was accused of having instigated the revolution. This accusation is preposterous in the eyes of any one who knows the actual conditions at Panama. Only the menace of action by us in the interest of Colombia kept down revolution; as soon as Colombia's own conduct removed such menace, all check on the various revolutionary movements (there were at least three from entirely separate sources) ceased; and then an explosion was inevitable, for the French company knew that all their property would be confiscated if Colombia put through her plans, and the entire people of Panama felt that if in disgust with Colombia's extortions the United States turned to Nicaragua, they, the people of Panama, would be ruined. Knowing the character of those then in charge of the Colombian Government, I was not surprised at their bad faith; but I was surprised at their folly. They apparently had no idea either of the power of France or the power of the United States, and expected to be permitted to commit wrong with impunity, just as Castro in Venezuela had done. The difference was that, unless we acted in self-defense, Colombia had it in her power to do us serious harm, and Venezuela did not have such power. Colombia's wrongdoing, therefore, recoiled on her own head. There was no new lesson taught; it ought already to have been known to every one that wickedness, weakness, and folly combined rarely fail to meet punishment, and that the intent to do wrong, when joined to inability to carry the evil purpose to a successful conclusion, inevitably reacts on the wrongdoer.

For the full history of the acquisition and building of the canal see "The Panama Gateway," by Joseph Bucklin Bishop (Scribner's Sons). Mr. Bishop has been for eight years secretary of the commission and is one of the most efficient of the many efficient men to whose work on the Isthmus America owes so much.

## Chapter XV

### THE PEACE OF RIGHTEOUSNESS

There can be no nobler cause for which to work than the peace of righteousness; and high honor is due those serene and lofty souls who with wisdom and courage, with high idealism tempered by sane facing of the actual facts of life, have striven to bring nearer the day when armed strife between nation and nation, between class and class, between man and man shall end throughout the world. Because all this is true, it is also true that there are no men more ignoble or more foolish, no men whose actions are fraught with greater possibility of mischief to their country and to mankind, than those who exalt unrighteous peace as better than righteous war. The men who have stood highest in our history, as in the history of all countries, are those who scorned injustice, who were incapable of oppressing the weak, or of permitting their country, with their consent, to oppress the weak, but who did not hesitate to draw the sword when to leave it undrawn meant inability to arrest triumphant wrong.

All this is so obvious that it ought not to be necessary to repeat it. Yet every man in active affairs, who also reads about the past, grows by bitter experience to realize that there are plenty of men, not only among those who mean ill, but among those who mean well, who are ready enough to praise what was done in the past, and yet are incapable of profiting by it when faced by the needs of the present. During our generation this seems to have been peculiarly the case among the men who have become obsessed with the idea of obtaining universal peace by some cheap patent panacea.

There has been a real and substantial growth in the feeling for international responsibility and justice among the great civilized nations during the past threescore or fourscore years. There has been a real growth of recognition of the fact that moral turpitude is involved in the wronging of one nation by another, and that in most cases war is an evil method of settling international difficulties. But as yet there has been only a rudimentary beginning of the development of international tribunals of justice, and there has been no development at all of any international police power. Now, as I have already said, the whole fabric of municipal law, of law within each nation, rests ultimately upon the judge and the policeman; and the complete absence of the policeman, and the almost complete absence of the judge, in international affairs, prevents there being as yet any real homology between municipal and international law.

Moreover, the questions which sometimes involve nations in war are far more difficult and complex than any questions that affect merely individuals. Almost every great nation has inherited certain questions, either with other nations or with sections of its own people, which it is quite impossible, in the present state of civilization, to decide as matters between private individuals can be decided. During the last century at least half of the wars that have been fought have been civil and not foreign wars. There are big and powerful nations which habitually commit, either upon other nations or upon sections of their own people, wrongs so outrageous as to justify even the most peaceful persons in going to war. There are also weak nations so utterly incompetent either to protect the rights of foreigners against their own citizens, or to protect their own citizens against foreigners, that it becomes a matter of sheer duty for some outside power to interfere in connection with them. As yet in neither case is there any efficient method of getting international action; and if joint action by several powers is secured, the result is usually considerably worse than if only one Power interfered. The worst infamies of modern times — such affairs as the massacres of the Armenians by the Turks, for instance — have been perpetrated in a time of nominally profound international peace, when there has been a concert of big Powers to prevent the breaking of this peace, although only by breaking it could the outrages be stopped. Be it remembered that the peoples who suffered by these hideous massacres, who saw their women violated and their children tortured, were actually enjoying all the benefits of "disarmament." Otherwise they would not have been massacred; for if the Jews in Russia and the Armenians in Turkey had been armed, and had been efficient in the use of their arms, no mob would have meddled with them.

Yet amiable but fatuous persons, with all these facts before their eyes, pass resolutions demanding universal arbitration for everything, and the disarmament of the free civilized powers and their abandonment of their armed forces; or else they write well-meaning, solemn little books, or pamphlets or editorials, and articles in magazines or newspapers, to show that it is "an illusion" to believe that war ever pays, because it is expensive. This is precisely like arguing that we should disband the police and devote our sole attention to persuading criminals that it is "an illusion" to suppose that burglary, highway robbery and white slavery are profitable. It is almost useless to attempt to argue with these well-intentioned persons, because they are suffering under an obsession and are not open to reason. They go wrong at the outset, for they lay all the emphasis on peace and none at all on righteousness. They are not all of them physically timid men; but they are usually men of soft life; and they rarely possess a high sense of honor or a keen patriotism. They rarely try to prevent their fellow countrymen from insulting or wronging the people of other nations; but they always ardently advocate that we, in our turn, shall tamely submit to wrong and insult from other nations. As Americans their folly is peculiarly scandalous, because if the principles they now uphold are right, it means that it would have been better that Americans should never have achieved their independence, and better that, in 1861, they should have peacefully submitted to seeing their country split into half a dozen jangling confederacies and slavery made perpetual. If unwilling to learn from their own history, let those who think that it is an "illusion" to believe that a war ever benefits a nation look at the difference between China and Japan. China has neither a fleet nor an efficient army. It is a huge civilized empire, one of the most populous on the globe; and it has been the helpless prey of outsiders because it does not possess the power to fight. Japan stands on a footing of equality with European and American nations because it does possess this power. China now sees Japan, Russia, Germany, England and France in possession of fragments of her empire, and has twice within the lifetime of the present generation seen her capital in the hands of allied invaders, because she in very fact realizes the ideals of the persons who wish the United

States to disarm, and then trust that our helplessness will secure us a contemptuous immunity from attack by outside nations.

The chief trouble comes from the entire inability of these worthy people to understand that they are demanding things that are mutually incompatible when they demand peace at any price, and also justice and righteousness. I remember one representative of their number, who used to write little sonnets on behalf of the Mahdi and the Sudanese, these sonnets setting forth the need that the Sudan should be both independent and peaceful. As a matter of fact, the Sudan valued independence only because it desired to war against all Christians and to carry on an unlimited slave trade. It was "independent" under the Mahdi for a dozen years, and during those dozen years the bigotry, tyranny, and cruel religious intolerance were such as flourished in the seventh century, and in spite of systematic slave raids the population decreased by nearly two-thirds, and practically all the children died. Peace came, well-being came, freedom from rape and murder and torture and highway robbery, and every brutal gratification of lust and greed came, only when the Sudan lost its independence and passed under English rule. Yet this well-meaning little sonneteer sincerely felt that his verses were issued in the cause of humanity. Looking back from the vantage point of a score of years, probably every one will agree that he was an absurd person. But he was not one whit more absurd than most of the more prominent persons who advocate disarmament by the United States, the cessation of up-building the navy, and the promise to agree to arbitrate all matters, including those affecting our national interests and honor, with all foreign nations.

These persons would do no harm if they affected only themselves. Many of them are, in the ordinary relations of life, good citizens. They are exactly like the other good citizens who believe that enforced universal vegetarianism or anti-vaccination is the panacea for all ills. But in their particular case they are able to do harm because they affect our relations with foreign powers, so that other men pay the debt which they themselves have really incurred. It is the foolish, peace-at-any-price persons who try to persuade our people to make unwise and improper treaties, or to stop building up the navy. But if trouble comes and the treaties are repudiated, or there is a demand for armed intervention, it is not these people who will pay anything; they will stay at home in safety, and leave brave men to pay in blood, and honest men to pay in shame, for their folly.

The trouble is that our policy is apt to go in zigzags, because different sections of our people exercise at different times unequal pressure on our government. One class of our citizens clamor for treaties impossible of fulfilment, and improper to fulfil; another class have no objection to the passage of these treaties so long as there is no concrete case to which they apply, but instantly oppose a veto on their application

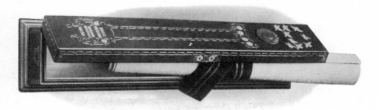

Nobel Prize Diploma in Case.

when any concrete case does actually arise. One of our cardinal doctrines is freedom of speech, which means freedom of speech about foreigners as well as about ourselves; and, inasmuch as we exercise this right with complete absence of restraint, we cannot expect other nations to hold us harmless unless in the last resort we are able to make our own words good by our deeds. One class of our citizens indulges in gushing promises to do everything for foreigners, another class offensively and improperly reviles them; and it is hard to say which class more thoroughly misrepresents the sober, self-respecting judgment of the American people as a whole. The only safe rule is to promise little, and faithfully to keep every promise; to "speak softly and carry a big stick."

A prime need for our nation, as of course for every other nation, is to make up its mind definitely what it wishes, and not to try to pursue paths of conduct incompatible one with the other. If this nation is content to be the China of the New World, then and then only can it afford to do away with the navy and the army. If it is content to abandon Hawaii and the Panama Canal, to cease to talk of the Monroe Doctrine, and to admit the right of any European or Asiatic power to dictate what immigrants shall be sent to and received in America, and whether or not they shall be allowed to become citizens and hold land — why, of course, if America is content to have nothing to say on any of these matters and to keep silent in the presence of armed outsiders, then it can abandon its navy and agree to arbitrate all questions of all kinds with every foreign power. In such event it can afford to pass its spare time in one continuous round of universal peace celebrations, and of smug self-satisfaction in having earned the derision of all the virile peoples of mankind. Those who advocate such a policy do not occupy a lofty position. But at least their position is understandable.

It is entirely inexcusable, however, to try to combine the unready hand with the unbridled tongue. It is folly to permit freedom of speech about foreigners as well as ourselves — and the peace-at-any-price persons are much too feeble a folk to try to interfere with freedom of speech — and yet to try to shirk the consequences of freedom of speech. It is folly to try to abolish our navy, and at the same time to insist that we have a right to enforce the Monroe Doctrine, that we have a right to control the Panama Canal which we ourselves dug, that we have a right to retain Hawaii and prevent foreign nations from taking Cuba, and a right to determine what immigrants, Asiatic or European, shall come to our shores, and the terms on which they shall be naturalized and shall hold land and exercise other privileges. We are a rich people, and an unmilitary people. In international affairs we are a short-sighted people. But I know my countrymen. Down at bottom their temper is such that they will not permanently tolerate injustice done to them. In the long run they will no more permit affronts to their National honor than injuries to their national interest. Such being the case, they will do well to remember that the surest of all ways to invite disaster is to be opulent, aggressive and unarmed.

Throughout the seven and a half years that I was President, I pursued without faltering one consistent foreign policy, a policy of genuine international good will and of consideration for the rights of others, and at the same time of steady preparedness. The weakest nations knew that they, no less than the strongest, were safe from insult and injury at our hands; and the strong and the weak alike also knew that we possessed both the will and the ability to guard ourselves from wrong or insult at the hands of any one.

It was under my administration that the Hague Court was saved from becoming an empty farce. It had been established by joint international agreement, but no Power had been willing to resort to it. Those establishing it had grown to realize that it was in danger of becoming a mere paper court, so that it would never really come into being at all. M. d'Estournelles de Constant had been especially alive to this danger. By correspondence and in personal interviews he impressed upon me the need not only of making advances by actually applying arbitration — not merely promising by treaty to apply it — to questions that were up for settlement, but of using the Hague tribunal for this purpose. I cordially sympathized with these views. On the recommendation of John Jay, I succeeded in getting an agreement with Mexico to lay a matter in dispute between the two republics before the Hague Court. This was the first case ever brought before the Hague Court. It was followed by numerous others; and it definitely established that court as the great international peace tribunal. By mutual agreement with Great Britain, through the decision of a joint commission, of which the American members were Senators Lodge and Turner, and Secretary Root, we were able peacefully to settle the Alaska Boundary question, the only question remaining between ourselves and the British Empire which it was not possible to settle by friendly arbitration; this therefore represented the removal of the last obstacle to absolute agreement between the two peoples. We were of substantial service in bringing to a satisfactory conclusion the negotiations at Algeciras concerning Morocco. We concluded with Great Britain, and with most of the other great nations, arbitration treaties specifically agreeing to arbitrate all matters, and especially the interpretation of treaties, save only as regards questions affecting territorial integrity, national honor and vital national interest. We made with Great Britain a treaty guaranteeing the free use of the Panama Canal on equal terms to the ships of all nations, while reserving to ourselves the right to police and fortify the canal, and therefore to control it in time of war. Under this treaty we are in honor bound to arbitrate the question of canal tolls for coastwise traffic between the Western and Eastern coasts of the United States. I believe that the American position as regards this matter is right; but I also believe that under the arbitration treaty we are in honor bound to submit the matter to arbitration in view of Great Britain's contention — although I hold it to be an unwise contention — that our position is unsound. I emphatically disbelieve in making universal arbitration treaties which neither the makers nor any one else would for a moment dream of keeping. I no less emphatically insist that it is our duty to keep the limited and sensible arbitration treaties which we have already made. The importance of a promise lies not in making it, but in keeping it; and the poorest of all positions for a nation to occupy in such a matter is readiness to make impossible promises at the same time that there is failure to keep promises which have been made, which can be kept, and which it is discreditable to break.

During the early part of the year 1905, the strain on the civilized world caused by the Russo-Japanese War became serious. The losses of life and of treasure were frightful. From all the sources of information at hand, I grew most strongly to believe that a further continuation of the struggle would be a very bad thing for Japan, and an even worse thing for Russia. Japan was already suffering terribly from the drain upon her men, and especially upon her resources, and had nothing further to gain from continuance of the struggle; its continuance meant to her more loss than gain, even if she were victorious. Russia, in spite of her gigantic strength, was, in my judgment, apt to lose even more than she had already lost if the struggle continued. I deemed it probable that she would no more be able successfully to defend Eastern Siberia and Northern Manchuria than she had been able to defend Southern Manchuria and Korea. If the war went on, I thought it, on the whole, likely that Russia would be driven west of Lake Baikal.

But it was very far from certain. There is no certainty in such a war. Japan might have met defeat, and defeat to her would have spelt overwhelming disaster; and even if she had continued to win, what she thus won would have been of no value to her, and the cost in blood and money would have left her drained white. I believed, therefore, that the time had come when it was greatly to the interest of both combatants to have peace, and when therefore it was possible to get both to agree to peace.

I first satisfied myself that each side wished me to act, but that, naturally and properly, each side was exceedingly anxious that the other should not believe that the action was taken on its initiative. I then sent an identical note to the two powers proposing that they should meet, through their representatives, to see if peace could not be made directly between them, and offered to act as an intermediary in bringing about such a meeting, but not for any other purpose. Each assented to my proposal in principle. There was difficulty in getting them to agree on a common meeting place; but each finally abandoned its original contention in the matter, and the representatives of the two nations finally met at Portsmouth, in New Hampshire. I previously received the two delegations at Oyster Bay on the U.S.S. Mayflower, which, together with another naval vessel, I put at their disposal, on behalf of the United States Government, to take them from Oyster Bay to Portsmouth.

As is customary — but both unwise and undesirable — in such cases, each side advanced claims which the other could not grant. The chief difficulty came because of Japan's demand for a money indemnity. I felt that it would be better for Russia to pay some indemnity than to go on with the war, for there was little chance, in my judgment, of the war turning out favorably for Russia, and the revolutionary movement already under way bade fair to overthrow the negotiations entirely. I advised the Russian Government to this effect, at the same time urging them to abandon their pretensions on certain other points, notably concerning the southern half of Saghelien, which the Japanese had taken. I also, however, and equally strongly, advised the Japanese that in my judgment it would be the gravest mistake on their part to insist on continuing the war for the sake of a money indemnity; for Russia

Peace Commission at Portsmouth.

was absolutely firm in refusing to give them an indemnity, and the longer the war continued the less able she would be to pay. I pointed out that there was no possible analogy between their case and that of Germany in the war with France, which they were fond of quoting. The Germans held Paris and half of France, and gave up much territory in lieu of the indemnity, whereas the Japanese were still many thousand miles from Moscow, and had no territory whatever which they wished to give up. I also pointed out that in my judgment whereas the Japanese had enjoyed the sympathy of most of the civilized powers at the outset of and during the continuance of the war, they would forfeit it if they turned the war into one merely for getting money — and, moreover, they would almost certainly fail to get the money, and would simply find themselves at the end of a year, even if things prospered with them, in possession of territory they did not want, having spent enormous additional sums of money, and lost enormous additional numbers of men, and yet without a penny of remuneration. The treaty of peace was finally signed.

As is inevitable under such circumstances, each side felt that it ought to have got better terms; and when the danger was well past each side felt that it had been over-reached by the other, and that if the war had gone on it would have gotten more than it actually did get. The Japanese Government had been wise throughout, except in the matter of announcing that it would insist on a money indemnity. Neither in national nor in private affairs is it ordinarily advisable to make a bluff which cannot be put through — personally, I never believe in doing it under any circumstances. The Japanese people had been misled by this bluff of their Government; and the unwisdom of the Government's action in the matter was shown by the great resentment the treaty aroused in Japan, although it was so beneficial to Japan. There were various mob outbreaks, especially in the Japanese cities; the police were roughly handled, and several Christian churches were burned, as reported to me by the American Minister. In both Russia and Japan I believe that the net result as regards myself was a feeling of injury, and of dislike of me, among the people at large. I had expected this; I regarded it as entirely natural; and I did not resent it in the least. The Governments of both nations behaved toward me not only with correct and entire propriety, but with much courtesy and the fullest acknowledgment of the good effect of what I had done; and in Japan, at least, I believe that the leading men sincerely felt that I had been their friend. I had certainly tried my best to be the friend not only of the Japanese people but of the Russian people, and I believe that what I did was for the best interests of both and of the world at large.

George von Lengerke Meyer,
Ambassador Extraordinary and
Plenipotentiary to Russia.

During the course of the negotiations I tried to enlist the aid of the Governments of one nation which was friendly to Russia, and of another nation which was friendly to Japan, in helping bring about peace. I got no aid from either. I did, however, receive aid from the Emperor of Germany. His Ambassador at St. Petersburg was the one Ambassador who helped the American Ambassador, Mr. Meyer, at delicate and doubtful points of the negotiations. Mr. Meyer, who was, with the exception of Mr. White, the most useful diplomat in the American service, rendered literally invaluable aid by insisting upon himself seeing the Czar at critical periods of the transaction, when it was no longer possible for me to act successfully through the representatives of the Czar, who were often at cross purposes with one another.

As a result of the Portsmouth peace, I was given the Nobel Peace Prize. This consisted of a medal, which I kept, and a sum of $40,000, which I turned over as a foundation of industrial peace to a board of trustees which included Oscar Straus, Seth Low and John Mitchell. In the present state of the world's development industrial peace is even more essential than international peace; and it was fitting and appropriate to devote the peace prize to such a purpose. In 1910, while in Europe, one of my most pleasant experiences was my visit to Norway, where I addressed the Nobel Committee, and set forth in full the principles upon which I had acted, not only in this particular case but throughout my administration.

I received another gift which I deeply appreciated, an original copy of Sully's "Memoires" of "Henry le Grand," sent me with the following inscription (I translate it roughly):

"PARIS, JANUARY, 1906.

"The undersigned members of the French Parliamentary Group of International Arbitration and Conciliation have decided to tender President Roosevelt a token of their high esteem and their sympathetic recognition of the persistent and decisive initiative he has taken towards gradually substituting friendly and judicial for violent methods in case of conflict between Nations.

"They believe that the action of President Roosevelt, which has realized the most generous hopes to be found in history, should be classed as a continuance of similar illustrious attempts of former times, notably the project for international concord known under the name of the 'Great Design of Henry IV' in the memoirs of his Prime Minister, the Duke de Sully. In consequence they have sought out a copy of the first edition of these memoirs, and they take pleasure in offering it to him, with the request that he will keep it among his family papers."

The signatures include those of Emile Loubet, A. Carnot, d'Estournelles de Constant, Aristide Briand, Sully Prudhomme, Jean Jaurés, A. Fallières, R. Poincaré, and two or three hundred others.

Of course what I had done in connection with the Portsmouth peace was misunderstood by some good and sincere people. Just as after the settlement of the coal strike, there were persons who thereupon thought that it was in my power, and was my duty, to settle all other strikes, so after the peace of Portsmouth there were other persons — not only Americans, by the way, — who thought it my duty forthwith to make myself a kind of international Meddlesome Mattie and interfere for peace and justice promiscuously over the world. Others, with a delightful non-sequitur, jumped to the conclusion that inasmuch as I had helped to bring about a beneficent and necessary peace I must of necessity have changed my mind about war being ever necessary. A couple of days after peace was concluded I wrote to a friend: "Don't you be misled by the fact that just at the moment men are speaking well of me. They will speak ill soon enough. As Loeb remarked to me to-day, some time soon I shall have to spank some little international brigand, and then all the well-meaning idiots will turn and shriek that this is inconsistent with what I did at the Peace Conference, whereas in reality it will be exactly in line with it."

To one of my political opponents, Mr. Schurz, who wrote me congratulating me upon the outcome at Portsmouth, and suggesting that the time was opportune for a move towards disarmament, I answered in a letter setting forth views which I thought sound then, and think sound now. The letter ran as follows:

OYSTER BAY, N.Y.,
September 8, 1905.

*My dear Mr. Schurz:* I thank you for your congratulations. As to what you say about disarmament — which I suppose is the rough equivalent of "the gradual diminution of the oppressive burdens imposed upon the world by armed peace" — I am not clear either as to what can be done or what ought to be done. If I had been known as one of the conventional type of peace advocates I could have done nothing whatever in bringing about peace now, I would be powerless in the future to accomplish anything, and I would not have been able to help confer the boons upon Cuba, the Philippines, Porto Rico and Panama, brought about by our action therein. If the Japanese had not armed during the last twenty years, this would indeed be a sorrowful century for Japan. If this country had not fought the Spanish War; if we had failed to take the action we did about Panama; all mankind would have been the loser. While the Turks were butchering the Armenians the European powers kept the peace and thereby added a burden of infamy to the Nineteenth Century, for in keeping that peace a greater number of lives were lost than in any European war since the days of Napoleon, and these lives were those of women and children as well as of men; while the moral degradation, the brutality inflicted and endured, the aggregate of hideous wrong done, surpassed that of any war of which we have record in modern times. Until people get it firmly fixed in their minds that peace is valuable chiefly as a means to righteousness, and that it can only be considered as an end when it also coincides with righteousness, we can do only a limited amount to advance its coming on this earth. There is of course no analogy at present between international law and private or municipal law, because there is no sanction of force for the former, while there is for the latter. Inside our own nation the law-abiding man does not have to arm himself against the lawless simply because there is some armed force — the police, the sheriff's posse, the national guard, the regulars — which can be called out to enforce the laws. At present there is no similar international force to call on, and I do not as yet see how it could at present be created. Hitherto peace has often come only be-cause some strong and on the whole just power has by armed force, or the threat of armed force, put a stop to disorder. In a very interesting French book the other day I was reading how the Med-iterranean was freed from pirates only by the "pax Britannica," established by England's naval force. The hopeless and hideous blood-shed and wickedness of Al-giers and Turkestan was stopped, and could only be stopped, when civilized na-tions in the shape of Russia and France took possession of them. The same was true of Burma and the Malay States, as well as Egypt, with regard

Nobel Peace Prize Medallion

This is a direct reproduction of the reverse of the medallion which measures 2⁹⁄₁₆ inches in diameter. On the edge appeared the words Parlamentum Norvegiæ MCMVI.

to England. Peace has come only as the sequel to the armed inter-ference of a civilized power which, relatively to its opponent, was a just and beneficent power. If England had disarmed to the point of being unable to conquer the Soudan and protect Egypt, so that the Mahdists had established their supremacy in northeastern Africa, the result would have been a horrible and bloody calamity to mankind. It was only the growth of the European powers in military efficiency that freed eastern Europe from the dreadful scourge of the Tartar and partially freed it from the dreadful scourge of the Turk. Unjust war is dreadful; a just war may be the highest duty. To have the best nations, the free and civilized nations, disarm and leave the despo-tisms and barbarisms with great military force, would be a calamity compared to which the calamities caused by all the wars of the nine-teenth century would be trivial. Yet it is not easy to see how we can by international agreement state exactly which power ceases to be free and civilized and which comes near the line of barbarism or des-potism. For example, I suppose it would be very difficult to get Russia and Japan to come to a common agreement on this point; and there are at least some citizens of other nations, not to speak of their governments, whom it would also be hard to get together.

This does not in the least mean that it is hopeless to make the effort. It may be that some scheme will be developed. America, for-tunately, can cordially assist in such an effort, for no one in his senses would suggest our disarmament; and though we should continue to perfect our small navy and our minute army, I do not think it necessary to increase the number of our ships — at any rate as things look now — nor the number of our soldiers. Of course our navy must be kept up to the highest point of efficiency, and the replacing of old and worthless vessels by first-class new ones may involve an increase in the personnel; but not enough to interfere with our action along the lines you have suggested. But before I would know how to ad-vocate such action, save in some such way as commending it to the attention of The Hague Tribunal, I would have to have a feasible and rational plan of action presented.

It seems to me that a general stop in the increase of the war navies of the world *might* be a good thing; but I would not like to speak too positively offhand. Of course it is only in continental Europe that the armies are too large; and before advocating action as regards them I should have to weigh matters carefully — including by the way such a matter as the Turkish army. At any rate nothing useful can be done unless with the clear recognition that we object to put-ting peace second to righteousness.

Sincerely yours,
THEODORE ROOSEVELT.

HON. CARL SCHURZ, Bolton Landing,
   Lake George, N.Y.

In my own judgment the most important service that I ren-dered to peace was the voyage of the battle fleet round the world. I had become convinced that for many reasons it was essential that we should have it clearly understood, by our own people especially, but also by other peoples, that the Pacific was as much our home waters as the Atlantic, and that our fleet could and would at will pass from one to the other of the two great oceans. It seemed to me evident that such a voyage would greatly benefit the navy itself; would arouse popular interest in and enthusiasm for the navy; and would make foreign nations accept as a matter of course that our fleet should from time to time be gathered in the Pacific, just as from time to time it was gathered in the Atlantic, and that its presence in one ocean was no more to be accepted as a mark of hostility to any Asiatic power than its presence in the Atlantic was to be accepted as a mark of hostility to any European power. I determined on the move without consulting the Cabinet, precisely as I took Panama without consulting the Cabinet. A council of war never fights, and in a crisis the duty of a leader is to lead and not to take refuge behind the generally timid wisdom of a multitude of councillors. At that time, as I happen to know, neither the English nor the German authorities believed it possible to take a fleet of great battleships round the world. They did not believe that their own fleets could perform the feat, and still less did they believe that the American fleet could. I made up my mind that it was time to have a show down in the matter; because if it was really true that our fleet could not get from the Atlantic to the Pacific, it was much better to know it and be able to shape our policy in view of the knowledge. Many persons publicly and privately protested against the move on the ground that Japan would accept it as a threat. To this I answered nothing in public. In private I said that I did not believe Japan would so regard it because Japan knew my sincere friendship and admiration for her and realized that we could not as a Nation have any intention of attacking her; and that if there were any such feeling on the part of Japan as was alleged that very fact rendered it imperative that that fleet should go. When in the spring of 1910 I was in Europe I was interested to find that high naval authorities in both Germany and Italy had expected that war would come at the time of the voyage. They asked me if I had not been afraid of it, and if I had not expected that hostilities would begin at least by the time that the fleet reached the Straits of Magellan? I answered that I did not expect it; that I believed that Japan would feel as friendly in the matter as we did; but that if my expectations had proved mistaken, it would have been proof positive that we were going to be attacked anyhow, and that in such event it would have been an enormous gain to have had the three months' preliminary preparation which enabled the fleet to start perfectly equipped. In a personal interview before they left I had explained to the officers in command that I believed the trip would be one of absolute peace, but that they were to take exactly the same precautions against sudden attack of any kind as if we were at war with all the nations of the earth; and that no excuse of any kind would be accepted if there were a sudden attack of any kind and we were taken unawares.

My prime purpose was to impress the American people; and this purpose was fully achieved. The cruise did make a very deep impression abroad; boasting about what we have done does not impress foreign nations at all, except unfavorably, but positive achievement does; and the two American achievements that really impressed foreign peoples during the first dozen years of this century were the digging of the Panama Canal and the cruise of the battle fleet round the world. But the impression made on our own people was of far greater consequence. No single thing in the history of the new United States Navy has done as much to stimulate popular interest and belief in it as the world cruise. This effect was forecast in a well-informed and friendly English periodical, the London *Spectator*. Writing in October, 1907, a month before the fleet sailed from Hampton Roads, the *Spectator* said:

"All over America the people will follow the movements of the fleet; they will learn something of the intricate details of the coaling and commissariat work under warlike conditions; and in a word their attention will be aroused. Next time Mr. Roosevelt or his representatives appeal to the country for new battleships they will do so to people whose minds have been influenced one way or the other. The naval programme will not have stood still. We are sure that, apart from increasing the efficiency of the existing fleet, this is the aim which Mr. Roosevelt has in mind. He has a policy which projects itself far into the future, but it is an entire misreading of it to suppose that it is aimed narrowly and definitely at any single Power."

I first directed the fleet, of sixteen battleships, to go round through the Straits of Magellan to San Francisco. From thence I ordered them to New Zealand and Australia, then to the Philippines, China and Japan, and home through Suez — they

From a painting by Henry Reuterdahl.

The Fleet in the Straits of Magellan.

stopped in the Mediterranean to help the sufferers from the earthquake at Messina, by the way, and did this work as effectively as they had done all their other work. Admiral Evans commanded the fleet to San Francisco; there Admiral Sperry took it; Admirals Thomas, Wainwright and Schroeder rendered distinguished service under Evans and Sperry. The coaling and other preparations were made in such excellent shape by the Department that there was never a hitch, not so much as the delay of an hour, in keeping every appointment made. All the repairs were made without difficulty, the ship concerned merely falling out of column for a few hours, and when the job was done steaming at speed until she regained her position. Not a ship was left in any port; and there was hardly a desertion. As soon as it was known that the voyage was to be undertaken men crowded to enlist, just as freely from the Mississippi Valley as from the seaboard, and for the first time since the Spanish War the ships put to sea overmanned — and by as stalwart a set of men-of-war's men as ever looked through a porthole, game for a fight or a frolic, but withal so self-respecting and with such a sense of responsibility that in all the ports in which they landed their conduct was exemplary. The fleet practiced incessantly during the voyage, both with the guns and in battle tactics, and came home a much more efficient fighting instrument than when it started sixteen months before.

The best men of command rank in our own service were confident that the fleet would go round in safety, in spite of the incredulity of foreign critics. Even they, however, did not believe that it was wise to send the torpedo craft around. I accordingly acquiesced in their views, as it did not occur to me to consult the lieutenants. But shortly before the fleet started, I went in the Government yacht Mayflower to inspect the target practice off Provincetown. I was accompanied by two torpedo boat destroyers, in charge of a couple of naval lieutenants, thorough gamecocks; and I had the two lieutenants aboard to dine one evening. Towards the end of the dinner they could not refrain from asking if the torpedo flotilla was to go round with the big ships. I told them no, that the admirals and captains did not believe that the torpedo boats could stand it, and believed that the officers and crews aboard the cockle shells would be worn out by the constant pitching and bouncing and the everlasting need to make repairs. My two guests chorused an eager assurance that the boats could stand it. They assured me that the enlisted men were even more anxious to go than were the officers, mentioning that on one of their boats the terms of enlistment of most of the crew were out, and the men were waiting to see whether or not to reënlist, as they did not care to do so unless the boats were to go on the cruise. I answered that I was only too glad to accept the word of the men who were to do the job, and that they should certainly go; and within half an hour I sent out the order for the flotilla to be got ready. It went round in fine shape, not a boat being laid up. I felt that the feat reflected even more credit upon the navy than did the circumnavigation of the big ships, and I wrote the flotilla commander the following letter:

May 18, 1908.

*My dear Captain Cone:*

A great deal of attention has been paid to the feat of our battleship fleet in encircling South America and getting to San Francisco; and it would be hard too highly to compliment the officers and enlisted men of that fleet for what they have done. Yet if I should draw any distinction at all it would be in favor of you and your associates who have taken out the torpedo flotilla. Yours was an even more notable feat, and every officer and every enlisted man in the torpedo boat flotilla has the right to feel that he has rendered distinguished service to the United States navy and therefore to the people of the United States; and I wish I could thank each of them personally. Will you have this letter read by the commanding officer of each torpedo boat to his officers and crew?

Sincerely yours,

THEODORE ROOSEVELT.

LIEUTENANT COMMANDER HUTCH. I. CONE, U.S.N.,

Commanding Second Torpedo Flotilla,

Care Postmaster, San Francisco, Cal.

There were various amusing features connected with the trip. Most of the wealthy people and "leaders of opinion" in the Eastern cities were panic-struck at the proposal to take the fleet away from Atlantic waters. The great New York dailies issued frantic appeals to Congress to stop the fleet from going.

The head of the Senate Committee on Naval Affairs announced that the fleet should not and could not go because Congress would refuse to appropriate the money — he being from an Eastern seaboard State. However, I announced in response that I had enough money to take the fleet around to the Pacific anyhow, that the fleet would certainly go, and that if Congress did not choose to appropriate enough money to get the fleet back, why, it would stay in the Pacific. There was no further difficulty about the money.

It was not originally my intention that the fleet should visit Australia, but the Australian Government sent a most cordial invitation, which I gladly accepted; for I have, as every American ought to have, a hearty admiration for, and fellow feeling with, Australia, and I believe that America should be ready to stand back of Australia in any serious emergency. The reception accorded the fleet in Australia was wonderful, and it showed the fundamental community of feeling between ourselves and the great commonwealth of the South Seas. The considerate, generous, and open-handed hospitality with which the entire Australian people treated our officers and men could not have been surpassed had they been our own countrymen. The fleet first visited Sidney, which has a singularly beautiful harbor. The day after the arrival one of our captains noticed a member of his crew trying to go to sleep on a bench in the park. He had fixed above his head a large paper with some lines evidently designed to forestall any questions from friendly would-be hosts: "I am delighted with the Australian people. I think your harbor the finest in the world. I am very tired and would like to go to sleep."

The most noteworthy incident of the cruise was the reception given to our fleet in Japan. In courtesy and good breeding, the Japanese can certainly teach much to the nations of the Western world. I had been very sure that the people of Japan would understand aright what the cruise meant, and would accept the visit of our fleet as the signal honor which it was meant to be, a proof of the high regard and friendship I felt, and which I was certain the American people felt, for the great Island Empire. The event even surpassed my expectations. I cannot too strongly express my appreciation of the generous courtesy the Japanese showed the officers and crews of our fleet; and I may add that every man of them came back a friend and admirer of the Japanese. Admiral Sperry wrote me a letter of much interest, dealing not only with the reception in Tokio but with the work of our men at sea; I herewith give it almost in full:

28 October, 1908.

*Dear Mr. Roosevelt:*

My official report of the visit to Japan goes forward in this mail, but there are certain aspects of the affair so successfully concluded which cannot well be included in the report.

You are perhaps aware that Mr. Denison of the Japanese Foreign Office was one of my colleagues at The Hague, for whom I have a very high regard. Desiring to avoid every possibility of trouble or misunderstanding, I wrote to him last June explaining fully the character of our men, which they have so well lived up to, the desirability of ample landing places, guides, rest houses and places for changing money in order that there might be no delay in getting the men away from the docks on the excursions in which they delight. Very few of them go into a drinking place, except to get a resting place not to be found elsewhere, paying for it by taking a drink.

I also explained our system of landing with liberty men an unarmed patrol, properly officered, to quietly take in charge and send off to their ships any men who showed the slightest trace of disorderly conduct. This letter he showed to the Minister of the Navy, who highly approved of all our arrangements, including the patrol, of which I feared they might be jealous. Mr. Denison's reply reached me in Manila, with a memorandum from the Minister of the Navy which removed all doubts. Three temporary piers were built for our boat landings, each 300 feet long, brilliantly lighted and decorated. The sleeping accommodations did not permit two or three thousand sailors to remain on shore, but the ample landings permitted them to be handled night and day with perfect order and safety.

At the landings and railroad station in Yokohama there were rest houses or booths, reputable money changers and as many as a thousand English-speaking Japanese college students acted as volunteer guides, besides Japanese sailors and petty officers detailed for the purpose. In Tokyo there were a great many excellent refreshment places, where the men got excellent meals and could rest, smoke and write letters, and in none of these places would they allow the men to pay anything, though they were more than ready to do so. The arrangements were marvelously perfect.

As soon as your telegram of October 18, giving the address to be made to the Emperor, was received, I gave copies of it to our

Ambassador to be sent to the Foreign Office. It seems that the Emperor had already prepared a very cordial address to be forwarded through me to you, after delivery at the audience, but your telegram reversed the situation and his reply was prepared. I am convinced that your kind and courteous initiative on this occasion helped cause the pleasant feeling which was so obvious in the Emperor's bearing at the luncheon which followed the audience. X., who is reticent and conservative, told me that not only the Emperor but all the Ministers were profoundly gratified by the course of events. I am confident

Senator Lodge.

that not even the most trifling incident has taken place which could in any way mar the general satisfaction, and our Ambassador has expressed to me his great satisfaction with all that has taken place.

Owing to heavy weather encountered on the passage up from Manila the fleet was obliged to take about 3500 tons of coal.

The Yankton remained behind to keep up communication for a few days, and yesterday she transmitted the Emperor's telegram to you, which was sent in reply to your message through our Ambassador after the sailing of the fleet. It must be profoundly gratifying to you to have the mission on which you sent the fleet terminate so happily, and I am profoundly thankful that, owing to the confidence which you displayed in giving me this command, my active career draws to a close with such honorable distinction.

As for the effect of the cruise upon the training, discipline and effectiveness of the fleet, the good cannot be exaggerated. It is a war game in every detail. The wireless communication has been maintained with an efficiency hitherto unheard of. Between Honolulu and Auckland, 3850 miles, we were out of communication with a cable station for only one night, whereas three [non-American] men-of-war trying recently to maintain a chain of only 1250 miles, between Auckland and Sydney, were only able to do so for a few hours.

The officers and men as soon as we put to sea turn to their gunnery and tactical work far more eagerly than they go to functions. Every morning certain ships leave the column and move off seven or eight thousand yards as targets for range measuring fire control and battery practice for the others, and at night certain ships do the same thing for night battery practice. I am sorry to say that this practice is unsatisfactory, and in some points misleading, owing to the fact that the ships are painted white. At Portland, in 1903, I saw Admiral Barker's white battleships under the searchlights of the army at a distance of 14,000 yards, seven sea miles, without glasses, while the Hartford, a black ship, was never discovered at all, though she passed within a mile and a half. I have for years, while a member of the General Board, advocated painting the ships war color at all times, and by this mail I am asking the Department to make the necessary change in the Regulations and paint the ships properly. I do not know that any one now dissents from my view. Admiral Wainwright strongly concurs, and the War College Conference recommended it year after year without a dissenting voice.

In the afternoon the fleet has two or three hours' practice at battle maneuvers, which excite as keen interest as gunnery exercises.

The competition in coal economy goes on automatically and reacts in a hundred ways. It has reduced the waste in the use of electric light and water, and certain chief engineers are said to keep men ranging over the ships all night turning out every light not in actual and immediate use. Perhaps the most important effect is the keen hunt for defects in the machinery causing waste of power. The Yankton by resetting valves increased her speed from 10 to 11½ knots on the same expenditure.

All this has been done, but the field is widening, the work has only begun.

*      *      *      *      *      *      *

C. S. SPERRY.

When I left the Presidency I finished seven and a half years of administration, during which not one shot had been fired against a foreign foe. We were at absolute peace, and there was no nation in the world with whom a war cloud threatened, no nation in the world whom we had wronged, or from whom we had anything to fear. The cruise of the battle fleet was not the least of the causes which ensured so peaceful an outlook.

President Roosevelt and the Gun Pointers of the U.S. Battleship Missouri.

When the fleet returned after its sixteen months' voyage around the world I went down to Hampton Roads to greet it. The day was Washington's Birthday, February 22, 1907. Literally on the minute the homing battlecraft came into view. On the flagship of the Admiral I spoke to the officers and enlisted men, as follows:

*"Admiral Sperry, Officers and Men of the Battle Fleet:*

"Over a year has passed since you steamed out of this harbor, and over the world's rim, and this morning the hearts of all who saw you thrilled with pride as the hulls of the mighty warships lifted above the horizon. You have been in the Northern and the Southern Hemispheres; four times you have crossed the line; you have steamed

The Return of the Fleet; entering Chesapeake Bay.

through all the great oceans; you have touched the coast of every continent. Ever your general course has been westward; and now you come back to the port from which you set sail. This is the first battle fleet that has ever circumnavigated the globe. Those who perform the feat again can but follow in your footsteps.

"The little torpeo flotilla went with you around South America, through the Straits of Magellan, to our own Pacific Coast. The armored cruiser squadron met you, and left you again, when you were half way round the world. You have falsified every prediction of the prophets of failure. In all your long cruise not an accident worthy of mention has happened to a single battleship, nor yet to the cruisers or torpedo boats. You left this coast in a high state of battle efficiency, and you return with your efficiency increased; better prepared than when you left, not only in personnel but even in material. During your world cruise you have taken your regular gunnery practice, and skilled though you were before with the guns, you have grown more skilful still; and through practice you have improved in battle tactics, though here there is more room for improvement than in your gunnery. Incidentally, I suppose I need hardly say that one measure of your fitness must be your clear recognition of the need always steadily to strive to render yourselves more fit; if you ever grow to think that you are fit enough, you can make up your minds that from that moment you will begin to go backward.

"As a war machine, the fleet comes back in better shape than it went out. In addition, you, the officers and men of this formidable fighting force, have shown yourselves the best of all possible ambassadors and heralds of peace. Wherever you have landed you have borne yourselves so as to make us at home proud of being your countrymen. You have shown that the best type of fighting man of the sea knows how to appear to the utmost possible advantage when his business is to behave himself on shore, and to make a good impression in a foreign land. We are proud of all the ships and all the men in this whole fleet, and we welcome you home to the country whose good repute among nations has been raised by what you have done."

# APPENDIX A

## THE TRUSTS, THE PEOPLE,
## AND THE SQUARE DEAL

[Written when Mr. Taft's administration brought suit to dissolve the steel corporation, one of the grounds for the suit being the acquisition by the Corporation of the Tennessee Coal and Iron Company; this action was taken, with my acquiescence, while I was President, and while Mr. Taft was a member of my cabinet; at the time he never protested against, and as far as I knew approved of my action in this case, as in the Harvester Trust case, and all similar cases.]

The suit against the Steel Trust by the Government has brought vividly before our people the need of reducing to order our chaotic Government policy as regards business. As President, in Messages to Congress I repeatedly called the attention of that body and of the public to the inadequacy of the Anti-Trust Law by itself to meet business conditions and secure justice to the people, and to the further fact that it might, if left unsupplemented by additional legislation, work mischief, with no compensating advantage; and I urged as strongly as I knew how that the policy followed with relation to railways in connection with the Inter-State Commerce Law should be followed by the National Government as regards all great business concerns; and therefore that, as a first step, the powers of the Bureau of Corporations should be greatly enlarged, or else that there should be created a Governmental board or commission, with powers somewhat similar to those of the Inter-State Commerce Commission, but covering the whole field of inter-State business, exclusive of transportation (which should, by law, by kept wholly separate from ordinary industrial business, all common ownership of the industry and the railway being forbidden). In the end I have always believed that it would also be necessary to give the National Government complete power over the organization and capitalization of all business concerns engaged in inter-State commerce.

A member of my Cabinet with whom, even more than with the various Attorneys-General, I went over every detail of the trust situation, was the one time Secretary of the Interior, Mr. James R. Garfield. He writes me as follows concerning the suit against the Steel Corporation:

"Nothing appeared before the House Committee that made me believe we were deceived by Judge Gary.

"This, I think, is a case that shows clearly the difference between destructive litigation and constructive legislation. I have not yet seen a full copy of the Government's petition, but our papers give nothing that indicates any kind of unfair or dishonest competition such as existed in both the Standard Oil and Tobacco Cases. As I understand it, the competitors of the Steel Company have steadily increased in strength during the last six or seven years. Furthermore, the per cent of the business done by the Steel Corporation has decreased during that time. As you will remember, at our first conference with Judge Gary, the Judge stated that it was the desire and purpose of the Company to conform to what the Government wished, it being the purpose of the Company absolutely to obey the law both in spirit and letter. Throughout the time that I had charge of the investigation, and while we were in Washington, I do not know of a single instance where the Steel Company refused any information requested; but, on the contrary, aided in every possible way our investigation.

"The position now taken by the Government is absolutely destructive of legitimate business, because they outline no rule of conduct for business of any magnitude. It is absurd to say that the courts can lay down such rules. The most the courts can do is to find as legal or illegal the particular transactions brought before them. Hence, after years of tedious litigation there would be no clear-cut rule for future action. This method of procedure is dealing with the device, not the result, and drives business to the elaboration of clever devices, each of which must be tested in the courts.

"I have yet to find a better method of dealing with the anti-trust situation than that suggested by the bill which we agreed upon in the last days of your Administration. That bill should be used as a basis for legislation, and there could be incorporated upon it whatever may be determined wise regarding the direct control and supervision of the National Government, either through a commission similar to the Inter-State Commerce Commission or otherwise."

Before taking up the matter in its large aspect, I wish to say one word as to one feature of the Government suit against the Steel Corporation. One of the grounds for the suit is the acquisition by the Steel Corporation of the Tennessee Coal and Iron Company; and it has been alleged, on the authority of the Government officials engaged in carrying on the suit, that as regards this transaction I was misled by the representatives of the Steel Corporation, and that the facts were not accurately or truthfully laid before me. This statement is not correct. I believed at the time that the facts in the case were as represented to me on behalf of the Steel Corporation, and my further knowledge has convinced me that this was true. I believed at the time that the representatives of the Steel Corporation told me the truth as to the change that would be worked in the percentage of the business which the proposed acquisition would give the Steel Corporation, and further inquiry has convinced me that they did so. I was not misled. The representatives of the Steel Corporation told me the truth as to what the effect of the action at that time would be, and any statement that I was misled or that the representatives of the Steel Corporation did not thus tell me the truth as to the facts of the case is itself not in accordance with the truth. In *The Outlook* of August 19 last I gave in full the statement I had made to the Investigating Committee of the House of Representatives on this matter. That statement is accurate, and I reaffirm everything I therein said, not only as to what occurred, but also as to my belief in the wisdom and propriety of my action — indeed, the action not merely was wise and proper, but it would have been a calamity from every standpoint had I failed to take it. On page 137 of the printed report of the testimony before the Committee will be found Judge Gary's account of the meeting between himself and Mr. Frick and Mr. Root and myself. This account states the facts accurately. It has been alleged that the purchase by the Steel Corporation of the property of the Tennessee Coal and Iron Company gave the Steel Corporation practically a monopoly of the Southern iron ores — that is, of the iron ores south of the Potomac and the Ohio. My information, which I have every reason to believe is accurate and not successfully to be challenged, is that, of these Southern iron ores the Steel Corporation has, including the property gained from the Tennessee Coal and Iron Company, less than 20 per cent — perhaps not over 16 per cent. This is a very much smaller percentage than the percentage it holds of the Lake Superior ores, which even after the surrender of the Hill lease will be slightly over 50 per cent. According to my view, therefore, and unless — which I do not believe possible — these figures can be successfully challenged, the acquisition of the Tennessee Coal and Iron Company's ores in no way changed the situation as regards making the Steel Corporation a monopoly.* The showing as to the percentage of production of all kinds of steel ingots and steel castings in the United States by the Steel Corporation and by all other manufacturers respectively makes an even stronger case. It makes the case even stronger than I put it in my testimony before the Investigating Committee, for I was scrupulously careful to make statements that erred, if at all, against

---

*My own belief is that our Nation should long ago have adopted the policy of merely leasing for a term of years mineral-bearing land; but it is the fault of us ourselves, of the people, not of the Steel Corporation, that this policy has not been adopted.

my own position. It appears from the figures of production that in 1901 the Steel Corporation had to its credit nearly 66 per cent of the total production as against a little over 34 per cent by all other steel manufacturers. The percentage then shrank steadily, until in 1906, the year before the acquisition of the Tennessee Coal and Iron properties, the percentage was a little under 58 per cent. In spite of the acquisition of these properties, the following year, 1907, the total percentage shrank slightly, and this shrinking has continued until in 1910 the total percentage of the Steel Corporation is but a little over 54 per cent, and the percentage by all other steel manufacturers but a fraction less than 46 per cent. Of the $54\frac{3}{10}$ per cent produced by the Steel Corporation $1\frac{9}{10}$ per cent is produced by the former Tennessee Coal and Iron Company. In other words, these figures show that the acquisition of the Tennessee Coal and Iron Company did not in the slightest degree change the situation, and that during the ten years which include the acquisition of these properties by the Steel Corporation the percentage of total output of steel manufacturers in this country by the Steel Corporation has shrunk from nearly 66 per cent to but a trifle over 54 per cent. I do not believe that these figures can be successfully controverted, and if not successfully controverted they show clearly not only that the acquisition of the Tennessee Coal and Iron properties wrought no change in the status of the Steel Corporation, but that the Steel Corporation during the decade has steadily lost, instead of gained, in monopolistic character.

So much for the facts in this particular case. Now for the general subject. When my Administration took office, I found, not only that there had been little real enforcement of the Anti-Trust Law and but little more effective enforcement of the Inter-State Commerce Law, but also that the decisions were so chaotic and the laws themselves so vaguely drawn, or at least interpreted in such widely varying fashions, that the biggest business men tended to treat both laws as dead letters. The series of actions by which we succeeded in making the Inter-State Commerce Law an efficient and most useful instrument in regulating the transportation of the country and exacting justice from the big railways without doing them injustice — while, indeed, on the contrary, securing them against injustice — need not here be related. The Anti-Trust Law it was also necessary to enforce as it had never hitherto been enforced; both because it was on the statute-books and because it was imperative to teach the masters of the biggest corporations in the land that they were not, and would not be permitted to regard themselves as, above the law. Moreover, where the combination has really been guilty of misconduct the law serves a useful purpose, and in such cases as those of the Standard

Oil and Tobacco Trusts, if effectively enforced, the law confers a real and great good.

Suits were brought against the most powerful corporations in the land, which we were convinced had clearly and beyond question violated the Anti-Trust Law. These suits were brought with great care, and only where we felt so sure of our facts that we could be fairly certain that there was a likelihood of success. As a matter of fact, in most of the important suits we were successful. It was imperative that these suits should be brought, and very real good was achieved by bringing them, for it was only these suits that made the great masters of corporate capital in America fully realize that they were the servants and not the masters of the people, that they were subject to the law, and that they would not be permitted to be a law unto themselves; and the corporations against which we proceeded had sinned, not merely by being big (which we did not regard as in itself a sin), but by being guilty of unfair practices towards their competitors, and by procuring unfair advantages from the railways. But the resulting situation has made it evident that the Anti-Trust Law is not adequate to meet the situation that has grown up because of modern business conditions and the accompanying tremendous increase in the business use of vast quantities of corporate wealth. As I have said, this was already evident to my mind when I was President, and in communications to Congress I repeatedly stated the facts. But when I made these communications there were still plenty of people who did not believe that we would succeed in the suits that had been instituted against the Standard Oil, the Tobacco, and other corporations, and it was impossible to get the public as a whole to realize what the situation was. Sincere zealots who believed that all combinations could be destroyed and the old-time conditions of unregulated competition restored, insincere politicians who knew better but made believe that they thought whatever their constituents wished them to think, crafty reactionaries who wished to see on the statute-books laws which they believed unenforceable, and the almost solid "Wall Street crowd" or representatives of "big business" who at that time opposed with equal violence both wise and necessary and unwise and improper regulation of business — all fought against the adoption of a sane, effective, and far-reaching policy.

It is a vitally necessary thing to have the persons in control of big trusts of the character of the Standard Oil Trust and Tobacco Trust taught that they are under the law, just as it was a necessary thing to have the Sugar Trust taught the same lesson in drastic fashion by Mr. Henry L. Stimson when he was United States District Attorney in the city of New York. But to attempt to meet the whole problem not by administrative governmental action but by a succession of lawsuits is hopeless from the standpoint of working out a permanently satisfactory solution. Moreover, the results sought to be achieved are achieved only in extremely insufficient and fragmentary measure by breaking up all big corporations, whether they have behaved well or ill, into a number of little corporations which it is perfectly certain will be largely, and perhaps altogether, under the same control. Such action is harsh and mischievous if the corporation is guilty of nothing except its size; and where, as in the case of the Standard Oil, and especially the Tobacco, trusts, the corporation has been guilty of immoral and anti-social practices, there is need for far more drastic and thoroughgoing action than any that has been taken, under the recent decree of the Supreme Court. In the case of the Tobacco Trust, for instance, the settlement in the Circuit Court, in which the representatives of the Government seem inclined to concur, practically leaves all of the companies still substantially under the control of the twenty-nine original defendants. Such a result is lamentable from the standpoint of justice. The decision of the Circuit Court, if allowed to stand, means that the Tobacco Trust has merely been obliged to change its clothes, that none of the real offenders have received any real punishment, while, as the New York *Times*, a pro-trust paper, says, the tobacco concerns, in their new clothes, are in positions of "ease and luxury," and "immune from prosecution under the law."

Surely, miscarriage of justice is not too strong a term to apply to such a result when considered in connection with what the Supreme Court said of this Trust. That great Court in its decision used language which, in spite of its habitual and severe self-restraint in stigmatizing wrong-doing, yet unhesitatingly condemns the Tobacco Trust for moral turpitude, saying that the case shows an "ever present manifestation . . . of conscious wrong-doing" by the Trust, whose history is "replete with the doing of acts which it was the obvious purpose of the statute to forbid, . . . demonstrative of the existence from the beginning of a purpose to acquire dominion and control of the tobacco trade, not by the mere exertion of the ordinary right to contract and to trade, but by methods devised in order to monopolize the trade by driving competitors out of business, which were ruthlessly carried out upon the assumption that to work upon the fears or play upon the cupidity of competitors would make success possible." The letters from and to various officials of the Trust, which were put in evidence, show a literally astounding and horrifying indulgence by the Trust in wicked and depraved business methods — such as the "endeavor to cause a strike in their [a rival business firm's] factory," or the "shutting off the market" of an independent tobacco firm by "taking the necessary steps to give them a warm reception," or forcing importers into a price agreement by causing and continuing "a demoralization of the business for such length of time as may be deemed desirable" (I quote from the letters). A Trust guilty of such conduct should be absolutely disbanded, and the only way to prevent the repetition of such conduct is by strict Government supervision, and not merely by lawsuits.

The Anti-Trust Law cannot meet the whole situation, nor can any modification of the principle of the Anti-Trust Law avail to meet the whole situation. The fact is that many of the men who have called themselves Progressives, and who certainly believe that they are Progressives, represent in reality in this matter not progress at all but a kind of sincere rural toryism. These men believe that it is possible by strengthening the Anti-Trust Law to restore business to the competitive conditions of the middle of the last century. Any such effort is foredoomed to end in failure, and, if successful, would be mischievous to the last degree. Business cannot be successfully conducted in accordance with the practices and theories of sixty years ago unless we abolish steam, electricity, big cities, and, in short, not only all modern business and modern industrial conditions, but all the modern conditions of our civilization. The effort to restore competition as it was sixty years ago, and to trust for justice solely to this proposed restoration of competition, is just as foolish as if we should go back to the flintlocks of Washington's Continentals as a substitute for modern weapons of precision. The effort to prohibit all combinations, good or bad, is bound to fail, and ought to fail; when made, it merely means that some of the worst combinations are not checked and that honest business is checked. Our purpose should be, not to strangle business as an incident of strangling combinations, but to regulate big corporations in thoroughgoing and effective fashion, so as to help legitimate business as an incident to thoroughly and completely safeguarding the interests of the people as a whole. Against all such increase of Government regulation the argument is raised that it would amount to a form of Socialism. This argument is familiar; it is precisely the same as that which was raised against the creation of the Inter-State Commerce Commission, and of all the different utilities commissions in the different States, as I myself saw, thirty years ago, when I was a legislator at Albany, and these questions came up in connection with our State Government. Nor can action be effectively taken by any one State. Congress alone has power under the Constitution effectively and thoroughly and at all points to deal with inter-State commerce, and where Congress, as it should do, provides laws that will give the Nation full jurisdiction over the whole field, then that jurisdiction becomes, of necessity, exclusive — although until Congress does act affirmatively and thoroughly it is idle to expect that the States will or ought to rest content with non-action on the part of both Federal and State authorities. This statement, by the way, applies also to the question of "usurpation" by any one branch of our Government of the rights of another branch. It is contended that in these recent decisions the Supreme Court legislated; so it did; and it had to; because Congress had signally failed to do *its* duty by legislating. For the Supreme Court to nullify an act of the Legislature as unconstitutional except on the clearest grounds is usurpation; to interpret such an act in an obviously wrong sense is usurpation; but where the legislative body persistently leaves open a field which it is absolutely imperative, from the public standpoint, to fill, then no possible blame attaches to the official or officials who step in because they have to, and who then do the needed work in the interest of the people. The blame in such cases lies with the body which has been derelict, and not with the body which reluctantly makes good the dereliction.

A quarter of a century ago, Senator Cushman K. Davis, a statesman who amply deserved the title of statesman, a man of the highest courage, of the sternest adherence to the principles laid down by an exacting sense of duty, an unflinching believer in democracy, who was as little to be cowed by a mob as by a plutocrat, and moreover a man who possessed the priceless gift of imagination, a gift as important to a statesman as to a historian, in an address delivered at the annual commencement of the University of Michigan on July 1, 1886, spoke as follows of corporations:

"Feudalism, with its domains, its untaxed lords, their retainers, its exemptions and privileges, made war upon the aspiring spirit of humanity, and fell with all its grandeurs. Its spirit walks the earth and haunts the institutions of to-day, in the great corporations, with the control of the National highways, their occupation of great domains, their power to tax, their cynical contempt for the law, their sorcery to debase most gifted men to the capacity of splendid slaves, their pollution of the ermine of the judge and the robe of the Senator, their aggregation in one man of wealth so enormous as to make Crœsus seem a pauper, their picked, paid, and skilled retainers who are summoned by the message of electricity and appear upon the wings of steam. If we look into the origin of feudalism and of the modern corporations — those Dromios of history — we find that the former originated in a strict paternalism, which is scouted by modern economists, and that the latter has grown from an unrestrained freedom of action, aggression, and development, which they commend as the very ideal of political wisdom. *Laissez-faire*, says the professor, when it often means bind and gag that the strongest may work his will. It is a plea for the survival of the fittest — for the strongest male to take possession of the herd by a process of extermination. If we examine this battle cry of political polemics, we find that it is based upon the conception of the divine right of property, and the preoccupation by older or more favored or more alert or richer men or nations, of territory, of the forces of nature, of machinery, of all the functions of what we call civilization. Some of these men, who are really great, follow these conceptions to their conclusions with dauntless intrepidity."

When Senator Davis spoke, few men of great power had the sympathy and the vision necessary to perceive the menace contained in the growth of corporations; and the men who did see the evil were struggling blindly to get rid of it, not by frankly meeting the new situation with new methods, but by insisting upon the entirely futile effort to abolish what modern conditions had rendered absolutely inevitable. Senator Davis was under no such illusion. He realized keenly that it was absolutely impossible to go back to an outworn social status, and that we must abandon definitely the *laissez-faire* theory of political economy, and fearlessly champion a system of increased Governmental control, paying no heed to the cries of the worthy people who denounce this as Socialistic. He saw that, in order to meet the inevitable increase in the power of corporations produced by modern industrial conditions, it would be necessary to increase in like fashion the activity of the sovereign power which alone could control such corporations. As has been aptly said, the only way to meet a billion-dollar corporation is by invoking the protection of a hundred-billion-dollar government; in other words, of the National Government, for no State Government is strong enough both to do justice to corporations and to exact justice from them. Said Senator Davis in this admirable address, which should be reprinted and distributed broadcast:

"The liberty of the individual has been annihilated by the logical process constructed to maintain it. We have come to a political deification of Mammon. *Laissez-faire* is not utterly blameworthy. It begat modern democracy, and made the modern republic possible. There can be no doubt of that. But there it reached its limit of political benefaction, and began to incline toward the point where extremes meet. . . . To every assertion that the people in their collective capacity of a government ought to exert their indefeasible right of self-defense, it is said you touch the sacred rights of property."

The Senator then goes on to say that we now have to deal with an oligarchy of wealth, and that the Government must develop power sufficient enough to enable it to do the task.

Few will dispute the fact that the present situation is not satisfactory, and cannot be put on a permanently satisfactory basis unless we put an end to the period of groping and declare for a fixed policy, a policy which shall clearly define and punish wrong-doing, which shall put a stop to the iniquities done in the name of business, but which shall do strict equity to business. We demand that big business give the people a square deal; in return we must insist that when any one engaged in big business honestly endeavors to do right he shall himself be given a square deal; and the first, and most elementary, kind of square deal is to give him in advance full information as to just what he can, and what he cannot, legally and properly do. It is absurd, and much worse than absurd, to treat the deliberate law-breaker as on an exact par with the man eager to obey the law, whose only desire is to find out from some competent Governmental authority what the law is, and then to live up to it. Moreover, it is absurd to treat the size of a corporation as in itself a crime. As Judge Hook says in his opinion in the Standard Oil Case: "Magnitude of business does not alone constitute a monopoly . . . the genius and industry of man when kept to ethical standards still have full play, and what he achieves is his . . . success and magnitude of business, the rewards of fair and honorable endeavor [are not forbidden] . . . [the public welfare is threatened only when success is attained] by wrongful or unlawful methods." Size may, and in my opinion does, make a corporation fraught with potential menace to the community; and may, and in my opinion should, therefore make it incumbent upon the community to exercise through its administrative (not merely through its judicial) officers a strict supervision over that corporation in order to see that it does not go wrong; but the size in itself does not signify wrong-doing, and should not be held to signify wrong-doing.

Not only should any huge corporation which has gained its position by unfair methods, and by interference with the rights of others, by demoralizing and corrupt practices, in short, by sheer baseness and wrong-doing, be broken up, but it should be made the business of some administrative governmental body, by constant supervision, to see that it does not come together again, save under such strict control as shall insure the community against all repetition of the bad conduct — and it should never be permitted thus to assemble its parts as long as these parts are under the control of the original offenders, for actual experience has shown that these men are, from the standpoint of the people at large, unfit to be trusted with the power implied in the management of a large corporation. But nothing of importance is gained by breaking up a huge inter-State and international industrial organization *which has not offended otherwise than by its size*, into a number of small concerns without any attempt to regulate the way in which those concerns as a whole shall do business. Nothing is gained by depriving the American Nation of good weapons wherewith to fight in the great field of international industrial competition. Those who would seek to restore the days of unlimited and uncontrolled competition, and who believe that a panacea for our industrial and economic ills to is be found in the mere breaking up of all big corporations, simply because they are big, are attempting not only the impossible, but what, if possible, would be undesirable. They are acting as we should act if we tried to dam the Mississippi, to stop its flow outright. The effort would be certain to result in failure and disaster; we would have attempted the impossible, and so would have achieved nothing, or worse than nothing. But by building levees along the Mississippi, not seeking to dam the stream, but to control it, we are able to achieve our object and to confer inestimable good in the course of so doing.

This Nation should definitely adopt the policy of attacking, not the mere fact of combination, but the evils and wrong-doing which so frequently accompany combination. The fact that a combination is very big is ample reason for exercising a close and jealous supervision over it, because its size renders it potent for mischief; but it should not be punished unless it actually does the mischief; it should merely be so supervised and controlled as to guarantee us, the people, against its doing mischief. We should not strive for a policy of unregulated competition and of the destruction of all big corporations, that is, of all the most efficient business industries in the land. Nor should we persevere in the hopeless experiment of trying to regulate these industries by means only of lawsuits, each lasting several years, and of uncertain result. We should enter upon a course of supervision, control, and regulation of these great corporations — a regulation which we should not fear, if necessary, to bring to the point of control of monopoly prices, just as in exceptional cases railway rates are now regulated. Either the Bureau of Corporations should be authorized, or some other governmental body similar to the Inter-State Commerce Commission should be created, to exercise this supervision, this authoritative control. When once immoral business practices have been eliminated by such control, competition will thereby be again revived as a healthy factor, although not as formerly an all-sufficient factor, in keeping the general business situation sound. Wherever immoral business practices still obtain — as they obtained in the cases of the Standard Oil Trust and Tobacco Trust — the Anti-Trust Law can be invoked; and wherever such a prosecution is successful, and the courts declare a corporation to possess a monopolistic character, then that corporation should be completely dissolved, and the parts ought never to be again assembled save on whatever terms and under whatever conditions may be imposed by the governmental body in which is vested the regulatory power. Methods can readily be devised by which corporations sincerely desiring to act fairly and honestly can on their own initiative come under this thoroughgoing administrative control by the Government and thereby be free from the working of the Anti-Trust Law. But the law will remain to be invoked against wrongdoers; and under such conditions it could be invoked far more vigorously and successfully than at present.

It is not necessary in an article like this to attempt to work out such a plan in detail. It can assuredly be worked out. Moreover, in my opinion, substantially some such plan must be worked out or business chaos will continue. Wrongdoing such as was perpetrated by the Standard Oil Trust, and especially by the Tobacco Trust, should not only be punished, but if possible punished in the persons of the chief authors and beneficiaries of the wrong, far more severely than at present. But punishment should not be the only, or indeed the main, end in view. Our aim should be a policy of construction and not one of destruction. Our aim should not be to punish the men who have made a big corporation successful merely because they have made it big and successful, but to exercise such thoroughgoing supervision and control over them as to insure their business skill being exercised in the interest of the public and not against the public interest. Ultimately, I believe that this control should undoubtedly indirectly or directly extend to dealing with all questions connected with their treatment of their employees, including the wages, the hours of labor, and the like. Not only is the proper treatment of a corporation, from the standpoint of the managers, shareholders, and employees, compatible with securing from that corporation the best standard of public service, but when the effort is wisely made it results in benefit both to the corporation and to the public. The success of Wisconsin in dealing with the corporations within her borders, so as both to do them justice and to exact justice in return from them toward the public, has been signal; and this Nation should adopt a progressive policy in substance akin to the progressive policy not merely formulated in theory but reduced to actual practice with such striking success in Wisconsin.

To sum up, then. It is practically impossible, and, if possible, it would be mischievous and undesirable, to try to break up all combinations merely because they are large and successful, and to put the business of the country back into the middle of the eighteenth century conditions of intense and unregulated competition between small and weak business concerns. Such an effort represents not progressiveness but an unintelligent though doubtless entirely well-meaning toryism. Moreover, the effort to administer a law merely by lawsuits and court decisions is bound to end in signal failure, and meanwhile to be attended with delays and uncertainties, and to put a premium upon legal sharp practice. Such an effort does not adequately punish the guilty, and yet works great harm to the innocent. Moreover, it entirely fails to give the publicity which is one of the best by-products of the system of control by administrative officials; publicity, which is not only good in itself, but furnishes the data for whatever further action may be necessary. We need to formulate immediately and definitely a policy which, in dealing with big corporations that behave themselves and which contain no menace save what is necessarily potential in any corporation which is of great size and very well managed, shall aim not at their destruction but at their regulation and supervision, so that the Government shall control them in such fashion as amply to safeguard the interests of the whole public, including producers, consumers, and wage-workers. This control should, if necessary, be pushed in extreme cases to the point of exercising control over monopoly prices, as rates on railways are now controlled; although this is not a power that should be used when it is possible to avoid it. The law should be clear, unambiguous, certain, so that honest men may not find that unwittingly they have violated it. In short, our aim should be, not to destroy, but effectively and in thoroughgoing fashion to regulate and control, in the public interest, the great instrumentalities of modern business, which it is destructive of the general welfare of the community to destroy, and which nevertheless it is vitally necessary to that general welfare to regulate and control. Competition will remain as a very important factor when once we have destroyed the unfair business methods, the criminal interference with the rights of others, which alone enabled certain swollen combinations to crush out their competitors — and, incidentally, the "conservatives" will do well to remember that these unfair and iniquitous methods by great masters of corporate capital have done more to cause popular discontent with the propertied classes than all the orations of all the Socialist orators in the country put together.

I have spoken above of Senator Davis's admirable address delivered a quarter of a century ago. Senator Davis's one-time partner, Frank B. Kellogg, the Government counsel who did so much to win success for the Government in its prosecutions of the trusts, has recently delivered before the Palimpsest Club of Omaha an excellent address on the subject; Mr. Prouty, of the Inter-State Commerce Commission, has recently, in his speech before the Congregational Club of Brooklyn, dealt with the subject from the constructive side; and in the proceedings of the American Bar Association for 1904 there is an admirable paper on the need of thoroughgoing Federal control over corporations doing an inter-State business, by Professor Horace L. Wilgus, of the University of Michigan. The National Government exercises control over inter-State commerce railways, and it can in similar fashion, through an appropriate governmental body, exercise control over all industrial organizations engaged in inter-State commerce. This control should be exercised, not by the courts, but by an administrative bureau or board such as the Bureau of Corporations or the Inter-State Commerce Commission; for the courts cannot with advantage permanently perform executive and administrative functions.

Brass Buddha.
Presented to President Roosevelt
by Dalai Lama.

# APPENDIX B

## THE CONTROL OF CORPORATIONS AND "THE NEW FREEDOM"

In his book "The New Freedom," and in the magazine articles of which it is composed, which appeared just after he had been inaugurated as President, Mr. Woodrow Wilson made an entirely unprovoked attack upon me and upon the Progressive party in connection with what he asserts the policy of that party to be concerning the trusts, and as regards my attitude while President about the trusts.

I am reluctant to say anything whatever about President Wilson at the outset of his Administration unless I can speak of him with praise. I have scrupulously refrained from saying or doing one thing since election that could put the slightest obstacle, even of misinterpretation, in his path. It is to the interest of the country that he should succeed in his office. I cordially wish him success, and I shall cordially support any policy of his that I believe to be in the interests of the people of the United States. But when Mr. Wilson, after being elected President, within the first fortnight after he has been inaugurated into that high office, permits himself to be betrayed into a public misstatement of what I have said, and what I stand for, then he forces me to correct his statements.

Mr. Wilson opens his article by saying that the Progressive "doctrine is that monopoly is inevitable, and that the only course open to the people of the United States is to submit to it." This statement is without one particle of foundation in fact. I challenge him to point out a sentence in the Progressive platform or in any speech of mine which bears him out. I can point him out any number which flatly contradict him. We have never made any such statement as he alleges about monopolies. We have said: "The corporation is an essential part of modern business. The concentration of modern business, in some degree, is both inevitable and necessary for National and international business efficiency." Does Mr. Wilson deny this? Let him answer yes or no, directly. It is easy for a politician detected in a misstatement to take refuge in evasive rhetorical hyperbole. But Mr. Wilson is President of the United States, and as such he is bound to candid utterance on every subject of public interest which he himself has broached. If he disagrees with us, let him be frank and consistent, and recommend to Congress that all corporations be made illegal. Mr. Wilson's whole attack is largely based on a deft but far from ingenuous confounding of what we have said of monopoly, which we propose so far as possible to abolish, and what we have said of big corporations, which we propose to regulate; Mr. Wilson's own vaguely set forth proposals being to attempt the destruction of both in ways that would harm neither. In our platform we use the word "monopoly" but once, and then we speak of it as an abuse of power, coupling it with stock-watering, unfair competition and unfair privileges. Does Mr. Wilson deny this? If he does, then where else will he assert that we speak of monopoly as he says we do? He certainly owes the people of the United States a plain answer to the question. In my speech of acceptance I said: "We favor strengthening the Sherman Law by prohibiting agreements to divide territory or limit output; refusing to sell to customers who buy from business rivals; to sell below cost in certain areas while maintaining higher prices in other places; using the power of transportation to aid or injure special business concerns; and all other unfair trade practices." The platform pledges us to "guard and keep open equally to all, the highways of American commerce." This is the exact negation of monopoly. Unless Mr. Wilson is prepared to show the contrary, surely he is bound in honor to admit frankly that he has been betrayed into a misrepresentation, and to correct it.

Mr. Wilson says that for sixteen years the National Administration has "been virtually under the regulation of the trusts," and that the big business men "have already captured the Government." Such a statement as this might perhaps be pardoned as mere rhetoric in a candidate seeking office — although it is the kind of statement that never under any circumstances have I permitted myself to make, whether on the stump or off the stump, about any opponent, unless I was prepared to back it up with explicit facts. But there is an added seriousness to the charge when it is made deliberately and in cold blood by a man who is at the time President. In this volume I have set forth my relations with the trusts. I challenge Mr. Wilson to controvert anything I have said, or to name any trusts or any big business men who regulated, or in any shape or way controlled, or captured, the Government during my term as President. He must furnish specifications if his words are taken at their face value — and I venture to say in advance that the absurdity of such a charge is patent to all my fellow-citizens, not excepting Mr. Wilson.

Mr. Wilson says that the new party was founded "under the leadership of Mr. Roosevelt, with the conspicuous aid — I mention him with no satirical intention, but merely to set the facts down accurately — of Mr. George W. Perkins, organizer of the Steel Trust." Whether Mr. Wilson's intention was satirical or not is of no concern; but I call his attention to the fact that he has conspicuously and strikingly failed "to set the facts down accurately." Mr. Perkins was not the organizer of the Steel Trust, and when it was organized he had no connection with it or with the Morgan people. This is well known, and it has again and again been testified to before Congressional committees controlled by Mr. Wilson's friends who were endeavoring to find out something against Mr. Perkins. If Mr. Wilson does not know that my statement is correct, he ought to know it, and he is not to be excused for making such a misstatement as he has made when he has not a particle of evidence in support of it. Mr. Perkins was from the beginning in the Harvester Trust but, when Mr. Wilson points out this fact, why does he not add that he was the only man in that trust who supported me, and that the President of the trust ardently supported Mr. Wilson himself? It is disingenuous to endeavor to conceal these facts, and to mislead ordinary citizens about them. Under the administrations of both Mr. Taft and Mr. Wilson, Mr. Perkins has been singled out for special attack, obviously not because he belonged to the Harvester and Steel Trusts, but because he alone among the prominent men of the two corporations fearlessly supported the only party which afforded any real hope of checking the evil of the trusts.

Mr. Wilson states that the Progressives have "a programme perfectly agreeable to monopolies."

The plain and unmistakable inference to be drawn from this and other similar statements in his article, and the inference which he obviously desired to have drawn, is that the big corporations approved the Progressive plan and supported the Progressive candidate. If President Wilson does not know perfectly well that this is not the case, he is the only intelligent person in the United States who is thus ignorant. Everybody knows that the overwhelming majority of the heads of the big corporations supported him or Mr. Taft. It is equally well known that of the corporations he mentions, the Steel and the Harvester Trusts, there was but one man who took any part in the Progressive campaign, and that almost all the others, some thirty in number, were against us, and some of them, including the President of the Harvester Trust, openly and enthusiastically for Mr. Wilson himself. If he reads the newspapers at all, he must know that practically every man representing the great financial interests of the country, and without exception every newspaper controlled by Wall Street or State Street, actively supported either him or Mr. Taft, and showed perfect willingness to accept either if only they could prevent the Progressive party from coming into power and from putting its platform into effect.

Mr. Wilson says of the trust plank in that platform that it "did not anywhere condemn monopoly except in words." Exactly of what else could a platform consist? Does Mr. Wilson expect us to use algebraic signs? This criticism is much as if he said the Constitution or the Declaration of Independence contained nothing but words. The Progressive platform did contain words, and the words were admirably designed to express thought and meaning and purpose. Mr. Wilson says that I long ago "classified trusts for us as good and bad," and said that I was "afraid only of the bad ones." Mr. Wilson would do well to quote exactly what my language was, and where it was used, for I am at a loss to know what statement of mine it is to which he refers. But if he means that I say that corporations can do well, and that corporations can also do ill, he is stating my position correctly. I hold that a corporation does ill if it seeks profit in restricting production and then by extorting high prices from the community by reason of the scarcity of the product; through adulterating, lyingly advertising, or over-driving the help; or replacing men workers with children; or by rebates; or in any illegal or improper manner driving competitors out of its way; or seeking to achieve monopoly by illegal or unethical treatment of its competitors, or in any shape or way offending against the moral law either in connection with the public or with its employees or with its rivals. Any corporation which seeks its profit in such fashion is acting badly. It is, in fact, a conspiracy against the public welfare which the Government should use all its powers to suppress. If, on the other hand, a corporation seeks profit solely by increasing its products through eliminating waste, improving its processes, utilizing its by-products, installing better machines, raising wages in the effort to secure more efficient help, introducing the principle of coöperation and mutual benefit, dealing fairly with labor unions, setting its face against the underpayment of women and the employment of children; in a word, treating the public fairly and its rivals fairly: then such a corporation is behaving well. It is an instrumentality of civilization operating to promote abundance by cheapening the cost of living so as to improve conditions everywhere throughout the whole community. Does Mr. Wilson controvert either of these statements? If so, let him answer directly. It is a matter of capital importance to the country that his position in this respect be stated directly, not by indirect suggestion.

Much of Mr. Wilson's article, although apparently aimed at the Progressive party, is both so rhetorical and so vague as to need no answer. He does, however, specifically assert (among other things equally without warrant in fact) that the Progressive party says that it is "futile to undertake to prevent monopoly," and only ventures to ask the trusts to be "kind" and "pitiful"! It is a little difficult to answer a misrepresentation of the facts so radical — not to say preposterous — with the respect that one desires to use in speaking of or to the President of the United States. I challenge President Wilson to point to one sentence of our platform or of my speeches which affords the faintest justification for these assertions. Having made this statement in the course of an unprovoked attack on me, he cannot refuse to show that it is true. I deem it necessary to emphasize here (but with perfect respect) that I am asking for a plain statement of fact, not for a display of rhetoric. I ask him, as is my right under the circumstances, to quote the exact language which justifies him in attributing these views to us. If he cannot do this, then a frank acknowledgment on his part is due to himself and to the people. I quote from the Progressive platform: "Behind the ostensible Government sits enthroned an invisible Government, owing no allegiance and acknowledging no responsibility to the people. To destroy this invisible Government, to dissolve the unholy alliance between corrupt business and corrupt politics, is the first task of the statesmanship of the day. . . . This country belongs to the people. Its resources, its business, its laws, its institutions, should be utilized, maintained, or altered in whatever manner will best promote the general interest." This assertion is explicit. We say directly that "the people" are absolutely to control in any way they see fit, the "business" of the country. I again challenge Mr. Wilson to quote any words of the platform that justify the statements he has made to the contrary. If he cannot do it — and of course he cannot do it, and he must know that he cannot do it — surely he will not hesitate to say so frankly.

Mr. Wilson must know that every monopoly in the United States opposes the Progressive party. If he challenges this statement, I challenge him in return (as is clearly my right) to name the monopoly that did support the Progressive party, whether it was the Sugar Trust, the Steel Trust, the Harvester Trust, the Standard Oil Trust, the Tobacco Trust, or any other. Every sane man in the country knows well that there is not one word of justification that can truthfully be adduced for Mr. Wilson's statement that the Progressive programme was agreeable to the monopolies. Ours was the only programme to which they objected, and they supported either Mr. Wilson or Mr. Taft against me, indifferent as to which of them might be elected so long as I was defeated. Mr. Wilson says that I got my "idea with regard to the regulation of monopoly from the gentlemen who form the United States Steel Corporation." Does Mr. Wilson pretend that Mr. Van Hise and Mr. Croly got their ideas from the Steel Corporation? Is Mr. Wilson unaware of the elementary fact that most modern economists believe that unlimited, unregulated competition is the source of evils which all men now concede must be remedied if this civilization of ours is to survive? Is he ignorant of the fact that the Socialist party has long been against unlimited competition? This statement of Mr. Wilson cannot be characterized properly with any degree of regard for the office Mr. Wilson holds. Why, the ideas that I have championed as to controlling and regulating both competition and combination in the interest of the people, so that the people shall be masters over both, have been in the air in this country for a quarter of a century. I was merely the first prominent candidate for President who took them up. They are the progressive ideas, and progressive business men must in the end come to them, for I firmly believe that in the end all wise and honest business men, big and little, will support our programme. Mr. Wilson in opposing them is the mere apostle of reaction. He says that I got my "ideas from the gentlemen who form the Steel Corporation." I did not. But I will point out to him something in return. It was he himself, and Mr. Taft, who got the votes and the money of these same gentlemen, and of those in the Harvester Trust.

Mr. Wilson has promised to break up all trusts. He can do so only by proceeding at law. If he proceeds at law, he can hope for success only by taking what I have done as a precedent. In fact, what I did as President is the base of every action now taken or that can be now taken looking toward the control of corporations, or the suppression of monopolies. The decisions rendered in various cases brought by my direction constitute the authority on which Mr. Wilson must base any action that he may bring to curb monopolistic control. Will Mr. Wilson deny this, or question it in any way? With what grace can he describe my Administration as satisfactory to the trusts when he knows that he cannot redeem a single promise that he has made to war upon the trusts unless he avails himself of weapons of which the Federal Government had been deprived before I became President, and which were restored to it during my Administration and through proceedings which I directed? Without my action Mr. Wilson could not now undertake or carry on a single suit against a monopoly, and, moreover, if it had not been for my action and for the judicial decision in consequence obtained, Congress would be helpless to pass a single law against monopoly.

Let Mr. Wilson mark that the men who organized and directed the Northern Securities Company were also the controlling forces in the very Steel Corporation which Mr. Wilson makes believe to think was supporting me. I challenge Mr. Wilson to deny this, and yet he well knew that it was my successful suit against the Northern Securities Company which first efficiently established the power of the people over the trusts.

After reading Mr. Wilson's book, I am still entirely in the dark as to what he means by the "New Freedom." Mr. Wilson is an accomplished and scholarly man, a master of rhetoric, and the sentences in the book are well-phrased statements, usually inculcating a morality which is sound although vague and ill defined. There are certain proposals (already long set forth and practiced by me and by others who have recently formed the Progressive party) made by Mr. Wilson with which I cordially agree. There are, however, certain things he has said, even as regards matters of abstract morality, with which I emphatically disagree. For example, in arguing for proper business publicity, as to which I cordially agree with Mr. Wilson, he commits himself to the following statement:

"You know there is temptation in loneliness and secrecy. Haven't you experienced it? I have. We are never so proper in our conduct as when everybody can look and see exactly what we are doing. If you are off in some distant part of the world and suppose that nobody who lives within a mile of your home is anywhere around, there are times when you adjourn your ordinary standards. You say to yourself, 'Well, I'll have a fling this time; nobody will know anything about it.' If you were on the Desert of Sahara, you would feel that you might permit yourself — well, say, some slight latitude of conduct; but if you saw one of your immediate neighbors coming the other way on a camel, you would behave yourself until he got out of sight. The most dangerous thing in the world is to get off where nobody knows you. I advise you to stay around among the neighbors, and then you may keep out of jail. That is the only way some of us can keep out of jail."

I emphatically disagree with what seems to be the morality inculcated in this statement, which is that a man is expected to do and is to be pardoned for doing all kinds of immoral things if he does them alone and does not expect to be found out. Surely it is not necessary, in insisting upon proper publicity, to preach a morality of so basely material a character.

There is much more that Mr. Wilson says as to which I do not understand him clearly, and where I condemn what I do understand. In economic matters the course he advocates as part of the "New Freedom" simply means the old, old "freedom" of leaving the individual strong man at liberty, unchecked by common action, to prey on the weak and the helpless. The "New Freedom" in the abstract seems to be the freedom of the big to devour the little. In the concrete I may add that Mr. Wilson's misrepresentations of what I have said seem to indicate that he regards the new freedom as freedom from all obligation to obey the Ninth Commandment.

But, after all, my views or the principles of the Progressive party are of much less importance now than the purposes of Mr. Wilson. These are wrapped in impenetrable mystery. His speeches and writings serve but to make them more obscure. If these attempts to refute his misrepresentation of my attitude towards the trusts should result in making his own clear, then this discussion will have borne fruits of substantial value to the country. If Mr. Wilson has any plan of his own for dealing with the trusts, it is to suppress all great industrial organizations — presumably on the principle proclaimed by his Secretary of State four years ago, that every corporation which produced more than a certain percentage of a given commodity — I think the amount specified was twenty-five per cent — no matter how valuable its service, should be suppressed. The simple fact is that such a plan is futile. In operation it would do far more damage than it could remedy. The Progressive plan would give the people full control of, and in masterful fashion prevent all wrongdoing by, the trusts, while utilizing for the public welfare every industrial energy and ability that operates to swell abundance, while obeying strictly the moral law and the law of the land. Mr. Wilson's plan would ultimately benefit the trusts and would permanently damage nobody but the people. For example, one of the steel corporations which has been guilty of the worst practices towards its employees is the Colorado Fuel and Iron Company. Mr. Wilson and Mr. Bryan's plan would, if successful, merely mean permitting four such companies, absolutely uncontrolled, to monopolize every big industry in the country. To talk of such an accomplishment as being "The New Freedom" is enough to make the term one of contemptuous derision.

President Wilson has made explicit promises, and the Democratic platform has made explicit promises. Mr. Wilson is now in power, with the Democratic Congress in both branches. He and the Democratic platform have promised to destroy the trusts, to reduce the cost of living, and at the same to increase the well-being of the farmer and of the workingman — which of course must mean to increase the profits of the farmer and the wages of the workingman. He and his party won the election on this promise. We have a right to expect that they will keep it. If Mr. Wilson's promises mean anything except the very emptiest words, he is pledged to accomplish the beneficent purposes he avows by breaking up all the trusts and combinations and corporations so as to restore competition precisely as it was fifty years ago. If he does not mean this, he means nothing. He cannot do anything else under penalty of showing that his promise and his performance do not square with each other.

Mr. Wilson says that "the trusts are our masters now, but I for one do not care to live in a country called free even under kind masters." Good! The Progressives are opposed to having masters, kind or unkind, and they do not believe that a "new freedom" which in practice would mean leaving four Fuel and Iron Companies free to do what they like in every industry would be of much benefit to the country. The Progressives have a clear and definite programme by which the people would be the masters of the trusts instead of the trusts being their masters, as Mr. Wilson says they are. With practical unanimity the trusts supported the opponents of this programme, Mr. Taft and Mr. Wilson, and they evidently dreaded our programme infinitely more than anything that Mr. Wilson threatened. The people have accepted Mr. Wilson's assurances. Now let him make his promises good. He is committed, if his words mean anything, to the promise to break up every trust, every big corporation — perhaps every small corporation — in the United States — not to go through the motions of breaking them up, but really to break them up. He is committed against the policy (of efficient control and mastery of the big corporations both by law and by administrative action in coöperation) proposed by the Progressives. Let him keep faith with the people; let him in good faith try to keep the promises he has thus repeatedly made. I believe that his promise is futile and cannot be kept. I believe that any attempt sincerely to keep it and in good faith to carry it out will end in either nothing at all or in disaster. But my beliefs are of no consequence. Mr. Wilson is President. It is his acts that are of consequence. He is bound in honor to the people of the United States to keep his promise, and to break up, not nominally but in reality, all big business, all trusts, all combinations of every sort, kind, and description, and probably all corporations. What he says is henceforth of little consequence. The important thing is what he does, and how the results of what he does square with the promises and prophecies he made when all he had to do was to speak, not to act.

# APPENDIX C

## THE BLAINE CAMPAIGN

In "The House of Harper," written by J. Henry Harper, the following passage occurs: "Curtis returned from the convention in company with young Theodore Roosevelt and they discussed the situation thoroughly on their trip to New York and came to the conclusion that it would be very difficult to consistently support Blaine. Roosevelt, however, had a conference afterward with Senator Lodge and eventually fell in line behind Blaine. Curtis came to our office and found that we were unanimously opposed to the support of Blaine, and with a hearty good-will he trained his editorial guns on the 'Plumed Knight' of Mulligan letter fame. His work was as effective and deadly as any fight he ever conducted in the *Weekly*." This statement has no foundation whatever in fact. I did not return from the convention in company with Mr. Curtis. He went back to New York from the convention, whereas I went to my ranch in North Dakota. No such conversation as that ever took place between me and Mr. Curtis. In my presence, in speaking to a number of men at the time in Chicago, Mr. Curtis said: "You younger men can, if you think right, refuse to support Mr. Blaine, but I am too old a Republican, and have too long been associated with the party, to break with it now." Not only did I never entertain after the convention, but I never during the convention or at any other time, entertained the intention alleged in the quotation in question. I discussed the whole situation with Mr. Lodge before going to the convention, and we had made up our minds that if the nomination of Mr. Blaine was fairly made we would with equal good faith support him.

# Index

CHRONOLOGY

NOTE ON THE TEXTS

NOTES

# *Chronology*

1858    Born October 27 at 28 East 20th Street, New York City, second child of Theodore Roosevelt and Martha Bulloch Roosevelt. (Grandfather Cornelius Van Schaack Roosevelt, born 1794, founded a prosperous plate-glass importing business and then made successful investments in Manhattan real estate and banking. Father, born 1831, worked for the family firm of Roosevelt & Son while involving himself in civic and philanthropic affairs, including the Children's Aid Society and the YMCA. Mother, born 1835, came from a family of slave-owning Georgia planters. Parents met in 1850 when father visited the Bulloch family home in Roswell, Georgia, and were married there on December 22, 1853. Their first child, Anna, was born on January 18, 1855.) Household includes aunt Anna Bulloch and grandmother Martha Stewart Elliott Bulloch.

1860    Brother Elliott born on February 28.

1861    Father does not enlist in the Union Army because of the objections of his wife, who supports the Confederacy, but does help establish an allotment system allowing Union soldiers to send a portion of their pay home to their families. (His work on the Allotment Commission will keep him away from home for much of the first two years of the war as he lobbies the government and visits army camps.) Sister Corinne born on September 27.

1862    Roosevelt begins to suffer acute asthma attacks, usually at night. Uncle James Bulloch, a Confederate naval officer, arranges the construction of commerce raiders in British shipyards, and uncle Irvine Bulloch serves on the Confederate raider *Alabama*.

1863–65    Father hires a substitute to avoid conscription. Roosevelt begins to be tutored at home by his aunt Anna Bulloch. Grandmother Martha Bulloch dies in October 1864. Roosevelt watches funeral procession for Abraham Lincoln on April 25, 1865, from the window of his grandfather's house at Broadway and 14th Street. Attends Presbyterian services with his family.

1866–68    Continues to suffer from severe asthma attacks as well as frequent headaches and stomach pain. Becomes friends with Edith Kermit Carow (b. 1861), a playmate of his sister Corinne, who is tutored along with the Roosevelt children. Enjoys reading and becomes fascinated with natural history. Father plays leading role in founding the New York Orthopedic Hospital.

1869–70    Father helps found the American Museum of Natural History. Family sails for England on May 12, 1869. They visit with James and Irvine Bulloch in Liverpool, then tour England, Scotland, Belgium, the Netherlands, the German Rhineland, Switzerland, northern Italy, Austria, Bavaria, Prussia, and France. Roosevelt keeps a detailed diary during the trip and takes long walks in the Alps despite his health problems. Family spends winter in Italy, then returns to France and England before sailing from Liverpool on May 14, 1870. Roosevelt continues to be tutored at home along with his siblings and begins lifting weights. Father joins in founding of the Metropolitan Museum of Art.

1871       Grandfather Cornelius Van Schaack Roosevelt dies on July 17, leaving an estate valued at between $3 million and $7 million. Family vacations in Adirondacks and White Mountains.

1872–73    Roosevelt is given a shotgun and his first set of spectacles, which greatly improve his vision. Becomes an enthusiastic bird hunter and studies taxidermy. Family sails for England on October 16, 1872, and travels through Belgium, the Netherlands, Germany, France, and Italy before arriving in Alexandria, Egypt, on November 28. In Cairo they charter a boat, then sail up the Nile as far as Aswan; during the Nile trip Roosevelt shoots almost 200 birds. Family tours Palestine, Lebanon, and Syria before sailing to Greece and Turkey and then traveling up the Danube, arriving in Vienna on April 19, 1873. While father returns to the United States and mother and Anna go to Paris, Roosevelt, Elliott, and Corinne spend five months living with a German family in Dresden. Returns to New York on November 5, 1873, and moves into new family home at 6 West 57th Street.

1874      Studies for Harvard College entrance examinations. Family begins spending summer in Oyster Bay on the north shore of Long Island; Edith Carow becomes a frequent visitor.

1876      Father becomes active in Republican reform politics. Roosevelt enters Harvard in late September. Moves into boarding house at 16 Winthrop Street, Cambridge, where he will live throughout his college years. Studies Greek, Latin, German, geometry, physics, and chemistry during his freshman year.

1877      Asthma improves. Studies rhetoric, German, French, Anglo-American history, vertebrate physiology and anatomy (taught by William James), and botany during his sophomore year. Father falls ill in December.

1878      Father dies of stomach cancer on February 9; Roosevelt describes his death in his diary as "the blackest day of my life." Inherits $125,000. Goes on hunting trip in northern Maine in late summer and continues to enjoy rowing at Oyster Bay and in Cambridge. Studies German, Italian, forensics, logic, metaphysics, political economy, geology, and zoology during his junior year. Meets Alice Hathaway Lee (b. 1861), cousin of his college friend Richard Saltonstall, at her home in Chesnut Hill, Massachusetts, on October 18.

1879      Returns to northern Maine in March for winter hunting trip and climbs Mt. Katahdin in late summer. Studies Italian, forensics, political economy, geology, and zoology during his senior year.

1880      Becomes engaged to Alice Lee on January 25. Writes senior thesis, "The Practicability of Equalizing Men and Women Before the Law," and begins naval history of the War of 1812. Graduates from Harvard on June 30, ranking 21 in a class of 177. Goes hunting in Minnesota with Elliott in the summer. Marries Alice Lee on October 27 at the Unitarian Church in Brookline, Massachusetts. After honeymoon at Oyster Bay, they move into the family home on West 57th Street. Roosevelt enters Columbia Law School.

1881        Sails for Europe with Alice on May 12. During their
            trip they visit Ireland, England, France, Italy, Austria,
            Switzerland, Germany, the Netherlands, and Belgium; in
            Switzerland Roosevelt climbs the Matterhorn. Returns to
            New York on October 2. Nominated as the Republican
            candidate for the state assembly in the 21st District on Oc-
            tober 28. Defeats Democrat William Strew 3,502–1,974 in
            the election on November 8.

1882        Assembly meets in Albany on January 3. Roosevelt accuses
            state supreme court judge T. R. Westbrook of corrupt
            dealings with financier Jay Gould and succeeds in having
            the assembly authorize an investigation of Westbrook.
            Supports bill to ban home manufacture of cigars after
            touring tenements in New York City with labor leader
            Samuel Gompers. Sister Corinne marries Douglas Robin-
            son in April. *The Naval War of 1812* is published to favor-
            able reviews. Effort to impeach Westbrook fails when
            assembly approves committee report clearing him of seri-
            ous wrongdoing. Assembly session ends on June 2. Roo-
            sevelt ends his legal studies. Moves with Alice to house at
            55 West 45th Street. Reelected to the assembly on No-
            vember 7 with 63 percent of the vote.

1883        Assembly meets January 2. Roosevelt is elected Republi-
            can minority leader. Works with Democratic governor
            Grover Cleveland to pass a civil service reform bill; the bill
            prohibiting home cigar manufacture also becomes law. In
            a speech in the assembly Roosevelt calls Jay Gould and his
            associates "the most dangerous of all classes, the wealthy
            criminal class." Assembly session ends May 4. Roosevelt
            plans to build a house in Oyster Bay. In early September
            he travels to the Dakota Badlands along the Little Missouri
            to hunt buffalo and invests $14,000 in two cattle ranches
            near Medora (investment will eventually total $85,000).
            Returns to New York in late September. Reelected to
            the assembly with 67 percent of the vote on November 6.
            Elliott marries Anna Hall on December 1. Roosevelt is
            defeated in voting for Republican assembly leader on
            December 31.

1884    Assembly session begins January 1. Roosevelt leads inves-
        tigation into corruption in New York City. Alice moves
        back to West 57th Street while awaiting the birth of their
        first child. Alice Lee Roosevelt is born on February 12.
        Roosevelt returns to New York City from Albany on Feb-
        ruary 13. His mother dies of typhoid fever at 3 A.M. on
        February 14, and his wife dies of kidney failure at 2 P.M.
        the same day. Roosevelt writes in his diary: "The light has
        gone out of my life." Gives Alice to his sister Anna to raise
        and sells his house on West 45th Street. Wins passage of
        bill giving the mayor of New York the power to make ap-
        pointments independently of the aldermen. Declines
        renomination for the assembly. Forms lifelong friendship
        with Henry Cabot Lodge of Massachusetts, a fellow sup-
        porter of Senator George Edmunds for the Republican
        presidential nomination. Roosevelt and Lodge attend the
        Republican convention in Chicago, June 3–7, where they
        unsuccessfully try to prevent the nomination of James G.
        Blaine. After the convention they declare their support for
        Blaine, angering the Republican reformers ("mugwumps")
        who consider Blaine corrupt and support Democratic can-
        didate Grover Cleveland. In late July Roosevelt goes to
        the Dakota Badlands and begins building a house on the
        Elkhorn Ranch north of Medora. Hunts grizzly bears, elk,
        and deer in the Big Horn Mountains of Wyoming. Cam-
        paigns for Blaine in New York and Massachusetts. Cleve-
        land wins election on November 4. Roosevelt goes to the
        Badlands, then returns to New York in December and
        stays with his sister Anna.

1885    Travels to the Badlands in April and rides the range
        during the spring roundup. Returns to New York in June
        and spends eight weeks with Anna and Alice at Saga-
        more Hill, newly finished house in Oyster Bay built for
        $45,000. *Hunting Trips of a Ranchman* published in July.
        Visits Elkhorn Ranch in August. Returns in September
        to New York, where he encounters Edith Carow while
        visiting his sister Anna. They become secretly engaged on
        November 17.

1886    Travels to the Elkhorn Ranch in March. With two ranch
        hands, Roosevelt pursues three thieves down the Little
        Missouri and captures them. Works on biography of
        Thomas Hart Benton. Returns to New York in July, then

goes hunting in the northern Idaho mountains in the late summer. Nominated as Republican candidate for mayor of New York on October 15. In election on November 2, Democrat Abram Hewitt receives 90,552 votes; independent Labor candidate Henry George, 86,110; and Roosevelt, 60,435. Sails for England on November 6. Marries Edith Carow at St. George's, Hanover Square, London, on December 2. They begin their honeymoon in France.

1887     Visits Italy, France, and London with Edith before returning to New York on March 27. Travels to Dakota Badlands in April and learns that more than half his cattle died in the unusually harsh winter of 1886–87. Ends active participation in ranching, though he will return to Elkhorn Ranch during hunting trips. (When he finally liquidates his cattle investments in 1898, Roosevelt will calculate his total loss at about $20,000.) Moves into Sagamore Hill with Edith and Alice. *Life of Thomas Hart Benton* published. Son Theodore Roosevelt Jr. (Ted) born September 13. Hunts in the Dakota Badlands in November. Returns to New York, where he founds the Boone and Crockett Club, dedicated to the hunting, study, and conservation of large American game mammals (will serve as its president until 1894).

1888     *Gouverneur Morris* published. Roosevelt begins work on a multi-volume history of American westward expansion, and becomes a prolific writer of magazine articles on politics, literature, history, natural history, and other subjects (many of his books will also be serialized). Hunts in northern Idaho in August and September. *Essays in Practical Politics*, collecting two essays on New York state and municipal politics, published. Campaigns for Republican nominee Benjamin Harrison in Illinois, Michigan, and Minnesota. Harrison defeats Grover Cleveland on November 6. *Ranch Life and the Hunting Trail* published in December.

1889     Works on *The Winning of the West*. President Harrison appoints Roosevelt as one of three members of the Civil Service Commission, and he takes office on May 13. Travels to Indianapolis and Milwaukee to investigate corruption in the Post Office. The first two volumes of *The Winning of the West*, covering the period from 1769 to

1783, are published in June. Hunts grizzlies in Montana in August. Son Kermit Roosevelt born October 10. Roosevelt rents house at 1820 Jefferson Place N.W., Washington, D.C., where he is joined in December by his wife and children. Becomes part of social circle that includes Lodge, John Hay, House Speaker Thomas Reed, and Henry Adams.

1890    Continues work on Civil Service Commission, but is frustrated by lack of funds and authority (the commission can only recommend the dismissal of corrupt officeholders). House committee investigates his conduct during the Milwaukee Post Office investigation but eventually exonerates him. Reads *The Influence of Sea Power upon History, 1660–1783*, by Alfred Thayer Mahan; the book strengthens his belief in the need for a larger navy. Visits Yellowstone National Park in September on behalf of the Boone and Crockett Club. Becomes increasingly concerned by Elliott's worsening alcoholism and deteriorating mental condition.

1891    Visits Baltimore to investigate involvement of federal officeholders in primary elections, then writes 146-page report calling for the dismissal of 25 postal employees. *History of the City of New York* published. Learns that Elliott has fathered a child with Katy Mann, a servant, and attempts unsuccessfully to have him declared legally insane. Daughter Ethel Carow Roosevelt born August 13. Hunts elk in the northern Rockies in September. Moves to 1215 19th Street N.W. in Washington.

1892    Travels to France in January to see Elliott and succeeds in getting him to place his assets in a trust, enter a sanitarium, and agree to live apart from his family for at least two years. Calls for a congressional investigation into Postmaster General John Wanamaker's failure to dismiss the 25 Baltimore postal workers cited in his 1891 report. Hunts wild pigs in southern Texas. Testifies before the House Civil Service Reform Committee, which issues report on June 22 severely criticizing Wanamaker. Roosevelt investigates corruption on Indian reservations in the northern plains in September. Cleveland defeats Harrison in the presidential election on November 8.

1893    Roosevelt remains in office at the request of President
        Cleveland. Publishes *The Wilderness Hunter*.

1894    Son Archibald Bulloch Roosevelt (Archie) born April 9.
        Elliott dies on August 14 from a seizure during delirium
        tremens; Roosevelt writes to his sister Anna: "he was
        hunted by the most terrible demons that ever entered
        a man's body and soul." The third volume of *The Win-
        ning of the West*, covering the period from 1784 to 1790, is
        published.

1895    Appointed to the New York City Police Commission by
        Republican reform mayor William Strong on April 17.
        Takes office on May 6 and is elected president of the four-
        member commission. Forces the resignation of Chief
        Thomas Byrnes, who is widely suspected of corruption,
        on May 27. Begins making night tours to check on police-
        men walking their beats. Orders strict enforcement of law
        closing saloons on Sundays, a policy that proves highly
        unpopular among traditionally Republican German-
        American voters. Publishes *Hero Tales from American His-
        tory*, a book for children written with Henry Cabot Lodge.
        Sister Anna marries William Sheffield Cowles, an Ameri-
        can naval officer, in November.

1896    Roosevelt continues efforts to expand and modernize
        the police department, but is frustrated when opposition
        by Commissioner Andrew Parker and Chief Peter Con-
        lin blocks the promotion of senior officers he favors.
        Fourth volume of *The Winning of the West*, covering
        years from 1791 to 1807, published. Hunts pronghorn in
        North Dakota in late summer, then campaigns for Re-
        publican nominee William McKinley in New York, Illi-
        nois, Michigan, Minnesota, New Jersey, Delaware, and
        Maryland. McKinley defeats William Jennings Bryan on
        November 3.

1897    Appointed Assistant Secretary of the Navy by President
        McKinley on April 6 and takes office on April 19. Serves
        as deputy to Secretary John D. Long, but soon takes the
        leading role in the department. Becomes an advocate
        within the administration for the annexation of Hawaii
        and intervention in Cuba. Gives widely reported speech
        at the Naval War College in Newport, Rhode Island, on

June 2 in which he calls for the rapid expansion of the navy and praises the willingness to wage war: "It is through strife, or the readiness for strife, that a nation must win greatness." Publishes *American Ideals*, a collection of essays and speeches. Serves as acting secretary during Long's summer vacation in August and September. Secures appointment of Commodore George Dewey as commander of the Asiatic Squadron. Son Quentin Roosevelt born on November 19.

1898    Battleship *Maine* is destroyed in Havana harbor on February 15 by an explosion that kills 262 of its crew. On February 25 Roosevelt alerts all squadrons to prepare for possible war with Spain and orders Dewey to attack the Philippines if war is declared. Edith falls dangerously ill, but recovers after undergoing surgery for an abdominal abscess on March 7. War with Spain is declared on April 25. Roosevelt resigns from the navy department and is appointed deputy commander of the First U.S. Volunteer Cavalry with the rank of lieutenant colonel; his friend Leonard Wood is made the regimental commander. Arrives in San Antonio, Texas, on May 15 and trains with the regiment, which soon becomes known as the Rough Riders. Regiment sails from Florida for Cuba on June 14. It lands at Daiquirí on June 22 and fights in skirmish at Las Guásimas on June 24. Wood is made a brigade commander on June 30 and Roosevelt becomes the regimental commander. On July 1 Roosevelt leads the Rough Riders in successful attacks on Kettle Hill and San Juan Hill during the battle for San Juan Heights. The regiment serves in the siege lines outside Santiago until the city surrenders on July 17. Armistice ending hostilities between Spain and the United States is signed on August 12. Regiment lands in Montauk, Long Island, on August 15 and is mustered out on September 15. Roosevelt is nominated for governor by the Republican state convention on September 27 and campaigns by train throughout the state. In the election on November 8, Roosevelt receives 661,715 votes, and Democratic candidate Augustus van Wyck, 643,921. Peace treaty is signed in Paris on December 10 under which Spain cedes Puerto Rico, Guam, and the Philippines to the United States and renounces all claim to Cuba. Roosevelt begins his two-year term as governor on December 31.

1899         Makes appointments to office in consultation with U.S. Senator Thomas Platt, the boss of the state Republican machine. Insurrection against American rule begins in the Philippines on February 4. Roosevelt supports taxation of corporate transit and utility franchises, a measure strongly opposed by Platt. Franchise tax bill is passed on April 28 at the end of a session in which Roosevelt also wins passage of legislation improving sweatshop conditions, strengthening factory inspections, and limiting the working hours of women, children, and state employees. Recalls legislature in May and secures passage of a strengthened version of the franchise tax bill. Greeted by enthusiastic crowds while traveling to Rough Riders reunion in Las Vegas, New Mexico, in late June. *The Rough Riders* is published in early summer. Vice-President Garret Hobart dies on November 21.

1900         Despite opposition from Platt, Roosevelt replaces the state superintendent of insurance, who had received large unsecured loans from a New York bank. *Oliver Cromwell* published. Roosevelt wins passage of conservation legislation and works to preserve state forests and wildlife through administrative measures. Opposes Hay-Pauncefote treaty, Anglo-American agreement signed on February 5 that permits the United States to build and maintain a canal across Central America, because it does not allow the U.S. to fortify the canal. (Treaty is ratified with amendments by the Senate in December 1900, but then rejected by the British in March 1901.) Movement to nominate Roosevelt for vice-president is backed by Platt, who wishes to remove him from the governorship. Roosevelt attends Republican national convention in Philadelphia, where on June 21 he is unanimously nominated for vice-president. While McKinley remains at home in Canton, Ohio, during the campaign, Roosevelt travels 21,000 miles and makes 673 speeches in 24 states, defending the annexation of the Philippines and attacking Democratic nominee William Jennings Bryan. *The Strenuous Life*, a collection of essays, is published during the campaign. On November 6 McKinley is reelected with 292 electoral votes, while Bryan receives 155.

1901         Hunts cougars in Colorado. Takes oath of office as vice-president on March 4 and presides over the Senate until its adjournment on March 9. Spends spring and summer at Sagamore Hill; with few official duties, he considers resuming his legal studies. William Howard Taft becomes the first civil governor of the Philippines on July 4 as American troops continue to fight Filipino guerillas. President McKinley is shot by Leon Czolgosz, an anarchist, in Buffalo, New York, on September 6 and dies from his wounds on September 14. Roosevelt takes the oath of office as president in Buffalo on the afternoon of September 14. Keeps George Cortelyou, who had served McKinley, as his presidential secretary, and retains McKinley's cabinet: John Hay (secretary of state), Lyman Gage (secretary of treasury), Elihu Root (secretary of war), Philander Knox (attorney general), Charles Emory Smith (postmaster general), John Long (secretary of the navy), Ethan Hitchcock (secretary of the interior), and as secretary of agriculture, James Wilson (the only cabinet member to serve throughout Roosevelt's presidency). Invites Booker T. Washington to have dinner with the Roosevelt family at the White House on October 16; the dinner is widely condemned in the South as a move toward "social equality." Although Roosevelt continues to consult with Washington and has other African-Americans as guests at White House receptions, he does not have dinner with an African-American again while president. Secretary of State John Hay signs a second treaty with Lord Pauncefote on November 18 after Britain agrees to permit fortification of a future canal. In his first annual message to Congress, December 3, Roosevelt calls for the creation of a department of commerce and labor, the regulation of large corporations, forest conservation, federal irrigation of western lands, and the expansion of the navy (during his presidency the battleship fleet is increased from 17 to 27 ships). Forms close relationship with Gifford Pinchot, chief of the Bureau of Forestry in the Department of Agriculture.

1902      Lyman Gage and Charles Emory Smith both retire; Roosevelt appoints Leslie Shaw as secretary of the treasury and Henry Payne as postmaster general. Department of Justice files anti-trust suit on March 10 against the Northern Securities Company, a recently formed holding company that controls the three major railroads in the northwestern United States. John Long retires and is replaced as secretary of the navy by William Moody. In response to recent allegations of widespread American atrocities in the Philippines, Roosevelt defends the general conduct of U.S. troops during the insurrection while ordering an investigation. Anthracite coal miners in Pennsylvania go on strike on May 12. U.S. administration of Cuba ends May 20 under terms that restrict Cuban sovereignty. Roosevelt signs bill on May 22 creating Crater Lake National Park in Oregon; during his presidency the number of national parks increases from five to ten. On June 17 he signs the National Reclamation Act, which provides for the first federal irrigation projects; 24 projects are established in 14 western states during his presidency. Congress rejects proposal for a Nicaraguan canal while approving plan for building one through the isthmus of Panama, the route favored by Roosevelt, and authorizes the administration to enter into negotiations with Colombia (at the time Panama is a Colombian state). Leaves Washington in early July and goes to Sagamore Hill, where he will spend every summer during his presidency. Officially declares an end to the Philippine insurrection on July 4 after fighting ends in the northern and central islands of the archipelago. (U.S. troops will continue to fight Moro rebels in the southern Philippines until 1913.) Orders Brigadier General Jacob Smith to be retired from the army for his brutal actions in the Philippines; several other officers charged with atrocities are acquitted by military courts. Appoints Oliver Wendell Holmes, chief justice of the Massachusetts Supreme Judicial Court, to the U.S. Supreme Court on August 11. During a visit to Pittsfield, Massachusetts, on September 3, the presidential carriage is struck by a trolley car, killing a Secret Service agent and throwing Roosevelt onto the pavement. Continues speaking tour, but undergoes two operations in late September to treat his injured left leg. Returns to Washington, staying at 22 Jackson Place while the White House undergoes extensive renovations. Meets with United Mine Workers president John Mitchell and mine owners on October 3 in attempt to avert a winter coal shortage. After extensive negotiations, Roosevelt names an investigating commission on October 16 and the miners return to work on October 23. (Commission report on March 18, 1903, results in settlement favorable to the miners, but not in union recognition.) Moves back into the White House on November 4.

Makes hunting trip to Mississippi during which he refuses to shoot a bear tied to a tree (cartoon depicting the incident inspires the term "teddy bear"). Nominates Dr. William Crum, an African-American, as collector of customs in Charleston, South Carolina; the appointment is resisted by southern senators, and Roosevelt makes a series of recess appointments until Crum is finally confirmed in 1905. On December 9 Britain and Germany begin a naval blockade of Venezuela in an attempt to force its government to pay its foreign debt. Concerned about possible German expansion in Latin America, Roosevelt reinforces the U.S. fleet in the Caribbean and obtains the agreement of Germany to submit the dispute to international arbitration (blockade ends in February 1903).

1903    Hay-Herrán treaty, signed January 22, provides for a canal zone six miles wide under Colombian sovereignty but with American regulations and courts. After Roosevelt insists that dispute over the Alaska-Canada border not be arbitrated by outside powers, the Hay-Herbert treaty is signed on January 24, providing for a commission with American, Canadian, and British members. Congress establishes Department of Commerce and Labor, February 14, and Roosevelt appoints George Cortelyou as its first secretary; William Loeb succeeds Cortelyou as Roosevelt's secretary. Congress also passes legislation reorganizing the army and establishing a general staff, a measure advocated by Roosevelt and Elihu Root, and the Elkins Act, prohibiting railroads from giving or receiving rebates. Roosevelt appoints William Day, a federal appellate judge from Ohio, to the Supreme Court on February 19. Creates the first national wildlife refuge on March 14; will establish 54 other wildlife refuges by executive order on federally owned land during his presidency. Leaves Washington April 1 on western trip during which he visits 25 states and travels 14,000 miles. Goes camping in Yellowstone National Park with nature writer John Burroughs and in Yosemite National Park with John Muir. Returns to Washington on June 5. Colombian senate rejects canal treaty on August 12. Alaska-Canada border commission proposes settlement favorable to the United States on October 20. Roosevelt appoints Public Lands Commission to study the use of federal lands. Rebellion in Panama begins on November 3. U.S. Navy prevents Colombia

from sending reinforcements, and on November 14 the
United States formally recognizes the new Panamanian
regime. On November 18 Hay signs a convention with
Panamanian envoy Philippe Bunau-Varilla; under its terms,
the United States guarantees Panamanian independence,
while Panama cedes perpetual sovereignty over a zone ten
miles wide in return for $10 million and an annuity of
$250,000 (financial terms are the same as those in the ear-
lier treaty with Colombia).

1904    Roosevelt appoints William Howard Taft as secretary
of war when Root returns to his law practice. Russo-
Japanese War begins on February 8. Senator Mark Hanna
of Ohio, Roosevelt's main rival for leadership of the Republican party, dies on February 15. Supreme Court rules
5–4 for the government in the Northern Securites anti-
trust case on March 14. Roosevelt orders warships to
Tangier after Ion Perdicaris, a former American citizen,
is kidnapped in Morocco on May 18 by Raisuli, a Berber
insurgent. Republican national convention nominates
Roosevelt by acclamation on June 23, chooses Senator
Charles Fairbanks of Indiana as the vice-presidential candidate, and makes Cortelyou national chairman of the
party. Perdicaris is released by Raisuli on June 24. Roosevelt appoints Victor Metcalf to succeed Cortelyou as
secretary of commerce and labor, names Secretary of the
Navy William Moody as attorney general when Knox is
elected to the Senate, and replaces Moody with Paul
Morton. Democrats nominate Alton B. Parker, a New
York judge, for president on July 9. In accordance with
tradition, Roosevelt does not actively campaign. Postmaster General Henry Payne dies on October 4; Roosevelt appoints Robert Wynne as his successor. In
election on November 8 Roosevelt wins 336 electoral
votes and 56 percent of the popular vote; Parker receives
140 electoral votes. Roosevelt declares on election night
that he will not seek another term. In his annual message
to Congress, December 6, states that in cases of "chronic
wrongdoing" or general lawlessness in Latin America the
United States should be prepared to intervene and exercise "an international police power" in order to prevent
European intervention. (Policy becomes known as the
Roosevelt Corollary to the Monroe Doctrine.) Injures
left eye while boxing with a military officer at the White

House; over the course of several years he loses sight in the affected eye.

1905    Signs bill on February 1 creating the U.S. Forest Service within the Department of Agriculture and giving it authority over national forest reserves previously controlled by the Department of the Interior. Names Gifford Pinchot as its first chief; during his presidency Roosevelt expands the forest reserves from 43 million to 194 million acres. On February 7 the United States and the Dominican Republic sign a diplomatic protocol under which the U.S. assumes responsibility for collecting Dominican customs and managing the payment of its foreign debt. After the Senate twice adjourns without voting on its ratification, Roosevelt continues to implement the protocol by executive action (American management of Dominican customs and debt payments continues until July 31, 1907). Roosevelt is inaugurated on March 4. Appoints George Cortelyou to succeed Robert Wynne as postmaster general. Gives away niece Eleanor Roosevelt at her marriage to her fifth cousin, Franklin Delano Roosevelt, in New York on March 17. Leaves Washington on western trip, April 3; hunts wolves in Oklahoma and bears in Colorado before returning to the capital on May 11. After the Japanese win decisive naval victory in Tsushima Strait, May 27–28, they ask Roosevelt to mediate peace with Russia, and he agrees. Czar Nicholas II accepts mediation offer on June 7. Roosevelt makes his first visit to Pine Knot, a small wooden cabin near Charlottesville, Virginia, that Edith has bought for him; returns for seven more short visits during his presidency. Kaiser William II writes to Roosevelt warning of a possible war between Germany and France over foreign intervention in Morocco. Roosevelt suggests holding an international conference to resolve the dispute, and Germany and France agree (conference opens in Algeciras, Spain, on January 16, 1906). John Hay dies on July 1, and Roosevelt names Elihu Root as his successor. Appoints Charles Bonaparte as secretary of the navy after Paul Morton resigns over controversy concerning his past actions as a railroad executive. Russo-Japanese peace negotiations begin at the Portsmouth, New Hampshire, navy yard on August 9. Roosevelt follows the talks from Sagamore Hill and helps persuade the Japanese not to press for an indemnity and to claim only the southern half of Sakhalin Island. Becomes the first president to descend in a submarine when he dives in Long Island Sound on August 25 onboard the *Plunger*. Peace treaty is signed at Portsmouth on September 5. *Outdoor Pastimes of an American Hunter* published in October. In his annual message to Congress, December 5, Roosevelt calls for legislation regulating railroad rates and protecting food and drugs against adulteration and fraudulent labeling.

1906    Daughter Alice marries Nicholas Longworth, a Republican congressman from Ohio, at the White House on February 17. Algeciras conference on Morocco ends on April 6 with the signing of an agreement favorable to France. Roosevelt orders an investigation of the meatpacking industry after reading Upton Sinclair's *The Jungle*. Signs Antiquities Act, June 8, giving the president authority to create national monuments on federally owned land; Roosevelt will establish 18 national monuments during his presidency. Signs the Hepburn Act, giving the Interstate Commerce Commission power to regulate railroad rates, June 29; the Pure Food and Drug Act, June 30; and a federal meat inspection act, June 30. Roosevelt follows investigation into incident in Brownsville, Texas, where on August 13 one white man is shot to death and two others are wounded, allegedly by black soldiers from the 25th Infantry Regiment. Orders American intervention in Cuba on September 28 after the Cuban government collapses (occupation lasts until a new government is inaugurated on January 28, 1909). Decision by the San Francisco board of education on October 11 to segregate Japanese schoolchildren causes crisis in U.S.-Japanese relations. Roosevelt orders the dishonorable discharge of 167 black soldiers for not identifying the alleged perpetrators of the Brownsville shootings, November 5, and subsequently defends decision from public criticism by Republican senator Joseph Foraker and others. Inspects the construction of the canal in Panama, November 14–17, becoming the first president to leave the continental United States while in office. Justice Department files suit to dissolve Standard Oil of New Jersey (company is dissolved in 1911 after the Supreme Court rules for the government). Appoints Attorney General William Moody to the Supreme Court on December 3, leading to cabinet reorganization in which Charles Bonaparte replaces Moody, Victor Metcalf replace Bonaparte as secretary of the navy, and Metcalf is succeeded as secretary of commerce and labor by Oscar Straus, who becomes the first Jewish cabinet member. Roosevelt is awarded the Nobel Peace Prize on December 10 for his role in the Portsmouth Treaty.

Replaces Ethan Hitchcock with James Garfield as secretary of the interior and Leslie Shaw with George Cortelyou as secretary of the treasury; George von Lengerke Meyer succeeds Cortelyou as postmaster general. In February Roosevelt reaches "gentlemen's agreement" with the Japanese government, under which San Francisco ceases segregation of Japanese schoolchildren in return for severe restrictions on Japanese immigration to the continental United States. Appoints Inland Waterways Commission on March 14 to study the use and control of river systems. During the spring and summer Roosevelt begins actively supporting Taft's bid to win the Republican presidential nomination. Administration files anti-trust suit against the American Tobacco Company in July (in 1911 the Supreme Court orders the company to be broken up). Roosevelt's advocacy of progressive policies and assertions of executive power lead to increasing tension with conservative Republicans in Congress. Collapse of the Knickerbocker Trust Company on October 22 causes major financial panic. Cortelyou works with financier J. P. Morgan to avert further bank failures, and on November 4 Roosevelt gives his approval to the acquisition of Tennessee Coal and Iron by U.S. Steel after being told the purchase will prevent the collapse of a major brokerage house (transaction is later criticized as being unduly favorable to U.S. Steel). Economic situation improves in November after Cortelyou issues $150 million in government bonds. Roosevelt orders 16 battleships on around-the-world cruise to demonstrate American naval power to Japan and other nations, and goes to Hampton Roads, Virginia, on December 16 to view the departure of the "Great White Fleet."

1908        Begins planning African hunting expedition to collect wild-life specimens for the Smithsonian. Holds national conservation conference at the White House, May 13–15, attended by governors from 45 states and territories. Names National Conservation Commission, with Gifford Pinchot as its chairman, on June 8; the commission conducts the first systematic national inventory of American natural resources. Republicans nominate Taft for president on June 18. Roosevelt appoints Luke Wright to succeed Taft as secretary of war. In the election on November 3, Taft wins 321 electoral votes and William Jennings Bryan 162.

1909    Roosevelt watches return of the Great White Fleet at Hampton Roads on February 22. Taft is inaugurated on March 4. Roosevelt and Kermit sail for British East Africa on March 23 and join expedition in Kenya on April 24. Shoots lion, elephant, rhinoceros, hippopotamus, buffalo, giraffe, zebra, and more than 20 different species of antelope while on safari. Travels to Uganda in December.

1910    Learns that Taft has dismissed Gifford Pinchot as head of the forestry service. Hunts in the Belgian Congo, then boards a steamer in southern Sudan and sails down the White Nile. Arrives on March 14 in Khartoum, where he meets Edith and Ethel. Lands in Naples on April 2, beginning European tour that takes him to Rome, Vienna, Budapest, Paris, Brussels, Amsterdam, and Copenhagen. Formally accepts Nobel Peace Prize in Christiana (Oslo) on May 5. Visits Stockholm and attends military maneuvers near Berlin with Kaiser William II. Serves as special American ambassador at the funeral of Edward VII in London on May 20. Returns to New York City on June 18, where he is greeted by a crowd of 100,000 people. Ted marries Eleanor Alexander in New York on June 20. Roosevelt becomes contributing editor to *The Outlook*. Endorses progressive positions in widely reported "New Nationalism" speech given at Osawatomie, Kansas, on August 31. *African Game Trails* published. Flies as passenger in airplane at St. Louis on October 11. Campaigns for Henry L. Stimson, the unsuccessful Republican candidate for governor of New York. *African and European Addresses* and *The New Nationalism* published.

1911    Writes series of articles for *The Outlook* on progressive nationalism as he becomes increasingly critical of Taft's administration. Goes on western speaking tour, March 8–April 16, during which he gives five lectures at the Pacific Theological Seminary in Berkeley (published as *Realizable Ideals* in 1912). Publishes "Revealing and Concealing Coloration in Birds and Mammals," a 112-page monograph, in the *Bulletin of the American Museum of Natural History*. Granddaughter Grace Roosevelt born August 17. Edith suffers serious head injury when she is thrown from her horse on September 30 and slowly recovers during autumn.

1912        Roosevelt declares his candidacy for the Republican nomination on February 21. Campaigns in 21 states during the spring and wins nine of the 12 Republican primaries, including the contest in Ohio, Taft's home state. Control of the party national committee allows Taft loyalists to unseat many Roosevelt delegates, and on June 22 Taft is renominated in Chicago as Roosevelt supporters walk out of the convention. Democrats nominate New Jersey governor Woodrow Wilson for president on July 2. Progressive Party convention meets in Chicago, August 15–17, nominates Roosevelt for president and California governor Hiram Johnson for vice-president, and adopts platform calling for woman suffrage, the direct election of U.S. senators, and legislation prohibiting child labor and limiting women's working hours. (Progressives become widely known as the "Bull Moose Party" after Roosevelt's frequent remark that he feels "as fit as a bull moose.") Roosevelt publishes *The Conservation of Womanhood and Children*. While campaigning in Milwaukee on October 14, Roosevelt is shot in the chest by a mentally unbalanced saloonkeeper; despite having a broken rib, he addresses a rally that evening for 90 minutes. Recovers in a Chicago hospital for eight days, then makes his final campaign speech in New York City on October 30. In the election on November 5, Wilson wins 42 percent of the popular vote and 435 electoral votes; Roosevelt, 27 percent and 88 electoral votes; Taft, 23 percent and eight electoral votes. Delivers address "History as Literature" in Boston on December 27 as he begins one-year term as president of the American Historical Association.

1913        Speaks at Progressive Party meetings. Daughter Ethel marries Richard Derby, a physician, in Oyster Bay on April 4. Roosevelt wins libel action on May 31 against George Newett, a Michigan newspaper editor who had accused him of frequent drunkenness. Hunts cougars in northern Arizona in late July. *An Autobiography* and *History as Literature* published. Sails for South America with

Edith on October 4. Gives speeches in Brazil, Uruguay, Argentina, and Chile, then crosses the Andes on horseback with Kermit in late November and travels through Argentina and Paraguay to Corumbá in southern Brazil. Joins Brazilian expedition led by Colonel Candido Rondon that is planning to explore the uncharted course of the Rio da Dúvida (River of Doubt) in western Brazil. Hunts jaguars and wild boars.

1914    Travels by boat to Tapirapuan, then by mule through the Mato Grosso to the headwaters of the Rio da Dúvida. Party of 22 men begin descent of the river, which the Brazilian government renames the Rio Roosevelt, on February 27. Grandson Richard Derby Jr. born March 6. Roosevelt injures his left leg on March 27. Suffering from abscesses, high fever, and severe dysentery, he recites Coleridge's "Kubla Khan" in his delirium and urges Kermit to leave him behind as the entire party becomes imperiled by a shortage of food and series of boat accidents. Expedition reaches Manaus on the Amazon on April 30, having lost three men during the trip. *Life Histories of African Game Animals*, written with Edmund Heller, published. Roosevelt returns to New York on May 19, his health permanently weakened. Attends wedding in Madrid on June 11 of Kermit and Belle Willard, the daughter of the American ambassador to Spain. Grandson Theodore Roosevelt III born June 14. Returns to New York in late June after visiting France and England. Leaves *The Outlook* and becomes a contributor to *Metropolitan* and the *Philadelphia North American*. At outbreak of war in Europe in early August Roosevelt is initially neutral, but he is soon angered by the German invasion of Belgium and reports of German atrocities. Makes more than 100 speeches for Progressive congressional candidates in the Midwest and Northeast during the fall campaign. *Through the Brazilian Wilderness* published.

1915    *America and the World War* published. Criticizes Wilson for ignoring the violation of Belgian neutrality, neglecting military preparedness, and failing to protect American citizens threatened by the civil war in Mexico. Travels in April to Syracuse, New York, where he is being sued for accusing Republican boss William Barnes of corruption. Publicly denounces the German sinking of the British liner *Lusitania* on May 7, in which 128 American passengers are killed, as an act of piracy and privately calls Wilson a coward for his attempts to avoid war with Germany. Acquitted in Barnes libel case on May 22. Becomes prominent public advocate of increased military preparedness. Goes hunting in Quebec in September. Grandson Cornelius Van Schaak Roosevelt born October 23.

1916    Grandson Kermit Roosevelt Jr. born February 16. Roosevelt visits British West Indies in February and March. Publishes *Fear God and Take Your Own Part*, collection of articles attacking Wilson's conduct of foreign policy, and *A Book-Lover's Holiday in the Open*. Declines presidential nomination of the Progressive Party on June 10 and endorses Republican candidate Charles Evan Hughes. Harshly criticizes Wilson while campaigning for Hughes in October. In the election on November 7 Wilson wins 277 electoral votes, Hughes 254.

1917    Germany resumes unrestricted submarine warfare against neutral shipping on February 1. Wilson sends war message to Congress on April 2, and the United States declares war on Germany on April 6. Roosevelt meets with Wilson at the White House on April 10 to request permission to raise a volunteer division and lead it into battle in France; the administration eventually declines the offer. Attends wedding in Boston on April 14 of Archie and Grace Lockwood. Granddaughter Ethel Roosevelt Derby born June 17. Ted and Archie are commissioned as officers and sail to France to serve with the 1st Infantry Division; Quentin sails for France in late July after training as a pilot on Long Island; and Kermit joins the British forces fighting the Turks in Mesopotamia (he will later serve as an artillery officer in France). Roosevelt continues to advocate progressive social policies while harshly criticizing the administration for failing to adequately equip American troops and for attempting to suppress criticism of its shortcomings. Publishes collection *The Foes of Our Own Household* in October and begins writing column for the *Kansas City Star*.

1918    Grandson Joseph Willard Roosevelt born January 16. Roosevelt has surgery in New York City on February 6 for severe ear infection and abscess related to Brazilian trip. Grandson Archibald Roosevelt Jr. born February 18. Roosevelt leaves hospital on March 4. Archie is severely wounded in the knee and arm by shell fragments on March 11. Quentin joins 95th Aero Squadron in June; on July 14 he is shot down and killed by German fighters near Reims. Ted is wounded in the leg on July 19. Archie returns from France on September 4. Roosevelt speaks at Liberty Loan rallies in September and October. Makes last public appearance on November 2, appearing with W.E.B. Du Bois at a benefit for Negro War Relief in New York City. *The Great Adventure: Present-Day Studies in American Nationalism* published. Suffering from rheumatism and gout, Roosevelt enters hospital in New York on November 11 as the war ends in Europe. Returns to Sagamore Hill on December 25.

1919        Dies in his sleep from a coronary embolism at 4:15 A.M. on January 6. After an Episcopal funeral service at Christ Church in Oyster Bay, he is buried in the nearby Youngs Memorial Cemetery on January 8.

# Note on the Texts

This volume collects two memoirs by Theodore Roosevelt, *The Rough Riders* (1899) and *An Autobiography* (1913). The texts printed here are taken from the first editions.

Theodore Roosevelt resigned as assistant secretary of the navy on May 6, 1898, the day on which he received his commission as lieutenant colonel of the First U.S. Volunteer Cavalry. His decision to help raise a regiment and fight in the Spanish-American War attracted attention in the press and the interest of several magazine editors. In a letter to Robert Bridges, assistant editor of *Scribner's Magazine*, written on May 21, 1898, from San Antonio, Texas, where his regiment was training, Roosevelt acknowledged an invitation to write about his war experiences for *Scribner's*. After mentioning that he had also received letters from *The Century Magazine* and *Atlantic Monthly*, Roosevelt continued: "If I do the job at all, I am going to do it thoroughly. Possibly I could make some such arrangement (provided neither the yellow fever nor a Mauser bullet catches me) as I have made before, namely, to have the thing appear in magazine form, that is, in popular form, first, yet when it comes out as a book to be in shape as a permanent historical work." After his return to the United States from Cuba in August, Roosevelt agreed to write a six-part series for *Scribner's*, for which he would be paid $1,000 for each installment. Following his election as governor of New York on November 8, 1898, he began dictating the articles to a stenographer at his home in Oyster Bay, Long Island, and continued work on the series in Albany after taking office there at the end of the year. In a letter to Bridges written on February 7, 1899, Roosevelt discussed his plans for book publication of *The Rough Riders*: "I shall put in the appendix the letters of recommendation of myself for the medal of honor, the Round Robin correspondence which you so kindly sent me and my report to the Secretary to which the officers of the regiment subscribed."

*The Rough Riders* appeared in *Scribner's* between January and June 1899 and was published in book form by Charles Scribner's Sons early in the summer of 1899. In the book version, each serial installment appeared as a separate chapter, and four appendices were added: the regimental muster-out roll; Roosevelt's report to Secretary of War Russell Alger on supply shortages during the Cuban campaign; an Associated Press report from August 1898 on the "round robin" letter sent by Roosevelt and other officers to General William Shafter, urging that the army be promptly returned to the United States to avoid further losses to malaria; and "Corrections," in which Roosevelt referred to, and in some cases excerpted, letters he had received in response to the *Scribner's* articles. (Though Roosevelt did not include letters recommending him for the Medal of Honor in the 1899 edition of *The Rough Riders*, several of these letters appear in appendix B to chapter VII of *An Autobiography*; see p. 513 and pp. 516–20 in this volume.)

There were 11 further printings of *The Rough Riders* during Roosevelt's lifetime, all between 1900 and 1911. Many of these printings appeared as part of collected sets of Roosevelt's works, such as the "Sagamore Edition" published by G. P. Putnam's Sons in 1900, the "Statesman Edition" published by the Review of Reviews Co. in 1904, and the "Elkhorn Edition" published by Scribner's in 1906. Some of the new printings contained additional ancillary material presented in appendices, including letters from officers commending Roosevelt's conduct; an account of the battle of San Juan by General Samuel Sumner; the texts of speeches Roosevelt made to his men at Montauk, Long Island, on September 4 and 13, 1898; his speech on "Yale Men in the Rough Riders," given at a Yale alumni dinner on May 3, 1899; and his address at a regimental reunion held in San Antonio, Texas, on April 7, 1905. This volume prints the text of the 1899 Charles Scribner's Sons edition of *The Rough Riders*.

Roosevelt decided to write his autobiography after the defeat of his third-party campaign for the presidency in 1912, and he had begun dictating the manuscript by January 4, 1913. During its composition he wrote to a number of his friends and associates, including Gifford Pinchot, Lemuel Quigg, and Leonard Wood, asking them to send him memoranda concerning events they had been involved in. Portions of the work appeared under the title "Chapters of a Possible Autobiography" in *The Outlook* between February 22 and December 27, 1913. *An Autobiography* was published by the Macmillan Company in November 1913. The Macmillan edition included the serial installments, with some additions and corrections, as well as considerable new material: the foreword, three new chapters (XI–XIII), and the appendices that follow chapters VII, VIII, XIV, and XV. No new editions of the book appeared during Roosevelt's lifetime. The present volume prints the text of the 1913 Macmillan edition of *An Autobiography*.

This volume presents the texts of the original printings chosen for inclusion here, but it does not attempt to reproduce nontextual features of their typographic design. The texts are presented without change, except for the correction of typographical errors. Spelling, punctuation, and capitalization are often expressive features and are not altered, even when inconsistent or irregular. The following is a list of typographical errors corrected, cited by page and line number: 34.36, peformed; 41.30, reasons; 41.39, its; 67.13, topic; 102.32, Ship; 110.31, gatlings; 116.9, that; 117.37, came; 148.2, Ayres; 206.4, Vagas; 207.2, Vagas; 229.15, ADNAH; 229.17, SUMMER; 231.40, The; 248.17, [line missing]; 249.29, Crater-Crater; 254.25, it if; 292.9, ground"; 299.3, crossing; 376.5, lantern-bearer.; 478.28, out-of-the way; 486.1, instead the; 498.37, every; 501.31 Fifty; 517.18, unnecessary; 609.21, questions,; 616.29, sugestions; 622.35, duty; 651.33, W J; 663.17, method; 671.14, Land; 679.1, Crater-Crater; 773.15, Colombia; 805.35, Franscico; 816.43, gulity.

# *Notes*

In the notes below, the reference numbers denote page and line of this volume (the line count includes headings). No note is made for material included in standard desk-reference books. Biblical quotations are keyed to the King James Version. Quotations from Shakespeare are keyed to *The Riverside Shakespeare*, ed. G. Blakemore Evans (Boston: Houghton Mifflin, 1974). Footnotes in the text are Roosevelt's own. For further biographical background and references to other studies, see Lewis L. Gould, *The Presidency of Theodore Roosevelt* (Lawrence: University Press of Kansas, 1991); Louis Auchincloss, *Theodore Roosevelt* (New York: Henry Holt and Company, 2001); Edmund Morris, *The Rise of Theodore Roosevelt* (revised edition, New York: The Modern Library, 2001) and *Theodore Rex* (New York: Random House, Inc., 2001); and Kathleen Dalton, *Theodore Roosevelt: A Strenuous Life* (New York: Alfred A. Knopf, 2002).

THE ROUGH RIDERS

9.1–21    Hark! I hear . . . drum.]   From "The Reveille" (1862).

12.5–10    Senator Lodge . . . Senator Frye]   Henry Cabot Lodge (1850–1924), Republican senator from Massachusetts, 1893–1924; Cushman Davis (1838–1900), Republican senator from Minnesota, 1887–1900; Redfield Proctor (1831–1908), Republican senator from Vermont, 1891–1908; Joseph Foraker (1846–1917), Republican senator from Ohio, 1896–1909; William Chandler (1835–1917), Republican senator from New Hampshire, 1889–1901; John Morgan (1824–1907), Democratic senator from Alabama, 1877–1907; William Frye (1830–1911), Republican senator from Maine, 1881–1911.

12.19–21    General Miles's . . . Apaches]   Wood (1860–1927) served with the American forces that pursued Geronimo and a small band of Chiricahua Apache through Arizona and northern Mexico from May 5 to September 8, 1886. The campaign ended when Geronimo surrendered to General Nelson Miles, the commander of the Department of Arizona; Geronimo and the Chiricahua were then sent to Florida under military guard.

15.4    Secretary Alger]   Russell Alger (1836–1907) was secretary of war, 1897–99; he later served as a Republican senator from Michigan, 1902–7.

15.27    New Mexico, Arizona, Oklahoma, and Indian Territory.]   In 1898 present-day Oklahoma was divided into Oklahoma Territory and Indian Territory. The two territories were merged and admitted as the state of Oklahoma in 1907. New Mexico and Arizona became states in 1912.

18.23–24      Krag-Jorgensen carbine]   A bolt-action weapon with a five-round magazine, the carbine was 41 inches long, weighed almost eight pounds, and fired a .30 caliber bullet.

20.10      Riel Rebellion]   Louis Riel (1844–1885), an advocate for Métis land rights in the Canadian Northwest, proclaimed a provisional government at Batoche, Saskatchewan, on March 18, 1885. After a skirmish between Métis insurgents and the Royal Canadian Mounted Police at Duck Lake on March 26, thousands of Canadian militiamen were called to service, and Batoche was captured on May 12, ending the rebellion. Riel was convicted of treason and hanged on November 16, 1885.

20.30–31      Lord Aberdeen's staff]   Lord Aberdeen was governor general of Canada, 1893–98.

22.33      Meagher's Brigade]   Union Army formation, also known as the Irish Brigade, that was originally composed of three regiments of Irish immigrants raised in New York by Brigadier General Thomas Meagher, who commanded the brigade from February 1862 to May 1863. The brigade served in the Second Corps of the Army of the Potomac for three years and had more than 4,000 men killed and wounded in action.

36.20–21      new model . . . Government cartridge.]   The 1895 Model Winchester could fire the same .30 caliber cartridge used in the Krag carbine.

48.9–10      Richard Harding Davis . . . Frederic Remington.]   Davis (1864–1916) was a correspondent for the New York *Herald*; Fox (1862–1919), a popular fiction writer, and Whitney (1862–1929), a well-known sportswriter, were correspondents for *Harper's Weekly*; Remington (1861–1909), an artist and sculptor, covered the war as an illustrator for the New York *Journal* and *Harper's Weekly*.

60.32      General Shafter]   William Shafter (1835–1906) commanded V Corps, the expeditionary force sent to Cuba in 1898.

63.7      dynamite gun]   The Sims-Dudley pneumatic gun, commonly known as a dynamite gun because it fired an explosive related to dynamite, used air compressed by a gunpowder charge to propel a projectile containing nitrogelatin. (Compressed air was utilized in the design because using gunpowder as the direct propellant would have caused the sensitive nitrogelatin to explode inside the barrel of the weapon.) The gun was soon made obsolete by the development of more stable high explosives that could be used with gunpowder propellant.

64.14      command . . . Park]   The U.S. Army administered Yellowstone National Park for the Department of the Interior from 1886 to 1919.

72.24      Edward Marshall]   Marshall (1870–1933) was a correspondent for the New York *Journal*.

78.37–38    "Albemarle" Cushing . . . ram]    Lieutenant William B. Cushing took a small launch up the Roanoke River in North Carolina on the night of October 27, 1864, and sank the ironclad *Albemarle* with a mine.

86.6–8    Whitman . . . flesh of kings'?]    See p. 230.3–7 in this volume.

90.13–14    the man who . . . the Fishes]    Hamilton Fish Jr. was the great-grandson of Elizabeth (Stuyvesant) Fish, a descendant of Peter Stuyvesant, and Nicholas Fish, a Revolutionary War officer, New York attorney, and friend of Alexander Hamilton. His grandfather Hamilton Fish was a congressman, 1843–45, governor of New York, 1849–50, senator, 1851–57, and secretary of state, 1869–77; his father, Nicholas Fish (1846–1902), served as a diplomat in Western Europe before joining the Harriman banking firm in New York.

103.17    "crowded hour"]    Cf. Thomas Osbert Mordaunt (1730–1809), "Verses Written During the War": "One crowded hour of glorious life / Is worth an age without a name."

124.16    Cossack posts]    Small outposts, usually made up of four men.

138.7–8    John Fox and Miss Murfree]    John Fox (1862–1919), author of *A Cumberland Vendetta and Other Stories* (1896) and *"Hell fer Sartain" and Other Stories* (1897) and a war correspondent (see note 48.9–10); Mary Noailles Murfree (1850–1922) published numerous story collections under the name Charles Egbert Craddock, including *In the Tennessee Mountains* (1884) and *The Young Mountaineers* (1897).

145.34    Turco-Greek war]    On April 17, 1897, Greece attacked Turkish forces in Macedonia. After a series of Turkish victories, an armistice was declared on May 20, and on December 4, 1897, a treaty was signed that required Greece to pay an indemnity.

162.30    immune regiments]    Regiments of U.S. Volunteer Infantry, recruited in the spring and summer of 1898 from among men supposed to be immune to tropical diseases. Six of the regiments were made up of southern whites and the remaining four of African-Americans. During the war four of the "immune" regiments were sent to Cuba, where their men proved to be no more resistant to disease than other soldiers; the remaining six stayed in the United States.

163.13    Wood's . . . Governor-General]    Wood was appointed military governor of the city of Santiago on July 20, 1898. He was subsequently made governor of the province of Santiago on October 7, 1898, and of Cuba on December 13, 1899, serving until the end of the first American occupation on May 19, 1902.

168.12    the Mosquito fleet]    Popular name for the United States Auxiliary Naval Forces, formed in response to fears of a Spanish naval attack on the eastern seaboard in the spring of 1898 and equipped with leased and purchased civilian vessels.

171.25–26    Peter Bell looked on primroses]    See William Wordsworth, *Peter Bell* (1819), ll. 248–50: "A primrose by a river's brim / A yellow primrose was to him, / And it was nothing more."

172.22    Archibald Forbes's . . . Pig-dog.]    In *Memories and Studies of War and Peace* (1895), British war correspondent Archibald Forbes (1838–1900) described how "Baron von und zu Steinfurst-Wallenstein," a young cavalry ensign, used his hunting rifle to kill a French sniper in the siege lines outside Paris on Christmas Eve in 1870. The sniper, who had previously killed several Germans, was referred to as a "pig-dog" by German soldiers in the story.

177.3    shown at Manila]    American troops defeated Filipino insurgents in the battle of Manila, February 4–23, 1899.

178.15    King's Mountain and the Thames]    The battles of King's Mountain, fought in South Carolina on October 7, 1780, and of the Thames, fought in Upper Canada (Ontario) on October 5, 1813, were both American victories.

225.4    General Miles]    Nelson Miles (1839–1925) was commanding general of the army, 1895–1903.

230.5–7    "Speak unto . . . of the earth."]    Ezekiel 39:17–18.

231.20    Mr. Stephen Bonsal]    Bonsal (1865–1951) reported on the Cuban campaign for the New York *Herald*.


AN AUTOBIOGRAPHY

252.11–12    Letters of Junius]    A series of pseudonymous letters published in the London *Public Advertiser*, 1769–72, that upheld Whig principles and criticized George III, prime minister Grafton, and the chief justice, Lord Mansfield.

252.16    the original *Edinburgh Review*]    The periodical began publication in 1802.

253.36–37    Falstaff's views . . . sack and bread]    See *Henry IV*, part 1, II.iv.528–41.

254.17    Revolutionary "President" of Georgia]    On April 15, 1776, the Georgia provincial congress adopted a temporary state constitution under which executive power was given to a "president and commander-in-chief of Georgia." Bulloch was elected president by the congress and served from May 1, 1776, until his death in February 1777.

256.20–21    the *Potiphar Papers*]    A collection of satirical sketches published by Curtis (1824–1892) in 1853.

262.34–35    Charles Loring Brace]    Brace (1826–1890) founded the Children's Aid Society in 1853 and served as its executive officer until his death.

264.32–33    genius . . . "Uncle Remus"]    Joel Chandler Harris (1848–1908) published *Uncle Remus: His Songs and Sayings*, the first in a series of collections, in 1881.

265.1    Colonel Newcome]    Character in the novel *The Newcomes* (1855) by William Makepeace Thackeray.

265.5    fight with the *Kearsarge*]    The U.S.S. *Kearsarge* sank the Confederate commerce raider *Alabama* off Cherbourg, France, on June 19, 1864.

266.36    Mayne Reid's]    Reid (1818–1883), an Irish novelist, wrote more than 50 adventure tales, many of them set in the American West and Mexico.

268.12–14    Ouida . . . "Under Two Flags."]    Ouida was the pen name of the English novelist Marie Louise de la Ramée (1839–1908); in *Under Two Flags* (1867) an English army officer joins the French Foreign Legion to avert a scandal.

269.3    *Our Young Folks*]    Illustrated monthly magazine published in Boston from January 1865 through October 1873.

269.20    "An Old-Fashioned Girl."]    A novel published by Louisa May Alcott in 1870.

269.22    Ballantyne's]    Scottish adventure novelist R. M. Ballantyne (1825–1894).

269.23    "Midshipman Easy."]    *Mr Midshipman Easy*, novel (1836) by Captian Frederick Maryatt (1792–1848).

271.20–21    Spencer Baird]    Baird (1823–1887) was professor of natural history at Dickinson College, 1846–50, assistant secretary of the Smithsonian Institution, 1850–78, and its secretary, 1878–87.

273.18    poor Smike]    A character in Charles Dickens' *Nicholas Nickleby* (1839).

277.39–40    Hart Merriam . . . Biological Survey]    Merriam (1855–1942) was chief of the biological survey of the Department of Agriculture, 1885–1910.

278.37–39    Herbert Croly's "Promise . . . "New Democracy"]    Croly (1869–1930) published *The Promise of American Life* in 1909; Weyl (1873–1919) published *The New Democracy* in 1912.

284.3    August Belmont]    August Belmont II (1853–1924), a banker and prominent horse breeder; his father, August Belmont (1816–1890), founded the family banking business and was the namesake of the Belmont Stakes.

285.4    Stewart Edward White]    White (1873–1946) was a novelist whose works included *The Claims Jumpers* (1901) and *The Blazed Trail* (1902). In

1904 Roosevelt appointed him special inspector of the federal forest reserves in California.

285.5–11     Sternberg . . . Forbes's]     See note 172.22.

297.13     Battling Nelson]     Oscar Nelson (1882–1954), a Danish-born American boxer, was the world lightweight champion, 1905–6 and 1908–10.

297.18     Bob Fitzsimmons]     Fitzsimmons (1863–1917), a New Zealander, defeated James Corbett for the heavyweight title in 1897, then lost the title to Jim Jeffries in 1899. He was also the light heavyweight champion, 1903–5.

298.31–32     Thomas Henry Barry]     Barry was president of the Army War College (then located in Washington, D.C.), 1905–7, and commander of the American intervention force in Cuba, 1907–9.

298.33     Robert Bacon]     Bacon (1860–1919) was assistant secretary of state, 1905–9, and served as secretary of state from January 27 to March 5, 1909, during the final weeks of the Roosevelt administration.

301.38     Leonard . . . Tientsin]     Leonard was wounded on July 13, 1900, during the Boxer Rebellion.

304.12     Johnny Hayes]     Hayes won the marathon at the 1908 London Olympics, the first one to be run on a course of 26 miles, 385 yards, with a time of 2 hours, 55 minutes, 18.4 seconds; his record was broken in 1909.

308.4–5     Professor Thayer]     James B. Thayer (1831–1902) was professor of law at Harvard from 1874 until his death. In an influential article published in 1893, Thayer advocated a rule of judicial review under which courts would overturn legislative acts only if their unconstitutionality was "very clear" and "not open to rational question."

315.4     the meat . . . Cæsar proud]     Cf. *Julius Caesar*, I.ii.149–50.

317.8     Arthur von Briesen]     Briesen (1843–1920), a German immigrant, was president of the New York Legal Aid Society, 1890–1916, and active in New York reform politics.

317.9     "Acht-und-Vierziger"]     From *acht und vierzig*, "eight-and-forty," i.e., the unsuccessful German revolution of 1848.

319.38     Henry George]     George (1839–1897), an American economist and social reformer, advocated levying a single tax on land as the solution to a variety of economic and social problems.

322.33     Stalwart and Half-Breed]     "Stalwarts" were Republicans who opposed civil service reform and the end of Reconstruction during the Hayes administration and who supported the attempt to nominate Ulysses S. Grant for a third term in 1880; Senator Roscoe Conkling of New York was one of the leaders of the Stalwart faction. "Half-Breeds" were supporters of strong protective tariffs, anti-inflationary "hard money" policies, and limited civil service reform; they had backed James G. Blaine for the 1880 nomination. (The term "Half-Breed," referring to their supposed "half-breed" Republicanism, originated with the Stalwarts.)

330.32    Francis Lynde Stetson]    Stetson (1846–1920) was a friend and adviser to Grover Cleveland who later served as legal counsel to J. P. Morgan.

339.15–16    Josh Billings's]    Pseudonym of American humorist Henry Wheeler Shaw (1818–1885). His first book, *Josh Billings, His Sayings*, was published in 1865.

340.15    Senator Miller]    Warner Miller (1838–1918) was a U.S. senator from New York, 1881–87.

341.2    Mr. Blaine]    James G. Blaine (1830–1893) served as a representative from Maine, 1863–76, as a senator, 1876–81, and as secretary of state in 1881 and from 1889 to 1892. He was Speaker of the House, 1869–75, and an unsuccessful candidate for the Republican presidential nomination in 1876 and 1880.

343.8–9    Mr. Bryce's "American Commonwealth,"]    *The American Commonwealth* (1888, revised 1910) by James Bryce (1832–1922). Bryce was professor of civil law at Oxford, 1870–93, a Liberal member of Parliament, 1880–1907, and British ambassador to the United States, 1907–13.

346.11    "gone, gone with lost Atlantis,"]    Rudyard Kipling, "Philadelphia," from *Rewards and Fairies* (1910).

374.7    David Harum, I "did it first,"]    Cf. *David Harum: A Story of American Life*, novel (1898) by Edward Noyes Westcott (1846–1898): "Do unto the other feller the way he'd like to do unto you, an' do it fust."

382.5–6    "accustomed . . . zymotic diseases."]    Cf. chapter XV, *The Diary of a Soldier of Fortune* (1910), a memoir of life in southern Africa by Stanley Portal Hyatt (1877–1914).

382.10    brace game]    Crooked game.

393.26    Gorman]    Arthur P. Gorman (1839–1906) was a senator from Maryland, 1881–99 and 1903–6, and chairman of the Democratic senate caucus, 1890–98; in 1893–95 the Democrats controlled the Senate.

400.14–15    Guiteau . . . Ballington Booth]    Charles Guiteau assassinated President Garfield in 1881; Ballington Booth (1857–1940) commanded the Salvation Army in the United States, 1887–96, then founded and led the Volunteers of America, 1896–1940.

406.30    Tom Reed's]    Thomas Reed (1839–1902) was a Republican representative from Maine, 1877–99, and served as Speaker of the House, 1889–90 and 1895–98.

407.12–14    Mr. Lorimer . . . improper methods]    William Lorimer (1861–1934) was a Republican representative from Illinois, 1895–1901 and 1903–9.

He was elected to the U.S. Senate in 1909 and served until July 13, 1912, when the Senate voted to invalidate his election on the grounds that it had been secured by bribery in the Illinois legislature.

407.31–38     "If the wicked . . . and live?"]   Ezekiel 18:21–23.

408.13     Senator Hanna]   Marcus Alonzo Hanna (1837–1904) was a Republican senator from Ohio, 1897–1904.

409.38     Senator Quay]   Matthew Quay (1833–1904) was a Republican senator from Pennsylvania, 1887–1899 and 1901–4.

411.4     Flight of a Tartar Tribe]   "The Revolt of the Tartars," a historical essay (1837) by Thomas De Quincy (1785–1859).

417.32     Frances Kellor]   Kellor (1873–1952) was a sociologist and reformer who worked for the protection of immigrants and black women migrating to Northern cities. She was director of the New York Bureau of Industries and Immigration, 1910–12, becoming the first woman to head a New York state agency. In 1912 she served as an adviser to Roosevelt during his Progressive campaign for president.

417.36     Mary Antin]   Antin (1881–1949), a Polish-Jewish immigrant, was a settlement worker in Boston. Her autobiography *The Promised Land* was published in 1912.

419.12–13     Kathleen Norris's . . . "Preliminaries"]   *Mother: A Story* (1911) by Kathleen Norris (1880–1963); *The Preliminaries and Other Stories* (1912) by Cornelia Comer.

439.21     "scorcher,"]   Fast bicyclist.

446.5–6     Governor Hill . . . Mr. Croker]   David Hill (1843–1910) was governor of New York, 1885–91, and a senator from New York, 1892–97. Richard Croker (1841–1922) was the head of Tammany Hall, 1886–1902.

446.40     Mulberry Street]   At the time police headquarters was at 300 Mulberry Street.

454.14     "flagrant man swine"]   From "Jenny" (1870), poem by Dante Gabriel Rossetti (1828–1882).

457.37     E. L. Godkin]   Edwin Lawrence Godkin (1831–1902) was the founder and editor of *The Nation*, 1865–1881, and of the New York *Evening Post* (into which *The Nation* was merged), 1881–99.

459.9–10     "peace was her passion,"]   Cf. Thomas Jefferson, in a letter to Scottish agronomist and member of Parliament Sir John Sinclair, June 30, 1803: "Peace is our passion, and the wrongs might drive us from it. We prefer trying *ever* other just principles, right and safety, before we would recur to war."

459.18–19     Mrs. Gummidge]   Character in Charles Dickens' *David Copperfield* (1850).

462.5      writings of Captain Mahan]   Captain Alfred Thayer Mahan
(1840–1914) was president of the Naval War College, 1886–89 and 1892–93.
His works include *The Influence of Sea Power upon History, 1660–1783* (1890),
*The Influence of Sea Power upon the French Revolution and Empire, 1783–1812*
(1892), and *The Interest of America in Sea Power, Present and Future* (1897).

463.10–11    revolt in Cuba]   The insurrection began on February 24, 1895.

466.16     trouble with Chile]   Two sailors from the cruiser U.S.S. *Baltimore* were killed in a fight with Chilean civilians in Valparasio on October 16,
1891. The incident was resolved on January 23, 1892, when the Chilean government agreed to pay an indemnity of $75,000 for their deaths.

467.23–24    investigation showed . . . outside.]   In a report published on
March 28, 1898, the U.S. Navy board of inquiry into the loss of the *Maine*
concluded that the explosion of the ship's magazines was caused by the det-
onation of an underwater mine.

469.35     acute philosopher Mr. Dooley]   The character of Martin Dooley,
an Irish saloonkeeper who commented on current events, was created by
Chicago journalist Finley Peter Dunne (1867–1936) in 1893; *Mr. Dooley in Peace
and War* (1898) was the first in a series of volumes collecting his columns.

479.39–40    Nogi's career . . . Washburn's little volume]   *Nogi: A Man
Against the Background of a Great War* (1913) by the American war correspondent Stanley Washburn (1878–1950). General Maresuke Nogi (1849–1912)
commanded the army attacking Port Arthur from June 1904 until the Russian surrender on January 2, 1905; both of his sons were killed during the
siege. Following the death of the Meiji Emperor in 1912, Nogi and his wife
committed seppuku (ritual suicide) as a demonstration of loyalty.

511.31–32    present Vice-President]   Thomas Marshall (1854–1925) was governor of Indiana, 1909–13, and vice-president, 1913–21.

512.1–2    the official report]   See pp. 514–15 in this volume.

525.11     Senator Platt]   Thomas Collier Platt (1833–1910) served as a representative, 1873–77, and in the senate in 1881 and from 1897 to 1909.

533.19     Gallio-like]   Gallio was the Roman proconsul in Achaia during the
time of Paul; see Acts 18:12–17.

533.21     Mr. Hughes]   Charles Evans Hughes (1862–1948) was nominated
for governor in 1906 and 1908 and served from 1907 to 1910.

541.34     my successor in the Governorship]   Benjamin B. Odell Jr. (1854–
1926) was a Republican congressman, 1895–99, and governor of New York,
1901–4.

549.6      Mr. John Hamlin]   A professional poker player in "Brown of
Calaveras" (1870) and other stories by Bret Harte (1836–1902).

549.15    George W. Perkins]    Perkins (1862–1920) was the chairman of the Progressive party national committee in 1912. From 1901 to 1910 he had been a senior financial adviser to J. P. Morgan.

571.33    "the green dance of summer"]    From "The Green Dancers," poem (1903) by Bliss Carman (1861–1929).

576.40–577.1    the Ettrick Shepherd]    Scottish poet James Hogg (1770–1835), so-called because he was a shepherd in the Ettrick Forest in southeastern Scotland.

577.10    Sir Edward Grey]    Grey (1862–1933) was a Liberal member of Parliament, 1884–1916, and foreign minister of Great Britain, 1905–16.

585.33    Proctor's]    American sculptor Alexander Proctor (1862–1950).

585.39    Macmonnies]    American sculptor Frederick MacMonnies (1863–1937).

586.7    Admiral Togo]    Heihachiro Togo (1848–1934) commanded the main Japanese fleet during the Russo-Japanese War and destroyed the Russian Baltic Fleet in the battle of Tsushima Strait, May 27–28, 1905.

586.11    John Hampden]    A leader of the parliamentary opposition to Charles I, Hampden (1594–1643) was killed in the English Civil War.

586.26    Carl Rungius]    Rungius (1869–1959), a German immigrant, was an American wildlife and landscape painter.

586.36    Lungren's]    American painter Fernand Lungren (1857–1932).

586.40    Hopkinson Smith]    American engineer, painter, and writer Francis Hopkinson Smith (1838–1915).

589.8–9    Heimskringla]    A collection of Norse sagas written by the Icelandic historian Snorri Sturluson (1178–1241).

589.15    Sutherland's . . . Moral Instinct,"]    *The Origin and Growth of the Moral Instinct* (1898) by Alexander Sutherland (1852–1902), an Australian journalist and former headmaster of Carlton College, Melbourne.

586.16    Lounsbury's]    Thomas Raynesford Lounsbury (1838–1915) was professor of English at the Sheffield Scientific School at Yale, 1871–1906, and wrote on Chaucer, Shakespeare, Cooper, and Browning.

590.11    Körner]    Karl Theodor Körner (1791–1813), German poet and dramatist who was killed fighting Napoleon.

590.12–13    the Bard of Dimbovitza]    *The Bard of Dimbovitza* (1911), a collection of Romanian folk songs by Helene Vacarescu, translated into English by Carmen Sylva (pen name of Queen Elizabeth of Romania) and Alma Strettel.

590.18–23    "Salammbo" . . . "Ingoldsby Legends"]    *Salammbô* (1862), historical novel of ancient Carthage by Gustave Flaubert; *Tom Brown's Schooldays* (1857) by Thomas Hughes; *The Two Admirals* (1842) by James Fenimore Cooper; *Quentin Durward* (1823) by Sir Walter Scott; Artemus Ward, pseudonym of American humorist Charles Farrar Browne (1834–1867); *The Ingoldsby Legends: or mirth and marvels, by Thomas Ingoldsby esquire* (1840), collection of tales and verse by Richard Harris Barham (1788–1845).

591.38–39    "The Semi-Attached Couple"]    Novel (1860) by Emily Eden (1797–1869).

596.38–39    Pete Hepburn]    William Peters Hepburn (1833–1916) was a Republican representative from Iowa, 1881–87 and 1893–1909, and the sponsor of the 1906 Railroad Rate Act.

602.21    "Hereward . . . Mannering,"]    Novel (1866) by Charles Kingsley about an 11th-century Saxon outlaw; novel (1815) by Sir Walter Scott.

602.28    Selous]    Frederick Coutney Selous (1851–1917), English hunter and explorer.

608.24–25    Aldrich and Hale]    Nelson Aldrich (1841–1915) was a Republican representative from Rhode Island, 1879–81, and a senator, 1881–1911. Eugene Hale (1836–1918) was a Republican representative from Maine, 1869–79, and a senator, 1881–1911.

608.27    Mr. Cannon]    Joseph Cannon (1836–1926) was a Republican representative from Illinois, 1873–91, 1893–1913, and 1915–23, and Speaker of the House, 1903–11.

609.31–35    Senator Turner . . . Senator Dolliver]    George Turner (1850–1932) was elected as a fusion candidate with Silver Republican, Democratic, and Populist support and served from 1897 to 1903. Robert Hitt (1834–1906) was a Republican representative, 1882–1906. Jonathan Dolliver (1858–1910) was a Republican senator from Iowa, 1900–10.

609.36–38    Congressman Cooper . . . Congressman Murdock]    Henry Cooper (1850–1931) was a Republican representative from Wisconsin, 1893–1919 and 1921–31. Albert Beveridge (1862–1927) was a Republican senator from Indiana, 1899–1911. Joseph Dixon (1867–1934) was a Republican representative from Montana, 1903–7, and a senator, 1907–13. Victor Murdock (1871–1945) was a Republican representative from Kansas, 1903–15.

610.1    Senator Clark]    James Clarke (1854–1916), a Democratic senator from Arkansas, 1903–16.

610.13–14    O. H. Platt . . . Cockrell]    Orville Hitchcock Platt (1827–1905) served in the senate from 1879 to 1905; Francis Marion Cockrell (1834–1915) served from 1875 to 1905.

614.8     Henry White]   White (1850–1927) served as a secretary in the London legation, 1883–93 and 1897–1905, as ambassador to Italy, 1905–7, and as ambassador to France, 1907–9.

616.34    Senator Fulton]   Charles Fulton (1853–1918), a Republican, served in the Senate from 1903 to 1909.

617.9     Senator Mitchell]   John Mitchell (1835–1905) was a Republican senator from Oregon, 1873–79, 1885–97, and 1901–5. He was convicted in 1905 of accepting payments in return for help in expediting land claims and died while the case was on appeal.

620.27    Mr. Mondell]   Franklin Mondell (1860–1939) was a Republican representative from Wyoming, 1895–97 and 1899–1923.

621.8     Mr. Ballinger]   Richard Ballinger (1858–1922) was accused in 1909 of failing to act against fraudulent coal-mine claims in Alaska. Although the majority report of a congressional investigating committee in 1910 exonerated him, Ballinger resigned in March 1911.

627.1     Mr. Tawney]   James Tawney (1855–1919) was a Republican representative from Minnesota, 1893–1911.

631.2–3   Senator Burton]   Joseph Burton (1852–1923), a Republican, served in the Senate from 1901 to 1906. Convicted in November 1905 of accepting payments to intercede in a mail-fraud investigation, Burton resigned his seat in June 1906 after the Supreme Court rejected his appeal and served five months in prison.

633.9–11   Haywood . . . Governor of Idaho]   Frank Steunenberg, who had used federal troops to suppress a miners' strike while governor of Idaho (1897–1901), was killed by a bomb on December 30, 1905. William Haywood, the general secretary of the Western Federation of Miners; Charles Moyer, its president; and George Pettibone, a union member, were arrested in Denver on February 17, 1906, and charged with the murder. Defended by Clarence Darrow, Haywood was acquitted on July 29, 1907. After Pettibone was acquitted early in 1908 the charges against Moyer were dropped.

648.12–13   Kansas City platform]   The Democratic national convention was held in Kansas City in 1900.

648.37    La Follette . . . his magazine]   *La Follette's Weekly Magazine*, which began publication on January 9, 1909. Its name was changed to *La Follette's Magazine* in January 1913, and in November 1914 it became a monthly; in 1929 the magazine was renamed *The Progressive*.

649.18    rebuker of 'muck-rakers']   Invoking the character of the Man with the Muck-rake in John Bunyan's *The Pilgrim's Progress*, Roosevelt said in a widely reported speech on April 14, 1906: "The men with the muck-rakes are often indispensable to the well-being of society; but only if they know when to stop raking the muck, and look upward to the celestial crown above them, to the crown of worthy endeavor." The speech led to the use of "muck-raking" to describe investigative journalistic exposés. (Roosevelt had previously used the phrase "the Man with the Muck-rake" in a speech at a private Gridiron Club dinner held on March 17, 1906.)

651.19   the Reclamation Act]   See Chronology, June 1902.

651.28   Francis G. Newlands]   A Democrat, Newlands (1848–1917) served in the House of Representatives, 1893–1903, and the Senate, 1903–17.

665.14   Bede]   James Bede (1856–1942) was a Republican representative from Minnesota, 1903–9.

669.25   Sir Wilfrid Laurier]   Laurier (1841–1919) was leader of the Liberal party, 1887–1919, and prime minister of Canada, 1896–1911.

669.32–33   colony of Newfoundland]   Newfoundland was a British colony separate from Canada until 1949, when it joined the confederation.

673.16   Thomas Watson]   Watson (1856–1922) was the Populist candidate for vice-president in 1896 and for president in 1904 and 1908. In 1905 he founded *Tom Watson's Magazine* (after 1907, *Watson's Jeffersonian Magazine*); in 1917 the journal was banned from the mails by the Post Office for its opposition to American involvement in World War I.

673.24   Henry Wallace]   Wallace (1836–1916) was the founder and editor of *Wallaces' Farmer*. His son, Henry C. Wallace (1866–1924) was secretary of agriculture, 1921–24; his grandson, Henry A. Wallace (1888–1965), was secretary of agriculture, 1933–40, and vice-president, 1941–45.

680.29   Frank Millet]   American painter and war correspondent Francis Millet (1846–1912).

688.33   Mr. Justice White]   Edward White (1845–1921) was an associate justice, 1894–1910, and chief justice, 1910–21.

689.14–15   the New York Bakeshop case]   In *Lochner* v. *New York* (1905) the Supreme Court ruled 5–4 that a state law regulating the hours of bakery workers violated the due process clause of the Fourteenth Amendment because it interfered with the right to enter into labor contracts.

694.14   Blifil and Black George]   Characters in *Tom Jones* (1749) by Henry Fielding.

694.38   Inter-State Commerce Commission]   The commission was established in 1887.

695.10   Senator Tillman]   Benjamin Tillman (1847–1918), known as "Pitchfork Ben," a Democrat, was governor of South Carolina, 1890–94, and a senator, 1895–1918.

695.13–14   a personal assault . . . South Carolina]   On February 22, 1902, Tillman criticized his junior Democratic colleague, John McLaurin

(1860–1934), for siding with the Republicans on a legislative matter and claimed that he had done so in return for committee assignments and control of federal patronage in South Carolina. McLaurin responded by calling Tillman's charge "a willful, malicious, and deliberate lie." Tillman then physically assaulted McLaurin, and blows were exchanged until the two men were separated. Both senators were officially censured on February 28 for their conduct; McLaurin did not seek reelection and served for only one term (1897–1903).

695.15–16    take action . . . certain land matters.]    Roosevelt had released documents indicating that Tillman had tried to acquire land in Oregon by improper means.

697.1–2    Commerce Court]    In 1910 Congress created a Commerce Court with jurisdiction over decisions by the Interstate Commerce Commission. A series of rulings by the court in favor of railroads made it politically unpopular, and in 1913 President Wilson signed a bill abolishing it.

698.27    Judge E. H. Gary]    Elbert Henry Gary (1846–1927), chairman of the board of directors of U.S. Steel, 1903–27, had served as a county judge in Illinois, 1882–90.

703.10    Frank Kellogg]    Kellogg (1856–1937) served as special government counsel in successful antitrust actions brought against Standard Oil and the Union Pacific Railroad. He was later a Republican senator from Minnesota, 1917–23, and secretary of state, 1925–29.

705.16    District-Attorney Stimson]    Henry Stimson (1867–1950) was U.S. attorney for the Southern District of New York, 1906–10. He later served as secretary of war, 1911–13 and 1940–45, and secretary of state, 1929–33.

705.28    Frankfurter]    Felix Frankfurter (1882–1965), who later served as an associate justice of the U.S. Supreme Court, 1939–62.

706.21–23    Both commutations . . . I left office.]    President Taft granted a commutation to Morse on January 18, 1912, and to Heike on March 2, 1913.

719.40–720.3    first employers' liability . . . the courts.]    The Employers' Liability Act of 1906 was declared unconstitutional by the Supreme Court in 1908 when the court ruled, 5–4, that the law exceeded the regulatory power of Congress by covering employees not directly engaged in interstate commerce. Congress then passed an act drafted to meet the Court's objections, and it was unanimously upheld in 1912.

730.33    Major-General Schofield]    Schofield (1831–1906) commanded the Army of the Ohio, 1864–65, and was commanding general of the army, 1888–95.

740.39    truck stores]    Company stores where workers bought inferior food and goods with scrip they received in lieu of cash wages.

750.40    John Morley]    Morley (1838–1923) was a Liberal member of Parliament, 1883–95 and 1896–1908, secretary of state for Ireland, 1892–95, and secretary of state for India, 1905–8. A prolific writer, his books included works on Gladstone, Cromwell, and Emerson.

754.5–6    Vladimir D. Simkhovitch]    Simkhovitch (1874–1959) was professor of economic history at Columbia University, 1905–44.

754.34    John Graham Brooks's "American Syndicalism"]    *American Syndicalism: The I.W.W.* (1913). Brooks (1846–1938) was the first president of the National Consumers' League and lecturer on social economics at the University of California, Berkeley.

764.34–35    After . . . Senate did act]    The executive agreement on customs collection was signed on February 7, 1905; the treaty was ratified by the Senate on February 25, 1907.

765.26    Hague Tribunal]    The Hague Permanent Court of Arbitration, established by the 1899 Hague peace conference.

766.9    French Panama Company]    The company was founded in 1879, went bankrupt in 1889, and was reorganized in 1894 with the aim of selling its concession to the United States.

775.14–15    Lieutenant-General Young]    Samuel Young (1840–1924) served as the army chief of staff from August 1903 until his retirement in January 1904.

777.38    "il gran rifiuto"]    "The great refusal." The passage is believed to refer to Celestine V, a hermit who was elected pope in 1294 but who resigned after five months to resume his ascetic life.

781.13–14    the Senate ratified the treaty]    The treaty was sent to the Senate on December 7, 1903, and ratified on February 23, 1904.

786.29–30    massacres of the Armenians . . . Turks]    In 1894–96 approximately 100,000 Armenians were killed in a series of massacres in the Ottoman Empire, and another 100,000 died from hunger and disease. Between 15,000 and 25,000 Armenians were killed in massacres in Adana and the surrounding region of southeastern Anatolia in April 1909.

787.7    "an illusion"]    In *The Great Illusion* (1910) the British journalist Norman Angell (1872–1967) argued that nations could not gain economic advantages through military power and conquest.

788.14    under the Mahdi for a dozen years]    Muhammad Ahmad (1844–1885), known as the Mahdi, led the revolt in the Sudan against Egyptian rule and captured Khartoum in January 1885. He died in June 1885 and was succeeded by 'Abd Allah ibn Muhammad al-Tai'ishi (1846–1899), known as the Khalifa, who ruled until his defeat in 1898 by an Anglo-Egyptian army led by Lord Kitchner.

791.15–16     M. d'Estournelles de Constant]    Paul d'Estournelles de Constant (1852–1924) was the French delegate to the Hague peace conferences of 1899 and 1907. He served in the chamber of deputies, 1895–1904, and the senate, 1904–24.

820.38     Dromios]    Identical twin brothers in Shakespeare's *The Comedy of Errors*.

822.14–15     Judge Hook]    William Hook (1857–1921) was a federal district judge in Kansas, 1899–1903, and a judge on the Eighth Circuit Court, 1903–21. In 1909 he wrote the decree dissolving the Standard Oil Company that was upheld by the Supreme Court in 1911.

834.7     his Secretary of State]    William Jennings Bryan served as secretary of state from March 1913 to June 1915.

836.3     "The House of Harper"]    The book was published in 1912.

836.4     Curtis]    George William Curtis (1824–1892), the author of *The Potiphar Papers*, was editor of *Harper's Weekly*, 1863–92, and president of the National Civil Service Reform League, 1881–92.

836.12     'Plumed Knight' of Mulligan letter fame]    In his speech nominating Blaine for president at the Republican convention on June 15, 1876, Robert G. Ingersoll described him as "a plumed knight" who "threw his shining lance" against former Confederate officers now serving as Democratic congressmen. In the spring of 1876 Blaine was accused of having engaged in improper transactions in railroad bonds while serving as Speaker of the House. During the subsequent investigation James Mulligan, a bookkeeper for Boston businessman Warren Fisher Jr., announced that he possessed letters written by Blaine to Fisher proving that Blaine had used the speakership for personal gain while speculating in bonds. Blaine retrieved the letters from Mulligan and after refusing to turn them over to the subcommittee investigating the charges, read them aloud in the House chamber on June 5 during a dramatic speech proclaiming his innocence. On July 10, 1876, the governor of Maine appointed Blaine to a vacant seat in the Senate, and the House investigation was discontinued.

*Library of Congress Cataloging-in-Publication Data*

Roosevelt, Theodore, 1858–1919.
    [Rough Riders]
      The Rough Riders; An autobiography / Theodore Roosevelt
        p. cm. — (Library of America ; 153)
      First work originally published: New York : C. Scribner's Sons,
1899. 2nd work originally published: New York : Macmillan, 1913.
      Includes bibliographical references.
      ISBN 1–931082–65–0 (alk. paper)
      1. United States. Army. Volunteer Cavalry, 1st — History.   2.
Spanish-American War, 1898 — Regimental histories.   3. Spanish-
American War, 1898 — Personal narratives.   4. Roosevelt,
Theodore, 1858–1919.   5. Presidents — United States — Biography.
I. Roosevelt, Theodore, 1858–1919. Theodore Roosevelt, an
autobiography.   II. Title: Theodore Roosevelt, an autobiography.
III. Title.   IV. Series.

E725.45ISt.R64   2004
973.8'93'092 — dc22
[B]                                 2004044195

# THE LIBRARY OF AMERICA SERIES

The Library of America fosters appreciation and pride in America's literary heritage by publishing, and keeping permanently in print, authoritative editions of America's best and most significant writing. An independent nonprofit organization, it was founded in 1979 with seed money from the National Endowment for the Humanities and the Ford Foundation.

*This book is set in 10 point Linotron Galliard,*
*a face designed for photocomposition by Matthew Carter*
*and based on the sixteenth-century face Granjon. The paper*
*is acid-free Domtar Literary Opaque and meets the requirements*
*for permanence of the American National Standards Institute. The*
*binding material is Brillianta, a woven rayon cloth made by Van*
*Heek-Scholco Textielfabrieken, Holland. The composition is by*
*Publishers' Design and Production Services, Inc. Printing*
*and binding by R.R. Donnelley & Sons Company.*
*Designed by Bruce Campbell.*